Judicial Review
A Thematic Approach

Judicial Review

A Thematic Approach

Brigid Hadfield
Editor

Gill & Macmillan

Gill & Macmillan Ltd
Goldenbridge
Dublin 8
with associated companies throughout the world
(c) Gill & Macmillan 1995
0 7171 2311 1

Index compiled by Elizabeth Ingham

Print origination by DTP Workshop, Dublin

Printed by ColourBooks Ltd, Dublin

Contents

Preface

It is a privilege to be asked to provide a short preface to this book. Its editor and one of its contributors is Brigid Hadfield. She has an encyclopaedic knowledge of Northern Ireland's administrative case law and a profound understanding of administrative law. Other contributors are also well known to me personally and held in high esteem because of the authority of their writing and research. The book's quality is, as you would expect, in keeping with the reputation of its contributors.

This book adopts what is, as far as I am aware, an entirely novel approach to the examination of administrative law. It examines the subject from a series of different perspectives and, as a result of doing so, identifies a number of themes which might not otherwise be appreciated. This is an approach which it is particularly appropriate to adopt when examining judicial review since within each of the jurisdictions with which this book is concerned, judicial review has grown like Topsy. The growth has been haphazard. It has depended essentially upon the cases which the accident of events has happened to bring before the courts. The introduction of a similar new procedure of judicial review, initially in England and Wales and subsequently in the other jurisdictions within the United Kingdom and the Republic of Ireland, has been the same catalyst which has stimulated this growth in each of these jurisdictions.

The principles which the vast volume of case law collectively reflect in each jurisdiction are by no means identical. In some instances the reason for this can be traced back to what was happening in a particular jurisdiction prior to the introduction of the judicial review procedure in that jurisdiction. Other explanations are the different constitutional and political situations in the different jurisdictions. An obvious example is the difference, which two of the contributors make clear exists, between Scotland and the Republic of Ireland on the one hand and England and Wales on the other, as to the public/private law divide. In a diluted form, the necessity for the continuation of the procedural divide between public and private law proceedings laid down in *O'Reilly v Mackman*[1] for England and Wales, despite vigorous academic criticism, has recently been accepted by the Law Commission but the other jurisdictions manage happily having rejected it. Ireland, having a written constitution, also provides useful precedents relating to the review of legislation which is a new role for the other jurisdictions which now have to take on this task as a result of their membership of the European Union. Quite apart from stark contrasts of this nature there are more subtle differences between the jurisdictions which the chapters on the Scottish and Irish jurisdictions make clear.

Unfortunately the majority of administrative lawyers practising in the High Court in London are abysmally unaware of the decisions in these jurisdictions. They are not entirely to blame for this. An examination of the case list of any of the standard textbooks on administrative law in England and Wales to which the profession and the judiciary regularly refer would provide confirmation of the limited reliance which their editors have placed on Scottish, Northern Ireland and the Republic of Ireland sources. When the virtues of this book become widely known, as they deserve to be, this situation should be alleviated. An aspect of the 'Thematic Approach' which is extremely important is to draw attention to the comparative lessons to be learnt from the Scottish and Irish authorities dealing with many of the areas of administrative law where the English courts are still struggling to find answers. In my case the two chapters dealing with these other jurisdictions would in themselves justify my acquiring this book since I confess that, until I read them, I was far less well informed than I should have been as to the developments north of the border and across the Irish Sea.

Another important theme of this book demonstrates how principles of administrative law which are of wide application have developed in a particular context. This is the case with prisons, not only in England and Wales but particularly in Northern Ireland where the numerous judicial review applications have helped to change the culture within prisons and at the same time contributed to the development of administrative law as a whole. The same is true of the Environmental (note not the out-dated title 'Planning'), Criminal, Local Government and Education fields, as the chapters dealing with these subjects make clear.

The remaining theme to which I would draw attention (although there are a number of others), is what I will call the 'pragmatic theme'. I detect this theme in the chapter which concentrates on the problems as to access to judicial review created, in particular, by the requirement to obtain leave to make the application. It is also present in the chapter which deals perceptively with judicial caution in the deployment of the powerful weapon of judicial review; in the chapter which explains the discomfort of the judiciary in the minefield of national security; and in the chapter which demonstrates how the judiciary in the case of certain areas of wide ranging social legislation have been sidelined in their normal role by the creation of intervening statutory review bodies.

I use the word 'pragmatic' to describe this theme because I regard these chapters as demonstrating the care which the judiciary has exercised and must exercise to confine itself to examining the legality of governmental activity and the care which the executive has in its turn exercised and must exercise not to abrogate judicial review. A fascinating feature of judicial review is the way it has required the courts and the executive to respect each others' roles. The courts must not impose their views as to policy on the executive and the executive must not prevent the courts upholding the rule of law. If this is to happen a pragmatic approach to the exercise of power is required by both since the task of maintaining the proper balance is a delicate one. These chapters show how the balance is just achieved in practice.

By comparison with some of its contemporaries, these themes are achieved in a commendably compact work. The book does this by providing material which is difficult to find elsewhere. Each of its contributors has specialist knowledge of the area about which they write. That knowledge is attractively displayed. Between them they provide a fresh and stimulating approach which I feel confident will be of benefit to all those interested in administrative law. The contributors are to be congratulated in fulfilling a real need. Certainly having been able to read the proofs I personally look forward to re-reading the work in its published form.

Lord Woolf
July 1995

Note
1. [1983] 2 AC 237

Introduction

The title of this book 'Judicial Review: A Thematic Approach' has been chosen in order to indicate what are at least three main themes within the book. First, given the growth in the number of judicial review applications, it seems to be of increasing importance to consider the way(s) in which the procedures and principles of judicial review operate within any given substantive context. The chapters, therefore, by Colin Reid, Paul Meredith, Paul Maguire, Peter Osborne, Stephen Livingstone and Brice Dickson seek to explore the operation of judicial review (and to gauge its impact) in the substantive areas indicated by the chapter titles—the environment, education, local government, the criminal process, prisons and national security (including aspects of judicial review in the fields of immigration and employment). Much research has recently been done, and continues to be done, with regard to the incidence of judicial review in England and Wales, in Northern Ireland and in Scotland, in terms of the subject areas of judicial review applications and the parties (not least here the respondents), in judicial review proceedings. It is, therefore, appropriate to begin to add to this kind of statistical analysis, analyses of the type provided by the six chapters mentioned. The themes chosen to be covered by these chapters are designed both to reflect areas where in the past there has been considerable resort to judicial review (as a proportion of leave applications) and also to indicate areas where there may be growth in the future (for example, the environment). They also reflect the fact that the incidence of judicial review is, of course, not identical in all the jurisdictions considered in this book.

This leads to the second theme of the book—the territorial theme. The book contains two chapters which expressly relate to one jurisdiction, namely the chapters by Christopher Himsworth and Gerard Hogan on, respectively, Scotland and the Republic of Ireland. Much can be learnt about trends in judicial review and the evolution of principles within one's own jurisdiction by considering what is happening in neighbouring jurisdictions and, it is hoped, by learning from both similarities and differences. The material on Northern Ireland, where the principles of judicial review and its procedure are virtually but not completely identical to those in England, is largely integrated (where relevant) into the text of the various chapters, although some material relates expressly to either England or Northern Ireland. The Appendix (dealing specifically with the Northern Ireland judicial review procedure and the case law thereon) is deliberately confined to Northern Ireland, mainly for comparative purposes with the better known (and more easily available) English material. All references to European Community Law and the jurisprudence relating to and stemming from the European Convention on Human Rights are dealt with, where relevant, in the individual chapters rather than considered independently. With regard to the former case law and now (increasingly?) the latter, this is how the judicial review principles are likely to grow and develop—as integrated, not divergent, systems. Thus the various jurisdictions within 'these islands', England and Wales, Scotland, Northern Ireland and the Republic of Ireland, should not be considered in isolation from each other— *a fortiori* should not be ignored—and the same is now true with regard to the evolving body of European administrative law principles.

The third 'theme' of the book is mainly to be found in the chapters by Maurice Sunkin, Andrew Le Sueur and Brigid Hadfield and that theme is the function of judicial review: what does it exist for? or for whom does it exist? The various answers of both judges and the government to these questions are considered.

The chapters themselves do not, of course, break down as simply as this threefold categorisation would suggest. Indeed, although each chapter is free-standing and there is very little overlap between any of them, the sequence for the chapters was designed so as to encourage the reader to proceed through the book as a whole (that is, the academic reader, at any rate, although it is both hoped and intended that the practitioner will find much of interest in the book).

Sir Stephen Sedley wrote in his review of the book *Judicial Review* edited by Michael Supperstone and James Goudie: 'odd though it may seem, judicial review has not yet made up its mind what it is or where it is going'.

It is our collective hope that this book will make a contribution to the debate on these issues.

Brigid Hadfield
Belfast
July 1995

List of Contributors

Brice Dickson is Professor of Law, University of Ulster at Jordanstown.

Brigid Hadfield is Professor of Public Law, The Queen's University of Belfast.

Christopher Himsworth is Senior Lecturer in Law, University of Edinburgh.

Gerard Hogan is Fellow of Trinity College, Dublin.

Andrew Le Sueur is Lecturer in Laws, University College London.

Stephen Livingstone is Reader in Law, University of Nottingham.

Paul Maguire is Lecturer in Public Law, The Queen's University of Belfast.

Paul Meredith is Senior Lecturer in Law, University of Southampton.

Peter Osborne is Lecturer in Public Law, The Queen's University of Belfast.

Colin Reid is Professor of Law, University of Dundee.

Maurice Sunkin is Reader in Law, University of Essex.

Acknowledgments

There are several people to whom I am particularly grateful for their assistance in the preparation of this book in addition, of course, to the individual authors whose ready co-operation (not least in terms of meeting deadlines) has been greatly appreciated.

I am very grateful to Lord Woolf who, in spite of considerable demands upon his time, so readily and kindly agreed to write the Preface to this book.

Finola O'Sullivan, Editor of Professional Books at Gill & Macmillan and Deirdre Greenan, also of Gill & Macmillan, have both given unstintingly of their professional expertise at various stages in the commissioning and production of the book.

My thanks also go to my colleague, Laura Lundy, out of discussions with whom the seeds for embarking upon this venture were sown.

Last, but by no means least, my thanks go to my secretary, Gina Inglis, who has given so willingly of her time and skills and whose continuous efficiency has made the task of editing this book so much easier.

Brigid Hadfield

Table of Cases

Table of Statutes

Table of Statutory Instruments etc.

Chapter One

The Problematical State of Access to Judicial Review

Maurice Sunkin

It is a principle of our law that every citizen has a right of unimpeded access to a court. In *Raymond v Honey* Lord Wilberforce[1] described it as a 'basic right'. Even in our unwritten constitution it must rank as a constitutional right.[2]

Procedurally the law is in good shape, with the possible exception of access to judicial review. Access is not of right, but is subject to the court's discretion.[3]

The public interest normally dictates that if the judicial review jurisdiction is to be exercised, it should be exercised very speedily and, given the constraints imposed by limited judicial resources, this necessarily involves limiting the number of cases in which leave to apply should be given.[4]

Introduction

The right of citizens to unimpeded access to the courts is as fundamental a constitutional right as any right can be in our unwritten constitution. It is an important facet of the 'constitutional ethic'[5] and of the rule of law.[6] It has been implicitly used to justify the courts overriding apparently plain words of primary legislation[7] and expressly to justify review of subordinate legislation.[8] It is protected by the principles of contempt of court[9] and by the European Convention on Human Rights.[10] As Professor Wade has remarked: 'The right of access to the courts is a matter that the courts . . . guard strictly.'[11]

Despite this pedigree, access to judicial review is one of the most problematical aspects of public law in the United Kingdom. The structure of the process presents the most visible image of the problem. In what sense, it may be asked, can we speak of a right to access when the ability to argue one's case is contingent upon obtaining the permission of a judge which may be granted or refused as a matter of discretion? Whilst the contingent nature of access is profoundly important, it only represents one facet of a problem that is deeply embedded in the theory and working culture of judicial review. A right can be protected and furthered by discretion if the

1

discretion is exercised on the basis that the right is a value which demands priority and respect unless substantial and principled justifications exist for its exclusion or limitation.[12] There would be less cause for concern were the right of access valued in this way. Despite its fundamental status in other areas of law, however, the interest in citizens gaining access to the courts to seek judicial review seems to be one interest amongst many.[13] Indeed, far from having any prior or special status as befits a right, it seems to be an interest that is particularly vulnerable in a system that is increasingly confronted by the need to ration scarce judicial resources amongst an apparently ever growing caseload.[14]

In this chapter I shall explore the problem of access at various levels of abstraction. I start by considering some of the most practical obstacles confronting applicants and would-be applicants. I then consider the prevailing attitudes to access in the light of the constitutional role of judicial review and the nature of rights in public law. This will show why the idea of a right of access fits uneasily with current attitudes. I shall then move on to consider arguments that are more positive and supportive of the notion of a right of access and assess their suitability to the system. Finally, I shall examine the prospect for inculcating a culture of access in the light of the Law Commission's recent recommendations for reform of judicial review.

Themes

Several themes recur throughout this chapter. One is the problem of locating a right of access in theories of liberal individualism of the type that is applicable in private law but which fits less easily with a system of public law that is increasingly concerned with public interests. Related to this is the problem of reconciling individual rights of access and the recent tendency towards according access to experienced and well-respected public interest litigants, such as Greenpeace and the World Development Movement. Such a trend has obvious functional advantages and is explicable in pluralist or communitarian terms which are clearly compatible with prevailing attitudes to judicial review. Does it, however, offer direct benefit to the vast majority of individual applicants who lack private law rights but are also unable to provide the court with the functional advantages of public interest litigants? Given that these applicants are the most vulnerable to current pressures to ration entry, do they have any constitutional tools with which to reinforce their right of access against the prevailing managerial pressures? I shall suggest that such tools do exist, but in so doing I shall be arguing that the real challenge is cultural. The challenge is to try to encourage reformers and judges to accept that rights, which are elsewhere regarded as fundamental, have a place in the public law system and that entry to the system is not simply a matter of largesse.

Before proceeding further I ought to define my field of concern more specifically. Access to courts is about being able to seek the court's protection of legally recognised rights and interests. In ordinary civil proceedings this generally implies that the plaintiff has the unhindered right to commence legal proceedings and to participate in any consequential hearing including, in particular, a hearing into the merits of the claim.[15] In judicial review proceedings in England, Wales and Northern Ireland the position is complicated by the requirement that leave of the court be obtained before proceeding to a substantive hearing.[16] The leave stage operates as a preliminary filter regulating the ability of applicants to get to court to have their case fully considered.

Some may argue that the principle that access to the courts should be unencumbered is satisfied because there is a right to seek leave. For the purpose of this chapter I am assuming, however, that a right of access includes the opportunity to obtain a full hearing on the merits and that leave is a potential barrier to this.[17] Nevertheless, it is important to recognise that, even for those who obtain permission to proceed, the leave stage may be a critically important and even determinative step in the proceedings. This may be so when an applicant for leave obtains interim relief which effectively disposes of the issue or when a favourable leave decision can be used to lever a favourable settlement out of a respondent.[18] Whilst there are no formal barriers to seeking leave, there are important practical obstacles to which I shall refer in passing.

It is implicit in what I have already said that this chapter is primarily concerned with the right of applicants and, in particular, individuals to gain access to judicial review. I am not here concerned with the rights of respondents to participate, for example, at the leave stage, or with the participation of third parties; both matters, though, raise issues of importance.[19]

I ought to add that I shall not focus on the issue of standing, although recent decisions have significant implications for access in general and deserve comment.[20] There is a tendency to exaggerate the importance of standing as a practical hurdle to access. In truth, standing is but one aspect of a broader picture of access and it is this broader picture that we need to keep in mind. Finally, this chapter is not concerned with the scope of judicial review, with justiciability[21] or with the grounds of judicial review.[22]

The Discretionary Nature of Access

The prevailing view is that access to judicial review is and ought to be a matter of discretion rather than of right.[23] This is said to be dictated by public policy considerations, including the need to secure the efficient management of the caseload; to ensure that hopeless applications are filtered out of the system; and to protect public administration.[24]

This, however, need not imply that access is not a value to be respected and promoted. The value of access, for example, might be reflected in the structure of the system by which access issues are to be determined and in the working culture of the judges. It might, for instance, be clear from the criteria used to determine access that judges approach cases assuming that applicants have a right of entry. This message might be repeated by the judges in their day-to-day work, as well as by official commentary on the system. Examining such material we might expect to find implicit, if not express, reference to the fundamental nature of such a right, and perhaps even to statements that access should only be denied if substantial contervailing issues of principle justify exclusion. If there was evidence of this cultural approach to access, it would matter less that the system is discretionary.

Unfortunately, if we sought evidence of such a view, we would look in vain.[25] The leave criteria, as they currently stand, have been widely criticised on the grounds that they are unclear and uncertain.[26] There is nothing in them to suggest that access is a right and at best they are neutral as to how judges should value access. Certainly, there is no express presumption that leave should be granted.[27] Moreover, I am aware of no judicial statement that judges should approach the leave discretion on the basis that applicants have a right to proceed to full hearing.[28] On the contrary, as the quotation from Lord Donaldson MR cited at the beginning of this chapter shows, there is good authority for the view that judges may turn away applications on general managerial grounds; it is, to say the least, difficult to reconcile this approach with the idea that access is a fundamental right.

The most authoritative recent official commentary on the procedure is that provided by the Law Commission in its 1994 Report.[29] Although the Law Commission is clearly aware of the practical problems facing many who seek access to judicial review,[30] there is little in its report to suggest that there is or ought to be a right of access, fundamental or otherwise. Citing the relevant public policy considerations impinging upon the judicial review procedure, the Law Commission refers to the 'private interest of individual litigants in obtaining a remedy for their grievances', but this interest is given no priority or particular weight as compared with other public interests such as the interest in good administration.[31] In fact the Law Commission goes on to say that 'in a case involving only public law issues the public policy interest in ensuring speed and certainty in administrative decision-making may be more important than the private interests of the individual litigant in obtaining a substantive hearing . . .'[32]

Whilst the Law Commission's recommendations may improve the overall working of the system, particularly in public interest cases, there is nothing in their recommendations to suggest that access for individual applicants is a right. From the point of view of access, the main thrust of the report is towards public interest litigation, and one is left with a feeling that judicial review is becoming too precious a system by which to pursue purely private interests.

This sketch presents an image of a system which is far less welcoming to individual applicants than some judges would have us believe.[33] Several other factors combine to reinforce these formal barriers to access and these also deserve a mention.

In considering these barriers it may be borne in mind that judicial review provides a classical example of the situation in which, to borrow Galanter's famous labels, 'one off' applicants who are also 'have nots' are regularly pitted against respondents who are likely to be 'repeat players' and 'haves'.[34] By far the majority of individual applicants are economically, socially and politically disadvantaged compared with those they are challenging. This inevitably places a premium on their having access to proper funding and to experienced professional assistance and representation.

Contrary to some impressions, judicial review can be extremely costly to use, and obtaining legal aid can be a serious problem.[35] Gaining access to appropriate legal advice and assistance can also be a hit or miss affair. Not only is there evidence that advice agencies regularly fail to identify potential judicial review challenges,[36] but even those seeking specialist legal advice may have trouble finding solicitors who profess an expertise in judicial review litigation. The problem is greatest outside London and the south-east, particularly in areas of law other than homelessness and immigration.[37]

Research shows that high proportions of applications, particularly in areas of law in which judicial review is heavily used, are processed by a small number of specialist firms of solicitors. It also shows, however, that many firms of solicitors are very infrequent users of the system.[38] The overall picture is one of a situation in which the scale and type of litigation is heavily dependent on the litigation strategies of small numbers of lawyers. One consequence is that access to the system seems to depend on whether potential applicants happen to have access to these lawyers.

We have no way of knowing how many potential judicial reviews are not made because litigants do not have access to appropriate advice and assistance. We do know, however, that a significant minority of applicants are litigants in person, and that these fare very badly in the system.[39] We also know that substantial numbers of applications are withdrawn, even after obtaining permission to proceed. Many of these will be settled. As yet, however, we have no data on whether there is a quantitative or qualitative link between settlement and the type of legal representation that applicants have obtained.[40]

A further reason why the quality of representation is so important lies in what may be described as the club-like nature of the system.[41] The discretionary nature of this centralised and specialist system depends very heavily on the understanding and assumptions which are shared by the judges and those practitioners who regularly appear before them. This, of itself, may well operate to the disadvantage of those who are represented in court by non-specialists, as well as to litigants in person.

My argument, then, is that the system does not accord a high value to rights of access. This is evident in the structure of the system, the working ethos of the judges and in official commentary on the system. The ethos is reinforced to the disadvantage of potential individual applicants by broader socio-legal and economic aspects of the process, including the need to ration judicial resources, centralisation, and the erratic distribution of appropriate legal advice and assistance.

I shall now turn to examine the link between this ethos and:

(a)   the constitutional role of judicial review;
(b)   the related conceptual nature of rights in public law; and
(c)   the pragmatic need to ensure efficient management of the caseload.

The Reasons Why Access is a Matter of Discretion

The constitutional role of judicial review and the low value attached to access

It has been observed that the theoretical and constitutional foundations of judicial review are rooted in what may be described as the imperium model of legal theory.[42] Essentially this model—which can be traced back through A.V. Dicey to Austin's command theory of law—assumes that the constitutional system can be understood as a hierarchy. At the top stands the sovereign lawmaker and below are the subordinate authorities of the state to whom legal duties and powers are delegated by the sovereign. Within this structure the judicial role is to ensure that these subordinate authorities do not exceed or abuse the powers which have been conferred upon them. In this way the courts play a policing role on behalf of the sovereign and are an integral part of the system concerned with controlling and regulating the agencies of government. Within this tradition the judicial role may be portrayed as being primarily concerned with applying the state's law to the state itself.[43]

Cotterrell points out that this 'top down' conception of a legal system is not inherently democratic and may indeed provide the basic centralised structure for authoritarian and even fascist regimes. The British system ultimately derives legitimacy, however, from the idea that sovereign power resides in a parliament that is politically accountable to the electorate.[44] Judicial review, therefore, derives its formal constitutional authority from this democratic base.

From the point of view of access this model has three main general implications. First, within imperium judicial review is primarily concerned with controlling and regulating the exercise of governmental power for the benefit of the process of governance itself, to ensure, in particular, that parliamentary purposes are implemented and that the system is legally efficient. The model is not concerned to further values or interests which are rooted in society or the community and which are not associated with the need to impose controls within the system. A right of access to the court in order to challenge government can, therefore, be asserted on the grounds that access furthers the courts' policing functions but not on the basis that access furthers the interest of citizens in obtaining redress against government per se.

Second, the legitimacy of judicial review ultimately flows from principles of parliamentary democracy. One of the reasons why the judicial role may be presented as being subservient is that courts lack an independent base of legitimate authority. This model provides little room for the suggestion that citizens have a right of access to courts derived from democratic principles. Such an idea would provide the judges with a source of legitimacy not derived from a delegation of power to them and would be incompatible with the overall structure of the system.

Third, it does not follow, however, that the issue of access is unimportant and irrelevant within the imperium model: only that access is important in so far as it furthers the ability of the courts to serve the functional needs of imperium, but not otherwise. How then does access serve these functional needs?

As well as triggering the courts into operation, access issues are relevant to ensuring that courts have a supply of appropriate instances from which to work. Since they are passive, courts have little direct control over the cases which are brought to them, although in judicial review the preliminary filter does give judges an opportunity to distinguish between applications which are more or less likely to provide a useful base for policing. It is implicit within the imperium model that decisions on such matters should be determined by judges according to their perception of the needs of the system. This, of course, is prima facie inconsistent with the idea that citizens have a right to demand access, for such a right would restrict judicial freedom and particularly the ability to decide how best to deploy scarce judicial resources.

Seen from the perspective of imperium, there would, for example, be little to gain by considering numerous individual applications which basically raise the same or similar errors involving the same or similar types of official body, however meritorious these might be on their individual merits. Lord Brightman's speech in *Puhlhofer v Hillingdon London Borough Council*[45] provides one of the best-known illustrations of this attitude. Here he castigated the homeless for making prolific use of judicial review and called upon judges to restrict access to applications, unless they were exceptional in some way. The use of the term 'prolific' to describe the numbers of cases is only explicable if Lord Brightman was concerned that many of the cases raised similar types of argument against similar (although not identical) authorities. In other words, looked at from the point of view of imperium, the cases essentially duplicated each other and did not further the policing function of the courts.

It does not, however, necessarily follow that the imperium model will lead to restrictions on access. On the contrary, the courts may be keen to attract certain types of cases and to encourage those considered best qualified to present high quality applications. In this context the only factor that is central to the imperium approach is that courts retain discretion over who is to be heard.

Standing provides some good examples of the way this discretion has been exercised. In the past it has tended to be assumed that those directly affected by official action are likely to be in the best position to pursue litigation and best placed to present the strongest arguments to the judges. In view of the likely costs that could flow from a potential increase in litigation, there appeared to be few functional gains to the judicial process to be achieved by liberalising standing.[46]

In a series of recent decisions the courts have roundly rejected this attitude and have acknowledged that there are functional benefits for the courts in adopting liberalised standing and allowing certain interest groups into court. These advantages were most clearly articulated by Otton J. in *R. v Pollution Inspectorate, ex parte Greenpeace (No. 2)*.[47]

Greenpeace challenged authorisation given to British Nuclear Fuels Ltd by the Pollution Inspectorate and the Minister of Agriculture to permit the discharge of radioactive waste from BNFL's premises at Sellafield during testing of BNFL's new thermal oxide reprocessing plant (THORP). Whilst referring to the health risks posed to local residents, Greenpeace based its claim to standing on the wider public interest in preventing the use of radioactive material and the disposal of radioactive waste. The challenge failed on its merits, but only after Otton J. had decided that Greenpeace had standing to bring the proceedings.

Approaching the matter primarily as one of discretion, he stressed the national and international standing of Greenpeace, its integrity and its concern for the environment. Referring to the membership of Greenpeace, he placed weight on the fact that 2,500 of its members came from the Cumbria region and that these people were 'inevitably concerned about (and had a genuine perception that there was) a danger to their health and safety from any additional discharge of radioactive waste . . .'[48]

Otton J. went on to say that if he denied standing to Greenpeace, it would be unlikely that there would be another potential applicant

> . . . able to command the expertise which is at the disposal of Greenpeace. Consequently, a less well-informed challenge might be mounted which would stretch unnecessarily the court's resources and which would not afford the court the assistance it requires to do justice . . . Greenpeace . . . with its particular experience in environmental matters, its access to experts in the relevant realms of science and technology (not to mention the law), is able to mount a carefully selected, focused, relevant and well-argued challenge.[49]

I have suggested that this decision illustrates the way functional considerations which are compatible with imperium can be used to justify granting access to an interest group espousing what it believes to be community based values. If this case can be analysed in this way, it shows that the lines between imperium and community based values and interests can become extremely blurred when courts are prepared to adopt a more activist approach to review. Room for argument no doubt exists as to whether such a decision is to be better understood as an example of an imperium based mentality exploiting a willing applicant or of a situation in which the applicant is exploiting the functional advantages it can offer. Probably both are relevant, but neither is likely to offer a complete explanation for the decision. They do suggest, however, that there may be some affinity between the imperium conception of judicial review and the public interest dimension of judicial review, and this may have significant implications for individuals who claim a right of access. Basically, it suggests that individual rights are likely to flounder when they run up against a public interest model of judicial review which is driven by a predominantly statist imperium approach or by more communitarian tendencies. This may pose the most serious challenge facing the argument that individuals have a right to access in public law. It is an issue to which I shall return.

Before moving on to consider the nature of rights in the imperium conception of public law, it is worth noting that the role of the Attorney General in representing the public interest fits well with an imperium conception of access.[50] As a member of the government the Attorney General is well placed to determine whether public interests would be served by litigation. Like the courts, his authority also derives from principles of parliamentary democracy but with the added bonus that he, like other members of the executive, is politically accountable for his actions. Moreover, in functional terms, the fact that the Attorney General is able to institute proceedings or to lend his name to a relator action reduces the need for rights of citizen access.[51] The major functional limitation of the Attorney General is that he is unlikely to litigate against government departments.[52]

The low value of access and the absence of individual rights in the imperium model of public law

The status of individual rights in imperium can be summarised very briefly. Within imperium it is misleading and inappropriate to talk about citizens having rights *as* individuals in public law, either in the substantive sense of having rights against potential respondents, or in the sense of having rights to get into court.[53] Public law is not about individual rights but about imposing legal controls within government. The existence of individual rights requiring particular respect would inhibit the freedom of judges to reconcile the competing public interests impinging upon their policing function.

This approach is reflected in the dominant trends in procedural and substantive public law and explains the importance of judicial discretion throughout the judicial review procedure, including the emphasis placed on the principle of procedural exclusivity.[54]

The need for managerial control over the system of access

So far the discussion has concentrated on prevailing theory and its conception of rights. There is, however, another very practical factor militating against a right of access. This is the fear that such a right would exacerbate difficulties in the management of the judicial review system. A right of access—even one mediated by judicial discretion—would surely lead to overload, to a crisis, and to collapse.[55] This, of course, would be in nobody's interest and would certainly not improve the lot of potential applicants.

Implicit in this concern is the assumption that a right of access would significantly contribute to the judicial review caseload and make management of the system more difficult. These assumptions are questionable. First, like many floodgates arguments, they fail to take account of the complex factors that combine to explain why litigation occurs. The judicial review caseload can be extremely erratic. It is susceptible to the effects of new legislation as well as to changes in administrative practice and policy; as we have seen, it is also dependent on decisions of individual lawyers. Each of these can produce relatively large changes in the scale of litigation over very short periods.[56] Against this background, the idea that there is a right of access is likely to have a minimal impact. Indeed, most lawyers and many members of the public may already assume that applications for leave to seek judicial review are currently considered on the basis that the right of access is a fundamental attribute of British legal culture.

As far as management is concerned, much depends on the nature of the right that is being considered. Abolition of a preliminary filter clearly would have management implications, although it is unclear what these would be.[57] Assuming, however, the continued existence of some sort of discretionary filter, it is arguable that the quality of management decisions would be enhanced if, for example, judicial discretion is confined and structured so as to require judges to presume that applicants have a right to gain access unless exclusion can be justified. Such an expectation, after all, is almost precisely what judges expect from officials when exercising their discretionary powers. In this sense the right of access would encourage reason and rationality in judicial decision-making at the leave stage.[58] It would also oblige the introduction of management systems that are open and designed to allow judges to provide principled justifications for their decisions. To this too I shall return.

The Right of Access?

I have argued that there is little support within dominant attitudes to the theory and practice of judicial review for a right of access. Does this mean that we should be prepared to allow the right to wither until our memory of it fades? Or perhaps the time has come to give it a decent burial beneath the soil of imperium, public interests, and managerialism?

In this part of the chapter I suggest that neither course is necessary, and burial would be premature; that there may yet be force and usefulness in the concept of a right of access in public law. I shall argue that the image of the system so far presented is incomplete and that there is room for a right of access in modern public law. Moreover, the need to recognise such a right and to have a clear conception of its scope and restrictions is growing in importance, and will continue to grow as resource pressures on the system increase and the lines between justice and management become more indistinct.

I shall consider the issues by reference to:

   (i)   the constitutional theory of judicial review; and

   (ii) the conceptual nature of rights in public law.

An alternative to imperium

Dominant attitudes towards judicial review may fit within the imperium model, but imperium provides too monochrome, bland and 'threadbare' an image of public law.[59] In particular, it underestimates what Cotterrell broadly describes as the community based conceptions of legal theory. From this perspective judicial review is concerned with protecting and promoting

> independent values of various kinds which are in some sense rooted in culture or society and which serve as an essential matrix for evaluation of govern-mental practices.[60]

Here the courts are guardians of 'values anchored in society and culture' rather than servants of parliament's will. Their role is to protect citizens against governmental abuse, to promote their rights and interests, to provide redress, and to ensure that government is fully accountable to the community for its actions.[61] Such concerns cannot be adequately explained in terms of the hierarchy of imperium.

The community based approach is reflected in and reinforced by the recent upsurge of interest in human rights[62] and the related argument that it is possible to develop a theory of individual rights in public law.[63] It may explain why the courts have abandoned the rigid *ultra vires* doctrine[64] and are developing more intrusive substantive principles of review.[65] The community based approach also provides a sounder explanation than does the imperium model for current concepts of fairness, including the developing principles relating to legitimate expectations.

There are widely different conceptions of what the community is, and considerable debate as to whether it is appropriate to speak in terms of community based values and rights. As I have already suggested, reference to public interests is a prime example of how slippery such a notion as community can be. Is the public interest, for instance, to be equated with community values or with official perceptions of the interests of the state or the system? Some assume the existence of a high level of consensus over community values and rights, and assume that the task of the judge is to discern these values and to apply them.[66] Others argue that consensus is a myth, that conflict and diversity are endemic in society,[67] and that consensus theories allow those in authority to impose their views on the system. Some will accept consensus over some matters but recognise that conflict is likely over other issues. Those who are sceptical about consensus may nonetheless espouse the need for procedures enabling individuals and groups to exert their claims, both in political and legal contexts.[68]

Despite this diversity, it is clear that community based theories are likely to be more hospitable than imperium to a right of access in public law. As can be seen, there are several strands of thinking which may be drawn on. I shall consider, for the moment, the claim that rights do have a place in contemporary public law.

Access in public law: a rights based approach

T.R.S. Allan has developed a theory of rights in public law that is particularly pertinent.[69] In essence, his case is that citizens have a right to expect government and official bodies to exercise their power properly and in accordance with the law. Whilst the imperium based approach assumes that obligations in public law are owed to the public in general rather than to individuals as individuals,[70] Allan argues that obligations, such as the duty not to abuse discretion and to act fairly, can properly be said to be obligations which are owed to individuals who are adversely affected by the governmental action.[71] His approach is located in the liberal concept of '. . . individual autonomy, or limited invulnerability to the exercise of power'.[72] This ultimately rests, Allan says, in a 'deep-seated commitment to the dignity of the individual'.[73]

Sir John Laws has recently lent his authority to the rights based approach to judicial review in the interesting context of an argument against introducing the European Convention on Human Rights into UK domestic law either by statute or by incorporation.[74] The thrust of his case is that it is unnecessary to strengthen our law by seeking the aid of the Convention because 'the common law is today able to accord a priority to fundamental rights comparable to their entrenchment in written sets of norms . . .'[75] Laws refuses to be drawn into defining precisely which rights qualify as fundamental. All he says by way of guidance on this critically important question is that the source of such rights 'is *not* statutory'. Assuming that identification is possible, he argues that when such rights are adversely affected by governmental action, it is legitimate for the courts to subject that governmental action to the most searching scrutiny to discover whether the action is justified. This requires

> ... an insistence that the decision-maker is not free to order his priorities as he chooses, confined only by a crude duty not to emulate brute beasts that have no understanding; an insistence that he accord the *first priority* to the right in question unless he can show a substantial, objective public justification for overriding it.[76]

Neither Allan nor Laws is specifically concerned with the right to access to the courts, but there is much in what they say to support its existence in public as well as in private law. If a conceptual image of such a right can be crafted, what form might it take and how might it fit within a culture that seems unwilling to accept a right of access? Who would be the beneficiaries of such a right, and upon what principles might it be located?

What form might the right of access take in public law?

Some preliminary points first. The characteristics of a right of access to judicial review must be determined by the nature of judicial review and its role within the constitutional system. This raises two very basic considerations. The first concerns the underlying focus of rights based theories themselves. If, as Allan argues, a rights based theory is ultimately founded on liberal conceptions of individual dignity, it must be asked whether an essentially liberal theory of right can provide an adequate basis for a right of access to a system which is patently and increasingly concerned with public interests?

The second basic consideration concerns the scope of the judicial role. The parameters of a right of access to the courts (including the range of beneficiaries and the qualifications needed to benefit from it) are inevitably determined by the scope of the court's jurisdiction. Rights of access cannot be claimed in respect of matters which are patently beyond the court's jurisdiction. This is not the same as saying, however, that there can *only* be a right of access when it is *clear* that jurisdiction exists.

Although the scope of any right is confined by jurisdiction, the question whether there is a right of access is logically distinct from the jurisdictional question. This is particularly important where issues of jurisdiction and justiciability are unclear or in a state of dynamic development as they have been in the context of judicial review over the past few years.[77] If there is a right of access to the court, it ought not to be defeated by uncertainty as to whether the court has jurisdiction. If this uncertainty exists in a particular case, the existence of a right of access implies that the applicant should be admitted into court and be allowed to present argument on the matter. Such an approach is compatible with the prevailing attitude to standing, which accepts that leave should only be refused on the grounds of standing in the clearest cases.[78] If there is a dispute about standing, it will normally be dealt with at the final hearing either as an aspect of the substantive issue or in relation to the grant of remedies.

It would be difficult to sustain the argument that a right of access could or should be absolute and unconditional. As well as the general limitations to which I have just referred, it is clear that other specific restrictions on the right of access may be imposed by statute or the courts. Limitation periods are an example of the former, and the right to strike out actions which are an abuse of process is an example of the latter.[79]

Restrictions may be imposed upon rights, but it is implicit, as Sir John Laws emphasises, that rights have a status that must be respected. At the very least this requires justification to be shown by those seeking their restriction or abrogation. The type of justification that will be legitimate depends on the nature of the body imposing the restriction, and its authority.

Dworkin's policy/principle distinction is helpful here.[80] Dworkin argues that parliament, and those to whom parliament delegates power, can limit rights on grounds of policy, but the courts have no authority to reach policy decisions. Their determinations on rights must, he argues, be rooted in principle. This approach provides a very useful way of considering the leave requirement. I shall consider this in more detail later, but broadly it suggests that parliament is free to impose hurdles to access if it feels there are policy reasons for doing so. Whilst judges can restrict access on grounds of principle, they can only do so on grounds of policy if they have been given authority to do so by parliament.

There is, of course, a well known thorny issue here, for this approach assumes an ability to distinguish between policy reasons for restricting access and principled reasons for doing so. Which side of the policy/principle divide, for example, would a refusal of leave on grounds that there are insufficient resources to deal with the case fall? This appears to be a policy consideration, but might the decision be justified on grounds of principle if the judge can show that granting leave to the particular applicant will adversely affect the progress of other more worthy cases? I would argue that managerial factors such as this should be used to exclude access only if they can be shown to be justified on grounds of principle, and that this requires not only that judges have access to the relevant information on the way the system is functioning, but also that parties have similar information at their disposal. This inevitably requires a far more sophisticated and open management system than currently exists.

Turning now to the conceptual nature of rights of access in public law: access rights may take one of two forms, or be a combination of the two forms. They may be either *collateral rights* or *autonomous rights*. The term collateral refers to the right of access as a necessary and implicit element in the protection of other more substantive rights. An autonomous right of access is a free standing right existing irrespective of the specific nature of the substantive claims being made.

Access as a collateral right

I shall start by considering the uncontroversial claim that there is a right of access to the courts to seek the protection of substantive rights which are recognised by private law.[81] It is self-evident that access to the courts is important in private law because it underpins the existence of legally recognised rights and interests. Such rights are of little value if citizens cannot get to court to have them enforced. It is this principle that underlies the decision of the European Court of Human Rights in *Golder v United Kingdom*[82] that Article 6 of the European Convention on Human Rights implicitly requires states to respect the right of access to courts in order to protect 'civil rights and obligations'. It also underpins the European Community law requirement that member states must ensure the effective protection of Community law rights.[83]

In these situations the right of access and the substantive rights reinforce each other: the substantive rights are protected by access rights and the access rights owe much of their importance to the existence of the substantive rights. Whilst this strengthens the claim for a right of access, however, it also imposes a limitation upon it.

If the right of access is a collateral right, its existence is dependent on the existence of other rights and interests which are recognised by the court. In private law the only real question is whether there is a cause of action in the particular case. Restrictions on access tend to be crafted into the substantive law by statute or by the common law. So, for example, a person suing for breach of statutory duty has to show that he or she is within the class that was intended to be protected by the statute and plaintiffs relying on the tort of negligence have to establish that they are owed a duty of care by the defendant. In contractual claims the principles of consideration and privity have a similar limiting affect on those able to avail themselves of the right of access. This link between the principles of substantive law and access rights works to reinforce the importance of access in the following way.

The process by which the substantive law is developed by the common law assumes that judicial decisions are taken after hearing full argument from both sides.[84] The process of development of these rights, therefore, implies participation by both the parties. In this sense access plays a role both in ensuring that plaintiffs are able to participate in defining the scope of their rights and in helping to ensure that the courts are presented with relevant argument. Whilst prospective plaintiffs will not have participated in the definition of their access rights, at least they will be aware of the general constraints that are likely to be imposed by the substantive law prior to embarking on their case.

If we move away from private law to public law, the claim for a collateral right of access becomes rather more tenuous, for it depends on judicial recognition of rights and interests to which access can be attached.

It is no longer true that the gateways to public law are shut to all who lack rights in private law,[85] but can those seeking entry without such rights demand to have the gates opened, or must they hope that the gatekeepers will exercise a favourable discretion and allow them in?

There is no doubt that judicial review will now protect interests that fall short of rights.[86] The principles of legitimate expectations provide a clear example of this; and as Allan and Laws have shown, there is also plenty of room for arguing that private law rights are not the only form of rights which the courts ought to respect.

These arguments are strongest where individuals can show that their direct property, financial and personal interests have been adversely affected by governmental action.[87] In such situations there is a sound foundation for a collateral right of access. There may even be a case for removing the issue of access from the realm of discretion altogether. Support for such a view may exist in the Law Commission's recommendation that 'any person who has been adversely affected by a decision should normally be given standing as a matter of course'.[88]

More difficult are those situations where the applicant cannot, or does not wish to, rely on any personal adverse impacts. For present purposes two types of case may be distinguished. One is where the applicant, possibly an unincorporated group or a corporation, claims to represent others who have been personally affected. Cane says that such applicants are claiming 'associational standing'. The other type of case is where applicants claim to represent public interests which are not identified with the interests of specific individuals.[89]

In the *Greenpeace* case, to which I have already referred, Greenpeace relied on both 'associational standing'[90] and its right to represent the general public interest. By contrast, in *R. v Secretary of State for Foreign Affairs, ex parte World Development Movement Ltd*[91] there was no claim to associational status. Here the World Development Movement successfully challenged the decision of the Secretary of State to grant aid to finance the Pergau Dam project in Malaysia on the grounds that the project was not economically sound within the meaning of section 1 of the Overseas

Development and Co-operation Act 1980. The Movement was granted standing even though its application was not based on a claim that the Movement had been directly affected by the Secretary of State's decision.

Collateral rights and 'associational' applicants

Whether those claiming associational status can rely on a collateral right of access may depend on their ability to establish that they truly represent the interests of those who would have a right of access had they pursued the litigation. Various tests can be developed to determine whether an applicant is competent to represent others. There might, for example, be a requirement that those represented be members of the association that is the applicant, or that they have a financial commitment to it. After discussing the US cases,[92] Cane argues that the key test is whether those represented have a democratic stake in the association. This involves the existence of mechanisms by which their views can be ascertained so that the courts can determine whether the views put forward by the association are a fair reflection of those it purports to represent.

The idea that representative applicants be able to show that they have a democratic system for eliciting the views of those they claim to represent is laudable. It assumes, however, that associations are only competent to represent others if they possess a particular organisational structure. This would impose a considerable restriction on the type of body that is competent to litigate. As Cane acknowledges, it would, for example, exclude some of the leading interest groups from taking cases on behalf of others, including the Child Poverty Action Group and Greenpeace which do not have internal structures which would satisfy this democratic stake test. Moreover, it would also prevent those who do not join organisations with these formal internal structures[93] (and this includes many who are likely to be the most vulnerable and in greatest need of representation), from benefiting from associational status. This democratic stake test would, therefore, substantially limit the benefits to be gained by liberal tests of standing.[94]

Two further comments may be made. The first is that the democratic stake test assumes the willingness and ability of judges to investigate these internal matters. It is questionable whether they would be prepared to investigate such matters at the leave stage; but more important than this, it is also questionable whether they should be encouraged to do so.

The second comment is that the democratic stake test implies an unnecessarily narrow concept of representation. Arguably the key question is whether individuals or groups are adversely affected in the ways being alleged and if so, whether the applicant can show that it is competent to represent the relevant arguments to the court. Representation and competence in this context ought to refer to an applicant's ability to show that the legal claims being asserted are representative of those that arise from the challenged action. This need not require them to persuade the court that they actually represent the views of the actual individuals who are adversely affected.[95] This being so, it would be an unnecessary restriction on access to demand applicants to show that they possessed a particular type of internal structure, or that they have taken specific steps to establish the views of individuals. Their ability to show these things may help their case, but they ought not be pre-conditions to entry into the legal system.

Collateral rights and 'public interest' applicants

More difficult still is the World Development Movement type situation where the applicant does not claim either a personal interest or to represent others who have been directly affected. Is there any basis upon which such an applicant can claim a right of access on the type of collateral principle that I am now discussing?[96] The problem here is to identify rights or interests to which a right of access might be attached.

We can again turn to Cane who suggests a possible approach. This is to search for an 'argument which would justify allowing *the public*, in the guise of a representative of the public interest, access to the judicial process'. Drawing an analogy with the individual rights theory, he argues that 'we need to start with the proposition that the citizenry as a whole has certain interests which should be more or less immune from governmental curtailment or encroachment'. He concludes that such 'fundamental rights and interests' of the 'citizenry' can be discerned and that it is the proper job of the courts to protect these interests against the government.[97] Adopting this reasoning, it may be argued that a right of access to the courts will exist in order to seek judicial protection of these fundamental rights and interests.

There are several difficulties with this approach in the context of the present discussion. First, and most profoundly, arguments based on liberal theories of dignity tend to exaggerate levels of consensus about the nature of rights within an increasingly communitarian yet pluralist public law system. In so doing they place considerable trust in the ability of judges to give effect to this consensus by defining what is fundamental and what is not. In practice there are likely to be real difficulties discerning which applicants are representing fundamental interests and which are not, particularly in areas of controversy. Would, for instance, an applicant seeking access to the courts in order to protect the life of an unborn baby be in the same position as an applicant seeking access in order to protect the life of a ten-year-old? Part of the problem is that ideas about fundamental citizenry rights are (like talk of public interests generally) extremely abstract and may be easily hijacked by those seeking to exploit them for their own purposes. We might approve of this if the expressed goal is to protect the environment,[98] but some of us might feel less easy where applicants employ citizenry interests, say, to assert a right to litigate in order to frustrate the growing power of Europe[99] or to limit trade union activity.[100]

One way of reducing these difficulties is to argue that the interest in ensuring that government complies with the law is itself a fundamental interest to which a right of access can be attached. Such an argument avoids the need to link a right of access to independent substantive rights, and in so doing, roots it in more process orientated notions of legal accountability. The argument amounts to a claim that there is a general right of access in order to ask the courts to adjudicate upon any justiciable issue in public law. There may be a sound argument here, but if so, it involves stretching the concept of a collateral right of access to a point where it is effectively no longer collateral at all.

Access as an autonomous right

I can again start by considering the uncontroversial situation in private law. So far I have assumed that in private law the right of access serves and is collateral to other recognised rights. This may be true, but it is important to appreciate that whilst connected, the two sets of rights—the access rights and the substantive rights—are logically distinct from each other. Indeed, they are very different types of rights and they play very different roles within the system. This can be seen at the most elementary level by considering a contractual situation. The duty imposed upon X to comply with its contractual obligation to Y has nothing to do with any duty there may be to ensure that Y can get to court to enforce the contract. Rights of access in private law are not the product of rights and duties between the parties. Their character and their constitutive foundation are totally different. Whilst one party may have a duty not to impede another party's litigation,[101] this duty is not related to the contractual relationship and is usually understood to be owed to the court. The right of access that is protected by this duty does not depend on the contract either. It is a right that derives from more fundamental constitutional sources, the precise nature of which need not be identified for the moment.

The suggestion then is that in private law an autonomous right of access can be discerned. This is independent of those private rights which it can be used to protect. We can go further and say that the right of access, in fact, is not a product of private law at all: rather, it is an inherent feature of the legal and constitutional system. Its importance is obvious in private law, partly because of the uncontentious nature of the rights involved and partly because it is accepted that the public interest and policy issues that might impinge upon access are to be reconciled through the medium of substantive hearings into the merits of particular cases.

A similar case can now be made for an autonomous right of access in public law benefiting applicants who can show that they have been adversely affected by the action being challenged. It would also benefit applicants who are able to show that they are competent to represent those who have been adversely affected. In these situations the autonomous right argument strengthens the case for a collateral right and in turn is strengthened by it. It does not, however, widen the scope of potential beneficiaries of a right of access. Can the argument for an autonomous right of access take us further? Might it also be used by those who do not rely on such adverse effects?

There are various ways in which an argument of this nature might be put, but its essence would be to assert the basic right of citizens and groups to call upon the courts to impose the rule of law on government, irrespective of any direct harm that might have been caused to them by governmental action. It might appeal to the principle underpinning the decisions on leave in both the *Greenpeace* and *Pergau Dam* cases that the courts should not allow governmental illegality to go unchallenged if a competent applicant is prepared and able to make a sound case that illegality has occurred.[102]

The claim might also find support in the approach adopted by Sir John Laws. There is much in what he says that seems to assume that the common law respects a fundamental right to gain access to the courts in order to have justiciable issues involving governmental illegality resolved (even where private law rights are not in issue). He reminds us, for example, that in *Anisminic v Foreign Compensation Commission*[103] the House of Lords applied the common law presumption that parliament does not intend to '. . . oust the court's power of review' to justify overriding 'the apparently plain words of an ouster clause'.[104] The clear implication is that Sir John Laws regards this decision as an illustration of the way fundamental rights—here access to the courts—have for long been recognised as being so deeply imbedded in the common law that they can only be explicitly limited by the clearest words of parliament.

One point should be emphasised. Each of these principles is compatible with either imperium or community based approaches. An argument for rights, however, has to claim that access is not a matter of pure discretion to be determined by judges in the light, for example, of their perception of the best interests of the system. This may lead to access, but only on the basis that access is a privilege. An argument for a right, therefore, has to assert that there is a community based value in ensuring that government is complying with the law and that this value imposes an obligation upon the courts to adjudicate upon credible legal claims. Upon what principles might such a claim be based?

The basis of the right of access

As we have seen, Allan bases his conception of rights in public law on the liberal theory of individual dignity. This approach may be satisfactory in situations where applicants are seeking to protect their individual inviolability by showing that they have been directly adversely affected. It is less adequate, however, where applicants do not rely on personal interests of this type. Cane has responded to this by arguing that the citizenry in general has rights. I have suggested, however, that this approach is also problematical, in particular because it underestimates the controversial nature of such rights.

A sounder and less artificial base for an autonomous right of access to the courts in public law might lie in democracy itself. Ideas of democracy extend beyond principles of parliamentary representation to embrace wider participative values including the right of citizens to participate more generally in political and legal affairs, irrespective of the nature of the substantive claims being asserted.[105] An argument for access rights based on such a conception of participative democracy might run as follows.

Although imperium denies the courts an independent base of democratic authority, it is now clear that the courts do play a central role in the democratic life of the system. The ability of citizens to participate in the work of the courts in ensuring that government is legally accountable is an important facet of this democracy. Moreover, the courts are themselves an important institution of power within the system, and for this reason alone citizens should have a right to gain access to them. I have argued that the right of plaintiffs to participate in the development of private law has been implicit in the nature of the private law system. Opportunities to participate in the development of public law are no less important in order to ensure, *inter alia,* that the courts are equipped to decide public interest issues.[106] By rooting access rights in democracy, it is possible to provide the expanding judicial review jurisdiction with a more reliable source of legitimacy than it currently possesses.[107]

My argument then is that there are several ways of constructing a theoretical, conceptual and constitutional base for a right of access in public law which can be asserted by those who claim to be adversely affected by governmental action, and by applicants who do not claim such injury. My preference is to base this right on democratic principles which demand that citizens be able to participate in the political and legal life of the community. Whatever its base, the right is confined by the parameters of jurisdiction and, therefore, can only be claimed by those able to make a credible case that an abuse of legal power has occurred. The right is not absolute and in practice its exercise will be mediated by judicial discretion. Its existence means that judges are obliged to treat the applicant's right of entry as having a priority over other interests so that it demands respect, unless judges can show a principled justification for excluding the case.

The Culture of Access and Reform

How might such a right be translated into the working practice of judicial review? The arguments I have discussed lend support to those who have argued against the imposition of the leave requirement and other preliminary filters to access.[108] That battle, however, appears to have been lost. Even so, arguments for a right of access still have an important part to play. They will help to provide a principled defence against the view that access is purely discretionary and is to be granted as a matter of largesse depending on the balance of unspecified public interests and managerial convenience. The call I am making is essentially for a cultural recognition of a right and for its furtherance and promotion by reformers, judges and administrators. It is relevant both to the design of the structure of the system and to the system's daily operation.

Unfortunately, as far as future reform of the structure of the system is concerned, the prospects are not good. Specific recommendations of the Law Commission fit very well with the culture of rights and participation.[109] These include its view that the criteria for refusing leave should be 'explicated clearly in the Rules';[110] its general attitude to the liberalisation of standing;[111] and its recommendations that judges should provide reasons for refusing leave.[112] The Law Commission's recommendations on procedural exclusivity[113] and its proposals on transfer into and out of judicial review will also limit the harshness of the principle and add welcome clarity.[114] Its recommendation that costs may be awarded out of central funds is also positive.[115]

The general tenor of the report, however, seems set to create a system which in several major respects will be even more inhospitable to the culture of access than the current system is. The nature of the proposed preliminary filter and the criteria for restricting access to substantive hearings are two prime examples.[116]

The preliminary filter: a legal stage or an administrative obstacle?

In the past it has generally been assumed that decisions on access to judicial review should be taken by judges in public as part of a judicial process. There are indications in the Law Commission's report that this view is now changing and that access is to become more akin to an administrative matter. Some history will help to put the significance of this shift of attitude into context.

When the leave procedure was first debated by the House of Lords in 1933, there was concern that the Bill contained no specific reference to the public nature of the process. Lord Atkin reminded the government that it had always been regarded as a matter of 'considerable moment' that applications to move for the prerogative writs be considered by judges in public.[117] Lord Hanworth, the Master of the Rolls, responded saying that the government was alive to the importance of this; and in due course the public nature of the process was enshrined in the Rules. In its 1976 report the Law Commission accepted both that leave applications ought to be dealt with in public and that decisions refusing leave should be taken by a three judge Divisional Court.[118] Chinks in the sanctity of the principle of openness first started to appear in the early 1980s when the written procedure for seeking leave was first introduced. Use of the written procedure, however, has up until now been voluntary, and applicants who are initially unsuccessful have the safeguard of being able to renew their applications in open court.

The Law Commission has recommended that several significant steps be taken away from these principles of openness. In particular, it recommends that the 'preliminary consideration' should be determined entirely on the papers, unless immediate interim relief is sought or it appears, on the basis of written material, to the Crown Office or a judge that a hearing is desirable in the interests of justice.[119] The use of civil servants in taking decisions about whether access issues should be determined in public or not is particularly significant, for it represents a step away from treating access as a judicial rather than an administrative matter.

The obligatory use of written procedures is likely, if existing data are a guide, to substantially increase the proportion of applicants who will be refused permission to proceed to a hearing.[120] If so, this will increase the importance of the right to renew. No doubt aware of this, and of the administrative costs involved in handling large numbers of renewals, the Law Commission has recommended that steps be taken to deter applicants from renewing. The Law Commission, for instance, reminds lawyers that they are under the professional duty to 'consider carefully whether it is reasonable to renew'.[121] Edge is given to this reminder by the recommendation that judges be given power to award costs against applicants who unsuccessfully renew their initial application in open court. This, says the Law Commission, will impose a 'discipline' on applicants.[122] Such proposals do not augur well for the culture of access.

The criteria for refusing access

In the face of criticism that the leave criteria are too vague and uncertain, and of suspicion that their stringency reflects the current state of the Crown Office list, the Law Commission has recognised the need to have the criteria spelt out more clearly.[123] Unfortunately, in its attempt to clarify, the Law Commission has settled on a form of words that appears to increase the potential burden facing applicants and to add a new dimension of uncertainty.

The Law Commission recognises that the preliminary filter is concerned with rejecting hopeless applications, but chooses neither to use 'hopelessness' nor 'arguability' in its proposed criteria. Instead, it imposes what appears to be a new test: the need to establish a 'serious issue to be tried'. By way of explanation of its thinking, it says that '[t]his reformulation recognises, *inter alia*, that one of the main purposes of having a filter is to protect public bodies from unmeritorious applications . . .'[124]

I have argued elsewhere that the arguability test is not without its problems.[125] Arguability, however, does have the virtue of requiring judges to focus on the specific merits of the application. The 'serious issue to be tried' test, in the form advocated by the Law Commission, is potentially a very different and more uncertain animal. The key problem lies in the word 'serious'. Is seriousness to be determined only by reference to the merits of the application, or is it to be assessed in the light of wider public interest considerations, including available judicial resources? Might an application which is serious in its own right be considered less than serious when compared with other applications, or when the issues in the case are considered against the desire to make efficient use of judge time? In its attempt to add clarity the Law Commission appears to have recommended replacing an imperfect arguability test—which at least is based on sound principle—with an even less certain and potentially more stringent test.

The source of the 'serious issue' test is worth commenting on since it appears that the Law Commission was influenced by an article that Andrew Le Sueur and I wrote.[126] In that article we argued that there should be a presumption in favour of granting leave and that leave should be refused, *inter alia*, if there were *no* serious issues to be tried. Our intention was to remove the burden from applicants and to lower the leave threshold. It seems that the Law Commission may have taken one part of our package and inverted it, so that what was originally a presumption in favour of leave has become a recommendation that applicants should have to surmount a new obstacle.

If the Law Commission was mainly concerned with filtering hopeless applications and did not intend to increase the burden or to add uncertainty, there are several alternative formulations of the leave criteria which seem better suited to achieve these objects than the 'serious issue' test. It could, for example, have recommended a test of 'hopelessness' or 'arguability'; or it could have simply dropped the word 'serious' and retained the obligation to show 'an issue to be tried'. This would fit well with the right of access and would be compatible with the approach advocated in this chapter. In particular, it would reduce suspicion that ease of access depends on the length of the Crown Office list.

Implementing a right of access and managerial freedom

No doubt the problem is that such a formulation would reduce judicial discretion in a way that is now considered unacceptable and impracticable in the light of the resource pressures on the system.

If this is so, one of the real challenges is to develop an approach to resource management that is compatible with a right of access, rather than one which is not. This would require a system that enables judges to take account of managerial needs when considering individual applications, and to apply these considerations on a principled basis. There are certain basic characteristics that such a system ought to possess. It ought, for example, to enable judges to take decisions on the basis of actual information about caseload pressures and trends rather than on the basis of their anecdotal impressions. This, in turn, requires judges to understand what the pressures really are and, of vital importance, how these pressures actually impact upon the particular decisions being taken. It is important also that applicants and their advisers have access to the relevant data and are in a position to comment upon it.

The problems in establishing such systems are not to be underestimated, but they are not insurmountable.

The first step is to build upon our current knowledge of the system to ensure that all users have available to them a regular flow of information, for example, about caseload trends, that is supported by a detailed analysis.

The aim should be to ensure that applicants are in a position to address managerial concerns as fully as possible and to enable judges to be more open about managerialism in the hope that this will reduce the tendency towards the use of hidden criteria.

Let me illustrate the way this might work. Suppose a judge is tempted to exclude a particular application partly because of concern about the pressure on the caseload. It would be inappropriate for the judge simply to resort to a generalised worry about delays or numbers of cases. It would be better, but not sufficient, for the judge to say that exclusion of this case would broadly benefit access of others. What the judge really needs, however, is access to data and analysis that shows in what way this case is likely to exacerbate delays or impose other pressures; and this should be used when providing a justification for denying access. Ideally, this information should be available to the applicant who may want to dispute the inferences which have been drawn on a renewal or on appeal. This of course requires both sophisticated management techniques and a culture that is amenable to access and the demands of principle. It requires, however, no more than judges expect of others who have power over citizens.

To Conclude

Those who say that the Law Commission's report shows an intent to render judicial review more permeable may be correct. The extent to which the system becomes more accessible to the general litigant will, however, depend on whether the current socio-legal and economic obstacles to access remain and on the attitudes which judges bring to bear to their discretionary decisions on access issues. There is no sign that the practical obstacles to gaining access to judicial review will diminish. As for judicial discretion, much depends on whether judges regard access to be a privilege available, in particular, to those able to provide functional benefits to a resource strapped legal system, or whether they take the view that access is a right. I have sought to argue that access to judicial review should be regarded as a right which is rooted in principles of democracy. I have also tried to show that this approach to access issues need not exacerbate pressure on judicial resources, but may well provide a sounder, more principled basis for caseload management.

I would like to thank Peter Cane, Richard Rawlings and Ian Loveland for allowing me to see papers prior to their publication in the forthcoming volume edited by Ian Loveland A special Relationship? American Influences on Public Law in the UK, *(Oxford) 1995. I would also like to thank Lee Bridges, Peter Cane, Richard Rawlings, Genevra Richardson and Bob Watt for their helpful comments on an earlier draft of this chapter.*

Notes

1. [1983] 1 AC 1, at 13.
2. Per Steyn LJ., *R. v Secretary of State, ex p. Leech* [1993] 4 All ER 539, at 548.
3. Lord Scarman, 'The Development of Administrative Law: Obstacles and Opportunities' [1990] PL 490, 492.
4. Per Lord Donaldson MR in *R. v Panel on Takeovers and Mergers, ex p. Guinness plc* [1990] 1 QB 146, at 177–8.
5. David Feldman, 'Public Interest Litigation and Constitutional Theory in Comparative Perspective' (1992) 55 MLR 44.
6. Cf. J. Raz, 'The Rule of Law and its Virtue' (1977) 93 LQR 195.
7. *Anisminic v Foreign Compensation Commission* [1969] 2 AC 147. See the Hon. Sir John Laws, 'Is the High Court the Guardian of Fundamental Constitutional Rights?' [1993] PL 59, at 78.
8. *Chester v Bateson* [1920] 1 KB 829; *R. v Secretary of State, ex p. Leech,* above, n. 2.
9. *Raymond v Honey* above, n. 1.
10. Art. 6. *Golder v United Kingdom* (1975) series A, n. 18 and 1 *EHRR* 524; and *Airey v Ireland* (1979) series A, No. 32 and 2 *EHRR* 305. On Art. 6 see further: P. Van Dijk and G.J.H. Van Hoof, *Theory and Practice of the European Convention on Human Rights* (Kluwer 2nd edn) p. 294; R. Beddard, *Human Rights and Europe* (3rd edn) ch. 7.
11. *Administrative Law* (7th edn 1994), H.W.R. Wade and C.F. Forsyth, p. 877.
12. R. Dworkin, *Taking Rights Seriously* (1977) esp. ch. 4.
13. Cf. the approach of Alan Boyle in 'Freedom of Expression as a Public Interest in English Law' [1982] PL 574.
14. As is evident from recent controversies surrounding access to treatment in the National Health Service, this is not a problem unique to judicial review or the legal system: *R. v Cambridge & Huntingdon Health Committee, ex p. B.: The Independent* 14 March 1995; *The Times* 15 March 1995; [1995] 2 All ER 129(CA).
15. Subject to limitation periods and technical procedural requirements. Of course, access to the courts may also be necessary in order to obtain interim relief or interlocutory orders.
16. There is no leave requirement in Scotland. The Law Commission has recommended that in future the procedure should be described as the 'preliminary consideration' stage. This, it believed, would help to remove the perception that applicants for judicial review are at a substantive disadvantage as compared with plaintiffs in private law proceedings. Law Commission, *Administrative Law: Judicial Review and Statutory Appeal,* Law Com., No. 226 (1994) paras 5.6–5.8. See, for comparison the chapters by C. Himsworth and G. Hogan, below. For comments on the Law Commission's recommendations, see below, n. 109.
17. It may be noted that *ex parte* applications for leave are not legal proceedings for the purposes of the award of costs, but *inter partes* hearings are: *Secretary of State for Wales v Rozhon* [1994] COD 111.
18. Settlement of cases which may raise important public law issues has implications for the effectiveness of judicial review as a system of control over government. Lee Bridges and I are currently co-directing an ESRC funded project on the Dynamics of Judicial Review Litigation. One of the concerns of this project is to study settlement in judicial review proceedings.

19. On third party intervention, see Carol Harlow and Richard Rawlings, *Pressure Through Law* (Routledge 1992), 310–314. There is currently a Public Law Project/Justice working party on third party interventions. A report is due by summer 1995.
20. In particular: *R. v Secretary of State for Foreign Affairs, ex p. Rees-Mogg* [1994] 1 All ER 457; *R. v Inspectorate of Pollution, ex p. Greenpeace (No. 2)* [1994] 4 All ER 329; *R. v Secretary of State for the Home Department, ex p. Fire Brigades Union* [1995] 2 All ER 244; *R. v Secretary of State for Foreign Affairs, ex p. World Development Movement Ltd* [1995] 1 All ER 611. On this case see Stephen Grosz, 'Pergau be Dammed' NLJ (1994) vol. 144, 1708. For recent discussions of standing see in particular Sir Konrad Schiemann, 'Locus Standi' [1990] PL 342; David Feldman, 'Public Interest Litigation and Constitutional Theory in Comparative Perspective' (1992) 55 MLR 44; Peter Cane, 'Standing, Representation and the Environment' in Ian Loveland (ed.) *A Special Relationship? American Influences on Public Law in the UK* (Oxford 1995); Peter Cane, 'Standing Up for the Public' [1995] PL 276. Also, *Public Interest Perspectives in Environmental Law*, Robinson and Dunkley eds (1995) Wiley Chancery, esp. chs 3, 10, and 11.
21. See A.P. Le Sueur, 'Justifying Judicial Caution: Jurisdiction, Justiciability and Policy', below.
22. Cf. P.P. Craig who refers to natural justice, standing and the ability to apply for relief as 'gateways to administrative law'. *Public Law and Democracy* (1990) Oxford University Press, p. 27.
23. Cf. Justice-All Souls, *Administrative Justice: Some Necessary Reforms* (1988) para. 6.23, p. 152. Whilst this chapter concentrates on judicial review, there are signs that similar issues are likely to become more pertinent in other proceedings as well. See *Access to Justice*, the Right Hon. Lord Woolf June 1995.
24. Law Comm., op. cit., n. 16 parts II and V.
25. Cf. the approach taken to access to the courts in environmental matters in the US and Switzerland. Note that there is a draft directive on Access to Justice in Environmental Matters currently before the European Commission: see Robinson and Dunkley, op. cit., n. 21, ch. 3.
26. e.g. Andrew Le Sueur and Maurice Sunkin, 'Applications for Judicial Review: The Requirement of Leave' [1992] PL 102.
27. Cf. Andrew Le Sueur and Maurice Sunkin, op. cit., n. 26.
28. But see Lord Diplock's statement that leave should be granted 'if, on a quick perusal of the material then available, the court thinks that it discloses what might on further investigation turn out to be an arguable case . . .' per Lord Diplock, in *IRC v National Federation of Self-employed and Small Businesses Ltd* [1981] 2 All ER 93, at p. 106 f–g. Cf. Lord Donaldson MR in *Winch v Jones* [1985] 3 All ER 97, at 102 c–d; and in *R. v Legal Aid Board, ex p. Hughes* 24 HLR (1992) 698.
29. Law Comm., op. cit., n. 16.
30. Particularly for those who do not live in London and the south-east, ibid., para. 2.28 (d).
31. ibid., paras 2.3–2.7.
32. ibid., para. 3.13.
33. Cf. Lord Woolf, *Protection of the Public: A New Challenge* (1990) p. 101 and Lord Justice Donaldson (as he then was) in *Parr v Wyre* BC [1982] HLR 71, at 80.
34. M. Galanter, 'Why the "Haves" Come Out Ahead: Speculations on the Limits of Legal Change' (1974) 9 *Law and Society Review* 95. Although typical, this representation of the relative strengths and experience of the parties does not always apply. It is not uncommon for applicants to be powerful and well resourced and it is not unknown for respondents to be relatively inexperienced. A well-directed challenge by an experienced pressure group against a public agency that has not been previously challenged, for example, would not fit within the generalisation.
35. Lee Bridges, 'Costs and Obtaining Legal Aid', ch. 3 in *An Applicant's Guide to Judicial Review*, Sweet & Maxwell (1995) (forthcoming); Stephen Grosz, 'Access to Environmental Justice in Public Law' in Robinson and Dunkley, op. cit., n. 20.

36. D. Forbes and S. Wright, *Housing Cases in Nine CABx*, unpublished (1990).
37. M. Sunkin, L. Bridges and G. Mészáros, *Judicial Review in Perspective: An Investigation of Trends in the Use and Operation of the Judicial Review Procedure in England and Wales* (1993) Public Law Project. See also B. Hadfield and E. Weaver, 'Judicial Review in Perspective (NI)' (1995) NILQ (forthcoming).
38. Sunkin *et al.*, ibid., ch. 3.
39. Sunkin *et al.*, ibid., at p. 76.
40. The ESRC funded research referred to above, n. 18, should throw light on this.
41. For a discussion of club principles in the context of judicial review, see Martin Loughlin, 'Courts and Governance', ch. 9 in P.B.H. Birks (ed.) *The Frontiers of Liability*, vol. 1 (1994). Also Andrew Le Sueur and Maurice Sunkin, op. cit., n. 26.
42. Roger Cotterrell, 'Judicial Review and Legal Theory' in *Administrative Law & Government Action*, Richardson and Genn (eds) (1994) Oxford University Press.
43. ibid., at p. 26.
44. See generally P.P. Craig, op. cit., n. 22, esp. ch. 2. For a discussion of judicial attitudes to democracy, see D. Feldman, op. cit., n. 5; also the Hon. Sir John Laws, 'Law and Democracy' [1995] PL 72.
45. [1986] AC 484 (HL); also *R. v Secretary of State for Home Affairs, ex p. Swati* [1986] 1 All ER 717. See M. Sunkin, 'What is Happening to Applications for Judicial Review' (1987) 50 MLR 46. See further B. Hadfield, below.
46. Sir Konrad Schiemann, op. cit., n. 20.
47. [1994] 4 All ER 329. See further Colin Reid, below.
48. ibid., 350 d–e.
49. ibid., e–j.
50. On the Attorney General, see generally J. Edwards, *The Attorney General, Politics and the Public Interest* (1984) Sweet and Maxwell. For a more specific discussion, see Sir Konrad Schiemann, op. cit., n. 20.
51. See Carol Harlow and Richard Rawlings, op. cit., n. 19, pp 144–5; *Gouriet v Union of Post Office Workers* [1977] 3 WLR 300; P. Mercer, 'The Gouriet Case: Public Interest Litigation in Britain and Canada' [1979] PL 214.
52. *IRC v National Federation of Self-employed and Small Businesses Ltd*, above, n. 28, per Lord Diplock, at 107.
53. See Sir Harry Woolf, 'Public Law-Private Law: Why the Divide? A Personal View' [1986] PL 220. Cf. M. Sunkin, 'Judicial Review: Rights and Discretion in Public Law' (1983) 46 MLR 645.
54. The principle requires litigants to use the judicial review procedure in public law matters. See in particular *O'Reilly v Mackman* [1983] 2 AC 237; *Roy v Kensington and Chelsea and Westminster FPC* [1992] 1 AC 624; Law Comm., op. cit., n. 16, pt III.
55. In 1991 Lord Woolf likened judicial review to a motorway where the 'tailback, or backlogs are becoming more disturbing. The use of judicial review has grown and is continuing to grow at a pace with which the present structure cannot cope.' Lord Woolf, Administrative Law Bar Association Annual Lecture, 4 November 1991.
56. M. Sunkin, 'The Judicial Review Caseload, 1987–1989' [1991] PL 490.
57. For example, we do not know how many litigants decide to apply for leave even though they do not intend to pursue their application to a substantive hearing.
58. The Hon. Sir John Laws, op. cit., n. 7.
59. Cotterrell reminds us that Hart ridiculed Austin's top-down conception of law as being 'threadbare': op. cit., n. 42, at p. 21.
60. ibid., at p. 19.
61. Cotterrell emphasises that the image of community which legal theory and practice presents is an essentially elitist image. The values enshrined in the common law, he points out, are not based on and do not necessarily reflect the actual values of the community, but the 'artificial reason' of the common law which represents the views and values of 'judicial decision-makers, legal experts and other opinion-forming elites':

ibid., at p. 30. The image of community is, therefore, not an image of 'popular participation' or an image of 'political society as a living community of people having the practical . . . means to establish and elaborate beliefs they can share'. ibid., at p. 32. See also Martin Loughlin, op. cit., n. 41.

62. See Lord Lester, 'European Human Rights and the British Constitution' in *The Changing Constitution* (3rd edn 1994) Jeffrey Jowell and Dawn Oliver (eds) Oxford University Press.

63. e.g. T.R.S. Allan, 'Pragmatism and Theory in Public Law' (1988) 104 LQR 422; T.R.S. Allan, 'Constitutional Rights and Common Law' (1991) vol. 11, n. 4, OJLS, 453; and see further T.R.S. Allan, *Law, Liberty and Justice* (1993) Oxford University Press. Also, the Hon. Sir John Laws, op. cit., n. 7; Peter Cane, 'Standing, Representation and the Environment', op. cit., n. 20.

64. Ian Harden and Norman Lewis, *The Noble Lie* (1986) (Hutchinson) esp. ch. 7; Dawn Oliver, 'Is the *Ultra Vires* Rule the Basis of Review?' [1987] PL 543.

65. J. Jowell and A. Lester, 'Beyond *Wednesbury*: Substantive Principles of Administrative Law' [1987] PL 368.

66. M. Cappelletti, *The Judicial Process in Comparative Perspective* (1989) Oxford Clarendon p. 131.

67. J.A.G. Griffith, 'The Political Constitution' (1979) 42 MLR 1.

68. For a discussion of process theories, see Genevra Richardson, *Law, Process and Custody: Prisoners and Patients* (1993), Weidenfeld and Nicolson, chs 2 and 3; see also her essay, 'The Legal Regulation of Process' in *Administrative Law & Government Action*, Genevra Richardson and H. Genn eds (1994) Oxford University Press.

69. T.R.S. Allan, op. cit., n. 63.

70. Sir Harry Woolf, op. cit., n. 53, at p. 221.

71. Also J.H. Grey, 'Discretion in Administrative Law' [1979] OHLJ, vol. 17, 107, esp pp 107–110.

72. T.R.S. Allan, 'Pragmatism and Theory in Public Law', op. cit., n. 63, at p. 436.

73. ibid., at p. 438.

74. The Hon. Sir John Laws, op. cit., n. 7.

75. ibid. See also his judgment in *ex p. B.*, above, n. 14.

76. Op. cit., n. 7, at p. 74 (notes omitted and emphasis added). In *ex p. B.*, above n. 14, Laws J., having referred to the right to life as a fundamental right vindicated by the common law, said that the first question to be considered was 'whether the respondents had taken a decision which interfered with the applicant's right to life and, if they had, whether they had a substantial public interest justification for doing so'.

77. See further A.P. Le Sueur, below.

78. *IRC v National Federation of Self-employed and Small Businesses Ltd*, above, n. 28; *R. v Monopolies and Mergers Commission, ex p. Argyll Group plc* [1986] 2 All ER 257, esp. Lord Donaldson MR at 265.

79. RSC Order 18, r. 19.

80. R. Dworkin, op. cit., n. 12.

81. The existence of this right is reflected by the general principle that permission of the court is not normally required in order to proceed to trial in private law.

82. See above, n. 10.

83. It has been argued that this principle may limit the power of parliament and the courts to restrict access by imposing narrow standing rules: see Peter Cane, 'Standing, Representation and the Environment' op. cit., n. 20. Whilst the ECJ has so far had little to say about standing in domestic law, recent decisions have indicated a greater tendency to become involved in the effectiveness of national enforcement, e.g. *R. v Secretary of State for Transport, ex p. Factortame* [1990] 3 CMLR 1.

84. Statute raises other issues since it is assumed that statutory rights are the product of political participation.

85. Cf. P.P. Craig, *Public Law and Democracy*, loc. cit., n. 22.

86. It is sometimes suggested that judges have been able to extend the scope of judicial review because of the controls which exist over access. Note that the scope of rights to which access may be claimed under Art. 6 of the European Convention on Human Rights has also been gradually extended. On this, see van Dijk and van Hoof and also Beddard, op. cit., n. 10.
87. Feldman, for example, has argued that liberal theory would imply that individuals should have the right to gain access to the courts in order to protect their own material interests, but access to protect or promote broader public interests or ideological concerns would be more problematic. David Feldman, op. cit., n. 5.
88. Law Comm., op. cit., n. 16, para. 5.20.
89. Peter Cane, 'Standing, Representation and the Environment' op cit., n. 20.
90. In so far as it was representing the interests of others.
91. [1995] 1 All ER 611. See further Colin Reid, below.
92. In particular, *Hunt v Washington State Apple Advertising Commission* (1977) 432 US 333.
93. Again, as Cane acknowledges.
94. According to Cane, applicants who cannot satisfy the democratic stake test might, nonetheless, be able to get to court as representatives of the public interest.
95. In this sense representation is more akin to the idea of a representative sample: see Anthony H. Birch, *The Concepts and Theories of Modern Democracy* (1993) Routledge, ch. 3. Cf. R. Rawlings, 'Legal Politics and Ratification of the Treaty on European Union' (pt 2) [1994] PL 367, at p. 371.
96. The Law Commission has recommended that in such cases standing should be a matter of discretion and should only be conferred if the judge considers this to be in the public interest. Law Comm., op. cit., n. 16 paras 5.21–5.22.
97. Peter Cane, 'Standing, Representation and the Environment', op. cit., n. 20. Like Laws he is unable to provide an exhaustive catalogue of these interests, but he includes by way of example: interests in securing the observance by government of basic constitutional principles such as the need to gain parliamentary approval to impose taxation; the interest in public and open justice; and freedom of information.
98. There is much current debate as to whether an interest in the environment would constitute a fundamental right. See generally Robinson and Dunkley, op. cit., n. 20.
99. In *R. v Secretary of State for Foreign and Commonwealth Affairs, ex p. Rees-Mogg* [1994] 1 All ER QB 552; the Divisional Court granted the applicant standing because he had a 'sincere concern for constitutional issues'.
100. *Gouriet*, above, n. 51.
101. The duty might ultimately be enforced by proceedings for contempt of court: see *Raymond v Honey*, above, n. 1; *ex p. Leech*, above n. 2.
102. See also Lord Diplock in *IRC v National Federation of Self-employed and Small Businesses Ltd* above, n. 28. Cf. *R. v Secretary of State for the Environment, ex p. Rose Theatre Trust Co.* [1990] QB 504 and particularly Schiemann J.'s statement that it is not the function of the courts 'to be there for every individual who was interested in having the legality of an administrative action litigated'.
103. [1969] 2 AC 147.
104. The Hon. Sir John Laws, op. cit., n. 7, at p. 78. See also his 'Law and Democracy', op. cit., n. 44.
105. See Genevra Richardson, above, especially her 'The Legal Regulation of Process', op. cit., n. 68.
106. A similar argument may be made regarding third party interventions.
107. Genevra Richardson develops a similar argument to support the view that citizens have a right to expect governmental institutions to comply with the principles of 'full process'. A right to gain access to the courts to enable judges to further these principles is implicit in her approach. See op. cit., n. 68.
108. e.g. Justice-All Souls, op. cit., n. 23, para. 6.23, p. 152.

109. For comments on the Law Commission's recommendations, see Carol Harlow, 'Public Interest Challenges: New Directions?', *Legal Action*, February 1995, p. 6; Richard Gordon QC, 'The Law Commission and Judicial Review: Managing the tensions between case management and public interest challenges' [1995] PL 11.
110. Law Comm., op. cit., n. 16, para. 5.14.
111. ibid., paras 5.16–5.22.
112. ibid., para. 5.36.
113. above, n. 54.
114. Law Comm., op. cit., n. 16, pt III.
115. ibid., paras 10.5–10.6.
116. Cf. Richard Rawling's view that the Law Commission's report shows a clear 'intent to render judicial review more permeable, at the initial stage of access to court'.
117. H.L. Debs, vol. 88, col. 119 (15 June, 1933). See Andrew Le Sueur and Maurice Sunkin, op. cit., n. 26, at p. 109.
118. Law Comm., 1976, Cmnd. 6407, para. 40.
119. Law Comm., op. cit., n. 16, para 5.9–5.11. See B. Hadfield and E. Weaver, op. cit., n. 37.
120. Sunkin *et al.* op. cit., n. 37, ch. 5.
121. Law Comm., op. cit., n. 16, at para. 5.12.
122. ibid., para. 10.3.
123. The Law Commission said that it does not propose departing from the existing grounds: ibid., para. 5.14.
124. ibid., para. 5.15.
125. Andrew Le Sueur and Maurice Sunkin, op. cit., n. 26.
126. See Richard Gordon QC, op. cit., n. 109, at p. 14.

Chapter Two

Judicial Review and the Environment

Colin T. Reid

This is in some ways a difficult time at which to be writing about judicial review and the environment. A few years ago this chapter would have had a different name and would have been devoted solely to a consideration of the role of the courts in the system of town and country planning, with the occasional reference to related matters such as the approval of new roads and the compulsory purchase orders made under the planning and related legislation. Today, however, the rise in concern for environmental issues is starting to manifest itself in increasing recourse to the courts across a much broader front of environmental law. This is not a one-sided phenomenon as litigation is being started both by those who feel that the law is not adequately protecting the environment and by those who consider that environmental controls are unduly restricting their freedom of action. As yet, though, it is difficult to discern any clear pattern to such litigation or to identify any particular 'environmental' features in the courts' handling of it. In a few years' time a clearer pattern may emerge, but at present only a fragmentary picture is apparent.

It follows that planning law remains the biggest influence on what is covered in this chapter, but I hope to be able to present a broader view of when and how judicial review is employed. A number of legal issues which are of general application but have been of particular significance in this field will then be considered, for example, restrictions on legal standing and the effect of provisions trying to prevent judicial review in the interests of certainty, and some features which appear more distinctive, for example, the increasing significance of European law.

One major point relating to procedure must be made at this stage. In the environmental field the courts are often called into action, not by means of a standard application for judicial review, but through an express statutory mechanism for challenging the validity of official decisions or actions. Thus most of the cases in which judges are asked to consider the legality of decisions in relation to planning matters reach them through the statutory procedure provided for such recourse to the courts.[1] Similar provisions are found in many other environmental regimes.[2] As these procedures fulfil exactly the same function as judicial review, for the purposes of this chapter, both are discussed together.[3]

There are, however, some significant aspects of the statutory procedures which must be mentioned. First, the right to challenge a decision is normally granted to a 'person aggrieved', and this may set a test for standing slightly different from that applying in the standard procedures. This is discussed more fully below in relation to Standing. Secondly, the statutory procedures are normally accompanied by fairly tight time-limits, so that the opportunity to question the validity of a decision is lost if the procedure is not invoked within, say, six weeks. Again this, and the courts' attitude to attempts to prevent any review of the legality of action once such time-limits have expired, are discussed below in relation to Exclusion of Review.

A third point is that the grounds on which the courts can intervene may be slightly different. The planning provisions, for example, allow two grounds on which the validity of decisions, notices or orders can be questioned. The first is that, in relation to an authority's failure to follow the prescribed procedural steps in making a decision, the statutory provisions say that the court should intervene only if the applicant has been 'substantially prejudiced by a failure to comply with any of the relevant requirements'.[4] In order to establish such prejudice there is no need to prove that the outcome would have been different if the procedure had been properly followed. It is sufficient that the applicant has suffered 'the loss of a *chance* of being better off'[5] and it has been said that 'where an applicant has been deprived of the exercise of a right conferred upon him by Parliament, that fact alone would appear . . . prima facie to indicate that he has suffered substantial prejudice'.[6] On the other hand, if a party makes no objection to an alleged irregularity at the time, this may weaken a subsequent argument that substantial prejudice has been caused.[7] The requirement to show prejudice may in practice, therefore, add little to the courts' general discretion to refuse a remedy even where some illegality has been discovered,[8] but does help to minimise the risk of proceedings being overthrown on the basis of a minor technicality which had no effect on the substance of what occurred.

The second aspect of the statutory formulation of the courts' powers is that the court is empowered to intervene where the order or action in question 'is not within the powers of this Act'.[9] Although there were arguments that this encompassed a narrower range of matters than the common law grounds on which action can be held to be *ultra vires*,[10] it is now generally accepted that the scope of the courts' powers in both cases is essentially the same. The current position was neatly expressed by Lord Dunpark in *Lithgow v Secretary of State for Scotland*:[11]

[if] a Minister exercises a statutory power in a manner prohibited by common law, that, in my opinion, is just as much a non-exercise of his statutory powers as the purported exercise of non-existent powers.

This broader approach has led to the courts tending to run together the two grounds of challenge in the statutory provisions, and in the '*Ashbridge* formula'[12] and other broad statements,[13] the courts in describing the scope of their powers to intervene under the statutory provisions have provided summaries which would be valid as a description of their powers at common law. The differences between statutory challenge to the validity of a decision and challenge at common law are, therefore, essentially ones of procedure, not substance.

Even where statutory procedures exist there may be room for applications for judicial review in the normal way.[14] Some decisions fall outside the scope of the statutory procedures described above; examples within the planning system include the Secretary of State's decision on whether to decide an appeal personally or to delegate it to a reporter,[15] or the decision of a reporter to award expenses against a party who has acted unreasonably.[16] In other cases the time-limit for using the statutory procedure may have expired,[17] or the courts may be prepared to entertain an application for judicial review as an exception to the general rule that where a statutory remedy is provided that is the method which should be used.[18] The fact that objectors do not have a right of appeal against a planning authority's decision to grant planning permission to a development, and hence do not have any statutory remedy to pursue, also gives rise to the use of judicial review as a means of challenging unwelcome decisions.[19]

The Use of Judicial Review

The nature of environmental law provides ample scope for judicial review to be invoked. Although there is a role for private law, most environmental law falls within the general public law category and is dominated by a range of regulatory systems. A standard pattern is for potentially harmful activities to be permitted only if prior authorisation has been obtained from a public authority which enjoys a broad discretion in determining whether and on what conditions authorisation is to be granted. Decisions will usually be reached only after some process of consultation, often including an opportunity for public involvement. The determinations of the authority may then be subject to an appeal procedure, usually to a Secretary of State or his delegates. Any regulatory system which is based on complex and detailed provisions and which includes a wide discretion vested in public authorities, statutory procedures for consultation and appeal, and opportunities for third parties to become involved, is bound to provide fertile ground for judicial review.[20] Even where the procedures and approvals are not in fact statutory, the courts may recognise their practical importance and allow review to proceed.[21]

A number of factors operate to inhibit or encourage the use of judicial review. Indeed, some may operate in both ways, since features which serve to reduce the likelihood of recourse to the courts in some cases may well give rise to additional grounds for challenge in others. This is true of the appeal and consultation procedures built into the various regulatory systems. By providing an opportunity for those who wish to become involved to have their say, it is hoped that the decisions which are made are ones which do not give rise to grievances, either because people are happy with an outcome which reflects their concerns, or because they are satisfied that even though the outcome is unwelcome their views have been properly taken into account in the decision-making process. On the other hand, the very opportunity to participate in the process may make people feel more strongly that their 'rights' are involved, encouraging recourse to the courts, while the proceedings themselves offer more scope for the authorities concerned to slip up in some way and, as a result, act unlawfully.

There are perhaps two main reasons why people consider it worth pursuing an action in the courts: the monetary value of the matter in question or the strength of their personal commitment to the issue. In the environmental field there are many situations where either or both is at stake. In financial terms, the future of property developments worth millions of pounds depends on the decisions of planning authorities and of the Secretary of State (or his reporters and inspectors) on appeal. If the outcome is unfavourable, there is a real commercial incentive to try every route possible to have the decision overturned and hope that a more acceptable decision can be made when the issue is reconsidered. Likewise, other forms of environmental control, for example, restrictions on heavy lorries in London unless they are fitted with additional noise suppressing equipment,[22] can impose considerable additional costs on industry and, therefore, justify recourse to the courts.

The financial background also operates as an incentive to others to turn to the courts. Especially in the planning field, it may be that there are rival plans for a particular sort of development in an area, or even on the same site, but it is clear that only one can in fact proceed (physically or in terms of commercial viability). The losers at any stage may, therefore, be tempted to go to the courts to try to protect their position and to give themselves a further opportunity to present their own case. Thus one finds many examples of decisions in favour of one developer being closely scrutinised by its rivals to see if there is any flaw which can lead to the decision being quashed and the issue being reopened,[23] or of rivals seeking to have any progress with other proposals delayed so as to allow their own plans to be considered.[24]

The financial consequences of delay may also be significant in prompting actions for judicial review. Those opposed to a particular development will know that if it can be delayed by a legal challenge to the permission authorising it, its viability may become questionable as a result of increased construction costs or simply the longer time before the development is in operation and thus producing a return on the capital outlays. This may lead to the development being abandoned or to further concessions being made in order to allow the development to proceed without delay. In different circumstances, judicial review can be used to delay effective enforcement action, allowing unauthorised activities to continue profitably or postponing the day when expensive alterations have to be made—the abuse of the legal procedures by the unscrupulous few determined to delay complying with the law for as long as possible has been a recurring problem in enforcing the planning system.[25]

Financial considerations are not the only motivation for court action. Many decisions stir up strong feelings. Whether the feelings are generated by an element of personal loss, for example when homes are to be compulsorily acquired to allow a new motorway to be built, by concern over the immediate consequences of a particular development,[26] or by a broader commitment to an environmental cause, for example, the recent litigation by Greenpeace against the thermal oxide nuclear reprocessing plant (THORP),[27] they are likely to lead to determined opposition to what are regarded as being harmful projects. There will often be a willingness to use all possible legitimate means to prevent or at least delay the project, a willingness often backed up by the personal involvement of those with professional skills to make the most of the opportunities presented and by at least some resources to finance legal action.

In some cases it is difficult to work out whether recourse to judicial review is the product of a determination born of deep passion to do everything possible to oppose a project to which the objectors can never be reconciled, or a symptom that there is something wrong with the decision-making procedures involved. Many of the regulatory systems in environmental law do include mechanisms to provide opportunities for third parties (neighbours, interest groups, commercial bodies) to be informed of proposals and to make representations before decisions are made. Yet these may fail to satisfy those affected by decisions and may even lead to greater frustration when the views which have been carefully prepared and put forward at the appropriate forum are not accepted, or even worse are overridden by policies or arguments which it is felt were not properly scrutinised during proceedings, a point noted in relation to public inquiries.[28] As a simple example from the planning system, many objectors consider it grossly unfair that the developer has a right of appeal against the refusal of permission or against the terms of any conditions, but the objectors have no right to appeal against the grant of permission or against the absence of conditions. For them, judicial review is the only way in which the decision can be considered again.

What must be emphasised is that judicial review is no substitute for the development of proper decision-making procedures which have the confidence of those affected. Recourse to judicial review may well be the outcome of frustration. Frustration that others do not accept what one passionately believes to be right can perhaps never be avoided, but frustration caused by the fact that one feels that one has never had a fair chance to put one's case or that the issue was in essence determined even before the formal, public consideration began is more serious and means of resolving it should be sought in a democratic system. Litigation is rarely an appropriate way of deciding issues where many parties are involved and the task of producing a final result, which is inevitably a balance between legitimate but irreconcilable interests, private and public, is inherently a political one.

It must be remembered that even a successful challenge may not in fact change the final outcome, because when the decision-making procedure is gone through properly, the same conclusion may be reached. Any challenges, however, will in fact force decision-makers to consider carefully what they have done and may well lead them to respond differently to any similar cases in future, seeking to avoid the grievances which have led them into court. Whether this will simply involve greater consultation or more careful adherence to the formalities of the procedure or will in fact lead to a reassessment of the relative weight of the conflicting interests, court action will affect the way in which decisions are taken in future, and this by itself may be a success for the challengers.

An unsuccessful challenge may also have practical consequences. The delay imposed while the litigation proceeds may itself be worth battling for, whether to an environmental group trying to prevent some environmentally damaging development or to a polluter seeking to delay effective enforcement action. The publicity which a legal challenge can generate, however weak the legal case, may also make recourse to the courts a worthwhile step, and may even lead to public and political pressures which will influence the way in which decisions are made in future.

One recent development which is likely to increase the use of the courts is the emergence of litigation at the instance of environmental interest groups. The apparent relaxation of the rules on standing (see below) has made this possible at the same time as interest groups become more aware of the possibilities of using the law to overturn particular proposals, to delay developments, or to attract publicity. Apart from actions raised by individual objectors who have banded together to form a group representing their common personal interests,[29] cases recently have involved Friends of the Earth challenging the government's response to the United Kingdom's failure to meet European standards in relation to drinking water,[30] Greenpeace challenging the decisions to authorise the thermal oxide reprocessing plant (THORP) at Sellafield,[31] and the Royal Society for the Protection of Birds challenging ministerial decisions in relation to the extent of Special Protection Areas under the European Birds Directive.[32]

As indicated above, planning law (coupled with the related legislation for roads, compulsory purchase and other aspects of development) continues to be by far the largest source of cases for the courts. A glance at the Table of Cases in any planning law textbook will reveal the significance of judicial decisions for the development of this area of law. On some topics much of this litigation has taken the form of the inevitable case-by-case refinement of definitions of words or phrases, such as 'development', which are crucial to the operation of the system but which, however formulated, could not hope to deal with all of the varied factual situations which arise in practice.[33] In other areas, though, the courts have made a major conceptual contribution to the development of the law, particularly the creation of the concept of 'the planning unit', the area of land to be considered when past and present uses of the land are being compared.[34] In determining the limits on the use of planning agreements[35] and the range of issues which qualify as 'material considerations',[36] the courts have played a key role in setting the boundaries of the authorities' powers to interfere with how owners treat their own land.

In these ways the courts have performed a vital public role. In other cases, though, and through no fault of their own, the courts have ended up as simply another forum through which those with strong differences of opinion seek to have their own way and to have unwelcome decisions on a specific issue overturned. Whether objectors are unhappy that their arguments have been overridden by an authority granting permission, developers unhappy that their plans have been refused or approved subject to conditions, or authorities unhappy that their view has been overturned by those higher in the administrative hierarchy, the real argument may be simply that the decision being challenged is wrong, and the legal argument directed at attacking its validity merely a way of getting the case before a court when other avenues have been exhausted. A difficulty is that cases which appear to fall into this latter category can sometimes produce issues which mean that the court's decision is not just the final word in a private argument, but is of significance for the system as a whole.

Planning is the source of most cases, but a broad range of topics has come before the courts. In addition to the issues mentioned above, the decision not to schedule the remains of a Shakespearean theatre as an ancient monument,[37] the award of a grant for an afforestation project[38] and various aspects of waste disposal, from the correct definition of 'deposit' to the contractual arrangements which a disposal authority can make,[39] have all generated court action. The Wildlife and Countryside Act 1981 has also given rise to actions challenging both the making of Nature Conservation Orders[40] and various decisions affecting rights of way in England and Wales,[41] while the validity of a local authority's decision to ban stag-hunting on its land has also been challenged.[42] As environmental concern develops into environmental activism, more cases across an ever-widening range of matters can be expected.

The potential for litigation is likely to be further enhanced by the greater availability of information on the environment. The European Directive on access to environmental information[43] has led to the creation of a large number of public registers making available details of applications, authorisations and monitoring results in several pollution control regimes[44] and also imposes a wider obligation to make information available.[45] Apart from the possibility of judicial review in relation to the operation of the information arrangements themselves (for example whether particular information falls within the classes which must be disclosed, or whether a decision to grant or refuse commercial confidentiality is lawful), the availability of such details will help those seeking to mount a challenge. In the past much environmental regulation was an essentially private process concerning the regulator and the regulated alone. The new arrangements for access to information have opened up the process to outside scrutiny, and it can be expected that the information will be used to provide the foundation on which a legal challenge can be based.

Standing

One issue which is of particular importance in determining the use of judicial review in the environmental field is that of legal standing.[46] The general rule is that only a person with some direct connection with the issue will be recognised as having sufficient standing to invoke the courts' powers of judicial review, a rule designed to prevent 'mere busybodies' from interfering in other people's business.[47] The difficulty in the environmental field is that in deciding whether somebody is a busybody or has a genuine interest in the matter, the law recognises only a limited range of interests, for example property rights, without taking cognisance of what might be claimed as the 'environmental rights' of the public which are infringed whenever environmental harm is done.

The difficulty can be demonstrated by considering the position in relation to wild birds. As wild creatures, they are not the property of anyone, and therefore nobody's legally recognised rights or interests are affected by anything that causes them harm. Many people may be very concerned about the fate of the birds, but in the past such concern has not been regarded as sufficient to justify permitting access to the courts when no legal interests are at stake. Thus individuals and pressure groups seeking to invoke the courts' assistance in protecting the environment may find that they fall at this first hurdle. The courts, however, do not always take a consistent view, and there are signs that a more generous approach may be developing. Any precise assessment of the legal position is, however, complicated by the fact that in many instances the standing of a party whose position may be arguable is not in fact contested, but is either wholly conceded or reserved for argument at a later stage which never in fact arises.

Within statutory procedures for recourse to the courts, the issue of standing is commonly addressed by a provision that it is a 'person aggrieved' who can refer matters to the courts.[48] 'The expression "a person aggrieved" is one which may vary in scope and meaning according to its context',[49] and it has been subject to considerable discussion.[50] The general trend, though, is clearly towards recognising a broadening range of grievances as justifying recourse to the courts.

The restrictive approach which used to hold sway limited the definition of 'person aggrieved' to 'the person with a legal grievance, that is to say, someone whose legal rights have been infringed',[51] but since the 1960s the courts have generally taken to heart the view of Lord Denning that the words 'are of wide import and should not be subjected to a restrictive interpretation'.[52] Accordingly, access to the courts has been granted to those who have appeared at a public inquiry only at the discretion of the inspector,[53] and to those who had played no part in appeal proceedings in relation to conditions in a grant of planning permission but had acquired the property before the appeal decision was announced.[54]

The right of all of those who have appeared at inquiries to qualify as 'persons aggrieved' has also been recognised in Scotland,[55] and a generous approach to the issue was adopted by a Scottish court in the case of *Cumming v Secretary of State for Scotland*.[56] Here the right to apply to the court was extended to a potential objector who had not in fact participated in the process leading to a grant of planning permission because the advertisement of the application did not accurately convey the substance of what was actually being sought—the 'road-side petrol station and service area' was in fact two filling stations on either side of the road, two restaurants, a forty bed motel and large car parks. The court recognised that there had been a transition from a restrictive interpretation of the words 'person aggrieved' to a more liberal one, and considered that as it was 'a cornerstone of planning legislation that planning proposals and decisions should be in the public domain . . . the public [should] be properly informed and given an opportunity, if they consider that they are adversely affected, to make appropriate representations about it'.[57] The court had doubts about the genuineness of the appellant's grievance, as he had probably known all about the proposal through other means, but as he had been deprived of the full opportunity to present his case he did qualify as a 'person aggrieved'.

This relaxation of the rules on standing in the statutory procedures has come at a time when the planning system as a whole has granted more recognition to the rights and interests of third parties.[58] In the general law on judicial review the position is less clear, and is partly affected by the procedural differences in the various jurisdictions, but again the trend has been towards an increasingly liberal approach.

One initial point of some difficulty is the issue of legal capacity. In England and Wales different views have recently been expressed on whether an unincorporated association has the capacity to seek judicial review.[59] The Law Commission has noted that it would cause a great deal of inconvenience and expense if pressure groups and interested bodies had to form themselves into limited companies solely to be able to apply for judicial review, and accordingly has recommended that unincorporated associations should be permitted to apply in their own name.[60] At present, though, the position is unclear. On the other hand, it seems that the fact of incorporation will not affect the issue of standing, even though in strict terms a new legal person has been created whose own individual standing, not that of the separate persons forming the corporate body, should be considered.[61] In Scotland the courts appear to look at the substance of any parties' interest in the matter, not simply their legal form. Accordingly if individuals who would have title to sue in the particular circumstances band together to form an unincorporated association, the association will enjoy standing to the extent that the individuals would personally.[62]

In Scotland the courts view the issue of title and interest to sue as a preliminary matter, to be determined before the substance of the case is considered,[63] and the two elements of the test may be treated separately, so that a party who is viewed as having title to sue may fail on the basis that in the particular circumstances he has no sufficient interest.[64] No comprehensive definitions exist, but as far as title is concerned reference is frequently made to Lord Dunedin's comment in *D. & J. Nicol v Dundee*

Harbour Trustees[65] that to have title a person 'must be a party (using the word in its widest sense) to some legal relation which gives him some right which the person against whom he raises the action either infringes or denies'. This idea has been given a broad interpretation and in *Wilson v Independent Broadcasting Authority*[66] it has been held that where a public body owes a duty to the public, individual members of the public may have title to sue.

Even if a person qualifies as having title to raise an issue, the court must also be satisfied that he or she has an interest to do so. This requires that the particular issue is of some real concern to the party, and not an academic issue or merely something which is being raised as a matter of general public spirited concern.[67] Such interest, though, need not be a formal, legal or property interest; for example, in *Kincardine and Deeside District Council v Forestry Commissioners*[68] it was held that a local authority had the requisite interest on the basis of its 'reasonable concern with a major project in their area which may affect the economy or amenity of the area generally'. Members of a conservation group are unlikely to have a legally recognised interest in all matters which are of concern to them, but if they can show a lasting and genuine concern in a particular topic or site, particularly if they have invested time, effort and money in it, they may in some cases be able to use this as demonstrating an interest to accompany their title as members of the public.

In England and Wales the procedural reforms to the process of judicial review swept away a number of restrictive rules on *locus standi* and replaced them with the general test that the applicant must demonstrate 'a sufficient interest in the matter to which the application relates'.[69] This test has generally been given a fairly liberal interpretation, and has been viewed as an issue which has to be considered as part of the broader consideration of the factual and legal circumstances of the case, not as a preliminary issue.[70] Some interest over and above that of the ordinary citizen has to be shown. If this is not possible, a party who does not have *locus standi* can attempt to persuade the Attorney General to instigate proceedings by way of a relator action, although the likelihood of success is small.[71]

Four decisions are of particular importance for the environmental field. In the first, a restrictive approach was taken; the next two illustrate ways in which conservation bodies and similar groups can become sufficiently involved in proceedings to establish their standing; and the fourth perhaps points to a much more generous approach by some courts. In *R. v Secretary of State for the Environment, ex parte Rose Theatre Trust Co.*[72] it was held that the ordinary citizen (and hence any group of citizens, whatever their concern over the issue) did not have sufficient interest to challenge the non-scheduling of an ancient monument, that is, the refusal to include it in the list of monuments granted legal protection. The same reasoning might well apply to prevent individuals or conservation groups challenging decisions relating to the many other forms of statutory designation or order provided for in the environmental field. It is uncertain whether the same result would have occurred in Scotland or whether the broader approach taken in *Wilson v Independent Broadcasting Authority*[73] might have enabled a challenge to be raised.

In *R. v Poole Borough Council, ex parte Beebee*[74] a grant of planning permission affecting a Site of Special Scientific Interest on lowland heath which offered a habitat for lizards was challenged by representatives of the Worldwide Fund for Nature and the British Herpetological Society. It was held that the society did have standing to challenge this decision because it had a long connection with the site through surveys and other research carried out there, because it had over the years made a significant financial input to the site, and because it was expressly connected with the permission granted since a condition therein stated that the society should be given the opportunity to catch and relocate lizards found on the site before development commenced. On the other hand, the Worldwide Fund for Nature, which had only an indirect connection with the site and had not even made representations in response to the initial planning application, would have had no standing on its own. The importance of establishing a real and direct connection with the particular site involved is clearly demonstrated here. It may well be that just as a legally aided pursuer sometimes raises an action in order to allow a pressure group to take action which it could not otherwise afford,[75] a small local environmental group may provide a means through which a case can be brought to court, perhaps with financial assistance from larger bodies which would not themselves have standing.

The third case is *R. v Swale Borough Council and Medway Ports Authority, ex parte Royal Society for the Protection of Birds*,[76] in which the delay in raising a challenge to certain planning decisions was held to have been too long for the court to entertain the case but where the standing of the applicants was acknowledged. This was based on the society's legitimate expectation that they would be consulted before decisions were taken, an expectation founded on undertakings given by the council. The courts will protect the legitimate expectations of parties that they will be consulted or otherwise involved in procedures once such expectations have been created by either the consistent past practice of an authority or its express promise.[77] The courts, however, are understandably reluctant to recognise expectations except in very clear cases. There is concern that if legally protected expectations are created too easily, public authorities, afraid that their future freedom of action will be hampered, will become too cautious in holding discussions and consultations with individuals and groups who have expressed some interest in particular issues, a general practice which benefits all parties.

The *Swale* case offers one example of the ways in which conservation groups and other concerned parties can become involved in proceedings in a way which clearly establishes their standing. In relation to planning decisions, the simplest way to become involved is through making representations in response to the initial application or at a public inquiry or other appeal proceedings, as it is well established that objectors have a clear right to ensure that proceedings have been conducted lawfully. The same will be true of involvement in other forms of proceedings where there are opportunities for objection or consultation.

Such involvement can transform someone from a concerned bystander, but a bystander nonetheless, into a legally interested party. For example, in *Patmor Ltd v City of Edinburgh District Licensing Board*[78] it was held that the holders of a gaming licence had no title in that capacity to challenge the grant of a licence to another company for similar premises in the area, despite their obvious concern as rival traders to limit competition, but did have title in their capacity as objectors to the new application, having formally taken advantage of the opportunity to submit representations when the application was advertised. The importance of becoming formally involved in proceedings is thus clear, and such involvement need not be onerous, as in most cases a simple letter making representations in response to the application for planning permission or other form of authorisation will suffice. The restrictive nature of the law on standing in the United Kingdom does stand in the way of greater use of the courts in all areas of environmental law, but in many circumstances the position can be improved by interested parties acting early enough to establish some direct connection with the issue.

A more generous approach to standing was taken in the fourth case to be considered, *R. v Inspectorate of Pollution, ex parte Greenpeace Ltd (No. 2)*,[79] in which it was held that Greenpeace did have standing to challenge the variations to the existing authorisations for radioactive waste necessary to permit testing of the thermal oxide reprocessing plant (THORP) at Sellafield. Otton J. emphasised that the issue was one on which the courts enjoyed discretion, and fell to be judged both at the threshold stage of applying for leave and when the court in the substantive hearing was deciding whether it was appropriate to grant a remedy in the particular circumstances. He recognised the national and international standing of Greenpeace and its integrity, he noted that it had 2,500 supporters in Cumbria who were inevitably concerned about dangers to their health, and he had no doubt that the issues raised were serious ones worthy of determination by a court. He also considered that allowing Greenpeace to have standing provided an effective way of dealing with the issue as opposed to leaving it in the hands of individual litigants who would lack equivalent expertise and might leave the respondents without an effective remedy in costs if the challenge failed. Greenpeace had further been treated as a consultee during the consultation process. He expressly declined to follow the decision in the *Rose Theatre* case and held that Greenpeace was not a 'mere' or 'meddlesome busybody', but 'eminently respectable and responsible' with a 'genuine interest'.[80]

This decision is interesting both for its rejection of the narrow approach taken in the *Rose Theatre* case, and for its emphasis that the matter of standing is one for the discretion of the courts, not only as a threshold issue, but also as a matter to be taken into account when the court decides what, if any, remedy it is appropriate to grant. Although other cases suggest that standing is a matter going to the jurisdiction of the court, it is still accepted that the merits of the challenge are 'an important if not dominant, factor when considering standing'[81]—a very different approach from that in Scotland. Otton J. stressed that the decision did not mean that Greenpeace and similar groups would automatically enjoy standing in future cases, but his decision is certainly significant for its recognition of the value to all those involved in disputed cases of allowing serious legal issues to come to court through the medium of an organised pressure group.

A similar view was taken in a different context in the more recent case of *R. v Secretary of State for Foreign Affairs, ex parte World Development Movement Ltd*,[82] where the importance of vindicating the rule of law, the importance of the issue raised, the likely absence of another responsible challenger, and the prominent role of the applicants in giving advice and assistance in the area, all contributed to the decision that a pressure group did have sufficient standing to challenge the legality of spending overseas development funds on a project known to be economically unsound (the Pergau Dam in Malaysia). If these decisions do represent a general willingness to allow standing to pressure groups (provided that they have a real and close interest in a particular issue), this is a very significant development indeed and makes it much more likely that judicial review in the courts will become a prominent feature of environmental law.[83]

The formal rules on standing are not, of course, the only hurdle to those seeking to mount a legal challenge. The costs involved can be a major obstacle. The imbalance between the resources of individual objectors and a large commercial undertaking promoting a project worth millions of pounds, or between interest groups dependent on voluntary funding and the government, may be significant even before legal action is contemplated, especially in relation to the ability to participate in public inquiries. When litigation is being considered, the applicants for review may not be able to take the risk of having to fund the other side's costs if they lose. Legal aid may be of little assistance, especially if there are several parties involved and the case has an element of 'public interest' as opposed to being purely to protect personal rights.[84] The Law Commission's recommendation is that when it is being decided whether legal aid should be granted, the wider public interest in having a case heard should also be considered, to the benefit of applicants who might otherwise be refused aid since, despite the public interest, they stand to gain only a trivial advantage from the proceedings.[85]

In this context it is interesting to note what was said about costs in the recent litigation arising out of the testing of the THORP plant at Sellafield. One factor which influenced Otton J. in granting Greenpeace the standing to pursue one action was that in the event of the challenge failing, it was more likely that costs could be recovered from them than if the challenge was mounted by individuals.[86] In the related action Greenpeace lost in the substantive hearing, but Potts J. exercised his discretion not to award costs against them on the basis that there had been a substantial public interest in the case and Greenpeace had been successful on one point, clarifying the law.[87] The potential unfairness of this to the winning party is dealt with by the recommendation of the Law Commission, that where judicial review proceedings are brought in the public interest, the judge should have the discretion to award the successful party's costs either against the other party or out of central funds.[88] If this recommendation is adopted, or the decision of Potts J. marks a general change in approach on this issue, a further obstacle to environmental litigation (and indeed to the use of judicial review in many areas) will be lifted.

The THORP litigation also raised a further issue of cost. In deciding whether to grant an interlocutory injunction, as was sought by Greenpeace at an early stage in the proceedings, one of the significant factors in weighing the balance of convenience is whether the party seeking the injunction has made an undertaking to pay, and will be able to pay, the damages due to the party restrained, should the latter be successful when the case is decided after the full hearing.[89] An injunction may be thought necessary to prevent others from acting on a public authority's decision while it is subject to judicial review (especially in view of the lengthy delays in reaching the courts), but the requirement to make and meet such an undertaking may provide a considerable barrier.

It is perhaps significant that in *R. v Secretary of State for the Environment, ex parte Royal Society for the Protection of Birds* [90] one of the factors influencing the court against granting any interim relief while the case was referred to the European Court of Justice was that the applicants had not sought an interim injunction, in relation to which they would 'undoubtedly' have been required to give an undertaking in damages, but were seeking to achieve the same result without the risk of incurring expenditure. The courts have stated that orders to preserve the status quo may be made without undertakings as to damages, but it has been emphasised that this will occur only in the most exceptional cases.[91] As environmental litigation becomes more frequent this may be an area which has to be further explored.[92]

Exclusion of Review

Another significant issue for judicial review in the environmental field is the extent to which recourse to the courts can be prevented by exclusion or ouster provisions. The tension between, on the one hand, providing the fullest opportunity for individuals to protect their rights and, on the other, ensuring that no uncertainty or delays are caused by decisions being challenged long after they have been made, is felt particularly acutely in this area where so many decisions are designed to be acted on. The whole point of a grant of planning permission or the making of a compulsory purchase order is to authorise action which may affect many people, which will usually be costly and which it may be impossible to undo. There may, therefore, be good reasons for wanting to limit the opportunities for judicial review and to confer finality at a fairly early stage in proceedings, especially as any delay is likely to impose a cost on those seeking to rely on the decision (for example, additional construction costs or a longer wait before a profitable use can commence) or to prolong any inconvenience or disruption which is to be cured.

The judicial response to provisions trying to oust the jurisdiction of the courts has been mixed. Two main strands of thought can be identified, each being able to look to authority from the House of Lords. One strand accepts the exclusion of the courts' powers of review. This can be illustrated by the decision in *Smith v East Elloe Rural District Council,*[93] where the House of Lords accepted that a provision saying that a compulsory purchase order should not, other than through the statutory recourse provided by the same legislation, 'be questioned in any legal proceedings whatsoever',[94] took effect to prevent the courts from reviewing the validity of an order. This was so even though the allegation was that the order had been made in bad faith and there were doubts over whether the statutory procedures would properly cover such a claim.

A different view was taken by the House of Lords in *Anisminic v Foreign Compensation Commission,*[95] where a determination made by the Commission was quashed despite a provision stating that determinations 'shall not be called in question in any court of law'.[96] The view taken here was that the protection granted to 'determinations' of the Commission could not extend to everything which purported to be a determination, and if a determination was so flawed as to be invalid, then it was a nullity and was not protected by the clause. In other words, the court was not calling a determination into question, but merely checking whether that which had been presented to it was in fact a 'determination'.[97] This approach clearly allows the court in effect to exercise its powers of judicial review without restriction, as all that the courts can ever do is check the validity of the decision before them, not question a decision which is valid.

These conflicting decisions of the House of Lords have caused problems for subsequent courts. For example, opposite conclusions have been reached by the Scottish and English courts on the question of whether an owner can by proceedings for judicial review challenge the validity of a planning enforcement notice on the ground that it has not been properly served, in the face of statutory provisions stating that a challenge on this ground can be made only by means of a statutory appeal.[98] Various attempts have been made to reconcile what has been said in the cases or to distinguish cases on their facts, but in essence the decisions reflect conflicting policy decisions between the merits of finality and certainty and those of ensuring that individuals are not deprived of a remedy against action interfering with their rights. It now seems, though, that a compromise is being broadly accepted.

This compromise, based largely on what Lord Denning MR (adopting the views of academic writers) said in *R. v Secretary of State for the Environment, ex parte Ostler*,[99] distinguishes between provisions which totally exclude the courts' jurisdiction and those which do allow for some form of challenge to the validity of the decision, but thereafter seek to exclude recourse to the courts. In the first situation, as in *Anisminic*, the courts will not accept that all decisions and purported decisions are immune from challenge. In the second, as in *East Elloe,* the courts will accept the statutory position as in effect a form of limitation clause. The compromise may not fit exactly what was said by the judges in *East Elloe* and *Anisminic*, but it does provide a workable way forward, and subsequent cases have generally adopted it or can be seen to fit within it.[100]

This approach attempts to strike a balance between the competing interests of securing finality and avoiding injustice, although the period available for challenge is commonly only six weeks. For developers waiting to get started on some major project, this delay before they can be wholly confident that the permission authorising their work is not at risk of being overturned will doubtless seem a long time; for owners who discover too late something which significantly affects their property, the time available for challenge will doubtless seem very short.

Consideration of this issue by the Justice-All Souls Review led to the majority conclusion that challenges after the six week period should still be permitted, provided that they were still prompt and that decisions would only be set aside if no innocent third party would suffer.[101] There was a dissenting view, however, presenting the argument that even this would undermine the legal certainty desired by those relying on the decisions, and there must be difficulties in working out how direct the suffering of a third party must be before this precludes intervention, for example, there may be no immediate 'victim', but many people suffer to some extent if a legal hitch delays the construction of a bypass to relieve a historic town centre which is being ruined by heavy traffic. The better way forward, in addition to endeavouring to ensure that the pre-decision and statutory procedures do in fact offer a real opportunity for grievances to be fully taken into account, may be to contemplate other remedies which will not undermine the official decision which is to be acted on yet will compensate those who have suffered a true injustice. This latter possibility, which has some support among judges and from the Law Commission, deserves to be properly examined.[102]

Grounds for Intervention

The grounds on which the courts can exercise their powers of judicial review in the environmental field are the same as in all other areas: illegality, irrationality and procedural impropriety, to adopt Lord Diplock's terminology in the *GCHQ* case.[103] These restrict the court to considering the formal limits of an authority's powers and the way in which decisions have been made, rather than their merits, and as such there is little that is specifically environmental about the arguments and issues in the cases. Within the broad development of administrative law, environmental cases have played a significant role in several areas, perhaps even a disproportionate role arising from the fact, noted above, that the money at stake in planning issues has resulted in a greater willingness to litigate in this area than in many others where the same regulatory issues arise.

The decision-making procedures within the planning system have offered plenty of opportunity for arguments based on natural justice. The formal procedural rules for appeal proceedings and inquiries should ensure that the basics of natural justice are observed, but there is scope for dispute on the margins. Thus in relation to inquiries, the courts have been called on to decide whether it is acceptable to refuse an adjournment when one party suffered a heart attack,[104] or when a party sought at very short notice to avoid a clash with a day of religious observance.[105] They have been asked to decide whether a prolonged lunch-hour offers a sufficient opportunity for a party at an inquiry to inspect and consider new documents submitted by others,[106] and whether it is acceptable for an inspector after a site visit to stay in a pub for an extra round of drinks with the representatives of one party when those of the other have left.[107]

The way in which new evidence received after an inquiry must be handled has been considered,[108] as has the extent to which an inspector can rely on his own unaccompanied site visit,[109] or a reporter base a decision on issues not fully canvassed in the representations made to him.[110] The role of cross-examination at inquiries has been discussed by the House of Lords[111] and planning cases have contributed to the developing jurisprudence on the circumstances in which the courts will protect the legitimate expectations of those affected by official decisions.[112] The role of the Secretary of State in deciding appeals, especially when he has expressed support for the general policy lying behind a particular issue[113] or has been previously involved in a case in another capacity,[114] has also given rise to litigation which has been significant for ministerial powers in general.

Other areas have been explored, for example, the effects of procedural flaws and the value of the distinction between mandatory and directory procedural requirements,[115] but all of the points raised here are merely examples to illustrate the contribution which cases in this field have made to administrative law in general.

Justifying Decisions

One issue which is worthy of particular note is the attention paid to whether there is any justification for the decisions reached by authorities. This issue has been given particular prominence by two features of the planning system, the express requirement that authorities in deciding planning applications have regard to 'material considerations', and the obligations to give reasons for many decisions. Both of these requirements expose to legal scrutiny the reasoning process behind a decision, and mean that the courts are in a position to delve more deeply into the justification for a decision than is normal in an area of discretionary decision-making.

Statutory provisions requiring the giving of reasons mean that there has been little cause to argue in the planning and environmental field about the scope of any common law duty to give reasons. Instead, argument has centred on the adequacy of the reasons which have been given, and many of the challenges to planning decisions, particularly against the outcome of appeals to the Secretary of State and his delegates, have been at least partly based on the argument that the decision letter does not properly reveal the reasoning process or does not adequately cover the issues raised. This has led to a considerable weight of case law on the subject,[116] with the courts keen to steer a course which ensures that the purposes of giving reasons are served but without the decisions 'being subjected to hypercritical textual analysis or criticism.'[117]

The overriding standard is that set in *Re Poyser and Mill's Arbitration*[118] that the reasons must be proper, adequate, intelligible, and must deal with the substantive issues raised. This does not mean that the reasons need to be lengthy,[119] but they must leave the informed reader in no real and substantial doubt as to the reasons for the decision and the material considerations which were taken into account in reaching it.[120] This, in turn, focuses attention on what are the material considerations which should be taken into account.

The requirement in general administrative law that decision-makers should have regard to all relevant considerations, and only to those which are relevant, always leaves the court with an element of discretion in determining what considerations are in fact relevant in the particular context. This determination can have a major influence not only on the outcome of particular cases but on the whole nature and scope of the administrative function in question, as it is in this way that the very broad discretion conferred by parliament by means of what are often very general provisions is channelled. It is the courts in determining what factors may properly be taken into account which will play the key role in deciding exactly what the purpose of a particular regulatory system is and which policy objectives can be pursued.

In the planning system the duty to have regard to all relevant considerations is given express form by the obligation to consider all 'material considerations',[121] but no statutory definition is given. Instead, the issue has been one for decision by the courts, and it is judicial review (including statutory challenges) which has provided the means for invoking their jurisdiction. By defining what considerations are material, the courts are in essence setting the limits to the grounds on which the whole regulatory system can intervene to restrict the use of land and property, and it is one of the ironies of environmental law that despite the volume of detailed legislation such key issues are left to judicial determination. This has the great merit of allowing the law to develop and to be flexible, but at the same time it inevitably leads to uncertainty.

Many issues have been held to qualify as material considerations, and as each case is decided on its own particular circumstances it can be difficult to draw clear lessons. There have been some attempts at fairly general definitions, for example, Cooke J.'s definition of material considerations as 'all considerations relating to the use and development of land',[122] but these tend to leave plenty of room for manoeuvre and argument. The planning textbooks offer their own lists,[123] but these differ in their precise formulations and are continually in need of amendment.

One area of particular interest at present is the extent to which matters which can be dealt with under other forms of environmental regulation can also be regarded as material for the purpose of planning decisions. There is inevitably a degree of overlap between what is relevant to a planning authority and to the pollution control authorities, especially where a formal environmental assessment of a proposal has been called for under the planning system, but some distinction must be drawn to prevent duplication and possible inconsistency. The issue is also one of political significance, as it will determine whether decisions are taken by an elected planning authority or by an official body which has no such political accountability to local residents. In *Gateshead Metropolitan Borough Council v Secretary of State for the Environment*[124] the Court of Appeal has decided that the possibility of harmful emissions from a proposed incinerator is a material consideration for planning purposes, but that the Secretary of State was entitled to decide that the controls exercised by Her Majesty's Inspectorate of Pollution under the Environmental Protection Act 1990 were adequate to deal with any concerns. This decision recognises the overlap between the different systems of regulation, and although the law is moving towards a more integrated approach to environmental control, such overlaps are likely to generate more litigation in future.

The courts are not left wholly free to determine what is 'material' as some factors are expressly identified as being ones to be taken into account, most notably the provisions of any relevant development plan. A major task for the courts has been to work out the proper role in decision-making of the various legally approved policy documents and many other forms of official guidance which are produced, for example, circulars and (National) Planning Policy Guidance Notes. As so much of the legislation in the environmental field is complex and accompanied by various forms of official guidance, this is an issue of importance not only for planning law.

The balance between the official policy documents and other material considerations, including local circumstances and the representations made by those affected by the proposed development, is of crucial importance to the balance of power within the whole system, especially as the opportunities for public involvement in the formulation of policy vary greatly. The public (which includes developers and other interest groups as well as the public at large) has most input when formal development plans are being prepared by planning authorities, and it is these development plans which are singled out for particular status. The legislation states that authorities must 'have regard to the provisions of the development plan'[125] in making their decisions, and this has been further strengthened by the requirement that decisions should be made 'in accordance with the plan unless material considerations indicate otherwise'.[126] Even here, though, the courts continue to make it clear that the outcome is for the planning authority or appellate body to decide on the basis of all the relevant factors, and although the development plan is important and there may even be a presumption that decisions will accord with it, there will be circumstances where other material considerations do justify a different response.[127]

This approach applies *a fortiori* in relation to other forms of guidance which differ from development plans in that they are not given express statutory status and are not preceded by formal procedural stages and opportunities for public and ministerial scrutiny. The general position was discussed by Woolf J. (as he then was) in *Gransden & Co. Ltd v Secretary of State for the Environment,*[128] where he made it clear that ministerial policies are material considerations. In order, however, to be a proper policy, and not an improper attempt to curtail the discretion conferred on the decision-maker, the policy must itself envisage that there will be exceptions and that it will not apply in every case. Moreover, the fact that the decision-maker is required to have regard to a policy does not mean that it must necessarily follow it, although departures should be accompanied by a clear explanation of why the particular case falls to be regarded as an exception.

The importance of policy guidance in modern administration is recognised by the courts' willingness in appropriate circumstances to consider directly the legality of a circular, even though by itself it decides nothing and has no formal legal effect.[129] The non-legal status of such documents is nevertheless kept firmly in mind and the courts have made it clear that, although circulars may be helpful in some circumstances, when it comes to defining the scope of legal duties and the meaning of the law, it is the legislation alone to which heed must be paid.[130]

By examining the scope of 'material considerations' and the manner in which relevant official guidance has to be taken into account, the courts are already going some way to scrutinising the reasoning leading to a decision. Judges always insist that it is for the statutory decision-maker, not the courts, to determine what weight is to be given to each of the relevant factors, and to decide how they are to be balanced in particular cases. Yet by going as far as they do in ensuring that all of the relevant matter has been considered, the courts are often subjecting the reasoning behind decisions to fairly close scrutiny, in some cases perhaps nearing the 'hard look' approach adopted by courts in the United States in the exercise of their powers of judicial review. Especially in the planning context, the courts can base their action on express provisions requiring the statement of reasons and regard to material considerations, but the same careful examination of the reasoning process may be appropriate in other areas, especially in the ever increasing range of circumstances where a statement of reasons[131] or justification[132] is required.

European Law

A further feature of judicial review cases in the environmental field is the increasingly significant role of European law. So much of our environmental law has been shaped by initiatives coming from within the European Union, or has to operate within a framework established there, that it is inevitable that the European dimension is appearing more frequently in the case law. In many cases it is not simply a question of determining the extent of the discretion enjoyed by authorities under British legislation, but also of ascertaining whether there are any provisions in European law which impose further limitations on the way in which that discretion can lawfully be exercised.

Cases have examined whether European law required that an environmental assessment be held before projects were granted permission to proceed,[133] have explored the nature of the Secretary of State's obligation to take remedial steps when the United Kingdom had been found to be in breach of European law in relation to water quality,[134] and have determined whether the precautionary principle enshrined in the European Community Treaty[135] creates an obligation on the Secretary of State in a domestic context.[136] The obligations of the Secretary of State in designating Special Protection Areas under the Birds Directive have been considered,[137] as has the existence of a requirement to provide justification when authorising practices entailing exposure to radiation,[138] and also the legality of an order restricting heavy lorries from using certain streets in London at night unless fitted with noise level suppressors, even though lorries without the suppressors met the relevant European Community construction standards.[139] If an expansive definition of environmental law is taken so as to include the regulation of marine fishing, a whole fleet of further cases can be embraced, including the central decision in *R. v Secretary of State for Transport, ex parte Factortame Ltd*,[140] which dealt with the registration of fishing boats entitled to fish in waters around the United Kingdom.

It is no accident that in the environmental field the European dimension has arisen in cases of judicial review. In other areas, European law has had a more direct impact as the Treaty and accompanying legislation have been held to confer rights on individuals which can be asserted in the courts. Litigation can, therefore, take the form of direct actions claiming a remedy for infringement of these rights.[141] This direct effect is only possible where the European provisions, whether in the Treaty or in a Directive, are clear and precise and render it certain exactly what rights and obligations should exist, without leaving discretion to the member states in implementing the measures. It has been suggested that some environmental measures may be regarded in this way, for example, certain precise prohibitions in the Birds Directive[142] or the requirement to hold an environmental assessment for a project which clearly falls within a category where such assessment is mandatory,[143] and more sweeping claims have occasionally been made,[144] but most environmental law tends not to operate in this way.

The Treaty provisions are phrased in too general a way to confer personal rights, or even to create definite obligations on the government.[145] The Directives which have been made are often very detailed, but again their form is not such as to confer rights on individuals, and their obligations are clearly placed on the member states, not on individuals. Even if individual rights were in fact created, for example, a right to air or water of certain quality, the fact that environmental controls operate largely through regulatory mechanisms rather than by direct obligations on potential polluters means that it is still likely that judicial review would be the appropriate mechanism for asserting these rights,[146] especially as it has been confirmed that the direct effect of Directives is restricted to vertical and not horizontal effect (that is, rights can be asserted against the state in all its manifestations, but not against private individuals or companies).[147]

Thus it is through judicial review that arguments will be made that ministers are bound to exercise their powers in certain ways in order to ensure that the country's European obligations are fulfilled. This aspect of environmental law is bound to increase as more of our environmental regulation has to operate within a European framework and as awareness spreads of the potential of introducing a European dimension to legal argument—the fact that the United Kingdom legislation gives a Secretary of State a broad discretion no longer settles the argument, and the compatibility of domestic measures with European ones should always be checked.

Specialisation

Any assessment of the suitability of judicial review as a means of determining environmental disputes inevitably touches on the broader arguments about the desirability of establishing an environmental court. This issue has generated a considerable amount of debate, including attention to the Australian experience where integrated tribunals are in operation.[148] One difficulty is that the discussion of an environmental court can reveal rather different ideas of what such a body should do, ranging from a tribunal to take over the appellate role currently fulfilled by the Secretary of State in the planning and other regulatory systems, to a full judicial body which through the one set of integrated proceedings could deal with all regulatory issues, any civil claims for compensation, and any criminal liability arising from a particular incident or state of affairs. The basic point which is consistently made, though, is that standard court procedures and personnel are not particularly appropriate for dealing with complex cases involving the assessment of scientific and technical issues.

This is not the place to rehearse all of the arguments, but two simple points can be made. The first is to note the *de facto* specialisation which already exists in relation to applications to the courts in England in planning matters. Large numbers of these cases are determined not by the full-time bench, whose experience may have been largely in quite different areas of law, but by QCs sitting as deputy judges.[149] This offers advantages in that the deputy judges are drawn from those with relevant experience, so that to some extent at least the decision is in the hands of a specialist court, familiar with the legal issues and the context in which they must be applied. The practice can also offer greater flexibility in the timetabling of cases, avoiding some of the delays which so cripple judicial review at present.

There may also be dangers. The widespread use of deputy judges may lead to inconsistency, both between individual judges who are not fully integrated into the judicial system and more seriously between the law as it is applied in the planning area and as it is applied in other areas of administrative law. A second danger is that decisions taken by the deputy judges somehow come to be seen as not sharing in the full magnificence of the Supreme Court and as a result the whole authority and standing of the court are diminished, a danger echoing the fear that establishing an environmental court might end up not enhancing the status of the law but marginalising the whole issue. Neither danger seems very real at present, and the quality of the decisions given and the existence of appeal to higher courts should maintain this position. It is, however, striking to note how far this *de facto* specialisation has developed without much comment and perhaps even without any grand design.[150]

The second point is simply to repeat something said earlier. Judicial review is not the appropriate process by which the final outcome of a complex dispute involving many parties with conflicting interests is determined. Any attempt, therefore, to address dissatisfaction with the process should not be confined to examining judicial review itself, but should look at the whole decision-making process and the opportunities for parties to participate and to be satisfied as far as possible that acceptable decisions have been reached. An environmental court of some sort may be one way of improving the position, but the other stages of the decision-making process should also be considered.

Conclusion

As indicated at the beginning of this chapter, any attempt at an overall assessment of judicial review and environmental law is difficult at present as there are two very different aspects to the subject. On one hand there is the large and well-developed corpus of material involving planning law and related matters. Here judicial review, whether through statutory references to the courts or the normal procedures, is an integral part of the operation of the system, and the courts are well used to handling such cases. Decisions in this area have made major contributions to both planning law and administrative law in general. Indeed, a study of the planning cases by themselves would possibly give an outsider as good an overall picture of judicial review in the United Kingdom as a study of any other single area.

On the other hand, there are the first signs of what may be a very significant development of judicial review as a major part of environmental law in general. In the past few years, as environmental issues have attracted more interest and as environmental law has developed as a serious subject in its own right, cases have started to come to the courts across the whole range of environmental issues, from nature conservation to waste disposal. Already there have been a number of significant successes for those challenging governmental decisions, for example, over night-flying at the London airports,[151] and even when cases have been lost, as in the THORP litigation,[152] both the publicity generated and the seriousness with which the legal issues have been considered have offered encouragement for further use of the courts.

Several factors combine to make it almost certain that the number of cases will increase. So long as the pattern for environmental controls continues to be that of imposing a fairly standard regulatory scheme, judicial review will continue to be the appropriate form in which to make legal challenges to the way in which such controls are being operated.[153] Continuing public concern over environmental issues will focus more attention on how such controls are in fact being operated, and the apparent relaxation of the rules on standing to allow pressure groups greater access to the courts will open the way for those with the determination, expertise and resources to mount effective legal actions. At the same time, as environmental controls become more stringent and thus have a greater effect on industry, one can expect those subject to the controls to turn to the courts in an attempt to escape what they regard as excessive, unjustified or simply unwelcome restrictions, as already occurs in the planning field.

Although the context may be new, many of these cases will raise no new issues and will simply require the application of the standard principles of administrative law. There are, however, some distinctive features which will have to be accommodated. The scientific and technical nature of many of the cases may seem to be a major feature, but is probably of little significance, as it is not for the courts to assess the correctness of technical decisions, merely to ensure that there is some evidence to support them, a task already familiar in relation to traffic predictions, noise assessments and other features of some planning cases. More significant, and already apparent in many of the recent cases, is the role of European Community law, both in terms of direct obligations on the government and as a limit on the way in which discretion can be exercised.

What remains to be seen is whether any specifically environmental concepts will emerge. In supervising the planning system, the courts have made a major contribution to the content of the law through the creation of such concepts as the planning unit. In the currently less-developed area of environmental law there is ample scope for judicial innovation. Acceptance of the precautionary principle as a starting point against which measures must be justified, or recognition of environmental 'rights' of the public or of individuals, to be set against the private property rights which have been traditionally recognised in the law, are examples of how courts could give effect to environmental activism. On the other hand, a very conservative adherence to the protection of traditional individual rights against interference by the state could impede the development of increased environmental protection, which to be truly effective must impose controls on individual and commercial freedom of action.

At present, we are observing the first trickles of judicial review in environmental law. We can be certain that these trickles will grow into a sizeable stream, if not a flood, in years to come. Whether this stream flows on to become a river in its own right, or simply merges with others to become part of the broader flow of administrative law in general, remains to be seen.

Notes

1. Town and Country Planning (Scotland) Act 1972, ss 232–3; Town and Country Planning Act 1990, ss 287-8.
2. e.g. Wildlife and Countryside Act 1981, sch. 11, para. 7; sch. 12, para. 8; sch. 15 para. 12.
3. They are likewise considered together in the recent report by the Law Commission, *Administrative Law: Judicial Review and Statutory Appeals* (Law Comm., No. 226;

1993–94 HC 669); several of the issues discussed here are covered in this report which recommends a number of significant reforms to the law in England and Wales.

4. Town and Country Planning (Scotland) Act 1972, s. 233(4); Town and Country Planning Act 1990, s. 288(5).

5. Browne J. in *Hibernian Property Co. Ltd v Secretary of State for the Environment* (1973) 27 P & CR 197, at 218.

6. Lord Cameron in *Wordie Property Co. Ltd v Secretary of State for Scotland* 1984 SLT 345, at 356.

7. *Midlothian District Council v Secretary of State for Scotland* 1980 SC 210.

8. A discretion which may be wider and which is certainly more openly referred to in England than in Scotland: M. Supperstone and J. Goudie, *Judicial Review* (1992) pp 349–53; *Hanlon v Traffic Commissioner* 1988 SLT 802, at 806.

9. Town and Country Planning (Scotland) Act 1972, s. 233(4); Town and Country Planning Act 1990, s. 288(5).

10. e.g. in *Smith v East Elloe Rural District Council* [1956] AC 736 it was suggested that allegations of bad faith could not be considered under this provision, and in *Hamilton v Secretary of State for Scotland* 1972 SC 72 that a failure to comply with natural justice fell outside its terms.

11. 1973 SLT 81, at p. 86.

12. Lord Denning MR in *Ashbridge Investments Ltd v Minister of Housing and Local Government* [1965] 1 WLR 1320, at 1326.

13. e.g. Forbes J. in *Seddon Properties Ltd v Secretary of State for the Environment* (1978) 42 P & CR 26, at 26–8; Lord President Emslie in *Wordie Property Co. Ltd v Secretary of State for Scotland* 1984 SLT 345, at 347–8.

14. M. Deans, 'Judicial Review in Planning' (1991) 32 SPLP 4, 33 SPLP 39.

15. *London and Clydeside Estates Ltd v Secretary of State for Scotland* 1987 SLT 459.

16. *Aberdeen District Council v Secretary of State for Scotland* 1993 SLT 1149.

17. *McDaid v Clydebank District Council* 1984 SLT 162; *R. v Greenwich London Borough Council, ex p. Patel* (1985) 51 P & CR 282; see below.

18. *R. v Hillingdon London Borough Council, ex p. Royco Homes Ltd* [1974] QB 720; *London and Clydeside Estates Ltd v Aberdeen District Council* 1980 SC (HL) 1.

19. e.g. *R. v Hammersmith and Fulham London Borough Council, ex p. People Before Profit Ltd* (1981) 80 LGR 322; *Inverness, Loch Ness and Nairn Tourist Board v Highland Regional Council* (1988) 24 SPLP 47.

20. One publisher considers that there are sufficient cases of sufficient interest to have launched a journal wholly devoted to this area, containing brief articles and a case digest: *Environmental Judicial Review Bulletin* launched by Wiley Chancery in September 1994.

21. *Kincardine and Deeside District Council v Forestry Commissioners* 1992 SLT 1180.

22. *R. v London Boroughs Transport Committee, ex p. Freight Transport Association Ltd* [1991] 1 WLR 828.

23. e.g. the disputes arising from rival plans to redevelop Aberdeen city centre (*Wordie Property Co. Ltd v Secretary of State for Scotland* 1984 SLT 345) and the trail of litigation over development on the 'golden mile' just east of Inverness (*Narden Services Ltd v Secretary of State for Scotland* (1993) 39 SPEL 48; *Mackenzie's Trustees v Highland Regional Council* 1995 SLT 218).

24. *Lakin Ltd v Secretary of State for Scotland* 1988 SLT 780.

25. See for example J. Rowan-Robinson, E. Young and I. McLarty, *The Enforcement of Planning Control in Scotland* (1984); R. Carnwath, *Enforcing Planning Control* (1989).

26. e.g. *R. v Secretary of State for Transport, ex p. Richmond-upon-Thames London Borough Council* [1994] 1 WLR 74 arising from opposition to the noise disturbance to be caused by new arrangements for night flying at the London airports; the revised plans proposed in the light of the objectors' success in that case have themselves been successfully challenged (*R. v Secretary of State for Transport, ex p. Richmond-upon-*

Thames London Borough Council, The Times, 29 December 1994, QBD; (1995) 7 ELM 52). See also the further litigation involving the same parties reported in *The Times*, 11 May 1995.

27. *R. v Inspectorate of Pollution, ex p. Greenpeace Ltd* [1994] 4 All ER 321; *R. v Inspectorate of Pollution, ex p. Greenpeace Ltd* (No. 2) [1994] 4 All ER 329; *R. v Secretary of State for the Environment, ex p. Greenpeace Ltd* [1994] 4 All ER 352.

28. e.g. *Bushell v Secretary of State for the Environment* [1981] AC 75.

29. e.g. *R. v Hammersmith and Fulham London Borough Council, ex p. People Before Profit Ltd* (1981) 80 LGR 322.

30. *R. v Secretary of State for the Environment, ex p. Friends of the Earth Ltd* [1994] 2 CMLR 760 QBD and *The Times*, 8 June 1995 CA.

31. *R. v Inspectorate of Pollution, ex p. Greenpeace Ltd* [1994] 4 All ER 321; *R. v Inspectorate of Pollution, ex p. Greenpeace Ltd (No. 2)* [1994] 4 All ER 329; *R. v Secretary of State for the Environment, ex p. Greenpeace Ltd* [1994] 4 All ER 352.

32. *R. v Secretary of State for the Environment, ex p. Royal Society for the Protection of Birds, The Times*, 10 February 1995, HL.

33. e.g. *Coleshill and District Investment Co. Ltd v Minister of Housing and Local Government* [1969] 1 WLR 746.

34. e.g. *Burdle v Secretary of State for the Environment* [1972] 1 WLR 1207.

35. e.g. *R. v Plymouth City Council, ex p. Plymouth and South Devon Co-operative Society Ltd* (1993) 67 P & CR 78.

36. See below at p. 53.

37. *R. v Secretary of State for the Environment, ex p. Rose Theatre Trust Co.* [1990] 1 QB 504.

38. *Kincardine and Deeside District Council v Forestry Commissioners* 1992 SLT 1180.

39. *R. v Metropolitan Stipendiary Magistrate, ex p. London Waste Regulation Authority* [1993] 3 All ER 113; *R. v Avon County Council, ex p. Terry Adams Ltd, The Times*, 20 January 1994 CA.

40. *North Uist Fisheries Ltd v Secretary of State for Scotland* 1992 SLT 333; *R. v Secretary of State for the Environment, ex p. Upton Brickworks Ltd* [1992] JPL 1044.

41. e.g. *R. v Secretary of State for the Environment, ex p. Simms and Burrows* (1989) 60 P & CR 105; *Fowler v Secretary of State for the Environment* (1991) 64 P & CR 16.

42. *R. v Somerset County Council, ex p. Fewings* [1995] 1 WLR 1037, CA.

43. Dir. 90/313.

44. e.g. Environmental Protection Act 1990, ss 20, 64, 122.

45. Environmental Information Regulations 1992, SI 1992, No. 3240.

46. The issues covered in this section are fully discussed in the contributions in Section II of D. Robinson and J. Dunkley, *Public Interest Perspectives in Environmental Law* (1995); see also C.T. Reid, *Nature Conservation Law* (1994) pp 21–8; J. Upson and D. Hughes, 'Locus Standi—an essential hurdle in judicial review of environmental action' (1994) 6 ELM 136.

47. See Sir K. Schiemann, 'Locus Standi' [1990] PL 342.

48. 'If any person . . . is aggrieved by . . .': Town and Country Planning (Scotland) Act 1972, s. 233(1); Town and Country Planning Act 1990, s. 288(1).

49. Lord MacDermott LCJ. in *R. (Nicholl) v Recorder of Belfast* [1965] NI 7, at 10.

50. See generally E. Young, ' "Aggrieved Persons" in Planning Law', 1993 SLT (News) 43.

51. Salmon J. in *Buxton v Minister of Housing and Local Government* [1961] 1 QB 278, at 285, relying on *In re Sidebotham* (1880) 14 ChD 458.

52. *Attorney General of the Gambia v N'jie* [1961] AC 617, at 634.

53. *Turner v Secretary of State for the Environment* (1973) 28 P & CR 123.

54. *Times Investment Ltd v Secretary of State for the Environment* (1990) 61 P & CR 98.

55. *Strathclyde Regional Council v Secretary of State for Scotland (No. 2)* 1990 SLT 149; *North East Fife District Council v Secretary of State for Scotland* 1992 SLT 373; the status of a planning authority as 'person aggrieved' may depend on the precise statutory context (*Strathclyde Regional Council v Secretary of State for Scotland* 1989 SLT 821).

56. 1993 SLT 228.
57. ibid., at 234–5.
58. Cf. the much more restrictive approach thirty years ago in *Simpson v Edinburgh Corporation* 1960 SC 313.
59. In *R. v Darlington Borough Council, ex p. Association of Darlington Taxi Owners, The Times,* 21 January 1994, QBD an unincorporated association was said to lack capacity, whereas it was stated in *R. v London Borough of Tower Hamlets, ex p. Tower Hamlets Combined Traders Association* [1994] COD 325 that in principle the unincorporated status of the body did not matter.
60. Law Commission, above, n. 3, pp 51–2.
61. *R. v Hammersmith and Fulham London Borough Council, ex p. People Before Profit Ltd* (1981) 80 LGR 322, at 333; *R. v Secretary of State for the Environment, ex p. Rose Theatre Trust Co.* [1990] 1 QB 504, at 521.
62. *Scottish Old People's Welfare Council, Petitioners* 1987 SLT 179, at 185.
63. *Scottish Old People's Welfare Council, Petitioners* 1987 SLT 179; in some cases, though, it is accepted that the issue of standing may not be separable from a consideration of the merits, *Gordon v Kirkcaldy District Council* 1989 SLT 507.
64. As in *Scottish Old People's Welfare Council, Petitioners* 1987 SLT 179.
65. 1915 SC (HL) 7, at 12–13.
66. 1979 SLT 279.
67. *Scottish Old People's Welfare Council, Petitioners* 1987 SLT 179.
68. 1992 SLT 1180.
69. Supreme Court Act 1981, s. 31(3); the same test applies in Northern Ireland: (Judicature (Northern Ireland) Act 1978, s. 18(4)).
70. *R. v Inland Revenue Commissioners, ex p. National Federation of Self-employed and Small Businesses Ltd* [1982] AC 617.
71. H.W.R. Wade and C.F. Forsyth, *Administrative Law* (7th edn) (1994) pp 601–610.
72. [1990] 1 QB 504.
73. 1979 SLT 279.
74. (1991) 3 JEL 293.
75. e.g. *McColl v Strathclyde Regional Council* 1983 SLT 616.
76. (1991) 3 JEL 135.
77. *Council of Civil Service Unions v Minister for the Civil Service* [1985] AC 374.
78. 1987 SLT 492 (affirmed 1988 SLT 850).
79. [1994] 4 All ER 329.
80. ibid., at 351.
81. Rose LJ. in *R. v Secretary of State for Foreign Affairs, ex p. World Development Movement Ltd* [1995] 1 All ER 611, at 620.
82. [1995] 1 All ER 611.
83. The Law Commission has proposed that there should be a broad test whereby cases could proceed where the court considers that it is in the public interest to allow the applicant to make the application; this would allow individuals to challenge decisions which affect the public at large and allow interest groups to take action where appropriate (Law Comm., above, n. 3, pp 41–4).
84. S. Cragg, 'Legal Aid and Environmental Judicial Review' (1994) 1 *Environmental Judicial Review Bulletin,* 7; C. Pugh and M. Day, *Toxic Torts* (1992) ch. 3; D. Robinson and J. Dunkley (eds) *Public Interest Perspectives in Environmental Law* (1995) pp 179–80, 185–7, 204–206.
85. Law Comm., above, n. 3, p. 88.
86. *R. v Inspectorate of Pollution, ex p. Greenpeace Ltd (No. 2)* [1994] 4 All ER 329, at 350.
87. See M. Purdue's commentary on *R. v Secretary of State for the Environment, ex p. Greenpeace Ltd* (1994) 6 JEL 337, at 342.
88. Law Comm., above, n. 3, pp 84–7.

89. *R. v Inspectorate of Pollution, ex p. Greenpeace Ltd* [1994] 4 All ER 321.
90. *The Times*, 10 February 1995 HL.
91. ibid.; *R. v London Borough of Lambeth and Caballito Properties Ltd, ex p. Sibyll Walker* (unreported, but quoted by M. Purdue at (1994) 6 JEL 343).
92. See M. Purdue's comment on the THORP litigation (1994) 6 JEL 337, at 342–4.
93. [1956] AC 736.
94. Acquisition of Land (Authorisation Procedure) Act 1946, sch. 1, para. 16.
95. [1969] 2 AC 147.
96. Foreign Compensation Act 1950, s. 4(4).
97. Interestingly, this decision led to a new statutory provision which did allow for questions of law and allegations of a breach of natural justice to be referred to the courts but otherwise extended the protection from challenge to 'anything which purports to be a determination' (Foreign Compensation Act 1969, s. 3).
98. *McDaid v Clydebank District Council* 1984 SLT 162; *R. v Greenwich London Borough Council, ex p. Patel* (1985) 51 P & CR 282.
99. [1977] QB 122.
100. e.g. *Pollock v Secretary of State for Scotland* 1992 SCLR 972; *R. v Cornwall County Council, ex p. Huntingdon* [1994] 1 All ER 694; see Law Comm., above, n. 3, pp 106–107.
101. Justice-All Souls, *Administrative Justice—Some Necessary Reforms* (1988) p. 175.
102. Law Comm., above, n. 3, pp 110–112.
103. *Council of Civil Service Unions v Minister for the Civil Service* [1985] AC 374.
104. *Gill & Co. (London) Ltd v Secretary of State for the Environment* [1978] JPL 373.
105. *Ostreicher v Secretary of State for the Environment* [1978] 3 All ER 82.
106. *Performance Cars Ltd v Secretary of State for the Environment* (1977) 34 P & CR 92.
107. *Cotterell v Secretary of State for the Environment* [1991] 2 PLR 37, [1991] JPL 1155.
108. *Hamilton v Secretary of State for Scotland* 1972 SC 72.
109. *London Borough of Southwark v Secretary of State for the Environment* [1987] JPL 36.
110. *Anduff Holdings Ltd v Secretary of State for Scotland* 1992 SLT 696.
111. *Bushell v Secretary of State for the Environment* [1981] AC 75.
112. *R. v Great Yarmouth Borough Council, ex p. Botton Bros Arcades Ltd* [1988] JPL 18; *R. v Swale Borough Council, ex p. Royal Society for the Protection of Birds* (1991) 3 JEL 135.
113. *Franklin v Minister of Town and Country Planning* [1948] AC 87.
114. *London and Clydeside Estates Ltd v Secretary of State for Scotland* 1987 SLT 459.
115. *Howard v Secretary of State for the Environment* [1975] QB 235; *London and Clydeside Estates Ltd v Aberdeen District Council* 1980 SC (HL) 1; *R. v London Borough of Lambeth Council, ex p. Sharp* (1986) 55 P & CR 232.
116. See M. Purdue, E. Young and J. Rowan-Robinson, *Planning Law and Procedure* (1989) pp 553–4.
117. Lord Cameron in *Wordie Property Co. Ltd v Secretary of State for Scotland* 1984 SLT 345, at 356; Lord Bridge expressed the same idea as follows: 'I should be sorry to see excessive legalism turn this requirement into a hazard for decision-makers in which it is their skill at draftsmanship rather than the substance of their reasoning which is put to the test' (*Save Britain's Heritage v Number 1 Poultry Ltd* [1991] 1 WLR 153, at 170–1).
118. [1964] 2 QB 467.
119. *Westminster City Council v Great Portland Estates plc* [1985] AC 661.
120. *Givaudan & Co. Ltd v Minister of Housing and Local Government* [1967] 1 WLR 250; *Wordie Property Co. Ltd v Secretary of State for Scotland* 1984 SLT 345.
121. Town and Country Planning (Scotland) Act 1972, s. 26(1); Town and Country Planning Act 1990, s. 70(2).
122. *Stringer v Minister of Housing and Local Government* [1970] 1 WLR 1281, at 1295.
123. e.g. N. Collar, *Planning Law* (1994) provides a list which runs from A–X but is 'not exhaustive' (pp 138–52).

124. [1994] 1 PLR 85, [1994] JPL B 118; see also *Aberdeen District Council v Secretary of State for Scotland* 1993 SLT 1325.
125. Town and Country Planning (Scotland) Act 1972, s. 26(1); Town and Country Planning Act 1990, s. 70(2).
126. Town and Country Planning (Scotland) Act 1972, s. 18A; Town and Country Planning Act 1990, s. 54A (both added by the Planning and Compensation Act 1991, ss 58 and 26).
127. M. Purdue, 'The Impact of Section 54A' [1994] JPL 399.
128. (1982) 54 P & CR 86.
129. *Gillick v West Norfolk and Wisbech Area Health Authority* [1986] AC 112; *Scottish Old People's Welfare Council, Petitioners* 1987 SLT 179.
130. *The Noble Organisation Ltd v Falkirk District Council* 1994 SLT 100 (sadly the Noble Organisation is not an aristocratic pressure group but a commercial firm operating amusement centres); *Re Cooper's Application* [1991] NI 257.
131. Statutory requirements to state reasons are increasingly common, and the common law appears to be moving gradually towards insisting on reasons in more and more circumstances (see P.P. Craig, 'The Common Law, Reasons and Administrative Justice' [1994] CLJ 282; C.R. Munro, 'The Duty to Give Reasons for Decisions', 1995 SLT (News) 5).
132. *R. v Secretary of State for the Environment, ex p. Greenpeace Ltd* [1994] 4 All ER 352.
133. e.g. *Kincardine and Deeside District Council v Forestry Commissioners* 1992 SLT 1180; *Twyford Parish Council v Secretary of State for the Environment* [1992] 1 CMLR 276.
134. *R. v Secretary of State for the Environment, ex p. Friends of the Earth* [1994] 2 CMLR 760 (QBD) and *The Times*, 8 June 1995, CA.
135. Art. 130r(2). This principle requires that once a potential risk to the environment has been identified, measures to combat it should be taken, even though the extent of the risk, or even its very existence, has not been scientifically established beyond doubt.
136. *R. v Secretary of State for Trade and Industry, ex p. Duddridge, The Independent*, 4 October 1994, QBD (and see 237 ENDS Report 41).
137. *R. v Secretary of State for the Environment, ex p. Royal Society for the Protection of Birds, The Times*, 10 February 1995, HL.
138. *R. v Secretary of State for the Environment, ex p. Greenpeace Ltd* [1994] 4 All ER 352.
139. *R. v London Boroughs Transport Committee, ex p. Freight Transport Association Ltd* [1991] 1 WLR 828.
140. [1990] 2 AC 85, [1991] 1 AC 603.
141. e.g. the famous case on sex discrimination, *Marshall v Southampton and South West Hampshire Area Health Authority (Teaching)* [1986] QB 401.
142. *Kincardine and Deeside District Council v Forestry Commissioners* 1992 SLT 1180, at 1187.
143. *Twyford Parish Council v Secretary of State for Environment* [1992] 1 CMLR 276.
144. See, for example, the comments of Advocate General Mischo in *Commission v Germany* (C-361/88) [1991] ECR I-2567, at 2591.
145. *R. v Secretary of State for Trade and Industry, ex p. Duddridge, The Independent*, 4 October 1994, QBD (and see 237 ENDS Report 41).
146. An interesting alternative still to be explored is the extent to which an individual suffering harm as the result of the government's failure to ensure that European environmental standards are in fact being met could claim compensation under the principle of *Francovich v Italy* (C-6/90, -9/90) [1991] ECR I-5357.
147. *Paola Faccini Dori v Recreb Srl* (C-91/92) *The Times*, 4 August 1994, ECJ.
148. Including: P. McAuslan, 'The Role of Courts and other Judicial Type Bodies in Environmental Management' (1991) 3 JEL 195; Sir H. Woolf, 'Are the Judiciary Environmentally Myopic?' (1992) 4 JEL 1; R. Carnwath, 'Environmental Enforcement: The Need for a Specialist Court' [1992] JPL 799; J. Rowan-Robinson,

'Environmental Protection—The Case for a new Dispute-Resolution Procedure' (1993) 38 JLSS 5; M. Grant (ed.) *Environmental Litigation: Towards an Environmental Court?* (1993); D. Robinson and J. Dunkley (eds) *Public Interest Perspectives in Environmental Law* (1995) chs 14–15.

149. Law Comm. above, n. 3, pp 165, 171–2.

150. Sir H. Woolf, 'Are the Judiciary Environmentally Myopic?' (1992) 4 JEL 1, at 10.

151. *R. v Secretary of State for Transport, ex p. Richmond-upon-Thames London Borough Council* [1994] 1 WLR 74 and *The Times*, 29 December 1994, QBD.

152. *R. v Inspectorate of Pollution, ex p. Greenpeace Ltd (No. 2)* [1994] 4 All ER 329; *R. v Secretary of State for the Environment, ex p. Greenpeace Ltd* [1994] 4 All ER 352.

153. Sir H. Woolf, 'Are the Judiciary Environmentally Myopic?' (1992) 4 JEL 1, at 7–8.

Chapter Three

Judicial Review and Education

Paul Meredith

Introduction

There can be few areas of social provision by the state where the level,
scope and nature of conflict has intensified to a greater extent in the past two
decades than education, and it should come as no surprise that one
consequence of this has been a marked growth in the incidence and variety
of judicial review. This growth in legal challenge has come about for many
reasons, but perhaps two may be identified as of particular importance: first,
the level of tension between the central department with responsibility for
education, the Department for Education (DFE), and local education
authorities, (LEAs), has risen to an unprecedented level, thus increasing
recourse to the courts as a means of mediation between the different levels
of government; and secondly, there has been strong encouragement since
1979 of individualism, freedom of choice, and consumerism as fundamental
principles promoting an ethos of individual rights enforceable against public
authorities.

It is, of course, true that tension between the central department and
LEAs has existed throughout the period following the enactment of the
Education Act 1944; indeed, in a real sense, the very essence of the central-
local relationship has been a creative and constructive tension, with each
level of government asserting the constitutional legitimacy of its role in the
policy and decision-making process.[1] In the past two decades, however, that
constructive tension has in a number of contexts erupted into open hostility
and legal challenge. This has happened notably in the context of the
comprehensive reorganisation of secondary schools, giving rise to one of
the landmark cases in modern English administrative law, the *Tameside* case
in 1976.[2] Since the early 1980s, similar tension has existed between the
central department and LEAs over taking surplus places out of use in the
light of the declining school population, a process which has given rise to
many bitter disputes over school closures, amalgamations and other forms
of structural reorganisation, leading in many cases to legal challenge.

The pressures exerted by central government on LEAs in the contexts of comprehensive reorganisation and reorganisation in the light of falling rolls, though real and in many cases greatly resented by LEAs which regarded such pressure as an assault on their legitimate strategic planning role, did not, however, directly undermine the fundamental basis of the institutional balance between the central department and LEAs established under the 1944 Act. Indeed, the very fact that many LEAs so successfully resisted such central pressures is evidence that that institutional balance remained essentially intact. Of greater long-term importance in terms of institutional structure has more recently been the undermining of LEAs' capacity for the strategic planning of the provision of schools in their respective areas brought about by permitting schools to apply to opt out of LEA control in favour of grant-maintained status.

Applications by individual schools to opt out have in many cases severely disrupted proposals put forward by LEAs for wide-ranging rationalisation of educational provision, and it is no surprise that this has given rise to substantial legal challenges. There is, furthermore, little doubt that there will be a major growth in judicial review in this context as the new Funding Agency for Schools, created under the Education Act 1993, incrementally assumes its strategic planning role in respect of the rationalisation of schools up and down the country: it is readily predictable that there will be major policy disagreements and demarcation disputes between LEAs and the Funding Agency, particularly at the stage when legal responsibility for ensuring sufficiency of educational provision is held jointly by the relevant LEA and the Funding Agency.[3] This type of radical structural change in the strategic planning process was bound to give rise to legal conflict as LEAs, jealous of their powers and fearful for their continuing existence, have invoked the protection of the courts to curb what they saw as the highly damaging consequences of the government's reforms.

Central government pressure on LEAs and structural reform of the institutional balance between central and local government are, therefore, among the foremost reasons for the growth of judicial review in the context of education in the past two decades. A second important reason has, however, been the adoption of the principles of individualism, freedom of choice and consumerism as a powerful driving-force behind educational reform since 1979. This fits well with the basic conception of judicial review as a means of upholding the interests of the individual against the abuse of discretion or procedural failure on the part of public authorities. Many applications for judicial review in the educational context during this period may be categorised as individual challenges in such spheres as choice of school and special educational needs. Some of these cases— particularly those relating to choice of school—raise profound considerations of conscience relating, for instance, to the religious or cultural or linguistic ethos of a school, and thereby bring into focus the nature and scope of fundamental rights and interests in education. Most of these types of individualised challenge relate essentially to the interests of the individual parent or child. Individual challenge has, however, also frequently arisen at the level of seeking to protect the interests of a particular school rather than a particular child: parental action groups or the governing bodies of schools have frequently sought to challenge proposals for school closures or amalgamations or other forms of structural reorganisation. School reorganisation has thus become a fertile ground for a wide range of pressure group activity involving the promotion of the interests of particular parents, particular sections of the community and particular schools, not infrequently conflicting with the wider interests of the community at large.

It will be clear from what has been written that the range and scope of judicial review in the context of education in the past twenty years has been wide ranging and disparate. No attempt will be made here to offer a comprehensive catalogue of legal challenges over educational disputes during this period: what follows will inevitably be highly selective, and will seek to identify only some of the spheres of conflict and trends that have arisen. First, we shall examine conflict over the reorganisation or rationalisation of schools, whether in the context of comprehensive reorganisation or falling rolls or schools seeking to opt out of LEA control: in these cases the legal conflict has either been between the different public authorities involved—the central department, the LEA concerned, or the governing body of the school or schools concerned; or else it has been launched by parental action groups seeking to avert the closure, amalgamation or reorganisation of a particular school. We shall then go on, secondly, to examine the nature of some of the more individualised types of legal challenge, focusing expressly on parental choice of school.

Legal Conflict over School Reorganisation and Rationalisation

The strategic planning partnership

The strategic planning of the provision of schools within their respective areas could legitimately be regarded as the core function of LEAs. It includes strategic planning as to the establishment of new schools, amalgamating existing schools, removing surplus places from use, closing schools down, formulating policy over the provision of single sex schools or selective schools, as well as many other crucial matters of immense importance to parents, pupils and local communities.

Under the balanced partnership between the central department and LEAs established by the Education Act 1944, LEAs were given a highly significant input into this strategic planning process, in recognition of their appreciation of and sensitivity towards local needs and preferences and of their local democratic accountability and legitimacy. LEAs were given under the 1944 Act the primary duty of ensuring the provision within their area of 'efficient education'[4] and 'sufficient' schools[5] and, most importantly, they were given the power of initiative in making proposals to the minister (later the Secretary of State) for the establishment or closure of schools[6] and, following the Education Act 1968, making significant changes in their character: a significant change in character might arise, for instance, by changing the age range of the school, changing the school from being single sex to coeducational or vice versa, or changing the admission arrangements by eradicating or introducing selection by reference to academic criteria. Although the Secretary of State had (and still retains)[7] the power of final determination of such proposals, the *initiative* power lay with the LEAs, and it was the LEAs, in consultation with the many interested parties involved, which would formulate the detailed proposals for reorganisation or rationalisation. Although the balance of power in the partnership between the Secretary of State and LEAs was never an even one, the Secretary of State always being regarded as the senior partner, LEAs unquestionably had a most significant role as initiators of proposals and in the formulation of their proposals. This is evidenced by the many different patterns of educational provision which developed throughout England and Wales in the decades following 1944.

Comprehensive reorganisation

The strategic planning partnership between the central department and LEAs has been subject to considerable strain, the structure and organisation of schools having been in a constant state of flux ever since 1944. Successive ministers of different political complexions have not hesitated to seek to impose their will on LEAs which often strenuously attempted to develop patterns of organisation not favoured by the centre. This is most graphically illustrated by the measures adopted by the Labour governments of 1964 to 1970 and 1974 to 1979 to bring about a radical change in the organisational structure of schools through the introduction of non-academically selective admissions to secondary schools, generally known as comprehensive reorganisation. The introduction of comprehensive reorganisation has been well catalogued elsewhere,[8] but it is worth recalling that the government's primary mechanism for promoting its policy was a succession of departmental circulars exerting considerable pressure on LEAs to submit reorganisation proposals under threat of various forms of financial pressure, notably the possible withholding of loan sanction for any proposed school building projects which were incompatible with comprehensive organisation.[9] Not until 1976 did the government resort to statutory endorsement of its policy, in the shape of the Education Act 1976, which for the first time enshrined the 'comprehensive principle' in statute[10] and empowered the Secretary of State to require the submission of reorganisation proposals,[11] a potentially lengthy process offering LEAs ample opportunity for delay and obstruction. Such tactics adopted by some LEAs ensured that comprehensive reorganisation was far from complete by the time of the 1979 general election and the subsequent repeal of the comprehensive principle by the Education Act 1979.[12]

Of all the many disputes between the central department and LEAs over comprehensive reorganisation in the 1960s and 1970s, perhaps the most prominent was the conflict over reorganisation in the Metropolitan Borough of Tameside in 1976, the key events of which took place before the coming into force of the Education Act of that year: *Secretary of State for Education and Science v Tameside Metropolitan Borough Council*.[13] Mr Fred Mulley as Secretary of State issued a direction under section 68 of the Education Act 1944 to the Conservative-controlled council which had been resisting full implementation of its predecessor (Labour-controlled) council's plans for comprehensive reorganisation which had already been approved by the Secretary of State under section 13 of the 1944 Act.[14] The section 68 direction was issued on the basis of the Secretary of State's satisfaction that the LEA had been acting 'unreasonably', in particular in relation to procedures for the selection of pupils for places in two grammar schools which would be retained under the proposals of the new Conservative-controlled LEA. The LEA, however, challenged the validity of the direction when the Secretary of State sought to enforce it by an order of mandamus. Though unsuccessful in the Divisional Court, the LEA's challenge was upheld unanimously by the Court of Appeal and House of Lords, applying the '*Wednesbury*' test[15] in deciding whether the Secretary of State had properly directed himself in law as to the alleged unreasonableness of the LEA's actions. This narrowed drastically the possibility of the Secretary of State issuing a section 68 direction, limiting it to circumstances where the Secretary of State was satisfied that the LEA was acting in a way in which no LEA could conceivably act. One view of this decision is that it amounted to a judicial usurpation of the legislative function through effectively rendering inoperable a statutory provision enacted with the object of enabling the Secretary of State in the final resort to take action by way of direction and control over educational provision,[16] and that the Court of Appeal and House of Lords had unwarrantably substituted their own appraisal of the reasonableness of the LEA's proposals for that of the Secretary of State, whose decision had been based on the accumulated expertise and advice of his department. As Professor Griffith has commented:

> In *Tameside* the minister had sound administrative reasons for believing that the local authority was acting unreasonably, but it was held that merely to have such reasons was insufficient.[17]

An opposing view is that the Secretary of State's direction had been based on no more than a difference of view as to educational policy, that the LEA's policy had received the endorsement of the local electorate in the May 1976 local elections, that for the Secretary of State to employ section 68 in order to impose his policy in place of that preferred by the LEA was a misuse of power, and that it evinced a misconstruction of the word 'unreasonable' in section 68. 'Unreasonable' was to be given its narrow public law meaning in accordance with the *Wednesbury* case. As stated by Lord Diplock:

> . . . In public law, 'unreasonable' as descriptive of the way in which a public authority has purported to exercise a discretion vested in it has become a term of legal art. To fall within this expression it must be conduct which no sensible authority acting with due appreciation of its responsibilities would have decided to adopt.[18]

In the *Tameside* case, the courts were inescapably enmeshed in a bitter political dispute between the central department and the LEA concerned. Whatever the outcome, they would inevitably have been accused of political partiality. In the event the Court of Appeal and House of Lords chose to apply the well-established *Wednesbury* definition of 'unreasonableness', equating the minister's power of intervention under section 68 with that of the courts to strike down executive action on the ground of unreasonableness. This rendered section 68 virtually inoperative, an outcome which could be regarded as running counter to parliament's intention of creating a specific measure for central control. One consequence has been that some later legislation has deliberately made central powers of intervention dependent upon ministerial satisfaction as to the existence of a pure state of fact rather than as to unreasonable conduct on the part of local authorities.[19] In practice, section 68 had been sparingly used before the *Tameside* case, chiefly in respect of cases involving the allocation of pupils to individual schools, and it has virtually never been invoked since *Tameside*. Even before *Tameside*, it is almost certainly the case that the government had been well aware of the potential difficulties involved in enforcing directions under the section. The inoperability of section 68 is, however, arguably of little practical significance in the light of the central department's undeniably dominant overall position. Given that dominance, although *Tameside* was a victory for one particular Conservative-controlled LEA at the time, it can scarcely be regarded as a major underpinning of local democracy and autonomy in educational policy-making. Indeed, the government continued to impose its policy of comprehensive reorganisation with even greater vigour following statutory endorsement of the comprehensive principle in the 1976 Act, and thereby achieved a substantial, though by no means complete, shift in the direction of non-selective entry to secondary schools by the end of the 1970s.

Falling rolls and the removal of surplus places

Similar pressure was brought to bear on LEAs during the 1980s—and continues into the 1990s—over the removal of surplus school places in the light of falling rolls,[20] and this too has caused considerable strain between the central department and many LEAs. Falling rolls have been the root cause of a great deal of structural upheaval in the provision of schools and of many legal challenges, largely by interest groups seeking to protect the interests of a particular school or schools. A most important further dimension to this structural reorganisation has, however, been added since the Education Reform Act 1988 by the possibility of schools opting out of LEA control in favour of grant-maintained status: a large proportion of the schools seeking to opt out have been those subject to structural threat under LEA proposals for rationalisation of provision in the light of falling rolls, and they have used opting out as a technique for averting closure, amalgamation or some other unwelcome form of reorganisation.

As with comprehensive reorganisation, the central department has used the device of the departmental circular to impose its preferred policy—the removal of surplus places in order to achieve economies. The pursuit of this policy by the central department has placed LEAs in the position of having to make agonising choices as to whether particular schools should be reduced in size, amalgamated or closed altogether; whether staff capacity should be reduced or redeployed, with extensive consequences for sustaining a viable curriculum; or whether, on the contrary, staffing resources should be maintained in order to improve staff-pupil ratios, and to make provision for an eventual upturn in pupil numbers. Many LEAs would have wished to approach these structural choices in their own way and in their own time in the light of their own political, social and educational priorities, yet the central department has not hesitated to use its legal, political and financial strength to impose its preferred option of taking surplus places out of use. This policy was spelled out in the clearest terms in a departmental circular in 1981 which stressed the need for 'much faster progress' towards removal of surplus places.[21] LEAs were required to conduct a review of their existing school stock and to submit to the Secretary of State their proposals for reduction in capacity. This requirement was coupled with a statement that the Secretary of State intended to take this information from LEAs into account when considering plans for educational expenditure in future years.[22] Central pressure on LEAs to reduce surplus capacity continued throughout the 1980s,[23] and indeed continues to this day.[24] From the early 1980s to the present, disputes over school closures and amalgamations have, indeed, been prominent on the local political agenda, and many pressure group campaigns have been organised in respect of particular schools or groups of schools. Many such groups have submitted detailed objections to proposals for reorganisation published by LEAs under section 12 of the Education Act 1980, and a significant number of disputes have been taken as far as the courts.

The statutory procedures under section 12 for the publication of proposals by the LEA, and the consideration of those proposals, and any objections submitted by interested parties, by the Secretary of State, are highly skeletal in form and offer little opportunity for legal challenge on grounds of procedural impropriety. Furthermore, the initial drawing up of the proposals by the LEA itself before their formal publication under section 12 was, before an important amendment requiring consultation with interested parties was introduced under the Education Act 1993,[25] entirely unregulated by statute, despite the fact that the gestation of these proposals could well involve highly complex processes of negotiation and deliberation over several years. This appeared to offer highly unpromising territory for judicial review, but this changed following an important challenge brought in 1985 by a group of parents of children in the London Borough of Brent on the ground that the LEA had failed adequately to consult them over the substance of their reorganisation proposals while they were at their formative stage before their formal publication under section 12: *R. v Brent London Borough Council, ex parte Gunning.*[26] On the evidence it was clear that the consultations had been seriously defective in material respects.[27] The difficulty was, however, that the process of drawing up the proposals was entirely non-statutory, the only requirements as to consultation at that time being in the form of a departmental circular[28] and an administrative memorandum[29] containing exhortations from the Secretary of State addressed to LEAs. The parents argued that the terms of these non-statutory administrative exhortations, coupled with a past practice of consultation, created a legitimate expectation that they would be fully and effectively consulted. Hodgson J. had no difficulty in holding that the parents did indeed have such a legitimate expectation:

> The parents had no statutory right to be consulted, but that they had a legitimate expectation that they would be consulted seems to be beyond question.[30]

The establishment of a clearly recognised legitimate expectation of consultation was a significant breakthrough for parental action groups seeking to challenge reorganisation proposals. The *Gunning* case was, furthermore, highly significant for its judicial clarification of the concept of consultation. Hodgson J. in his judgment cited with approval the four essential criteria for proper consultations set out in argument by Mr Stephen Sedley QC (as he then was) on behalf of the parents:

1. consultations must take place while the proposals are still at a formative stage;
2. the proposer must give sufficient reasons for any proposal to permit 'intelligent consideration and response';
3. 'adequate time' must be given for such consideration and response; and
4. the product of consultation must be 'conscientiously taken into account' in finalising any statutory proposals.[31]

These criteria were subsequently endorsed in two unreported school closure challenges in 1986, *R. v Sutton London Borough Council, ex parte Hamlet*[32] and *R. v Northamptonshire County Council, ex parte Tebbutt*,[33] and have very recently been endorsed in the context of the adequacy of consultation over closure of a local authority home for the elderly.[34] The first criterion—that the proposals be still at a genuinely *formative* stage when the consultation takes place—may in practice be extremely difficult to apply. This was illustrated in *Nichol v Gateshead Metropolitan Borough Council*,[35] where a parental action group complained that the LEA had failed to consult parents on each one of six separate possible patterns of school organisation in the area, but rather on only one of those patterns, the LEA having already made a clear decision of policy in favour of that one pattern. At first instance, McCowan J. held that this was in breach of the principle that consultation should take place at a truly formative stage in the planning process, the LEA having at the time of consultation been all but committed in principle to one pattern. The Court of Appeal, however, reversed McCowan J.'s decision, O'Connor LJ. taking the view that to require consultation over each possible organisational pattern would be 'in effect requiring a referendum': it was quite proper for the LEA to take an initial decision of policy in favour of one pattern, provided that it then proceeded to consult genuinely as to the detailed proposals within that pattern.

Judicial recognition of legally insufficient consultation as a basis for pressure group challenge to reorganisation proposals, even in the absence of any statutory requirement to consult, operated as a significant strengthening of parental interests and of the promotion of principles of due process. In the event, the absence of a statutory requirement as to consultation was subsequently remedied at least in part by section 229 of the Education Act 1993, an important amendment which would probably not have been introduced had it not been for the *Gunning* case and later challenges. The substance of section 229, however, could hardly be said to impose on LEAs an extensive and clear-cut duty of consultation: it requires LEAs, before publishing their proposals, to consult 'such persons as appear to them to be appropriate', and to 'have regard to any guidance given from time to time by the Secretary of State'. This hardly represents a secure guarantee of comprehensive consultation and due process in this most important area. For an elaboration of the actual content of consultation here, the *Gunning* case remains of considerable importance as the source of the 'Sedley criteria'.

A further most important legal basis of challenge to reorganisation proposals—one with wide consequences for LEAs seeking to perform their statutory obligation to ensure provision of sufficient schools in their area— has been that the proposals conflict with the LEAs' obligation under the Sex Discrimination Act 1975 to avoid discrimination between the sexes. One such challenge arose in Bristol: *R. v Secretary of State for Education and Science, ex parte Keating*.[36] The LEA, Avon County Council, had sought to overcome the problem of falling rolls by proposing the closure of the only single sex comprehensive school for boys in the city, while retaining two girls' single sex comprehensive schools, partly as a result of pressure from the city's substantial Muslim population. The applicants argued that the LEA, in carrying out its duty to secure the provision of sufficient schools,[37] had failed to comply with section 23 of the Sex Discrimination Act by performing an act which constituted sex discrimination. Their action had led to 'less favourable' treatment of boys living in the city. Taylor J. (as he then was) concluded in the *Keating* case that the LEA's proposals did indeed constitute unlawful discrimination: the lack of availability to boys of the option of single sex education, when that option was available to girls, could reasonably be regarded as the loss of an option of value and thus as less favourable treatment within the meaning of section 1(1)(a) of the Sex Discrimination Act.[38]

A most important challenge on similar grounds was brought in Birmingham, not over a school closure but over existing unequal provision of *selective* single sex schools: *Equal Opportunities Commission v Birmingham City Council.*[39] In 1987 there were eight selective secondary schools in the city of Birmingham, each of which was single sex. Of these, five were boys' schools (providing 390 admission places), and three were girls' schools (providing 210 admission places). One consequence of this was that girls with a test mark near the borderline had a substantially smaller chance of obtaining a grammar school education in Birmingham than boys with a comparable mark. The House of Lords, affirming the majority in the Court of Appeal, held that this was unlawful under section 23 of the Sex Discrimination Act read in conjunction with section 8 of the Education Act 1944. The difficulties posed by these successful challenges for LEAs in seeking to structure or rationalise their provision of schools may well be formidable. Birmingham City Council, following the House of Lords' decision, considered the possibility of closing down one of the boys' schools (Handsworth Grammar School), thereby bringing provision for girls and boys into a more even balance. As has been by no means uncommon, its threatened closure prompted the governors of Handsworth Grammar School to put forward proposals to opt out of LEA control in favour of grant-maintained status, proposals which were approved by the Secretary of State in October 1990. The Equal Opportunities Commission then made a further application for judicial review, seeking a declaration that the city council was obliged, in securing compliance with its obligations under the Sex Discrimination Act in the provision of schools, to take into account not only those schools in the area maintained by the LEA itself but also any grant-maintained schools in the area: *R. v Birmingham City Council, ex parte Equal Opportunities Commission (No. 2).*[40] The Court of Appeal, affirming the decision of the Divisional Court, held that the city council was so obliged, the 'pool' of available places to be taken into account including those in grant-maintained as well as LEA-maintained schools. The relevant 'pool' for comparison of available provision between the sexes was the pool of free places in single sex grammar schools; furthermore, that pool could possibly include assisted places in independent schools, although this final point was left undecided.[41]

There can be little doubt that compliance with their obligations under the Sex Discrimination Act poses intractable problems for LEAs and a potent ground of judicial review for parents and others minded to challenge LEA rationalisation proposals. Furthermore, the Court of Appeal's decision in the second Birmingham case to extend the pool of available places to the grant-maintained sector graphically emphasises how easily an LEA's carefully balanced reorganisation proposals may be thrown into disarray by one or more schools in the authority's area seeking to opt out, an important issue which will now be developed further in the broader context of opting out.

Opting out in favour of grant-maintained status

The possibility of schools opting out in favour of grant-maintained status has added a significant further dimension to the range of legal challenges over the reorganisation of schools. These include challenges brought by pressure groups of parents opposed to a particular governing body's proposal to opt out, as well as challenges brought by LEAs opposed to loss of control over maintained schools and anxious to preserve the structural integrity of their overall provision.

An early challenge arose in Birmingham over a proposal by the governors of Small Heath School—a coeducational county comprehensive school for pupils aged 11 to 16 years—to hold a ballot of parents on opting out. Parallel applications for judicial review were brought by the LEA—Birmingham City Council—and by a group of parents opposed to opting out: *R. v Governors of Small Heath School, ex parte Birmingham City Council*; *R. v Governors of Small Heath School, ex parte Kahn.*[42] The parental challenge related essentially to the content of the information which had been issued to parents concerning grant-maintained status and the manner of its dissemination. The parents unsuccessfully challenged the legal sufficiency of the dissemination of prescribed pre-ballot information about grant-maintained status[43] only in English, given the ethnic and linguistic diversity of the pupils and parents. They also unsuccessfully challenged the actions of certain of the governors, particularly the head teacher, by playing an active part in the campaign in favour of grant-maintained status. It was held by Woolf LJ. (as he then was) that there was no legal requirement preventing governors from doing this, particularly where their aim was to counteract inaccuracies and confusion then circulating as to the school's position under grant-maintained status. A specific challenge was directed towards the conduct of the head teacher and two teacher-governors who had distributed information leaflets to parents through the intermediary of the pupils and had explained the contents of the leaflets to the pupils: this, the parents submitted, was in breach of section 45 of the Education (No. 2) Act 1986, a statutory requirement relating to the secular curriculum, requiring that political issues be dealt with in a balanced manner. The invocation of section 45 in this context could be seen as somewhat strained, the section being essentially intended to operate as a restraint on the substantive content of the school curriculum. Woolf LJ. held, however, that even if section 45 could be invoked in this context, the evidence disclosed no breach as a 'perfectly objective' approach had been adopted in the presentation of the material to the pupils.

Though the parental challenges failed, the LEA achieved a short-lived victory in its challenge to the legal propriety of those governors who were also employees of the LEA participating in the deliberations of the governing body as to whether a ballot should be held, given that they had a pecuniary interest in the outcome, contrary to the Education (School Government) Regulations 1987.[44] The employee-governors were the head teacher, two elected teacher-governors and one of the elected parent-governors who happened to work at the school in a support capacity. Whether the regulations should have the effect of disqualifying those governors on account of a pecuniary interest depended on the court's perception of the consequences that would flow from the possible change in the school's status for the employee-governors' conditions of employment. Woolf LJ. upheld the LEA's challenge on this ground at first instance, following the Court of Appeal decision in *Bostock v Kay*[45] in which employee-governors had been held to have a disqualifying pecuniary interest in deliberations of the governing body as to whether the school should become a city technology college. On appeal by the Small Heath School governors, however, the Court of Appeal declined to follow its earlier decision in *Bostock v Kay*, on the basis that the change in status from LEA-maintained school to grant-maintained school rather than city technology college involved less radical alteration in the conditions of employment of the staff, even though the identity of the employer would change from the LEA to the governing body.

The parents in the *Small Heath* case used what they saw as a procedural defect in the dissemination of information leading up to the ballot as a means of giving vent to their opposition in principle to opting out and their conviction that this particular school could better serve the needs of the community if it remained within LEA control. The LEA, however, had a broader concern with the structural integrity of its overall provision of schools: judicial review of the governors' actions leading up to the parental ballot is certainly one potential means open to an LEA striving to maintain that structural integrity. Indeed, the statutory procedural requirements imposed on governors[46] in this context could be regarded as a procedural minefield giving rise to a range of possible avenues of legal challenge. A good further illustration of this is provided by *R. v Governing Body of Irlam and Cadishead Community High School, ex parte Salford City Council,*[47] in which the LEA challenged the legality of the precise timing of the governors' second resolution to hold a ballot of parents, on the basis that the date chosen had the effect of disenfranchising parents of children who would be joining the school at the start of the new school year in September 1992.[48] The LEA contended that the disenfranchisement of those parents frustrated the policy and object of the statutory provisions which were to maximise parental involvement in the decision to opt out, a challenge based essentially on the principles laid down in *Padfield v Minister of Agriculture,*

Fisheries and Food.[49] In the event the LEA challenge failed, Rose J. holding that there was nothing in the Education Reform Act which placed maximisation of parental involvement in 'a pre-eminent position'.[50]

The problem faced by LEAs of striving to maintain the structural integrity of their provision of schools is, however, perhaps at its most acute when the proposal for opting out is put forward by governors at the very time when the LEA is itself seeking to rationalise its provision, a coincidence of events which has frequently arisen and which was entirely predictable given that opting out is perceived by many governing bodies as a possible means of avoiding unwelcome structural change. A leading illustration[51] of this arose in the city of Bath in 1989.

The LEA—Avon County Council—had submitted to the Secretary of State a composite package of rationalisation proposals under section 12 of the 1980 Act. These proposals would have involved reducing the number of secondary schools serving Bath from six to five by the closure of Beechen Cliff Boys' School, creating a new sixth form college on the Beechen Cliff site to centralise sixth form provision in the city, and 'decapitation' of the five remaining secondary schools by restricting their age range from 11 to 16 years. The governors of Beechen Cliff School, adamant that the school should be preserved, then submitted proposals under section 62 of the Education Reform Act 1988[52] to the Secretary of State to opt out in favour of grant-maintained status. The procedural effect of this was to activate the provisions of section 73 of the 1988 Act[53] which required the Secretary of State to consider both sets of proposals (those of the LEA for reorganisation and of the governors for grant-maintained status) together on their merits, but to determine the grant-maintained status proposals first. If the governors' proposals were approved, the LEA's proposals in respect of *that* school would be bound to be rejected, but it *might* be possible to grant a modified approval of the remaining LEA proposals, provided that they remained sufficiently intact following the severance of the school accorded grant-maintained status from their midst.

In the event, the Secretary of State decided to approve grant-maintained status for Beechen Cliff School and to reject the LEA's composite package of proposals. Avon County Council were dismayed by the consequences of this decision for their wider proposals on which they had held extensive consultations and which had emerged only after a gestation period going back to the early 1980s, and brought an application for judicial review of the Secretary of State's determination: *R. v Secretary of State for Education and Science, ex parte Avon County Council.*[54] The Secretary of State's determination—which had been issued with virtually no supporting reasons—was struck down by Hutchison J. principally on the ground that the minister had misconstrued section 73 by giving the grant-maintained status application *priority* over the LEA's reorganisation proposals, whereas they should properly have been weighed against one another equally in the balance; he also held that the minister had failed to give proper consideration to the wider consequences for the remaining schools in Bath of his decision to permit Beechen Cliff School to opt out. The Secretary of State promptly took his determination back for reconsideration in the light of Hutchison J.'s judgment, but then made an identical determination afresh, this time, however, spelling out his reasoning at considerable length. He argued that Beechen Cliff was clearly a viable, well-established and popular school of proven worth with a strong sixth form; the LEA's proposals, on the other hand, involved the closure of Beechen Cliff, and, through centralisation of all sixth form provision in a single college, eliminated competition between schools and parental choice at sixth form level. Avon County Council again sought judicial review of the Secretary of State's determination: *R. v Secretary of State for Education and Science, ex parte Avon County Council (No. 2).*[55] Central to the LEA's challenge was that the Secretary of State had treated the grant-maintained status application as 'paramount', an argument similar to the unlawful priority argument which had been accepted by Hutchison J. in the first challenge. The LEA's second challenge, however, was received with much less enthusiasm: it was emphasised that the legislation had expressly left the determination of the issues to ministerial discretion and that it was perfectly proper for the minister to adopt policy preferences, provided that they were applied flexibly and in accordance with relevant considerations. The ministerial discretion in this context involved the exercise of 'judgment and evaluation' in the light of the department's policy and the minister's own educational philosophy. It was held that the challenge was fundamentally misconceived in the sense of seeking to challenge by way of judicial review what was in essence no more than a disagreement over educational policy.[56]

The importance of this case is that it is a classic expression of judicial restraint and a reflection of how difficult it may be for an LEA to challenge the substance of the Secretary of State's determination of opting out proposals, given that the legislation has vested the decision-making powers in the minister in such broad discretionary terms. In the absence of defective compliance with procedural requirements, LEAs are in an extremely weak position to challenge ministerial determination of opting out proposals and thus may well be forced to grapple with the intractable problem of dealing with the often highly disruptive consequences which flow from the severance of one or more schools from carefully balanced rationalisation proposals which may themselves be the product of years of detailed consultation and deliberation.

Concluding comments

Given that the organisation and structure of schools has been in a continuous state of flux since the coming into force of the Education Act 1944, it is no surprise that there has been a high incidence of legal dispute in this context. As we have seen, some disputes have focused more narrowly on the particular sectoral interests of parental pressure groups or governing bodies seeking to pursue their own interests; but others have focused more broadly on the relationship between the central department and LEAs. While fully recognising the importance of the first category to the participants involved, it is probably justifiable to regard the second category of disputes as the more important as they raise issues of broader constitutional importance in terms of the institutional balance of power between central and local government in education, and the role of the courts has been essentially as mediators between the two sectors of government. Increasing recourse to the courts as mediators is a direct result of the political polarisation that has developed in the context of education: the structural reorganisation of schools brought about by comprehensive reorganisation, by falling rolls, and more recently by the encouragement of governing bodies to opt out, has led to a breakdown in the broad consensus which formerly existed between central and local government over the governance of education. That consensus has largely broken down by virtue of sustained pressure by central government to secure its preferred educational objectives, frequently overriding the strongly held views of LEAs. This political polarisation has undoubtedly led to increased judicial intervention as LEAs have turned to the courts in an attempt to avert unwelcome central pressure. The deteriorating relationship between the central department and LEAs is, indeed, likely to become even more acute as more schools opt out in favour of grant-maintained status and the newly established funding authorities— the Funding Agency for Schools in England and the Schools Funding Council for Wales[57]—take over all-important strategic planning functions from LEAs. These planning functions flow from the duty to secure sufficient schools in each area,[58] which functions will be transferred incrementally to the funding authorities when given proportions of pupils in each area are in attendance at grant-maintained schools.[59] How long this process of transfer will take cannot be accurately predicted, particularly as few governing bodies are, at the time of writing, submitting proposals to opt out. Should the transfer of strategic educational planning from LEAs to the funding authorities become widespread, however, it can fairly be predicted that there will be a marked growth in the incidence of legal disputes and recourse to judicial mediation in this area. This is likely to be particularly true when planning responsibilities are *shared* between the relevant LEA and funding authority, a position which arises when between 10 and 75 per cent of pupils in the relevant area in the primary or the secondary sector are in attendance at grant-maintained schools,[60] when it is by no means improbable that the LEA and the funding authority will have different perceptions of how best to tackle critical structural problems.

Judicial review is, therefore, likely for the foreseeable future to remain of importance in the context of the strategic planning and reorganisation of schools. The courts here have played an important mediating role between central and local government during a period when the institutional balance of power has been shifting markedly in the direction of the centre. On the other hand, as a means of achieving a significant check upon that shift in institutional balance, the courts have had only very limited success. This is so essentially because of the political and legal strength of the central department: leaving aside the *Tameside* case, the central government has been able to rely upon generously phrased discretionary powers, in addition to potent extra-statutory mechanisms for exerting pressure on LEAs to fall in line with government policy. It is, however, wrong to evaluate the impact of judicial review simply in terms of the actual outcome of individual cases: the very prospect, let alone the actuality, of recourse to the courts operates as a restraining influence upon ill-considered structural change, and contributes towards the promotion of procedural propriety. Although judicial review has not been able ultimately to prevent the institutional imbalance brought about by accretion of power to the centre in the past two decades, it has nonetheless operated significantly as a restraining and moderating influence.

Judicial Review and the Promotion of Individualism

Introduction

There can be little doubt that government education policy since 1979 has strongly promoted the concepts of individualism, freedom of choice, parental participation, accountability and consumerism. This has been reflected in many different contexts, including statutory procedures underpinning parental choice of school, provision for children with special educational needs, provision for dealing with curricular complaints, the enhancement of parental and community representation on school governing bodies, the conferment of considerable extra responsibilities upon governing bodies, and the extension of the concept of 'charterism' to education in the form of the publication of *The Parent's Charter*. These initiatives, along with others, have cumulatively sought to promote an ethos of individualistic freedom, and this has been paralleled by an increase in recourse to the courts by individual parents or groups of parents in order to pursue a broad and diverse range of individual interests. The extent to which those interests have been upheld has, however, been somewhat limited, largely by the very nature of the relationship between individuals and the state in the provision of education. The statutory regime is such that it is seldom possible to discern enforceable individual rights in the educational context: rarely do Education Acts confer express and readily enforceable rights on parents or children; rather, they impose duties on LEAs or school governing bodies, but these duties tend to be heavily qualified. Though it may sometimes be possible to discern some individual rights as correlative to duties imposed on public authorities in the provision of education, it is rare that they are readily enforceable in law.

Despite this important caveat with regard to the enforceability of individual interests in education, a wide range of individual challenges have nonetheless been brought in the courts. In a short space it is impossible to attempt a comprehensive survey: rather, we shall focus selectively on instances of judicial review in the sphere of choice of school, an area of wide concern which raises some acute issues of individual conscience as well as more practical issues. It must, of course, be acknowledged that there are other vital areas of individual concern, of which perhaps provision for children with special educational needs is the most prominent. There has been a very high incidence of judicial review over special needs, although the establishment of the Special Educational Needs Tribunal under the Education Act 1993[61] may to an extent limit the flow of judicial review here.

Parental choice of school—background

Choice of school is a crucial area of individual concern over education where there has been considerable recourse to judicial review. It is an area which has been used by the government as a vehicle for promoting some prominent aspects of its educational philosophy—maximising individual freedom of choice so far as compatible with the provision of efficient education and avoidance of unreasonable expenditure; maximising the accountability of the providers of education to their consumers, particularly by subjecting schools to market forces; and maximising the range and diversity of schools. The government first sought to promote these goals by the establishment of a new statutory regime for school admissions in the Education Act 1980, including formal arrangements for the expression of parental preferences,[62] a heavily qualified duty on the part of LEAs and school governors to comply with the expressed parental choice,[63] and a new structure of Education Appeal Tribunals to determine disputes.[64]

Parental choice and the deliberations of Education Appeal Tribunals

The locally based Education Appeal Tribunals have in many areas been faced with the most intractable difficulties of resolving parental choice disputes, being forced to differentiate between like claimants for a most finite resource—a limited number of places in an oversubscribed school. They have operated with only the most skeletal statutory procedural guidance,[65] though subject to the supervision of the Council on Tribunals and guided by a *Code of Practice* drawn up by the Council in conjunction with the local authority associations.[66] Although non-statutory, the detailed guidance offered in the *Code of Practice* may be of considerable evidential significance in the event of the proceedings of a tribunal being challenged. The most authoritative guidance has, however, come from the courts: indeed, in this context judicial review has made a significant contribution to the development of due process and procedural propriety.

The most important judicial guidance was offered in 1984 by Forbes J. in *R. v South Glamorgan Appeals Committee, ex parte Evans.*[67] The critical element in Forbes J.'s judgment was his analysis of the decision-making process of an Education Appeal Tribunal in determining parental challenges to the denial of choice of school by an LEA. Under the Education Act 1980, the parents' preference may be denied by the LEA if compliance would prejudice the provision of efficient education or the efficient use of resources.[68] It was held by Forbes J. that the tribunal must adopt a two-stage approach to such a parental challenge: first, it must consider whether there exists evidence on which it can properly conclude that the admission of the individual child under appeal in the instant case would cause prejudice (either to the provision of efficient education or the efficient use of resources); and secondly, if it concludes that this is so, it must go on to carry out a discretionary balancing exercise to determine whether the degree of prejudice so caused is sufficient to outweigh the particular 'parental considerations' raised in the case—the parents' reasons for expressing their preference together with the LEA's published priority ranking criteria.[69]

Forbes J.'s clarification of the decision-making procedures of Education Appeal Tribunals has been of wide importance as it has served to instil a greater degree of analytical rigour into their deliberations. Indeed, the two-staged procedure has been incorporated into the Council on Tribunals' *Code of Practice,* and has been endorsed by Woolf J. (as he then was) in *R. v Commissioner for Local Administration, ex parte Croydon London Borough Council.*[70]

Procedural clarification of the deliberative processes of Education Appeal Tribunals has been one of the most significant contributions of judicial review in the context of choice of school. Another has been clarification of the extent of the duty of LEAs and governors to comply with expressed parental preferences under section 6(2) of the Education Act 1980. Parental preferences may be based on matters of pure practicality, including location of the family home in relation to the school; or they may be based on academic considerations, either where schools operate non-selective admissions procedures but are nonetheless perceived to have particular academic strengths, or where an admissions system based upon selection by reference to ability or aptitude is in operation;[71] or they may be based on issues of profound personal importance and conscience, including religion, culture, language or even perhaps the racial or ethnic ethos of the school. Choice of school disputes have thus drawn the courts into consideration of some highly delicate matters of fundamental conscience, in addition to rather more mundane—though nonetheless important—matters of geographical proximity and the significance of the location of LEA boundaries.

Parental choice based on cultural and linguistic considerations

The delicacy of the issues raised by parental choice can be illustrated by two disputes widely reported in the press—the Dewsbury and Cleveland disputes. There were some similarities between these cases, but they raised quite different legal points. In the *Dewsbury* case,[72] the LEA—Kirklees Borough Council—refused to comply with the preferences expressed by parents of some twenty-five children on the basis that their planned admissions quota had been reached and the preferred schools were thus oversubscribed. At that time (in 1987) LEAs were free to apply admissions quotas below a school's maximum physical capacity, and indeed this was widely practised in order to spread pupil intakes between schools for a combination of educational, social and economic reasons. These events pre-dated the introduction of open enrolment under the Education Reform Act 1988[73] which outlawed this practice. The parents had expressed preferences for two schools in Dewsbury where the majority of the children were white and which had a predominantly Christian ethos; the LEA, however, on the basis that the preferred schools were oversubscribed, had allocated the children instead to schools where some 85 per cent of the children came from Asian backgrounds. The parents' appeals to the local Education Appeal Tribunal were rejected, as were their complaints to the Secretary of State[74] who concluded that no intervention was possible as the LEA had acted neither unreasonably nor unlawfully. The aggrieved parents were outraged by the LEA's decisions, claiming that there was spare capacity in the preferred schools, and the dispute attracted a great deal of press publicity when the pupils concerned were denied entry to the chosen schools at the start of term and were then for some months educated privately on the premises of a public house in Dewsbury. Indeed, the case provoked a wide debate on the broader issue of multicultural education. In the meantime the parents applied for judicial review, challenging the rationality of the LEA's decisions as well as alleged non-compliance with procedural requirements. The parents powerfully expressed their view on the educational and cultural grounds (any racial motive on their part was strenuously denied throughout) that their children's interests would best be served by their being educated at the preferred schools; the LEA, on the other hand, argued that they had a broader duty to avoid excessive numerical imbalance between its schools and the longer-term educational and administrative problems that this would create.

The parental challenge to the rationality of the LEA's decisions would, indeed, have been extremely difficult to substantiate, given the widespread practice among LEAs at the time of imposing admissions quotas, and the educational and administrative reasons for so doing. In the event, no judicial determination of this central challenge was made, as the LEA conceded that there had been procedural defects in the application of its admissions quotas and the publication of details of those quotas. The case was, therefore, settled and the LEA acceded to the parents' requests. The *Dewsbury* case is, therefore, of somewhat narrow legal importance, although still an important illustration of the force of judicial review as a means of ensuring procedural propriety in the allocations process. It is, however, of wider social and educational importance as an illustration of the operation of planned admissions quotas, before the introduction of open enrolment, as a vital means of strategic educational planning on the part of LEAs by spreading pupil intakes on a rational and coherent basis. Whether this was done in order to promote a multicultural educational policy cannot be stated with certainty, but what is clear is that the LEA's denial of the parents' choice of school in Dewsbury would have been unlawful following the Education Reform Act 1988, as the LEA would have been bound to accede to the expressed parental preferences given that the chosen schools' standard numbers had not been reached.

In the *Dewsbury* case, the nature and quality of the expressed parental preferences and their underlying motivation were in fact peripheral to the legal debate which focused rather on the reasonableness of the LEA's decisions and questions of procedure. In the later case of *R. v Cleveland County Council, ex parte Commission for Racial Equality,*[75] however, the nature of parental preferences was directly in issue. In the *Cleveland* case, a primary school pupil's mother had requested that the LEA transfer her to a different school, and in her letter of request indicated her unhappiness that her daughter was currently in a class with predominantly Pakistani children, that she did not wish her to learn their language, and that she would prefer if she could attend a school where the majority of the children were white and where English would be the majority first language. The mother strenuously denied any racial motive behind her choice, emphasising that her preference was based on cultural and linguistic considerations alone. The LEA reluctantly acceded to her request, taking the view that it was its inescapable duty to do so under section 6(2) of the Education Act 1980. Given that the mother's preferred school was undersubscribed—below its standard number—it could not rely upon the exception in section 6(3)(a) of the 1980 Act, and none of the other provisos in section 6(3) applied. The Commission for Racial Equality, however, challenged the legality of the LEA's decision, principally on the ground that the LEA's duty under section 6(2) was *qualified* by its duty under section 18(1) of the Race Relations Act 1976. This provided that it was unlawful for an LEA, in carrying out any of its functions under the Education Acts, to do any act which constituted racial discrimination. The Commission's argument was, however, rejected: Parker LJ. in the Court of Appeal was persuaded by the apparent absurdity that a parent who chose to express no reason whatsoever for a preference would be in a stronger position than one who had expressed a reason that could conceivably be construed as racist in nature.[76] Nor did the LEA's failure to refuse admission of the pupil to the preferred school constitute an 'act' within the meaning of section 18(1): Parker LJ. held that 'act' should be given its ordinary meaning of the taking of a positive step, and that what the LEA had done was in the nature of a failure to act.[77] Nor did the LEA's failure to refuse admission amount to segregation of the pupil on racial grounds within the meaning of section 1(2) of the Race Relations Act, the only segregation consisting in the removal of the child from the first primary school, this having been the lawful act of the mother.[78]

The *Cleveland* case could well have the highly undesirable consequence of encouraging parental choice based on grounds which are essentially racist in nature. On the other hand, the considerations which underlie parental choice of school may be deeply personal, and may relate to aspects of private and family life which ought to be free from state interference. It would in any event be simple for parents to disguise their motives by the expression of other types of reasoning or by giving no reasons at all.

Parental choice based on religious considerations

Of all the many other factors which may condition parental choice of school, perhaps the most prominent are religious considerations. This is true throughout the United Kingdom, but is perhaps of especial significance in

Northern Ireland where there is a strong tradition of denominational education.[79] In respect of England and Wales, the existence of a substantial body of Church schools within the maintained sector was one of the central pillars of the 1944 Act: voluntary controlled and voluntary aided schools are established by voluntary bodies, but very largely funded by LEAs. The majority of schools in the voluntary sector are Church of England or Roman Catholic foundations, along with some other religious foundations including Methodist and Jewish. Muslims have for some years been seeking voluntary aided status for some of their schools currently operating in the independent sector, but this has so far been denied.[80] It may in due course be that such schools will be accorded grant-maintained status under the Education Act 1993.[81] The possibility of choosing a school with a particular religious or denominational ethos plainly adds a fundamental dimension to the nature and quality of choice of school for many parents. For this choice to be available to Anglicans, Roman Catholics, Methodists and Jews, but not, for example, to Muslims or some other religious groups, could be regarded as inherently unsupportable. Religious considerations being clearly a significant factor conditioning choice of school for many parents, voluntary schools and grant-maintained schools which are religious foundations are often heavily oversubscribed. They are also frequently in high demand by parents who do not adhere to the religious faith concerned, as they are often perceived to be schools with high standards of academic achievement and discipline.

The particular problems that can arise in respect of admissions to voluntary schools are well illustrated by *Choudhury v Governors of Bishop Challoner Roman Catholic Comprehensive School*:[82] the governors of a Roman Catholic voluntary aided girls' comprehensive school applied an admissions policy in the event of oversubscription under which they gave priority for admission to Roman Catholics and other Christians and those with sisters already at the school. The parents of two girls—one a Hindu, the other a Muslim—expressed a preference for the school, but were denied admission by virtue of the application of the governors' policy. The normal practice is for voluntary schools to draw up specific arrangements for admissions with LEAs under section 6(6) of the Education Act 1980, under which an LEA, if so requested by the governors of a voluntary aided school, shall make arrangements with the governors in respect of the admission of pupils for preserving the character of the school. These arrangements normally give priority to applicants with defined religious affiliations, in order to safeguard the school's religious character. Such schools may then refuse to admit pupils without such religious affiliations by virtue of section 6(3)(b) of the 1980 Act, which permits the governors to deny admission to a pupil where it would be incompatible with such arrangements. In the case of

Bishop Challoner School, however, no such formal statutory arrangements had been made, and the parents challenged the legality of the governors' policy in the absence of such arrangements. Their challenge was successful at first instance, but it was rejected by the Court of Appeal and the House of Lords: as the school was oversubscribed, the governors were entitled to deny the parents' preferences by virtue of section 6(3)(a) on the basis that to admit these children would be prejudicial to efficient education or the efficient use of resources. Where a voluntary aided school was oversubscribed, the governors were entitled to apply any reasonable policies they saw fit. Criteria which gave preference to children with defined religious affiliations designed to preserve the religious character of the school were perfectly reasonable. Formal arrangements under section 6(6) would have been necessary in order to rely upon such a religious affiliation policy only in the event of the school being undersubscribed.

It comes as no surprise that voluntary schools with recognised religious affiliations apply such policies in order to preserve their religious ethos, although many do admit children from other faiths where they have spare capacity. What was far less certain was whether it would be lawful for LEAs to apply religious affiliation as a criterion in respect of admissions to oversubscribed *county* schools. It is arguable that the underlying policy of the 1944 Act was that county schools should be non-denominational in character and that the application of religious affiliation as a criterion would be fundamentally inconsistent with this. Despite this, such a policy as applied by Lancashire County Council has recently been upheld in *R. v Lancashire County Council, ex parte F.*[83] The LEA's policy was that children who had attended a *Roman Catholic* primary school should be given a lower priority ranking for admission to oversubscribed county schools than children who had attended *county* primary schools. Kennedy LJ. noted that, because of arrangements made between the Roman Catholic diocesan authorities and the LEA under section 6(6) of the 1980 Act, very few non-Roman Catholic children could be accommodated in Roman Catholic schools, even if they wished to go there. In the light of this, and given heavy demand for the county school places, he found it impossible to hold that the LEA's policy was irrational.[84]

Not only is this hard to reconcile with the essential philosophy of county schools as non-denominational schools in which the religious affiliation of the children should be a wholly irrelevant consideration, but it conflicts with clearly stated guidance issued by the DFE on the matter. In a recent circular, it is emphasised that:

> ... The Secretary of State does not believe that it is reasonable for *non-denominational* schools to distinguish between applicants on the grounds of their faith or denominational background. He starts from the position that

oversubscription criteria in such schools which assign a lower priority to applicants of one faith or denomination as compared with another cannot be justified on educational grounds and are therefore unacceptable.[85]

Though not binding, clear and unambiguous policy guidance is most certainly a relevant consideration, and it is surprising that an LEA policy which runs manifestly counter to it and, arguably, to the policy of the 1944 Act in respect of county schools could be upheld.[86]

Parental choice based on geographical considerations

Religious affiliation, the cultural ethos, the ethnic or racial background of the pupils, the mixture of languages spoken in the children's homes, and many other considerations may condition parental choice in fundamental ways. Also of great importance, however, are geographical considerations and the delineation of catchment areas. Catchment areas raise issues of great sensitivity and concern:[87] the precise way in which they are drawn is not a matter of mundane practicality, as it may have a considerable impact on the social, cultural and ethnic ethos of the school. Indeed, the potential for social engineering through the delineation of catchment areas has long been recognised. LEA policies relating to proximity, catchment areas, feeder schools and, very importantly, the LEA area from which pupils are drawn have proved to be a fertile source of judicial review. A leading case with wide implications for LEA admissions policies in this context was *R. v Shadow Education Committee of Greenwich London Borough Council, ex parte Governors of John Ball Primary School*:[88] by virtue of section 6(5) of the 1980 Act, LEAs were placed under the same duty of compliance with parental wishes in relation to children living in the area of another LEA as in relation to children living in their own area. This could considerably enhance the reality of parental choice for those living close to the boundaries of two LEAs, in whose case it might make greater geographical sense to send their children to a school in the neighbouring LEA. It would be of particular significance where one or more schools was heavily oversubscribed, and it would be of great importance in London where each borough is its own LEA and the probability of living close to a borough boundary would be comparatively high. In the *Greenwich* case, the Shadow Education Committee—which had planning responsibilities pending the transfer of responsibility for education from the Inner London Education Authority to the London boroughs on 1 April 1990—decided to change the existing admissions policy under which there had been 'two-way traffic' of children between Lewisham and Greenwich schools: the Greenwich shadow authority decided to give priority in allocating places to oversubscribed schools to children living within its own area, with the consequence that children living in Lewisham would be unlikely to obtain places in Greenwich schools. The governors of John Ball School, a primary school in Lewisham, from which pupils had hitherto regularly transferred to secondary schools in Greenwich, argued that, while it was perfectly lawful for the Greenwich authority to adopt certain admissions policies to establish priority ranking—including geographical considerations such as the distance between home and school—it was unlawful in the light of section 6(5) to apply a policy which discriminated against children living in another borough. This would thwart the policy and objects of section 6(5), namely that extra-area children should rank equally with children living within the borough. The Greenwich authority, on the other hand, argued that imposition of a duty to give equal ranking to extra-area pupils might lead to a large influx of such pupils and make it impossible for the authority to meet its statutory obligation under section 7 of the 1944 Act to secure that efficient education was available to meet the needs of the population of its area: this would place the authority in an untenable position which could not have been intended by parliament. The Court of Appeal had little difficulty in rejecting the Greenwich argument, though it was conceded by Lloyd LJ. that he could 'see here the seeds of a theoretical difficulty'.[89] In practice, Lloyd LJ. commented, a large influx of extra-area pupils would be unlikely to occur, given the imposition of a proximity criterion. Furthermore, it was entirely likely that the 'two-way traffic' which had previously existed would continue. The Court of Appeal brushed aside the practical difficulties in favour of what they saw as the central issue—that the Greenwich policy was in conflict with the underlying object of section 6(5), which was to enhance choice by treating all pupils equally, irrespective of the LEA area in which they lived.

On one view of the *Greenwich* case, it might indeed seem wrong to discriminate against extra-area pupils; the equality of treatment policy could, however, give rise to serious problems for LEAs, especially in the case of highly favoured schools for which there is likely to be substantial competition from children both within and outside the area. There may well also be a high level of grievance among parents of children living within the authority area but denied places allocated to extra-area pupils.

Concluding comments

The application of virtually any policy by an LEA or by governors is indeed likely to give rise to friction and resentment. The many legal challenges which have been brought in the context of choice of school—of which only a small selection has been discussed here—serve to emphasise that the reality of parental choice is in many cases very weak. Parental choice as a concept has great political appeal, but the legal limitations on the duty to comply with expressed parental preferences are so broad as to undermine the reality of choice of school for many parents. The true extent of parental rights here was aptly expressed by Kennedy LJ. in *R. v Lancashire County Council, ex parte F*:[90]

> The applicant has no [civil] right to go to Highfield School. He only has a right to express a preference and if the school is oversubscribed, to have the local education authority respond in accordance with a published policy which is itself not unreasonable.[91]

This reduces the broad political rhetoric of parental choice to the legal reality of a very limited procedural right on the part of parents to express a preference, coupled with a wide discretion vested in LEAs and governors to apply any reasonable policies in the likely event of oversubscription. It is true that there are statutory rights of appeal, but the appeal bodies can do little in many cases beyond ensuring that the published policies have been properly applied. Judicial review over choice of school—as in other areas of individualised challenge—has essentially done little more than emphasise the extremely limited nature of individual rights in the context of state provision of education. It is true that it has promoted procedural propriety, notably in relation to the deliberations of Education Appeal Tribunals, and it has confined the range of permissible policies which may be applied by LEAs, notably by outlawing those discriminating against extra-area pupils, but it has not furthered the cause of parental rights in a significant way.

Conclusions

It is undeniable that there has been a marked growth in recourse to judicial review in the sphere of education in the past two decades. That would, however, be true of other important areas of social provision, though the availability of legal aid to children has been a significant factor in the growth of judicial review in education. Of greater importance is identification of the underlying reasons for that growth in judicial review— and evaluation of the significance of the impact of judicial review on the complex relationships between the many different parties involved in the provision of education.

This study has identified two underlying reasons for the growth of judicial review in education, both of which have a significant constitutional dimension. The first is the breakdown of consensus between central and local government; the second is the growing recognition of fundamental rights in education. The breakdown of consensus between central and local government has come about for many reasons and taken different forms, and is reflected in other important areas of state provision. Education is, however, one of the most prominent examples of the accretion of power towards the centre in the past two decades. As central government has sought to impose its will on LEAs in relation to policy matters of crucial significance, including comprehensive reorganisation and the eradication of surplus places, with the extensive structural reorganisation that these have inevitably given rise to, so LEAs have resorted to the courts as a means of moderation and mediation. This has also occurred in the context of schools opting out of LEA control in favour of grant-maintained status—a direct assault on the scope and nature of LEA functioning. To this there will be added a major new dimension as crucial strategic planning functions are transferred in time from LEAs to the new funding authorities. Whether judicial mediation has actually succeeded in significantly checking the accretion of power to the centre is, however, highly doubtful. It is true that LEAs have generally done badly in terms of the actual outcome of the cases, but the outcome of cases is an extremely crude measure of the significance of judicial review. What is much more important is the moderating influence of the courts: the prospect or threat of judicial review and the actuality of review in some cases have served to moderate central pressure and to instil a greater degree of procedural propriety and due process. Judicial review lies in reserve as a most important recourse for LEAs: the kind of institutional imbalance we are witnessing in the governance of education is a threat to democracy and, although the courts may not be able ultimately to prevent it, their moderating influence should not be underestimated.

The growing recognition of fundamental rights in education should come as no surprise. Education is absolutely crucial to the development of individual autonomy and to society; and education underpins other fundamental rights including freedom of speech. Without education, the intrinsic value of freedom of speech is greatly diminished. Within our constitutional and legal structure, however, these amount in essence to little more than political claims. There is only very limited recognition of enforceable rights in education legislation, and the courts have substantially failed to promote and develop the concept of rights in this—as in so many other—spheres. There is no clearer illustration of this than the reduction of the political rhetoric of choice of school to the minimal statutory right to express a reasoned preference coupled with a highly qualified duty on the part of LEAs and governors to comply. That judicial review here has largely failed to develop parental rights is, however, not surprising, given the unpromising nature of the statutory material with which the courts have had to grapple. The government in framing the legislation has deliberately avoided conferring clearly enforceable rights on the individual by giving the public authorities extensive discretion and highly qualified duties. Although judicial review has largely failed to develop individual rights in education, it would, however, be wrong to evaluate the contribution of the courts in an entirely negative way: they have done much to promote procedural propriety in many respects, and they have acted as an important moderating and mediating influence over the exercise of discretion, notably by LEAs and governors. These contributions have, furthermore, been achieved as much by the constant prospect or threat of judicial review as by the outcome of actual cases.

Notes

1. See M. Loughlin, 'The Restructuring of Central-Local Government Relations', ch. 10 of J. Jowell and D. Oliver, *The Changing Constitution* (3rd edn, 1994) at pp 260–1.
2. *Secretary of State for Education and Science v Tameside Metropolitan Borough Council* [1977] AC 1014.
3. Education Act 1993, s. 12(1)(a).
4. Education Act 1944, s. 7.
5. ibid., s. 8.
6. ibid., s. 13.
7. See now Education Act 1980, ss 12 and 13.
8. See R. Buxton, *Local Government* (2nd edn, 1973) ch. 8; C. Benn, *Half Way There: Report on the British Comprehensive School Reform* (2nd edn, 1972); I.G.K. Fenwick, *The Comprehensive School 1944–1970: The Politics of Secondary School Reorganisation* (1976).
9. See DES Circular 10/65, 'The Organisation of Secondary Education'; DES Circular 10/ 66, 'School Building Programmes'; DES Circular 4/74, 'The Organisation of Secondary Education'.
10. Education Act 1976, s. 1.
11. ibid., s. 2.
12. s. 1(1).
13. [1977] AC 1014.
14. Approval by the Secretary of State under s. 13 did not at that time carry with it a legal duty to implement the proposals. This was subsequently changed by s. 12(9), Education Act 1980.
15. *Associated Provincial Picture Houses v Wednesbury Corporation* [1948] 1 KB 223.
16. s. 1, Education Act 1944, as it was then framed, explicitly refers to the Secretary of State's power of direction and control over LEAs. See now ss 1–2, Education Act 1993.
17. John Griffith, *The Politics of the Judiciary*, (4th edn, 1991) p. 122.
18. [1977] AC 1014, at p. 1064.
19. See, for instance, Housing Act 1980, s. 23, interpreted in *Norwich City Council v Secretary of State for the Environment* [1982] 1 All ER 737, at p. 745 (per Kerr LJ.).
20. See P. Meredith, 'Falling Rolls and the Reorganisation of Schools' (1984) JSWL 208; P. Meredith, *Government, Schools and the Law* (1992) ch. 5.
21. DES Circular 2/81, 'Falling Rolls and Surplus Places' para. 19.
22. ibid., para. 29.

23. See DES Circular 3/87, 'Providing for Quality: the Pattern of Organisation to Age 19'.
24. See DFE Circular 23/94, 'The Supply of School Places'.
25. s. 229(1). This amendment was a direct result of the litigation discussed below.
26. (1986) 84 LGR 186; see P. Meredith, 'Legitimate Expectations and Schools Closures' 1988 PL 4; P. Meredith, *Government, Schools and the Law*, op. cit., n. 20, pp 127–32.
27. (1986) 84 LGR 168, at pp 189–95.
28. DES Circular 2/80, 'Procedure Affecting Proposals Made Under Sections 12–16 of the Education Act 1980', para. 5.1.
29. DES Administrative Memorandum 4/84, 'Proposals Made Under Sections 12–16 of the Education Act 1980', paras 9 and 10.
30. (1986) 84 LGR 186, p. 187.
31. ibid., p. 189.
32. 26 March 1986, per Webster J. See LEXIS transcript.
33. 26 June 1986, per Woolf LJ. See LEXIS transcript.
34. *R. v Devon County Council, ex p. Baker* [1995] 1 All ER 73, at p. 83 (per Dillon LJ.) and pp 91–2 (per Simon Brown LJ.).
35. (1989) 87 LGR 435.
36. (1986) 84 LGR 469.
37. Education Act 1944, s. 8.
38. (1986) 84 LGR 469, at p. 477.
39. [1989] 1 All ER 769. For Northern Ireland cases involving the impact of sex discrimination legislation on the selection procedure for grammar schools, see *In Re E.O.C. (No. 1)* [1988] 10 NIJB 44 and *In Re E.O.C. (No. 2)* [1988] 10 NIJB 88.
40. [1994] ELR 37 (QBD); [1994] ELR 282 (CA).
41. See [1994] ELR 282, at p. 297 (per Neill LJ.). For further consideration of the principle in the *Birmingham (No. 2)* case that the pool of available places extends to schools in the grant-maintained sector, see *R. v Northamptonshire County Council and Secretary of State for Education, ex p. K.* [1994] ELR 397.
42. *The Independent* Law Reports, 30 June 1989 (QBD); *The Independent* Law Reports, 3 August 1989 (CA). See also LEXIS transcripts. See P. Meredith, *Government, Schools and the Law*, op. cit., n. 20, pp 158–69.
43. Prescribed under Education Reform Act 1988, s. 61(3) and (4). See now Education Act 1993, s. 28(3).
44. S.I. 1987, No. 1359, para. 2, sch. 2.
45. (1989) 87 LGR 583.
46. Formerly under Education Reform Act 1988, ss 60–3; see now Education Act 1993, ss 24–32.
47. [1994] ELR 81.
48. See Education Reform Act 1988, s. 61(4), under which the qualifying date for eligibility to vote in the parental ballot was fourteen days after the second governors' resolution. See now Education Act 1993, s. 29(2).
49. [1968] AC 997.
50. [1994] ELR 81, at pp 87–8.
51. For a further illustration see *R. v Secretary of State for Education and Science, ex p. Newham London Borough Council* TLR, 11 January 1991. See also LEXIS transcript. This is discussed in P. Meredith, 'Opting-out Litigation: the Newham Experience' (1992) Education and the Law 69.
52. See now s. 32, Education Act 1993.
53. See now s. 273, Education Act 1993.
54. (1990) 88 LGR 716.
55. (1990) 88 LGR 737.
56. See LEXIS transcript of judgments of Ralph Gibson LJ. and Nicholls LJ. The report in (1990) 88 LGR 737 provides only extracts from the judgments.
57. See Education Act 1993, ss 3 and 4.

58. Imposed on LEAs under Education Act 1944, s. 8.
59. See Education Act 1993, s. 12.
60. ibid., s. 12(1)(a) and 12(4).
61. ibid., s. 177.
62. Education Act 1980, s. 6(1).
63. ibid., s. 6(3).
64. ibid., s. 7.
65. See sch. 2, Education Act 1980.
66. See *Code of Practice as to the Constitution and Procedures of Appeal Committees Established Under the Education Act 1980 and the Education Act 1981* (February 1985). Annex I provides guidance on their decision-making procedures.
67. Unreported: 10 May 1984. See P. Meredith, '*R. v South Glamorgan Appeals Committee, ex p. Evans*' (1985) JSWL 162.
68. See Education Act 1980, s. 6(3)(a).
69. These must be published under Education Act 1980, s. 8.
70. [1989] 1 All ER 1033, esp. at pp 1039–41.
71. See Education Act 1980, s. 6(3)(c), which provides that parental choice may be denied where it would be incompatible with the operation of selection on the basis of ability or aptitude. Academically selective admissions to secondary schools still operate in a number of LEAs in England and Wales and, indeed, a return to academic selection may become increasingly common. Selective admissions to secondary schools are also operated in Northern Ireland, and have there given rise to legal challenges: see, for instance, *In Re Gribbon* [1990] 6 NIJB 15; *In Re Ross*, unreported, 2 September 1994.
72. Though the parents applied for judicial review, the case was settled and thus unreported. See A. Bradney, 'The Dewsbury Affair and the Education Reform Act 1988' (1989) Education and the Law, 51. See also P. Meredith, *Government, Schools and the Law*, op. cit., n. 20, pp 37–9.
73. ss 26–32.
74. Under Education Act 1944, ss 68 and 99.
75. [1994] ELR 44. See N. Harris, 'Educational Choice in a Multi-Cultural Society' [1992] PL 522.
76. [1994] ELR 44, at pp 50–51.
77. ibid., p. 52. It was also held that the duty under s. 6(2) to comply with the parent's wishes was mandatory and that it was thus exempted from the application of s. 18 by virtue of s. 41(1)(a) of the Race Relations Act 1976.
78. ibid., p. 53.
79. The government has, however, sought in recent years to promote integrated schools in Northern Ireland: see Education Reform (Northern Ireland) Order 1989 (SI 1989 No. 2406, NI 20), pt VI. This Order was unsuccessfully challenged by bishops of the Roman Catholic Church on the basis that it was discriminatory on grounds of religious belief or political opinion, contrary to s. 17(1), Northern Ireland Constitution Act 1973: see *In Re Most Rev. Cahal Daly*, unreported, September 1990.
80. See *R. v Secretary of State for Education and Science, ex p. Yusuf Islam* [1994] ELR 111.
81. Under s. 49 'promoters' may put forward proposals for the establishment of new grant-maintained schools.
82. [1992] 3 All ER 277. See N. Harris, op. cit., n. 75, at pp 528–9.
83. [1995] ELR 33.
84. See ibid., at pp 40–41.
85. DFE Circular 6/93, para. 21.
86. See also *R. v Lancashire County Council, ex p. M.* [1994] ELR 478, in which Popplewell J. refused to quash a decision of an Education Appeal Tribunal which had applied this LEA policy.

87. This is well illustrated by *R. v Bradford Metropolitan Borough Council, ex p. Sikander Ali* [1994] ELR 299.
88. (1990) 88 LGR 589.
89. ibid., at p. 598.
90. [1995] ELR 33.
91. ibid., p. 40.

Chapter Four

Judicial Review and the Political Functioning of Local Government

Paul Maguire

Introduction

Local councils bear all the hallmarks of authorities subject to judicial review. They are statutory creations. Their powers and duties are acquired from parliament. Their actions affect the rights and interests of citizens. Their functions are governmental in nature. Apart from executive powers, they possess a limited lawmaking power. They also have certain revenue raising powers.

What distinguishes local authorities from other governmental authorities, however, according to Widdicombe[1] are its 'interlocking and complementary' attributes of pluralism, participation and responsiveness. It is local government *by* local communities rather than *of* local communities. Local authorities because of their elected composition have a political nature, which is both outward and inward looking. It is outward looking in that councils contribute to the national political system and reflect a patchwork pattern of points of local political power within the context of the unitary state; and it is inward looking in that councils offer a forum for the participation at local level of the community in local democracy, including the delivery of services. The language of the debate in local democracy not surprisingly, therefore, reflects notions of sensitivity, accountability and local initiative. It is to the political aspect of local government and its treatment by judges in judicial review that this chapter is directed. By auditing judicial responses to what might be described as the 'political functioning' of local authorities it is hoped that some general conclusions can be offered concerning the contribution which judicial review has made to the conserving, if not the fostering, of at least some of the special attributes of local government.

Before setting out, a number of points need to be acknowledged. First, judicial decisions in this sphere will nearly always be taken against a statutory backcloth. This has the consequence that the area of judicial discretion will usually be circumscribed. Secondly, it is relatively infrequently that judges openly address the vitality of the special attributes of local government as being relevant to their decisions. This is probably because a judicial favouring or disfavouring of these attributes may be thought by the judges themselves to be an unduly political posture to adopt. Finally, in the field of judicial review of local government activity in which the growth of case law has been marked, it is necessarily the case that the materials hereafter considered to illustrate the political functioning of local government and the weight given to them will reflect a selective judgment. Emphasis has been placed on considering the political freedoms described below, and discussion of the financial disputes of recent years involving central-local government relations and the courts has been eschewed as these have been discussed in full elsewhere.[2]

Political Freedoms

In what follows it is assumed that for political activity in local government to survive and/or prosper, certain freedoms will be important. These include the right for those involved, especially councillors, freely to meet and engage in debate; the right of councillors to have access to information; the right for political parties to operate within the local government arena and freely to organise and participate within the institutions of local authorities; and the right, especially of councils, freely to express and publicise their views and campaign on issues which they regard as being of public importance. In relation to these rights, while parliament will usually have provided a legal framework, the courts in judicial review have both filled in gaps in legislative provision and put meat on the bones of existing provisions. They have, moreover, stood over the shoulders of the main actors in local government for the purpose of review. How have the judges approached issues of these kinds?

Holding meetings

The life-blood of local government politics is the transaction of the authority's business at council meetings and at committees of the council. These are held in accordance with a statutory framework. In general, councils are required to hold an annual general meeting and such other meetings as the council thinks necessary. Committees meet as required.[3] Any interference with the pattern of holding meetings—in most councils the council itself will meet monthly with committee meetings dovetailing to meet the timing of the council meeting itself—will be controversial, especially so if the effect is that meetings are not being held or the business of the council is not being transacted. If the majority on the council are using their powers to prevent meetings taking place or to curtail the duration of these meetings, the rights of minority councillors may be put at risk. While the law provides a procedure by which a set number of councillors may requisition the chairman to hold a meeting,[4] if the chairman is associated with the majority group he or she may not be co-operative. While it might be thought unlikely that the majority on a council would use its powers in the fashion described, this is exactly what occurred in Northern Ireland, not just in an isolated instance but recurrently throughout the 1980s, and not just in one council but in all councils controlled by a particular party or group of parties. The main Unionist Parties, which together controlled most of the province's district councils, adopted a policy of adjourning meetings without transacting any or all of the business as a means of political protest. Initially the protest at the beginning of the 1980s was directed at the alleged inadequacy of the government's security policy. Later, however, the same tactic was used to protest against the presence of Sinn Féin councillors who had been elected to councils. Later still, after 1985, adjournments took place in protest at the Anglo-Irish Agreement. These last adjournments were the most widespread and had the effect of paralysing local government, with councils not transacting their business for a lengthy period.[5]

It was inevitable that councillors opposed to the adjournment policy would seek to circumvent or challenge it. In 1982 an attempt was made by a minority group of councillors to requisition the chairman of a council to hold a meeting on a date specified in the requisition before the next scheduled meeting of the council. The chairman responded (within the seven days from the receipt of the requisition as required by statute) by agreeing to the holding of a meeting to deal with the business contained in the requisition. He set the date and time of the requisitioned meeting, however, to coincide with the date and time of the next scheduled meeting of the council. This was not what the requisitionists wanted, as they had desired to clear the backlog of business produced by the adjournment of meetings and were also concerned that the next scheduled meeting would be adjourned in the same way as the last. Accordingly, they decided to send summonses to all members for a council meeting convened by themselves, taking the view that the chairman had 'refused' to call a meeting as required under the statutory procedure. At the date and time fixed by them the requisitionists duly arrived at the council's offices to find them locked. Moreover, none of the majority group's councillors appeared. In these circumstances, the requisitionists purported to hold a council meeting in an adjacent café and subsequently they went to court to attempt to establish the legality of the café meeting and the business transacted at it. The attempt failed both in the High Court and the Court of Appeal.[6]

In both courts the arguments centred on the statutory provisions relating to requisitioning of meetings and on the powers of the chairman. It was held that the chairman was not obliged to set the meeting at the date and time stipulated by the requisitionists; that once he had (within seven days of receipt of the requisition) set a date for a meeting, it was doubtful whether he could ever be said to have 'refused' to call a meeting and hence have enabled the requisitionists to call a meeting; and that the decision of the chairman as to the date and time of the meeting he called was a matter for his discretion which would only be reviewable in cases of 'clear abuse'.[7] Interestingly, little is said in the judgments about the overall political context of the dispute. No criticism of the adjournment of the council meetings as a mechanism of protest is made. The political effect on those councillors who did not share the majority's view regarding adjournments is unacknowledged. The implications of repeated adjournments for the efficiency of the council and its delivery of services to ratepayers are not drawn out or adverted to. The judgments read mainly as technical essays in statutory interpretation.

In 1986, however, the policy of Unionist controlled councils of adjourning meetings in protest at the Anglo-Irish Agreement was challenged head on in a judicial review (*Cook*) in which the applicants were members of a minority party on Belfast City Council. The resolution at each month's council meeting in addition to adjourning the meeting without the transaction of business contained authority to delegate the functions of the council to the town clerk for the period of the adjournment. It was argued by the applicants that this resolution was unlawful as being *Wednesbury* unreasonable and that, while there was a statutory power[8] available to the council to arrange for the discharge of any of its functions (subject to a small list of express exceptions) by an officer of the council, this power was being used for an improper purpose.

In both the High Court and the Court of Appeal[9] the resolution was held to be unlawful. On this occasion, however, the effect of the resolutions on the position of the minority councillors, on the efficiency of the transaction of council business and on the ratepayers and local democracy was clearly influential. In the Court of Appeal, Lord Lowry (then Lord Chief Justice) characterised the council's action as 'the negation of all the principles according to which local government is carried out through discussion and debate among elected representatives' and as 'completely unreasonable in the *Wednesbury* sense in the local government context'.[10] Further, in the High Court, Hutton J. (as he then was), having reviewed the affidavit evidence as to how the policies of the council were being stultified by the adjournments, interpreted the statutory powers to hold meetings and to delegate functions to officers as being intended by parliament to be used to assist the council in the efficient and effective carrying out of its functions. As they were being used not for this purpose but for that of demonstrating opposition to the Anglo-Irish Agreement, the resolutions were unlawful 'on the ground that power given for one purpose cannot be exercised for a different purpose'.[11]

Plainly, by 1986 the damage being done to local government in the province by these disruptive tactics was far more evident than in 1982. In fact the earlier decision from 1982 was not even cited in the 1986 judicial review.[12]

The scope of debate

It is widely recognised that local government bodies do occasionally discuss and pass resolutions on matters which, strictly speaking, may have little to do with the functions of their authority. These may be matters of central government policy or matters of international concern and the incentive for such debates and resolutions will usually be political: to let government know where the elected authority stands, to encourage the government to action, to show local concern on an issue and so on. Freedom of speech for a democratic institution will probably be asserted as a justification for such exercises, if one is required.

In terms of statutory provisions, no explicit limit is placed on the scope of debate in local authorities, unlike certain analogous bodies,[13] but does the common law doctrine of *ultra vires* serve to limit the authority's powers? This is an issue which arose in the *Cook* case which in another context has already been the subject of discussion. It arose because it was argued that Belfast City Council was acting *ultra vires* when it discussed and passed a resolution expressing opposition to the Anglo-Irish Agreement. The council also decided to spend a sum of money on the erection of a banner on the City Hall building saying 'Belfast Says No', of which more will be said later. The approach of Hutton J. (as he then was) to this issue, while recognising the 'great importance of protecting the right to freedom of speech',[14] was to equate the passing of a resolution by the council with any other 'act' by it. As 'acts' of the council are subject to the *ultra vires* doctrine, so also are resolutions; therefore, resolutions at common law are unlawful unless they relate or are incidental to or are consequent upon the statutory functions of the council. Hence the learned judge considered whether the Anglo-Irish Agreement had sufficient proximity to the council's work. As he held it did, it followed that the council's debate and resolution were not outside the scope of its powers, but would the opposite conclusion have resulted if the Anglo-Irish Agreement had failed to pass the proximity test? Hutton J.'s answer appears to be yes and this appears also to be the case even if the Local Government Act (Northern Ireland) 1972 had had an equivalent section in it to section 111(1) of its English counterpart.[15] This is because Hutton J. viewed the subsection as merely giving expression in statutory form to the common law's proximity doctrine.

Such an outcome seems difficult to reconcile with the goal of free speech, and if matters had rested there, complaints from local authorities about the restrictions arising from this judgment might have been expected; but Hutton J. did not rest there. As a further ground for regarding the council's debate and resolution as lawful he cited section 115 of the 1972 Act (section 137 in the English Act). This is the discretionary spending power which enables a council to expend its funds (up to a stated ceiling) 'for any purpose which in its opinion is in the interests (a) of the council; (b) of its district or any part of its district; (c) of the inhabitants of its district or of any part of its district'. The learned judge's view was that payments made pursuant to this section were not subject to the *ultra vires* doctrine. Thus if a council has power to make a payment under the section, it must also have power to pass a resolution directing the action in respect of which the payment is made and stating why the action is being taken.

As in this case the expenditure of money to express the council's opposition to the Anglo-Irish Agreement (by erecting a banner) was the outcome of the debate, the invocation of section 115 appears justifiable, but it is not explicitly stated whether the learned judge's view was that the existence of section 115 removed any restriction the common law may impose on the scope of debate within a local authority. Suppose the authority is debating a topic without any intention to consider the discretionary expenditure of money in relation to it at the end of the debate. If the topic is outwith the proximity test, would such debate and, say, the passage of a resolution on the topic be lawful? The *Cook* case, which appears to be the only authority directly relevant to the issue, is unclear on these points (which were not taken on appeal to the Court of Appeal). While it is easily understood that a legal challenge to the *vires* of a debate and resolution of a council without the expenditure of money or other positive action by the council will be a rarity, nonetheless the general issue is one of political importance, and if the special attributes of local government are to survive and prosper, it is one which requires at least clearer resolution.

Controlling meetings

In the heat of debate tempers are apt to rise with the political temperature. The control exercised by a council over its own proceedings requires a light touch. While a failure to assert order may lead to uproar or worse, an over-zealous exercise of control may have the effect of limiting participation and debate or of nullifying the views or expectations of elected representatives or others. It is appropriate to consider the control exercised over councillors separately from that exercised over the public at council meetings.

Normally the control of councillors during debate will be an issue ultimately to be resolved by the council itself acting under standing orders. At a meeting of Belfast City Council on 6 December 1984 passions were inflamed when a councillor made reference to 'the Union Jack, also known as the butcher's apron'.[16] This led to a motion being passed by the council suspending the councillor until he withdrew his statement. The offending councillor, who was a representative of a small minority party strongly antipathetic to the Unionist majority on the council, withdrew from the meeting. At each of the two following council meetings, when the councillor arrived he was asked to withdraw his earlier statement or apologise for it. He refused to do so and on both occasions he was escorted out of the chamber by police. The councillor, Mr Thomas McAnulty, sought judicial review of the legality of the council's motion suspending him. The relevant standing order under which the council had acted provided that in the event of a member being guilty of offensive conduct, the council may 'suspend such member for the remainder of the sitting and may, in addition, order the suspension to continue until submission of apology by the offending member'. Hutton J. ruled that this standing order was *ultra vires* as it went wider than the powers which the council possessed at common law. These were only those 'as are necessary to the existence of such a body, and the proper exercise of the functions which it is intended to execute' and these powers were 'protective and self defensive powers only, and not punitive'.[17] While the council did have power to suspend a member for the particular sitting in a case like this where the member had been guilty of offensive conduct, the need to protect its own proceedings did not require any greater penalty. The matter might well be different where a member had engaged in persistent and wilful obstruction of the business of the council. In this event, Hutton J. thought that 'there might well be a power at common law to suspend him from further meetings until he apologised because such a course would be reasonably necessary for the proper exercise of the council's functions'.[18] In drawing the line where he did, the learned judge clearly had in mind the democratic context in which the dispute arose. Powers of this nature, he said, were 'dangerously liable, in possible cases, to excess or abuse'. Likewise he acknowledged that powers of suspension constitute 'a serious interference with the rights of those local government electors who elected the applicant to have him speak and vote at council meetings'.[19] Moreover, the learned judge reviewed the code of punishments for infringement of the rules of debate at Westminster and noted that these had been described as 'a graduated code'.[20]

Clearly, if a local council were to draw up wide standing orders in this area and to police them vigorously, a great deal of damage could be inflicted to the ideals of local democracy and participation. Hutton J.'s judgment will represent a considerable brake upon any council so minded. Having said this, it is worthy of note that Hutton J. did indicate that, had the council's standing order been *intra vires*, he would have been unable to conclude that the resolution under challenge was *Wednesbury* unreasonable.

As regards the rights of the public to attend the proceedings of local government bodies, there is a detailed statutory code which is fully discussed elsewhere,[21] but these statutory provisions are expressly without prejudice to any power of exclusion to suppress or prevent disorderly conduct or other misbehaviour at a meeting.

In the case of *Francis*[22] a meeting of the Brent Health Authority was challenged as being invalid because the public, contrary to section 1 of the Public Bodies (Admission to Meetings) Act 1960, had been excluded from it. The reason for the exclusion was that, in view of a lengthy history of disorder at similar meetings, it appeared to the authority that it would not be possible to transact the business unless the public were excluded. The authority, therefore, relied on common law powers which it claimed to possess to exclude either before or during a meeting anyone whose behaviour was disruptive of the meeting. The authority said that as it could not determine from past experience which members of the public were or were not intent on disrupting the meeting, the only practical course was to exclude the public as a whole from it.

The court held that such powers did exist and had been preserved by the 1960 Act. The precise limits of the powers were not defined, Forbes J. being content to put the matter on a general footing. He said that 'there must exist a power to enable the business of the authority to be carried on in circumstances where it reasonably appeared that, if the requirements of keeping the meeting open to the public were followed, no business could possibly be transacted . . . because the meeting would be disrupted'.[23] The power, if abused, would be subject to judicial review on *Wednesbury* principles. In the circumstances, however, he viewed the authority as having acted reasonably with the consequence that its meeting was valid.

In *Assegai*[24] it was held that a resolution of Brent London Borough Council banning the applicant, who was a local Labour Party activist and a council-appointed school governor, from visiting any council premises was unlawful, both on procedural grounds and on the ground of unreasonableness. The applicant had a history of 'threatening and intimidatory behaviour towards members of the council'[25] and the council deemed that his presence on council premises was a risk both to members of the council and members of the public and was likely to interfere with the proper business of councillors, public and staff alike. In view of *Francis* the court accepted that there was power at common law to exclude either before or during a meeting anyone whose behaviour was disruptive of a meeting. Further, the court was of the view that the council also had power to exclude him from other council premises to which the public would ordinarily have access. The power to exclude, however, had to be exercised fairly, which generally would require that the council would give an indication of what it was proposing to do and an opportunity for the person affected to make representations as to why the proposed course of action should not be adopted. This had not occurred in this case and, accordingly, there had been a breach of the duty to act fairly. In the context of the *Francis* power of exclusion, the court noted that the requirements of a hearing might be impractical in certain circumstances, for example, due to reasons of urgency or because of the nature of the disruption which was taking place. These factors were not present in the applicant's case. Interestingly, the court concluded that the banning resolution was *Wednesbury* unreasonable. This primarily was because of its width. The resolution banned Dr Assegai from all the council's property irrespective of the circumstances and the court, in view of the applicant's past conduct, considered that the council's reaction was 'wholly out of proportion to what Dr Assegai had done'.[26] This was a clear pointer to the decision being unreasonable and, as the resolution lacked fair and sensible limits, it was unlawful on this ground also.[27]

Access to information

It is important for local democracy that an elected councillor is in a position to carry out his duties effectively. In this context access to information and to the places from which it can be obtained may raise sensitive political questions. A councillor may wish to gain sight of documents or files in the authority's control which would not in the normal course of his duties be disclosed to him. Likewise, as a means of obtaining information, he may wish to attend and observe a committee or subcommittee of which he is not a member. On several occasions the courts have had to adjudicate between the rights of the councillor and those of the council, and occasionally the context has been party political. In 1938 in a case[28] with no obvious party political edge to it, the court laid down the general principle: a councillor is entitled to the production of such documents as will enable him properly to carry out his duties as a councillor.

This principle was applied subsequently in cases without significant party political controversy.[29] In the last of these in 1983 the House of Lords[30] distinguished the position of a councillor who is a member of a committee whose papers he wishes to see from that of one who is not. In the former case, the councillor 'as a general rule will *ex hypothesi* have good reasons for access to all written material of such committee'. In the latter case, however, 'the outside councillor . . . has no automatic right of access to documentary material'.[31] A 'need to know' must be demonstrated ultimately, in a case of dispute, to the council itself whose decision is subject to judicial review on grounds of *Wednesbury* unreasonableness. In 1985 and 1986 these common law principles gave rise to judicial reviews of significant party political interest. In the first, that of *Gamper*,[32] a minority party councillor, who was both a member of the council's public services and housing committees, and who was also chairman of a district housing subcommittee, sought access to documents relating to a commercially sensitive subcommittee of the public services committee, composed of representatives of the majority party only, which dealt with policy and operational control of direct labour organisations including those dealing with housing. As he was concerned with a variety of housing-related problems, the applicant considered that he had a valid reason for his request. It was turned down, however, on the ground that the subcommittee's papers were confidential, and when the applicant sought to attend and observe the subcommittee's proceedings the subcommittee adjourned its meeting to prevent him from doing so. The court held that the council had acted unlawfully. In the first place, it had asked itself the wrong question. It has asked itself, said Lloyd LJ., 'whether the proceedings of the sub-committee are confidential' when the question it should have asked was 'whether, notwithstanding the confidential nature of the sub-committee's documents, the applicant had a "need to know"'.[33] Hence it had failed to take a relevant factor, the councillor's need to know, into account; but even if it had directed itself properly the council had, according to the learned judge, reached a conclusion that no reasonable council could have come to. The applicant had 'a legitimate and indisputable interest in the efficient running of the council'.[34] Wearing his various hats the applicant clearly had a need to know and the width of the prohibition imposed by the council, which covered all the subcommittee's papers, was unjustifiable, even if there were some documents which were so highly confidential that they could not be disclosed to members of the council. In relation to the issue of the applicant's right to attend to observe the proceedings of the subcommittee, the same considerations applied. On the need to know principle, the decision to exclude the applicant was similarly unlawful.

The implications of this decision for a majority group which sought to monopolise information concerning its authority were only being worked out when the case of *Chadwick*[35] arose in 1986. The applicant was a Liberal member of Sheffield City Council which was controlled by Labour. While the council's Policy committee, of which he was a member, was composed of councillors from a variety of parties, its Budget subcommittee was composed only of Labour councillors. This was because the purpose of this subcommittee was to serve as a forum in which members of the ruling group could work out their budgetary proposals, with the assistance and advice of council officials. Once finalised in the subcommittee, these proposals would be placed before the Policy committee and, ultimately, the council. As the council had been rate-capped in the preceding financial year, the applicant considered that the deliberations of the subcommittee were of particular importance and so he sought access to its papers and sought to attend its meetings. His view was that in order to evaluate the proposals emerging from the subcommittee, he needed to be aware of what information was before it, what options were open and what advice had been received from officials. Like *Gamper* before him, he found that his request for documents was refused and he was barred from attending to observe the subcommittee's deliberations. When he sought judicial review, the council argued that the existence of the subcommittee served the needs of the 'administration' or 'government' of the council and that it enured to the efficiency of the despatch of the authority's business. It was desirable, it was submitted, that the majority group should be able to develop its budgetary policies, with the assistance of officials, in private. Moreover, it was pointed out that similar arrangements existed for other parties on the council to consult officials privately for the purpose of formulating policy. If the applicant were to be granted access to the subcommittee and its documentation, it was argued, this would upset these arrangements with the effect that the majority group's deliberations would be driven into informal meetings of councillors, without officials, from which undoubtedly he could be excluded. Consequently, there would be a loss to the efficiency of operation of the authority.

Woolf J. (as he then was) held that the council had acted unlawfully. The council's justification for its decisions lay in the presumed need for confidentiality and secrecy in relation to the subcommittee's activities, but this need only arose because of the party political purpose served by the committee. If this purpose was unlawful, the requirement for confidentiality disappeared. The learned judge's view was that while the Policy committee had power to delegate its functions or part of them to the subcommittee and had power to exclude members of opposition parties from it, it was *ultra vires* for such a subcommittee to be designed to work out what should be the policy of a group of the members of the council rather than what should be the policy of the council itself. As a matter of law, it was 'not permissible for the council, by allowing the subcommittee to be used for party political purposes, to justify a need for confidentiality and secrecy which would not otherwise arise'.[36] The question, as before, was whether the applicant had a need to know. On this the learned judge had no doubt. He was entitled to the information he was seeking and it was reasonable for him to want to know what options had been considered before the subcommittee's recommended policy was chosen. If the council had not been influenced by the confidentiality factor which it had wrongly taken into account, it could not reasonably have taken the view that the applicant did not have a need to know. There was, in short, no justifiable basis for refusing access in this case. Moreover, if the councillor's attendance at the subcommittee's meetings was a convenient method of obtaining information, the learned judge could see no rational basis for refusing attendance. Interestingly, Woolf J. was not impressed by the council's submission that there could not be a need to know if the information in question could be obtained by some other means. Provided the councillor acted reasonably, he was not required to exhaust all other avenues by which he might obtain the information.

In *Strak*,[37] Woolf J. (as he then was) was of the opinion that informal consultative meetings between a party or parties and officials, outside the official committee structure, would not normally be subject to these access requirements, but the position might be different if informal channels in fact were being used for the taking of decisions which would bind the council.

Taken together, the decisions in *Gamper* and *Chadwick* may be viewed as vindications of the rights of the individual councillor when these have been threatened by broader party political considerations. In *Gamper* the desire to protect direct labour organisations for party purposes, it may be speculated, was the driving force behind the council's arrangements, whereas in *Chadwick* a model of government, not dissimilar to that at Westminster, was being promoted by the ruling group on the council. Hence it was natural for the policy-making function of the executive on the council (officials and councillors) to be carried on without the direct participation of opposition parties. As Woolf J. held, however, this model conflicted with existing legal requirements. While the tension between the needs of the individual councillor and those which drive party politics in local authorities in these cases was resolved largely in favour of the former, in other contexts the courts have been prepared to acknowledge to an appreciable degree the importance of party politics.

Party discipline

It is now well recognised that increasingly local authorities are organised on party political lines.[38] Local manifestos will be presented to the electorate. After elections, parties will jostle for control of the authority and party political programmes will be sought to be implemented. Party discipline will inevitably emerge as a feature of political life within the authority. Occasionally such discipline may abrade or be thought to abrade with the requirements of lawful decision-taking. A judicial review which illustrates the approach of the courts is *Baxter*.[39] The applicant sought review of a rating level decision on the basis that a number of the councillors among the voting majority had cast their votes contrary to their own personal views, these having been aired at a ruling group caucus meeting where they had not found favour with the majority in the party group. It was alleged that the councillors in question had fettered their discretion at the council meeting by regarding themselves as bound by the ties of party loyalty and discipline. The court, however, was slow to arrive at any such conclusion. The Court of Appeal had regard to the Labour group's standing orders and declared them not 'in any way objectionable'.[40] Likewise, the operation of, in effect, a whipping system and of caucus meetings was not disapproved of, provided it did not result in councillors fettering their discretion by elevating party requirements to a point where all other relevant factors were being excluded. Councillors were entitled, in arriving at their decision, to consider party loyalty and the need for the group to act cohesively as relevant factors, along with other relevant factors. To rule otherwise, thought Stocker LJ., would 'create many practical difficulties'[41] in the organisation of local government and, said Lord Donaldson MR, would 'by implication be criticising the system operating in Parliament itself'.[42] The court was satisfied on the evidence that the councillors concerned had not fettered their discretion but rather had properly exercised it, taking into account all relevant factors (including those of party loyalty and group cohesiveness). Of course, the weight to be given to individual factors was a matter for each councillor himself.

In *Jackson*,[43] decided some four years before *Baxter*, the approach of the court had been similar. Judicial review had been sought by a local conservationist seeking an order of prohibition in anticipation of a grant of planning permission by the Amber Valley District Council to a company which was seeking to develop a major amusement park on land owned by a county council. It was argued that any valid consideration of the planning application had been pre-empted by a Labour Party group meeting which had involved leading party figures in both the district and the county council, which were both controlled by Labour. The outcome of the meeting had been a decision to support the company's development. It was not in dispute that present at the meeting were sufficient members of the majority group on the district council to ensure that, by use of the party whips, the application would be approved. Notwithstanding this, Woolf J. (as he then was) dismissed the application. While he accepted that the Labour majority group on the district council had shown themselves to be 'politically predisposed'[44] in favour of the development, he did not regard this as disqualifying the council from dealing with the matter or as meaning that the application would not be treated fairly and lawfully. It was almost inevitable, he thought, now that party politics play so large a part in local government, that the majority group would decide on a party line in respect of the proposal. He went on: 'If this was to be regarded as disqualifying the district council from dealing with the planning application, then if that disqualification is to be avoided the members of the planning committee at any rate will have to adopt standards of conduct which I suspect will be almost impossible to achieve in practice.'[45] The council had to consider the objections to the planning application on their merits, despite the policy predisposition, but it was held that there was nothing to suggest that all material considerations would not be taken into account.

In the field of the licensing of the use of premises as sex establishments by local authorities, where councillors may, in advance of deciding on individual applications, have expressed strong general views on the subject or be party to a group policy, the law as expounded in *Jackson* has been applied. In *Quietlynn Limited*[46] Kennedy J. could see no objection to the Conservative group on Reading Borough Council deciding that it was not in favour of sex establishments, provided the group's policy was not applied over-rigidly.[47] Likewise, he did not regard the fact that a councillor had, a year before deciding a series of applications, written to a newspaper expressing his view that sex establishments should be banned altogether as meaning that he could not exercise discretion lawfully.

Manifestos

May political promises made in election manifestos to the electorate be regarded as having special prominence in the decision-making process? Decisions based on electoral mandates, when challenged, have produced inconsistent responses from the courts and contrasting judicial comments. The leading case is *Bromley*[48] decided by the House of Lords in 1983. In the Labour local election manifesto for the Greater London Council elections in 1981 the promise was made that within six months of winning the election the Labour group, if returned with a majority, would cut fares on London

Transport's buses and tubes by an average of 25 per cent. This, once in power, the Labour group did, notwithstanding a number of practical problems which had surfaced once the election was over. When the decision was challenged by Bromley London Borough Council (which had among others to contribute to the costs arising from it) it was argued that it was unlawful because the majority on the GLC had fettered their discretion by the commitment in their election manifesto and had regarded themselves as irrevocably committed to implementing it, come what may. While not all of the law lords dealt with this issue, which was not the sole issue in the case,[49] those who did considered that, on the facts, Bromley's contention was correct. Emphatically, their lordships held that while councillors were entitled, after the election, to have regard to their election promises and treat them as relevant considerations, they must not regard themselves as bound by them 'whatever the cost and other countervailing considerations may turn out to be'.[50] These last mentioned matters must be considered if discretion is to be exercised lawfully. Thus the legal rule appears unaffected by any special quality arising from the fact that the consideration at issue derives its importance from the electoral process.

In contrast, the relevance of an election manifesto and mandate in local government was viewed as a significant and legitimate element in the local authority's calculations in the *Tameside* case.[51] Following an election the political complexion of the authority changed (from Labour to Conservative) and, in turn, this led to a shelving of plans to 'comprehensivise' schools in the area in favour of maintaining some grammar schools. The Secretary of State for Education in a Labour government, which itself favoured comprehensive education, decided that the disruption caused by this change of local policy in Tameside meant that the newly elected council was 'acting or proposing to act unreasonably'.[52] Accordingly, he imposed directions on the authority to continue with the old council's proposals using default powers under the Education Act 1944. When the authority did not comply with them, the Secretary of State sought mandamus from the court to bring the authority to heel. In both the Court of Appeal and the House of Lords, however, it was unanimously held that the Secretary of State's directions were unlawful and invalid as it was considered that he had no grounds for concluding that the authority had acted or was proposing to act unreasonably. In both courts it was viewed as important that the fate of the council's school proposals had been a major issue at the local election and the desire of the new council to carry out the policy on which it was elected was regarded as a relevant factor, both to the authority and to the Secretary of State. Viscount Dilhorne referred to the fact that the council could claim to have obtained a mandate 'in the same way as a party which has won a general election can claim to have a mandate to carry out its manifesto',[53] while Lord Wilberforce went so far as to say that the newly elected council was in a sense bound to carry out the policy on which it was elected. Implicit in the change of policy sanctioned by the electorate was administrative disruption. 'So', said Lord Wilberforce, 'the mere possibility, or probability, of disruption cannot be a ground for issuing a direction to abandon the policy.'[54]

Taken as a whole, the speeches in the House of Lords may be read as conferring a special legitimacy upon the authority's action arising from its source: a political manifesto endorsed by the electorate. The fact that Tameside were an elected authority, moreover, was described as 'vital'.[55] The Secretary of State's intervention was, therefore, subjected to a high intensity form of review which permitted ministerial intervention only in limited circumstances and which on the facts before the House led to the invalidation of his directions.

If in the *Bromley* case the law lords had shared the view that the Labour group was in a sense bound to carry out the policy on which it was elected, it must be doubted whether they would have regarded the GLC's adherence to that policy as amounting to a fetter on their discretion.

Political control of the committee structure

An important facet of political life, now subject to specific statutory provision[56] but unregulated prior to 1986, is the extent to which the majority on the council can exercise political control over the committee structure. Interestingly, the courts when called upon to scrutinise this aspect of local government prior to 1986 had been remarkably non-interventionist. In *Lovelace*[57] the majority party on the council sought to steer a policy through a subcommittee in which it had met opposition by recomposing the subcommittee's membership so as to replace those councillors who were in opposition to the policy. The court viewed such action as lawful. The council was entitled to seek to ensure that its policy was followed in the committee and the removal of those opposed to it was for the lawful purpose of getting the committee to act consistently with the council's policy. The court, however, went on to state that it would be unlawful to remove a councillor from a committee for frivolous reasons or reasons not connected with the council's activities.

Perhaps even more striking is the case of *Crawford*[58] where the court refused to regard as unreasonable steps taken by a council to suspend political opponents from positions they had hitherto enjoyed in council committees, these steps being in retaliation for at least one member of the group of councillors concerned having published allegations which subsequently were neither withdrawn nor substantiated and which had been aimed at discrediting the majority group. Forbes J., in a judgment notable for its acceptance of party politics in local government, made it clear that a councillor had no right to membership of any committee of the council. The council was entitled to neglect to appoint any member of any particular political party to a committee, and if such a power were used so that one political party took the opportunity of excluding its opponents from committees, this was not *Wednesbury* unreasonable. The learned judge's view was that 'the question of whether a thing is unreasonable as we understand it in *Wednesbury* . . . has to be stretched pretty far when one is considering party political behaviour in the party political arena'.[59] The power of exclusion, however, did not run to exclusion of a councillor from the council itself. In the end the court in *Crawford* struck down the decision to suspend the councillors as it was held to be inconsistent with the council's own standing orders.

Emasculating opposition

Forbes J., as quoted above, was of the view *obiter* that the council could not exclude a councillor from the council itself. It is doubtful whether he had in mind any power of exclusion which might arise through the need to prevent disorder in debate. Rather, he probably had in mind the situation where a majority on the council might seek for political reasons to exclude a councillor or a group of councillors from the council itself and its work. In Northern Ireland this situation has arisen and has been the subject of judicial review. In the mid-1980s the ruling Unionist groups on several councils resented the presence of Sinn Féin councillors who supported the use of violence for political ends and the strategy of the 'armalite and the ballot box'. Accordingly, they employed a number of devices designed to emasculate the ability of these councillors to participate in the council's affairs. The chief device, tried in several councils, was to establish a committee of the council from which only Sinn Féin councillors were excluded, to which all the lawfully delegable business of the council was sent. In *Curran and McCann*,[60] however, the court held this action to be unlawful. While the council did have a statutory power to delegate a wide range of its activities to a committee,[61] this power could only be used for the better management and regulation of the council's business. It could not be used to exclude councillors from the work and activities of the council; but could the Sinn Féin councillors be excluded on foot of protective and self-defensive common law powers of the same nature as those recognised in the *McAnulty* case? It was submitted by the applicants that such powers were confined to dealing with disorder in the council chamber, but Hutton J. was not so sure. To this submission, he responded: 'In the great majority of cases where the powers require to be exercised the occasion which will give rise to their exercise will be disorder in the chamber, and if a council purported to exercise the powers in respect of the activities or policies of a councillor or his party outside the chamber I consider that such an exercise would very often be held by the Courts to be unnecessary and therefore invalid and unlawful.'[62] When, however, if at any time, would the exercise of the powers in the respect of the policies or activities of a councillor be legal? Hutton J.'s answer to this—though his phraseology at this point in his judgment indicates that he was (to use words later used in respect of it by Carswell J.) 'prepared . . . to countenance the possibility'[63] rather than to decide anything—would seem to be that the exercise of the powers would be legal if it flowed from the necessity to protect the existence of the council and the proper exercise of the functions it was intended to execute. It is difficult to envisage circumstances which would illustrate when and how this power might legally be used, but it is worthy of note that in a later case, commenting on this very question, Carswell J. (as he then was) was inclined (without deciding the matter) to the view that common law protective and self-defensive powers did not go outside the sphere of control by the council of its proceedings. He considered that a council did not have power 'either to expel or exclude councillors . . . on security grounds'.[64] This judicial difference of opinion may be of little practical significance in any case. In *Curran and McCann*, Hutton J. reached the general conclusion that it would be inappropriate for the wider exclusionary power to be implied by the common law. As the matter was one of general importance he thought that any decision in relation to it should be left to the legislature to take, rather than be one for individual councils to decide.

Clearly the power to exclude or expel a councillor from the council altogether, not just as an incident in the control of proceedings, is a Draconian one and it is not surprising that, even in the then extraordinary circumstances of Northern Ireland, judges have concluded that councils do not possess it. If the power did exist and was used, it is quite a different matter as to whether it could then be said that its use was unlawful as being *Wednesbury* unreasonable. As Forbes J. said, in the party political arena what is reasonable or not unreasonable may stretch pretty far. In both the cases of *Curran and McCann* and of *French*,[65] Hutton J. and Carswell J. respectively considered that a decision to exclude Sinn Féin councillors from the activities of the council, if power to take it did exist, could not be condemned as *Wednesbury* unreasonable. This view was arrived at after judicial notice was taken of the policy and objectives of Sinn Féin and of

Article 17 of the European Convention on Human Rights and the case law in respect of it.

Campaigning and persuading

Much of the meat of politics, local or national, involves the articulation, explanation and advocacy of policies which themselves have been arrived at through argument and debate. Local authorities will inevitably want to let the public know what they are doing and may wish to influence or persuade others of the correctness of their stances. These others may include the national government or the persuasion may be part of a broader national campaign. As creatures of statute, local authorities will have to be able to demonstrate a legal pedigree for expenditure on these activities, and with ample room in this context for political controversy, on occasions there has been resort to judicial review. Two cases in the early 1980s concern the interpretation of section 142 of the Local Government Act 1972 in England and Wales and its Scottish equivalent, section 88(2) of the Local Government (Scotland) Act 1973. While the statutory framework regarding the publication of information has changed since then,[66] the approach of the courts remains instructive. The language of the statutory provisions at issue enabled local authorities to publish 'information on matters related to local government'. In *Meek*[67] the issue for the court was whether the *Lothian Clarion* published by Lothian Regional Council was, having regard to its contents, properly to be viewed as within the terms of section 88(2) of the Scottish Act. The contents which had been written by the majority Labour group on the council tended to support various stances of the Labour group and to disparage the policy positions of the Conservative group of which Meek was a member. The applicant argued that the word 'information' meant factual information in the context of the statute and that, as the paper went beyond factual information and included explanations and justifications for policies adopted and criticisms of Conservative policies, its publication by the council was unlawful. Lord Ross rejected the applicant's argument. He could find nothing in the statute to confine 'information' in the manner suggested and his view was that when parliament conferred the power it 'must have appreciated that party politics do prevail in local government and that a majority group in a local authority might well select for publication information on matters related to local government which would show or tend to show the majority group in a favourable light'.[68] Lord Ross's interpretation, therefore, offered a licence to local authorities to use this power to explain and justify their policies by the publication of information about what was being done or not done in the council.

Moreover, the *Lothian Clarion*'s purpose could scarcely be viewed as confined to the aim of educating its readership about the council's activities as opposed to persuading them of the wisdom of the majority group's approach and policies.

Whether persuasion was a legitimate purpose to be served by the publication of information on matters related to local government was the issue raised by a subsequent judicial review of decisions of the Inner London Education Authority (ILEA) at the instance of *Westminster City Council*.[69] ILEA were opposed to the government's proposals in relation to rate-capping and decided on a programme of public information to increase public awareness of the proposals and their implications. The programme involved retaining an advertising agency at a cost of some £651,000 and the agency's plan was to mount a media and poster campaign designed not only to provide information but to persuade the public to support ILEA's point of view. The applicant, which in part contributed to the funds of ILEA, argued that it was *ultra vires* for the authority to engage, under the authority of section 141 of the English Act, in a campaign of this sort. Glidewell J. (as he then was) agreed. His analysis was that the authority had intended by their actions to serve the dual purposes of information and persuasion. While the former was a permissible purpose under the section, the latter was not, and as the latter purpose had materially influenced the decision-making process, the decisions were invalid. In the learned judge's view the authority was entitled under the section to give an account and description of its activities and costs and indeed could lawfully explain the government's proposals and their effects. It could not, though, engage in the business of persuasion. From the point of view of the outward looking aspect of local government politics, this decision, therefore, represents a clipping of the wings of authorities which wish to use resources in this way.

This point was underlined a short time later when an interlocutory injunction was granted to restrain a multi-million pound campaign, involving five advertising agencies, which had been mounted by the Greater London Council in its efforts to save itself from abolition by the government. Much of the material produced was viewed as being tainted by the impermissible purpose of persuasion and the 'say no to no say' campaign accordingly was stopped in its tracks.[70]

An alternative statutory basis for expenditure for political or campaigning purposes in the past had been the discretionary spending power. Expenditure on the erection of a banner saying 'Belfast Says No' was regarded as lawful on foot of this power in the *Cook* case which was discussed above, though such expenditure would, thought Hutton J., be subject to the test of unreasonableness. Amendments to the discretionary spending power which post-date *Cook* would make reliance on the power for party political purposes now unlawful.[71]

Requiring compliance with council views

On occasions councils have sought to enforce their views on political issues by means of penalising in one way or another individuals and agencies outside the council who have failed to conform to the council's requirements. Invariably when such tactics have been challenged by judicial review, the local authority has been viewed as acting unlawfully. The leading case is that of *Wheeler*[72] which was decided by the House of Lords in 1985. Leicester City Council was politically opposed to the system of apartheid in South Africa and was also opposed to a proposed English rugby football tour of South Africa. The city's rugby union club, which used a recreational ground controlled by the council, had three of its players chosen for the tour. In view of this, the council sought from the club an endorsement of its own views on the issue, and it asked the club to put pressure on the three players not to tour. While going a long way towards the council's views, the club in its response fell short of fully aligning itself with the council and the three players did in fact go on the tour. This led to the council, in the exercise of its discretion, deciding to ban the club from its recreational ground for twelve months. In doing this the council said that it took into account its duty[73] imposed by the Race Relations Act 1976 to promote good race relations. The House of Lords unanimously held that the authority had acted unlawfully. While it was accepted that the council was entitled to have regard to its duties under the Race Relations Act, Lord Roskill considered it to have acted both unreasonably and unfairly. The council was at liberty to seek to persuade others of the soundness of its views, but, however powerful, persuasion 'must not be allowed to cross that line where it moves into the field of illegitimate pressure coupled with the threat of sanctions'.[74] This is what had occurred in this case. As Lord Templeman put it, 'the club could not be punished because the club had done nothing wrong'.[75] A strong signal was, therefore, sent out to local authorities. Private individuals and organisations 'cannot be obliged to display zeal in pursuit of an object sought by a public authority and cannot be obliged to publish views dictated by a public authority'.[76]

That this ruling has rested uneasily with the political desire of some authorities has been evidenced by several later cases where the *Wheeler* authority has served to strike down local authority actions. In the *Times Newspaper* case[77] it was held unlawful for a number of local authorities to use their discretion under the Public Libraries and Museums Act 1964 in such a way as to ban Murdoch newspapers from the authorities' public libraries. This step had been taken as a reflection of the councils' political support for a dismissed workforce and their trade unions who were in industrial dispute with the publisher of the newspapers concerned. The object of the exercise, the court reasoned, was to punish the employer, and parliament, said the court, did not contemplate such action to be within the power conferred. Watkins LJ. put the matter bluntly when he said that 'no rational authority would for a moment have thought that such a ban was open to it to impose in discharge of its duties to service libraries'.[78]

In what verged on a rerun of the *Times Newspaper* case, on the application of the *Times Supplements Limited*[79] a resolution of Derbyshire County Council was set aside. The resolution, making use of discretion conferred by the Education (No. 2) Act 1986, sought to alter the council's practice of advertising its educational appointments in the *Times Educational Supplement* (TES) and sought to ban the placing of any advertisements of the authority in any publications owned by the applicants or Mr Murdoch. The court found that the purpose behind the resolution was retaliation for articles which had appeared in the *Sunday Times* (published by Murdoch Newspapers) which allegedly had libelled the leader of the majority group on the council. The court, moreover, could discern no educational ground for the resolution, as advertising in the national newspaper chosen to replace the TES by the council cost more to reach a more limited target readership. In these circumstances the court viewed the resolution as an abuse of power. In a scathing judgment, Watkins LJ. indicated that had it been necessary to do so, he would have been prepared to regard the resolution as perverse as 'it appeared to have no sensible or justifiable basis'.[80] Plainly, he considered that the passage of the resolution was as a result of a slavish and thoughtless adherence to the party line, contrary to the principles laid down in *Baxter.*

In the *Shell UK*[81] case a policy of boycotting the applicant's products as a way of pressurising the company to withdraw associated company interests from South Africa was adopted by Lewisham London Borough Council. This was part of a campaign which was intended to embrace a number of local authorities and was devised as a means of promoting good race relations in the same way as was Leicester Council's actions discussed above. The court, following the *Wheeler* decision, held that the purpose of the council in putting pressure on the company to procure withdrawal of associated companies from South Africa was unlawful as the applicant company had not in any way itself acted unlawfully. Moreover, 'the wish to change the Shell policy towards South Africa was inextricably mixed up with any wish to improve race relations in the borough and this extraneous and impermissible purpose has the effect of vitiating the decision as a whole'.[82] Accordingly, a declaration was made that the decision of the council was *ultra vires*.

When Liverpool City Council, because of its political antipathy to the government's Employment Training Scheme, decided on a policy of using its own discretionary powers in a manner which would aid only those who rejected participation in the government's scheme, this led almost immediately to judicial review. The court, again on the basis of *Wheeler*, had little difficulty in concluding that this policy was unlawful.[83] Emphasis, as in the other cases discussed above, was placed on the element of coercion or punishment involved. It was not legitimate for the council to attempt to force others, who themselves were acting lawfully, to toe its line. A remedy was, therefore, granted by the court even though the policy, while encapsulated in a council resolution, had actually to be applied in a concrete case.

Finally in a different vein to the line of cases just discussed but related to councils requiring others to comply with their views, it seems, from the judicial review in *Fewings*,[84] that elected local authorities are limited in the extent to which, in exercising statutory discretions, they may act on the basis of broad moral or ethical beliefs. In some contexts such beliefs may be viewed as relevant, but in others the courts may not regard them as such. The statutory language and perspective will probably be the crucial considerations in deciding on which side a case falls. In *Fewings* both at first instance and in the Court of Appeal[85] the decision of Somerset County Council to ban deer hunting over land owned by the authority was held to be unlawful. The council had purported to exercise a discretionary power given for the purposes of 'the benefit, improvement or development'[86] of the land in question. In the High Court, Laws J. took the view that this power imported the need for the council to act upon objective judgments about what would conduce to the better management of the land. As the learned judge considered that the council's decision had been taken purely as a result of the councillors' moral perceptions, rather than as a result of the weighing up of objective factors related to managing the land, the ban on hunting was quashed.

Notably, in the course of his decision Laws J. rejected an argument submitted to him that, in consequence of the decision-maker being a democratically elected body, he should construe the statutory conferral of power more widely than would be the case if the decision-maker was unelected. His view was that he could only have regard to the words parliament had used in providing the power, and that these words would bear the same construction whether the recipient of the power was elected or unelected.[87]

Conclusion

The picture which emerges from the above survey of cases on the political functioning of local government must be viewed in context and perspective. As acknowledged earlier, a selection only of relevant authorities has been discussed. It is, of course, hoped that these are a representative sample but case study technique, which necessarily in a sphere like local government involves delineating a single area, has obvious limitations. Likewise it is trite, but nonetheless important, to keep in mind that cases are creatures of their time. Fortunately all those dealt with here have been decided within the last twenty years. While the general political landscape during this period, which it is not proposed to describe here, provides a backcloth against which individual controversies may be viewed, significant for our purposes is the realisation that judges have been able to approach judicial review in the period under consideration with relative confidence and assurance. Following the rapid development and exposition of administrative law in the highest courts in the late 1960s and early 1970s, reviewers have been able to concentrate more on the application of existing principles to the facts of the case before them than on the establishment of new principles.

What then do these cases tell us about the operation of judicial review and about how judges have dealt with the political functioning of local government, given the attributes of this arena? Only answers in broad terms can be offered.

As regards the operation of judicial review, the most important message to emerge is that the task of applying judicial review principles to the facts of each case is anything but a mechanical one. This is so not only because the principles themselves are open-ended and flexible but also because the desires of individual judges differ. The process may be illustrated by considering the application of the review standard of unreasonableness. While the rhetoric and language used to describe this standard would suggest that only rarely would an authority be found to offend against it, the reality very often is different. This explains the contrast between the willingness of Forbes J. in *Crawford* to offer considerable latitude and the willingness to strike down as unreasonable the authority's actions in *Cook*, *Gamper*, *Chadwick*, *Times Newspapers* and *Wheeler*. Clearly, what is unreasonable to one judge may not be unreasonable to another, and deciding where to draw the line is a matter of degree affected by subjective considerations. The elasticity of the standard means that without obvious distortion it may be stretched in any direction. Certainly in the above survey there has been little to suggest that judges are reluctant to use this standard in an overtly political environment, though there are also examples, such as *Curran and McCann* and *French*, where restraint can be observed.

To a lesser extent, perhaps, the same factors can be seen in operation in relation to other principles of judicial review. Where the exercise of a statutory power is concerned, what is or is not a proper purpose will often be a delicate exercise in statutory interpretation, as is illustrated by the views of the judges in *Meek* and in *Westminster City Council*. While in the former case no objection was raised by either the parties or the court to the publication of literature which was clearly intended to persuade electors to a certain view, in the latter, dealing with the same statutory provision, such a purpose was held to be improper. A possible explanation for this sort of situation is that the controversy may be shaped by counsels' submissions or by procedural factors, but it may be naive to accept this where the implications of going one way rather than another are far reaching. More probably the desires of the judge and his willingness to manipulate the application of malleable concepts to the facts will be crucial. As is well depicted by the quotations above from the cases of *Bromley* and *Tameside*, the same principle of review—in these cases that which requires public authorities to avoid the fettering of discretion by manifesto commitments—may assume a sharply different flavour when applied to different situations.

It is, therefore, suggested that when the courts are applying the judge-made principles of review, considerable latitude is available to them.

As regards the political functioning of local government, the cases surveyed differentially impact on the attributes identified earlier. Inevitably there are currents and cross-currents. The attribute of responsiveness, which is concerned more with the relationship of the council with its population, is only tangentially touched upon, but in so far as it is, it is clear that for an authority to argue in a judicial review that it is acting in response to public demand in its area, whether as expressed in an election, as in *Tameside* or *Bromley*, or as divined by the elected representatives as, for example, the need to promote good race relations in *Wheeler*, will be no more than a factor which the court will consider among others. Indeed it will not necessarily be a forefront, as opposed to a background, factor in such consideration and there will be cases, as illustrated by *Fewings*, where councillors' perceptions of moral or ethical feelings in the locality will be identified by the court as irrelevant to the exercise of discretion.

The attributes of participation and pluralism have been more central to this study. Participation needs to be viewed at different levels. While at the level of individual councillor participation not all of the cases point in the same direction, on balance the cases surveyed have portrayed a willingness on the part of the courts to secure a broad measure of participation in the council's affairs to the individual councillor. When the individual councillor's ability to participate has been directly threatened, as in *Curran and McCann*, *French* and *McAnulty*, the courts have been careful to limit the scope of lawful interference. Hence the council majority cannot simply emasculate the councillor's ability to participate by the use of artificial devices designed to exclude him altogether and they cannot take disproportionate punitive action in response to disorder in the chamber. Equally, where the effect of majority action is to frustrate the whole operation of elected local government and so deprive all councillors of the ability to do what they were elected to do, such action is also unlawful, as *Cook* demonstrates. Where the issue has been the equipping of the individual councillor with necessary information to enable him to participate, the courts have also been protective. The 'need to know' principle has been rigorously policed and, as in *Gamper* and *Chadwick*, the judges have not interpreted the concept narrowly.

At the level of group participation and the acceptance of party politics in local government by the courts, much has depended on the context. Individual rights have in general prospered over group rights where the two are in conflict, even where as in *Chadwick* this has meant the destruction of politically agreed arrangements for the internal operation of the council. There have been exceptional cases where individual rights have been subordinated, of which *Crawford* and *Lovelace* are examples, but for illustrations of general acceptance of party politics a more favourable context is required. In *Meek* the court regarded it as important to read a statutory power against the backcloth of the party political nature of council affairs, and in *Baxter* and *Jackson*, as noted above, the court accepted party organisation and discipline without difficulty.

Finally, as regards the attribute of pluralism, little acknowledgment of it can be found in the cases surveyed. While *Tameside* might be regarded as an exception, as a general rule the notion of authorities representing outward looking and diverse sources of political power is restrained, rather than promoted. Examples are the curbing of the campaigning activities of ILEA in the *Westminster City Council* case; the inhibition on the tactics of councils which wish to persuade others to accept or adhere to their views, evidenced by *Wheeler*, *Fewings* and similar cases; and the proscription in *Cook* of 'go slow or stop' as a means of protest against the actions of central government. As *Cook* also showed, it is not even clear that local government authorities are entitled to discuss matters unrelated to their statutory responsibilities.

From the above survey it would be difficult, overall, to conclude that the judges in judicial review have used the considerable latitude available to them to conserve or foster the special attributes of local government.

Notes

1. Report of the Committee of Inquiry into the Conduct of Local Government Business, Chairman, Mr David Widdicombe QC, June 1986, Cmnd. 9797. The quotation is at para. 3.12.
2. See, for example, Loughlin, 'Innovative Financing in Local Government: The Limits of Legal Instrumentalism [1990] PL 372, [1991] PL 568; also P. Meredith, *Judicial Review and Education*, above.
3. For the position in England and Wales, see Bailey, 'Cross on Principles of Local Government Law' (1992) at 4.09 to 4.14. For the position in Northern Ireland, see Local Government Act (Northern Ireland) 1972, sch. 2.
4. ibid. for England and Wales 4.10; for Northern Ireland, sch. 2, para. 2(2).
5. Local authorities in Northern Ireland do not enjoy the same range of powers as similar authorities in Britain. This is partly as a result of the presence of devolved government in Northern Ireland, a position temporarily superseded by direct rule of the province, and partly as a result of the growth of non-elected statutory bodies, a growth encouraged by fear that local authorities might use their powers in a partial manner. The legal status and functioning of local authorities in Northern Ireland are, however, materially similar to their counterparts in Britain. In the period 1987–91, there were fourteen judicial reviews involving local authorities in Northern Ireland: see Hadfield and Weaver [1994] PL 12, at p. 13.
6. *Mallon v Armstrong* [1982] NI 112 (High Court); p. 119 (Court of Appeal).
7. Per Murray J., at p. 117.
8. S. 47A, Local Government Act (Northern Ireland) 1972.
9. *In Re Cook and Other's Application* [1986] NI 242 (High Court); [1986] NI 274 (Court of Appeal).
10. ibid., at p. 277.
11. ibid., at p. 263.
12. The adjournment campaign did not cease with the decision in *Cook*. Despite an order of mandamus being directed at the Belfast City Council to hold meetings to carry out the business and functions of the council, meetings were not held and this led to the council being held in contempt of court and fined: see [1986] NI 283. Special default powers as a temporary provision were also legislated for by the government: see Local Government (Temporary Provisions) (Northern Ireland) Order 1986. Under this Order the government could appoint a person to act for and on behalf of the authority when it appeared to it that an authority 'has failed or is unable or unwilling to exercise duly and effectively any of the functions vested in it'. These default powers were used to ensure that rates were set as required by law by eleven councils in February 1987 and on other occasions as well.
13. See, for example, the restriction contained in s. 3 of the Northern Ireland Act 1982 on the subjects which might be debated by the Northern Ireland Assembly.
14. [1986] NI 242, at p. 252.
15. The material words in s. 111(1) are as follows: 'a local authority shall have power to do any thing . . . which is calculated to facilitate, or is conducive or incidental to, the discharge of any of their functions'.
16. The councillor concerned claimed that the description originated among Scottish Highlanders during the Highland Clearances by the Duke of Cumberland following the Battle of Culloden in 1746.
17. *In Re McAnulty's Application* [1985] NI 37; quotations are found at p. 41.
18. ibid., at p. 47.
19. ibid., at p. 45.
20. This description is from Erskine May, *Parliamentary Practice* (20th edn) at p. 444 which deals with the disciplinary powers of the Chair under House of Commons standing orders.

21. See Bailey, n. 3 above, at 4.21–4.26.

22. *R. v Brent Health Authority, ex p. Francis* [1985] QB 869.

23. ibid., at p. 879.

24. *R. v London Borough of Brent, ex p. Assegai, The Times,* 18 June 1987; (1987) 151 LGR 891.

25. Wording of the challenged resolution.

26. Per Woolf LJ.

27. A second resolution had also been passed by the council dismissing the applicant from his position as school governor. It was held, in respect of this, that the council had power to dismiss but that procedurally it must be exercised in a fair manner. As on the facts no form of hearing before dismissal had been provided, this resolution was held to be unlawful.

28. *R v Barnes Borough Council, ex p. Conlan* [1938] 3 All ER 226.

29. For example, see *R. v Lancashire County Council Police Authority ex p. Hook* [1980] QB 603.

30. *R. v Birmingham City Council, ex p. O.* [1983] 1 AC 578.

31. ibid., at p. 594.

32. *R. v Hackney London Borough Council, ex p. Gamper* [1985] 1 WLR 1229.

33. ibid., at p. 1239.

34. ibid.

35. *R. v Sheffield City Council, ex p. Chadwick* (1985) 84 LGR 563.

36. ibid., at p. 572.

37. *R. v Hyndburn Borough Council, ex p. Strak* (1986) 150 LGRev p. 57.

38. See Widdicombe Report, n. 1 above, at para. 2.34.

39. *R. v Waltham Forest London Borough Council, ex p. Baxter* [1988] QB 419.

40. ibid., at p. 424.

41. ibid., at p. 427.

42. ibid., at p. 424.

43. *R. v Amber Valley District Council, ex p. Jackson* [1984] 3 All ER 501.

44. ibid., at p. 508.

45. ibid., at p. 509.

46. *R. v Reading Borough Council, ex p. Quietlynn Ltd* (1987) 85 LGR 387.

47. In this context, the comments contained in the Widdicombe Report, n. 1 above, at para. 6.72 are worth bearing in mind: 'where councillors follow the policy of their local party it is not possible to divine whether they do so because they place party loyalty above their own views, whether they fear de-selection or whether they are acting under instruction from their own party. As Elizabeth I reportedly said: "One cannot open a window into men's souls."' In *R. v Derbyshire County Council, ex p. The Times Supplements, The Times,* 19 July 1990, on which comment is made below, it is clear from the report that the court regarded the majority of the councillors as slavishly adhering to the party line in passing the resolution at issue; but there were other grounds for setting the resolution aside.

48. *Bromley London Borough Council v Greater London Council* [1983] 1 AC 768.

49. Other issues in the case related to interpretation of the Transport (London) Act 1969 and the ability of the GLC to subsidise public transport fares as an object of social policy and, further, the issue of the council's fiduciary duty to its ratepayers in connection with additional burdens falling on them resulting from the reduction of fares and the consequent loss of rate support grant. After *Bromley* a spate of similar cases arose: see, for example, *R. v Merseyside County Council, ex p. Great Universal Stores Ltd* (1982) 80 LGR 639; *R. v London Transport Executive, ex p. Greater London Council* [1983] QB 484.

50. [1983] 1 AC 768, at p. 853.

51. *Secretary of State for Education and Science v Tameside Metropolitan Borough Council* [1977] AC 1014.

52. S. 68, Education Act 1944. The word 'unreasonably' was interpreted by all the law lords except Lord Wilberforce as meaning *Wednesbury* unreasonable. This interpretation may have been influenced by the fact that s. 68 was a default or override power in the Secretary of State's hands.
53. [1977] AC 1014, at p. 1055.
54. ibid., at p. 1048.
55. ibid., at p. 1047 (Lord Wilberforce).
56. See ss 15 and 16 and sch. 1 of the Local Government and Housing Act 1989 providing for proportionality in the composition of formal committees of councils.
57. *R. v Greenwich London Borough Council, ex p. Lovelace* [1991] 1 WLR 506.
58. *R. v Rushmoor Borough Council, ex p. Crawford, The Times,* 28 November 1981.
59. ibid.
60. *In Re Curran and McCann's Application* [1985] NI 261. For a more recent illustration of the same principles in operation, see *In Re McCann's Application* [1992] 9 NIJB 1.
61. S. 18(1), Local Government Act (Northern Ireland) 1972.
62. [1985] NI 261, at p. 276.
63. *In Re French's Application* [1985] NI 310, at p. 319.
64. ibid., at p. 320.
65. Carswell J. expresses himself as agreeing with the reasoning of Hutton J. on this point (ibid, at p. 323). Hutton J. (at p. 272) states: 'If the Council had power to do so, it was not acting completely unreasonably in excluding Sinn Féin councillors because the exclusion would be in conformity with the intent of article 17 of the European Convention as Sinn Féin, by reason of its policy of supporting terrorist murder and violence, is a group engaged in activities aimed at the destruction of many of the most important rights and freedoms set forth in the Convention.'
66. See Local Government Act 1986.
67. *Meek v Lothian Regional Council* [1983] SLT 494.
68. ibid., at p. 495.
69. *R. v Inner London Education Authority, ex p. Westminster City Council* [1986] 1 WLR 28.
70. *R. v Greater London Council, ex p. Westminster City Council, The Times,* 22 January 1985.
71. See Local Government Act 1986, s. 3(3); and Local Government and Housing Act 1989, s. 36 and sch. 2. In Northern Ireland, see Local Government (Miscellaneous Provisions) (Northern Ireland) Order 1992, art. 41.
72. *Wheeler v Leicester City Council* [1985] AC 1054.
73. Race Relations Act 1976, s. 71.
74. [1985] AC 1054, at p. 1078 (Lord Roskill).
75. ibid., at p. 1079.
76. ibid., at p. 1080.
77. *R. v Ealing London Borough Council, ex p. Times Newspapers Ltd* (1986) 85 LGR 316.
78. ibid., at p. 329.
79. *R. v Derbyshire County Council, ex p. The Times Supplements Ltd, The Times,* 19 July 1990.
80. ibid.
81. *R. v London Borough of Lewisham, ex p. Shell UK Ltd* [1988] 1 All ER 938.
82. ibid., at p. 952 (Neill LJ.).
83. *R. v Liverpool City Council, ex p. Secretary of State for Employment* [1989] COD 404.
84. *R. v Somerset County Council, ex p. Fewings* (1994) 92 LGR 674 and (CA) [1995] 1 WLR 1037.
85. Leave to appeal to the House of Lords was granted.
86. S. 120(1)(b), Local Government Act 1972.
87. (1994) 92 LGR at p. 694.

Chapter Five

Judicial Review and the Criminal Process

Peter Osborne

The High Court exercises a supervisory jurisdiction over inferior courts, tribunals and personnel. This jurisdiction is exercised by way of judicial review, the purpose of which is to ensure that public bodies do not exceed their powers and do not abuse any discretion which they may have.

Discretion is an elemental feature of every criminal justice system in the common law world.[1] To a greater or lesser extent in different jurisdictions, the formal procedures of the criminal law and the substantive rules of evidence determine only the final stages of a criminal prosecution. Prior to the trial, decisions will have been taken by various actors in the criminal justice system which will impact upon the subsequent proceedings—the most basic illustration of this is the discretion whether to prosecute or not. Such discretions, which are exercised by the police and public prosecutors, have an enormous influence on those who are subject to them. Equally, the substantive criminal process, entailing formalised and often solemn procedures with onerous implications for those subjected to it, suggests an especial importance for procedural propriety and observance of the principles of fairness and natural justice. Such is the life blood of public law.

A number of themes are evident when one addresses the application of the judicial review procedure to the criminal process. It can initially be observed that the actors within the criminal justice system are broadly subject to the same controls as are other officers performing duties of a public nature, although this may be qualified on occasion by the ubiquitous 'public policy'. A further theme commonly identified is to ask 'To what extent will the civil courts regulate the criminal courts?' It is to these two central issues that this chapter will turn. When appropriate, potential avenues for development will be identified. The study encompasses the judicial review procedure as it has been applied to aspects of the criminal process in England and Wales and in Northern Ireland, additionally drawing upon the experiences of other jurisdictions as appropriate. Further, the ambit of this chapter is restricted to the substantive criminal process and excludes consideration of topics such as emergency laws and the treatment of prisoners, nor does it discuss in detail the position in neighbouring

128

jurisdictions such as the Republic of Ireland or Scotland, all of which are comprehensively dealt with in other chapters of this book. Neither will the order of habeas corpus be discussed in this chapter.

The approach taken, therefore, is to analyse three distinct stages of criminal procedure and then to conclude with some general observations. The sections which follow are:

1. Introduction;
2. Judicial Review of Police Powers;
3. Judicial Review of Prosecutors' Discretions;
4. Judicial Review and the Criminal Courts; and
5. Overview.

Introduction

Some preliminary points merit consideration.

Criminal Cause or Matter

The procedure of judicial review differs depending on whether the application is in a 'criminal cause' or in a 'civil cause', and merely an outline of the procedural differences will be addressed here.[2] These differences which are consequent upon this distinction are procedural rather than substantive, and principally relate to the route which the application will follow through the hierarchy of the courts. In England and Wales, applications relating to a criminal cause or matter will be made to a single judge by way of a 'table application' (i.e. on the papers) or an 'oral application', and may be renewed (not appealed) for an oral hearing before a Divisional Court if refused.[3] The question of leave must be conclusively determined at that point, with no further renewals or appeals if unsuccessful. Hearings of substantive judicial review actions are by the Divisional Court comprised normally of two judges. In Northern Ireland, jurisdiction in a criminal cause or matter is exercised also by a Divisional High Court, though applications for leave are directed to a single judge.[4]

As regards the nature of the distinction, Lord Esher expressed the view in the last century that the phrase in previous legislation should be interpreted widely, and thought it to apply to 'a decision by way of judicial determination of any question raised or with regard to proceedings, the subject matter of which is criminal, at whatever stage of the proceedings the question arises'.[5] Applications relating to criminal trials, however, may still be non-criminal causes or matters if the issue in dispute is far removed from any potential punishment.[6]

The empirical picture of judicial review and the criminal process

It is also interesting at the outset to consider the incidence of judicial review in respect of criminal causes or matters, and to this end the research of the Public Law Project is informative.[7] Writing in 1993, the authors of *Judicial Review in Perspective* noted that 'criminal matters account for a remarkably steady percentage of all leave applications, at between 13.4 per cent and 15.6 per cent', and specifically amounting in 1991 to 15 per cent and in 1992 to 13 per cent.[8]

Judicial Review of Police Powers

Baldwin has suggested that '[T]he pre-trial stages of the criminal process have proved curiously impenetrable to outside observers, despite the fact that this is the time when the vulnerability of defendants might most easily be exploited.'[9]

It is important to note initially the difference between the role of the police in Northern Ireland and their role in England and Wales. In England and Wales, the investigative and prosecutorial functions have been separated since 1986, when the Crown Prosecution Service (CPS) was established under the Prosecution of Offences Act 1985. The police in England and Wales now have a prosecutorial role in respect of trivial offences and minor road traffic offences only, the CPS being obliged 'to take over the conduct of all criminal proceedings . . . instituted by or on behalf of a police force (whether by a member of that force or by any other person)'.[10] This differs from the status of the Northern Ireland police, the Royal Ulster Constabulary (RUC), who continue to play a significant role in both the investigation and the prosecution of offences, and where both the structure of and the resources available to the Director of Public Prosecutions for Northern Ireland also differ significantly from those of his English counterpart.

Possibly more than any other actors in the criminal process, the police are endowed with an enormous latitude of discretion in the manner in which their duties are discharged. The police are invariably the 'front line' of the criminal justice system and as such the individual officer is to an extent a filter for potential entrants to it. When coupled with the paradox of discretion which is inherent in the police organisation, namely, that 'those lowest in the hierarchy enjoy maximum field discretion',[11] the susceptibility of the police to the process of judicial review might have been thought to be inevitable and comprehensive. The practical effectiveness of the review carried out by the courts over the general exercises of police discretion, however, is quite limited, though judicial review of police conformity to statutory and administrative criteria has been more fruitful.

Review of police policy and operations

The courts have for almost three decades shown a willingness to judicially review decisions of policy by police forces. In a seminal decision, all of the members of the Court of Appeal in *R. v Metropolitan Police Commissioner, ex parte Blackburn* (1968) concurred in the proposition that the Commissioner of the Metropolitan Police owes a duty to members of the public to enforce the law of the land. In confirming this duty, Lord Denning MR stated:

> [The Commissioner] must take steps so to post his men that crimes may be detected and that honest citizens may go about their affairs in peace. He must decide whether or no [*sic*] suspected persons are to be prosecuted; and, if need be, bring the prosecution or see that it is brought. But in all these things he is not the servant of anyone, save of the law itself. . . . The responsibility for law enforcement lies on him. He is answerable to the law and to the law alone. . . . But there are some *policy decisions* with which, I think, the courts can, if necessary, interfere.[12]

Salmon LJ. felt that 'In the extremely unlikely event . . . of the police failing or refusing to carry out their duty [to enforce the law], the court would not be powerless to intervene.'[13] Having admitted a willingness to intervene in the realm of police decisions on policy, however, it was also noted by their lordships that operational matters were effectively immune from review:

> Although the chief officers of police are answerable to the law, there are many fields in which they have a discretion with which the law will not interfere. For instance, it is for the Commissioner of Police for the Metropolis, or the chief constable, as the case may be, to decide in any particular case whether inquiries should be pursued, or whether an arrest should be made, or a prosecution brought. It must be for him to decide on the disposition of his force and the concentration of his resources on any particular crime or area. No court can or should give him direction on such a matter.[14]

This landmark recognition of the courts' willingness to review the policy decisions of the police was reinforced in subsequent applications by Mr Blackburn. In *R. v Metropolitan Police Commissioner, ex parte Blackburn (No. 3)*, for example, Lord Denning MR stated:

> [In *ex parte Blackburn* (1968)], we made it clear that, in the carrying out of their duty of enforcing the law, the police have a discretion with which the

courts will not interfere. There might, however, be extreme cases in which [the Commissioner] was not carrying out his duty. And then we would.[15]

The nature of police decisions which were envisaged as reviewable were failures to enforce the law at all, and so long as some measures were being taken to discharge this police duty, then the matter fell into the realm of 'operations' and as such was unreviewable. This is clearly illustrated in *R. v Metropolitan Police Commissioner, ex parte Blackburn* (1980),[16] in which Lawton LJ. suggested that the application was misconceived both on the facts and on the law. In a noteworthy dictum, his lordship cogently summarised the fundamental distinction between questions of policy and operational matters:

> This court may be able to make an order of mandamus if the Commissioner, or any Chief Constable, makes no attempt to enforce the law; but in my judgment this court has no jurisdiction to tell the Commissioner how he is to perform his duties . . . [C]ommonsense would be affronted if this court started to interfere in police matters relating to the disposal and management of resources of manpower and finance. Both are limited and have to be deployed in accordance with police experience. . . . The Commissioner has to decide, and should be left to decide, how many of his officers should be engaged in the many activities which have to be undertaken by the police and how they should do their jobs.

Hence, the courts will allow a very large degree of discretion to senior police officers in the operational manner in which they discharge their undoubted duty to enforce the law. For example, in *R. v Oxford (Chief Constable of the Merseyside Police), ex parte Levey,*[17] Lord Donaldson MR for a unanimous Court of Appeal suggested that the appellant's argument involved confusing the propriety of policing policies with their effectiveness, when they were in reality 'two quite different matters'.

> There is no doubt [about the] duty of the Chief and other constables to keep the peace and enforce the law. Nor is there any doubt about the jurisdiction and readiness of courts to intervene by mandatory, prohibitory or declaratory orders, if it is established that they are failing in their duty . . . However, Chief Constables have the widest possible discretion in their choice of the methods whereby they will discharge this duty.[18]

Lord Donaldson MR indicated the very low likelihood of a successful challenge being mounted to an exercise of a chief constable's policy discretion, when he concluded:

> . . . such is the necessary width of a Chief Constable's discretion as to the method of policing which he will adopt and such, in general, is the conscientiousness of such officers, that only in very rare cases will it be possible to make a convincing prima facie case of breach of duty.[19]

It can thus be seen that there are a number of areas of police activity upon which the courts will not trespass by way of judicial review. The courts will not review operational decisions of the police by, for example, making orders as to how and when to exercise powers in specific situations. The judicial view taken is that the police themselves are the best judges of what was or is best in any given operational scenario. Hence in *R. v Chief Constable of Devon and Cornwall, ex parte Central Electricity Generating Board*,[20] the court refused mandamus to compel the police to remove demonstrators from certain land upon which the board wished to conduct drilling tests—it was an operational decision in which the courts would not intervene.

It would thus appear that so long as the police are doing *something* to enforce the law and therefore to discharge their duty, then that will satisfy the courts—it is only when a policy has been adopted to do *nothing* that the courts will intervene. Even then, however, the limited scope of the available remedies such as mandamus further weaken the effectiveness of the process of judicial review as a control over police policy discretion, in that mandamus would for example merely require that the law be enforced generally, though the operational manner in which that would be achieved would be left to the police themselves. It would seem likely that a declaration that a chief constable was failing in his or her duty to enforce the law would provide no more promise than exists with the remedy of mandamus, because such a declaration in itself would do no more than effectively place a moral onus on the chief constable to enforce the law; as before, how that enforcement is pursued would appear to be a matter of operational discretion.

Though the distinction between the spheres of 'policy' and 'operations' is in theory neat, it is in fact difficult on occasion to make an intelligible contrast between the two. Yet an ability to make that distinction is crucial, as upon it will depend the susceptibility to judicial review of the particular police decision. For example, in *ex parte Levey*, the Court of Appeal declined to impugn a police decision effectively to restrict policing of a geographical area to a special police unit with the effect that the applicant suffered loss when other officers were unable to pursue into that area criminals who had stolen his property. Far from being an abdication of his duty, the chief constable's decision was a reasoned and considered policy response to particular social problems. It was significant to the court, however, that *something* was being done by the police, and it seems probable that a day will come when the courts will be called upon to attach practical meaning to this apparent distinction in their jurisdiction to review decisions to do nothing at all to enforce the law (which is reviewable), and decisions to do 'very little' to enforce the law (which, as an operational matter, is apparently unreviewable). At the root of the distinction is probably a requirement that the police do not unduly fetter their own independence to act in response to the crime prevention and detection needs of the community, as the prevailing circumstances demand. A decision entirely to stop policing a particular urban area irrespective of the circumstances which may come to prevail is unquestionably reviewable. Can it be said, however, that a decision to 'reduce' policing of that same urban area to only one patrol a year is really any different from 'none'? If it is accepted that there is nothing more than a token difference between the two decisions, then the inquiry becomes an exercise in identifying the threshold at which 'nothing' becomes 'something'—and that in effect is review of the operational decisions of the police. If to provide only one patrol a year to an area is 'nothing', then is one patrol per month sufficient? The maintenance of the jurisdictional distinction between policy and operational decisions of the police is an example of a principle which appears fine in theory, but which withers in the face of reality. This aspect of the supervisory jurisdiction of the High Court would appear to be an appropriate occasion for an expression of the courts' willingness to assume jurisdiction to review, but with the characteristic discretion as to the granting of a remedy in any given case. This distinction between the jurisdiction to review and the exercise of discretion within that jurisdiction is fundamental to the process of judicial review and surfaces in a number of aspects of this and other chapters of the book.[21] As matters presently stand, however, the maintenance of this highly artificial distinction is regrettable, and the admission by the courts of their jurisdiction to review operational decisions by the police on at least the minimal grounds of unreasonableness and fairness is advocated.

Review of police conformity to statutory and administrative criteria

Thus the courts have been willing to subject to the process of judicial review policy decisions of the police, though not decisions which are in the sphere of 'operations'. More recent years, however, have seen a burgeoning body of case law on the judicial review of police conformity to statutory and administrative criteria, such as the provisions of the Police and Criminal Evidence Act 1984 (PACE).[22] Thus, where statute ascribes specific functions to the police which are to be exercised on the basis of stated criteria, adherence to those criteria can be judicially reviewed. Hence, the High Court in Northern Ireland has been willing to review, though on the facts unwilling to grant relief against, decisions of senior police officers exercising their powers under article 4 of the Public Order (NI) Order 1987.[23]

The courts have also shown a willingness to inquire into the non-adherence by the police (and other agencies) to non-statutory policies, such as the policy of considering cautions rather than prosecuting. In *R. v Chief Constable of the Kent Constabulary, ex parte GL*[24] it was held by the Divisional Court that a failure to apply such a settled policy could impugn an individual decision which was made regardless of or clearly contrary to that policy, the immediate case concerning a published policy of diverting juveniles from prosecution. This case is discussed below on the topic of judicial review and prosecutorial discretions.

The provisions of PACE have been a fruitful source of applications for judicial review in recent years, and the adherence to statutory requirements by the police and other agencies with an involvement in the criminal process has been successfully challenged on numerous occasions. This has particularly been so in the context of police investigative powers. Examples are illustrative.

In *R. v Central Criminal Court, ex parte A.J.D. Holdings Ltd,*[25] the Divisional Court struck down a judicial warrant issued for the purpose of seizing documents on the applicant company's premises, because the warrant was in wider terms than was the information which purportedly founded it.[26] The earlier decision in *R. v Reading Justices, Chief Constable of Avon and Somerset and Another, ex parte South West Meat Ltd*[27] affords an illustration of those rare occasions on an application for judicial review when damages will be awarded. In *ex parte South West Meat*, the police had obtained a search warrant even though the applicant had previously co-operated with the investigating officers of the Meat Intervention Board, with whom the police were liaising. Further, the police had conducted no independent enquiry and their involvement was merely nominal. The officers of the Board, who had no such power to do so, searched the applicant company's premises and retained possession of the seized materials, once again unlawfully. The Divisional Court regarded the actions of the police and the government-funded Meat Intervention Board as oppressive, arbitrary and unconstitutional, 'a deplorable abuse of power by public officials' and which merited an award of exemplary damages.[28]

Similarly, police powers of detention have on a number of occasions been reviewed. For example, in *R. v Slough Justices, ex parte Stirling*[29] the Divisional Court held that out of time applications under PACE, section 43 for further detention after the statutory thirty-six hour period had expired should not normally be entertained if the magistrates court to which application is made is of the view that it would have been reasonable to have made the application in time.

The question of access to legal advice has been litigated by way of judicial review in two principal contexts, namely the denial by the police of that access, and police exclusion of particular advisers from police stations. PACE provides in section 58 and Code C, section 6[30] that 'a person arrested and held in custody in a police station or other premises shall be entitled, if he so requests, to consult a solicitor privately at any time'. That right is not unqualified, however, and section 58 further provides that access to legal advice may be delayed if certain criteria are met.[31] Analogously, in *R. v Chief Constable of South Wales, ex parte Merrick*[32] the Divisional Court reviewed a policy by the police and the local clerk to the justices that solicitors' access to clients who were being detained in cells in the courthouse should be severely curtailed after 10 a.m. Ralph Gibson LJ. for the court recognised a common law right analogous to section 58 of PACE, with the effect that a person remanded in cells in a courthouse should be permitted to consult a solicitor as soon as was practicable; each request for access to a prisoner or for access to a solicitor had to be assessed by the police on its individual merits and the adoption of a general policy denying access was declared by the court to be a breach of the applicant's common law rights. The discretionary provisions enabling the police to deny access to a solicitor under section 45 of the Northern Ireland (Emergency Provisions) Act 1991 have also been litigated. For example, in *In Re McKenna*[33] the Northern Ireland Divisional Court held that a decision of a police superintendent to delay access to a solicitor was clearly one by an official affecting public law rights and was, therefore, susceptible to judicial review. Significantly, the court held that the possibility that judicial review of police denial to those in detention of access to legal advice might hamper the practical administration of the criminal law was no reason for the court to exercise its discretion to refuse review.[34] Further, a solicitor who has been refused access to his or her client would have *locus standi* in his or her own right to challenge the decision to defer access. In subsequent litigation on the same provision, Hutton LCJ. in *In Re Duffy*[35] in the Northern Ireland Divisional Court held that it was unlawful for the police to deny the applicant access to his solicitor when that solicitor had given what were in the view of the court sufficient undertakings to the police to eliminate the ground of 'innocent transmission of information to terrorists', the claimed justification for denying that access.

A second category of litigation concerning legal advice has been the challenges to police decisions to exclude particular legal advisers from advising in particular police areas. For example, in *R. v Chief Constable of Avon and Somerset, ex parte Robinson,*[36] the Divisional Court accepted as legitimate an instruction from the respondent chief constable to his custody officers that the presumption of integrity applicable to solicitors did not apply to clerks. This instruction was followed by further advice that four named clerks in the applicant's employment should on very few occasions be allowed access to persons in custody; significantly, however, the final decision was left to the individual officer to be determined on the facts of each individual case. The Divisional Court declined to intervene as the 'general instruction' did not mandate any decision by custody officers in any particular case, further holding that it was permissible for the police to deny clerks access if of the view that their visit might hinder the investigation of a crime. Similarly, in *R. v Chief Constable of Leicestershire, ex parte Henning*,[37] the Divisional Court declined to intervene in what was effectively a police 'blacklisting' of the applicant legal adviser from attending police stations in the force area. The court reviewed the decision of the deputy chief constable (who had issued the direction) on the traditional grounds of alleged *Wednesbury* unreasonableness[38] and bad faith, although finding that the decision was neither unreasonable in that sense nor was it contaminated by bad faith. Leave to appeal has been granted.[39]

Fairness and abuse of process

The courts have imposed a general requirement of fairness upon the police and other agencies in the investigative and prosecutorial system. The imposition of this requirement is an exercise of the individual court's inherent jurisdiction to prevent an abuse of its process, and has in recent years been applied to almost all facets of the investigation, prosecution and trial of criminal offences. Though a long-established jurisdiction at common law, the power to intervene and restrain abuses of process could in the terminology of judicial review be regarded as a variety of the requirement of procedural propriety associated with the principle of 'fairness', as an abuse of process necessarily implies that there is a want of fairness—the 'rules' are not being observed. The jurisdiction to stay proceedings as an abuse of process is, however, with contempt of court, one of the two original inherent jurisdictions at common law and is, therefore, available both by way of application for judicial review for a remedy such as certiorari, and on application to a court of trial or an appellate court.[40] This topic will be discussed in greater detail in the section on judicial review of the criminal courts, but initial brief mention is appropriate at this stage in respect of the influence of this principle on the exercise of police powers; further mention will also be made in the next section on the review of prosecutorial discretions.

Examples of stays for abuse of process on the grounds of police impropriety at the investigative stage are legion in the area of extradition. For example, in *R. v Horseferry Road Magistrates Court, ex parte Bennett*,[41] the House of Lords confirmed that a 'disguised extradition' which brought a defendant before the English courts from South Africa was a matter of which the courts could, and should, take cognisance. Bennett, a New Zealand citizen, was wanted in England in relation to alleged deception offences. He was arrested in South Africa, and was placed by South African police on a flight to London, on a pretext of deporting him to New Zealand. On arrival in London, Bennett was arrested and charged with the alleged deception offences. The House of Lords, with one dissentient, had no hesitation in staying the prosecution as a blatant abuse of the courts' processes by the police. Lord Griffiths, having noted that the fairness of any trial of Bennett would not in fact be compromised, nonetheless opined:

> If the court is to have the power to interfere with the prosecution in the present circumstances it must be because the judiciary accept a responsibility for the maintenance of the rule of law that embraces a willingness to oversee executive action and to refuse to countenance behaviour that threatens either basic human rights or the rule of law . . . My Lords, I have no doubt that the judiciary should accept this responsibility in the field of criminal law . . .

> The High Court in exercise of its supervisory jurisdiction has power to enquire into the circumstances by which a person has been brought within the jurisdiction and if satisfied that it was in disregard of extradition procedures it may stay the prosecution and order the release of the accused.[42]

Lord Lowry regarded it as 'essential to the rule of law that the court should not have to make available its process and thereby indorse . . . unworthy conduct when it is proved against the executive or its agents, however humble in rank . . .'[43]

It can, therefore, be seen that the courts have with little hesitation demonstrated a willingness to review the exercise of police powers. Yet between the willingness to review decisions not to enforce the law at all (a willingness underwritten by copious dicta), and the willingness to review the exercise of powers where that exercise may not be in conformity with stated policy or principles of general fairness, there apparently remains the amorphous unreviewable category of police operational decisions, as exemplified in *ex parte Blackburn* (1980) and *ex parte Levey*. The survival of this wholly artificial distinction between policy and operational decisions of the police, in light of the abundant recent case law on the review of police statutory and common law discretions, is doubted by the author. As is stressed elsewhere in this book,[44] however, the recognition of a jurisdiction to review decisions and the favourable exercise of discretion within that review are distinct issues, the latter not necessarily flowing from the former.

Judicial Review of Prosecutors' Discretions

A fundamental aspect of the administration of criminal justice in many common law jurisdictions (such as England and Wales and Northern Ireland) is the latitude of discretion which is entrusted to the officers of state in the discharge of their functions. Hence, for example, one of the key aspects of the role of the prosecutor in England and Wales and in Northern Ireland is the discretion which he or she exercises, primarily in the decision on whether or not to prosecute and whether or not to continue a prosecution. This emphasis on the discretionary nature of the prosecutorial function differs fundamentally from systems which exist in some other jurisdictions where, for example the latitude of discretion may be considerably less.[45] Lord Shawcross, speaking in 1951 (when Attorney General for England and Wales), indicated the extent of this discretion which exists in England and Wales and in Northern Ireland in oft-quoted and cogent terms:

> It has never been the rule of this Country—I hope it never will be—that suspected criminal offences must automatically be the subject of prosecution. Indeed the very first Regulations under which the Director of Public Prosecutions worked provided that he should . . . prosecute 'wherever it appears that the offence or the circumstances of its commission is or are of such a character that a prosecution in respect thereof is required in the public interest'. That is still the dominant consideration.[46]

There are innumerable examples of the exercise of this discretion, for by definition it is deployed in every decision to prosecute, not to prosecute, to continue a prosecution and to discontinue a prosecution. Amongst reported instances where this may clearly be seen is the decision of the Divisional Court in *Arrowsmith v Jenkins*.[47] The court there declined to address the appellant's complaint that she had been prosecuted when others who had previously engaged in like behaviour on other occasions had not been prosecuted. The court in *Arrowsmith v Jenkins* restricted itself to considering whether there had been a transgression of the law and when satisfied of that fact would not enquire further into the exercise of discretion in previous cases which may have involved similar behaviour; as Parker LCJ. said, that issue 'has nothing to do with this court'.[48] In similar vein, it has recently been confirmed by Hidden J. that there is no principle in public law that different persons have to be treated in the same way.[49]

The exercise of this prosecutorial discretion, be it by the police or by some other prosecution agency, is a matter of obvious significance to those accused of criminal offences—notwithstanding the fact that all of the technical 'proofs' of a crime may be present,[50] a prosecution need not necessarily follow. This can be for a variety of reasons, such as the age of the alleged offender (juvenile or advanced years), or a large number of other considerations, such as the staleness of the charge and the degree of participation in the offence alleged against the prospective defendant. The exercise of this important discretion to prosecute is regulated in part by the *Code for Crown Prosecutors*,[51] which was drafted by the Crown Prosecution Service in England and Wales, and which carries a persuasive weight with the DPP for Northern Ireland. The significance of the *Code* is that it is a set of criteria, in the public domain, against which decisions of prosecutors may be gauged. The availability of set criteria and policy documents is a valuable aid to a litigant pursuing a remedy in the field of public law, and is a point to which a return will be made below.

As discussed above, the exercise of police powers has for a number of decades been amenable to the process of judicial review. Particular significance may be attached to those earlier cited decisions in view of the fact that the police in England and Wales were prior to 1985 invested with powers both of investigation and prosecution in the vast majority of cases. For that reason, these authorities may be viewed as the seeds of judicial review of the discretion of prosecutors more generally. Recent years have, however, seen a newly acknowledged jurisdiction for the courts to review the decisions of other prosecutors. This developing jurisdiction was signalled by early indications, such as the Court of Appeal decision in *Raymond v Attorney General*,[52] where the court was of the view that it would not interfere with the DPP's decision to intervene in a private prosecution and abort it unless the decision was manifestly such that it could not have been honestly and reasonably arrived at, effectively admitting a jurisdiction to review prosecutorial decisions on the basis of *Wednesbury* unreasonableness. Other indications of the expanding jurisdiction were discernible. For example, in *R. v General Council of the Bar, ex parte Percival*[53] the Divisional Court was expressly of the opinion that no ground of public policy should inhibit it from conferring upon itself a jurisdiction to review a decision of the Bar Council's Professional Conduct Committee concerning the prosecution of a senior barrister on a charge less serious than that which the complainant, who was the accused's Head of Chambers, believed was warranted by the facts.[54]

The rationale for the jurisdiction to review decisions of prosecutors is one rooted soundly in general principles of public law. Decisions of prosecutors are decisions made by public officials which potentially impact both directly and significantly upon the individual, be he or she the defendant in criminal proceedings or, alternatively, the victim of a crime the suspected perpetrator of which the DPP does not intend to prosecute. Taken at this level and coupled with the large latitude of discretion which public prosecutors enjoy, their decisions were an obvious candidate for judicial review. The only obstacle was the presumed immunity which they enjoyed, justified usually by the perceived exigencies of 'public policy'.

After the tentative indications in *Raymond v Attorney General* of a narrow jurisdiction to review and after the judicial acknowledgment of the more comprehensive jurisdiction to review non-state prosecutors in the guise of the Bar Council's disciplinary tribunal in *ex parte Percival*, a number of watershed decisions in this area of the law have recently been handed down. Taken together, the decisions in the conjoined applications in *R. v Chief Constable of Kent, ex parte GL*; *R. v Director of Public Prosecutions, ex parte RB*[55] and that in *R. v Inland Revenue Commissioners, ex parte Mead*[56] are important precedents in the jurisprudence of judicial review and the criminal process. These decisions are clear acknowledgments by the Divisional Court that decisions of state prosecutors and state prosecution agencies, such as the Crown Prosecution Service (*ex parte RB*) and the Commissioners of Inland Revenue (IRC) (*ex parte Mead*), are by no means immune from the process of judicial review.[57] Indeed, Lawton LJ. had long before expressed the *obiter* view that although 'the courts have never interfered with the exercise of the Director [of Public Prosecution's] discretion . . . it does not follow that they could not do so if he refused or failed to perform his public duties or acted corruptly or unfairly'.[58] Further, the recent case law has illustrated that the jurisdiction to review the decisions of prosecutors has not been restricted to the basic decision on whether to prosecute or not, or whether or not to continue a prosecution—they have also examined, for example, the decision of the police on whether or not to administer a caution.[59] This newly acknowledged jurisdiction is not, however, without criteria and limitations.

In *ex parte GL*, the Divisional Court held that a decision to prosecute a juvenile was reviewable if it was clearly contrary to established policy guidelines, in *GL*'s case the Home Office *Guidelines relating to the Cautioning of Juveniles*. Watkins LJ. also made *obiter* comment to the effect that judicial review of the decision to prosecute an adult would not be available, as he felt that this would be 'opening too wide the door of review'; '[j]uveniles', his lordship felt, 'and the policy with regard to them are . . . in a special position'.[60] It has previously been suggested by the author that Watkins LJ.'s reasoning in this regard was flawed,[61] and indeed it was subsequently held in *R. v Inland Revenue Commissioners, ex parte Mead* that there was no reason why the *ratio decidendi* in *ex parte GL* should be restricted to juveniles; Stuart-Smith LJ. held that the principles were equally applicable to adults.[62] *Ex parte Mead* held that public law principles demanded that an authority charged with the duty of exercising its discretion (as the IRC were in this case) had to do so fairly and consistently. 'Fairness' in the case of prosecutions demands that each case has to be considered on its merits, fairly and dispassionately, and have applied to it the criteria for prosecution or the prosecution policy which are used by the relevant authority (be it, for example, the DPP or the IRC). Stuart-Smith LJ. declined to impugn the IRC policy of selective prosecution; in relation to his lordship's judgment, it has been said: '. . . while not questioning the policy *of* selective prosecution, he did stress that any decision should be in accordance with the policy *for* selecting prosecution'.[63]

Policies of selective prosecution have previously received the imprimatur of the courts in respect of a body of judicial review litigation regarding the enforcement (or not, as the case may be) of the law as then contained in the Shops Act 1950.[64] Hence, for example, Donaldson LJ. in *R. v Braintree District Council, ex parte Willingham*[65] held that the respondent council had an obligation to enforce the law, this entailing 'a duty to institute and carry on such proceedings in respect of contraventions as may be necessary to secure observance'.[66] More recently in *R. v Kirklees Metropolitan Borough Council, ex parte Tesco Stores Ltd*[67] the applicants failed to have the court impugn the respondent council's policy of prosecuting only larger commercial enterprises rather than 'smaller' undertakings; McCowan LJ. regarded the policy as 'both fair and sensible' in view of the council's limited resources. Such judicial responses to policies of selective prosecution signify judicial endorsement of prosecutorial discretion and entail a recognition of the independence which is necessary to underwrite that discretion. To hold otherwise would be to require mandatory prosecutions.

Allegedly unfair practices and improper motives by the prosecution received the attention of the Divisional Court in *R. v Havering Justices, ex parte Gould*,[68] when the Court regarded the applicant as having an arguable case that the recommencement of an incorrectly discontinued earlier prosecution against her was as a response to her taking civil action against the police. Merely involving the granting of leave, however, the decision is of modest value, signifying only that the applicant had an arguable case. Indeed, on the facts, Waterhouse J. warned that 'the applicant should not be unduly optimistic about her prospect of success'.[69] This, however, is probably more indicative of the future exercise of the court's discretion than it is of the view which may be adopted on the question of jurisdiction to review. Nonetheless, in view of the limited body of authorities in this developing area of law, pronouncements on applications for leave can take on an enhanced authority,[70] and the granting of leave is an important signal that the court may be willing to agree with the substantive arguments. If on the facts of *ex parte Gould* it were established that the prosecution was reactivated in response to the applicant having sued the police, then it would seem inevitable, and wholly proper, that it be stayed or that the decision be quashed.

The prominence which published policies have come to play in the judicial review of the fundamental prosecutorial discretions arguably reached a jurisprudential Rubicon in the key decision in *R. v DPP, ex parte Tasmin C.*[71] It has previously been suggested by the author that the 'real test' of the courts' willingness to review prosecutorial discretion would be the quashing of a decision by the DPP not to prosecute;[72] the issue was touched upon by Nolan J. in *R. v DPP, ex parte Langlands-Pearse,*[73] though then only in the context of an unsuccessful application for leave. *Ex parte Tasmin C.* concerned judicial review of the decision of the DPP not to prosecute the appellant's husband for alleged offences of non-consensual buggery committed against her. The decision not to prosecute had been made after consideration by the CPS of the second edition of the *Code for Crown Prosecutors,* the view being formed that the facts did not justify a criminal prosecution as the evidential sufficiency requirements of the *Code* were not regarded as satisfied.[74] Kennedy LJ. identified the parameters to the courts' jurisdiction to review in cases such as *Tasmin* C:

> . . . it seems to me that in the context of the present case this court can be persuaded to act if and only if it is demonstrated to us that the Director of Public Prosecutions acting through the Crown Prosecution Service arrived at the decision not to prosecute:
>
> 1. because of some unlawful policy (such as the hypothetical decision in *Blackburn* not to prosecute where the value of goods stolen was below £100); or
> 2. because the Director of Public Prosecutions failed to act in accordance with her own settled policy as set out in the *Code*; or
> 3. because the decision was perverse. It was a decision at which no reasonable prosecutor could have arrived.

While noting the ample dicta to the effect that the courts should exercise restraint when discretion has been vested in others,[75] the court was nonetheless of the view that there had been an erroneous interpretation and application of the *Code for Crown Prosecutors* to the facts of the case. As the court could not be certain that the same decision would have been reached had the *Code* been correctly interpreted and applied, the decision of the DPP not to prosecute was quashed and remitted to her to be decided again in light of the present judgment. Kennedy LJ. further noted:

> [The applicant] is entitled to say that the decision was unreasonable in that it failed to have regard to a material consideration. Primarily however I base my decision on what seems to have been a patent failure to act in accordance with the settled policy as set out in the *Code*.

In view of the significant role played by the existence of the *Code for Crown Prosecutors* in the laudable decision in *ex parte Tasmin C.*, it is a matter of added concern that the most recent edition of the *Code*, that published in June 1994, has been considerably reduced in length and content. Much of the detail in the edition of the *Code* which was litigated in *ex parte Tasmin C.* has been removed to the internal, unpublished CPS manuals,[76] and the scope for successful review of prosecutorial decisions under the current third edition must be regarded as correspondingly reduced.[77] *Ex parte Tasmin C.*, however, has taken the law considerably further than the earlier jurisprudence, and completes a portfolio of precedents which collectively hold that:

1. General policies of non-prosecution are reviewable;[78]
2. Decisions on the choice of charge are reviewable, though there is not yet any precedent in respect of such decisions of the police or the DPP;[79]
3. A decision to prosecute a juvenile which has been made in contravention of a settled policy is reviewable;[80]
4. A decision to prosecute an adult will be gauged against both settled policies and general public law criteria and is reviewable;[81]
5. A decision to reactivate a prosecution, which has been regarded by both parties as discontinued and which may be motivated by an improper purpose or bad faith, is probably reviewable;[82] and
6. A decision not to prosecute in an individual case is reviewable.[83]

The authorities thus point to a relatively comprehensive theoretical framework of control over the exercise of prosecutorial discretion— decisions by prosecutors not to prosecute, to prosecute and on how any prosecution is conducted, are susceptible to the supervisory jurisdiction of the High Court.[84] The emergence of published policies in recent years has been the catalyst for the development of judicial review of such various aspects of the prosecutorial function. The common thread has been the prosecution's adherence to or deviation from a stated policy—in *ex parte GL*, a policy of diverting juveniles from prosecution; in *ex parte Mead*, a policy of selective prosecution; and in *ex parte Tasmin C.*, the general prosecution policy as set out in the second edition of the *Code for Crown Prosecutors*. Hilson has pointed out the importance of review based on a failure to adhere to settled policy, for the standard of proof must be lower and the likelihood of a successful challenge in such a case must be higher than would exist in an allegation of prosecutorial *mala fides* or *Wednesbury* unreasonableness: '[w]here there is a policy . . . the issue before the courts is much more clear cut: either the decision was contrary to the policy or it was not'.[85]

Questions of fairness would also apply to the ascription of improper motives to the prosecutor, a further consideration from the general field of public law. Thus, hypothetically, a decision by the IRC to prosecute an individual may indeed be perfectly in conformity with the IRC's prosecution criteria; but if it can be established that the prosecution is motivated by a desire by the IRC's masters to place pressure on the individual in question, then that seemingly valid exercise of discretion would be contaminated on a number of grounds, not least impropriety, unfairness in the *ex parte Mead* sense, and possibly also general *mala fides*; a court would not be slow to grant certiorari in such circumstances, although the question of discharging the high burden of proof is a distinct matter.

What then are the criteria for the successful review of a decision by a prosecutor? They would appear to be fourfold:[86]

1. There must exist a policy regarding the exercise of the particular discretion.
2. The policy must be open, in that it is ascertainable by the public; it need not, however, be a document in the 'public domain'. This could be, in relation to the decision to (or not to) prosecute, the *Code for Crown Prosecutors*, or, in relation to the decision to caution, the police guidelines on cautioning. Such documents, however, as are in the public domain frequently tell only part of the story, and are often supplemented by internal memoranda as, for example, with the Crown Prosecution Service's *Policy Manual* and *Practice and Procedure Manual*, both of which are internal documents.
3. The provisions must be sufficiently detailed to enable a considered evaluation of the challenged decision to be made.[87]
4. There must be a transgression of a recognised head of relief within administrative law, such as *mala fides*, procedural irregularity, *Wednesbury* unreasonableness, taking into account irrelevant considerations, failing to take into account relevant considerations, failing properly to apply a settled policy, and so forth. To this must be added Stuart-Smith LJ.'s dictum from *ex parte Mead* to the effect that there may be review for an 'unfair' exercise of discretion.[88]

It is the author's view that in the absence of such published policies as have recently been litigated, the development of judicial review in this field would be stunted and inadequate. The case law would most probably be limited in a similar respect to that which presently pertains in the Republic of Ireland, where no such published policies exist in the public domain. Hence while in *The State (McCormack) v Curran*[89] the Irish Supreme Court, *obiter*, was willing to countenance the review of the discretion exercised by the Irish Director of Public Prosecutions on the basis of *mala fides* or on the basis of influence by an improper motive or policy, it has more recently been signalled in *H. v DPP*[90] that *Curran's* case sets the outermost parameters of that newly recognised jurisdiction. In *H.*, the Supreme Court held that the jurisdiction to review the exercise of discretion by the DPP was limited to the manner identified in *Curran*'s case. This jurisdictional contrast neatly illustrates what would possibly have been an alternative body of jurisprudence in England and Wales had the authorities of that jurisdiction not published policies for the regulation of various discretionary powers which they exercise. To the author, this would have been a regrettable scenario.

A balance must be struck, however, for it is also the case that the fine detail of many prosecutorial policies must by necessity be kept secret. This would include policies on the allocation of resources to the prosecution of particular offences, for example, burglary, which may be particularly prevalent at various times or in various geographical areas. Indeed, such policies are arguably envisaged by the *Code for Crown Prosecutors* which provides in paragraph 6.4(n) that a factor tending in favour of a prosecution is that 'the offence, although not serious in itself, is widespread in the area where it was committed'. By analogy with the earlier cited authorities on police operational independence and the courts' endorsement of policies of selective prosecution, such disproportionate allocation of prosecutorial resources would probably not be susceptible to judicial review so long as it did not stray into the forbidden territory of a complete failure to enforce the law at all.[91] The earlier mentioned balance which must be struck, however, is that there must be sufficient information in the public domain to enable an aggrieved person to assess the decision of the prosecutor, and for a court to review that exercise of discretion. Achieving this equilibrium is not an easy task, but is nonetheless one which must be accomplished.

The discussion in this section has thus far focused on the two principal discretions of the prosecutor, namely, whether to prosecute or not (and the related discretion of whether to continue a prosecution or not) and, secondly, if a prosecution is undertaken, then on which charge. There are, however, numerous other prosecutorial discretions which have also been subject to the process of judicial review, and of which brief mention will now be made.

The police, sometimes in conjunction with the CPS or the DPP for Northern Ireland, will on occasion confer a 'witness indemnity', that being an undertaking that the witness will not be prosecuted if he or she assists in the prosecution of others.[92] Such was the case in *R. v Croydon Justices, ex parte Dean*,[93] where the applicant had admitted to doing acts with intent to impede the apprehension of suspected murderers, but was promised by the police that, as he was a prosecution witness, he had the protection of the police. The CPS, however, subsequently decided to charge him *inter alia* with the destruction of evidence. Stuart-Smith LJ. for the Divisional Court held that the prosecution of the applicant after such an assurance had been given to him was an abuse of the process of the court for which certiorari would be granted. His lordship cited McMullan V-P in the Hong Kong Court of Appeal to the effect that '. . . there is a clear public interest to be observed in holding officials of the State to promises made by them in full understanding of what is entailed by the bargain'.[94] In a point of procedural significance developed below, however, the view was also expressed in *ex parte Dean* that those seeking to challenge the exercise of a prosecutorial discretion as being an abuse of process, if there is contested evidence, should normally make application to the court of trial rather than move by way of judicial review under Order 53. Nonetheless, on the facts, the judicial review proceedings had been properly instituted and the relief was granted, quashing the applicant's committal for trial.

There are many further illustrations of prosecutorial discretions which will not be developed here.[95] It is, however, noted elsewhere in this book that in judicial review proceedings, leave or a remedy may be denied if there was an adequate and effective alternative remedy available to the applicant.[96] The adequacy and the effectiveness of the alternative remedy are important, for only if an alternative boasts both of these attributes will the court be justified in effectively penalising the applicant for his or her haste in pursuing a remedy by way of judicial review rather than by way of the alternative route which was open to him or her. It must, therefore, be examined what such alternative remedies would be in this field. Two potential concerned parties in an allegedly or arguably unsatisfactory exercise of prosecutorial discretion are likely to be the defendant who is to be prosecuted, or the victim/complainant where a decision is taken not to prosecute, or merely to caution instead of prosecute.

The alternative remedies available to an aggrieved defendant are most obviously to await trial in due course, and then to make submissions that the prosecution is an abuse of process, that there is a technical irregularity, and so forth. As the courts have frequently said, however, the alternative remedy must be both adequate and effective, and if an individual is, for example, incarcerated in a remand centre, with the trial a number of weeks or months away, then he or she is surely entitled to apply for judicial review to challenge what he or she maintains is a procedural unfairness in the circumstances of his or her detention. As Lord Mustill has said in connection with the related point of an erroneous committal to trial:

> For the moment I am unwilling to go further than to doubt whether, in a case where it is quite obvious that the committal proceedings disclose no offence, the court is powerless to protect the defendant from the stress, labour and expense (not to speak of the possible loss of liberty) entailed by having to wait until the end of the prosecution's case at trial before the obvious conclusion is drawn.[97]

While judicial review should not be the first port of call for an aggrieved defendant, neither need it be the final option available—much will be determined by the circumstances of each case and the degree of unfairness which the defendant has suffered.

Victims and complainants who are dissatisfied with the decisions of prosecutors can often pursue the alternative course of a private prosecution at common law.[98] The enduring power of private prosecution has been said to provide 'a useful and effective safeguard against "improper inaction" by the prosecuting authority'.[99] Hence, for example, the Divisional Court in *R. v Bow Street Stipendiary Magistrate, ex parte South Coast Shipping Co. Ltd*[100] held that where the DPP could have instituted proceedings against a person on the ground that it was appropriate that she do so having regard to the importance and difficulty of the case but has decided not to do so,[101] then any other person may prosecute privately in respect of the same matter. The theory underlying private prosecutions, however, does not accord with the reality, and it is submitted that they are not the constitutional safeguard which they are often hailed to be. For example, such actions are not legally aided, and a situation in which the option of a private prosecution (particularly for an indictable offence) was in fact available only to those victims with substantial economic resources could well be envisaged. Further, a significant qualification has apparently been placed on the principle in *ex parte South Coast Shipping*, because the Divisional Court in *R. v Tower Bridge Metropolitan Stipendiary Magistrate, ex parte Chaudhry*[102] has more recently held that a magistrate would be justified in refusing to issue a summons to a private prosecutor where the DPP has considered and specifically decided against prosecuting the charge for which the private prosecutor is seeking that summons, as to issue the summons would negate the public prosecutor's discretion.[103] *Ex parte South Coast Shipping* was regrettably not cited in *ex parte Chaudhry,* and the decisions seem difficult to reconcile. The present position would nonetheless appear to be that private prosecutors have no entitlement to the issue of a summons where the DPP has decided against prosecuting the same person for the same offence arising from the same facts, though the magistrate retains a residual discretion to issue the summons if there is apparent bad faith on the part of the prosecutor. When this refinement is combined with the observation that section 6(2) of the Prosecution of Offences Act 1985[104] entitles the DPP to intervene in any prosecution and discontinue it if she sees fit, the adequacy and effectiveness of a private prosecution as an alternative remedy must be doubted. Accordingly, it is probable that the High Court would regard itself as the sole adequate and effective alternative remedy for a victim aggrieved by the exercise of prosecutorial discretion. This view is fortified by the decision in *ex parte Tasmin C.*, where the possibility of the applicant having pursued a private prosecution was adverted to by Kennedy LJ. though no suggestion was made that she may not have exhausted her alternative remedies by failing to prosecute privately in the face of the DPP's unwillingness to do so. It is the author's opinion that this is the better view.

More significant difficulties arise in connection with the inherent jurisdiction of the courts to stay proceedings as an abuse of their process, a topic which has been mentioned previously in this chapter; the following section will deal with the generally available alternative remedies including an application to a court of trial.

Notwithstanding the promise which emanates from decisions such as *ex parte Blackburn* (1968 and 1973) *ex parte GL, ex parte Mead* and *ex parte Tasmin C.*, it has recently been commented that

> [t]he doctrine of constabulary independence, which applies to all enforcement agencies and not just the police, [remains] virtually impregnable . . . The consequence is almost complete autonomy for law enforcement bodies in all enforcement and prosecution decisions . . .[105]

Ultimately, there must be a considerable degree of trust reposed in the integrity of prosecutors, for even in systems of mandatory prosecution there is a small latitude of discretion available, for example, in respect of prosecutors' assessment of the cogency and strength of the evidence.[106] The increasing willingness of the courts to supervise the exercise of these fundamentally important discretionary powers, however, is reassuring, though the small number of cases in which review has been successful, relative to the massive number of crimes detected and thus the number of exercises of prosecutorial discretion, is less heartening.

Judicial Review and the Criminal Courts

Judicial review of the criminal courts accounts for a large proportion of judicial review business, amounting to between 12 per cent and 15 per cent of all applications.[107]

The position regarding the judicial review of the criminal courts differs between Northern Ireland and England and Wales. While in both jurisdictions, judicial review unquestionably lies against the magistrates court and accordingly that aspect will be dealt with in tandem, there are sufficient distinctions and uncertainties in other respects to warrant separate treatment of the two jurisdictions in the latter portion of this section.

The criteria for the quashing by way of certiorari of the decisions of an inferior court were set out by Lord Lowry LCJ. (as he then was) in the Northern Ireland Divisional Court in *In Re Quinn's Application*[108] and subsequently in *In Re McNally (a Minor)*.[109] Lord Lowry considered 'the question whether a sentence imposed by an inferior court can be quashed on certiorari for being harsh and oppressive (although within the lawful statutory limit).' His lordship engaged in a comprehensive review of the law on the topic, which does not accord with the trend of jurisprudence concerning the judicial review of inferior courts in England and Wales, and which will be developed below.

Judicial review of the magistrates court

It is a well-established principle that magistrates' court proceedings are generally reviewable by the Queen's Bench Divisional Court; as but one of innumerable examples, the court in *R. v Bradford Justices, ex parte Wilkinson*[110] granted certiorari against magistrates for their failure to accede to the applicant's request, at his trial, for the issue of witness warrants to compel the attendance of witnesses who were vital to his defence. Breaches of natural justice and fair procedures, the previously mentioned inherent abuse of process discretion, irrationality, excess of jurisdiction, and so forth, are all relatively long-established criteria for the assumption of jurisdiction by a Divisional Court in its general supervisory capacity over tribunals and inferior courts.

The jurisdiction to review the decisions of inferior courts for their non-jurisdictional errors of law, however, has in recent years raised some interesting issues. The topic has been treated by the author in detail elsewhere,[111] and the minutiae of the background will not be repeated here. Suffice it to say in this present context that the law concerning judicial review for errors of law has undergone profound change in recent decades, moving from a traditional position that such errors were reviewable only if they went to the jurisdiction of the tribunal. This distinction between jurisdictional and non-jurisdictional errors of law was based on the premise that where there were 'jurisdictional parameters to the conferment of power',[112] then a tribunal or inferior court was only reviewable where its error of law had led to it exceeding that jurisdiction (i.e. acting *ultra vires*) or was apparent on the face of the record, as the correct interpretation of the law was a condition precedent to the tribunal or inferior court's assumption of jurisdiction; but if the tribunal or inferior court had correctly construed the jurisdictional parameters of its power, then its errors of law, when made within that jurisdiction, were unreviewable. *R. (Blakeney) v Roscommon Justices*[113] illustrates the time-honoured reluctance which the courts expressed to interfere with errors of law within jurisdiction. That case concerned a committal for trial which was not objectively sustainable on the evidence, but as it was an error within jurisdiction, the decision was not quashed even though 'the witnesses for the prosecution, as well as for the defence, distinctly disproved the charge'.[114] As was commented by Lord Reid in *R. v Governor of Brixton Prison, ex parte Armah*:

> If a magistrate or any other tribunal has jurisdiction to enter on the enquiry and to decide a particular issue, and there is no irregularity in the procedure, he does not destroy his jurisdiction by reaching a wrong decision. If he has jurisdiction to go right he has jurisdiction to go wrong. Neither an error in fact nor an error in law will destroy his jurisdiction.[115]

The seeds of reform were sown in the seminal decision of *Anisminic Ltd v Foreign Compensation Commission*,[116] where a majority of the House of Lords considerably enlarged the categories of jurisdictional error. Their lordships were nonetheless most careful to insist that the traditional distinction did remain. The principle in *Anisminic*, though initially resisted, was accepted, developed and applied to inferior courts in a series of significant decisions including *O'Reilly v Mackman*,[117] *R. v Greater Manchester Coroner, ex parte Tal*,[118] *Page v Hull University Visitor*[119] and *Neill v North Antrim Magistrates' Court*.[120] With few exceptions, any error of law by an inferior court was apparently reviewable.[121]

This distinction between jurisdictional and non-jurisdictional errors of law, however, while almost entirely eroded in England and Wales, has resurfaced recently in Northern Ireland. This complication in the jurisprudence is caused by the decision of the previous Lord Chief Justice of Northern Ireland, Lord Lowry, who in forthright dicta in *In Re McNally (a Minor)*[122] said in relation to the judicial review of inferior courts that he would uphold the distinction between errors of law within jurisdiction, and those errors which were 'jurisdictional'. Though decided in 1986, judgment was delivered only in 1992, and it is thus uncertain whether the decision in *In Re McNally (a Minor)* should be viewed in the context of the common law as it stood in 1986, or whether the judgment was intended to reflect the law in Northern Ireland in more recent times. Irrespective of that point, it is regrettable that the judgment in *In Re McNally (a Minor)* was not available to the House of Lords in *Neill*, or indeed in the later decision in *Page*, for it would have been a clear and persuasive argument against the significant extension to the jurisdiction to review for errors of law by inferior courts and tribunals, although the author would not necessarily accord with the views expressed by Lord Lowry therein.

It might have been thought that in light of the developments in case law in recent years, it was likely that the decision in *In Re McNally (a Minor)* would be regarded as a 'missed opportunity', a relic of 1986. Hutton LCJ., the present Lord Chief Justice of Northern Ireland, has, however, more recently in the coincidentally named *In Re McNally*[123] made *obiter* comment to the effect that he would be slow to exercise the court's discretion to grant certiorari on the facts of the case in view of the judgment of Lord Lowry in *In Re McNally (a Minor)*, holding as it does that an error of law within jurisdiction can be quashed only if the error is apparent on the face of the record. His lordship, however, did 'not express a concluded opinion on the point.' A definitive determination of the issue in the Northern Ireland jurisdiction and the elimination of the uncertainty caused by *In Re McNally (a Minor)* would be welcome.

Judicial review and the Crown Court and the County Court

In Northern Ireland, judicial review does not lie against the Crown Court, as it is a superior court; in England and Wales, in contrast, the Crown Court is susceptible to judicial review in matters other than those 'relating to trial on indictment'.[124] By way of further contrast, the County Courts in Northern Ireland have an appellate criminal jurisdiction.

The general power of the High Court under the Supreme Court Act 1981, section 31, to conduct judicial reviews is, thus, qualified in respect of the review of decisions of the Crown Court. The question of what is a matter 'relating to trial on indictment' has, therefore, proved a fruitful source of litigation in England and Wales, and a considerable body of case law has developed regarding this term; that case law will not be reviewed here, and is comprehensively discussed in the leading texts.[125] Some general principles are, however, discernible; Lord Bridge in *In Re Smalley (Smalley v Warwick Crown Court)*[126] suggested that the phrase encompasses both decisions taken in the course of the trial on indictment and all decisions which affect the conduct of the trial, even if taken before the trial has commenced, and Lord Browne-Wilkinson in *R. v Manchester Crown Court, ex parte DPP*[127] suggested that in determining the issue it is helpful to ask whether the decision sought to be reviewed arises 'in the issue between the Crown and the defendant formulated by the indictment (including the costs of such issue)'. Thus an order discharging a jury,[128] an application to the trial judge to stay the prosecution as an abuse of process,[129] and the decision of the Crown Court judge on the question of jurisdiction to try an indictment[130] are examples of matters relating to trial on indictment; in contrast, the listing of cases in the Crown Court[131] and the making of a legal aid contribution order are not.[132]

Aside from the undoubted general jurisdiction to review magistrates courts for their errors of law (*pace In Re McNally (a Minor)* in Northern Ireland) and the fairness and legality of their procedures in the context of their parent legislation, and so forth, a small number of recurring complaints have been litigated by way of judicial review of magistrates' decisions. These will now be briefly dealt with.

Judicial review and legal aid

A decision by a magistrate to refuse legal aid is subject to judicial review just as any other decision is, as discussed above. The standard remedies by way of judicial review would be to petition the court for orders of both certiorari (to bring up and quash the refusal of aid) and mandamus (to require that the decision be reconsidered). As in so many of the other contexts considered in this book, it must be remembered that the judge on an application for judicial review would not normally say whether or not the decision was intrinsically right, but rather only whether it was properly made. Hence, in *In Re McAuley's Application,* Hutton LCJ. noted that:

> It is the position that this court does not sit as a court of appeal and it is not the function of this court to substitute its view for that of the magistrate. Nevertheless, if this court is satisfied that a magistrate has erred, in the sense that he has not taken account of the matters of which he should have taken account, then this court can intervene where there has been such a wrongful exercise of the magistrate's discretion.[133]

Therefore, if unreasonableness is alleged, then unless the refusal of legal aid was a decision which no reasonable magistrate could have reached, the decision may well be unimpeachable. There are, however, reported cases in which such review has been successful. For example, in *R. v Derby Justices, ex parte Kooner,*[134] the Divisional Court quashed a refusal by the magistrates to grant a legal aid certificate for both solicitor and counsel in respect of committal proceedings for a murder charge. The decision was unreasonable, in that the Divisional Court was of opinion that a charge of murder was always sufficiently grave to call for legally aided representation by both professions (if the criteria for inadequate means were also met). The reasonableness or otherwise of a refusal to grant legal aid was addressed by Carswell J. (as he then was) in 1992 in *In Re McKinney's Application.*[135] In refusing the application, his lordship adverted to the yardstick by which these decisions will be judged when he said that 'We do not consider that the case was so clear that no reasonable magistrate would have refused legal aid in the circumstances.'[136] In the previously mentioned *In Re McAuley's Application*, however, Hutton LCJ. granted certiorari against the resident magistrate's decision on the basis of the *Wednesbury* decision in his refusal to grant legal aid to a defendant (whose means were greater than the legal aid threshold), and who was charged with offences which were likely to result in a custodial sentence; the resident magistrate had neglected to take into account a material consideration in his failure to properly apply the Widgery criteria for legal aid.

More likely to succeed than a claim of unreasonableness would be a petition based on the magistrate's flawed consideration of the circumstances of the application. For example, the magistrates in *ex parte Kooner* had admittedly also taken irrelevant considerations into account, in that (in their subjective view) counsel at an earlier remand hearing had wasted court time with 'irrelevant' cross-examination. Such a decision need not be 'unreasonable' in the objective sense, but if it is established that the decision was influenced, or may have been influenced, by irrelevant factors, or by a failure to look at the entire circumstances, then the decision is flawed and should be struck down.

Needless to say for the sake of completeness, factors such as bad faith on the part of the magistrate, as with the exercise of discretion by any other figure, would contaminate the decision; however, the likelihood of such a factor both existing and being provable are surely remote.

Sentencing

Sentencing by magistrates has been a contentious issue in the case law on judicial review. There is authority that a sentence which is 'harsh and oppressive', though within the statutory limits, may be impugned either by way of judicial review or an appeal by way of case stated, although the current formulation is that the sentence must be by any acceptable standard 'truly astonishing'.[137] Notwithstanding these restrictive dicta, the jurisdiction to review sentences remains an important element of the High Court's supervisory jurisdiction. As will be discussed below, however, it may in many circumstances be advisable to proceed by way of statutory appeal rather than by way of a case stated or an application for judicial review.

Judicial review or case stated?

It will be recalled that the granting of judicial review is influenced by the availability of alternative remedies, and this issue has been touched upon in the various preceding sections. In respect of criminal proceedings where issue is taken with the proceedings in the inferior court, then a statutory appeal will normally lie, such as against conviction and sentence. A point of some significance in the present context, however, is whether a person aggrieved by a decision of a magistrates court should seek relief by way of judicial review or by way of case stated or, as mentioned, by way of a statutory appeal. This can be a crucial issue, for if a court in an application for judicial review forms the opinion that the applicant should more properly have moved by way of statutory appeal or by way of case stated, then the discretionary remedy may be denied. For example, in *R. v Ealing Justices, ex parte Scrafield*[138] the Divisional Court held in refusing judicial review that the more appropriate method of challenging a sentence imposed by justices was to appeal to the Crown Court (the County Court in Northern Ireland) as opposed to the High Court by way of judicial review or case stated. It was held in *R. v Greater Manchester Justices, ex parte Aldi GmbH & Co. KG*[139] that it is not generally appropriate to challenge by way of case stated or judicial review justices' interlocutory decisions; however, it may be appropriate to do so where the information is amended to substitute one defendant for another.

The case stated procedure is a long-established method of appealing the decision of a magistrate to the High Court (England and Wales)[140] or to the Court of Appeal (Northern Ireland).[141] There is also a distinction between the position in Northern Ireland and that pertaining in England and Wales in that a magistrates court in Northern Ireland may state a case during the course of proceedings (for example, on the question of jurisdiction), while in England and Wales a case may be stated only after the case has been conclusively determined.[142]

There are a number of similarities between the two procedures of judicial review seeking certiorari and an appeal by way of case stated; in seeking certiorari, the applicant is trying to quash a decision of the magistrate for a specific reason, and this will commonly be the situation also with a case stated when it will be claimed that the magistrate has made an error of law or a mistake in exercising jurisdiction. In turn, there are a number of differences between judicial review seeking mandamus or prohibition and an appeal by way of case stated; an applicant for either of these prerogative remedies argues that the magistrates have made an error in failing to exercise their jurisdiction, or should be prevented from exercising a jurisdiction which it is alleged they do not have. It is appropriate to distil these observations into points of principle.[143]

1. A case may only be stated from 'summary proceedings', thus excluding, for example, committal proceedings and remand hearings and trials on indictment.[144] Hence, where the dissatisfaction stems from a pre-trial element of procedure, such as a remand hearing or committal proceedings, or the imminent 'transfer for trial' procedure in England and Wales,[145] a prerogative remedy is in fact the only available option.

2. Further to the previous point, certiorari is the appropriate remedy where the rules of natural justice have been broken; this is because the case

stated procedure is effectively restricted to the facts as found proved by the magistrates and the issues of law arising from those facts, and questions of the jurisdiction of the inferior court. Nonetheless, the decision on which option to pursue (certiorari or case stated) can be difficult. There are dicta to the effect that where both are available, the preference should be for a case stated—*R. v Ipswich Crown Court, ex parte Baldwin*.[146] There is, however, older authority to the effect that a serious breach of natural justice will always warrant an application for *certiorari* rather than an appeal by way of case stated; Viscount Caldecote CJ. said in *R. v Wandsworth Justices, ex parte Read*:

> It remains to consider the argument that the remedy of *certiorari* is not open to the applicant because others were available. It would be ludicrous in such a case as the present for the convicted person to ask for a case to be stated. It would mean asking this court to consider as a question of law whether the justices were right in convicting a man without hearing his evidence. That is so extravagant an argument as not to merit a moment's consideration. As to the right of appeal to quarter sessions, it may be that the applicant could have had his remedy if he had pursued that course, but I am not aware of any reason why, if in such circumstances as these, he preferred to apply for an order of *certiorari* to quash his conviction, the court should be debarred from granting his application. . . .[147]

It is also well settled that if a decision is to be challenged on a point of law and where the identification of the facts is critical, then case stated is the more appropriate remedy than judicial review.[148] It is also implicit in the judgment of Evans LJ. in *R. v Ealing Justices, ex parte Scrafield*[149] that the order in which the remedies should be considered by those aggrieved by a decision of an inferior court are to initially consider a statutory appeal, then an appeal by way of case stated and only then an application for judicial review.

3. A major difference between an appeal by way of case stated and an application for judicial review is that a court may on a case stated supplant its decision for that of the inferior court, while in an application for judicial review the process is not an appeal, but rather is an examination of the manner in which the decision was reached. Accordingly, the result of a successful challenge by way of judicial review to a decision by a magistrate, for example, would probably be the quashing of the decision and an order that it be retaken in light of the proper considerations. The High Court will not generally say what the correct decision would be, for that would merely be an exercise of its subjective judgment and would blur the important distinction between judicial review as the supervisory jurisdiction of the High Court and the function of 'appeal', the latter of

which is no part of the judicial review jurisdiction;[150] as Lord Hailsham LC has pointed out in an oft-quoted dictum: 'Two reasonable [people] can perfectly reasonably come to opposite conclusions on the same set of facts without forfeiting their title to be regarded as reasonable.'[151]

Judicial review and abuse of process

It will be recalled from earlier sections of this chapter that the courts have been willing to draw upon their inherent jurisdiction to prevent abuses of process to give relief by way of judicial review as well as by way of application to the examining magistrates or the trial judge; indeed, many of the leading modern authorities on that topic stem from the Crown Office list.[152] Therefore, the possibility of relief being granted by a court of trial on application to the trial judge must be regarded as an alternative remedy which will be assessed by a court in judicial review proceedings when formulating its opinion on whether it would be appropriate to award a discretionary remedy. In an effort to stem the tide of applications for judicial review on the grounds of abuse of process, Lord Lane CJ. said in *Attorney General's Reference (No. 1 of 1990)*:

> We would like to [stress] . . . a point which is sometimes overlooked, namely that the trial process itself is equipped to deal with the bulk of complaints which have in recent Divisional Court cases founded applications for a stay.[153]

It was similarly stated in *R. v Barnet Magistrates, ex parte Wood*[154] that only in exceptional cases should committal proceedings be quashed once an indictment has been signed and the defendant arraigned. More detailed guidelines have, however, been provided by the Divisional Court in *R. v Croydon Justices, ex parte Dean,* where Staughton LJ. said:

> If it is necessary for the disputed issues of fact in this case to be resolved by oral evidence, I consider that we should decline to deal with it by way of judicial review, and should leave it to the Crown Court to decide whether there is abuse of process. It is only if we can decide the point on the undisputed facts, together with any other facts that we feel bound to accept as true, that we should undertake the task.[155]

Hence, where an abuse of process is alleged, then unless the factual background to the application is undisputed, the proper remedy for an aggrieved person is to make application to the court of trial for a stay of the prosecution, and should move by way of judicial review only where the factual background is agreed or where the court would be bound to accept one version as true. A court in considering whether there will be an abuse of process will not be fettered by rigid criteria, but rather will examine all aspects of the case in deciding whether in all the circumstances it would be unfair to permit the prosecution to proceed; if it would be unfair, then it is likely that the prosecution will be stayed.

Overview

The judicial review procedure does not offer a panacea to criminal law practitioners for their clients' every ill; indeed, the courts have in recent years given strong indications that the procedure is not to be invoked lightly in the criminal domain, exemplified by the strong emphasis which has been placed on the necessity of pursuing alternative remedies.[156] While not a panacea, however, the supervisory jurisdiction of the High Court has been an essential and overdue development in the accountability of authorities within the criminal justice system who, arguably, previously were insufficiently so. The author holds that this is particularly true of the police and of the Crown Prosecution Service.

As has been suggested, success in relation to many of the potential avenues of claim is by no means certain, for the simple reason that they are frequently challenges to the exercise of discretion. It is apposite also to recall that the procedure of judicial review recognises a fundamental distinction between its jurisdiction to review, and a favourable exercise of the court's discretion in that review.[157] These points, when coupled with the important observation that judicial review is review and is not an appeal, tend to circumscribe the instances in which a court will be willing to interfere with the exercise of discretion by the police, a prosecutor or an inferior court, as being *Wednesbury* unreasonable—the threshold of proof in the criminal domain is, as in other areas of administrative law, very high. The chances of success, however, against the challenged authority in the face of a demonstrable failure to apply its settled policy, consideration by it of irrelevant considerations, or its patent failure to take into account relevant considerations, and so forth, are greater, and litigants such as Mrs Tasmin C. have had their notable successes.

It could be said that one of the significant attractions of the judicial review mechanism is the opportunity which it affords concerned parties to vent their beliefs in a judicial forum regarding what they believe to be an improper exercise of power by a public authority. Judicial review is an important procedural safeguard for a large and often diverse category of people who come into contact with the organs and officers of state in the criminal process, such as defendants, victims and relatives of fatal victims, police authorities, prisoners, and so forth. To that extent, applicants who fail in their petition due to a judicial reluctance to exercise discretion in favour of granting a remedy for allegedly improper action or inaction may feel that they have nonetheless won a moral victory—they have called the public authority to account and may believe that they have humbled it in a small respect.[158] This symbolic role should not be underrated, though Pyrrhic victories have only a limited attraction and usefulness, and success on the substantive question is surely the real gauge of procedural merit.

It will also be readily appreciated that in respect of many of the matters discussed in this and in other contributions to this book, a knowledge of 'principle' is often merely half the task for practitioners—in order to avail of these remedies, it will also be necessary to secure sufficient, admissible evidence to persuade the judge of the suspicions held in regard to the decision which it is wished to challenge. That, regrettably, has been and looks set to continue to be a difficult chore.

'Floodgates' is a word the use of which has been *de rigueur* in modern writings on the developing jurisdiction of judicial review, and has encapsulated a fear which has conditioned the views of judges on occasion. If the process of judicial review develops too wide a jurisdiction, then it will rapidly become a victim of its own success, the theory goes. To an extent, the research evidence tends to support this view, with recent years showing a burgeoning judicial review case-load.[159] The increasing use of the procedure, however, and the developing supervisory jurisdiction of the court are welcomed by the author as indicative of a vibrant jurisprudence and an earnest interest on the part of people to call in aid the High Court as its guardian against unfair or improper action or inaction which historically may well have been overlooked as being beyond the court's jurisdiction. If this expanding jurisdiction is to be characterised as a 'flood', then the author would suggest that it is indicative of a preceding 'drought', where often there existed a vacuous area of responsibility of a public body for whose mistakes and errors no remedy existed or where a remedy was denied for unduly technical reasons which could themselves compound any injustice.[160]

In conclusion, therefore, the civil courts have indeed shown an increased willingness to take to themselves a supervisory jurisdiction over both the inferior criminal courts and the personnel of the criminal justice system. Developments in the field of judicial review and the criminal process have kept apace with the rapid developments in administrative law more generally over the past three decades. Remarkable though the expansion in the jurisdiction of the High Court in this sphere has been in recent years, however, it seems likely that these are yet 'early days' for the public law influence in criminal law and procedure.

Notes

1. See generally D. Galligan, *Discretionary Powers: A Legal Study of Official Discretion* (1986); R. Pattenden, *Judicial Discretion and Criminal Litigation* (1990); K. Davis, *Discretionary Justice* (1969); and K. Hawkins, *Uses of Discretion* (1992).
2. Rules of the Supreme Court 1977, Order 53; Rules of the Supreme Court (NI) 1980, Order 53. See further the Appendix by Paul Maguire, below.
3. On this see G. Aldous and J. Alder, *Applications for Judicial Review: Law and Practice of the Crown Office* (1993) pp 151–2.
4. RSC Order 53, r. 3(4)(a).
5. *Ex p. Woodhall* (1888) 20 QBD 832. See also *Amand v Secretary of State for Home Affairs* [1943] AC 147.
6. *R. v Southamption Justices, ex p. Green* [1975] 2 All ER 1073.
7. M. Sunkin *et al.*, *Judicial Review in Perspective: An Investigation of Trends in the Use and Operation of the Judicial Review Procedure in England and Wales* (1993). See also B. Hadfield and E. Weaver, 'Judicial Review in Perspective: Trends in the Use of Judicial Review in Northern Ireland' (1995) 46 *Northern Ireland Legal Quarterly* (forthcoming).
8. ibid., p. 6. It is possible that people who wish to challenge decisions of personnel within the criminal justice system or an inferior court may themselves be in custody at the time. It is, therefore, important to note the availability of bail where an application for judicial review has been lodged, a decision to grant bail being within the inherent jurisdiction of the court. See *R. v Secretary of State for the Home Department, ex p. Turkoglu* [1988] QB 398, RSC Order 79 and RSC(NI), Order 79.
9. J. Baldwin, *Pre-Trial Justice* (1985) p. 1.
10. Prosecution of Offences Act 1985, s. 3(2)(a).
11. C. Kemp et al., *Negotiation Nothing: Police Decision-making in Disputes* (1992) p. 3.
12. [1968] 2 QB 118, 136–7 (emphasis added).
13. ibid., p. 139. The court found it unnecessary to exercise its discretion in *ex p. Blackburn* 1968, as the challenged policy decision had been voluntarily revoked prior to the appeal.
14. ibid., p. 136.
15. [1973] 1 QB 241, 254.
16. Unreported Court of Appeal (Civil Division) 6.3.1980 (no. 414/78).
17. *The Independent*, 31 October 1986; *The Times*, 1 November 1986; Court of Appeal (Civil Division) 30 October 1986.
18. However, Lord Donaldson MR also added an important qualification to this principle, to the effect that '[a]ny police officer who finds that his chosen policing methods are ineffective will be under a duty to re-examine them and consider whether any and, if so, what alteration is required . . .'
19. *Ex p. Levey* concerned a policy decision by the Chief Constable of Merseyside to introduce special policing arrangements for the Toxteth area of Liverpool, which was claimed by the appellant to amount to declaring the area to be a 'no go' region for the purposes of policing. Though special policing arrangements had indeed been implemented for Toxteth, Lord Donaldson MR held that it was a considered response to a significant social problem in the aftermath of the notorious Toxteth riots, and was in conformity with the recommendations of Lord Scarman's Report on the Brixton riots of 1981. Of particular interest to the readers in Northern Ireland in what is at the time of writing a recently unprecedented environment of non-violence, Lord Donaldson MR in *ex p. Levey* conceded that 'there can be only one standard of law enforcement, but that methods of achieving that could and should be tailored to suit the diverse special needs and characteristics of different communities'.
20. [1982] QB 458.
21. See for example the section on 'Overview' below, and A. le Sueur, *passim*.

22. Police and Criminal Evidence (NI) Order 1989.
23. *Re Murphy* [1991] 5 NIJB 72 (QBD) and 88 (CA); *Re Armstrong*, unreported, NI QBD 27.8.1992, Nicholson J. See also B. Hadfield, 'Public Order Police Powers and Judicial Review' [1993] CrimLR 915.
24. (1991) [1993] 1 All ER 756.
25. [1992] CrimLR 669.
26. PACE 1984, ss 15(6)(b) and 16.
27. [1992] CrimLR 672.
28. Contrast *R. v Milton Keynes Magistrates Court, ex p. Roberts* [1995] CrimLR 224, where it was held not to be an abuse of process for trading standards officers to act against the applicant in conjunction with employees of an interested motor car company, which company had indemnified the officers against compensation claims arising under the Trade Descriptions Act 1968. However, 'if a prosecutor did indeed make himself the creature of a private interest in exercising his powers, then that conduct would at least be prima facie abusive'.
29. [1987] CrimLR 576.
30. Police and Criminal Evidence (NI) Order 1989, art. 59 and Code C, s. 6.
31. See particularly PACE 1984, sub-ss 58(4), 58(6), 58(8) and 58(8A).
32. [1994] 2 All ER 560.
33. [1992] 1 NIJB 1.
34. The court in *McKenna* explained the previous decision in *In Re O'Neill* (Unreported, NI QBD 1991, Carswell J.) as holding that an application for judicial review of the deferment of access to legal advice will be entertained only if the hearing takes place during the currency of the deferment of access, as such review after the period of deferment has ended would be of no practical benefit.
35. [1991] 7 NIJB 62.
36. [1989] 2 All ER 15.
37. Unreported Divisional Court, 3 December 1993.
38. *Associated Provincial Picture Houses Ltd v Wednesbury Corporation* [1948] 1 KB 223.
39. Unreported Court of Appeal (Civil Division) 8 July 1994.
40. For what is generally regarded as the seminal decision on the abuse of process jurisdiction in criminal procedure, see *Connolly v DPP* [1964] AC 1254; see also A. Choo, *Abuse of Process and Judicial Stays of Criminal Proceedings* (1993).
41. [1993] 3 All ER 138.
42. ibid., at pp 150, 152.
43. ibid., at p 163.
44. See for example A. le Sueur, *passim*.
45. See for example L. Leigh and L. Zedner, *A Report on the Administration of Criminal Justice in France and Germany* (Royal Commission on Criminal Justice, Research Study No. 1: HMSO 1992) and Van Den Wyngaert *et al.*, *Criminal Procedure Systems in the European Community* (1993).
46. HC Debates, vol. 483, col. 681, 29 January 1951. This excerpt from the speech of Lord Shawcross was cited in previous editions of the *Code for Crown Prosecutors*, though it has been omitted from the current third edition. See also A. Sanders and R. Young, *Criminal Justice* (1994) pp 207 ff.
47. [1963] 2 QB 561.
48. ibid., at p. 566.
49. *R. v Special Adjudicator, ex p. Kandasamy* [1994] ImmAR 333, echoing the decision of Stuart-Smith LJ. in the Divisional Court in *R. v Inland Revenue Commissioners, ex p. Mead* [1993] 1 All ER 772, discussed below.
50. For example, that an individual may have dishonestly appropriated the property of another with the intention permanently to deprive, contrary to s. 1 of the Theft Act 1968 (Theft Act (NI) 1969).
51. *The Code for Crown Prosecutors* (3rd edn, 1994).

52. [1982] QB 839.

53. [1990] 3 All ER 137.

54. The applicant in *ex p. Percival* was nonetheless denied relief upon the facts, since the court felt that the Professional Conduct Committee had acted within discretion and had not transgressed any of the traditional criteria for judicial review, such as by acting unreasonably or with procedural irregularity.

55. [1993] 1 All ER 756.

56. [1993] 1 All ER 772.

57. See generally on this: P. Osborne, 'Judicial Review of Prosecutors' Discretion: The Ascent to Full Reviewability' (1992) 43 *Northern Ireland Legal Quarterly*, 178; and C. Hilson, 'Discretion to Prosecute and Judicial Review' [1993] CrimLR 739.

58. *Selvarajan v Race Relations Board* [1976] 1 All ER 12, 21.

59. See *R. v Chief Constable of Kent, ex p. GL* n. 24, n. 55, above. The entitlement of the police to issue a caution as an alternative to prosecution is governed by published criteria in line with Home Office recommendations, and all police forces including the RUC operate such schemes in respect of both juveniles and adults.

60. *Ex p. GL*, at p. 771.

61. See P. Osborne, 'Judicial Review of Prosecutors' Discretion: The Ascent to Full Reviewability' (1992) 43 *Northern Ireland Legal Quarterly*, 178; see also D. Birch, *Commentary* at [1991] CrimLR 841, 842.

62. Popplewell J. dissenting. Kelly LJ. had also said in an *obiter dictum* in the Northern Ireland Divisional Court that 'In my view the test which [Watkins LJ.] was prepared to apply to the prosecution of juveniles should also apply to adults.' *In re McKenna* [1992] 1 NIJB 1.

63. C. Hilson 'Discretion to Prosecute and Judicial Review' [1993] CrimLR 739, 742.

64. See now the Sunday Trading Act 1994.

65. (1983) 81 LGR 70.

66. ibid., at p. 78.

67. Unreported Divisional Court, 27.7.1993 (CO/467/93).

68. Unreported Divisional Court, 7.4.1992 (CO/340/02).

69. The author has been advised that the application in *ex p. Gould* was settled and did not proceed beyond the leave stage.

70. See for example the decision of Nolan J. (as he then was) in *R. v DPP, ex p. Langlands-Pearse* [1991] COD 92.

71. Unreported Divisional Court, 18.2.1994 (CO/642/93).

72. See P. Osborne, 'Judicial Review of Prosecutors' Discretion: The Ascent to full Reviewability' (1992) 43 *Northern Ireland Legal Quarterly*, 178, 196.

73. [1991] COD 92. The case, which arose out of the *Marchionesse* tragedy on the River Thames, related to the applicant's desire to compel the DPP to prosecute an individual for manslaughter in addition to what was viewed as a lesser offence under s. 24(4)(b) of the Merchant Shipping Act 1970 (as substituted by s. 30 of the Merchant Shipping Act 1980).

74. It was held that the Crown Prosecutor had misapplied the evidential sufficiency criterion within the *Code*, and had effectively overlooked the fact that the alleged buggery was non-consensual.

75. See for example Lord Brightman in *R. v. Hillingdon London Borough Council, ex p. Puhlhofer* [1986] 1 AC 484 and Lord Lowry in *R. v Secretary of State for the Home Department, ex p. Brind* [1991] 1 AC 696.

76. See A. Ashworth and J. Fionda, 'The New Code for Crown Prosecutors: (1) Prosecution, Accountability and the Public Interest' [1994] CrimLR 894 and R. Daw, 'The New Code for Crown Prosecutors: (2) A Response' [1994] CrimLR 904.

77. The launch of the third edition of the *Code* was accompanied by an *Explanatory Memorandum* which contains some slight development of the points in the new shorter *Code*; however, the status of the *Explanatory Memorandum* within the CPS is

unknown, though its purpose 'is to explain to crown prosecutors and other CPS staff what changes have been made, and why', (*Explanatory Memorandum*, para. 1.2). This retrograde step is paradoxically against a commendable trend which is apparent in the Inland Revenue, where for example internal guidance manuals in respect of certain rental reliefs and on the Enterprise Investment Scheme have recently been released into the public domain—see (1995) 145 *New Law Journal* 58.

78. Decisions to not enforce the law; see for example *R. v Metropolitan Police Commissioner, ex p. Blackburn* [1968] 2 QB 118.

79. See for example *R. v General Council of the Bar, ex p. Percival* [1990] 3 All ER 137. Though there are not to date any precedents for the review by the High Court of the selection of charge by the police or the DPP, by analogy with case law on the decision to prosecute and through having noted the existence of *Charging Standards for Criminal Offences* in the public domain, it is submitted that the extension of judicial review into this area is inevitable. The Crown Prosecution Service have since 1994 begun to introduce such published charging standards for various commonly committed offences—see for example the *Charging Standards for Offences Against the Person*, discussed at (1994) 144 *New Law Journal* 1168.

80. *R. v Chief Constable of Kent, ex p. GL* [1993] 1 All ER 756.

81. *R. v Inland Revenue Commissioners, ex p. Mead* [1993] 1 All ER 772.

82. *R. v Havering Magistrates Court, ex p. Gould*, unreported, Divisional Court 7 April 1992 (CO/340/02)(application for leave only).

83. *R. v DPP, ex p. Tasmin C.* unreported, Divisional Court 18 February 1994 (CO/642/93).

84. The research of the Public Law Project shows that the DPP was the respondent in 11 per cent of the applications against non-departmental public bodies over the study period. See M. Sunkin *et al. Judicial Review in Perspective* (1993) p. 28. See also B. Hadfield and E. Weaver, 'Judicial Review in Perspective: Trends in the Use of Judicial Review in Northern Ireland' (1995) 46 *Northern Ireland Legal Quarterly* (forthcoming).

85. C. Hilson, 'Discretion to Prosecute and Judicial Review' [1993] CrimLR 739, 743.

86. I am indebted to C. Hilson for his analysis in 'Discretion to Prosecute and Judicial Review' [1993] CrimLR 739, which has informed the present discussion of this aspect of the issue.

87. It is sadly the case that public servants can to a certain extent frustrate litigation over their decisions by maintaining secrecy in their deliberations. It is, however, fair to say that there is an increasing tendency on the part of agencies of government to voluntarily publish and release policy documents—the *Code for Crown Prosecutors*, published pursuant to section 10 of the Prosecution of Offences Act 1985, is an example in point, although as has previously been noted the reduction in the detail contained in the most recent edition of that document is regrettable.

88. *Ex p. Mead*, at p. 783. While it is true that this consideration has long been a part of the general jurisprudence of judicial review, *ex p. Mead* is the first occasion of its application as a yardstick by which the exercise of prosecutorial discretion could be gauged.

89. [1987] ILRM 225.

90. [1994] 2 ILRM 285.

91. See the section on 'Judicial Review and Police Powers', above.

92. The *Code for Crown Prosecutors* in paras 10.1 and 10.2 provides in part that a prosecution should only rarely be undertaken when the CPS has previously communicated to the suspect that there will not be a prosecution.

93. [1993] 3 All ER 129.

94. [1984] HKLR 411, 417–18.

95. A further example of the judicial review of the exercise of a prosecution discretion is *R. v DPP ex p. Warby* [1994] Crim. LR 281 which concerned an unsuccessful challenge to the refusal by the CPS to disclose evidence prior to a committal hearing, it being claimed that the refusal was in contravention of the *Attorney General's Guidelines*

(1981) 74 CRAppR 302. See also in respect of summary trials, *R. v Bromley Magistrates Court, ex p. Smith and Wilkins; R. v Wells Magistrates Court, ex p. King* [1995] CrimLR 248.

96. See for example A. le Sueur, *passim* and the Appendix by Paul Maguire.

97. *Neill v North Antrim Magistrates Court* [1992] 4 All ER 846, 858.

98. See s. 6(1) of the Prosecution of Offences Act 1985 and art. 5(3) of the Prosecution of Offences (NI) Order 1972. The entitlement to prosecute privately is subject to a number of qualifications such as the frequent requirement under particular statutes that the *fiat* of the Attorney General or the DPP be obtained prior to commencing a prosecution, and the possible procedural requirement that a private prosecutor in an indictable offence must brief solicitor and counsel to prosecute on his or her behalf in the Crown Court— *R. v George Maxwell (Developments) Ltd* [1980] 2 All ER 99. It appears, however, that this common law procedural rule may in more recent times have been abrogated by statute, the Divisional Court holding that by reason of s. 27 (2) (5) of the Courts and Legal Services Act 1990, the Crown Court could allow a private prosecution to be conducted in person—*R. v Southwark Crown Court, ex p. Tawfick, Crown Prosecution Service Intervening* [1994] 12 CL 223.

99. Per Lloyd LJ. in *R. v Bow Street Stipendiary Magistrate, ex p. South Coast Shipping Co. Ltd* [1993] 1 All ER 219, 222, citing the *Royal Commission on Criminal Procedure* (Cmnd. 8092 (1981)), para. 7.50.

100. [1993] 1 All ER 219.

101. Prosecution of Offences Act 1985, s. 3(2)(b).

102. [1994] 1 All ER 44.

103. See particularly Kennedy LJ. at pp 51, 52. The court certified a point of law of general public importance for the consideration of the House of Lords.

104. See art. 5(3) of the Prosecution of Offences (NI) Order 1972.

105. A. Sanders and R. Young, *Criminal Justice* (1994) pp 211–12.

106. See for example Van Den Wyngaert *et al.*, *Criminal Procedure Systems in the European Community* (1993).

107. M. Sunkin *et al.*, *Judicial Review in Perspective* (1993) p. 27.

108. [1987] NI 325.

109. Although decided in 1986, this judgment was reported only in 1992. See n. 122 below.

110. [1990] 2 All ER 833.

111. See P. Osborne, 'The Floodgates of Judicial Review: Once More Unto the Breach' (1993) 44 Northern Ireland Legal Quarterly, 233.

112. Per Bailey, Jones and Mowbray, *Cases and Materials on Administrative Law* (1992) at p. 194.

113. [1894] 2 IR 158.

114. Per Holmes J., at p. 177. However, some doubt has been cast over the decision by the speech of Lord Mustill in *Neill v North Antrim Magistrates Court* [1992] 4 All ER 846.

115. [1968] AC 192, 234.

116. [1969] 2 AC 147.

117. [1983] 1 AC 237.

118. [1985] QB 67.

119. [1993] 1 All ER 97.

120. [1992] 4 All ER 846.

121. Notable exceptions to this proposition that there is general review for errors of law include university visitors, who apparently remain immune from judicial review for non-jurisdictional errors (*Page v Hull University Visitor*, n. 119, above), and the views of variously composed English Divisional Courts which have striven to avoid the implications of the House of Lords decision in the Northern Ireland appeal in *Neill v North Antrim Magistrates Court*, n. 120, above: see for example *R. v Nottingham Justices, ex p. Cunningham and Attaway* (unreported, Divisional Court 7 April 1993 (CO/3117/92, CO/3104/92)), where the Divisional Court said that *Neill* was not of

direct application to England and that the court would not exercise its discretion so as to order certiorari on the basis of the inadmissibility or insufficiency of evidence upon which an accused person had been committed for trial. It is interesting to note the similarities in the views propounded by Watkins LJ. in *ex p. Cunningham and Attaway* and those of Lowry LCJ. in the Northern Ireland case of *In Re McNally (a Minor)* (discussed below).

122. [1992] 11 NIJB 100.
123. Unreported, Northern Ireland Divisional Court 30.4.1993.
124. Supreme Court Act 1981, s. 29(3).
125. See for example Archbold, *Criminal Pleading, Evidence and Practice*, paras 2–195 ff. and *Blackstone's Criminal Practice*, para. 24.30.
126. [1985] AC 622.
127. (1994) 98 Cr App R 461.
128. *Ex p. Marlowe* [1973] CrimLR 294.
129. *R. v Manchester Crown Court, ex p. DPP* (1993) 97 CrAppR 203, overturning *R. v Central Criminal Court, ex p. Randle* (1991) 92 CrAppR 323.
130. *R. v Manchester Crown Court, ex p. DPP* (1994) 98 CrAppR 461.
131. *R. v Southwark Crown Court, ex p. Commissioners of Customs and Excise* (1993) 97 CrAppR 266.
132. *Sampson v Crown Court at Croydon* (1987) 84 CrAppR 376.
133. [1992] 4 NIJB 1 at pp 6–7.
134. [1971] 1 QB 147.
135. [1992] 9 NIJB 86.
136. Carswell J. (as he then was) then detailed the procedure which he felt should govern applications for legal aid in future times, the most important aspect being that the prosecution, and not the defence, should be expected to appraise the resident magistrate of the seriousness of the alleged offence: see p. 92.
137. *R. v St Alban's Crown Court, ex p. Cinnamond* [1981] QB 480; *Universal Salvage v Boothby* (1983) 5 CrAppR (S) 428; *R. v Croydon Crown Court, ex p. Miller* (1986) 85 CrAppR 152; and *Tucker v DPP* [1992] 4 All ER 901. Watkins LJ. (who in *ex p. Miller* endeavoured to restrict the ambit of *ex p. Cinnamond* to cases where the sentence was 'truly astonishing') has also expressed the view that the decision in *ex p. Cinnamond* is wrong—*Arthur v Stringer* (1987) 84 CrAppR 361, 368.
138. *The Times*, 29 March 1993.
139. [1995] 1 CL 93.
140. Magistrates Courts Act 1980, s. 111(1).
141. Magistrates Courts (NI) Order 1981, art. 146(1). The ambit of the case stated jurisdiction in Northern Ireland is wider than that in England and Wales; while the English Act prescribes the grounds for stating a case as relating to decisions which are wrong in law or which are in excess of jurisdiction, the Northern Ireland provision encompasses any point of law involved in the determination of the proceeding or any issue as to the court's jurisdiction.
142. See *Streames v Copping* [1985] QB 920 and Valentine and Hart, *Criminal Procedure in Northern Ireland* (1989) para. 17.26 ff.
143. See also the Law Commission Report on *Administrative Law: Judicial Review and Statutory Appeals* (Law. Comm. No. 226; October 1994), which in part recommends the replacement of appeals to the High Court by way of case stated with an appeal on a point of law.
144. Both the County Court in Northern Ireland when exercising its criminal appellate jurisdiction and the Crown Court in England and Wales when doing likewise may also state a case respectively for the opinion of the Court of Appeal in Northern Ireland (County Courts (NI) Order 1980, art. 61) or the Divisional Court in England and Wales (Supreme Court Act 1981, s. 28).

145. See the Criminal Justice and Public Order Act 1994, s. 44 and sch. 4, substituting ss 4 to 8 of the Magistrates Court Act 1980.

146. [1981] 1 All ER 596.

147. [1942] 1 KB 281, 284.

148. See for example *R. v Morpeth Ward Justices, ex p. Ward* (1992) 95 CrAppR 215 and *In Re McNally* (unreported, Northern Ireland Divisional Court 30 April 1993).

149. *The Times*, 29 March 1993.

150. However, there are important provisions in s. 21 of the Judicature (Northern Ireland) Act 1978 which entitle the court when issuing *certiorari* 'to remit the matter to the lower deciding authority concerned, with a direction to reconsider it and reach a decision in accordance with the ruling of the court or [to] reverse or vary the decision of the lower deciding authority', thereby entitling the court to supplant its decision for that of the lower court.

151. *Re W.* [1971] AC 682, 700. In similar vein, Carswell J. stated in *In Re Glór Na nGael* [1991] 3 NIJB 1, at p. 13 that 'Judicial review is not an appeal from [an administrative] decision, and is not concerned with its merits, but only with the manner in which it has been reached . . .'

152. See for example *R. v Telford Justices, ex p. Badhan* [1991] 2 All ER 854; *R. v Croydon Justices, ex p. Dean* [1993] 3 All ER 129; and *R. v Horseferry Road Magistrates' Court, ex p. Bennett* [1993] 3 All ER 138.

153. [1991] 3 All ER 169, 175.

154. [1993] CrimLR 78.

155. [1993] 3 All ER 129, 135.

156. See for example *Attorney General's Reference (No. 1 of 1990)* [1991] 3 All ER 169, and the cases discussed above regarding statutory appeals and appeals by way of case stated.

157. The discretionary nature of the remedies is neatly illustrated in *R. v Kirklees Metropolitan Borough Council, ex p. Tesco Stores Ltd*, Unreported, Divisional Court 27.7.1993 (CO/467/93), where McCowan LJ. held that even if there was legal substance in the applicant's case, he 'would still not have thought it an appropriate case in which to grant the relief sought having regard to [the applicant's] plain unwillingness to comply with the law as laid down in the Shops Act 1950'.

158. M. Sunkin *et al., Judicial Review in Perspective* n. 7 above, doubt from their data whether judicial review is in truth a powerful weapon in the hands of the citizen and ranged towards central government, as statistics indicate that it is used more against local authorities than against central authorities. See p. 101. The authors' research also shows that while the 'vast majority' of applications are brought in the name of an individual (84–88%), it should not be presumed that all such individuals were acting for themselves rather than, for example, for a special interest grouping.

159. See for example the research of the Public Law Project, which highlights growing delays in the procedure—M. Sunkin *et al., Judicial Review in Perspective*, pp 56 ff., and the Law Commission Consultation Paper No. 126, 1993, *Administrative Law: Judicial Review and Statutory Appeals*, para. 2.14.

160. In this vein the author would highlight the receding distinction between jurisdictional and non-jurisdictional errors of law.

Chapter Six

The Impact of Judicial Review on Prisons

Stephen Livingstone

Introduction

Prisons are often seen as one of the successes of judicial review. They are frequently viewed as an area where judicial review litigation has brought about significant changes in the operation of a major bureaucracy. One can point to changes in rules and practices within the prison system which have been changed as a result of judicial review actions. Moreover, it can be argued that the values which judicial review seeks to inculcate, values of formality, transparency and accountability in decision-making, have now become the values by which the prison service operates and have displaced a more authoritarian style of management. These are significant, and to a large extent genuine, achievements. Yet its interaction with prisons also reveals a darker side of judicial review, of its inability to subject arbitrary power to the norms of the rule of law, of the compromises that law makes with power. Examination of the interaction of judicial review with the prison environment is an important site at which to study the *tension* between law and administration, of how each can influence the other.

Judicial Review and Prisons: The Development of Jurisdiction

The first success of judicial review in relation to prisons was for judicial review to be admitted at all. As late as 1972 Lord Denning MR was observing that the courts would not entertain claims from 'disgruntled prisoners'.[1] Although the *Becker* case concerned a civil action, attempts to extend the High Court's jurisdiction over administrative action around the same time met with just as little success. In the case of *Fraser v Mudge*[2] (in which a declaration and injunction were sought) Lord Denning MR again observed that allowing prisoners to seek the courts' assistance in overseeing a disciplinary hearing by a governor[3] could not be allowed.[4] In these decisions the operation of prisons and, in particular, the administration of discipline within them, was analogised to the operation of the military. Speed of decision-making and the need to reinforce the authority of those

167

exercising discipline were emphasised. Judicial review, especially some of the specific values associated with concepts of natural justice, were seen as simply inappropriate to this environment.

The change came with the decision of the Court of Appeal in *R. v Board of Visitors Hull Prison, ex parte St Germain*.[5] Therein the court recognised that certiorari was available to quash the decision of the board of visitors exercising disciplinary powers. While *St Germain* marked a breakthrough it was a cautious one. Shaw LJ. alone appeared prepared to reject entirely the idea that prisons should be treated differently from other areas of administration when it came to the issue of the courts' *jurisdiction*, as opposed to the exercise of their discretion to grant a remedy. His brethren based their decision more on the quasi-judicial nature of boards of visitors and appeared to suggest that the military analogy might retain some validity when it came to the exercise of governors' disciplinary powers. It was a view that was endorsed by the English Court of Appeal in *R. v Deputy Governor Camphill Prison, ex parte King*,[6] but not by its sister court in Northern Ireland. In the case of *R. v Governor of the Maze Prison, ex parte McKiernan*[7] the Northern Ireland Court of Appeal took the view that *St Germain* did extend to the exercise of disciplinary powers by governors. In the *Leech*[8] case the House of Lords resolved the dispute in favour of the view held in Belfast and indicated some support for lower court decisions that a duty to act fairly might extend to a governor's exercise of non-disciplinary powers. This view was subsequently endorsed by the House of Lords in *R. v Deputy Governor of Parkhurst, ex parte Hague*.[9]

With the *Hague* case the wheel appeared to have come full circle. Now any decision taken within the prison system appears to be subject to judicial review. Yet the issue of jurisdiction may not have gone away for ever. Since 1993 a number of prisons have been contracted out to the private sector.[10] It might be argued that these bodies, as private rather than public bodies, should not be subject to judicial review jurisdiction. The point has yet to be tested, but as the operators of these contracted out prisons are clearly exercising public functions (all the prisoners they hold have been committed by the courts and the prison service retains ultimate responsibility for the operation of contracted out prisons) it seems that they should be susceptible to judicial review.[11]

Application of Judicial Review to Areas of Prison Administration

Having established jurisdiction, courts have gone on to consider the lawfulness of the actions of prison administrators. In doing so they have not only reviewed the lawfulness of present actions by those charged with the administration of prisons, but have also given indications of what is required in order to ensure that prisons operate in conformity with the law.

Access to lawyers, the courts and the outside world

While in most areas of prison administration the impact of judicial review has been via notions of natural justice and the duty to act fairly, issues of *ultra vires* have featured significantly in cases concerning the prisoner's access to the world outside the prison. The first example is the decision in *Raymond v Honey*,[12] wherein the House of Lords held that a prisoner could not be prevented from sending documents to the High Court in order to pursue a claim for contempt of court against the governor. In addition to the case being notable for Lord Wilberforce's broad statement of principle that a prisoner 'retains all civil rights which are not taken away expressly or by necessary implication', it also witnessed judicial observations that the right of access to the courts was such a fundamental right that it could only be removed by primary legislation expressly indicating that this was parliament's intention. Neither standing orders, nor the prison rules they purported to interpret, could achieve this.

The *Raymond v Honey* decision was invoked by the Court of Appeal in *R. v Secretary of State for the Home Department, ex parte Anderson*.[13] The policy challenged in *Anderson* was the successor to that in *Raymond v Honey*. Rather than prohibit prisoners from submitting civil claims to the courts, Prison Rule 33(1) required that they simultaneously be submitted to internal grievance procedures. When Anderson failed to do this his letter to his lawyer was stopped. He argued that this too inhibited his access to the courts and that no statute had authorised this. The argument found favour with the Court of Appeal, which observed that most prisoners would need legal assistance if their claims were to be fairly considered by the courts.

After the *Anderson* case all restrictions on a prisoner's correspondence with his or her lawyer were removed. Once a prisoner became a party to legal proceedings[14] the prison rules provided that his or her correspondence with a lawyer could not be read or stopped, though it could be examined to see that no contraband was contained in it. Correspondence with lawyers before legal proceedings were taken, however, indeed where they were never even contemplated, remained subject to censorship until the decision in *R. v Secretary of State for the Home Department, ex parte Leech*.[15] Therein Leech, a veteran prisoner litigant, successfully challenged what was then Prison Rule 33(3) as *ultra vires* the 1952 Prison Act in so far as it permitted censorship of a prisoner's correspondence with his or her lawyer. As in *Anderson* the Court of Appeal ruled that such a power to censor correspondence inhibited the prisoner's access to the courts and that section 47 of the Prison Act 1952 (which empowers the Secretary of State to make rules for the management of prisons) did not explicitly authorise such a limitation on access.

With the decision in *Leech* the courts completed the task of removing restrictions on the prisoner's ability to seek judicial oversight of his or her treatment. In many ways these cases complement the cases establishing jurisdiction, for they ensure not only that the courts are competent to inquire into the lawfulness of official actions taken in prisons, but also that prisoners will be able to bring such claims before the courts. They are a way of making jurisdiction effective. They reinforce the message that it is the judiciary rather than the bureaucrats who will decide upon the lawfulness of what happens in prisons and are a further rejection of the idea that the prison is a totally closed society. While these cases on access to courts and lawyers amount to significant gains for prisoners seeking an effective means of challenging what they see as injustices done to them within the prison, they may be just as important, in terms of outcome, in the struggle between the courts and the administration.

Judicial review actions have played a less prominent role as regards prisoners' ability to communicate with someone other than their lawyer. Here the European Commission and Court of Human Rights have played a larger role.[16] The Strasbourg decisions have led to an overall reduction in the level of censorship and to significant changes in the way such censorship is administered. Judicial review actions have not featured prominently with regard to other aspects of contact with the outside world, such as visits or home leave. What litigation there has been relates mainly to Northern Irish prisoners and has been largely unsuccessful. Thus in *McCartney v Governor HM Prison Maze*[17] the decision of the Secretary of State for Northern Ireland to deny a prisoner a visit from a Sinn Féin councillor was upheld despite the absence of a specific claim of a threat to prison security in relation to this visit. In *R. v Secretary of State for the Home Department, ex parte McComb*[18] a Northern Irish prisoner's attempt to obtain transfer from England, to be nearer to his family, was rejected on the grounds that section 26(1) of the Criminal Justice Act 1961 gave the Home Secretary a broad discretion as regards decisions to transfer and that it was a relevant consideration in exercising this discretion that the prisoner would benefit from a substantial increase in remission if transferred to Northern Ireland.[19]

As we shall see, the prisoners involved in these cases were not the first or the last to see that while the courts have cleared the way for challenges against the actions of prison administrators they tend to endorse those actions once the challenges have been heard.

Formal disciplinary powers

It was in the area of formal disciplinary powers that judicial review made its initial breakthrough in relation to prisons and it is in this area that its impact has been greatest. There can be little doubt that the extensive disregard of some of the most basic elements of fair procedure in the board of visitors hearings which led to the *St Germain* cases—all of which was faithfully recorded in longhand by prison officials—played a significant part in leading the courts to reverse their non-interventionist policy with regard to prisons. The case arose out of three days of extensive riots at Hull Prison in 1976. Subsequently prisoners from Hull were dispersed around the country and a panel of the Hull Board (specially convened to deal with the charges) travelled around England holding adjudications. Ultimately they heard over 500 charges against 185 prisoners. Nearly all were found guilty and severe punishments of up to 720 days loss of remission were ordered. Dispersal alone made it difficult for the prisoners to conduct their defence as it rendered almost impossible the task of identifying and consulting witnesses. Such difficulties were compounded by the board's refusal to allow them to call any witnesses or to cross-examine even hearsay evidence against them.

After *St Germain (No. 1)* had made the breakthrough as regards establishing the courts' jurisdiction to review the actions of boards of visitors, it was *R. v Hull Prison Board of Visitors, ex parte St Germain (No. 2)*[20] which began to spell out what the courts regarded as satisfying natural justice in the context of prison disciplinary hearings. *St Germain (No. 2)* indicated that prisoners should normally be entitled to call witnesses (at least where these were not being called simply to delay and disrupt the hearing) and that they should be entitled to cross-examine hearsay evidence given against them. Since then a large number of judicial review actions have sought to challenge the procedural fairness of board and, more recently, governors' disciplinary hearings. Decisions resulting from such actions have established a number of requirements which must be satisfied if the hearing is to be deemed a fair one. These include decisions that prisoners should be entitled to call witnesses[21] and that if the authorities are aware of a witness relevant to the prisoner's case they should inform that prisoner.[22] Prisoners do not have a general right to see all statements made by prison officers prior to the hearing,[23] but should be entitled to see such statements where a discrepancy exists between what a witness claims at the hearing and what he said in a previous statement.[24] Disciplinary hearings must operate to a standard of proof beyond reasonable doubt that the charges are proven[25] and where any ambiguity exists as to the meaning of a disciplinary charge (notably as to whether a mental element is required by the definition of the offence), this should be interpreted in favour of the prisoner.[26] Courts have also indicated that the requirement in the prison rules that charges must be heard the next day is a mandatory one and that only in exceptional cases can this requirement be departed from.[27]

Perhaps the most protracted litigation struggle in the area of prison discipline arose over the issue of whether prisoners should be entitled to legal representation when facing disciplinary charges. In *Fraser v Mudge* the Court of Appeal had plainly said that they were not, but this case was decided before the courts accepted the idea that judicial review could lie against the actions of those involved in administering the prisons. When the issue arose again in the post-*St Germain* climate the court was to give it a more sympathetic hearing. In the case of *R. v Secretary of State for the Home Department, ex parte Tarrant* Webster J. distinguished *Fraser v Mudge* on the grounds that its rejection of a right to legal representation did not provide an answer to the question as to whether the board of visitors had a discretion to grant representation. He concluded that they did and that, in so far as the board had refused to consider the prisoners' request for legal representation, those adjudications could automatically be quashed. Where a board did give consideration to a request, Webster J. outlined six factors which they ought to take into account.[28] Moreover on some charges, notably mutiny charges as in this case, he added that no reasonable board could refuse representation to prisoners such as the applicants. Contrary to the expectations of many, *Tarrant* did not lead to the establishment of a *general right* to legal representation, at least before boards of visitors. In 1988 in its decision in *Hone and McCartan v Maze Prison Board of Visitors*[29] the House of Lords rejected the idea of a *right* to representation, but endorsed the view that a *discretion* to allow representation existed in each case. Even before the *Hone* case the courts had suggested that in most cases boards exercising their discretion to deny representation would be safe from review.[30] Governors, who have always heard over 90 per cent of disciplinary adjudications and now hear all of such adjudications in England and Wales, (though not in Northern Ireland), must consider requests for legal representation.[31] They will, however, usually be entitled to conclude that it is not necessary, and only in exceptional cases might they be found to have exercised their discretion unreasonably if they failed to grant it.[32]

Discretionary powers for the management of prisons

This section is concerned with, for example, powers to classify prisoners, transfer them between prisons, search their persons and cells, and remove prisoners from association 'for the maintenance of good order and discipline'.[33] Prison administrators see these powers as central to effective prison management as they provide a way of avoiding or of dealing with potential conflicts in the prison.[34] Without them the authorities may find themselves powerless to intervene in dealing with situations of conflict or intimidation. Yet such powers also carry the risk that they will be used arbitrarily as an informal discipline system, lacking the safeguards against error in the formal discipline system, or will be used to harass and control prisoners whom the authorities find disagreeable.[35]

The courts have proved reluctant to grant applications for judicial review in this area. In particular, they have generally rejected the idea that anything like the same level of procedural guarantees to ensure fair decision-making, such as have been recognised with regard to disciplinary adjudications, should apply to the exercise of these discretionary powers. An attitude of judicial 'hands off' can first be discerned in the case of *Payne v Home Office*.[36] Therein Cantley J. in the Divisional Court rejected the claim that a prisoner who was classified category A should be entitled to be informed of the material which went before the category A committee or make representations to the committee or be given reasons as to why he remained classified as category A. A similar view was expressed in the removal of association case of *Williams v Home Office (No. 2)*.[37] Although Williams was removed from association to a special unit for a period of ninety days (renewable for another ninety days), where he was only allowed out of his cell for one hour a day, Tudor Evans J. saw no need to require any form of a hearing either before the governor's initial decision to segregate or when the board of visitors came to review the segregation after one month. Although *Williams* may be seen as a relic of the days when courts tended only to impose procedural duties in respect of 'judicial' as opposed to 'administrative' decision-making, the same cannot be said of *R. v Deputy Governor Parkhurst Prison, ex parte Hague*. There the Court of Appeal upheld the *Williams* ruling that a prisoner had no right to a hearing in respect either of the governor's initial decision to segregate or of the subsequent decision of the board of visitors to extend that segregation after seventy-two hours. The Court of Appeal also overturned a finding of the Divisional Court that a prisoner was entitled to a statement of reasons as to why he had been removed from association or continued to be removed from association.[38] The same court, however, did find that Hague's continued segregation was unlawful as he had immediately been placed in segregation (or 'on Rule 43' as it is usually described in prison) on arriving in Wormwood Scrubs Prison from Parkhurst. This was in pursuance of Circular Instruction 10/74 which provided for 'disruptive' prisoners to be moved 'on the ghost train' from the segregation units of one prison to another. The court granted judicial review in respect of this aspect of the decision-making process as it involved the refusal by the ('receiving') governor to exercise *his* discretion as to whether or not removal from association was necessary for the maintenance of good order and discipline in that prison.[39]

Cases on inter-prison transfer[40] and the removal of a baby from her mother in prison[41] also display a lack of judicial willingness either to overrule low level decision-making within the prison system or even to impose a higher level of procedural guarantees in respect of such decision-making. This is despite the fact that a decision to transfer, for example, can have a major impact on a prisoner's life. It will often amount to a significant upheaval in the prisoner's circumstances, may make it much more difficult for the prisoner's family to visit and can involve a sharp decline in the living conditions in which a prisoner serves his sentence. Although conceptualised as a fairly low level 'administrative' decision, its impact may be severe.

Recently, however, the courts have shown signs of moving away from this stance, at least where the discretionary decision in question has an impact on the prisoner's chances of release. Perhaps the most significant case in this respect is *R. v Secretary of State for the Home Department, ex parte Duggan*.[42] *Duggan* also involves the issue of classification, but here the Divisional Court overturned *Payne* to the extent that it indicated that reasons were never required in respect of classification decisions. Duggan, who had initially been classified as a category A prisoner on reception into prison to serve a life sentence in 1984, continued to be classified as category A after a meeting of the category A committee in 1993. He was given no reasons for this, nor had he been able to see the material which the category A committee examined. Concentrating especially on the fact that continuing category A status considerably diminished Duggan's chances of parole, Rose LJ. concluded that the decision to continue so to classify him had not been a fair one. He indicated that Duggan should receive at least the gist of the material before the category A committee (although identities of informants could be protected) and he was entitled to reasons for the decision not to reduce his security classification. The decision can be viewed rather narrowly as suggesting that because classification can have such a significant impact on a prisoner's chances of release, a serious liberty interest is implicated and a prisoner is entitled to the same procedural safeguards as attend release decisions. It might also be seen, however, as indicating that the courts are prepared to enter into the thicket of low level administrative decision-making in prisons, at least to suggest some minimal procedural guidelines. Whether its impact will be extended beyond category A classification decisions into areas such as segregation or transfer remains to be seen.[43]

Prison conditions

Problems relating to prison conditions are well documented in the United Kingdom. Regular reports from Her Majesty's Inspector of Prisons, Judge Tumin, have recounted a story of overcrowding, poor sanitation, dirty conditions and security problems. The European Committee on Torture, carrying out an inspection under the mandate of the European Convention on Torture, Inhuman and Degrading Treatment, declared conditions at three English prisons to be 'degrading'.[44] Although some of these concerns were alleviated by reforms subsequently undertaken and by a decreasing prison population in the wake of the Woolf Report, by the mid-1990s prison numbers were creeping up again and the conditions issue seems unlikely to go away.

There is a limited amount that courts can do to alleviate such conditions by way of judicial review since they have no legal standards on which to bite. The prison rules provide only cursory directions as to conditions. That on medical care, for example, does not even contain the commitment that such care should accord with professional standards generally prevailing in the community. Despite making promises to introduce a minimum code of standards for prison accommodation the Home Office has never produced one. Even those prison rules which might provide a guide to standards are subject to exceptions. Prison Rule 23(2) in England, for example, indicates that a certificate given under the rule may specify the maximum number of prisoners who can sleep in the room. It then goes on to add, however, that 'the number so specified shall not be exceeded without the leave of the Secretary of State'. This is hardly much of a safeguard since it is the Secretary of State, rather than a prison governor or the board of visitors, who is most likely to be happy to decree an increase. In any case, judicial decisions holding that prison rules in most cases are to be regarded as directory rather than mandatory have undercut any legal force that they might have been seen as possessing.

Within the limited scope thus left to them, the courts have shown little interest in imaginative strategies that might have developed judicial oversight of prison conditions. Claims framed in both judicial review and negligence have fallen on deaf ears. Thus in the *Williams* case, discussed above, Tudor Evans J. displayed some concern as to the nature of the conditions in the control unit, but concluded that no remedy was available.

In *Hague* the House of Lords rejected an argument that prison conditions could become so intolerable as to entitle the prisoner to pursue an action for false imprisonment. Citing section 12 of the Prison Act, which provides that a prisoner may be lawfully confined in any prison, the House of Lords concluded that this disposed of any claims of unlawful imprisonment once a prisoner had been committed to prison by the courts. This was despite the fact that the prisoner was not necessarily claiming that they should be released from custody entirely because of the intolerable conditions, merely that they should be moved to more tolerable conditions. In the same case the House of Lords appeared to indicate that the Home Office might not even be vicariously liable for assaults by prison officers in the tort of misfeasance in public office. In the more recent decision of *Racz v Home Office*,[45] however, the Lords indicated that it remained a question for the trial court whether the officers' acts were entirely unconnected with their duties, and only if they could be said to be unconnected would a claim for misfeasance in public office necessarily fail. To complete this depressing pattern in relation to conditions, Pill J., in the case of *Knight v Home Office*,[46] refused to hold that the prison medical service was subject to the same standards of care which applied to the NHS.

One decision which did suggest a role for the courts in reviewing prison conditions was that of the Court of Appeal in *R. v Secretary of State for the Home Department, ex parte Herbage (No. 2)*.[47] Therein the court indicated, though only on a discovery application, that prison conditions could amount to 'cruell and unusuall punishments', prohibited by the Bill of Rights 1688, and that invoking the prison rules would not be sufficient to justify such treatment. In doing so, the Court of Appeal appeared prepared to countenance a broader reading of the Bill of Rights than had been contemplated by Tudor Evans J. when the same question was raised in *Williams*. There he had indicated that treatment had to be both cruel and unusual. The Court of Appeal approach seemed to envisage a more holistic approach to the issue. In the United States, invocation of the prohibition on cruel and unusual punishments in the Eighth Amendment to the Constitution has been the vehicle by which extensive prison reform litigation has been launched against dangerous, unsafe and overcrowded prisons. As a result of this litigation, part or all of the prison system in over forty states has been operating under court order. While views on the impact of such litigation vary, and its work has often been undone by a sharply rising prison population, a recent study concluded that it had largely been successful in producing significant improvements in prisoner safety, living conditions and medical care. Moreover, such improvements were unlikely to have been produced without litigation acting at least as a catalyst for change within the state prison bureaucracy.[48]

Ironically it is in the newly privatised sector of the prison service that the most interesting legal developments with respect to prison conditions could occur in the United Kingdom. When prisons are put out to tender, the prison service negotiates a detailed contract with the private company, a tender which often contains detailed specifications on things like time out of cell, sanitation and the numbers to be housed in each cell. The prison service has refused to publish these contracts on the grounds of 'commercial confidentiality', but tender documents—which often correspond closely to the final contract—are published and several contracts are now in the public domain. Such documents could be seen to give rise to 'legitimate expectations' on the part of prisoners that certain standards will be maintained and could entitle them to pursue judicial review actions if they are not maintained, either against the contractor or the prison service, which has a duty to monitor standards.

Release from prison

Since the late 1980s, procedures in respect of release from prison have been the fastest growth area of judicial review. Much of the prompting has come from a series of decisions of the European Court of Human Rights, which decisions have indicated the need for a judicial element in the decision whether to release prisoners, at least as regards those sentenced to discretionary life sentences.[49] The domestic courts, however, have also played a part and have shown themselves increasingly willing to scrutinise in detail the way in which decisions to release, or more often not to release, are made.

The beginning of the story is a familiar one. In the case of *Payne v Lord Harris of Greenwich*[50] the Court of Appeal indicated that while the Parole Board, which makes recommendations to the Secretary of State on release, was under a duty to act fairly, this duty did not extend to showing the prisoner material which went before the board, or to allowing him to make representations in person to the board, or to giving him reasons as to why his release was refused. The *Payne* decision stood in the way of any development of procedural requirements in relation to release decisions until the 1987 decision in *R. v Secretary of State for the Home Department, ex parte Handscomb*.[51]

The *Handscomb* case seized on the distinction made in the application of the life sentence scheme between the period served for retribution and deterrence, the 'tariff period', and the period served because the prisoner was still considered a risk to the public, the 'risk element'. Home Secretaries had developed the practice of consulting the judiciary as to the tariff period and of generally refusing to allow release before at least that period was served. The Divisional Court agreed with this philosophy, especially in respect of discretionary lifers, but found unreasonable the Home Secretary's practice of waiting for up to four years before making the first referral of the prisoner's case to the parole board and of waiting a similar period before he consulted the Lord Chief Justice and the trial judge (if available) about the appropriate tariff. The court concluded that it would be much more rational if the Home Secretary were to consult the judiciary immediately as to the tariff and, if he agreed with their recommendation, set the first referral to the parole board at a period shortly before the tariff period expired. The presumption at this hearing would be that the prisoner should be released unless there was evidence that he was a danger to the public. The *Handscomb* court also indicated a belief that the Home Secretary would be subject to judicial review if he disagreed with the judicial estimate of the tariff, but subsequent decisions have indicated that the statutory framework envisages ultimate decisions about both tariff and risk elements being taken by the Home Secretary, at least as regards mandatory lifers.

The Home Secretary's decision on how and when to set the tariff has been the subject of subsequent judicial reviews. The most significant perhaps is the House of Lords' decision in *Doody* v *Secretary of State*.[52] Therein their lordships rejected the *Handscomb* view that the Secretary of State was bound by the tariff period set by the judiciary. When dealing with mandatory lifers, they considered that section 35 of the Criminal Justice Act 1991 (a statute heavily influenced by European and judicial review developments) entitled the Home Secretary to depart from the judicial review of the tariff. If he did so, however, the duty of fairness required that a prisoner should be shown at least the gist of the material on which the Home Secretary relied in making his decision (again this should be done without putting anyone's safety at risk), an opportunity to make representations about the appropriate tariff, and reasons as to why the Home Secretary was departing from the judicial view. Also in *R.* v *Secretary of State for the Home Department, ex parte Pegg*[53] the parole board was held to have erred when it failed to give reasons for departing from a recommendation of a local review committee that the prisoner be released after a year in open conditions.

Other decisions have focused more on the procedure in relation to the risk element once a prisoner has served the required tariff period. In the *Benson*[54] case the Divisional Court indicated that the parole board and the Home Secretary must focus on the issue of whether the prisoner was dangerous and that, where the Home Secretary relied on factors which were not relevant to this issue, they would be prepared to quash his decision. In the case of *R. v Parole Board and Home Secretary, ex parte Wilson*[55] the Court of Appeal finally overruled *Payne*, at least with regard to discretionary lifers, and indicated that they should be entitled to see material that went to the Parole Board. They should also be given reasons for refusal to release. *Wilson* was decided after parliament had passed the Criminal Justice Act 1991, which provided that the Home Secretary had to accept the judicial estimate of the tariff and refer a discretionary lifer's case to the parole board when that period expired. Before the Discretionary Lifer Panels (DLPs) of the Parole Board, each of which is chaired by a judge, a prisoner has the right to be legally represented, see the material which went to the parole board and to be given reasons for any adverse decision. These rules do not apply in the case of mandatory lifers.[56] The case to which *Wilson* related, however, was begun under the pre-1991 scheme and in giving judgment the Court of Appeal indicated that it found the different treatment of mandatory and discretionary lifers illogical. This view was echoed by the Divisional Court in *R. v Parole Board, ex parte Creamer and Scholey*.[57] In *Doody* the House of Lords observed that parliament had not taken the opportunity to alter the law as significantly for mandatory lifers in 1991 but also that, following the *Wilson* decision, the Home Secretary had indicated that procedures in relation to what information went to the Parole Board and the opportunity for mandatory lifers to make representations in respect of this would be brought into line with the situation for discretionary lifers.

Since the introduction of the Criminal Justice Act 1991 the courts have been involved in scrutinising the adequacy of reasons given by the Parole Board for refusals to release life sentence prisoners. In the case of *R. v Parole Board, ex parte Creasey*[58] the board was held to have given inadequate reasons to a discretionary life prisoner who had remained in prison nine years after the expiry of his tariff, while in *R. v Secretary of State for the Home Department, ex parte Raja and Riaz*[59] the Divisional Court considered the Home Secretary's disclosure of information in a case where he set mandatory life sentence tariffs ten years higher than the trial judge as being 'woefully inadequate'. These decisions suggest that the courts will continue to have a role in scrutinising the fairness of decision-making in respect of the release of life sentence prisoners and that they are likely to continue to inject elements of 'transparency' into this decision-making. Courts are clearly uncomfortable with the idea that whereas determinate sentence prisoners have their sentences determined in open court, with a full opportunity for them to participate in the decision, are given reasons for it and have an opportunity to challenge it, the release of indeterminate sentence prisoners has been shrouded in secrecy. The effect of their intervention has clearly been to formalise the process more and, notably in the case of discretionary lifers, to introduce a more judicial element into it.

The Impact of Judicial Review on Prisons

The formal legal impact of judicial review on prisons may be viewed as limited. Despite a decade of active litigation the Prison Rules 1964 remain in force in England, although they have been modified as to disciplinary adjudications and correspondence with lawyers, and the Prison Act has been left unchanged since 1952. The latest version of the Prison Rules in Northern Ireland, which came into force in March 1995, does show some evidence of having been modified to take account of the impact of judicial review (notably as regards the provision for delaying disciplinary adjudications discussed above), but the alterations are limited. Even the more detailed guidelines on the conduct of adjudications remain in standing orders.

The one major legislative change which can be traced to the impact of litigation is the change in the regime for the release of life sentence prisoners reflected in the Criminal Justice Act of 1991. Although judicial review litigation clearly played a part in bringing this about, the more significant litigation was that pursued through the European Court of Human Rights. The European Court's decisions in *Weeks* and in *Thynne, Wilson and Gunnell* made the continuation of a purely administrative approach to the release of discretionary life sentence prisoners untenable. Had the court decided the other way in the mandatory life sentence case of *Wynne*, it is likely that the mandatory life sentence for murder would have come to an end.[60] As it is, neither political pressure nor judicial review litigation in the United Kingdom seems likely to bring this about.

The Criminal Justice Act might also be seen to be reflecting something of a trend. Arguably it has always been that decisions of the European Court of Human Rights have had a greater impact on prison administration and prison law than domestic judicial review litigation. Sometimes, indeed, it seems that Europe has prodded the domestic courts into action that might not otherwise have been taken. Thus it was the cases of *Golder*[61] and *Silver*[62] that first produced a reconsideration of the rules and practice on access to the courts and on censorship some time before the domestic courts took up the issue in *Raymond v Honey* and *ex parte Anderson*. The trial court in *ex parte Leech* (in relation to reading correspondence with lawyers) decided against the prisoner. By the time the Court of Appeal came to rule on the issue they had the benefit of the European Court of Human Rights decision in *Campbell v United Kingdom*[63] which held such restrictions to be a breach of Article 8. The *Tarrant* court delivered its ruling on the issue of legal representation in the knowledge that the European Commission of Human Rights had already indicated that in some circumstances denial of legal representation at disciplinary hearings could amount to a breach of Article 6(3) of the Convention. This decision was subsequently affirmed by the court in *Campbell and Fell v United Kingdom*.[64] Indeed had the court upheld the Commission decision that boards of visitors were not an impartial tribunal as required by Article 6(1), it is likely that the role of boards in hearing disciplinary charges in England would have come to an end much earlier than 1992. As it was, boards continued in this function in part because the Home Office concluded that they could live with the consequences of judicial review of such decisions, especially after the courts indicated that there was no right to legal representation at a board adjudication. It was only the impact of the 1990 riots and the conclusions in the Woolf Report to the effect that concerns did exist as to the impartiality of board hearings that the system was changed.[65]

Moving away from the impact of judicial review on the statutory framework to examine how it has affected both the administrative rules and the day-to-day practices of prisons, it is worth noting that we lack a detailed empirical study of the impact of judicial review on prison life. There is nothing in the United Kingdom which matches the work on the Canadian system, for example.[66] Such work would be especially valuable in investigating whether a formalisation of the disciplinary process has led to greater use of informal disciplinary mechanisms such as segregation or transfer.[67] It might also tell us whether judicial review has had an impact on the culture of prison management, perhaps encouraging greater openness and information sharing, and on how prisoners relate to the prison administration. What evidence there is does suggest a legalising of prison culture. There is the formalisation of release procedures for life sentence prisoners, the publishing of standing orders,[68] the revising of the *Disciplinary Manual*,[69] the creation of a prisons ombudsman to investigate complaints, and the introduction of prisoners 'compacts'. The last point, however, demonstrates a fear of too much legalisation as the prison service has refused to call such arrangements 'contracts'. All these developments fit in with an increasingly bureaucratic emphasis in prison management that no doubt reflects a decline in the belief that prison can actually do anything, positive or negative, to change prisoners' behaviour once they are released. They are also developments, however, that sit well with judicial review developments, stressing the need for clear criteria, formalisation and consistent decision-making in prison administration.

It is arguably this emphasis on process that is judicial review's most enduring impact on prison administration. The courts have been happiest when ensuring prisoners access to the courts, reforming the quasi-criminal process of prison disciplinary proceedings and the quasi-sentencing function of life sentence release. In other words their impact has been greatest on the parts of prison administration that can be most closely analogised to the legal process. Judicial review has had less impact on either the framework of policy-making in relation to prisons or on the exercise of low level discretionary powers deemed essential to prison management. As regards the former, the decision in *In Re Findlay*[70] stands out as a clear example of judicial abdication. Therein the House of Lords rejected the claim of four life sentence prisoners that they had a legitimate expectation of consultation before the Home Secretary altered parole policy in such a way that they would have to serve a considerably longer time in prison. Indeed the House of Lords held that the Home Secretary did not even have an obligation to consult the Parole Board.[71] As regards the latter point, we have seen that the courts have consistently shown a reluctance to recognise any procedural restrictions on the exercise of discretionary powers to classify, segregate or transfer. There is nothing in the common law which requires such an approach, and indeed Canadian courts, even before the advent of the Charter of Rights and Freedoms in 1982 gave them a clearer doctrinal basis on which to operate, recognised that the duty to act fairly might require some sort of a hearing before segregation decisions took place and an account of reasons afterwards.[72] Courts in the United Kingdom have not taken this view, but this is perhaps not wholly surprising for judicial review remains largely a doctrine that is marginal to administration. It operates primarily to correct aberrations in bureaucratic decision-making but ultimately tends to find itself powerless before the arbitrariness which is often the normality of prison life. This is perhaps why it has had so little impact on prisoners' living and working conditions, a field that probably is best left to the more detailed investigative work of bodies like the European Committee on Torture or Her Majesty's Chief Inspector of Prisons.

If the main impact of judicial review is to lead to the formalisation of the prison environment, then it may already have passed its high water mark.[73] As prison management becomes more bureaucratised, perhaps even extending to the use of discretionary powers, there may be less of a role for the courts to play. This might alter if statute did create some form of a code of standards, the enforcement of which the courts might then oversee. Without such a legislative framework it seems unlikely that the courts will wish to become involved in the detailed examination of prisoners' living and working conditions, even though such problems are likely to bedevil the prison system for some time to come. This, however, does not mean that judicial review is worthless, for, in addition to its instrumental role in forcing revision of prison rules and practices, judicial review also plays a symbolic role of throwing light on what is still largely a closed world. Judicial reviews have often succeeded in extracting from the prison service a much more detailed explanation of why decisions were taken, and on what information, than was initially provided to the prisoner.[74] A case like *Williams*, which wholly failed in court, nevertheless brought to light the control unit regime and ultimately led to its disbandment.[75] Prisoners, who often find the experience of prison a deeply powerless and debilitating one, have found in judicial review a means of exercising some power and of requiring the authorities to listen to their concerns.[76] This is no doubt why prisoners have remained such prominent exponents of judicial review.[77] To the prison authorities such a use of judicial review seems irritating and disruptive, but given the Woolf Report's stress on the corrosive impact of a sense of injustice among prisoners, of their concerns not being properly considered, the safety valve value of judicial review is one which it would be unwise to ignore.[78]

Notes

1. *Becker v Home Office* [1972] 2 QB 407. Earlier attempts to subject actions of prison administrators to legal regulation, on the basis of breaches of the prison rules, had failed when the courts ruled that the rules were merely directory and that breach of them was not intended to give rise to civil liability. See *Arbon v Anderson* [1943] KB 252.
2. [1975] 3 All ER 78.
3. Fraser sought to restrain the board of visitors from proceeding with the disciplinary hearing until he had been given the opportunity to obtain legal representation.
4. See also *Payne v Home Office*, unreported 2 May 1977, in which an application for a declaration that a decision to classify a prisoner as category A without a hearing was in breach of natural justice, was rejected. Cantley J. observed that any application of a general principle of a right to be heard would 'seriously hamper and in some circumstances could frustrate the efficient and proper government of prisons'.
5. [1979] QB 425.
6. [1985] QB 375.
7. [1985] 6 NIJB 6.
8. *R. v Deputy Governor of Parkhurst, ex p. Leech* [1988] AC 533.
9. [1992] 1 AC 154.
10. At the start of 1995 there were four contracted out prisons.
11. Even on the authority of decisions such as *R. v Jockey Club, ex p. Aga Khan* [1993] 1 WLR 909, the activities of contracted out prisons would appear to be within the purview of judicial review.
12. [1983] 1 AC 1.
13. [1984] QB 778.
14. This was defined in *Guilfoyle v Home Office* [1981] 1 QB 309 as being when a writ is issued.
15. [1993] 4 All ER 539.
16. Such as in the cases of *Golder v United Kingdom* Series A, No. 18 (1975) 1 EHRR 524 and *Silver v United Kingdom* (1983) 5 EHRR 347.
17. [1987] 11 NIJB 94.
18. *The Times*, 15 April 1991.

19. As a prisoner in England McComb was entitled to one-third remission on his sentence. In Northern Ireland he would be entitled to 50 per cent.
20. [1979] 3 All ER 545.
21. In addition to *St Germain (No. 2)* this principle has been affirmed in *R. v Board of Visitors, ex p. Moseley, The Times*, 23 January 1981 and (in respect of a governor's hearing) *ex p. Watkins*, unreported 4 December 1991.
22. See *R. v Board of Visitors Blundeston Prison, ex p. Fox-Taylor* [1982] 1 All ER 646.
23. See *R. v Board of Visitors Albany Prison, ex p. Mayo*, unreported 18 March 1985.
24. See *R. v Board of Visitors Wandsworth Prison, ex p. Raymond, The Times*, 17 June 1985.
25. See *R. v Secretary of State for the Home Department, ex p. Tarrant* [1984] 1 All ER 799.
26. See *R. v Board of Visitors Highpoint Prison, ex p. McConkey, The Times*, 23 September 1982.
27. See *R. v Board of Visitors Dartmoor Prison, ex p. Smith* [1986] 3 WLR 61. Northern Irish courts have been especially assiduous in regard to this rule, consistently rejecting the idea that hearings could not take place on Saturdays as no governor was available; see *In Re Jordan's Application* [1992] 2 NIJB 81. In response Rule 36(2) of the 1995 Prison and Young Offenders Centre Rules (Northern Ireland) provides that the charge will not have to be heard the next day if that day is a 'Saturday, Sunday or Public Holiday'.
28. [1984] 1 All ER 799, at pp 816–17. These were (1) the seriousness of the charge and the potential penalty, (2) the likelihood that difficult points of law would arise, (3) the capacity of a prisoner to present his own case, (4) difficulty for prisoners to locate and interview witnesses before the hearing, (5) need for reasonable speed in deciding cases, (6) need for fairness between prisoners and between prisoners and prison officers.
29. [1988] 1 All ER 381.
30. See for example *R. v Board of Visitors Blundeston Prison, ex p. Norley* unreported 4 July 1984; *R. v Board of Visitors Risley Remand Centre, ex p. Draper, The Times*, 24 May 1988.
31. *In Re Carroll's Application* [1987] 10 NIJB 23.
32. In *In Re Reynolds's Application* [1987] 8 NIJB 82 Higgins J. suggested that only where a prisoner was clearly unable to conduct his or her defence, for example, where the prisoner was mentally subnormal, would a governor be under a duty to grant representation. See also *In Re Carroll*, n. 31, above, and *In Re Baker* NICA April 1994 (unreported), per Nicholson J.: 'the aim [of a governor's adjudication] is to do speedy and simple justice. As a result it is rare for the prisoner to need legal representation. But the penalties for breach of discipline include loss of remission for a period not exceeding twenty-eight days. This is not a light punishment. Speed and simplicity must be subordinate to justice.'
33. This last power being contained in r. 43 in the Prison Rules in England and Wales and in r. 32 in Northern Ireland.
34. Indeed some cases in the United States have held prison authorities to be in breach of constitutional requirements in part because they had no classification system. This resulted in some prisoners being subject to excessive security while others were subject to little security. It also created the potential for more experienced criminals to dominate, intimidate and injure less serious offenders.
35. The potential of such misuse is evidenced by the *Hague* case. On discovery, documents were produced which showed one reason why Hague was regarded as someone who should be removed from association for reasons of good order and discipline was that he had pursued so many legal actions against the prison service.
36. Unreported 2 May 1977. Category A prisoners are those 'whose escape would be highly dangerous to the public or the police or the security of the State'; consequently they endure a more restrictive regime than those prisoners in the other categories.

37. [1982] 1 All ER 1211.
38. The Northern Irish courts reached a similar view in *McKernan v Governor of Belfast Prison* [1983] NI 83.
39. The decision of the CA in *Hague* is in [1990] 3 All ER 687. Also before the case reached the House of Lords (see [1991] 3 All ER 733) the Home Office withdrew CI 10/74, replacing it with CI 26/90 and CI 37/90. These do require that prisoners segregated under r. 43 should be given reasons and suggest that a member of the board of visitors should speak to the prisoner before any decision on whether or not to continue segregation. See Livingstone and Owen: *Prison Law: Text and Materials* (1993) pp 223–7. The level of reasons required can be rather brief. In *R. v Governor of HM Prison Long Lartin, ex p. Ross, The Independent*, 9 June 1994 it was held that telling a prisoner that he was 'disruptive' was sufficient to satisfy the requirements of CI 37/90 with regard to inter-prison transfer.
40. *R. v Secretary of State for the Home Department, ex p. McAvoy* [1984] 3 All ER 417.
41. *R. v Secretary of State for the Home Department, ex p. Hickling and JH (a minor)* [1986] 1 FLR 543.
42. [1994] 3 All ER 277.
43. Some of the analysis is very suggestive as regards segregation decisions. Rose LJ. appeared to take the view that as the prisoner's record clearly justified initial category A classification there was no need to furnish material on which the decision was made. However, as a prisoner might be of excellent behaviour in prison the decision was less obvious when it came to subsequent reviews. Similarly, the need for speed may justify a governor in allowing no hearing in respect of initial decisions to segregate, but the position may be otherwise when it comes to reviews by boards of visitors.
44. See *Report to the United Kingdom Government on the Visit to the United Kingdom carried out by the European Committee for the Prevention of Torture and Inhuman or Degrading Treatment or Punishment* CPT/Inf (91) 15. For a graphic account of conditions in British prisons see Stern, *Bricks of Shame* (1987).
45. [1994] 1 All ER 97.
46. [1990] 3 All ER 237.
47. [1987] 1 All ER 324.
48. See Sturm, 'The Legacy and Future of Corrections Litigation' (1994) 142 *University of Pennsylvania Law Review*, 639.
49. These cases include *Weeks v United Kingdom*, Series A, No. 114 (1987) 10 EHRR 293 (recall of discretionary lifer without judicial hearing violates Art. 5(4)), *Thynne, Wilson and Gunnell v United Kingdom*, Series A, no. 190 (1990) 13 EHRR 666 (decision not to release discretionary lifer after expiry of tariff period without judicial hearing violates Art. 5(4)). But see also *Wynne v United Kingdom*, Series A, No. 294-A (1994): no violation where decision not to release mandatory lifer was taken without any opportunity for judicial hearing.
50. [1981] 1 WLR 754.
51. (1988) 86 CrAppRep 59.
52. [1993] 3 All ER 92.
53. *The Times*, 11 August 1994.
54. *R. v Secretary of State for the Home Department, ex p. Benson, The Times*, 21 November 1988.
55. [1992] QB 740.
56. Nor do they apply in Northern Ireland, to which the Criminal Justice Act does not extend and where the Secretary of State has not made a formal separation of tariff and risk elements in relation to either mandatory or discretionary lifers.
57. Unreported 21 October 1992.
58. Unreported 28 April 1994.
59. Unreported December 1994.
60. For details, see n. 49, above.

61. *Golder v United Kingdom*, Series A, No. 18 (1975) 1 EHRR524.
62. *Silver v United Kingdom*, Series A, No. 61 (1983) 5 EHRR 347.
63. Series A, No. 233 (1992) 15 EHRR 137.
64. Series A, No. 80 (1984) 7 EHRR 165.
65. For a discussion of these changes see Livingstone, 'The Changing Face of Prison Discipline' in Player and Jenkins, eds, *Prisons After Woolf: Reform Through Riot* (1993) pp 97–111. In Northern Ireland boards of visitors adjudications were retained in the 1995 Rules although the maximum period for loss of remission has been reduced to ninety days. This might still encounter difficulties with Art. 6 of the Convention.
66. Notably the work of Michael Jackson on the impact on prisons in British Columbia. See 'Justice Behind the Walls—A Study of the Disciplinary Process in a Canadian Penitentiary' (1974) 12 *Osgoode Hall LJ.* 1, and 'The Right to Counsel in Prison Disciplinary Hearings' (1986) 20 *University of British Columbia LR* 221.
67. A possibility discussed in Loughlin, 'The Underside of the Law: Judicial Review and the Prison Disciplinary System' (1993) 46 *Current Legal Problems* 23, at pp 49–50.
68. Again a development prompted by the *Silver* decision indicating that censorship of prisoners' correspondence, based on a prison rule that correspondence could be stopped if it was 'objectionable', was too vague to be a restriction 'prescribed by law', as required by Art. 8(1) of the Convention. Standing orders provide more detail on when letters can be stopped.
69. The 1995 version of which comes complete with a summary of significant judicial review decisions on adjudications in appendix 4.
70. [1985] AC 318.
71. For a thorough criticism of the *Findlay* decision see Richardson, *Law, Process and Custody: Prisoners and Patients* (1993) pp 178–9.
72. See for example *Morin v National Special Handling Review Committee* [1985] 2 SCR 662 and for a discussion Livingstone, 'Designing a Statutory Framework for Prison Administration: The Experience of the Corrections and Conditional Release Act 1992' (1995) *Anglo-American Law Review* (forthcoming).
73. For a view that this is so, see Richardson, 'From Rights to Expectations' in Player and Jenkins (eds) *Prisons After Woolf: Reform Through Riot* (1993) pp 78–96.
74. The example of the *Hague* case has already been given. Another recent example was that of *R. v Governor of Long Lartin Prison, ex p. Ross, The Independent*, 9 June 1994 where the prisoner was initially simply told that he was regarded as 'disruptive'. The judicial review elicited the information that he was regarded as one of a number of prisoners who were having a destabilising effect on the wing as revealed in the reports of a number of prison officers.
75. Especially after the applicant's solicitor gave documents which were read out in open court to a journalist who wrote several articles on the topic. The solicitor was subsequently prosecuted for contempt, leading to a further European human rights case and ultimately a friendly settlement. See *Home Office v Harman* [1983] AC 260 and *Harman v United Kingdom* (friendly settlement reported in *Stocktaking* 1986).
76. See Taylor, 'Bringing power to particular account: Peter Rajah and the Hull Board of Visitors' in Carlen and Collinson (eds) *Radical Issues in Criminology* (1980) p. 28.
77. Especially in Northern Ireland where Hadfield and Weaver found that 42 per cent of all judicial review applications in 1987–91 emanated from the prisons, see 'Trends in Judicial Review in Northern Ireland' [1994] *Public Law* 12. See further the chapter by Brigid Hadfield, below.
78. For one view of a prison governor recognising this, see Coyle, letter in Prison Reform Trust *Prison Report*, No. 30, p. 28 (1995): 'From the inside, one sometimes feels that prisons must be the most inspected, audited, overseen set of institutions in the country. That is as it should be, since we are the most abnormal institutions in the country, charged with depriving human beings of their liberty.'

Chapter Seven

Judicial Review and National Security

Brice Dickson

Introduction

One of the most important objectives of any government is to ensure the security of the state. In seeking to achieve this objective the government will inevitably rely upon a wide variety of institutions and will insist upon many of the activities of these institutions being kept secret so that enemies of the state cannot learn how to undermine its defences. Undeniably such secrecy *can* be in the public interest. When it is truly at stake, national security *is* a vital matter.

The difficulty, of course, is determining when national security is truly at stake. There is also the problem of who should be the final arbiter of that issue, for something which may seem to one group of people to be a relatively minor matter may to others take on a much greater significance. It is natural to expect persons who are charged with the task of safeguarding national security to adopt a cautious attitude: they will usually be unwilling to run any risks with security because they know that if a breach does occur the consequences may be extremely serious and they could ultimately be held responsible.

The principal aim of this chapter is to explore in some detail, by reference to case law drawn from different contexts, whether the procedure of judicial review can be used to regulate the government's reliance upon the concept of national security. Can the procedure ensure, for instance, that national security is not employed as a blanket cover for secret operations in an attempt to render executive action automatically immune from legal challenge? Conversely, can it ensure that where secrecy is genuinely required it is legally guaranteed? The rise and rise of judicial review in recent years might lead casual observers to suppose that its utility in this context is clearly demonstrable. Unfortunately this optimism would be misplaced. Such advances as have been made in this area are comparatively minor in scope. The law is still something of a blunt instrument and has not yet adopted a noticeably nuanced approach.

National Security and the Rule of Law

Whenever a judge is asked to grant an application for judicial review in spite of the respondent's reliance on the concepts of national security, what he or she really has to decide is the strength of society's commitment to that great organising principle known as 'the rule of law'. This principle connotes different things to different people, but at its heart in today's modern world is surely the idea that—as far as possible—every act performed within society must be capable of being labelled either lawful or unlawful. The label does not always have to be applied by a judge—it can be enough if there is some demonstrably fair process of adjudication available—but obviously the involvement of a judge will more easily legitimise the labelling process. In accordance with this basic idea there must be no, or at any rate very few, matters which are non-justiciable: whoever performs the act, whatever the circumstances in which that performance takes place, an act must be capable of measurement against established criteria in order that a final determination may be made as to whether it is lawful or not.

That judicial review applications play such a crucial role in the implementation of the rule of law has been recognised for decades. Most recently the point was eloquently repeated by Laws J. writing extra-judicially:

> The prospect of judicial examination of public decisions to test their reasonableness has none of the arresting quality of a Bateman cartoon; it is regarded as an elementary necessity, a function of the rule of law itself.[1]

For a similar statement from the academic community one need only turn to the standard text by de Smith and Brazier:

> [The courts] do stand in a very real sense as the ultimate arbitrator of the balance between the demands of effective government and individual interests.[2]

In the United Kingdom, however, one of the greatest obstacles to a full-blown application of the rule of law is the traditional allegiance to the age-old doctrine of parliamentary sovereignty,[3] supposedly a bedrock principle of our unwritten constitution and one that continues to be defended despite the fact that because parliament is in practice almost totally controlled by the government of the day, even if recalcitrant backbenchers can sometimes influence the extent of that control, it is in reality the government, not parliament, which seeks to assert legal infallibility. In addition, the government of the day continues to be able to exercise residual *prerogative* powers in areas traditionally out of bounds to parliament. Mercifully the legal systems of the United Kingdom have rejected the notion of government infallibility. Judicial review of government decisions is nowadays fairly commonplace,[4] but a government is still able to hide behind the rule that, once it has succeeded in getting its decisions passed into law in the form of a parliamentary Act, it is home and dry as far as a challenge in the courts is concerned. The imperviousness of Acts to judicial review remains the biggest obstacle to the complete florescence of the rule of law in Britain today and is itself a severe blow to the credibility of judicial review as a mechanism for ensuring justice.

We should remember that for this obstacle to be overcome society does not need to await the adoption of a completely new written Constitution. Instead judges have it within their power to begin developing their own principles against which parliamentary Acts can be measured. In 1969 the highest court in the land dealt a body-blow to so called 'ouster' clauses, through which parliament sometimes seeks to preclude judicial review,[5] and in 1992 the House of Lords took another momentous step when it decided that judges can, albeit in limited circumstances, refer to *Hansard* when deciding how to interpret statutory language.[6] Moreover, the *Factortame* and *ex parte EOC* decisions mean that the operation of an Act can be suspended if it contravenes European Community law.[7] It would not, therefore, be a completely revolutionary development if the House of Lords were to decide in the near future that whenever parliament enacts primary legislation it must adhere to certain fundamental principles. Indeed this has already been recognised by a serving law lord, Lord Woolf:

> ... ultimately there are even limits on the supremacy of Parliament which it is the courts' inalienable responsibility to identify and uphold. They are limits of the most modest dimensions which I believe any democrat would accept. They are no more than are necessary to enable the rule of law to be preserved.[8]

Another serving law lord, Lord Browne-Wilkinson, has suggested that control is already operating by virtue of the principles contained in the European Convention on Human Rights.[9] Likewise Laws J., in the article referred to above, puts forward the general thesis that, even without the incorporation of the European Convention on Human Rights into domestic British law, judges in Britain have at their disposal a variety of tools for developing the common law so as to ensure that it reflects the propositions enshrined in that Convention.[10] With particular reference to judicial review, Laws J. suggests as follows:

> We should apply differential standards in judicial review according to the subject-matter, and to do so deploy the tool of proportionality, not the bludgeon of *Wednesbury*. A function of this is to recognise that decision-makers whose decisions affect fundamental rights must inevitably justify what they do by giving good reasons; and the judges should not construe statutes

which are said to confer power to interfere with such rights any more favourably than they would view a clause said to oust their own jurisdiction.[11]

It remains to be seen whether in discrete areas of the law his Lordship's fellow judges will adhere to this way of thinking. His path may be the preferred way forward, but are judges already programmed to go down a different track, one which calls for a less interventionist attitude on their part? Certainly if judges were to adopt tools such as a doctrine of proportionality, a duty to give reasons and a presumption against statutes interfering with rights, they would find themselves dealing with an even wider range of sensitive issues in judicial review applications than they do at the moment.[12] The potential for conflicts of opinion between executive bodies and the judiciary, not to mention between parliament and the judiciary, would be greatly enhanced, and one particular area where we could expect clashes to arise would be in the interpretation of national security.

In the present state of the law the phrase 'national security' is an extremely vague one which can mean different things to different people and can cover a multitude of sins. There is no definition of it in any legal dictionary, bar one or two of the most modern ones which simply repeat the *dicta* in the *GCHQ* case[13] to the effect that national security is a non-justiciable issue. Neither Stroud's *Judicial Dictionary of Words and Phrases*[14] nor Butterworths' *Words and Phrases Legally Defined*[15] include the phrase. *Brownlie's Law of Public Order and National Security*[16] and other specialist books on judicial review[17] are equally unhelpful in this regard. What can be said, though, is that national security is not itself an activity; it is rather an objective which other activities are intended to achieve. In principle, therefore, it should not be cited in isolation as the justification for keeping judges away from particular matters: if judicial involvement is not desirable it must be because the activities in question— not their goal—are deemed incapable of assessment by a judge. If the courts are to take seriously their concern to uphold the rule of law they must begin to 'unpack' the phrase 'national security' and decide which of the particular activities it embraces are or are not justiciable and in what circumstances.[18]

We shall now explore the current law on judicial review and national security by looking in turn at cases concerning prerogative powers, exclusion orders, immigration, employment and inquests. Fortunately the unpacking process mentioned above has already been commenced, even if only very tentatively. We still await a more systematic judicial dissection of the concept of national security.

Prerogative Powers

In a great number of situations where challenges to administrative action are rebuffed on the ground that national security is at stake, respondents will seek to strengthen their argument by indicating that what was done was an exercise of the Crown prerogative. Until recently the prevalent view was that prerogative powers represented an absolute no-go area for judicial review.[19] In fact, case law shows that this combination of circumstances does not necessarily guarantee the failure of an application for judicial review. The law is not completely black or white in this context.

The first important case on the point was *The Zamora*[20]. It was there that one of the most forthright judicial statements on national security was issued, one which many judges have cited with approval in subsequent cases:

> Those who are responsible for the national security must be the sole judges of what the national security requires. It would be obviously undesirable that such matters should be made the subject of evidence in a Court of law or otherwise discussed in public.[21]

Like all *obiter dicta* this statement must be read in context. In the first place Lord Parker was not saying that no evidence of any description could be adduced in relation to national security, only that whether or not something was required by national security should not be the subject of evidence. He and his fellow judges in the Privy Council actually held that although judges could not second-guess the government on what was required by national security, they could nevertheless require evidence to be adduced showing that the government was indeed relying on considerations of national security when it took certain steps.

In the second place, in the very dispute before them the Privy Council rejected the government's case. At first instance the judge in the Prize Court had made an order allowing the requisition of copper found on board a ship which had been arrested *en route* from the United States to Sweden during the First World War. The affidavit of the Director of Army Contracts merely stated that it was desired on behalf of His Majesty to requisition the copper. On appeal the Privy Council held, somewhat remarkably given the circumstances of the time and the make-up of the court,[22] that the judge's order had to be set aside 'because the judge had before him no satisfactory evidence that such a right [of requisition] was exercisable'. Indeed the Privy Council added, though again this was arguably *obiter*, that whereas a prerogative Order in Council declaring a blockade would *prima facie* justify the condemnation of vessels attempting to enter blockaded ports, it would not preclude evidence being adduced to show that the blockade was ineffective and, therefore, unlawful. Similarly, the court said that an Order in Council authorising reprisals would be conclusive as to the facts recited showing that a case for reprisals existed, but would not preclude the right of the court to hold that the use of such reprisals was unlawful because they entailed a degree of inconvenience on neutral parties which was unreasonable in all the circumstances of the case.

It can be seen, therefore, that even in 1916 judges were not prepared blindly to accept the government's reliance on national security. A comparable independence of spirit was displayed in the *GCHQ* case some seventy years later.[23] There the main issue was whether the exercise of prerogative powers over the civil service could be judicially reviewed, an Order in Council having been issued by the Minister for the Civil Service[24] which banned trade unions from the government's Communications Headquarters at Cheltenham without any prior consultation with the unions themselves. The House of Lords held that the power's exercise could be challenged but that as soon as the minister in question produced evidence to show that the action was taken on grounds of national security no court could attempt to assess the reliability of that evidence. The position was well summed up by Lord Fraser:

> The question is one of evidence. The decision on whether the requirements of national security outweigh the duty of fairness in any particular case is for the Government and not for the courts; the Government alone has access to the necessary information, and in any event the judicial process is unsuitable for reaching decisions on national security. But if the decision is successfully challenged, on the ground that it has been reached by a process which is unfair, then the Government is under an obligation to produce evidence that the decision was in fact based on grounds of national security.[25]

On one reading of the last sentence in Lord Fraser's statement, the obligation to produce evidence arises only if the government's decision is successfully challenged on the ground of unfairness. No such limitation was mentioned in *The Zamora*, however, and the better view is that Lord Fraser was referring only to the circumstances of the particular case before him, where the complaint was that no proper consultation had occurred before the minister's action was announced.

Lord Scarman went slightly further in his speech than any of his brethren. He observed that the question as to what is required in the interest of national security can arise in different forms:

> The question may arise in ordinary litigation between private persons as to their private rights and obligations: and it can arise, as in this case, in proceedings for judicial review of a decision by a public authority. The question can take one of several forms. It may be a question of fact which Parliament has left to the court to determine: see for an example section 10 of

the Contempt of Court Act 1981.[26] It may arise for consideration as a factor in the exercise of an executive discretionary power. But, however it arises, it is a matter to be considered by the court in the circumstances and context of the case.[27]

Lord Scarman went on to say that in the last type of case (where the interest of national security is a factor to be considered in the review of the exercise of executive discretionary power):

> . . . the court will accept the opinion of the Crown or its responsible officer as to what is required to meet [the interest of national security], unless it is possible to show that the opinion was one which no reasonable minister advising the Crown could in the circumstances reasonably have held.[28]

The fact that in the House of Lords two grounds were mentioned as being capable of founding a challenge to the Crown's reliance on national security—unfairness and unreasonableness—is some evidence of a chink existing in what used to be widely considered as an impervious brick wall,[29] and while it is possible to characterise the judges' refusal to go behind the government's reliance on national security on the facts of this particular case as 'timorous',[30] the *GCHQ* judgments did clearly have an impact on the government in so far as they brought home to ministers that there was always a judge looking over their shoulders, even on matters traditionally located within the sphere of governmental prerogative powers.[31] The case seems to have been the prelude to a spate of other applications for judicial review aimed at challenging administrative decisions taken by the government.[32]

It is worth remembering that both of the cases just discussed were civil cases. Do the judges adopt a similar hands-off attitude to the concept of national security whenever the context is a criminal trial? At first glance they do, even though the consequences can then be much more serious in that the refusal to go behind the government's definition of national security may mean a defendant receiving a lengthy prison sentence.[33] In *Chandler v DPP*[34] supporters of the Campaign for Nuclear Disarmament (CND) were charged with conspiring to commit a breach of section 1 of the Official Secrets Act 1911 by entering a prohibited place (an RAF base in Essex) for a purpose 'prejudicial to the safety or interests of the state', namely, sitting in front of aircraft in an attempt to prevent them taking off. Havers J. would not allow the defendants to call evidence to show that their purpose was not prejudicial to the interests of the state (they believed it would be beneficial to the United Kingdom if it gave up nuclear armament). The accused were accordingly convicted by the jury and sent to prison. The House of Lords saw nothing wrong with the approach adopted by the judge, Lord Reid saying that in his opinion it was clear:

that the disposition and armament of the armed forces are and for centuries have been within the exclusive jurisdiction of the Crown and that no one can seek a legal remedy on the ground that such discretion has been wrongly exercised.

The same judge did, however, say, in the passage immediately preceding the above, that he did not subscribe to the view that the government or minister must always or even as a general rule have the last word about what is or is not *in the public interest*, and Lord Radcliffe agreed that Ministers of State did not have any inherent general authority to prescribe to the courts what is or is not prejudicial to *the interests of the state*.[35] It seems that, while each judge considered the disposition and armament of the armed forces to be a subject worthy of ring-fencing against judicial interference, they were not prepared to accord similar status to all other subjects affecting the safety or interests of the state. Furthermore, in *R. v Ponting*,[36] despite a direction to the jury by McCowan J. that the interests of the state were synonymous with the interests of the government, the defendant was acquitted of breaching section 2(1) of the Official Secrets Act 1911[37] after he had sent documents to an MP because he believed the government was deliberately misleading parliament over the sinking of the Argentinian warship *General Belgrano* during the Falklands campaign. This remarkable example of 'jury equity' lends further support to the view that the government of the day does not in law have a monopoly over the definition of state security interests.

Nor, it seems, do the police, at any rate not when, on behalf of the state, they choose to perform their duty to detect and prevent crime by tapping telephones. In *Malone v Metropolitan Police Commissioner*[38] a man whose telephone had been tapped sought to sue the police for breach of confidence. In the High Court he lost but he then took his case to Strasbourg (there was no suggestion that he had first to pursue the fruitless task of appealing all the way through the British court system to the House of Lords). The European Court of Human Rights decided that the English law on telephone-tapping was not 'laid down with reasonable precision in accessible legal rules that sufficiently indicated the scope and manner of exercise of the discretion conferred on the relevant authorities',[39] and this meant that the court did not have to decide whether the tapping was 'necessary in a democratic society in the interests of national security, [or] public safety [or] . . . for the prevention of disorder or crime'.[40]

The European Court's decision led to the enactment of the Interception of Communications Act 1985,[41] section 2 of which permits the Secretary of State to issue a warrant requiring a telephone to be tapped if the Secretary of State considers that the warrant is necessary (a) in the interests of national security, (b) for the purpose of preventing or detecting serious crime, or (c) for the purpose of safeguarding the economic well-being of the United

Kingdom. Section 2(3) goes on to say that when deciding whether a warrant is necessary the Secretary of State must take into account whether the information which is sought could reasonably be acquired by other means. Section 7 of the Act creates a tribunal with powers to investigate applications from any person who believes that his or her phone has been tapped and, in particular, power to investigate whether there has been any contravention of section 2. In drawing conclusions from the investigation the Tribunal is enjoined to apply 'the principles applicable by a court on an application for judicial review'.[42] There is also a Commissioner, appointed by the Prime Minister, to keep under review the carrying out by the Secretary of State of the functions conferred by (*inter alia*) section 2[43] and the Commissioner has stated that in doing this job he too will apply the principles of judicial review.[44] These provisions, therefore, permit a further degree of second-guessing of government activity in this sphere, though presumably the Tribunal and Commissioner cannot probe any more deeply than a judge could do. The question, then, is to what extent can a judge probe?

Before the Interception of Communications Act 1985 was brought into force a further case concerning telephone-tapping came before the courts. In *R. v Secretary of State for the Home Department, ex parte Ruddock*[45] one of the leaders of the CND (later to become a Labour MP) challenged the Home Secretary to say whether or not her telephone and those of two of her colleagues were being tapped. A suggestion to that effect had been made in a Channel 4 television programme by a former employee of the Home Office, Cathy Massiter. The Home Secretary declined to confirm whether or not tapping had occurred and argued that the court should not investigate the matter. In support of both positions he relied upon the government's prerogative powers to intercept communications in the interests of national security and to determine for that purpose what the interests of national security actually required.[46] Although on the facts Ms Ruddock did not succeed in obtaining a declaration that the Home Secretary had not followed published criteria on telephone-tapping, nor that he had been guilty of misfeasance in public office, Taylor J., as he then was,[47] did say that he would accept the Home Office's plea of national security only if it were supported by cogent evidence. His words are so important that they are worth citing in full:

> I do not accept that the court should never inquire into a complaint against a minister if he says that his policy is to maintain silence in the interests of national security. To take an extreme and one hopes unlikely example, suppose an application were put before the court alleging a warrant was improperly issued by a Secretary of State against a political opponent, and suppose the application to be supported by the production of a note in the

minister's own hand acknowledging the criteria did not apply but giving instructions that the phone be tapped nevertheless to see if anything discreditable could be learnt. It could not be sensibly argued that the department's invariable policy of silence should require the court meekly to follow suit and decline to decide such a case. At the other extreme, I recognise there could occur a case where the issue raised was so sensitive and the revelations necessarily following its decision so damaging to national security that the court might have to take special measures (for example sitting in camera or prohibiting the mention of names). Conceivably (although I would reserve the point) in an extreme case the court might have to decline to try the issues. But in all such cases, cogent evidence of potential damage to national security flowing from the trial of the issues would have to be adduced, whether in open court or in camera, to justify any modification of the court's normal procedure. Totally to oust the court's supervisory jurisdiction in a field where *ex hypothesi* the citizen can have no right to be consulted is a Draconian and dangerous step indeed. Evidence to justify the court's declining to decide a case (if such a course is ever justified) would need to be very strong and specific.[48]

Even if read in the narrow context of powers to tap telephones, these are strong words indeed. They demonstrate a pronounced reluctance on the part of judges to cede jurisdiction to government ministers. Indeed that a judicial review application was brought at all in the *Ruddock* case indicates how far the law on national security had moved by 1986. When coupled with the references to principles of judicial review in the 1985 Act, the dicta of the future Lord Chief Justice show that the law *can* control governmental reliance upon national security. There is no immediately apparent reason why similar control could not be exercised in other contexts where national security raises its head. This is not to say that such a reason can never exist, but if it does it needs to be clearly articulated so that a serious judicial evaluation of its weight can be undertaken. This is, in effect, what happened in the recent case of *R. v Secretary of State for the Home Department, ex parte Leech*[48a], where the Court of Appeal held that rule 33(3) of the Prison Rules 1964 was *ultra vires* the Prison Act 1952. The judges found that, although section 47(1) of the 1952 Act did by necessary implication confer a power to make prison rules for the examining of correspondence to and from prisoners in the interests (*inter alia*) of national security, rule 33(3) went too far in that it authorised the governor to stop any letter or communication 'on the ground that its contents are objectionable or that it is of inordinate length'. In the context of invasions of privacy, therefore, judges are prepared to challenge the government's interpretation of what is required in the interests of national security if this interpretation is clearly exorbitant.

The view that it no longer matters, as far as judicial review is concerned, whether the source of the power being judicially reviewed is the Crown prerogative, legislation or the common law has been convincingly presented by Munro.[49] He makes it clear that what really counts is the subject matter being dealt with by the power, not the source of the power, and as authority he cites the apposite words of Lord Roskill in the *GCHQ* case (which no doubt Taylor J. had in mind when deciding the *Ruddock* case):

> It must, I think, depend on the subject matter of the prerogative power which is exercised . . . Prerogative powers such as those relating to the making of treaties, the defence of the realm, the prerogative of mercy, the grant of honours, the dissolution of Parliament and the appointment of Ministers as well as others are not, I think, susceptible to judicial review because their nature and subject matter is such as not to be amenable to the judicial process.[50]

Whilst one can applaud this statement of principle one must also express regret that Lord Roskill did not thoroughly apply it to the facts before him by holding that he could not interfere with the government's decision to ban trade unions at GCHQ because the subject matter in issue was the defence of the realm, not because the government had asserted that such a step was necessary in the interests of national security. The former, it is submitted, is a much more acceptable category to put forward as falling exclusively within the competence of the government of the day. Merely to assert something 'in the interests of national security' is not a specific enough justification for ousting the jurisdiction of the courts, whether the context be telephone-tapping, the banning of unions or the requisitioning of ships. National security is the goal which activities such as defending the realm seek to achieve, in the same way, for example, as preserving friendly relations with other states is the goal pursued by treaty-making. National security is not itself an 'activity' worthy of automatic immunity from judicial scrutiny, nor is it a 'power', let alone a prerogative power. The protection of national security is an end, not a means to an end. This basic flaw in governmental reliance on the concept of national security is more fully exposed in other contexts, especially the context of judicial review of exclusion orders issued under emergency powers.

Emergency Powers and Exclusion Orders

'Emergency powers' is not usually a term of art in British law.[51] Usually they are conferred by legislation initiated not after a proclamation of emergency but as a government reaction to its assessment that society is seriously threatened by the actions of a disaffected or dangerous organisation. Examples of such legislation are the Official Secrets Act 1911[52] and the anti-terrorism Acts of recent years—the Northern Ireland (Emergency Provisions) Acts (the EPAs) and the Prevention of Terrorism (Temporary Provisions) Acts (the PTAs).[53] Such Acts inevitably infringe human rights, but supposedly for the sake of a greater good.

When judicially reviewing emergency powers, the courts seem content to apply the standard criteria listed by Lord Diplock in the *GCHQ* case— procedural impropriety, irrationality and illegality, but commentators still assert that the principles upon which judges review administrative action should, and do, differ depending on the particular context in which the action is taken.[54] Bonner, in his leading monograph on emergency powers, has to concede that the exact state of the law is still unclear in this area:

> Much may depend on judicial attitudes to the suitability for judicial control of the subject area concerned and to the respective worth of the particular interests advocated for protection by protagonists before them and on the identity of the decision-maker. It cannot be gainsaid that this is a policy or value-laden area of law in which it may be more difficult than in other areas to predict the outcome of cases.[55]

Further factors may combine to make the law uncertain in this context. The range of persons recognised as having *locus standi* to challenge an emergency measure may be restricted because fewer persons could be said to have a 'legitimate expectation' of prior consultation. It may also be more difficult to launch a challenge because there may not be a fully reasoned decision on which such a challenge can bite, and the concepts of bad faith, irrationality and procedural impropriety all take on a less elastic interpretation when the process being examined has been played out against the backcloth of an emergency. In short, the very circumstances of an emergency will tend to make it less likely that a successful challenge to executive action can be mounted. The paradox is that it is in the context of emergencies that a particularly penetrating application of the principles of judicial review may be called for if basic rights are to be fully protected.[56]

For present purposes there is one clutch of emergency law cases which casts especial light on the ability of the judicial review procedure to get behind a government's reliance on national security. These are the cases relating to exclusion orders. Under the Prevention of Terrorism (Temporary Provisions) Act 1989 an exclusion order is issued by a Secretary of State. The recipient can make representations to the Secretary of State and may be granted, if he or she so requests, an interview with a person nominated by the Secretary of State as an adviser.[57] There is no provision for routinely involving a judge.

The first significant challenge to this procedure was issued in 1987 by a Mr Stitt. His application for judicial review was summarily rejected by an English Divisional Court on the basis that the power to issue the order was exclusively the preserve of the Secretary of State. To begin with, Watkins LJ. replied to counsel's argument that terrorism did not necessarily raise issues of national security:

> One should say, I think, as plainly as can be, that terrorism goes to the security of the State. It strikes at the security of the people too, and that is so, whether it is violence which comes from without or within.[58]

Macpherson J. took the same line:

> The Secretary of State is in my judgment, in these circumstances which plainly involve security and the safety of individuals who may have been concerned, the only person to judge the matter.[59]

Counsel for Mr Stitt then argued that, because the issue of an exclusion order is a quasi-criminal procedure, the Home Secretary is obliged to give particulars:

> . . . not fine details, such as one would expect in an actual criminal process, but sufficient information to someone like the applicant to let him know what kind of terrorist he is and when he is supposed to have carried out his terrorist activities, and, broadly speaking, the nature of them.[60]

Again Watkins LJ. could not accept this. He was 'overwhelmingly' of the view that the Home Secretary is absolutely right not to give reasons when making an exclusion order under this legislation, and in coming to this conclusion he was greatly influenced by the words of Lord Shackleton in his earlier review of the PTA:

> Information which is specific about a person's participation in an act of terrorism may be known to only two or three people. It could, without difficulty, be traced back to its source if it became known to the subject of the exclusion order or to a wider circle of his associates and friends.[61]

The result was the same on both counts when a further challenge was made to an exclusion order five years later in *ex parte O'Neill*.[62] In this case, however, although Rose J. showed little hesitation in dismissing the application, feeling himself bound by the Divisional Court's decision in *Stitt*, he did end his judgment by agreeing with counsel that in such cases it was not enough for the Home Secretary to rely upon 'a general blanket claim that national security applies'. He said that some more details were required, but that in the case before him this requirement was satisfied by the following passage in the affidavit of a Home Office official:

> It was not possible for the applicant (nor is it ever possible for any person against whom such an order is made) to be informed, in greater detail than is set out in the exclusion order, of the reasons why the order was made or the information which led to it being made or why the order could not be revoked. This is because to do so might well lead to the discovery of sources of information available and so possibly compromise police operations and/or put at risk the lives of informants or their families . . .[63]

It would appear, therefore, that it is not enough merely to cite the phrase 'national security' as a justification for automatically declining to review an exclusion order. There must be further evidence that the exclusion is justified because of information supplied by an informer. In both *Stitt* and *O'Neill* there *was* such evidence, not in the exclusion orders themselves but in letters sent separately by the Home Office. In the absence of such evidence, it is submitted, it would not be enough, in law, for the government to assert that an exclusion order has been imposed because a person is suspected of being involved in terrorism or for reasons of national security. Something more specific is called for than the mere incantation of the statutory phrase. A suspicion of involvement in terrorism may in some cases derive not from an informer's information but from police observations or forensic evidence, and in those instances the subject of the order should be allowed to know more details and to comment on the information. Only in genuine cases of informer evidence should secrecy be required, and even then one has to wonder whether the judge has to be kept completely in the dark. It would, of course, be possible to allow the judge to view the evidence in private. Although this immediately runs the risk of implicating the judiciary in executive acts, thereby potentially destroying their reputation for impartiality, such a risk is already run through using judges as Commissioners under the Interception of Communications Act 1985 and the Security Service Act 1989.[64]

If judges have the legal right to go behind the government's assertion that national security is involved in an exclusion order, even to the limited extent just outlined, the correlative duty on the government's part is to express the reasons underlying their assertion. At present, of course, the duty to give reasons for administrative actions does not generally exist in British law. According to received wisdom, which will no doubt change in the near future, the duty to give reasons arises only where fundamental rights are at stake or where the decision taken is aberrant.[65] Cases involving exclusion orders are obviously cases where the fundamental right of free movement is at stake and one would, therefore, expect reasons to be issued in such instances. Moreover, when the law requires reasons to be given it also requires them to be meaningful: they must be proper, adequate reasons which will not only be intelligible but also deal with the substantial points which have been raised.[66] In the present writer's opinion this entails the government saying not just that exclusion is required in the interests of national security but that it is required because the government has evidence from a source, which must remain anonymous, that the excluded person is or has been involved in terrorist acts. In most cases it would not be unreasonable to expect the government to give examples of such acts, or a rough indication of the period during which they were supposedly committed.

In 1994 three further cases raised a fresh challenge to the exclusion order phenomenon, this time by relying on provisions in European Community law. The first was *ex parte Gallagher*[67], followed less than six months later by a case brought on behalf of the President of Sinn Féin, Gerry Adams.[68] Both of these applications for judicial review were stayed pending a reference of questions to the European Court of Justice in Luxembourg. In the third case, *ex parte McQuillan*, the judge stayed the proceedings until the European Court of Justice had returned its answers to the questions posed in the two earlier cases. Unfortunately, it now appears that none of these cases will ultimately be decided by a European ruling, for in April 1995 judges in England accepted a Home Office application to have the reference in the *Adams* case withdrawn, his exclusion order (like McQuillan's) having been lifted in October 1994.[69]

To understand the legal issues arising in these three cases one has to remember that under the PTA the Secretary of State must exercise his power to make exclusion orders:

> in such a way as appears to him expedient to prevent acts of terrorism ... connected with the affairs of Northern Ireland[70]

and he must first be satisfied that the person to be excluded:

(a) is or has been concerned in the commission, preparation or instigation of acts of terrorism to which this Part of this Act applies; or

(b) is attempting or may attempt to enter [Great Britain, Northern Ireland or the United Kingdom] with a view to being concerned in the commission, preparation or instigation of such acts of terrorism.[71]

For present purposes 'terrorism' is defined as 'the use of violence for political ends, [including] any use of violence for the purpose of putting the public or any section of the public in fear'.[72] There is no reference anywhere in the Prevention of Terrorism Act to the need to protect national security, nor is that phrase always employed in the correspondence entered into by the government with the excluded person. This is, however, the phrase around which argument has centred in these three cases.

In *ex parte McQuillan* counsel for the applicant argued that the court could in principle re-examine the Home Secretary's decision even where national security was an element in the balance. She wanted to know what were the national security matters weighed by the Secretary of State and what contrary weight he had given to the applicant's fears that if he remained in Northern Ireland rather than move to Great Britain he would be attacked by loyalist paramilitaries and thus be in danger of losing his right to life.[73] Counsel for the Secretary of State argued that the courts' power to go behind an assertion of national security, and to examine the relevant documents, was confined to criminal cases (itself a revealing concession) and to public interest immunity claims in civil cases which did not raise a national security issue. He further suggested that, because the exclusion order procedure was statutory, nothing could be added to it.

Both sides also argued over European Community law, which of course takes precedence over domestic law. Article 48 of the Treaty of Rome guarantees freedom of movement for workers within the territory of member states of the Community, but 'subject to limitations justified on grounds of public policy, public security or public health'.[74] In turn, what can count as 'public security' is defined by EC Directive 64/221, Article 6 of which provides that the person concerned is to be told the grounds of public security on which the decision in his or her case is based unless this would itself be contrary to the interests of state security. In addition, Article 223.1.a of the Treaty of Rome exempts a state from having to supply information if it considers disclosure to be 'contrary to the essential interests of its security'.

In his judgment in *ex parte McQuillan* Sedley J. said that, because the Home Secretary's power to issue exclusion orders was so Draconian, 'the courts would scrutinise his reasoning closely and draw the boundaries of rationality tightly around his judgment'.[75] He thought the courts would be particularly keen to balance both sides with great care in a case which called the right to life into question (as here, where Mr McQuillan feared assassination). Although his personal view was that the reasons given for exclusion orders did not necessarily amount to reasons of national security at all, the learned judge felt constrained by the doctrine of precedent to follow the earlier decisions in such cases (including *ex parte Adams* and *ex parte Gallagher*) and, therefore, not to go behind the order.

Sedley J. did not feel able to refer any further questions to the European Court of Justice. He believed that the questions already referred in *ex parte Adams* and *ex parte Gallagher* covered all the relevant points. In *ex parte Adams* the questions asked whether Article 8a(1) of the Maastricht Treaty conferred additional rights of free movement to those in Article 48 of the Treaty of Rome and, if so, whether these rights are directly effective so that citizens may invoke them before national courts.[76] In addition the English Divisional Court wanted to know whether Article 8a(1) applies to situations which are wholly internal to a member state and how the principle of proportionality is to be applied when the right of free movement clashes with interests of national security. In *ex parte Gallagher* the questions posed were whether the person nominated to advise the Secretary of State under schedule 2 of the PTA is a 'competent authority' for the purposes of EC Directive 64/221 and whether article 9 of that Directive prohibits the Secretary of State from making an exclusion order until he has received the opinion of a competent authority (under the PTA an order is made *before* the nominated adviser becomes involved). An opinion of the European Court of Justice on all of these points would be received with great interest.

It is worth noting that the key concept in European Community law, both in Article 48 of the Treaty of Rome and in EC Directive 64/221, is, for present purposes, 'public security'. This is surely a more sensible phrase to employ than 'national security' for, despite what the judges said in *ex parte Stitt*, it is not immediately obvious that terrorism, whether or not it is connected with the affairs of Northern Ireland, always raises questions of national security. Surely it cannot be said that national security is put at risk with each and every terrorist act? Possibly what has prompted the use of the phrase is the involvement of the internal security service (MI5) in the fight against terrorism. The existence of that service has recently been officially recognised by the Security Service Act 1989, section 1(2) of which provides that its function shall be:

> the protection of national security and, in particular, its protection against threats from espionage, terrorism and sabotage, from the activities of agents of foreign powers and from actions intended to overthrow or undermine parliamentary democracy by political, industrial or violent means.

It is interesting, however, that during the Bill's Second Reading in the House of Commons the Home Secretary explained the reference to national security as follows:

> By its very nature, the phrase refers—and can only refer—to matters relating to the survival or well-being of the nation as a whole, and not to party-political, sectional or lesser interests.[77]

It is possible to deduce from this comment that the phrase 'national security' in the 1989 Act should not be interpreted as embracing activities of paramilitary organisations affecting the survival or well-being of only one part of the United Kingdom, but it must be conceded that this argument would run counter to the interpretation of the 1989 Act adopted by the Commissioner appointed thereunder, Stuart-Smith LJ.[78] It would also contradict the government's stance when, before the European Court of Human Rights in *Brannigan and McBride v UK*[79], it vigorously—and successfully—defended its derogation notice under the European Convention on Human Rights on the basis that there was a public emergency 'threatening the life of the nation'.

Immigration

Claims of national or public security are frequently raised in the context of immigration or deportation disputes. An early example is *R. v Brixton Prison Governor, ex parte Soblen*.[80] There the applicant challenged a deportation order on the basis that the Secretary of State had acted for an improper purpose, namely, to comply with a request by the United States, rather than because deportation was 'conducive to the public good'[81] in the United Kingdom. The Court of Appeal held that deportation was an act of an executive, not of a judicial or quasi-judicial, character and so Mr Soblen was not entitled to an opportunity to submit representations against the making of the order or to challenge in any court the Home Secretary's discretion to issue the order,[82] but here too the ban on judicial supervision was said not to be absolute.[83] In the words of Lord Denning MR:

> The court cannot compel the Home Secretary to disclose the materials on which he acted, but if there is evidence on which it could reasonably be supposed that the Home Secretary was using the power of deportation for an ulterior purpose, then the court can call on the Home Secretary for an answer: and if he fails to give it, it can upset his order.[84]

Donovan LJ. was even more explicit, saying the applicant may:

> sow such substantial and disquieting doubts in the mind of the court about the bona fides of the order he is challenging that the court will consider that some answer is called for. If that answer is withheld, or, being furnished, is found unsatisfactory, then, in my view, the order challenged ought not to be upheld, for otherwise there would be virtually no protection for the subject against some illegal order which had been clothed with the garments of legality simply for the sake of appearances . . .[85]

In a subsequent case, *R. v Secretary of State for Home Affairs, ex parte Hosenball*,[86] the Court of Appeal appeared less willing to intervene, even to the limited extent conceded in *Soblen*. It affirmed the decision of a three judge Divisional Court that Mr Hosenball, an American journalist, should be deported from Britain because that was conducive to the public good. In an affidavit on behalf of the Secretary of State it was deposed that the Secretary of State had personally considered Mr Hosenball's request for further information of the allegations against him but had decided that it was not in the interests of national security to disclose such information. Mr Hosenball complained that there had been a breach of the rules of natural justice and applied for an order of certiorari to quash the deportation order.

Without referring to his judgment in the *Soblen* case, Lord Denning MR admitted that if this had been a case in which the ordinary rules of natural justice had to be observed, he would have directed some criticism at the Home Office. He continued, however, as follows:

> But this is no ordinary case. It is a case in which national security is involved: and our history shows that, when the state itself is endangered, our cherished freedoms may have to take second place. Even natural justice may suffer a setback. [He then cited dicta from two wartime cases, *R. v Halliday, ex parte Zadig*[87] and *Liversidge v Sir John Anderson*[88] and went on:] That was said in time of war. But times of peace hold their dangers too. Spies, subverters and saboteurs may be mingling amongst us, putting on a most innocent exterior. They may be endangering the lives of the men in our secret service, as Mr Hosenball is said to do. If they are British subjects, we must deal with them here. If they are foreigners, they can be deported. The rules of natural justice have to be modified in regard to foreigners here who prove themselves unwelcome and ought to be deported.[89]

Cumming-Bruce LJ. spoke in similarly uncompromising terms:

> In my view, the field of judicial scrutiny, by reference to the enforcement of the rules of natural justice, is an extremely restricted field in the sphere of the operations necessary to protect the security of the state. There is a certain range of such operations which depend for their efficacy entirely on secrecy, and they are none the less important for that reason.[90]

It is noteworthy that in a parallel case the European Commission of Human Rights held that a state was not required to grant a hearing to an alien whom the public authorities of that state had decided to deport on grounds of security:

> . . . this constitutes an act of state falling within the public sphere and . . . does not constitute a determination of civil rights or obligations within the meaning of article 6 [of the European Convention on Human Rights].[91]

Despite the judicial attitude displayed in *ex parte Hosenball*, the applicant in *N.S.H. v Secretary of State for the Home Department*,[92] who was a stateless person of Palestinian descent, again tried to challenge the Home Secretary's decision that he should not be granted indefinite leave to remain in the United Kingdom on the grounds of national security. The Home Secretary relied upon Article 33.2 of the UN's Convention Relating to the Status of Refugees, which allows a refugee to be sent away from a country, even to a place where his or her life might be under threat, if there are reasonable grounds for regarding him or her as a danger to the security of that country. Dillon LJ. held that the Home Secretary had 'sufficiently particularised' the grounds on which he regarded the applicant as a danger to the country's security. These had appeared in a letter sent to the applicant and in affidavits from Home Office officials; they referred to the applicant's former membership of the Palestine Popular Struggle Front and to his clandestine negotiations with members of the Provisional IRA.

Dillon LJ. concluded that the Home Secretary had 'shown enough to make it clear that there was no basis on which the Divisional Court could properly quash [the Home Secretary's] decision that there were reasonable grounds for regarding [the applicant] as a danger to the security of the United Kingdom'.[93] The judge's conclusion was based on the assumption that some evidence had to be produced for the decision, even if the court could not ask for chapter and verse. Neill LJ. operated from the same starting point:

> It may well be that, save perhaps in most exceptional circumstances, it would not be sufficient for the Secretary of State merely to state that there were reasonable grounds for regarding a person as a danger to the security of the country without giving any information whatever as to the nature of the activities relied upon.[94]

In *Manzoor Hussain v Secretary of State for the Home Department*[95] the applicant sought to have quashed a decision of the Home Secretary of November 1992 whereby the latter had refused to revoke an order made against the applicant under the Immigration Act 1971 excluding him from the United Kingdom. The order had been made on the ground that the applicant's presence in the United Kingdom was not conducive to the public good for reasons of national security. When the matter came before Hutchison J. affidavit evidence was supplied on behalf of the Home Secretary which set out in more detail the reasons why the Home Secretary was refusing to revoke the order:

> The reason for the making of the exclusion order in 1984 was that the Applicant was known to be engaged with others in the supply of arms and other services to a foreign Government involved in international terrorism, including terrorism directed against United Kingdom interests. It would not be in the interests of national security to give further details of the information which formed the basis of the Secretary of State's decision, but the matters taken into account by the Secretary of State went beyond the matters in connection with which the Applicant was charged with others and acquitted in 1983.[96]

The applicant's counsel argued that these reasons were still totally inadequate, and contrasted them with the more expansive reasons given by the Secretary of State in the *N.S.H.* case,[97] but the Court of Appeal had little difficulty in holding that the Home Secretary's affidavit was perfectly sufficient:

> It is not necessary for him to have gone beyond the formula that he there employed. I am very much alive to [counsel's] point that it is all too easy for anybody in the position of swearing an affidavit . . . to simply use a formula, a mere matter of words on each occasion which defeats the applicant's case. However, in the present application I do not find that to be the case.[98]

Farquharson LJ. did, however, stress that the court's inability to go into questions of national security was dependent upon the executive affording 'sufficient material' to justify the case they are putting. This presupposes a readiness to review the interpretation of national security if no evidence at all were submitted.

In *R. v Secretary of State for the Home Department, ex parte Cheblak*[99] the applicant, a Lebanese citizen born in Palestine in 1944, had been living in the United Kingdom since 1975 and had been granted indefinite leave to remain in 1987. In January 1991, however, on the outbreak of hostilities in the Gulf, he was served with a notice that he was to be deported and was immediately detained. He applied for a writ of *habeas corpus* and for leave to apply for judicial review, but he failed on both counts. During the course of the High Court hearing counsel for the Home Secretary said she was authorised to give further information as to the nature of the allegations against the applicant:

> The Iraqi Government has openly threatened to take terrorist action against unspecified Western targets if hostilities break out in the Gulf. In the light of this, your known links with an organisation which we believe would take such action in support of the Iraqi regime would make your presence in the United Kingdom an unacceptable security risk.[100]

The Court of Appeal decided that it could not go behind this assessment of the national security position. Having cited the *Hosenball* case, Lord Donaldson MR stressed that:

> In accepting, as we must, that to some extent the needs of national security must displace civil liberties, albeit to the least possible extent, it is not irrelevant to remember that the maintenance of national security underpins and is the foundation of all our civil liberties.[101]

With the greatest of respect, this smacks of over-simplification. It reveals a touching belief that everything the government undertakes in the name of national security must be in furtherance of existing liberties. It takes no account of the possibility that the government may be underhand, or simply misguided. On the other hand, Lord Donaldson MR was right to point out that under the Immigration Act 1971 a person who is to be served with a deportation order can make representations (in writing and in person) to an independent advisory panel presided over by a senior judge[102] and that this panel is itself 'susceptible of judicial review if, for example, it could be shown to have acted unfairly within its terms of reference'.[103] So, although all three judges in *Cheblak* were prepared to renounce jurisdiction to inquire into matters of national security, they nonetheless expected applicants to be given *some* evidence for a deportation order and *some* opportunity to challenge it. Of course the question remains why can a judge review the government's assessment of national security matters when sitting on independent advisory panels, but not when sitting to hear judicial review applications?

In *R. v Secretary of State for the Home Department, ex parte Chahal*[104] the applicant, an Indian Sikh, had again been issued with a deportation order on the ground that this was conducive to the public good and in the interests of national security. He then claimed political asylum but the Home Secretary rejected the claim. The rejection was successfully judicially reviewed before Popplewell J. who, remarkably, said that the Home Secretary must reconsider the matter in the light of a report by Amnesty International on the persecution of Sikhs in India.[105] After the Home Secretary had reconsidered the case, and again rejected the asylum claim, the applicant sought judicial review once more. This time it was argued on behalf of the Secretary of State that, once he had reached the conclusion that deportation was conducive to the public good, it did not matter whether the applicant was a refugee and entitled to asylum. Both the judge at first instance, Potts J., and the Court of Appeal held that in law this was not so.

The judges relied on rule 161 of the Immigration Rules, which states that nothing in the rules is to be construed as requiring action contrary to the United Kingdom's obligations under the 1951 Convention on the Status of Refugees (and the later Protocol thereto). Article 32(1) of that Convention provides that states shall not expel a refugee lawfully in their territory save on grounds of national security or public order. Article 33(1) then provides that no state shall expel a refugee to the frontiers of territories where his life or freedom would be threatened on account of his race, religion, nationality, membership of a particular social group or political opinion, but Article 33(2) adds that Article 33(1) shall not benefit a refugee whom there are reasonable grounds for regarding as a danger to the security of the country in which he is. In *Chahal* Staughton LJ. agreed with academic writers that the threat to life or freedom in Article 33(1) had to be balanced by the Home Secretary against the danger to the security of the country in Articles 32(1) and 33(2), despite a dictum to the contrary in the *N.S.H.* case.[106]

On the facts of *Chahal* Staughton LJ. and his fellow judges decided that the Home Secretary had in fact conducted the necessary balancing exercise. The court then said that it was not possible for it to consider whether the decision reached after that exercise was irrational or perverse, but it seemed to suggest that the reason why this review was impossible was not that the court was always precluded from questioning a decision involving consideration of national security but simply that the Home Secretary had sufficiently indicated the nature of the evidence which had led him to regard the applicant as a risk to national security.[107] The implication is that if the evidence had not been made available a judicial review might have succeeded. The courts, thus, are still refusing to conduct a balancing exercise themselves but are insistent that the body which took the challenged decision must itself be able to demonstrate that such an exercise was conducted before the decision was made.

The attitude and tone of the judges in *ex parte Chahal* can be interpreted as supporting the view that the most recent cases on immigration are gradually moving away from the strict non-interventionist stance adopted in earlier cases such as *Soblen* and *Hosenball*. In this context also the judges are requiring *some* evidence to back up a reliance upon national security, even if not as much evidence as applicants' counsel would wish. This mirrors the position currently applying in the context of prerogative powers and PTA exclusion orders, although in immigration cases the authorities seem more willing to provide details of the reasons for their actions. Whether it be as a result of the influence of international standards (as enshrined in the Refugee Convention) or because of pressures emanating from other legal contexts, there is emerging a more enlightened approach whereby in the immigration context the word of a government minister is no longer taken as gospel without further ado. The courts are still some way off from making their own substantive assessment of when national security is truly at stake—and they may well never get that far, probably quite rightly—but it is submitted that they are tentatively feeling their way towards ensuring that requirements of procedural fairness are meaningfully fulfilled. As yet no duty to give detailed reasons has been explicitly imposed, but faltering steps in that direction can be detected.

Employment Cases

Two of the cases already discussed under the heading of prerogative powers were in fact employment disputes.[108] But national security can also become an issue in the more specific context of employment discrimination. Legislation on this matter has proliferated during the past three decades,[109] but a little known fact is that all of the existing laws contain a provision which permits discrimination if security or public safety is at stake.[110] A typical example is article 53 of the Sex Discrimination (NI) Order 1976:

(1) Nothing in Part III of this Order shall render unlawful an act done for the purpose of safeguarding national security or of protecting public safety or public order.

(2) A certificate signed by or on behalf of the Secretary of State and certifying that an act specified in the certificate was done for a purpose mentioned in paragraph (1) shall be conclusive evidence that it was done for that purpose.

These are the words which were in issue in the important case of *Johnston v Chief Constable of the Royal Ulster Constabulary*.[111] The Chief Constable had refused to renew the contracts of part-time female police reservists for the reason that he needed reservists who could use firearms and his policy was not to arm female officers. The Secretary of State for Northern Ireland endorsed the Chief Constable's view by issuing a certificate under article 53(2) to the effect that such discrimination was required in the interests of national security. The industrial tribunal in Northern Ireland thought that this raised a question under EC law, namely, whether it breached the provisions of EC Directive 76/207 on the implementation of the principle of equal treatment for men and women with regard to access to employment, vocational training and promotion. Accordingly, the tribunal referred the matter to the European Court of Justice in Luxembourg.

The ECJ responded by saying that a provision such as article 53(2), with its reference to 'conclusive evidence', was contrary to the principle of effective judicial control laid down in Article 6 of the 1976 Directive. Article 6 requires all member states to introduce into their national legal systems:

such measures as are necessary to enable all persons who consider themselves wronged by failure to apply to them the principle of equal treatment . . . to pursue their claims by judicial process after possible recourse to other competent authorities.

The ECJ also declared that Article 2(2) of the Directive, which allows member states to exclude from the Directive's field of operation those occupational activities for which the sex of the worker constitutes a determining factor, had to be interpreted strictly. On receipt of this judgment the tribunal in Belfast looked again at the Chief Constable's arguments and concluded that there was no good reason for refusing to renew these particular contracts. The women concerned received a total of nearly £1 million compensation and the Chief Constable was even ordered to pay their legal costs, a most unusual outcome in a tribunal hearing.

Whilst this case was not one of judicial review, the same result would doubtless have occurred if the application had been to the High Court in Belfast using that procedure, rather than to an industrial tribunal for unlawful discrimination. The case illustrates the subordinate position of British law to EC law, but of course its impact is limited to legal questions about which EC law has something to say. There is a great deal of EC law on sex discrimination, and on discrimination based on nationality,[112] but otherwise the scope for controlling the use of the national security criterion under EC rules is limited.[113] To date, no such challenge in the field of religious or political discrimination has been successful. In this context the certificates are known as section 42 certificates because that is the section in the Fair Employment (NI) Act 1976 which authorises their issue.[114] The leading case is *R. v Secretary of State for Northern Ireland, ex parte Gilmore.*[115] Mr Gilmore had applied for a post as residential social worker at St Patrick's Training School on the Glen Road in Belfast. He appears to have been recommended for appointment by the Training School's Board of Management but when it sought the approval of the Northern Ireland Office, which it was required by law to do,[116] this was refused. Mr Gilmore concluded that the refusal was on account of his former prominence in student politics as a member of the Workers' Party. In a letter the NIO denied this but said that the lack of approval was 'for reasons of public safety and public order'.

The judge, Carswell J. (as he then was), who has a reputation for not being over-sympathetic to judicial review applications, was careful to distinguish between two decisions being challenged. The first was the NIO's refusal to approve of the applicant's appointment; the second was its decision to issue the section 42 certificate. In relation to the first decision Carswell J. stated it to be clear that:

> section 42 of the 1976 Act cannot apply to issues which are not referable to complaints of unlawful discrimination contrary to the terms of the Act. In so far as the applicant's case may depend upon arguments not so referable, the Secretary of State's certificate certainly could not constitute conclusive evidence of any matter or preclude judicial review of the decision . . . [117]

He went on to say that if the applicant alleged unlawful political discrimination, then the certificate would appear to be a conclusive answer to it—unless the certificate is itself held invalid. In expansion of this he canvassed the various ways in which a challenge might be mounted. He found it unnecessary to issue a categorical decision on whether such challenges could ever be successful—because it was not necessary to do so in order to answer the question posed to him in the preliminary point of law with which he was then dealing—but after surveying some relevant authorities[118] he felt that he should state his view in the interests of limiting the issues:

> In my opinion the applicant cannot make the case that the decision to give the certificate was perverse or irrational or made without any rational justification . . . Nor do I think that it could be attacked on the *Wednesbury*[119] grounds, if there were evidence giving a foundation for such an attack.

The learned judge did, however, leave open the possibility that the decision could be challenged on the ground that it had not been taken in good faith, citing in support the words of Lord Loreburn LC. in *Board of Education v Rice*:[120]

> In such cases the Board of Education will have to ascertain the law and also to ascertain the facts. I need not add that in doing either they must act in good faith and fairly listen to both sides, for that is a duty lying upon everyone who decides anything.

In Northern Ireland the Fair Employment Agency, now the Fair Employment Commission, has been consistently in favour of the repeal of section 42. While the present Commission accepts that from time to time decisions must be taken on the basis of national security considerations, it is concerned at the conclusive nature of the certificate, at the apparent lack of safeguards to ensure the system is not discriminatory and at the absence of any mechanism of review. Since 1976 section 42 has had the effect of preventing thirty-nine persons from proceeding with complaints they had initiated, six of these being cases where national security alone was invoked.[121] Only in one instance was a complainant able to pursue the claim further, namely where the Ministry of Defence admitted that in carrying out its vetting procedures it had checked the name only of the Catholic applicant for the job in question: vetting is permitted, but not of one religious group only![122]

The only comparable case to have been decided in England is *R. v Director of GCHQ, ex parte Hodges*.[123] Here Mr Hodges, who had been employed at GCHQ for more than four years, had his positive vetting clearance withdrawn because of 'the frequency and nature of his homosexual relationships and the social circles which he frequented in consequence of his homosexual inclinations'. When he appealed against this decision the fact that he had allowed his name to be disclosed to the press and public comments to be made on the circumstances of his case was taken by the management as confirmation of their serious doubts as to his discretion and reliability. The Director of GCHQ swore an affidavit to the effect that the positive vetting arrangements stemmed from recommendations of the Security Commission as a result of serious leaks of information which prejudiced national security. Counsel for Mr Hodges argued (a) that Mr

Hodges was not treated fairly in that he had not been given a copy of the notes made by the officer who conducted an interview with him, and (b) that the matters of fact upon which the decision was based did not in any way justify such a decision (i.e. *Wednesbury* unreasonableness).

Glidewell LJ. dealt with the case by relying upon the House of Lords' pronouncements in the *GCHQ* case, the case where he himself, at the High Court stage, had allowed the trade union to succeed.[124] He noted that only Lord Scarman suggested that the courts might intervene if it were possible to show that the opinion was one which in the circumstances could not reasonably have been held. Glidewell LJ., with some reluctance, found himself bound by such high authority, but he did nevertheless state his personal view in case the opinion of Lord Scarman were to be adopted as the correct law. This view was that it was not possible to say that the Director of GCHQ had arrived at an unreasonable, absurd or irrational decision.

The judge went on to say, having cited relevant dicta from Lord Fraser and Lord Roskill in the *GCHQ* case, that the same inability to intervene did not apply to the question of fairness. He noted that, whether they were obliged to or not, GCHQ did supply Mr Hodges and his solicitor with a résumé of the facts elicited at an interview in November 1986 and an account of the reasons for the various decisions taken in connection with Mr Hodge's vetting. He went on:

> Those facts having been disclosed, and there being no suggestion that their disclosure is not in the national interest, the question whether or not fairness— the rules of natural justice as they are sometimes called—required that GCHQ should go further and disclose the notes taken in November 1986 is one that on the face of it did not itself involve national security.[125]

The learned judge then examined what the rules of natural justice required and held that on the facts before him they had been satisfied:

> What is appropriate is that a person who is having a privilege withdrawn from him shall be given an indication of what is alleged against him; be told in general terms the facts upon which the initial decision has been based; shall be given an opportunity to correct those facts and comment upon them; shall be given an opportunity to present any arguments which he wishes to present; and shall not be taken in any sense by surprise. In my view all those characteristics were contained in the procedure followed by GCHQ in this case.[126]

The government's reliance upon national security can also come under scrutiny if, in its capacity as employer, it issues a Public Interest Immunity Certificate to seek to keep secret some information which the employee is trying to discover. This is what occurred in *Balfour v Foreign and*

Commonwealth Office,[127] where the former British vice-consul in Dubai was challenging his dismissal from the diplomatic service for allegedly accepting £5,000 from an Iranian businessman whom police suspected of being a terrorist. The Court of Appeal dismissed Mr Balfour's application for discovery of classified documents which he thought would clear his name (his defence being that he had been asked to befriend the Iranian businessman by an officer from MI6). Russell LJ. cited with apparent approval Lord Diplock's statement in the *GCHQ* case that national security 'is *par excellence* a non-justiciable question'.[128] He added:

> There must always be vigilance by the courts to ensure that public interest immunity of whatever kind is raised only in appropriate circumstances and with appropriate particularity, but once there is an actual or potential risk to national security demonstrated by an appropriate certificate the court should not exercise its right to inspect.[129]

When the application came on for hearing at an industrial tribunal the position of Mr Balfour was made even more difficult by the members of the tribunal deciding that the evidence should be heard in private: the chairman said that the cover of agents could be blown if evidence was heard in public, even though he conceded that 'much of the evidence has no national security implications'.[130]

Nor is the European Convention on Human Rights of any real assistance in this context. In *Leander v Sweden*[131] the European Court of Human Rights unanimously held that the vetting in question had not breached Article 8 of the Convention because every state enjoys a wide margin of appreciation as regards the requirements of national security. Similarly, in *Esbester v UK* the European Commission declared inadmissible a complaint to the effect that vetting procedures under the Security Service Act 1989 were not in compliance with the requirements of Article 8. In particular the European Commission considered that 'the protection of national security' was a sufficient definition of the Security Service's functions and that those functions were subject to express limitations as well as to supervision by a Commissioner and a Tribunal.[132]

From this review of four British cases in the employment field— *Johnston*, *Gilmore*, *Hodges* and *Balfour*—it is possible to draw the conclusion that a decision not to employ someone on grounds of national security cannot be impugned unless (a) there is a principle of EC law which can be called in aid, (b) the decision can be shown to have been taken in bad faith, or (c) it can be shown that the principles of natural justice—if applied at all—have not been complied with fully. Limited though they may be, these are more extensive grounds for review than exist in any of the other contexts examined in this chapter. There is no obvious reason why this should be so, for although the right to earn a living is an extremely important right, it can hardly be said to rank noticeably higher than, say, the right to liberty or to freedom of movement. It is possible that the ethos of equal opportunities, which so imbues the anti-discrimination legislation in the employment field, has exerted a positive influence.

Inquests

At inquests a full investigation of the circumstances surrounding a death is sometimes said to be impossible because national security interests are involved. Although the important cases on this point are connected with the Troubles in Northern Ireland, for the most part they have revolved around the question of what precisely is the scope of an inquest and on this there are two important recent English decisions. These have confirmed that the purpose of an inquest is limited and that it should not be used as an excuse for a general inquiry into extraneous matters, including matters connected with national security.

In *R. v Coroner for Western District of East Sussex, ex parte Homberg*[133] five people had died after a fire had broken out in a flat. The fire had been started deliberately by a man who later killed himself but the next-of-kin of the fire victims wanted the inquest to investigate as well the absence of fire escapes in the building. In the Divisional Court Simon Brown LJ. rejected their application for a fresh inquest. He concluded that none of the purposes identified by the Broderick Committee in 1971 as served by a coroner's inquiry would be fulfilled by an 'elaborate approach to the identification of so called secondary causes and their inclusion within the actual verdict'.[134] He added:

> The duty to inquire 'how' the deceased died does not to my mind properly encompass inquiry also into the underlying responsibility for every circumstance which may be said to have contributed to the death.[135]

This conclusion is perhaps strange, given that the third of the five purposes listed in the Broderick Report is 'to draw attention to the existence of circumstances which, if unremedied, might lead to further deaths', but it is consistent with what the Divisional Court has said on other occasions.[136]

The same approach was adopted by the English Court of Appeal in *R. v North Humberside and Scunthorpe Coroner, ex parte Jamieson*,[137] where the inquest related to the death of a prisoner who had hanged himself. He had previously warned the prison authorities that he intended to take his own life and the next-of-kin sought to have the inquest consider the prison authorities' alleged lack of care. Sir Thomas Bingham MR firmly rejected the application, saying that, apart from identifying the deceased and the place and time of death, the purpose of an inquest was to decide how he or she died:

> 'How' is to be understood as meaning 'by what means'. It is noteworthy that the task is not to ascertain how the deceased died, which might raise general and far-reaching issues, but 'how . . . the deceased came by his death', a more limited question directed to the means by which the deceased came by his death . . . There can be no objection to a verdict which incorporates a brief, neutral, factual statement . . . but such verdict must be factual, expressing no judgment or opinion . . . [138]

In a recent Northern Irish case, *ex parte McNeill*, the Lord Chief Justice placed considerable store by these two English authorities. The case concerned the death of three men who in January 1990 were shot by one or both of two British soldiers while the men were in the act of robbing a bookmaker's premises in Belfast. As was their right under the law,[139] the two soldiers elected not to give oral evidence at the inquest, but their statements were to be read to the jury. The coroner directed, however, that four other soldiers who were present at the incident should attend to give oral evidence,[140] but the Secretary of State for Defence signed a Public Interest Immunity Certificate (PIIC) in relation to three of these four soldiers.[141] In this certificate it was asserted that the terrorist campaigns of violence in the United Kingdom, and in particular within Northern Ireland, threatened national security in a direct and immediate way. The Secretary of State added that there were special units of the armed forces in Northern Ireland which carry out security and intelligence work, that the three soldiers in question were members of these units, and that the very nature of the units' work required secrecy if it was to be effective. He, therefore, wanted the soldiers to give their evidence behind a screen, hidden from all present except the coroner, the jury and the legal representatives of any properly interested persons. The coroner, however, refused to accept this certificate, ruling that PIICs were not appropriate in situations where there are no documents and only oral evidence is envisaged. McCollum J. quashed this decision on an application for judicial review brought by the Ministry of Defence and the Court of Appeal upheld the judge's decision.

It is difficult to quarrel with the judgments of McCollum J. and of the Court of Appeal in so far as they show that PIICs *can* be an appropriate vehicle of objection even in relation to oral evidence[142] but, although the coroner lost, the case is still remarkable on at least two fronts: first, because the PIIC in question went into considerable detail, both as to the categories of information which public interest required to be protected from disclosure and as to the bases upon which such protection was founded, and secondly, because the Court of Appeal, especially Sir Brian Hutton LCJ., attempted an examination of the ambit of the term 'national security'. To some extent the latter seems to have been a consequence of the former: the relative openness of the Ministry of Defence prompted a more refined differentiation on the part of the court.

Of particular relevance was the following passage in the PIIC:

> The disclosure of, or evidence about, the nature and activities of the special units of the Armed Forces in Northern Ireland or about the identity and physical appearance of their members would substantially impair the operational effectiveness and efficiency of the units and put at risk the lives of their members and their families.[143]

Relying on this, counsel for the Ministry of Defence argued that the minister's certificate that a certain procedure would harm national security was conclusive. Hutton LCJ., however, did not accept that a judicial balancing exercise, between the need for open and public justice and the claims for national security, was automatically precluded. Having cited dicta from *Conway v Rimmer*,[144] the *GCHQ* case[145] and *Balfour v Foreign and Commonwealth Office,*[146] he noted that these were all cases where the claim of national security was advanced against the claim of an individual plaintiff or trade union. The case before him, he went on, was not of this latter kind:

> Here the claim is itself a fundamental principle based on the well-being of the community, and that is the principle of open justice. In my opinion the judgments . . . in *Attorney General v Leveller Magazine* . . . make it clear that where the claim of national security is raised in such a way that it may conflict with the principle of open justice, the courts must balance the claims and decide whether there should be a restriction of the principle of open justice in order to meet the claims of national security.[147]

He then proceeded to quote his own words in the earlier case of *Doherty v Ministry of Defence*,[148] another case on the screening of witnesses:

> . . . the question whether a witness should be screened is a matter relating primarily to the administration of justice which has to be determined by the court, and . . . the court is not precluded from determining that issue because of a certificate of the Secretary of State in relation to matters of national security.[149]

The Lord Chief Justice then went further by analysing the phrase 'national security' itself. He noted that the cases where statements had been made to the effect that courts are not equipped to assess and evaluate matters of national security were cases 'where the area of national security involved was at a high level', in relation, for example, to the plans of a submarine,[150] to the security of United Kingdom military and official communications,[151] or to the location of British intelligence agents in the Middle East.[152] He then wondered whether the principle should apply with the same force to the activities of two or three soldiers engaged in security duties in Northern Ireland, and he again referred to his own earlier judgment in *Doherty v Ministry of Defence*,[153] where he had expressly reserved his opinion on the question to what extent the plea of 'national security' could be raised in respect of the whole range of activities of army units combating terrorism in Northern Ireland. He now answered that question by deciding that the activities of three or four undercover soldiers:

> are towards the bottom of the scale of matters coming within the concept of national security and are activities which a court is competent to assess and the importance of which a court is entitled to balance against the importance of the requirement of justice.

The Lord Chief Justice then remitted the case back to the coroner for a new decision on whether the witnesses should indeed be screened.[154] MacDermott LJ. and Nicholson J. issued short concurring judgments, the former saying that 'a Certificate founded on grounds of public interest relating to national security should relate with appropriate particularity to the individuals in respect of whom the Certificate is issued . . .'[155]

As luck would have it, Nicholson J. found himself issuing a judgment in another judicial review of an inquest less than a month later. This was *In Re Toman*,[156] where the Chief Constable was seeking to have set aside writs of *subpoena* directing him to submit copies of the Stalker and Sampson Reports to the inquest.[157] These were reports prepared by police officers for transmission to the Director of Public Prosecutions, and the Secretary of State for Northern Ireland issued a PIIC certifying that it was in the public interest that information of this nature should not be revealed because its publication would be likely to cause serious harm to the fight against terrorism and thereby prejudice the interests of national security. In particular, the PIIC identified two grave concerns in relation to national security. One was the integrity and efficacy of the relevant security forces in their efforts to counter the terrorist threat and the other was the protection of the lives and safety of those involved, of their families and of persons who have provided or may provide information and intelligence to the security forces.

The learned judge asked himself whether the public interest in the integrity of the criminal investigation process outweighed the public interest in the disclosure of information which may assist the coroner at his inquests. He held that it did, because the Stalker and Sampson Reports were not relevant to the coroner's inquiry (all the evidence submitted to those inquiries having also been submitted to the inquest) and their disclosure would be an abuse of the process of the court. He also held that there was evidence that national security would be imperilled by the production of the reports and so the writs of *subpoena* had to be set aside. In the process of coming to his conclusions Nicholson J. referred to *Thorburn v Sir John Hermon*,[158] a case in England where Chief Superintendent Thorburn, who had been Mr Stalker's deputy during his inquiry in Northern Ireland, had sued the former Chief Constable of the RUC for alleged defamation during a Channel 4 news programme in June 1990 and in the process had sought disclosure of the Stalker and Sampson Reports. Otton J. held that he was not entitled to order disclosure, on the grounds of national security, but he added that even if he was so entitled he did not think that the plaintiff's interest in this case tilted the balance against the public interest founded on the integrity of the criminal investigation process:

> I am satisfied that the integrity of the process of criminal investigation requires that there should be freedom of communication between senior police officers conducting inquiries . . . and the DPP for Northern Ireland without fear that those documents will be subject to scrutiny and analysis in private litigation at some later date.[159]

Nicholson J., like Hutton LCJ. before him, was thus prepared to engage in a balancing exercise, even if he found it very easy to come down in favour of 'the integrity of the criminal investigation process' as against the disclosure of information which would imperil national security. Both judges upheld the government's reliance upon national security, but only after carefully considering (a) whether there was *prima facie* evidence that national security was indeed at stake, (b) how far up the scale of national security the activities in question were, and (c) what weight should be given to countervailing interests.

Conclusion

It is indisputable that in nearly every situation where a court is faced with a governmental claim that a decision was taken on the grounds of national security the court will be very loath to question that decision in any way. But in each of the five contexts examined in the course of this chapter there are signs that occasionally the judges are prepared to assert themselves more forcibly. At the moment it seems impossible to identify principles which will in all circumstances justify such assertiveness, but the main candidates for that status are the doctrines of proportionality, good faith and natural justice.

We may also be on the verge of a greater judicial willingness to get to the bottom of what is actually meant by national security in different contexts: while judges are prepared to concede that there will always be some areas of responsibility in which they should never be implicated, they apparently want the government to be more precise in its justifications for keeping judges at arm's length. They seem increasingly aware that there are activities which may in theory touch upon national security but which do not in practice put that security at risk even when further details are disclosed in court.

It is arguable that only in the most incontrovertible instances of threats to national defence should judges *not* have a say in deciding the legality of initially secret operations. To require them to abstain from intervention in less crucial matters is to chip away at the centrality of the rule of law. Adapting the words of Lord Donaldson MR cited earlier,[160] we can say that maintaining judicial control over decisions on national security is the surest foundation for all our civil liberties.

Notes

1. Sir John Laws, 'Is the High Court the Guardian of Fundamental Constitutional Rights?' [1993] PL 59. Laws J. was formerly a Treasury Devil who represented the government in many judicial review applications to which it was the respondent. See also his 'Judicial Remedies and the Constitution' (1994) 57 MLR 213. For other recent affirmations of the important role to be played by judges see the Hon. Beverley McLachlin, 'The Role of Judges in Modern Commonwealth Society' (1994) 110 LQR 260 and A. Lester QC, 'English Judges as Law Makers' [1993] PL 269.
2. *Constitutional and Administrative Law* (7th edn, 1994) at p. 580.
3. In the eyes of another distinguished practitioner, Michael Beloff QC, it is the sovereignty of parliament which means that 'in the new millenium the rule of law will *not* be superseded by the rule of Laws'. See 'Judicial Review—2001: A Prophetic Odyssey' (1995) 58 MLR 143, 147.
4. Recent examples include *R. v Secretary of State for the Environment, ex p. Hammersmith and Fulham LBC* [1991] AC 521 (review of government's decision to cap councils' community charges); *R. v British Coal Corporation and Secretary of State for Trade and Industry, ex p. Vardy and others* [1993] ICR 720 (review of Mr Heseltine's decision to close 10 coal collieries); *R. v Secretary of State for Transport, ex p. Richmond-upon-Thames LBC* [1994] 1 All ER 577 (review of decision to permit more night flying at London's airports); *R. v Secretary of State for the Home Department, ex p. Bentley* [1994] 2 WLR 101 (review of Home Secretary's refusal to grant a pardon); *R. v Secretary of State for Foreign and Commonwealth Affairs, ex p. Rees-Mogg* [1994] 2 WLR 115 (review of government's decision to ratify the Maastricht Treaty); *R. v Secretary of State for the Home Department, ex p. Hickey (No. 2)* [1995] 1 All ER 490 (review of Home Secretary's decision not to refer an alleged miscarriage of justice to the Court of Appeal); *R. v Secretary of State for Foreign Affairs, ex p. World Development Movement Ltd* [1995] 1 All ER 611 (review of Mr Hurd's decision to grant development aid to the Pergau dam project); *R. v Secretary of State for Home Affairs, ex p. the Fire Brigades Union* [1995] 2 All ER 244 (review of Home Secretary's decision to impose a new victims' compensation scheme).
5. *Anisminic v Foreign Compensation Commission* [1969] 2 AC 147.
6. *Pepper v Hart* [1992] 3 WLR 1032; for interesting comments see Sir Nicholas Lyell, '*Pepper v Hart*: The Government Perspective' (1994) 15 Statute LR 1; Lord Lester,

'*Pepper v Hart* Revisited', ibid., p. 10; J.C. Jenkins, '*Pepper v Hart*: A Draftsman's Perspective', ibid., p. 23.

7. *Factortame Ltd v Secretary of State for Transport (No. 2)* [1991] 1 AC 603 (the Merchant Shipping Act 1988); *R. v Secretary of State for Employment, ex p. EOC* [1994] 2 WLR 409 ('threshold' provisions in the Employment Protection (Consolidation) Act 1978).

8. '*Droit public*—English Style' [1995] PL 57, 69. Cf. Laws J. in 'Law and Democracy' [1995] PL 72, 92: 'Ultimate sovereignty rests, in every civilised constitution, not with those who wield governmental power, but in the conditions under which they are permitted to do so.'

9. 'The Infiltration of a Bill of Rights' [1992] PL 397.

10. He himself applied this philosophy in the high-profile case of *R. v Cambridge District Health Authority, The Times*, 15 March 1995, where he required a health authority to reconsider its decision not to continue funding treatment for a very ill young girl.

11. Above, n. 1, at p. 78.

12. Cf. *R. v Cambridge District Health Authority*, above, n. 10, where the CA reversed Laws J.'s decision on the same day: see [1995] 2 All ER 129.

13. [1985] AC 374, discussed in the next section.

14. 5th edn, 1986. Nor is there any mention of the phrase in Francis Bennion's *Statutory Interpretation* (2nd edn, 1992).

15. 3rd edn, 1988 and Supplements.

16. 1981.

17. See e.g. M. Fordham, *Judicial Review Handbook* (1994); G. Aldous and J. Alder, *Applications for Judicial Review* (2nd edn, 1993); R. Clayton and H. Tomlinson, *Judicial Review: A Practical Guide* (1993); M. Sunkin, L. Bridges and G. Mészáros, *Judicial Review in Perspective* (1993).

18. See generally K.D. Ewing and C.A. Gearty, *Freedom Under Thatcher: Civil Liberties in Modern Britain* (1990) ch. 5 ('The National Security State'). A particularly useful account is provided in L. Lustgarten and I. Leigh, *In from the Cold—National Security and Parliamentary Democracy* (1994), pp 323–334.

19. See e.g. I. Harden and N. Lewis in *The Noble Lie: The British Constitution and the Rule of Law* (1986) p. 200: 'There can be no doubt that the exclusion of prerogative powers from judicial review has left unstructured by law a number of aspects of administration which are no different in principle from others governed by statute.'

20. [1916] 2 AC 77.

21. At p. 107, per Lord Parker in the Judicial Committee of the Privy Council.

22. A point emphasised by Lord Fraser in the *GCHQ* case [1985] AC 374, 402G.

23. *Council of Civil Service Unions v Minister for the Civil Service* [1985] AC 374. For illuminating comments see C. Forsyth, 'Judicial Review, the Royal Prerogative and National Security' (1985) 36 NILQ 25.

24. Mrs Thatcher, as she was then, *qua* Prime Minister.

25. [1985] AC 374, 402C.

26. This section provides: 'No court may require a person to disclose, nor is any person guilty of contempt of court for refusing to disclose, the source of information contained in a publication for which he is responsible, unless it be established to the satisfaction of the court that disclosure is necessary in the interests of justice or national security or for the prevention of disorder or crime.' Lord Scarman himself unsuccessfully proposed a version of this (omitting the reference to 'interests of justice') when the Contempt of Court Bill was debated in the House of Lords. The Commons inserted the section as it stands, the reference to 'interests of justice' being included in order to preserve the decision of the House of Lords in *British Steel Corporation v Granada* [1980] 3 WLR 774.

27. [1985] AC 374, 404.

28. ibid., at p. 406H.

29. Cf. the metaphor used by Sir John Laws in [1993] PL 59 at 76: 'There are of course situations where it is the court's duty to safeguard the security of the state, as much of the public interest immunity litigation shows; though recent political initiatives as regards openness for the Security Services suggest that it is not necessarily best served by a blank wall with no doors or windows.'

30. Simon Lee, *Judging Judges* (1988) p. 69.

31. *The Judge Over Your Shoulder* was the title of a pamphlet first produced for civil servants in 1987 by the Treasury Solicitor's Department in conjunction with the Cabinet Office's Development Division. A new edition was issued in 1994.

32. See the cases cited above, n. 4.

33. This is an issue which may be touched upon in the forthcoming Report by Scott LJ. into the 'Arms for Iraq' affair.

34. [1964] AC 763.

35. If the same facts were to be tried today the court would be entitled to apply *Pepper v Hart* in order to look at the purpose behind s. 1 of the 1911 Act; as D. Thompson points out in [1963] PL 201, parliament had been assured by two attorneys-general and a Lord Chancellor that s. 1 was intended to apply to cases of espionage only.

36. [1985] CrimLR 318.

37. Under which it was an offence to disclose official information to anyone other than a person to whom it was, in the interest of the state, one's duty to communicate it. S. 2 was eventually replaced by s. 2 of the Official Secrets Act 1989.

38. [1979] Ch 344.

39. *Malone v United Kingdom* (1985) 7 EHRR 14, at para. 70 of the judgment.

40. Art. 8(2) of the European Convention on Human Rights.

41. I.J. Lloyd (1986) 49 MLR 86.

42. S. 7(4). See further, generally, the chapter in this book by Brigid Hadfield.

43. S. 8(1)(a).

44. Report of the Commissioner for 1989 (Lloyd LJ.) Cm. 1063, para. 4. Lloyd LJ. also states that the newly appointed Security Service Commissioner (Stuart-Smith LJ.) intends to apply the principles of judicial review and that the two Commissioners are to consult together to ensure that they apply the principles of judicial review broadly the same way.

45. [1987] 1 WLR 1482; I. Leigh [1987] PL 12.

46. The government retains a prerogative power to maintain law and order: *R. v Secretary of State for the Home Department, ex p. Northumbria Police Authority* [1988] 1 All ER 556.

47. He later became the Lord Chief Justice of England.

48. [1987] 2 All ER 518, at 526h–527b.

48a.[1993] 4 All ER 539.

49. *Studies in Constitutional Law* (1987) at pp 175–182. See also the chapter in this book by Andrew Le Sueur.

50. [1985] AC 374, 418.

51. The Payments for Debt (Emergency Provisions) Act (NI) 1971 did say that its provisions were to continue in force 'until six months after the end of the period of the present emergency', which was in turn defined as 'the period beginning with 1st October 1971 and ending on such date as the [Secretary of State] may by Order in Council declare to be the date on which the emergency that was the occasion of the enactment . . . came to an end'. During the debate on the proposed Act in the Stormont parliament it was acknowledged that the emergency in question was the rent and rates strike begun in certain parts of Northern Ireland in 1971 as a protest against the introduction of internment without trial. That strike was called off in 1976, but the Act was not repealed until 1991.

52. The Act passed through all of its Commons stages in less than an hour. Its origins are explored in the Report of the Franks Committee on section 2 of the Official Secrets Act 1911, Cmnd. 5104, 1972, ch. 4 and appendix III.

53. The first of the EPAs, which apply only in Northern Ireland, was passed in 1973. The stimulus was the grave political violence in Northern Ireland which in 1972 left 467 people dead, 321 of them civilians. The latest EPA dates from 1991; it must be renewed every year but will expire for good, unless replaced by a similar Act, in June 1996. The first of the PTAs, which apply throughout the United Kingdom, was passed in a hurry in 1974, immediately after the Birmingham pub bombings in November of that year which killed 21 civilians; the latest version dates from 1989 and expires in March of each year unless renewed (as to date it always has been).

54. Special considerations apply to actions taken during a period of declared martial law.

55. *Emergency Powers in Peacetime* (1985) at p. 53 (footnote omitted).

56. It was for this reason that non-governmental organisations meeting in Sicily in 1984 devised the Siracusa Principles, nos 30 and 31 of which call upon governments not to invoke national security as a reason for imposing limitations to prevent merely local or relatively isolated threats to law and order or as a pretext for imposing vague or arbitrary limitations.

57. Sch. 2 to 1989 Act.

58. *R. v Secretary of State for the Home Department, ex p. Stitt* (28 January 1987; unreported, but see LEXIS). Counsel for the Home Secretary was Mr Laws, later appointed to the bench and author of the article cited above, n. 1.

59. See the LEXIS Report.

60. See the LEXIS Report.

61. Cmnd. 7324 (1978) para. 52.

62. *R. v Secretary of State for the Home Department, ex p. O'Neill* (13 February 1992; unreported except on *LEXIS*).

63. See the LEXIS Report.

64. Lloyd LJ. served as Commissioner under the 1985 Act for six years; currently Sir Thomas Bingham MR fulfils the role. Stuart-Smith LJ. has served as Security Service Commissioner since the post was created by the Security Service Act 1989.

65. *R. v Civil Service Appeal Board, ex p. Cunningham* [1991] 4 All ER 310; *Doody v Secretary of State for the Home Department* [1994] 1 AC 531; *R. v Higher Education Funding Council, ex p. Institute of Dental Surgery* [1994] 1 WLR 242; *R. v London Borough of Islington, ex p. Hinds* (15 July 1994; unreported except on LEXIS). See generally P. Craig, 'The Common Law, Reasons and Administrative Justice' (1994) 53 CLJ 283.

66. *Re Poyser & Mills Arbitration* [1964] 2 QB 467.

67. 10 February 1994; unreported except on LEXIS.

68. *R v Secretary of State for the Home Department, ex p. Adams* (29 July 1994; unreported except on LEXIS).

69. *Ex p. Adams, The Independent, 28 April 1995.* The European Commission has intimated that in its opinion exclusion orders do not comply with EC legal standards: *The Guardian,* 6 March 1995.

70. S. 4(1) and (2).

71. S. 5(1) for entry into Great Britain; s. 6(1) for entry into Northern Ireland; s. 7(1) for entry into the United Kingdom.

72. S. 20(1).

73. Guaranteed by Art. 2 of the European Convention on Human Rights.

74. Art. 48.3.b.

75. p. 38 of the unrevised judgment.

76. Art. 8a(1) provides that: 'Every citizen of the Union shall have the right to move and reside freely within the territory of the Member States, subject to the limitations and conditions laid down in this Treaty and the measures adopted to give it effect.'

77. *Hansard* (1988–89), HC Debs., vol. 143, col. 1105 (15 December 1988). Immediately prior to this Mr Hurd said, 'I think that the term "national security" is now well

recognised and understood in statute' and at col. 1108 he observed that at col. 1105 he had 'defined it rather carefully and at rather greater length than previously'.

78. For his reports to date see Cm. 1480 (1990), Cm. 1946 (1991), Cm. 2174 (1992) and Cm. 2523 (1993). In this regard Stuart-Smith LJ. has not deviated from the views of the Commissioners appointed under the Interception of Communications Act 1985, Sir Thomas Bingham MR and Lloyd LJ. In his report for 1988 (Cm. 652, para. 10) Lloyd LJ. writes: '[National security] is narrower than the term "public interest" . . . but it is obviously wider than the three heads of counter-terrorism, counter-espionage and counter-subversion . . . Further than that I do not think it would be wise or indeed possible to go in defining what is covered by national security. Each case must be judged on its merits.'

79. (1994) 17 EHRR 539.

80. [1963] 2 QB 243; see Heuston, *Essays in Constitutional Law* (2nd edn, 1964) at pp 182–3 and more generally, L. Lustgarten and I. Leigh, n. 18 above, ch. 7.

81. Aliens Order 1953, art. 20(2)(b); Lord Denning said (at p. 301) that this provision supplanted and replaced the Royal Prerogative on the matter.

82. Lord Denning (at p. 298) thought there might be a right to make representations prior to the deportation order being executed and at the end of the case counsel told the court that the Attorney-General had said such an opportunity would be given to Mr Soblen.

83. Cf. *Bonsignore v Oberstadtdirektor der Stadt Köln* [1975] ECR 297, where the European Court of Justice in effect held that the deportation of a national of a member state could be prevented if it was ordered for a purpose other than one connected with the personal conduct of the individual concerned.

84. [1963] 2 QB 243, 302.

85. ibid., p. 308.

86. [1977] 1 WLR 766.

87. [1917] AC 260.

88. [1942] AC 206.

89. [1977] 1 WLR 766, 778F–H.

90. ibid., p. 787G.

91. *Agee v UK*, 17 December 1976; applic. No. 7729/76; cited by Lord Denning at [1977] 1 WLR 766, at 779A–C. Lord Denning used this finding as support for his view that when national security is at stake even the rules of natural justice may have to be modified to meet the position. Art. 6(1) of the European Convention says that 'In the determination of his civil rights and obligations . . . everyone is entitled to a fair and public hearing . . . by an independent and impartial tribunal established by law.'

92. [1988] Imm AR 389.

93. ibid., p. 396.

94. ibid., p. 397.

95. [1993] Imm AR 353.

96. ibid., p. 356.

97. Above, n. 92.

98. ibid., p. 357, per Farquharson LJ.

99. [1991] 1 WLR 890.

100. ibid., p. 896D.

101. ibid., pp 906H–907A.

102. At that time this was Lloyd LJ.

103. Above, n. 99, at p. 907G.

104. [1995] 1 All ER 658; [1994] ImmAR 107.

105. Decision of 2 December 1991 (unreported).

106. [1988] ImmAR 389.

107. The applicant was said to be a leading adherent of the extreme London-based faction of the International Sikh Youth Federation, which has close links with Sikh terrorists in the

Punjab. He was alleged to have been centrally involved in the organisation, planning and financing of terrorism both in India and the United Kingdom.

108. The *GCHQ* case, above, n. 23 and *R. v Ponting*, above n. 36.
109. e.g. Race Relations Act 1965, as amended; Equal Pay Act 1970 and Sex Discrimination Act 1975; Rehabilitation of Offenders Act 1974. In Northern Ireland the Fair Employment (NI) Acts of 1976 and 1989 extended the law's protection to victims of discrimination on the basis of religious or political belief. At the time of writing a Bill is going through parliament making discrimination against disabled persons unlawful in the workplace.
110. See too the Trade Union and Labour Relations (Consolidation) Act 1992, ss 183(6) and 275. For a discussion of security vetting in employment, see I. Linn, *Application Refused: Employment Vetting by the State* (The Civil Liberties Trust, 1990) and L. Lustgarten and I. Leigh, n. 18 above, ch. 6.
111. [1987] QB 129.
112. The freedom of movement for workers conferred by Art. 48 of the Treaty of Rome must not be denied to any person on the basis of his or her nationality if he or she is a national of a member state of the EC (Art. 48.2). This was the principal reason for the ECJ's condemnation of the Merchant Shipping Act 1988 in the *Factortame* case, above, n. 7.
113. See the previous section for the relevance of EC law in challenges to exclusion orders under the PTA.
114. S. 42(1): 'This Act shall not apply to an act done for the purpose of safeguarding national security or of protecting public safety or public order.' S. 42(2): 'A certificate signed by or on behalf of the Secretary of State and certifying that an act specified in the certificate was done for a purpose mentioned in subsection (1) shall be conclusive evidence that it was done for that purpose.'
115. 10 April 1987; unreported except on LEXIS.
116. Under r. 15(1) of the Training School Rules (NI) 1952.
117. See the LEXIS report.
118. Apart from the *GCHQ* case and *The Zamora*, these were *R. v Secretary of State for Foreign Affairs, ex p. Trawnik* (1986, unreported; CA), where a challenge was unsuccessfully made to a decision by the government on whether a country was a state for the purposes of the State Immunity Act 1978, and *R. v Registrar of Companies, ex p. Central Bank of India* [1986] QB 1114, where a party failed to overturn the registrar's registration of a company by showing that the registrar had been supplied with inadequate and incorrect information (s. 98(2) of the Companies Act 1948 said that the registrar's certificate of registration was conclusive evidence that the requirements of the Act had been complied with).
119. *Associated Provincial Picture Houses v Wednesbury Corporation* [1948] 1 KB 223. Carswell J. earlier states that he takes these principles to be that a challenge can be made if the respondent took into account improper considerations or left out of account considerations to which he or she ought to have had regard.
120. [1911] AC 179, 182.
121. For information on the FEC and section 42 I am indebted to an unpublished dissertation submitted to the Faculty of Law at Queen's University, Belfast, by Drusilla Hawthorne: *Security Vetting, National Security and Fair Employment* (June 1994).
122. *Lynas v Ministry of Defence*, 14 January 1988, Belfast Recorders Court; see Hawthorne, above, n. 121, at pp 76–8. At pp 79–95 Hawthorne provides details of *Tinnelly v Northern Ireland Electricity*, a decision of the High Court on an application for judicial review in December 1991; despite strongly criticising NIE, McCollum J. felt bound to uphold the s. 42 certificate as in the *Gilmore* case.
123. Divisional Court, 20 July 1988; *The Independent*, 21 July 1988; *The Times*, 26 July 1988; reported also on LEXIS.
124. Though national security was not one of the issues at the High Court stage.
125. See the LEXIS Report.

126. ibid.
127. [1994] 2 All ER 588; [1993] ICR 663.
128. [1985] AC 374, 412.
129. [1994] 2 All ER 588, 596f.
130. *The Independent*, 2 March 1995; see the Employment Appeal Tribunal Rules 1993, r. 29(2)(a).
131. (1987) 9 EHRR 433. Art. 8 concerns respect for a person's private and family life.
132. This case is discussed, along with those of Vanessa Redgrave, Patricia Hewitt and Harriet Harman MP, in the Report of the Security Service Commissioner (Stuart-Smith LJ.) for 1993, Cm. 2523, paras 7–40.
133. 26 January 1994; unreported.
134. ibid. The Broderick Report was the Report of a Committee on Death Certification and Coroners, Cmnd. 4810 (1971).
135. p. 22 of the judgment, as cited by Hutton LCJ. in *ex p. McNeill*, 17 June 1994, at p. 47 of that judgment.
136. e.g. during the judicial review of the inquest into the Hillsborough football stadium disaster: *R. v Coroner for South Yorkshire, ex p. Stringer*, 5 November 1993; unreported.
137. April 1994, unreported; the Divisional Court decision is reported in *The Times*, 23 July 1993; see too *Jervis on Coroners* (11th edn, 1993) paras 13.33 to 13.40; the case is also cited by Hutton LCJ. in *ex p. McNeill*, 17 June 1994, at p. 49.
138. p. 27 of the judgment.
139. R. 9(2) of the Coroners (Practice and Procedure) Rules (NI) 1963. This had earlier been the subject of extensive litigation culminating in the decision of the House of Lords in *McKerr v Armagh Coroner* [1990] 1 All ER 865.
140. The coroner has this power under r. 8(1) of the 1963 Rules.
141. On Crown privilege in general in this context see *Jervis on Coroners* (11th edn, 1993), paras 12.142 to 12.148.
142. The authorities cited in support of this proposition included dicta in *R. v Lewes Justices, ex p. Home Secretary* [1973] AC 388, 400D (Lord Reid), 405B (Lord Morris) and 407E (Lord Simon); and in *Conway v Rimmer* [1968] AC 910, 952 (Lord Reid).
143. Para. 4, cited on p. 4 of the CA's unofficial judgment.
144. [1968] AC 910.
145. [1985] AC 374.
146. [1994] 2 All ER 588; [1994] 1 WLR 681.
147. pp 31–32 of the CA's unofficial judgment. In *AG v Leveller Magazine Ltd* [1979] 1 All ER 745 the House of Lords acquitted three magazines of contempt after they had published the name of a witness in committal proceedings despite an order from the magistrates not to do so.
148. [1991] 1 NIJB 68.
149. p. 34 of the unofficial CA judgment. For other Northern Irish cases on the screening of witnesses see *R. v Murphy and Maguire* [1990] 7 NIJB 44; and *R. v Millar and others* (1992; Judge Hart; unreported).
150. *Duncan v Cammell Laird & Co.* [1942] AC 624.
151. The *GCHQ* case: *CCSU v Minister for the Civil Service* [1985] AC 374.
152. *Balfour v Foreign and Commonwealth Office* [1994] 2 All ER 588; [1994] 1 WLR 681.
153. [1991] 1 NIJB 68.
154. Hutton LCJ. asked the coroner to bear in mind the content of a letter which the Court of Appeal had received from an official in the Lord Chancellor's Department in London, in which information was contained as to the frequency with which witnesses were screened in trials in England.
155. p. 4 of his unofficial judgment.
156. 11 July 1994; unreported.

157. These were of course reports written by senior English police officers into alleged shoot-to-kill incidents in south Armagh in the early 1980s.
158. 21 February 1992; unreported except on LEXIS.
159. Cited by Nicholson J. in *In Re Toman*, at p. 21 of his unofficial judgment.
160. See text, above at n. 101.

Chapter Eight

Justifying Judicial Caution: Jurisdiction, Justiciability and Policy

A.P. Le Sueur

Introduction

British administrative lawyers frequently tell the story of the 'expansion' of judicial review. This involves descriptions and analysis of the growing sophistication and 'intrusiveness' of the substantive grounds of review[1] and reference to the overall increase in the number of Order 53 applications.[2] This chapter focuses on another often told part of the narrative: the adjectival law. In recent years the High Court seems to have assumed greater powers to grant remedies, while at the same time relaxing some of the procedural obstacles which used to face applicants wanting to challenge the legality of governmental action.

The story line is well known. First during the mid-1980s the court extended its supervisory powers into new types of decision-making bodies[3] and kinds of decision-making by developing a new test for the amenability to judicial review based on function rather than source of power. In doing so it abandoned the notion that the principle of ultra vires is the constitutional basis for judicial review.[4] Around this time the court rather subverted provisions in the Supreme Court Act 1981 dealing with standing and delay (devices designed as procedural protections for respondents) by deciding that these were not matters which could be adequately dealt with at the leave stage (as section 31 suggested), but should instead be considered at the full hearing.[5] Then in 1990, prompted by the European Court of Justice, the court took on power to grant injunctions against Ministers of the Crown, initially only where Community law rights were asserted by an applicant[6] but then shortly afterwards even in cases where only domestic law issues were at stake.[7] For good measure, it was also held that the court had jurisdiction to make a finding of contempt against a minister who disobeys an order made, or undertaking given, during judicial review proceedings.[8] In addition, the court has permitted an expansion of 'judicial review' outside the confines of Order 53 proceedings against the spirit of the exclusivity principle set down in *O'Reilly v*

Mackman[9] in 1982: tribunals may now consider questions as to the validity of administrative action or delegated legislation[10] and public law issues may be raised in ordinary civil proceedings.[11] The effect of this has, again, been to deprive public bodies in some circumstances of the special procedural protections (short time limit, standing, etc.) afforded by Order 53. In the latest development of the plot, during the mid-1990s the rules on standing have been relaxed to the point where they probably no longer present any real obstacle to respectable people or groups with serious allegations of unlawful governmental action.[12] Lord Diplock's reasoning in favour of standing for pressure groups in the landmark *National Federation* case,[13] which differed markedly from that of the other members of the House on this point, is now looked on with more favour than the majority approach in that case.

Continuing judicial caution

This essay sets out to explore an alternative facet of this story of expansion: the situations in which the High Court, exercising its supervisory role, sometimes remains reticent about intruding into some types of governmental decisions; in other words, how the court itself draws boundaries around its power to review.[14] The main focus is on the types of reasoning used by the court to justify non-intervention.

In outline, the trend can be described as follows. In a variety of ways, the High Court has extended its jurisdiction (that is, legal powers) to judicially review governmental action and grant remedies to applicants. This increased legal power does not, however, mean that the court has necessarily become more intrusive: while the court has contrived to give itself more power, it has retained a strong discretion as to when, how and whether to use this power. A predisposition towards caution in the use of its review powers and remedies is accepted by many judges, practitioners and academic writers. The motivations for this cautious stance include judicial perceptions about the legitimacy of their role, an awareness of the constitutional position of the court *vis-à-vis* democratically elected institutions and the Executive, and fears about the impact of court intervention on the quality of public administration in certain contexts. Perhaps the 'expansion' of judicial review is illusory.

Leaving aside the substantive grounds of review (which can be drawn so as to create greater or lesser degrees of intrusiveness into governmental decision-making), three main types of reasons are used by the court to justify the ways it draws the boundaries around the reach of judicial review.

(a) The court may hold that it does not have jurisdiction to review certain types of action, hear a particular applicant or grant a specific remedy.

(b) The court may hold that an impugned decision is not justiciable.

(c) The court may invoke a variety of public policy reasons to justify non-intervention.

Although these different techniques are interconnected, it is useful to regard them as different and distinct.

In short, the tendency has been for the court no longer to regard the reach of judicial review as being constrained by jurisdictional considerations (*law*); the main constraints are now *conceptual* and *policy* ones. 'Jurisdiction' has been robbed of most of its effectiveness as a boundary setting device: the court now rarely finds itself without appropriate legal power to review a decision or grant a remedy if it wishes to do so. More and more, 'non-justiciability' and 'public policy' are used to justify the court's decisions to intervene or not intervene. The former concept remains undeveloped and the court is apt to misapply it in the special context of judicial review, and the use of public policy arguments to justify non-intervention creates a challenge for many of the explanatory theories of judicial review. There is also an apparent tension here: non-justiciability is invoked by the court because it says that adjudicative procedures and also the judges themselves, by their upbringing and experience, are ill equipped to weigh up competing policy considerations;[15] yet in exercising its public law powers (for instance, deciding whether or not to grant relief to an applicant who has shown governmental action to be unlawful) the court claims that its task is 'to strike a balance between the conflicting public interests that arise'.[16]

The Opportunities for Non-Intervention

The court's self-imposed caution about over-intrusion into governmental decisions is a complex phenomenon which takes place at various stages of the judicial review process. The Order 53 procedure presents the court with a series of opportunities in which to exercise caution, if it so chooses, through the use of procedures and remedies.

At the outset, the court may refuse to embark on adjudicating an applicant's complaint of administrative invalidity. This happens at the leave stage in which the respondent public body does not normally participate. Generally it can be said that different judges may apply different tests as to the 'threshold' of arguability needed for leave to be granted: for some the requirement may only be *potential* arguability; for others that the application will very probably succeed at the full hearing. More specifically, in a series of decisions the court has held that leave in some types of cases should not be given unless the applicant's case raises some issue of 'general public importance' or there are 'special circumstances' over and above a run of the mill allegation of irrationality or procedural impropriety. Sentiments such as these have been expressed in judicial review applications in a very wide range of contexts including: refusal of entry to the United Kingdom by officials unconvinced that a person is a 'genuine visitor'[17] or 'genuine student'[18] within the meaning of the Immigration Act 1971; decisions of local authorities under the homeless persons legislation;[19] decisions by social service departments to place a name on a child protection register;[20] the refusal to make a grant or loan from the social fund set up by the Social Security Act 1986;[21] reports of the commission responsible for recommending changes to the boundaries of local government areas;[22] decisions to deport people on the grounds of national security;[23] and decisions of examining magistrates to commit an accused person for trial.[24]

During the interlocutory stage of proceedings, caution is evident in relation to the court's attitude towards granting discovery and interim relief. Under RSC Order 24 (which applies in Order 53 applications) discovery is refused 'unless the court is of the opinion that the order is necessary either for disposing fairly of the cause or matter or for saving costs'.[25] The court has (in the words of the Law Commission) 'created a climate considered unfavourable to applications for discovery in judicial review'.[26] Without access to documents an applicant may find it impossible to establish grounds for review such as the taking into account of irrelevant factors.[27] In its 1994 report, the Law Commission recommended 'a slightly more liberal application' of the existing discovery rules, but stopped short of recommending any change to the rules themselves.[28]

Caution is also evident in the court's approach to interim relief. First, for a long time it was thought that interlocutory injunctions could not be granted against the Crown or ministers[29] (though now they can be).[30] On a more general level, the approach advocated by the House of Lords in the private law case of *American Cyanamid Co. v Ethicon Ltd*[31] has been modified in relation to judicial review challenges. First, damages will rarely be an adequate remedy for either the applicant or (in the event that the interim injunction turns out to have been wrongly granted) the respondent. The court, therefore, must consider the 'balance of convenience' in most cases. Judges have shown themselves reluctant to grant interim relief on the grounds that what is challenged is legislation affecting large numbers of people or that third parties are affected in some other way.[32]

When an application is argued at a full hearing, caution can take many forms. Many are to do with the ways in which the court applies the substantive grounds of judicial review to the particular context before it and its willingness to review errors of fact—matters which have to fall outside the scope of this chapter.[33] There are several other opportunities for non-intrusion to occur. First, cross-examination of deponents is very rarely allowed.[34] Secondly, the court may be asked to rule that the applicant does not have standing:[35] however in almost all reported cases in which the respondent has raised this as an issue, the court has nevertheless gone on to rule on the substantive case even if standing is denied.[36] In practice, therefore, while the rules of standing have in the past provided judges with the opportunity to make statements in favour of non-intrusion, in reality lack of standing rarely provides any *real* ground for non-intervention. Thirdly, there exists a presumption as to the validity of administrative decisions and delegated legislation (*omnia praesumuntur rite esse acta*). Finally, it should be noted that, as in almost all other types of litigation, the applicant bears the evidential burden of proof in establishing the factual and legal grounds on which relief is sought.[37]

At the conclusion of the full hearing, the court may be wary of over-intrusion in the form of relief (if any) it is prepared to grant.[38] Caution at its most extreme may prompt a court to refuse to make any formal order in favour of an applicant who has established grounds that a governmental decision is unlawful: each year some applicants who have succeeded in showing that administrative action is unlawful are nevertheless turned away with no remedy from the court. No data exists to show how often remedies are withheld in this way, but a survey of cases summarised in the *Crown Office Digest* shows that the issue of withholding a remedy arises on average in approximately 6 per cent of all applications for judicial review.

If relief is granted, then from the perspective of a respondent, declarations are the least intrusive of all the judicial review remedies because they are prospective and non-coercive.[39] A declaration is also likely to give the respondent the most scope for deciding how to comply with the court's order. Next is certiorari which, though quashing the respondent's decision, normally leaves it free to reconsider the matter and, if appropriate, make the same substantive decision. Next comes an order of prohibition (or a prohibitory injunction): this intrudes to the extent that it prevents the respondent carrying out certain action, though it retains freedom to do other action. Most interventionist is an order of mandamus (or a mandatory injunction) which requires specific action to be done. On occasion this may have the effect of substituting the court's judgment for that of the official decision-maker.

These, then, are the main opportunities for the High Court to exercise caution and lean on the side of non-intrusion into allegedly unlawful governmental decisions.

A Predisposition Towards Caution?

A court which prefers to be cautious would establish a high threshold test at the leave stage, rarely grant interim relief or discovery, use the standing and delay rules to prevent otherwise possibly meritorious cases from being argued, and often withhold from successful applicants any formal relief or, at least, be careful about granting a remedy (like mandamus) which is considered to be 'intrusive'. A court which has a commitment to intervention would do the opposite of these things. The current stance of the court towards caution and intervention lies *somewhere* between these two extremes poles. Considerable care, however, is needed about making sweeping generalisations. Over time, different judges have established reputations among practitioners for their different attitudes towards caution. Recent research has also revealed considerable variations in the proportions of leave applications granted and refused by different judges.[40] Also, as already noted, an attitude of caution is advocated in relation to some types of administrative decision, such as those relating to homelessness, but not others.[41] The picture is, therefore, patchy; but it is clear that for many judges, in many contexts, adjectival law provides an important tool for erring on the side of caution.

Holding these caveats in mind, however, it seems to be the case that in general there is something of a predisposition towards caution in the way the court develops and applies adjectival law in judicial review and that this sort of caution is often regarded as welcome. Evidence of acceptance of judicial caution in the legal community may be found in the 1994 Law Commission Report, where a fair degree of support for caution in relation to some topics is described: for example, a majority of those who responded agreed that the court ought to have discretion to refuse remedies and that this was not a cause for concern;[42] and a third of respondents considered the present restrictive approach to discovery fully justified.[43]

Some academic writers have also welcomed this restraint, both as to the reach of the substantive grounds of review and in relation to the adjectival matters which are the focus of this chapter. Cranston, for instance, has recently contended that 'the courts should tread more warily than they sometimes have in applying and extending the grounds of judicial review'.[44] He also argues that liberal rules on standing are not necessarily desirable. In a recent book, Fordham elevates the fact of judicial caution to a 'principle', stating that 'The law of judicial review is the product of the forces of vigilance and deference.'[45] He is, however, careful to argue that the courts do and should err on the side of 'deference' in which 'reviewing courts acknowledge (1) that their stance should primarily be one of restraint; and specifically (2) that each public body has and must retain its own field of judgment, within which it is entrusted with responsibility and choice'.[46] Fordham argues that questions as to the discovery of documents and the discretionary refusal of remedies must also be informed by the principle of judicial deference.

The judicial motivation for caution

Even though the main purpose of this chapter is to examine the techniques of reasoning used by the courts to justify non-intervention and intervention, something does need to be said briefly about a closely connected subject— the *motivations* for the court to favour caution. The case law and extra-judicial writing reveal two interconnected sets of concerns. One is about the constitutional position of the court: there is a need for an appropriate allocation of tasks between the courts and administrators, and the courts and democratic institutions and processes. Orthodox constitutional doctrines such as the 'rule of law' and the 'separation of powers' are invoked. Fordham states that 'there is a constitutional dimension here: as vigilance corresponds to the rule of law, deference is underpinned by the separation of powers',[47] though for Sir John Laws, 'the limits on the jurisdiction of the courts . . . are simply a function of the rule of law: the judges are no more than anyone else entitled to exercise power which legally belongs to another'.[48] Another motivation towards caution is the judges' fears about the practical impact of judicial review, either generally or in the particular case before the court. The anxieties relate to the potential for the court's intervention to disrupt sensitive administrative decisions or to encourage more applications for judicial review which would further stretch the court's limited resources.[49] These two general concerns—with the constitutional limits of the court's role and the possibility of judicial overkill—are linked and merge. The connections are highlighted by the notion of 'partnership' developed by Lord Donaldson MR during the late 1980s: for him, there had developed 'a new relationship between the courts and the administration' which was a 'partnership based on a common aim, namely, the maintenance of the highest standards of public administration'.[50]

Three Modes of Judicial Reasoning

To return, then, to the main focus of this chapter—the techniques of reasoning used by the court to justify its decisions to intrude or not to intrude (in the senses described above) into allegedly unlawful governmental action. A court may use one or more of the following methods of justification for not intruding:

(a) It can say that it does not have jurisdiction to hear an application or grant relief; or

(b) that the case raises an issue which is not justiciable; or

(c) reasons of public policy are invoked in order not to intrude into an allegedly unlawful governmental decision.

In several important respects, these are plainly distinct bases for justifying non-intrusion. When the court says it has *no jurisdiction* to intervene, it is invoking a legal rule. The High Court has at its disposal only certain statutory and common law powers to determine issues and make formal orders during and at the conclusion of judicial review proceedings. The court has some scope for altering its jurisdiction by reinterpreting the statutes which give them these powers or impose restrictions.[51] Common law in relation to jurisdiction is developed incrementally and the doctrine of precedent is applied and there is a search for principle. The judges, therefore, need to justify the limits to the court's jurisdiction by using reasoning based on legal rules rather than appealing directly or mainly to the desirability of change for reasons of public policy.[52]

When a court characterises a governmental decision as *non-justiciable* on the basis that the court and its adjudicative process are ill suited to resolving the dispute with the public body, it is using a conceptual device broader than applying a legal rule: the question whether an issue is justiciable or not cannot be resolved merely by relying on the doctrine of precedent or legal analysis of statutory provisions, nor is it merely a question of public policy. The concept of justiciability rests on essential or inherent limits of the adjudicatory process rather than the artificial legal limits set by the technique of delimiting the court's jurisdiction in a particular way. A question may be justiciable yet not within the court's jurisdiction, for example, an alleged breach of rules of natural justice by the Jockey Club as against one of its members.[53] An ouster clause in an Act of Parliament may also, rightly or wrongly, remove a justiciable issue from the court's jurisdiction.

A third judicial technique for justifying non-intervention is for the court to give reasons of *public policy* for its decision. Here the court's reasoning rests not on legal argument and precedent, nor on any necessary conceptual boundaries to its work. Instead, the judges look to the practical repercussions of intervening, both on the court itself and on the respondent public body. Using this technique, the court may withhold from scrutinising a governmental decision, or from making a formal order, giving reasons such as fear that to do so would have a detrimental impact on the quality of decision-making by that public body or that intervention would place a strain on the court's own resources.

Discretion

There has sometimes been a failure to differentiate clearly between these different bases, even using the terms jurisdiction and justiciability interchangeably. This results in muddled thinking and may open the way to sleight of hand. What the techniques have in common is that they each enable the court to exercise 'discretion', in the sense that the judge may exercise power in more than one way.[54] The court has often been keen to stress the discretionary nature of its decisions to intervene or not intervene,[55] but the court *never* has a completely free choice; discretion is always limited to some extent, though in different ways in relation to each of the three constraints. For instance, there is discretion as to how a statutory provision establishing the court's jurisdiction is to be interpreted, but this discretion is limited because the issue is a 'legal' one. Discretion in relation to non-justiciability is limited by a conceptual framework. Discretion as to public policy considerations is limited by judicial perceptions of the legitimacy of their role.

Jurisdiction: The Legal Constraints

In recent years the 'jurisdiction' of the court, its *legal power* to intervene, has expanded: as we have seen, more types of decision-making bodies are now subject to review; the fact that a decision is taken in exercise of prerogative powers is no longer a bar to review; lack of standing is rarely a problem for applicants; injunctive relief may now be granted against ministers and contempt proceedings commenced, and so forth. The court has thus effectively removed many of the *legal constraints* on its powers and alternative devices—principally 'justiciability' and 'public policy'—are now used to justify the decision to intervene or not intervene in cases. (I argue later that these techniques of justification place fewer constraints on the court's discretion and for this, and other reasons, the trend away from using 'jurisdiction' as a boundary-setting device ought to be viewed with circumspection.) When the court itself[56] makes a decision about the extension, maintenance or contraction of its jurisdictional powers, this ought to be justified primarily on the basis of legal argument, rather than merely by a general appeal to the desirability of changing or keeping the current confines of judicial review. The court has occasionally lost sight of this and broad considerations of public policy are sometimes used to justify such decisions.[57]

More fundamentally, the recent and rapid development of judicial review has cast doubt on orthodox perceptions of the nature of the court's jurisdiction. The traditional approach is to say that the application for judicial review procedure 'lacks an independent scope of its own';[58] and so the court's power to review a given decision is determined by its jurisdiction to award whichever of the *particular remedies* of certiorari, prohibition and mandamus are sought by the applicant. The argument is that section 29(1) of the Supreme Court Act 1981 provides that 'The High Court shall have jurisdiction to make orders of mandamus, prohibition and certiorari in those classes of cases in which it had power to do so immediately before the commencement of this Act.'[59] Prior to section 29 and its precursors, the circumstances in which the High Court (and its predecessors) had jurisdiction to grant the prerogative orders and writs was determined by the common law. So when, as in a case like *R. v Panel on Take-overs and Mergers, ex parte Datafin plc,*[60] the court must decide whether to extend its supervisory powers, it needs to use case law technique and ask whether the particular remedy sought by the applicant (for example, an order of certiorari) has in the past been granted in similar or analogous circumstances. In this, though, the court had preserved to itself quite a degree of discretion because, as Lord Parker CJ. put it, '. . . the exact limits of the ancient remedy by way of certiorari have never been and ought not to be specifically defined. They have varied from time to time being extended to meet changing conditions.'[61] Nevertheless, in this approach to jurisdiction the exercise takes place within the constraints of quite narrow forms of legal argument.

An alternative approach is to assert that the court now has a *general* 'supervisory' or 'public law' jurisdiction, not one defined by the scope of the individual remedies of certiorari, mandamus and prohibition. Sir John Laws, writing extra-judicially, states boldly that 'we now possess a jurisdiction in which every public body is in principle subject to the supervision of the court as regards every decision it makes'.[62]

A number of interconnected trends and events have made it possible to speak of a general jurisdiction to review, independent of the scope of the prerogative order sought by the applicant in any given application for judicial review. One is the erosion of the technical differences between the circumstances in which each of the prerogative orders may be granted; for example, for a period the court confined certiorari and prohibition to the supervision of decisions which were judicial in character, whereas no such limitation applied to orders of mandamus. Another is that certiorari, prohibition and mandamus have come to be regarded merely as forms of relief to be used in flexible ways to give effect to the court's judgment, rather than as devices which in themselves determine the power of the court to embark on a review in the first place. Good illustrations of this flexible approach to the availability of different forms of relief come from challenges to allegedly ultra vires statutory instruments. For a long time it was thought that the only appropriate remedy was a declaration. Then it was held that the court would, in appropriate circumstances, grant certiorari to quash delegated legislation.[63] Most recently the court has indicated that it is 'not inconceivable' that a mandatory order might be granted against a minister directing that he lay a statutory instrument before parliament.[64]

A further step along the road to the court's abandonment of the prerogative orders as fetters on jurisdiction came in the House of Lords' decision in *R. v Secretary of State for Employment, ex parte Equal Opportunities Commission,*[65] where it was held that an applicant may in Order 53 proceedings apply for a declaration even in circumstances where the court would have no jurisdiction to grant one of the prerogative orders. (On behalf of the respondent, it had been argued that section 31(2) of the Supreme Court Act 1981[66] prevented the court granting a declaration in the case because certiorari could not be ordered to quash an Act of Parliament, nor had the Secretary of State made any 'decision' capable of being quashed.)[67] According to Lord Browne-Wilkinson, *O'Reilly v Mackman*[68] made it clear that under Order 53 any declaration as to public rights which could formerly be obtained in civil proceedings in the High Court could now also be obtained in judicial review proceedings.[69]

Perhaps the most significant impetus in the development of a general 'public law jurisdiction' has been the Court of Appeal's decision in *R. v Panel on Take-overs and Mergers, ex parte Datafin plc.*[70] The tests of 'public functions' and 'public law consequences' propounded in that case have been seen by the court as providing a *general* principled basis for its supervisory jurisdiction in judicial review cases. (Whether the court has, in fact, managed in subsequent cases to articulate and develop such a coherent basis is a rather different question.) No longer is it necessary to cite and closely analyse authorities to show whether the court has jurisdiction (say) to grant mandamus in similar or analogous situations; one asks instead whether the decision was made by a body carrying out public functions.

Standing

The particular issue of standing illustrates well the general trend (just described) in the court's approach to its jurisdiction. The requirement that an applicant for judicial review have standing is a jurisdictional issue: section 31(3) of the Supreme Court Act 1981 specifies that the applicant have a 'sufficient interest in the matter to which the application relates' before the court may review the matter. A respondent public body may not simply agree that an applicant has *locus standi.*[71] In recent years, however, the court has dismantled the standing requirement. In 1982 it decided that it was undesirable to decide issues of standing at the leave stage—despite the apparently clear words to the contrary used in section 31(6) of the 1981 Act. Today standing is very rarely the reason for any application failing at the leave stage.[72] This has deprived the device of standing of any real ability to constrain the court from embarking on a judicial review. Now standing is an issue discussed, if at all, at the full hearing. Yet here it rarely prevents the court from passing judgment on the legality of the impugned governmental decision. Even if standing is denied, the court will almost always go on (or even begin)[73] to deal with the grounds of the applicant's case. Recent decisions have shown the court to be extremely reluctant to deny it has jurisdiction to hear applications made by individuals[74] or pressure groups[75] who have genuine concern. If standing has any function left today, it is to act as a constraint on which particular form of relief will be granted; but as Cane has noted, this connection between sufficiency of interest and form of relief is misconceived.[76]

The issue of standing also illustrates how the new approach to jurisdictional issues allows the court to use public policy considerations to justify decisions to intervene or not intervene. The recent liberalisation of the standing requirement has not been explained by the court primarily on the basis of principle (for example, that there ought to be a presumption in favour of standing because there is a fundamental right of access to justice). Rather, the court has clearly had in mind, and has articulated, policy factors: faced with a choice between hearing a case brought by an ordinary individual, the court prefers 'expert' litigants; pressure groups should be allowed to litigate because this is better for the successful public body who will be able to recover costs from the group but not from a legally aided individual. Little effort has been given to interpreting the words 'sufficient interest' or considering the principles which lie behind them. As Schiemann J. said in the *Rose Theatre* case, 'these words must have some meaning'.

For many proponents of judicial review, the joy at the liberalisation of the standing rules has led them to overlook how exactly this has been achieved. The court has taken a cavalier attitude towards precedent in this context: inconvenient authorities have been overlooked; earlier cases such as *Rose Theatre* have not been convincingly distinguished or overruled; and reasons of policy rather than principle have been to the fore of explanations for the change. For these reasons, the new liberal regime towards standing lacks a firm foundation. Above all, the court's almost total disregard of the legislative intent of section 31(3) of the 1981 Act must call into question the legitimacy of the effective abandonment of the sufficient interest requirement.[77]

Jurisdiction: a summary

The court has been startlingly effective in removing blocks in its mind about the proper extent of its legal powers: standing requirements have been largely jettisoned, new types of decision-making made subject to review (even though they do not emanate from statutory powers), injunctions and contempt extended to ministers, relief made available in a more flexible way, and so forth. The result is that as a boundary-setting device, the notion of the court's jurisdiction has lost most of its force. With the creation of a 'public law jurisdiction', and more particularly the abandonment of any effective standing requirements and the new attitude towards flexible forms of relief, the court has expanded its powers to intervene. The court now has the legal power to review almost anything and grant any remedy at the behest of any applicant (though whether it actually exercises these powers is another matter). This enlargement of power needs to be viewed with circumspection. The court's appropriation of greater legal powers does not necessarily mean that they will be used—the court has been careful to maintain its discretion not to intervene (for example, through the power to withhold relief in any given application). Another reason for caution about the trend is that the newer modes of reasoning which are being brought in to replace 'jurisdiction' as boundary-setting devices remain undeveloped and controversial: 'justiciability' (the conceptual as opposed to legal limits of the court's power to intervene) is misunderstood; and even if it is acceptable for judges to justify decisions on the basis of public policy, serious doubts exist as to whether existing procedures and judicial experience equip the court to evaluate policy considerations in quite so central a way.

Justiciability

The court may give as its reason for not reviewing a governmental decision that the issue raised by the application is not 'justiciable'. Little effort has been given to developing a coherent and principled conceptual basis for non-justiciability.[78] Justiciability is the notion that some types of governmental decision ought not to be reviewed by the High Court because 'their nature and subject matter is such as not to be amenable to the judicial process'.[79] More specifically, justiciability refers to the conceptual boundaries of what tasks the court may perform, given the nature of its procedure (adjudication) and its personnel (judges rather than specialist administrators or democratically accountable politicians). As a matter of analysis, there are some types of decision which simply cannot be performed adequately by a court—such as decisions about the appropriate allocation of finite public funds. Such decisions cannot be made using formal legal argument and proof. Thus; although the terms 'jurisdiction' and 'justiciability' are sometimes used interchangeably, they really are distinct: the former concerns the 'artificial' legal limits of the court's power; the latter rests on the essential or inherent limits of the judicial review process. There have been quite rapid changes in judicial opinion as to whether an impugned decision is, or is not, justiciable. For example, in *GCHQ* Lord Roskill listed 'prerogative powers such as those relating to the making of treaties, the defence of the realm, the prerogative of mercy, the grant of honours, the dissolution of Parliament and the appointment of ministers as well as others' as examples of non-justiciable decisions. Yet within ten years, one of these, the Home Secretary's refusal to grant a royal pardon (or mercy), has been held to be amenable to judicial review challenge.[80]

In this chapter it is not possible to do more than highlight a few of the problems associated with the way non-justiciability is invoked by the court to set the boundaries to judicial review. The focus will be on one kind of potentially non-justiciable issue, the discretionary allocation of public funds. Some of the problems can be seen in *R. v Secretary of State for the Home Department, ex parte P.*[81] where the Court of Appeal held that while it had jurisdiction to hear an application for judicial review of decisions taken under prerogative powers by the Home Secretary in relation to the Criminal Injuries Compensation Scheme (CICS), the particular issue raised was not justiciable.

Two women who had been the victims of sexual abuse during their childhood challenged the validity of a rule made by the Secretary of State on entitlement to compensation. Under the original rules for the CICS, offences committed against a member of an offender's family living with him at the time of the crime were excluded altogether ('the same roof rule'). In 1979 the rules were altered, though not retrospectively, with the effect that child victims of sex abuse could claim compensation. The applicants had suffered abuse before 1979, and when they applied for compensation they were turned down.

The applicants argued that the 1979 cut-off date was unlawful on several grounds, including irrationality, and that it discriminated against women (who are the great majority of victims of domestic violence). In the Court of Appeal Neill LJ. rejected the applicants' cases on the ground that the decision to continue excluding the pre-1979 same roof crimes from the CICS was not justiciable. He stated:[82]

> The ground of complaint is that the decision to maintain the old exclusion rule in force in respect of offences committed before 1 October 1979 is arbitrary and irrational. It is therefore necessary to take note of the warning given by Lord Diplock in relation to a complaint of irrationality where the decision is one taken in the exercise of prerogative powers. He said . . . .

'While I see no *a priori* reason to rule out "irrationality" as a ground for judicial review of a ministerial decision taken in the exercise of "prerogative" powers, I find it difficult to envisage in any of the various fields in which the prerogative remains the only source of the relevant decision-making power a decision of a kind that would be open to attack through the judicial process upon this ground. Such decisions will generally involve the application of government policy. The reasons for the decision-maker taking one course rather than another do not normally involve questions to which, if disputed, the judicial process is adapted to provide the right answer, by which I mean that the kind of evidence that is admissible under judicial procedures and the way in which it has to be adduced tend to exclude from the attention of the court competing policy considerations which, if the executive discretion is to be wisely exercised, need to be weighed against one another—a balancing exercise which judges by their upbringing and their experience are ill qualified to perform.'

With these words in mind (Neill LJ. continued) one looks at the decisions in issue in this case. In my judgment they fall within the class of decision which Lord Diplock had in mind. These decisions involve a balance of competing claims on the public purse and the allocation of economic resources which the court is ill equipped to deal with. In the language of the late Professor Fuller in his work 'The Forms and Limits of Adjudication' decisions of this kind involve a polycentric task. The concept of a polycentric situation is perhaps most easily explained by thinking of a spider's web: 'A pull on one strand will distribute tensions after a complicated pattern throughout the web as a whole. Doubling the original pull will, in all likelihood, not simply double each of the resulting tensions but rather create a different complicated pattern of tensions. This would certainly occur, for example, if the double pull caused one or more of the weaker strands to snap': 1978 (92) Harvard Law Review 353, at p. 395.

The Secretary of State had to make a judgment as to how to allocate the resources at his disposal. It will be remembered that in respect of claims after 1979 a time limit of three years was imposed between the relevant offence and the date of a claim. I cannot see that a different time limit, say two years, could have been attacked. Such a decision would not have been 'justiciable'. Similarly, I cannot see that the decision to continue the pre-1979 exclusion can be regarded as a 'justiciable' issue on the facts of the present case. As Lord Wilberforce said in *Buttes Gas v Hammer* [1982] AC 888, 938B, in a case involving relations with a foreign state, the court has 'no judicial or manageable standards by which to judge' the issue. In attempting to review the Secretary of State's decision in this regard the court would be 'in a judicial no-man's-land'.

One flaw in Neill LJ.'s analysis is its failure to distinguish sufficiently between (a) the task of the Secretary of State in making the original decision, and (b) the task of the court in judicially reviewing that decision.[83]

The focus of Fuller's analysis in the article cited by Neill LJ. was mainly upon the limits of adjudication *as a method of original decision-making* by officials and governmental agencies. An analogy is useful here. In his famous article, Fuller gives, as an illustration of a polycentric problem unsuited to adjudication, the decision by a team manager to assign players on a football team to their positions. To adopt this as an analogy, on an application for judicial review the court is not in the position of a team manager but rather the referee. As Lord Donaldson MR put it in a judicial review challenge to decisions taken by the Secretary of State for the Environment to cap the amount of community charge which some local authorities could levy:[84]

> [Politicians, press and public] should appreciate that we [sc. the court] are not concerned with whether the new system of local taxation is or is not 'a good thing'. Nor are we concerned with the merits or demerits of particular aspects of this system or with the wisdom displayed by the Secretary of State in taking actions which we have been called upon to examine. These are matters for Parliament not for us.
>
> The role of the judiciary is essentially that of a referee . . . The powers and duties of the Secretary of State and the local authorities were governed by rules. In the football World Cup, which is engaging the attention of so many at the present time, the moves made by the players and the tactics employed by the teams were matters entirely for them. The referee was only involved when it appeared that some player had acted in breach of the rules. The referee could then stop play and take some remedial action, but it was not for him to express any view on the skill of the players or how he would have acted in their position. Still less, following a breach of the rules, did he take over the position of one of the players. So too with the judiciary.

So, except in a very indirect and trivial sense, the court on an application for judicial review is not allocating economic resources.[85] This is the task of the original decision-making body (or sometimes, a court or tribunal hearing an appeal on the merits). The primary role of the court in judicial review is different: it is to set the parameters within which (for example) resources may lawfully be allocated. The Court of Appeal in *ex parte P.* was not, therefore, being called upon 'to balance the competing claims on the public purse and the allocation of economic resources'—at least not directly. Neill LJ. lost sight of the fact that they were meant to be supervising the Secretary of State's task rather than doing it themselves.

For this reason, the approach adopted by Evans LJ. (with whom Peter Gibson LJ. concurred) in *ex parte P.* is to be preferred:[86]

> I gratefully adopt Neill LJ.'s analysis of the issues of jurisdiction and justiciability, and it is only with regard to the latter that I have difficulty in agreeing with his conclusion that the issues raised by these applications are

'non-justiciable', or 'not amenable to judicial process' (per Lord Roskill in *CCSU*). In short, I do not regard the facts that the scheme may be described as the distribution of 'bounty' on behalf of the Crown and that moneys are granted to the Home Office by Parliament for this purpose, either as justifying an unfair or irrational scheme, if such was the case, or as precluding the courts from exercising their constitutional powers of judicial review in an appropriate case. . . .

If it is permissible to infer a Parliamentary intention from the annual grant of funds, then in my judgment the inference must be that the money was intended to be distributed in a fair and rational manner, rather than otherwise, and that the courts were expected to exercise their powers so far as is lawful to ensure that this is done . . . . It is alleged that this decision was both irrational and discriminatory against women, because the majority of victims of domestic or household violence are female. The preliminary question, however, is whether by reason of the subject matter it is non-justiciable and therefore not amenable to judicial review, and within the category of cases described in *CCSU*, *Everett* and *Bentley*.

This category includes 'matters of high policy' (per Taylor LJ. in *Everett*). Examples given are 'matters so vital to the survival and welfare of the nation as the conduct of relations with foreign states' (per Lord Diplock in *CCSU* at p. 410B) and in the domestic sphere executive decisions which involve 'competing policy considerations' (per Lord Diplock in the passage already cited). It is difficult to see how the decision to exclude previous 'same roof' incidents from the 1979 scheme, or even the decision to revise the scheme in the light of the 1978 Working Party report, can be said to come within the category of 'high policy' decisions.

In substance, the submission on behalf of the Home Secretary appears to rest upon the financial aspects to which I shall refer further below. It is said that the 'policy' decision involved a choice between competing claims upon the public purse. There is no evidence to this effect, or otherwise to explain the decision as there was for example in *CCSU*. Whilst the court should be careful not to extend the scope of judicial review beyond its proper limits, nevertheless in my judgment when an issue as to jurisdiction [*sic*] is raised it should decide the issue as best it can on the material before it.

It does not seem inevitable or even likely that there was some financial constraint which led to the exclusion which is complained of. If a fixed amount of funds was available to implement the scheme, then this did not justify an unfair (irrational) as opposed to a fair distribution under the scheme. It is the nature of the scheme which is complained of and, far from being non-justiciable, the decisions to introduce and continue a scheme to be administered by an independent body of persons on a judicial or quasi-judicial basis seem to me to be almost the epitome of an executive or administrative decision which is amenable to review by the courts.

Evans LJ.'s approach is not, however, without its own difficulties. Writing about justiciability more generally, Galligan has expressed scepticism: 'the suggestion that, by concentrating on aspects of procedure and background constraints, judicial review can avoid violating the non-justiciable elements of discretionary decisions is open to question'.[87] In a complex argument, Galligan contends that 'virtually any aspect of a decision, no matter how closely it relates to the merits, can be characterized as one relating to the minimum requirements of rationality or purpose'.[88]

If the notion of justiciability is to replace jurisdiction as a major boundary-setting device for judicial review, it will be necessary for the court to develop a considerably more sophisticated understanding of the concept than emerges from the current case law. First, it will be important for the court to appreciate that there is a need to differentiate between its own role in supervising a decision-taker and the task of the decision-taker himself. Secondly, the richness of the notion of justiciability needs to be recognised—especially when the objection to reviewing an administrative decision is, as in *ex parte P.*, that it is 'polycentric'. For Fuller a decision-making task was not *either* polycentric *or* not polycentric; rather there was a spectrum. 'There are polycentric elements in almost all problems submitted to adjudication.'[89]

A third matter is the relationship between the conception of justiciability currently being considered and the ways in which the principles of judicial review are applied in a given case. In *ex parte P.* all the members of the Court of Appeal (Neill LJ. on the assumption that he was wrong on the issue of justiciability) held that the applicants had not made out their case on irrationality or any of the other grounds they relied upon. Neill LJ. said he could 'see no material on which the court could decide that no Secretary of State acting rationally could have maintained in force the pre-1979 rule in respect of claims for offences committed before 1 October 1979'. Would there have been such willingness to categorise the issue as non-justiciable if the rule-making power of the minister had in fact been used 'in bad faith, or for an improper motive, or that the consequences . . . were so absurd that he must have taken leave of his senses'?[90] In other contexts, such as judicial review of the allocation of funds by central to local government, the court has recognised the need for caution—but it achieved this by being cautious about the application of review principles, especially *Wednesbury* unreasonableness,[91] rather than refusing to consider the application at all on the basis of non-justiciability. In *ex parte P.*, Neill LJ.'s view appears to be that the court could never find appropriate standards against which to judge the legality of the Secretary of State's discretionary rule-making powers. Yet if the House of Lords can conceive of common law standards—extreme bad faith, improper purpose and manifest absurdity—against which ministerial decisions on local government funding can be reviewed, it is difficult to see why the same is not true in the context of decisions about the entitlement of individuals to benefit from the CICS. Even in cases involving strongly discretionary ministerial decisions about the allocation of public funds, the court should be prepared to adjudicate on a matter rather than abdicate responsibility by turning it away as non-justiciable. The court retains ample scope for caution and for giving due weight to the principle of parliamentary sovereignty in the way it sets the standards of legality in any given context. Erecting the fence of non-justiciability in front of cases like these fails to recognise how far judicial review has evolved since cases such as *Liversidge v Anderson*,[92] where a court 'more executive minded than the executive'[93] declined to intervene on the ground that discretionary decisions were inherently non-justiciable and so beyond the pale of review.

Public Policy

The argument so far is that the court has extended its jurisdiction (that is, its legal powers) and that the attempts to replace this legal boundary with a conceptual one (justiciability) have raised problems. In exercising caution about over-intrusion, the court can also use a third type of justification to set the boundary of judicial review: public policy.[94] In its 1994 report on adjectival aspects of judicial review, the Law Commission placed 'public policy' at the forefront of its general considerations:[95]

> The way in which individual aspects of the supervisory jurisdiction by way of judicial review operate in practice, most particularly in relation to procedural exclusivity, time limits and interim relief, shows that policy is a continual theme in the public law sphere. Judicial review often involves values and policy interests, which must be balanced against and may transcend the individual interests, which are normally the subject of litigation between private citizens.

For Dworkin, 'arguments of policy justify a political decision by showing that the decision advances or protects some collective goal of the community as a whole'.[96] In the context of judicial review, policy arguments are quite often used by the court to justify its decision not to intervene in a particular case. One example of this is the reasoning behind the Court of Appeal's decision that extreme caution was needed before granting leave to review decisions relating to child protection registers for fear (it seems) that this would be detrimental to good administration.[97] Policy reasons are also invoked at the other end of the judicial review process—the grant or refusal of relief to an applicant who has satisfied the court that a governmental action is unlawful. This is normally described by saying that public law remedies are 'discretionary'.[98] The use here of the term 'discretion' rather obscures the different reasons for refusing relief to an otherwise successful applicant. The court has 'discretion', in the sense that it has freedom to choose between alternatives,[99] in most of its decisions during the judicial review process and it is not synonymous with the court using public policy considerations. Sometimes public policy considerations for refusing relief have been embodied in legislation. For example, relief may be refused because the applicant delayed in making the application for judicial review: the court is empowered to do this under section 31(6) of the Supreme Court Act 1981. There is little problem for the court here in so far as it can be seen to be giving effect to policy judgments made by parliament (in the present example, that a person may be denied a legal right by the court because to do so will prevent some community goal being harmed, such as the need for certainty in public administration).

More problematic are situations where the court (say) refuses leave or declines to grant relief for 'policy' reasons which are not (unlike delay) expressly authorised by statute, but which emerge from the court's own evaluation of what is to the public benefit. One illustration of this is *R. v Governors of Bacon's School, ex parte ILEA and Southwark LBC*.[100] The Divisional Court held in favour of the applicants that a resolution made by school governors to convert a voluntary aided secondary school into a city technology college[101] was flawed because of the pecuniary interest of one of the governors. It declined, in its 'discretion', however, to grant relief for two reasons. First, it said that the resolution passed would have been taken in any event.[102] Secondly, the court considered the practical disadvantages which would flow from granting relief. It thought that the administrative inconvenience which would result from striking down the resolution outweighed the need to provide a sanction for breach of rules about pecuniary interest. Simon Brown J. pushed aside doubts expressed by Glidewell LJ. in an earlier case[103] as to whether administrative inconvenience was a sound and relevant reason for refusing relief, and 'declined to sacrifice the children's future on the altar of the rules' sanctity'. For Simon Brown J., 'the fact remains that this Court exercising its public law jurisdiction *does* have a discretion and must, in exercising that discretion, seek to strike a balance between the conflicting public interests that arise in a case like this'. This seems paradoxical given the court's protestations—under the rubric of justiciability—that it is ill suited to make evaluations of competing policy considerations. The court's approach to justiciability is premised on conceptions of adjudication and the judicial function associated with private law models of litigation in which the judge is a neutral and disinterested umpire who reaches a decision on the basis of analysis and application of legal rules.[104] Yet the prominence given to the 'policy role' of the court—both by judges themselves and the Law Commission—present a challenge to this conception.

An even more problematic public policy justification of the court's own making for non-intervention is that to intervene would have a detrimental impact on the court's own resources. Rose J. hinted at this in *R. v Football Association Ltd, ex parte Football League Ltd* [105] when he decided, as a matter of law, that the court had no jurisdiction to review the FA. He added this, however:[106]

> It would be . . . a misapplication of increasingly scarce judicial resources [to review bodies regulating sports]. It will become impossible to provide a swift remedy, which is one of the conspicuous hallmarks of judicial review, if the courts become even more swamped with such applications than they are already. This is not, of course, a jurisprudential reason for refusing judicial review, but it will be cold comfort to the seven or eight other substantive applicants and the many more *ex parte* applicants who have had to be displaced from the courts' lists in order to accommodate the present litigation to learn that, though they may have a remedy for their complaints about the arbitrary abuse of executive power, it cannot be granted to them yet.

Lord Donaldson MR has been even more frank as to his views of the relevance of insufficient numbers of judges to decisions as to whether or not to grant leave to apply for judicial review:[107]

> The public interest normally dictates that if the judicial review jurisdiction is to be exercised, it should be exercised very speedily indeed and, given the constraints imposed by limited judicial resources, this necessarily involves limiting the number of cases in which leave to apply should be given.

This stance poses several difficulties which have been considered elsewhere—not least that it is difficult to square with notions of the independence of the judiciary[108] and the rise of 'managerialism'.[109]

More generally, a number of different objections can be levelled at the way in which the court uses public policy arguments of its own making to justify caution in judicial review cases. First, the court's use of public policy justifications is much less confined, structured or able to be checked than are decisions justified in terms of jurisdiction. Appellate courts are rarely prepared to overturn the decision of a first instance judge to withhold a remedy on public policy grounds. Secondly, the High Court and the adjudicative process is also not equipped to make decisions based on considerations of complex public policy (such as the likely impact of a judicial decision) compared with its ability to deal with the legal issues of the limits of its jurisdiction.

Public policy justifications also present a challenge to constitutional explanations of judicial review. One, only beginning to emerge in modern case law, is based on 'rights'. The increasing importance of legal rights and the court's role in protecting them is being accepted by the court, not only in the context of European Community law,[110] but, more generally, many judges have been developing an interest in articulating reasoning based explicitly on 'rights' both in cases[111] and extra-judicial writing.[112] The importance of this development may be lost if the court asserts power to trump rights for reasons of public policy such as administrative inconvenience. Further, even if one accepts that it may sometimes be appropriate for the court 'to strike a balance between the conflicting public interests', there must—as we have already noted—be doubts as to how institutionally competent the court is to do this given its procedures and personnel.[113] Public policy justifications also challenge another perspective on judicial review, the notion that the primary constitutional function of the court ought to uphold the sovereignty of parliament through the use of the ultra vires doctrine.

The Future Agenda

This chapter has attempted to outline the trends in the ways the court justifies the boundaries of judicial review. Less importance is now attached to jurisdictional limits (the legal constraints of the court) as these have largely been pruned away. The constraints on intervention can now be explained on the basis of the inherent limits of the adjudicatory process (justiciability) and public policy. For Loughlin:[114]

> Modern law no longer possesses a conceptual unity; in so far as we wish to address the unity of law we must talk in terms of a functional unity. Law's distinctiveness today lies in its function . . . the limits of judicial review are derived from the judiciary's sense of the function of the activity within the overall structures of governance.

The shifts we have noted in the ways the court articulates its justifications for intervention and non-intervention seem to support this. Justiciability and policy allow questions about the court's own function to be addressed explicitly in a way which arguments about the court's *legal* boundaries (jurisdiction) do not. This has caused problems on two levels. The first is immediate and practical. How is a lawyer to argue a case before the court when what is sought is, in effect, to alter the boundaries of review? Take, for instance, judicial review of decisions made by the Attorney General. Hitherto, the court has taken the view that such decisions are not reviewable.[115] In any future legal challenge to the Attorney General, how should the court justify its decision? Is it still sufficient to give a 'legal' justification—that there is no precedent for granting a prerogative order or declaration against the law officer and *therefore* the court will not do so? Or will the court need to explain, in terms of justiciability and public policy, why, in 'functional' terms, the court should or should not review in such a case? The problem with the latter is that lawyers and judges may lack the skills to do the latter adequately.

Recent writing about judicial review suggests two quite different routes forward. For some, the answer is to accept that judicial review has grown— or ought to grow—in a way distinct from a model of private law litigation as a contest between two parties with the court as a disinterested arbiter making its decision on the basis of analysis and application of legal rules to the court having a more expansive constitutional role as a regulatory force in government, in which it is able properly to address issues of policy.[116] As Loughlin puts it, 'today it seems that the courts are critically involved in the management of public business; *res justicia* . . . plays no significant role in the modern world of judicial review'. The response of some writers, such as Griffith[117] and Allison,[118] is to advocate institutional reforms, such as the creation of some sort of Director of Civil Proceedings,[119] more oral testimony to improve the court's fact finding ability, the increased use of *amicus* briefs and expert evidence, to equip the court better for its policy tasks. The result of this may well be that the constitutional function of the court becomes little different from that of a parliamentary select committee; that law becomes a less distinct enterprise, just another way of talking about political controversies. An alternative route is to assert that 'law' *is* distinct from policy and politics and that at the core of the court's work should be the protection of legal rights of individuals (including group rights) rather than evaluating what is in the collective interest.

May be it is too easy for criticism to be levelled at the Law Commission's recent report on judicial review remedies and procedures as timid and limited in its scope. The report contains some useful and practical proposals for improving the present procedural system. It is fair to point out, however, that trends and tensions in the case law and academic writing, some of which have been described here, require deep and strategic thinking about the future of judicial review and what it is *for*.

I am grateful to my colleagues Professors Jeffrey Jowell and Dawn Oliver and Dr Stephen Guest for their helpful comments and criticisms of an earlier draft of this chapter.

Notes

1. For interesting recent accounts of how the grounds of review can be moulded to achieve greater or lesser degrees of 'intensity', see P.P. Craig, *Administrative Law* (3rd edn, 1994) pp 433–45 and Ian Yeats, 'Findings of Fact: The Role of the Courts', ch. 6 in

Genevra Richardson and Hazel Genn (eds) *Administrative Law and Government Action* (1994).

2. For detailed analysis of the judicial review case load, see M. Sunkin 'What is Happening to Applications to Judicial Review?' (1987) 50 MLR 432 and [1991] PL 490; and B. Hadfield and E. Weaver, 'Trends in Judicial Review in Northern Ireland' [1994] PL 12. See also Sunkin, L. Bridges and G. Mészáros, *Judicial Review in Perspective: An Investigation of Trends in the Use and Operation of the Judicial Review Procedure in England and Wales* (1993, revised edition 1995); the authors summarise some of their findings in 'Trends in Judicial Review' [1993] PL 443. See also B. Hadfield and E. Weaver, 'Trends in Judicial Review in Northern Ireland' [1994] PL 12 and T. Mullen, K. Pick and T. Prosser, 'Trends in Judicial Review in Scotland' [1995] PL 52.

3. Such as non-statutory self-regulatory bodies: see *R. v Panel on Take-overs and Mergers, ex p. Datafin plc* [1987] QB 815; *R. v Advertising Standards Authority, ex p. The Insurance Service plc* (1990) 2 AdminLR 77; *R. v LAUTRO, ex p. Kendall, The Independent*, 16 December 1993.

4. See further Dawn Oliver, 'Is the *Ultra Vires* Rule the Basis of Judicial Review?' [1987] PL 543.

5. *R. v I.R.C., ex p. National Federation of Self-employed and Small Businesses Ltd* [1982] AC 617 (standing); *R. v Dairy Produce Quota Tribunal, ex p. Caswell* [1990] 2 AC 738 (delay).

6. *R. v Secretary of State for Transport, ex p. Factortame (No. 2)* [1991] 1 AC 603.

7. *M v Home Office* [1993] 3 WLR 433.

8. *Loc. cit.*

9. [1983] 2 AC 237.

10. *Foster v Chief Adjudication Officer* [1993] 1 All ER 705 (HL).

11. See *Roy v Kensington and Chelsea and Westminster Family Practitioner Committee* [1992] 1 AC 624.

12. *R. v Inspectorate of Pollution, ex p. Greenpeace (No. 2)* [1994] 4 All ER 329; *R. v Secretary of State for Foreign Affairs, ex p. Rees-Mogg* [1994] 1 All ER 457; *R. v Secretary of State for Foreign Affairs, ex p. World Development Movement Ltd* [1995] 1 All ER 611. Lack of standing is very rarely the sole reason given for refusing leave: see A.P. Le Sueur and M. Sunkin, 'Applications for Judicial Review: The Requirement of Leave' [1992] PL 102, 120.

13. *R. v IRC, ex p. National Federation of Self-employed and Small Businesses* [1982] AC 617.

14. Other recent and rather broader treatments of the problem of setting appropriate boundaries around judicial review include: Martin Loughlin, 'Courts and Governance', ch. 9 in P.B.H. Birks (ed) *The Frontiers of Liability*, vol. 1 (1994); Ross Cranston, 'Reviewing Judicial Review', ch. 3 in Genevra Richardson and Hazel Genn, *Administrative Law and Government Action* (1994); Sir John Laws, 'Law and Democracy' [1995] PL 72; and Michael J. Beloff, 'Judicial Review–2001: A Prophetic Odyssey' (1995) 58 MLR 143 (the text of this chapter was completed before the publication of Beloff's article).

15. See further, p. 240 below.

16. See *R. v Governors of Bacon's School, ex p. ILEA and Southwark LBC* [1990] COD 414.

17. *R. v Secretary of State for the Home Department, ex p. Swati* [1986] 1 WLR 477 (CA).

18. *R. v Secretary of State for the Home Department, ex p. Davendranath Doorga* [1990] ImmAR 98; [1990] COD 109 (CA).

19. *Puhlhofer v Hillingdon London Borough Council* [1986] AC 484 (HL).

20. *R. v London Borough of Harrow, ex p. D.* [1990] Fam. 133 (CA).

21. *R. v Social Fund Inspector, ex p. Waris Ali* [1993] COD 263 (Brooke J.); *In the Matter of an Application by Maureen Friel for Judicial Review* (unrep. decision of the High Court of Northern Ireland, NICC050). See further Brigid Hadfield, below.

22. *R. v Boundary Commission, ex p. Hart District Council,* 9 December, 1987 (unrep.); *R. v Local Government Commission, ex p. Cambridgeshire District Council and Cambridgeshire County Council* [1995] COD 149.

23. *R. v Secretary of State for the Home Department, ex p. Cheblak* [1991] 1 WLR 890 (CA).

24. *R. v King's Lynn Justices, ex p. Holland* [1993] 2 All ER 377.

25. Order 28, r. 13(1).

26. See Law Com. no. 226, 1994, para. 7.7. See also Justice-All Souls Review of Administrative Law, *Administrative Justice: Some Necessary Reforms* (1988) para. 6.32. For recent decisions in which discovery was refused, see *R. v Secretary of State for the Environment, ex p. Islington London Borough Council and London Lesbian and Gay Centre* [1992] COD 67 and *R. v Secretary of State for Foreign Affairs, ex p. World Development Movement Ltd* [1995] 1 All ER 611. See also Appendix by Paul Maguire.

27. The courts have, on the other hand, become more interventionist in deciding whether documents may be withheld on the ground of public interest immunity: see generally Rt Hon. Lord Justice Simon Brown, 'Public Interest Immunity' [1994] PL 579. See also Brice Dickson, above; but because discovery is so rarely ordered *in any event*, issues of public interest immunity have not arisen very often in judicial review cases.

28. Op. cit., para. 7.12.

29. See *R. v Secretary of State for Transport, ex p. Factortame* [1990] 2 AC 85.

30. Above, text accompanying notes 7 and 8.

31. [1975] AC 396. See further Woolf, Jowell and de Smith, *Judicial Review of Administrative Action* (1995) ch. 17.

32. See Law Com. no. 226, 1994, para. 6.30: 'Some consultees considered that greater care is needed before awarding interim relief where delegated legislation or, where European Community rights are involved, primary legislation was the subject of a challenge . . . It is undoubtedly the case that courts will be very much more reluctant to grant interim orders in such cases.' The Law Commission Report went on to say that although 'there are differences between the review of legislative and administrative powers we do not consider that statute or the rules should create a jurisdictional difference between the two in the context of interim relief' (para. 6.31).

33. See n. 1, above.

34. See Lord Lowry in *Roy* (n. 11 above): 'oral evidence and discovery although catered for by the rules are not part of the ordinary stock in trade of the prerogative jurisdiction'. cf. J.A.G. Griffith, 'Judicial Decision-making in Public Law' [1985] PL 564 where it is argued that there ought to be greater use of oral testimony in judicial review cases.

35. On which, see below.

36. See e.g. *R. v Secretary of State for the Environment, ex p. Rose Theatre Trust Co. Ltd* [1990] 1 QB 504. This is the inevitable product of the approach to standing set down in the *National Federation* case (above, n. 5) where the House of Lords held that in most cases the issue could only satisfactorily be determined by looking in detail at the factual and legal matrix of the application.

37. The position was different before the introduction of the leave requirement for the prerogative orders in 1933; under the old rule nisi and absolute procedure the burden of proof was on the respondent at the full hearing: see A.P. Le Sueur and M. Sunkin, 'Applications for Judicial Review: the Requirement of Leave' [1992] PL 102, 108. Today, the 'burden of proof' (in one sense) can in a few situations be shifted on to the respondent public body; e.g. when it refuses to give the court reasons for administrative action, the court may presume that there are no valid ones: see *Padfield v Minister of Agriculture, Fisheries and Food* [1968] AC 997 (HL).

38. For an interesting analysis of the intrusiveness of remedies, in the context of the USA, see Peter H. Schuck, *Suing Government: Citizen Remedies for Official Wrongs* (1983) ch. 1.

39. For judicial comment on the intrusiveness of the different remedies, see *National Federation* (above, n. 5) and *Rose Theatre* (above, n. 36). In these and other cases the issue of standing has been linked to the intrusiveness of the remedy, so that it is said that a person may have 'sufficient interest' for a declaration but not for (say) mandamus. P. Cane has argued this linkage is erroneous as the sufficiency of the applicant's interest should relate to the application and not the particular remedy sought: see 'Statutes, Standing and Representation' [1990] PL 307.

40. See M. Sunkin, L. Bridges and G. Mészáros, *Judicial Review in Perspective: An Investigation of Trends in the Use and Operation of the Judicial Review Procedure in England and Wales* (1993, revised ed, 1995)

41. Cf. the 'anxious scrutiny' approach adopted when an applicant alleges an infringement of a fundamental human right such as the right to life (*Bugdaycay v Secretary of State for the Home Department* [1987] 1 AC 514) and freedom of movement (*R. v Secretary of State for the Home Department, ex p. McQuillan, The Independent*, 23 September 1994). See further Brice Dickson, above.

42. Law Com. No. 226, 1994, para. 8.17. The report does not reveal how large a majority this is; nor whether support came equally from different kinds of responders (government lawyers, private practitioners, academics etc.).

43. Op. cit., para 7.8. Two-thirds favoured a more liberal approach.

44. Cranston, op. cit., n. 14, p. 45.

45. Fordham, *Judicial Review Handbook* (1994) p. 94.

46. ibid., p. 85

47. ibid., p. 86.

48. 'Law and Democracy' [1995] PL 72 at 78. See further D.J. Galligan, *Discretionary Powers* (1990) p. 228.

49. See below.

50. *R. v Lancashire County Council, ex p. Huddleston* [1986] 2 All ER 941, 945. See also *R. v Monopolies and Mergers Commission, ex p. Argyll plc* [1986] 1 WLR 763, 774.

51. e.g. as to whether Crown Proceedings Act 1947 barred the court granting an injunction against a minister on an application for judicial review: see *M v Home Office* (above, n. 7).

52. On the methods of the common law in this context, see Martin Loughlin, 'Courts and Governance' in PHB Birks (ed.) *The Frontiers of Liability*: Vol. 1 (1994).

53. *R. v Jockey Club, ex p. HH Aga Khan* [1993] 1 WLR 909.

54. See A. Barak, *Judicial Discretion* (1989) p. 7.

55. See e.g. Lord Diplock in *National Federation* (above, n. 5) who said of the statutory words 'sufficient interest' that these are 'ordinary English words which, on the face of them, leave the court an unfettered discretion to decide what in its own good judgment it considers to be "a sufficient interest", on the part of an applicant in the particular circumstances of the case before it' and that Order 53 is intended 'to leave the court a wide discretion as to what interlocutory directions, including orders for discovery, were appropriate to the particular case'.

56. Different considerations apply, of course, when parliament considers how and where to set boundaries to the court's powers by legislation, e.g. through the use of ouster clauses.

57. As in the relation to standing, on which see below.

58. See C. Forsyth, 'The Scope of Judicial Review: "public duty" not "source of power"' [1987] PL 356, 359 and N. Bamforth, 'The Scope of Judicial Review: still uncertain' [1993] PL 239.

59. Cf. Judicature (Northern Ireland) Act 1978, s. 18(2)(b) and the Appendix on the Judicial Review Procedure in Northern Ireland, below.

60. [1987] QB 815.
61. *R. v Criminal Injuries Compensation Board, ex p. Lain* [1967] 2 QB 864.
62. Sir John Laws, 'Law and Democracy' [1995] PL 72 at 75, 76. He adds that the only 'true' exception is the Queen in parliament enacting primary legislation, though of course the courts now have power to review this in so far as it is inconsistent with European Community law.
63. In *R. v Secretary of State for Social Security, ex p. Association of Metropolitan Authorities* [1986] 1 WLR 1 certiorari was assumed to be available to quash a statutory instrument on housing benefit but was refused by the court in its discretion. Certiorari was granted in *R. v Secretary of State for Health, ex p. United States Tobacco International* [1991] 3 WLR 529.
64. *R. v HM Treasury, ex p. British Telecommunications plc* [1995] COD (forthcoming).
65. [1994] 2 WLR 409.
66. 'A declaration may be made or an injunction granted . . . in any case where an application for judicial review, seeking that relief, has been made and the High Court considers that, having regard to—(a) the nature of the matters in respect of which relief may be granted by orders of mandamus, prohibition or certiorari; (b) the nature of the persons and bodies against whom relief may be granted by such orders; and (c) all the circumstances of the case—it would be just and convenient for the declaration to be made or the injunction granted, as the case may be.'
67. Quite often applications in which certiorari is sought are dismissed on the ground that no 'decision' had been made: see e.g. *R. v Leicestershire Education Authority, ex p. Cannon* [1991] COD 120 (father denied contact with children requested LEA supply him with information about their progress; LEA replied outlining its policy) and *R. v Devon County Council ex p. L.* [1991] 2 FLR 541 (social workers allegedly disseminating information to the effect that the applicant was a child abuser; local authority refused to act).
68. See Lord Diplock [1982] 3 All ER 1124, at p. 1133.
69. Cf. Richard Gordon QC, 'Judicial Review and Equal Opportunities' [1994] PL 217.
70. [1987] QB 815.
71. *R. v Secretary of State for Social Services, ex p. Child Poverty Action Group* [1990] 2 QB 540 (CA).
72. Le Sueur and Sunkin, 'Applications for Judicial Review: the requirement of leave' [1992] PL 102, 120.
73. Schiemann J., while acknowledging that it would be logical to deal with the issue of standing first, nevertheless began by dealing with the merits of the applicant's case in *R. v Secretary of State for the Environment, ex p. Rose Theatre Trust Co. Ltd* (above, n. 36).
74. See *R. v Secretary of State for Foreign Affairs, ex p. Rees-Mogg* [1994] 1 All ER 457. Lord Rees-Mogg, a former editor of *The Times*, had standing because of 'sincere concern for constitutional issues'.
75. See *R. v Secretary of State for the Environment, ex p. Greenpeace Ltd (No. 2)* [1994] 4 All ER 352 ; *R. v Secretary of State for Foreign Affairs, ex p. World Development Movement Ltd.* n. 12 above. The *WDM* case was a significant step forward in the trend towards liberalising the requirement of standing because, unlike Greenpeace's challenge to the legality of testing of the THORP plant, none of WDM's members were directly affected as individuals by the decision to grant overseas aid funds to build the uneconomic Pergau dam hydroelectric power station in Malaysia. See further Colin Reid above.
76. Above, n. 39.
77. Cf. Judicature (Northern Ireland) Act 1978, s. 18(4).
78. See Cranston, op. cit., n. 14, p. 50. He notes that the 'English courts have never refined their ideas of justiciability at a level of principle', and comments later at p. 75 that 'the notion that justiciability is a matter of discretion, or can be dealt with on a case-by-case basis, is not especially helpful'. Craig has noted that 'justiciability is a word not

frequently used in our jurisprudence' (in the sense of judicial decisions): P.P. Craig, *Administrative Law* (3rd edn 1994) p. 537.

79. Per Lord Roskill in *CCSU v Minister for the Civil Service* (above). D.J. Galligan has argued that the term may also be understood in a different sense 'to indicate that for certain kinds of *policy reasons* there is to be no review, such as the fact that the decision is of a political nature or is politically sensitive, or it is wartime or an emergency of some kind, or there is some strong reason for leaving the decision to some other authority': *Discretionary Powers* (1990) p. 241 (emphasis added). For the purposes of this chapter, reasoning such as this is considered directly under the heading 'Public policy': see later.

80. *R. v Secretary of State for the Home Department, ex p. Bentley* [1994] 2 WLR 101 (DC). See further B.V. Harris, 'Judicial Review of the Prerogative of Mercy?' [1991] PL 386.

81. [1995] 1 All ER 870.

82. [1995] 1 All ER 870, beginning at p. 881c.

83. A similar weakness arguably afflicts J. Allison's interesting article 'The Procedural Reason for Judicial Restraint' [1994] PL 452. At p. 459 Allison does comment that 'the adjudicative court hearing applications for judicial review does not itself make allocations in regard to public law rights but it does review administrative decisions that have serious repercussions for the allocation of resources'. But this does not really capture the importance of the distinction between original decision-making, appellate and supervisory functions.

84. *R. v Secretary of State for the Environment, ex p. Hammersmith and Fulham and others* [1990] 3 WLR 898, at 933–4.

85. Cf. the different situation where an applicant seeks mandamus to compel a local authority or other public body to comply with a specific mandatory statutory *duty* to provide a service.

86. [1995] 1 All ER 870, beginning at p. 882j.

87. *Discretionary Powers*, pp 246–7.

88. ibid., p. 247.

89. Lon Fuller, op. cit. in text at p. 242.

90. See Lord Scarman in *Nottinghamshire County Council v Secretary of State for the Environment* [1986] AC 240, at 247, and also approach of the Court of Appeal in *R. v Cambridge District Health Authority, ex p. B.* [1995] 2 All ER 129.

91. This reaches further into the substance of a decision than do allegations of illegality or procedural impropriety.

92. [1942] AC 206.

93. ibid., per Lord Atkin (dissenting) at p. 244.

94. See generally John Bell, *Policy Arguments in Judicial Decisions* (1983).

95. Law Com., No. 226, 1994, para. 2.1 (footnotes omitted).

96. *Taking Rights Seriously* (1977) p. 82.

97. *R. v Harrow Council, ex p. D.* [1990] Fam. 133.

98. See e.g. Sir Thomas Bingham, 'Should Public Law Remedies be Discretionary?' [1991] PL 64.

99. See A. Barak, *Judicial Discretion* (1989) p. 7.

100. *The Times*, 12 April, 1990; [1990] COD 414 (DC). See also Paul Meredith, above.

101. See Education Reform Act 1988, s. 105.

102. For discussion of the difficulties associated with this factor for refusing relief, see Law Com., No. 226, 1994, para. 8.18 where the Law Commission notes that the 'factor of merit is sometimes considered under the guise of the inevitability of the outcome' and that 'it is normally incompatible with the court's reviewing function for the merits of a case to be taken into account in exercising discretion whether to grant relief or not'.

103. *R. v Governors of Small Heath School, ex p. Birmingham City Council, The Times*, 14 August, 1989 and [1990] COD 23 (CA).

104. See generally the work of Abram Chayse, 'The Role of the Judge in Public Law Litigation' (1976) 89 HarvLR 1281 on the shift in the USA from private law to public law styles of litigation.

105. [1993] 2 All ER 833.

106. ibid., p. 849.

107. *R. v Panel on Take-overs and Mergers, ex p. Guinness plc* [1990] 1 QB 146, 177–8.

108. See Lord Browne-Wilkinson [1988] PL 44 and Sir Francis Purchas, 'What is happening to judicial independence?' (1994) 144 *New Law Journal* 1306.

109. See Purchas, op. cit. and Loughlin, op. cit. who notes (at p. 110) that 'the judiciary are beginning to examine the system of judicial review not just by reference to conceptual considerations but, having regard to issues of economy, efficiency and effectiveness, also by reference to value-for-money audit criteria'.

110. It has to be doubted whether the right of the court to withhold relief from an otherwise successful applicant can amount to the provision of an 'effective remedy'.

111. See e.g. Steyn LJ.'s judgment in *R. v Secretary of State for the Home Department, ex p. Leech* [1993] 4 All ER 720, Sedley J. in *R. v Secretary of State for the Home Department, ex p. McQuillan* (above, n. 41) and Laws J.'s judgment in *R. v Cambridge District Health Authority, ex p. B, The Times*, 15 March, 1995 (overruled by the CA on the same day).

112. See e.g. Lord Browne-Wilkinson 'The Infiltration of a Bill of Rights' [1992] PL 397, Sir John Laws, 'Is the High Court the Guardian of Fundamental Constitutional Rights?' [1993] PL 59.

113. For discussion of the court's limitations in handling 'policy' see e.g. J.A.G. Griffith, 'Judicial Decision-Making in Public Law' [1985] PL 564 and J. Allison, 'The Procedural Reason for Judicial Restraint' [1994] PL 452.

114. Loughlin, op. cit., pp 110–11.

115. See *Gouriet v Union of Post Office Workers* [1978] AC 435 (challenge to refusal to consent to relator action). In *R. v Attorney General, ex p. Ferrante* [1995] COD (forthcoming) Popplewell J. held that the ratio of *Gouriet* was of general application and not confined to relators. In *R. v Attorney General, ex p. Lisa and Michelle Taylor* (unrep.) Schiemann J. granted leave to move for judicial review of the Attorney General's decision not to commence contempt proceedings against newspapers which had published material prejudicial to the applicants' trial for murder: see *The Times*, 7 December, 1994. (See now *The Independent*, 3 August, 1995. (Ed.))

116. See e.g. Abram Chayse, 'The Role of the Judge in Public Law Litigation' (1976) HarvLR 1281; J.A.G. Griffith, 'Judicial Decision-making in Public Law' [1985] PL 564; Loughlin, op. cit.; and J. Allison, 'The Procedural Reason for Judicial Restraint' [1994] PL 452.

117. Op. cit.

118. Op. cit.

119. Also advocated by Lord Woolf: see *Protection of the Public—a New Challenge* (1990), p. 109.

Chapter Nine

Judge-proofing Reviewable Decisions— Should the Judges be Trusted with Review?

Brigid Hadfield

Introduction

When the government proposed by clause 43 of the Administration of Justice Bill 1985 to remove the right of an applicant for judicial review to 'appeal' a refusal of leave to the Court of Appeal, two Lords Justices of Appeal spoke out from the Bench against the proposal—and then subsequently apologised to the Lord Chancellor who stated it to be 'utterly improper . . . for a Court of Appeal judge or any other judge speaking on the Bench to criticise matters passing through parliament'.[1]

The clause nevertheless was eventually defeated by the House of Lords acting in its legislative capacity.[2] Lord Denning, speaking in the debate on the clause and borrowing words from Lord Scarman, called the clause a 'constitutional monstrosity' and then proceeded to provide a potted twentieth-century history in order to indicate why clause 43 endangered justice for the citizen under the law.[3] These are the salient features of his speech. During the First World War 'government interfered more and more, with ministers' powers in regulations for this, that and the like', protected by clauses 'which said that their decisions were not to be invoked or inquired into by the courts of law'. Lord Hewart's *The New Despotism* (1929) and the (Donoughmore) Committee on Ministers' Powers (1932) 'brought to book many of those excesses of government departments. That was overtaken because during the last World War . . . more and more regulations were brought in and more and more powers were given to Ministers and authorities, and when the welfare state came in we had all the tribunals under the national health Acts and the planning inquiries, and so on. There was much disquiet because no one could control the causes or misuse of power'. The stress which the Franks Committee (1957) laid upon openness, fairness and impartiality for tribunal adjudications and the requirements of the Tribunals and Inquiries Act 1958, however, did a 'great deal to remedy the abuses and misuses of power'.

Lord Denning then referred to a number of Court of Appeal cases in order to illustrate the importance of the Court of Appeal in the judicial review procedure, namely, *Re Gilmore*,[4] *R. v Hull Prison Board of Visitors, ex parte St Germain (No. 1)*[5] and *R. v Secretary of State for Foreign and Commonwealth Affairs, ex parte Indian Association of Alberta*.[6] He concluded by echoing Lord Diplock:[7]

> In a way it has been the greatest development in our judicial system whereby we have been enabled to control the misuse and abuse of power by any of the public authorities. If they misinterpret the law, if they decide most unreasonably, if they go wrong in one way or the other, the courts now have control over them.[8]

It is now highly unlikely that the provisions of the Rating and Valuation Act 1925 would ring many bells. Yet this was the Act which, along with others, caused Lord Hewart, then the Lord Chief Justice of England, to attack the 'new despotism', for this Act both conferred extensive discretionary powers upon the relevant minister and also empowered him by order to modify the provisions of the Act itself as he thought expedient. This is the essence of Lord Hewart's concern:

> A little inquiry will serve to show that there is now, and for some years past has been, a persistent influence at work which, whatever the motives or the intentions that support it may be thought to be, undoubtedly has the effect of placing a large and increasing field of departmental authority and activity beyond the reach of the ordinary law. Whether this influence ought to be encouraged, or whether it ought rather to be checked and limited, are questions into which, for the moment, it is not necessary to enter. But it does at least seem desirable that the influence itself should be clearly discerned, that its essential nature and tendency should be quite plainly exhibited, and that its various methods and manifestations should not be allowed to continue and multiply under a cloak of obscurity. The citizens of a State may indeed believe or boast that, at a given moment, they enjoy, or at any rate possess, a system of representative institutions, and that the ordinary law of the land, interpreted and administered by the regular Courts, is comprehensive enough and strong enough for all its proper purposes. But their belief will stand in need of revision if, in truth and in fact, an organized and diligent minority, equipped with convenient drafts, and employing after a fashion part of the machinery of representative institutions, is steadily increasing the range and the power of departmental authority and withdrawing its operations more and more from the jurisdiction of the courts.[9]

Lord Hewart's main aim was thus the primarily descriptive one indicated by the opening and closing sentences of this quotation—to show the extent to which (an increasingly large amount of) governmental power was beyond the reach of the ordinary courts of law. Although the title of his book indicates the nature of his conclusion, he rightly isolated as a separate question the issue of whether such a development should be encouraged or checked.[10]

It is certainly easy to claim the high moral constitutional ground in terms of arguing against a limited jurisdiction for the courts *vis-à-vis* the exercise of governmental power, especially in the context of a constitutional framework and particularly a parliamentary system which essentially facilitates the vesting of extensive powers in the government of the day.[11] The courts have not always resisted governmental arrogations of exclusive power, particularly during the fifty years ending in 1964—Lord Atkin's *cri de coeur* in *Liversidge v Anderson*[12] best illustrates that. The great quartet of 1960s House of Lords decisions, *Ridge*, *Padfield*, *Anisminic* and *Conway v Rimmer*,[13] swept out the era of judicial passivity and compliance, however, and heralded in an era of judicial activism, greatly assisted by the procedural reforms of the end of the next decade. Lord Hewart would have approved of the 1960s judicial rejection of the argument that the lawfulness of 'administrative' action should not be measured by the principles of natural justice, of the rejection of totally unfettered discretionary power (at least outside time of war or other national emergency), of the rejection of absolute ouster clauses, and of the rejection of the unthinking invocation and acceptance of 'Crown privilege'. In his chapter on 'some leading cases' Lord Hewart had affirmed that '[mere] expediency is not enough to displace the principle that the courts are bound to administer justice in public';[14] deplored the decision of the House of Lords in *Local Government Board v Arlidge*[15] (the 'effect of the decision seems to be that where judicial functions are vested in a minister or government department, parties to the proceedings have none of the securities against injustice which they enjoy in judicial proceedings before the courts');[16] and approved of *R. v Electricity Commissioners*[17] (the 'case is important as showing that the court is not precluded by this form of legislation from intervening if the government department exceeds the limits of its authority').[18]

The importance of the role of the courts as the custodian of the lawfulness of the decision-making of public bodies, so clearly (re-)established during the 1960s, cannot and should not be underestimated. To vindicate the rule of law,[19] to prevent public bodies from becoming autocratic,[20] to provide at least a partial counterpoise to an exceedingly powerful executive branch of government,[21] are all of immense significance. This is perhaps particularly so where the executive can, through parliament, reverse unwelcome decisions of the courts, even (if thought desirable or expedient) retrospectively. This is a power exercised only rarely but exercised nonetheless, most notably in the War Damages Act 1965,[22] the Northern

Ireland Act 1972[23] and the National Health Service (Invalid Direction) Act 1980.[24] The general way in which the courts ensure that the citizen has access to the courts[25] is by the court establishing that it has *jurisdiction* to entertain the particular action, leaving whatever judicial caution there may be to manifest itself in the exercise of the court's *discretion*. This thus enables the court to take the high ground of ensuring that, potentially at least, the exercise of no type of public power is beyond the reach of the courts, whilst facilitating the court's own deference, as and when it thinks it appropriate, to the public body's powers.[26]

Whatever else may be stated for or against this approach, it certainly facilitates the courts in discharging two main functions. First, it enables the judges to be and to become worthy successors to the spirit of the court in *Entick v Carrington*.[27] Although debates concerning the over-concentration of power in the hands of the executive can lead elsewhere than to a debate about the merits of judicial review *per se*—electoral reform, a reformed second (legislative) chamber, reform of aspects of parliamentary procedure, a Bill of Rights and so forth—nevertheless the courts do have an important role to play in the field of civil liberties and fundamental freedoms (whether or not assisted by the jurisprudence of the European Commission and European Court of Human Rights and certainly assisted by the jurisprudence of the European Court of Justice and the fundamental principles of European Union law).

The second (although unquantifiable) role which the courts can pre-eminently discharge is that of being a public forum for the ventilation of specific, often personal grievances—publicity acting as a potential if not actual brake or limit upon the exercise of public power. Both of these functions, it is suggested, one primary, the second an incident of judicial power, are both worthy of preservation and in the case of the former, enhancement.

There is, however, another way of considering the value of judicial review. Lord Hewart, as indicated above, kept separate the description of the concentration of power in the hands of central government from the question whether such a tendency should be encouraged, or checked and limited. Although in terms of the broad principles already articulated, many would agree that the courts have a role to play, it does not necessarily mean that all questions as to the lawfulness of public body decision-making should be resolved by the courts by means of the judicial review procedure. There *may* be more preferable ways of resolving such issues than through the courts. This important issue has, in many ways unfortunately, been subsumed under or submerged by the debate on the merits of tribunals versus the courts, in the context of adjudicating upon departmental decision-making. This debate came to a head, essentially in the 1950s, leading to the institution of the Franks Committee on Administrative Tribunals and Enquiries, to consider *inter alia* 'the constitution and working of tribunals other than the ordinary courts of law, constituted under any Act of Parliament by a Minister of the Crown or for the purposes of a Minister's functions'.[28] The opening paragraphs of the Report on the scope and nature of the inquiry remain important:

> Our terms of reference involve the consideration of an important part of the relationship between the individual and authority. At different times in the history of this country it has been necessary to adjust this relationship and to seek a new *balance between private right and public advantage, between fair play for the individual and efficiency of administration.*[29]

The debates are too well known to be rehearsed in detail here. Franks, following Donoughmore,[30] identified the advantages of tribunals over courts as including 'cheapness, accessibility, freedom from technicality, expedition and expert knowledge of their particular subject'.[31] Tribunals, however, it was urged, should nevertheless be regarded as a part of the machinery of adjudication and not administration, and therefore their procedures should meet the criteria of 'openness, fairness and impartiality', as thus defined:

> In the field of tribunals openness appears to us to require the publicity of proceedings and knowledge of the essential reasoning underlying the decisions; fairness to require the adoption of a clear procedure which enables the parties to know their rights, to present their case fully and to know the case which they have to meet; and impartiality to require the freedom of tribunals from the influence, real or apparent, of departments concerned with the subject-matter of their decisions.[32]

It is, in the light of what follows in this chapter, worth juxtaposing this quotation beside the definition of a 'true judicial decision' as provided by the Donoughmore Committee:

> A true judicial decision presupposes an existing dispute between two or more parties, and then involves four requisites:
>
> (1)   the presentation (not necessarily orally) of their case by the parties to the dispute;
>
> (2)   if the dispute between them is a question of fact, the ascertainment of the facts by means of evidence adduced by the parties to the dispute and often with the assistance of argument by or on behalf of the parties on the evidence;
>
> (3)   if the dispute between them is a question of law, the submission of legal argument by the parties; and
>
> (4)   a decision which disposes of the whole matter by a finding upon the facts in dispute and an application of the law of the land to the facts so

found, including where required a ruling upon any disputed questions of law.[33]

The Donoughmore Committee continued:

> It is obvious that if all four of the above-named requisites to a decision are present, if, for instance, a Minister, having ascertained the facts, is obliged by the statute to decide solely in accordance with the law, the decision is judicial. The fact that it is not reached by a court so-called, but by a Minister acting under statutory powers and under specialised procedure, will not make the decision any the less judicial.[34]

The Franks Committee, in the quotation emphasised above, sought to consider tribunals in the context of the balance between 'fair play for the individual and efficiency of administration'. In the years since Franks (and the Tribunals and Inquiries Acts 1958 and 1971) judicial review has been perceived as the prime forum (or prime generalist forum, as against the specialist concerns of tribunals) for the weighing of these different interests.[35] In order, however, to probe further into the overall value of judicial review, consideration will be given, in the light of the need for this balance, to the merits of an internal review system which has entrusted the application of traditional judicial review principles to neither the courts nor to tribunals.

The Social Fund

The salient elements of the Social Fund (introduced to assist those in need and with a low income) for our purposes can be sketched briefly. The Social Fund was introduced by the Social Security Act 1986 (see now the Social Security Administration Act 1992 and the Social Security Contributions and Benefits Act 1992).[36] The Social Fund is in two parts, the first (controlled by regulations and not cash limited) concerns maternity, funeral and cold weather payments. This part of the Social Fund carries a right of appeal to an independent Social Security Appeal Tribunal. The second part of the Social Fund, which is our sole concern here, is both discretionary and cash limited (not demand led) and covers Community Care *Grants*, Budgeting *Loans* and Crisis *Loans*. Applications for payments out of the discretionary part of the Social Fund are considered by a Social Fund Officer, who is required by the legislation, when determining whether or not to make an award to the applicant, to have regard to 'all the circumstances of the case' and in particular

- the nature, extent and urgency of the need;
- the existence of resources from which the need may be met;
- the possibility that some other person or body may wholly or partly meet it;
- the state of the local office budget; and
- directions and guidance issued by the Secretary of State.[37]

This last requirement is of immense significance, virtually changing a highly discretionary scheme—as far as the legislative framework is concerned—into a highly regulated system with only residual discretion located in a Social Fund Officer. It should also be noted that the directions, which are mandatory, issued by the Secretary of State are not subject to any parliamentary control.[38] In *R. v Secretary of State for Social Services and the Social Fund Inspector, ex parte Stitt, Sherwin and Roberts*,[39] Woolf LJ. (as he then was) referred to the distinction between directions and guidance and continued:

> Directions . . . have to be followed and are therefore equivalent to delegated legislation: unusual delegated legislation, because they are not subject to any form of direct Parliamentary control. There is no requirement for the directions to be laid before Parliament after they have been made and, unlike Statutory Instruments, they are not subject either to the positive or negative resolution procedures.

The directions, however, cover a wide range of issues, often in detail, many of the provisions giving rise to potentially difficult questions of interpretation or meaning. A few examples may be given: 'help the applicant . . . to re-establish himself *in the community* following a stay in institutional or residential care'; 'ease exceptional pressures on the *applicant and his family'* (both direction 4); 'mobility needs' (direction 23, on excluded items for crisis loans); a 'medical, surgical, optical, aural or dental *item or service*' (direction 12 on excluded items for budgeting loans); the meaning of *housing* (cf. accommodation?) costs (direction 29, for example, also on excluded items). It should be noted that the directions do not come replete with interpretation clauses; the reverse is the case, although no doubt the (judicially indicated) best approach for those administering the Social Fund to adopt is 'a common sense' approach, not involving a departure 'from the ordinary meaning' of the words.

An application to the Social Fund is, as stated, determined by a Social Fund Officer (SFO). If the applicant is dissatisfied with the outcome of this determination, he or she can apply to have the determination reviewed by the SFO; and if the SFO is not minded to review the decision wholly in favour of the applicant, the SFO must offer him or her (accompanied if so desired by a friend or representative) an interview. If, on review, the SFO does not revise the determination in the applicant's favour (by, for example, making rather than refusing an award; or by reducing the amount to be repaid), then a further review is (as from April 1994) provided by a Social Fund Review Officer (SFRO). The SFRO's decision may be 'reviewed' by a Social Fund Inspector (SFI).

It is, at this point, that the scheme becomes particularly pertinent to the value of judges in the judicial review process. Social Fund Inspectors (appointed by the Social Fund Commissioner,[40] 'from persons made available to the Commissioner by the Secretary of State'[41]) have, under the department's SFI directions 1 and 2, both review and appeal powers. SFI direction 1 reads:

> In reviewing a determination, a social fund inspector must have full regard initially to
>
> (a) whether the SFO applied the law correctly in arriving at his decision or review.
>   In particular:
>   • that the decision is sustainable on the evidence;
>   • that the SFO took all relevant considerations into account and did not take irrelevant considerations into account;
>   • that the SFO interpreted the law including Secretary of State directions correctly;
> (b) whether the SFO acted fairly and exercised his discretion to arrive at a conclusion that was reasonable in the circumstances, i.e. a decision that a reasonable SFO could have reached;
> (c) whether the required procedural steps have been followed; that the applicant had sufficient opportunity to put his case; and there has been no bias.

That is the review power. SFI direction 2 grants the appeal power:

> If in reviewing a determination initially, [an SFI] is satisfied that the decision was reached correctly, having regard to the factors in direction 1, the [SFI] in reviewing the determination *thereafter* must have full regard to
>
> (a) all the circumstances, including the state of the budget and local priorities that existed at the time the original decision was made;
> (b) any new evidence which has since been produced; and
> (c) any relevant change of circumstances.

On a review, an SFI has the power (a) to confirm the determination made by the SFO; (b) to make any determination which an SFO could have made; (c) to refer the matter (back) to an SFO for determination.

Against the decision of an SFI there is no appeal on the merits, although under section 66(5) an SFI may review a determination already made by himself or herself or by some other SFI.

The Social Fund Commissioner (who is appointed by the Secretary of State) has under section 65 of the Administration Act (in addition to the appointment of the SFIs) the following duties:

   (a) to monitor the quality of decisions of SFIs and to give them such advice and assistance as he or she thinks fit to improve the standards of their decisions;

   (b) to arrange such training of SFIs as he or she considers appropriate;

   (c) to carry out such other functions in connection with the work of SFIs as the Secretary of State may direct; and

   (d) to report annually in writing to the Secretary of State (who is under a duty to publish the report) on the standards of reviews by the SFIs.

Under the scheme as originally proposed by the government, no right of appeal to an independent tribunal—for example, the Social Security Appeal Tribunal—*or to SFIs* was provided for a dissatisfied claimant. The government's reasons (given in the White Paper on the Reform of Social Security which preceded the Act) for refusing any right of independent appeal to a tribunal were as follows. The government accepted:

> that there must be a means of reviewing decisions where individual claimants are unhappy with the outcome. But any such system must also be consistent with flexibility and control of the social fund. The Government's view is that a formal system on the lines of the adjudication system for other social security decisions is not appropriate for reviewing the exercise of judgment by [SFOs]. Decisions which turn on whether it is reasonable to give or deny help in a particular case lend themselves far less readily to a separate, external assessment than do matters which turn on more specific criteria such as the amount of contributions paid or the income received. A necessary feature of any social fund review system is that it should operate quickly and effectively on the basis of knowledge and experience of local circumstances.[42]

This line of reasoning was rejected by many, not least the Council on Tribunals:

> The people most affected by this proposal are among the most vulnerable in our society. Very good reasons are needed before the abolition of the right to an independent appeal in such circumstances, an appeal which has existed for over fifty years. It would probably be the most substantial abolition of a right of appeal to an independent tribunal since the Council on Tribunals were (sic) set up by Parliament in 1958, following the Franks Report. It is for these reasons that we are so critical of this [highly retrograde] proposal.[43]

Although the government's response—the introduction of the Social Fund Inspector level of review—did not meet with the Council on Tribunal's satisfaction, it was at least an acknowledgment that the system as originally envisaged was deficient in the protection of an individual claimant's interests.

('Rights', in the context of a highly discretionary scheme, controlled by government directions and guidance essentially unsupervised by parliament, does not seem the most apposite word.) According to the factors to be weighed in the Franks formula—'fair play for the individual and efficiency of administration'—the original scheme was weighted too heavily towards the latter. The question remains as to whether the institution of the SFIs has redressed the balance adequately. The system has attracted much comment, particularly in terms of the weighing of the respective merits of the SFI system with those of tribunal adjudications,[44] and in terms of the extent to which the SFIs can meet the Franks' criteria of openness, fairness and impartiality. Specifically, concern has been expressed about the extent to which the SFI system ('independent review service' is its current name in Great Britain)[45] can be regarded not only as *functionally* adjudicative but also factually independent of the government. Factors usually mentioned on this latter point include, for example, the fact that the Social Fund Commissioner is appointed by the Secretary of State (not the Lord Chancellor), that the SFIs are appointed by the Commissioner from persons 'made available by the Secretary of State', and that the SFIs operate under directions issued by the Secretary of State.[46] The system probably has adequate flexibility as to allow a Commissioner with sufficient determination and commitment to achieve and to maintain a high degree of *de facto* independence. It is also clear, of course, that flexibility can break either way.

On the extent to which the SFI *system* is truly *adjudicative* (rather than administrative), consideration has to be given to various factors, including the desirability of having legal questions (see SFI directions 1 and 2 above) decided by non-lawyers (albeit with legal advice available). Essentially the government has decided to entrust these questions to non-lawyers, leaving the courts (through judicial review) to play, as will be seen, a residual, indeed marginal, role.[47]

The procedure followed by an SFI in the two stage, review then appeal, process is a 'paper' review on all the documentation, of which the applicant receives a full copy, and on which he or she (or his or her) representative can make comments. There is *no* oral hearing, although (exceedingly) rarely an SFI may visit an applicant in the course of the determination. Full reasons are given for the decision reached by the SFI.[48] There is, of course, no system of precedent to facilitate consistency of decision-making as between different SFIs, although, anyway, consistency would operate against the government's commitment to flexibility in terms of responsiveness to local individual needs.

In 1993/1994, the Independent Review Service received 26,433 applications for review, an increase of 11.4 per cent on 1992/1993 and an increase of 64.5 per cent on the two years previously. Inspectors confirmed

37.9 per cent of the decisions, referred back 14.2 per cent and made their own determination in 47.9 per cent of the cases.[49]

As far as the Commissioner's monitoring role is concerned, the overriding test employed by the Commissioner is 'that the decision should withstand a Judicial Review challenge'. Of the 150 cases examined by the Commissioner, she found 85.3 per cent (128) to be of an acceptable standard, leaving the balance of 14.7 per cent (22) deficient in terms of the 'stringent judicial review' test.[50]

There have been very few judicial reviews of Social Fund Inspectors' decisions[51] (and query—who should be named as the respondent?), and in general terms, the courts have indicated (whilst not necessarily always finding for the respondent) a 'hands-off' approach. So, for example, Brooke J. in *ex parte Waris Ali et al.*[52] said:

> . . . how obvious it is that Parliament intended the management of the social fund to be left to the control of an expert body of people.[53] Decision after decision in the House of Lords over the last fifteen years has made it clear that when Parliament entrusts an expert body of people, whether they be tribunals or civil servants, or, as here, a combination of civil servants and independent inspectors, with the task of fulfilling the intentions of Parliament in a specialist sphere, the courts should be very slow to interfere.[54]

In the conjoined case of *ex parte Semplis*[55] Brooke J. also said of the SFI's decision:

> I have to remind myself that this is not a judgment of a court. This is a decision by an [SFI] who is directing himself in the course of his highly specialist duties in relation not only to the facts of the case before him but also to the directions which he is bound to apply and the guidance which he is under a duty to take into account . . . In my judgment there is nothing to be gained by these courts interfering with decisions by experts in their field provided it is tolerably clear that the decision which they reached was in conformity with the law. This was a decision for the [SFI] provided that he complied with the directions and took such account of the relevant guidance as he considered desirable or necessary. It is his decision and not mine . . .[56]

The issues which have, however, arisen before the courts on judicial review of SF decisions have been of a routine nature[57] as far as the principles of review are concerned, essentially involving the meaning to be given to key phrases or the status or impact of local or national guidance. That said, however, this albeit limited input into the system is nevertheless of importance—a system largely insulated from external perceptions of 'legality', 'fairness' and 'reasonableness', and 'good administration'[58] needs at least an occasional transfusion of ideas or the application of a goad or a tap on the shoulder—whichever metaphor one prefers—in terms of both an impetus for growth and the joint formulation of standards of good administration on the one hand and of external validation and the enhancement of transparency of decision-making on the other.[59]

It remains the case, however, that in the context of the Social Fund, the interests of the citizen depend very heavily upon the work of the SFIs. If in the context of such dealings with the state the adjudicative or judicial model is regarded as the most appropriate, then it is at least arguable that the procedure followed by the SFIs goes a not insignificant way towards meeting the Donoughmore definition of 'judicial' (provided above) and the Franks criteria (as defined) of openness, fairness and impartiality as deemed appropriate for tribunal adjudication. This is not to say, however, that SFI determinations are truly comparable with a tribunal hearing, nor that SFIs are as well equipped (in terms of training, knowledge or expertise) to deal with judicial review principles as are the courts. The point is, however, that the SFI system with sufficient training, monitoring and legal back-up is not as deficient as might at first blush appear. In fact it can be phrased more positively. The combination of SFI directions 1 and 2—review, then appeal—may cause some difficulties in terms of its classification, but together they do facilitate an extensive re-examination of SFO decisions. The system, however, needs resources, both financial and legal, to work, it needs governmental respect for the maintenance, at all levels and in all aspects, of the independence of the Review Service, it needs a Social Fund Commissioner committed to the values encapsulated in judicial review as well as to management[60] and efficiency (what is an effective system is perhaps harder to resolve), and it needs at least an occasional input from the judges themselves to ensure the formulation of principles of general application in what is a highly localised/individual system.

The Northern Ireland Office, Prisoners and Judicial Review

The directions to the Social Fund Inspectors invest them with, in effect, judicial review powers, in the execution of which they are facilitated by the Social Fund Commissioner's statutory duties. The system which has been described in the preceding section should now be contrasted with rule 45 of the Prison and Young Offenders Centre Rules (Northern Ireland) 1995.[61] Rule 45 provides as follows:

(1) A prisoner may petition the Secretary of State in respect of an award made by a governor or by the board of visitors.[62]

(2) A petition will only be permitted under this section where it alleges that—
(a) the facts established did not justify a finding of guilt;

(b) the governor or board of visitors misapplied the prison rules or failed to follow the principles of natural justice;

(c) the award was more severe than was merited by the findings; or

(d) any combination of the above.

(3) The petition will be considered on its merits and a response in writing sent to the prisoner as soon as possible.

(4) Where a petition is upheld any of the remedies provided for under rule 44(1) may be applied as appropriate.

Rule 44(1) is thus incorporated into rule 45 which is a new prisons rule in Northern Ireland. Rule 44 is in substance a pre-existing rule but it contains —as from 1995—a new power. Rule 44, under which the Secretary of State acts *suo motu* (or by implication in response to a prisoner's petition—at least prior to 1995 when the right was expressly granted in Northern Ireland by rule 45—or in response to a successful leave application by a prisoner) provides that:

(1) The Secretary of State may quash any finding of guilt or remit any punishment or mitigate it.

The power to quash is the new power.

(2) Subject to any directions of the Secretary of State, the governor may remit or mitigate any punishment by a governor . . .

(3) In this rule mitigate means reducing the punishment or substituting another punishment which is, in the opinion of the Secretary of State [or] the governor . . . less severe.

The importance of these rules will be considered in the context of the high incidence of Northern Ireland cases involving judicial review of prison disciplinary decisions. In England, prisons cases now account for a very small overall percentage of judicial reviews. Maurice Sunkin in his analysis of 'What is happening to applications for judicial review?'[63] in England showed that the number of applications made during three six-month samples in 1983, 1984 and 1985 for prisoners cases was 34, 42 and 64 respectively.[64] In the years 1987 to 1989 inclusive, however, the figures had dropped to 17 (1.1%), 25 (2%) and 16 (1%) respectively.[65] By contrast, in Northern Ireland the five year period from 1987 to 1991 inclusive witnessed a total of 216 prisoners' leave applications—42.4 per cent of the overall total of judicial review applications in the five year period. Of these prisons cases, over 70 per cent—some 152 cases in all—involved challenges to the decisions of prison governors on disciplinary adjudications.[66] (Very few cases now involve judicial review of a board of visitors disciplinary decisions.)[67]

Some overall context should be provided for these figures. The prison population in Northern Ireland during this time averaged nearly 2,000,[68] including both men and women in the four prisons (Belfast (Crumlin Road), Maze, Maghaberry, Magilligan) and the young offenders at Hydebank Wood Young Offenders Centre. The following illustrative figures for disciplinary hearings held in the prisons in three years are:

1989–90	1,479	(702 at Belfast; 89 at Maze; 204 at Magilligan; 71 at Maghaberry; 321 at the YOC; and 92 at the female section of Maghaberry (now Mourne House));
1990–91	1,249	(711; 16; 131; 66; 311 and 14 respectively); and
1991–92	803	(411; 20; 193; 36; 106; and 37 respectively).[69]

The disciplinary charges brought against the prisoners included violence, damage to property, idleness, trafficking or possession of prohibited articles, insubordination, refusing to work, fouling of the cell and abusive language. The disciplinary hearings thus, potentially, could entail difficult legal concepts such as duress, possession (especially where the object was in a room occupied by more than one person and the evidence did not point to a connection with one person specifically or to joint possession), and the proving of issues arising out of co-ordinated campaigns, as well as entail specific procedural issues such as representation at the hearing or the calling of defence witnesses. The penalties (called *awards*) which may be imposed by a prison governor include cellular confinement, loss of privileges, earnings or remission (all of a limited amount or duration, although not necessarily insignificant to the prisoner), warnings or a caution.

Under the new rule 45 of the Prison Rules, a prisoner's first port of call regarding a challenge to the disciplinary hearing is now—or is arguably now—rule 45. The first matter to note about rule 45 is that it *seemingly* vests the judicial review jurisdiction (or large amounts of it) in the hands of civil servants[70] in the Prison Service Headquarters of the Northern Ireland Office. The knowledge which the civil servants will possess about or the training they will be given on the evolving judicial review principles, the expertise they will bring to bear, the factors they will take into account, their processes of reasoning—all (in so far as they will be publicly known) have to be compared with the salient features of the open review system provided by the High Court and its expertise. (In Northern Ireland, approximately two-thirds of all judicial reviews are heard by the same judge.) Any weighing of their respective merits would have to consider (whatever the outcome in any given case) the interests of the particular prisoner specifically and of prisoners generally, in terms of the overall principles used to influence the decision on the particular petition; the interests of the adjudicating governor and of the prison service generally; and the wider public interest in the administration of and adjudication in the disciplinary system operating in the prisons.

These are only general, first impression points, however, and they must be explored more fully. In the memoranda—notes on the proposed new rules when in draft—issued by the Prison Service Headquarters of the NIO as part of consultation with the public on the draft rules, rules 44 and 45 were explained as follows:[71]

> Rule 44, *Remission and Mitigation of awards*, removes a lacuna from the rules by giving the Secretary of State the power to quash an award. Under the 1982 Rules, he could only remit the punishment or mitigate it.
>
> *New Rule—Petition against Award*
>
> Rule 45, Petition against awards, sets out for the first time in the rules the right of a prisoner to appeal [*sic*] against a disciplinary award. *This right becomes a part of the disciplinary process.*[72] The right of petition does not give a right to a re-hearing of the case but does require that the record of the case be examined to ensure that any award made was justified on its merits and produced in accordance with proper procedure. Petitions will be considered at Prison Service Headquarters and where they are upheld the award may be quashed, remitted or mitigated.

Some light may be cast on the new power in rule 44 (power to quash) and the substantively new rule 45 by reference to certain pertinently directed dicta from both Northern Ireland and England in two cases involving judicial review of a governor's decision at a time when the Secretary of State had no power to *quash* any finding of guilt. The issue pertinent to our purposes is, in Northern Ireland, whether the (then implicit) remedy of petitioning the Secretary of State, absent such a power, could be regarded as an adequate and effective alternative remedy so as to preclude the applicant from seeking judicial review—at least until such an avenue had been exhausted. (Judicial review would then, if sought, lie against the Secretary of State's decision on the prisoner's petition.) In *In Re McKiernan*[73] Lord Lowry, then Lord Chief Justice of Northern Ireland, said: 'If the right to apply to the Secretary of State can be called "a right of appeal", it is only a right of appeal against sentence and provides no other relief . . .'[74]

This was a point considered more fully by the House of Lords in *Leech v Parkhurst Prison Governor*[75] in which Lord Bridge of Harwich (speaking with regard to the English position) said, in the context of the adequacy of the remedy of petitioning the Secretary of State:

One manifest inadequacy of the remedy by petition is the absence of any power in the Secretary of State to quash the adjudication. This may seem of minor significance. If the award has been remitted, it may perhaps be of little consequence that the adjudication of guilt has not been set aside. But, when the prisoner's record shows merely that the punishment awarded for an offence has been remitted by the Secretary of State, those who have to take account of the record, as for example when the prisoner's eligibility for parole is under consideration, will not know in a case such as that of *Leech*, that the proceedings leading to the award were wholly invalid, and it is at least possible that the record may operate to his prejudice. This is a lacuna in the rules which can readily be cured by amendment and it is very desirable that it should be. If the Secretary of State had power to quash the adjudication as well as power to remit the award, it would be difficult to suppose that the court, as a matter of discretion, would be likely to grant judicial review to a prisoner who had not petitioned the Secretary of State, save in a case of urgency where the prisoner's release was imminent but would be delayed by loss of remission ordered by the disputed award.[76]

Clearly, therefore, the inclusion of the new power in rule 44, both in its own right and as coupled with the express powers of the (new) rule 45, is a direct response to these judicial dicta and the two rules together have clearly enhanced the value to a prisoner of the right to petition—at least as far as available remedies are concerned. What, however, of the substance of rule 45? Can it be regarded, in its totality, as an adequate and effective remedy which must be pursued rather than judicial review of the governor's decision, leaving judicial review to be sought, if at all, with regard to the Secretary of State's ultimate decision on the prisoner's petition under rule 45? If the memorandum note to rule 45 is observed, the answer seems obvious. The memorandum, as quoted above, stated that the right to petition the Secretary of State 'becomes a part of the disciplinary process'. If this is so, then it would be very easy for a court to refuse a prisoner who had not invoked rule 45 leave to bring a judicial review against the governor's award on the ground either that as the disciplinary process was incomplete the review application was premature or that there was no *final* decision or determination to be reviewed. (Such arguments would not necessarily apply with regard to, for example, situations where prohibition might be the appropriate remedy.)

If, however, rule 45 is to be regarded as an *alternative* remedy to judicial review rather than as the final part of the disciplinary process—and the rule itself does not state the latter to be the case, although it is in part IV of the rules on Discipline and Control[77]—then can it be regarded as an adequate and effective alternative such as to preclude recourse to the courts (as a general rule at least) immediately after the governor's adjudication? It is clear that the existence of an alternative remedy will not suffice to oust the *jurisdiction* of the court in judicial review;[78] therefore, as far as the exercise and the extent of the court's *discretion* are concerned Lord Donaldson MR, in *R. v Epping and Harlow General Commissioners, ex parte Goldstraw,* said:

> . . . it is a cardinal principle that, save in the most exceptional circumstances, that jurisdiction will not be exercised where other remedies were available and have not been used.[79]

The word 'exceptional' should not, however, mask the fact that the alternative remedies (which would include but not be confined to statutory appellate procedures) must be adequate, effective, suitable or appropriate to deal with the issues raised by the complainant. Various reasons lie behind the exhaustion of alternative remedies rule: for example, the expertise possessed by the alternative appellate body, the desire (or need) not to overload the courts with judicial review applications, and (where the alternative procedure has been provided by parliament) the need (or desire) of the courts not to usurp that procedure.[80]

The need for the alternative remedy to be adequate was emphasised by the House of Lords in *Leech,*[81] discussed above. Lord Bridge said:

> In a case . . . where the ground of challenge to the governor's award was an alleged misconstruction of the prison rule under which the prisoner was charged, it is apparent that, subject to any question of urgency, the court can just as well adjudicate on the point at issue by judicial review of the Secretary of State's decision on the petition as by judicial review of the award itself. But such a case is likely to be exceptional. Most challenges are likely to relate to the conduct of the proceedings by the governor . . . In such a case I do not see how a petition to the Secretary of State can possibly provide an adequate remedy . . . [The] matter will come before a civil servant in the Home Office who will consider on the one hand the prisoner's petition, on the other hand the relevant records and reports supplied by the governor.[82]

Lord Bridge then considered the likelihood, where there was an issue of fact, of the civil servant accepting the governor's account as against the prisoner's account, and the difficulty (in terms of experience and lack of procedural machinery) facing the civil servant in resolving any issue of fact, and then continued:

> If the Court's jurisdiction is limited to considering an application for judicial review of the Secretary of State's decision on a prisoner's petition, the court will have to accept the Secretary of State's findings as a barrier to prevent the use of its own procedure and powers to ascertain the facts on which the validity of the governor's adjudication essentially depends. This cannot be an adequate substitute for judicial review of the award itself.[83]

Lord Bridge's conclusion to this part of his speech contained this memorable sentence: 'If a prisoner has a genuine grievance arising from disciplinary proceedings unfairly conducted, his right to petition a *faceless authority in Whitehall*[84] for a remedy will not be of much comfort to him.'[85] Lord Bridge also stressed the probability that any damage to prison discipline that might result from a frivolous and vexatious use of the judicial review procedure would be substantially offset by 'the advantages which access to the court [would] provide for the proper ventilation of genuine grievances'[86] and perhaps also by the effect that the availability of the court's supervisory role would have on the conduct of disciplinary hearings. Lord Oliver expressed himself in similar terms:

> A review of a governor's decision by, effectively, a civil servant with access only to the paper record, even assuming that the Secretary of State has the power . . . not only to remit an award but to expunge a conviction, must in its very nature be less than satisfactory in most cases.[87]

This is essentially what the position now is in Northern Ireland— assuming that prisoners use the procedure, or that the courts refuse judicial review leave applications until they do, leaving prisoners (and adjudicating governors?) to seek a review of the Secretary of State's decision. Rule 45 certainly limits the grounds on which the Secretary of State can entertain a petition[88]—this 'right . . . to appeal . . . which [is] part of the disciplinary process'—but in essence the rule requires civil servants (at what level of seniority?) to exercise what is in effect a judicial review expertise—and this may well, of course, reduce the number of leave applications being brought —or brought successfully—by prisoners in Northern Ireland. There is little value in overstating the position. When a prisoner applicant does obtain the leave of the court, he or she may also obtain *interim relief*[89] which can effectively remove the substantive impact on the prisoner of the disciplinary award. Also, where leave is granted, the Secretary of State may choose to exercise his powers under (what is now) rule 44. The new procedure does, however, indicate that, for whatever reason, the government is prepared to entrust civil servants with the judicial review powers, thereby diminishing the impact of the factors mentioned by Lord Bridge in *Leech*: the value of the court as an open forum for the ventilation of genuine grievances and the value of the *courts'* supervisory role and evolving principles in and to the governor's adjudicative processes. Public ventilation of grievances is, of course, not always welcome. Rule 45 might also help to 'unclog' the courts, and possibly even save the legal aid money expended on judicial review (leave) applications brought by prisoners.

Judicial Review and the Homeless

Judicial review has been seen to play a marginal role for social fund applicants, who also lack the right to appeal to a specialist tribunal. Prisoners in Northern Ireland have certainly made use of the judicial review procedure, but the pattern may be about to change because of the government's new prison rules. Consideration is now given to a third category of people whom many would also regard as being marginalised in 'mainstream' society, namely, the homeless.

During the debate on the Courts and Legal Services Bill in January 1990, the Lord Chancellor referred to a government review of the homelessness legislation and then stated:

> . . . following the review the Government are anxious that the legislation shall, in future, be administered in a quicker, fairer and more consistent manner. The Government proposes to issue a new code of guidance to local authorities in connection with homelessness provisions,[90]

encouraging local authorities which had not already done so to introduce internal appeal systems to deal with complaints by homeless applicants. The Council on Tribunals, particularly anxious to ensure that financial considerations did not militate against adequate safeguards (especially those as provided by an expert, independent tribunal) for individuals and the public at large, dealt with this statement by the Lord Chancellor in their Annual Report for 1989–90.[91] They stated:

> We have consistently taken the view that the important influence of the subject matter here on the lives of those affected demands a decision from an independent adjudicative body, and we regard some kind of internal administrative review to be adopted by local authorities at their discretion . . . as highly unsatisfactory. We reiterate here . . . and observe that this is a prime instance where, on account of the importance of the issues at stake for the individuals concerned, it would be appropriate to provide the necessary resources for an independent adjudication approach by a body properly constituted for the purpose. We stress that . . . no process of internal review can in any sense be regarded as a proper substitute for a right of appeal.[92]

In the absence of an appeal to a specialist tribunal, the only recourse open to a dissatisfied complainant under the internal system would be leave to apply for a judicial review. The Council on Tribunals was not, however, unduly impressed with the value of judicial review:

> . . . as well as being cumbersome and expensive, [it] often cannot address the point at issue, [and] is not an appropriate remedy for dealing with this kind of dispute.[93]

Here, however, as is well known, the courts, whatever the merits or demerits of judicial review, are reluctant to become too embroiled.[94] The figures on judicial review and homelessness in England are considered by Maurice Sunkin, Lee Bridges and George Mészáros in their Public Law Project report of 1993,[95] but it is not intended to deal with the English position here; rather the position in Northern Ireland will be considered. One paragraph of their report is, however, particularly pertinent:

> Given the lack of an independent appeal right against local authority decisions on homelessness, applicants denied accommodation must rely on local authorities' own internal review procedures, or have immediate resort to judicial review. While the frequent use of judicial review in this area is perfectly understandable from the perspective of the applicants, *the way in which some local authorities use the procedure as a substitute for tighter internal scrutiny of decisions* and as an additional hurdle into accommodation requires much more critical attention from judicial and legal commentators than it has so far received.[96]

In Northern Ireland, in the five year period from 1987 to 1991 inclusive, there were five housing cases *in total* (an average of 1 per cent overall). Two cases were brought with regard to compensation following the making of a vesting order, one involved review of the residence requirements for applicants to the waiting list, and only two cases[97] were brought (both in 1989) with regard to the homeless persons provisions of the Housing (NI) Order 1988, under the provisions of which the Northern Ireland Housing Executive assumed statutory responsibility for dealing with homelessness in 1989.[98]

The Northern Ireland Housing Executive (which is a non-elected public body with responsibility for the allocation of public housing throughout Northern Ireland) does operate an *internal* review/appeal system.[99] No public information is available either on the grounds for making an appeal/review request or on the grounds upon which the decision will eventually be reached. Almost certainly, however, the process will involve a consideration of the factors taken into account in the original decision, its 'reasonableness' and the procedure according to which it was taken. Approximately 10,000 people per annum present themselves for housing, of which 4,000 are accepted as meeting the legislative criteria.[100] Those who are not accepted by the relevant district manager as meeting the criteria are entitled to appeal first to the appropriate regional housing manager[101] and (if that appeal is unsuccessful) to the Director of Housing and Planning in Belfast. If this final appeal is unsuccessful, the applicant may then, if he or she wishes, seek leave to apply for a judicial review.

Analysis of NIHE Homeless Appeals 1989–1994[102]

Period Ending	Total Number of Appeals	Total 1st Stage	Total 2nd Stage	1st Altered	2nd Altered
MARCH 90	63	53	24	16	6
MARCH 91	96	84	41	25	8
MARCH 92	122	103	50	34	9
MARCH 93	198	184	73	63	22
MARCH 94	163	146	69	44	20

It should be noted that in all instances above the total number of appeals differs from the number of first stage appeals. This is due to applicants, who have been turned down under the legislation, appealing the decision, but providing new information at this stage. In these instances the case is looked at again by the district manager, taking into account the new information. In these cases the appeal is not counted as a first stage appeal. Given the lack of any general information concerning grounds of appeal, reasons for accepting or rejecting the appeal, factors taken into account during the appeal/review process and so forth, it is not possible to provide anything other than stark description. Certainly it would appear that this kind of internal review (whatever its detailed nature) fits in with the government's[103] own preferences concerning the handling of homelessness applications. The government has announced its intention now to 'require' each local authority 'to establish a formal mechanism whereby a person can challenge a decision by the authority's officers on the homelessness application'. The motive which lies behind this is 'to lessen the present reliance on judicial review'.[104] It is likely that the Northern Ireland experience—or in terms of judicial reviews of homelessness cases, lack of experience—would serve as a justification for them in pursuing this aim although the arguments on the need for an independent adjudicative body, such as the creation of a specialist tribunal, instead of an *internal* review, are not likely to be dissipated rapidly.[105]

Conclusion

As far as the three substantive areas considered in this chapter are concerned, the government has in essence indicated a preference that the *primary* method for the resolution of 'review' issues should be by administrators rather than judges (or tribunals), leaving the judges with a secondary or residual role.[106] This is what may be referred to as the bureaucratisation of judicial review principles—and it is probably easier (and more acceptable) to attempt to achieve this at the current time (rather than earlier), given that a body of principles and illustrative case-law has evolved. The more routine the issues become, the more they can be accommodated into a bureaucratic rather than a court/judicial structure, always provided that scope is left for the infusion of judicial values into the system which should not be insulated from evolving principles of review or allowed to develop in accordance only with 'internal' values such as management efficiency.

The three substantive areas of the Social Fund, prison disciplinary adjudications and homelessness are not themselves identical, other than with regard to the partial 'exclusion' of judicial review. There are often very significant differences between them. With regard to both the Social Fund and homelessness issues, the courts have not always manifested unbridled enthusiasm at being involved, often for very good reason. The resource implications, their lack of expertise, the problems of delay in the judicial review system itself having an impact upon applicants in very difficult personal circumstances—all of these create a different situation from that created by the (usually) narrower legal/procedural issues raised by prison governors' adjudications (in contrast with other kinds of prisons cases). The level of expertise of SFIs (with the management role and standards of the Social Fund Commissioner) may be very different from that achieved by the NIO civil servants or the NI Housing Executive managers who will have a multiplicity of responsibilities in addition to the review/appeal ones with which they have been entrusted.

It has, further, not been the aim of this chapter to provide a dichotomy or polarisation between the judicial and the bureaucratic/administrative exercise of review powers. In both the Social Fund and homelessness areas, very strong arguments may be presented for the establishment of a specialist tribunal. Moreover, it is not being argued that the SFIs, NIO civil servants or NI Housing Executive managers will *necessarily* decide cases 'less accept-ably' than the courts—indeed in terms of speed,[107] efficiency, fact finding and responsiveness to local needs, their procedures may be better than those of the courts on judicial review. There is no reason—whether judicial review is available or not—why administrative bodies should not continuously seek to improve their own internal scrutiny procedures.

The two issues being aired in this chapter concern, first, the 'Franks formula'—'fair play for the individual and efficiency of administration'. Where the administration itself also 'adjudicates', then fair play for the individual may become—or may be perceived as having become—a subordinate, not co-equal factor.[108] The second issue being aired concerns the values of judicial review as formulated by the courts. Although such values may be overestimated—particularly in terms of the impact they may have on any given administrative structure—they should not be underestimated either.

Martin Partington, in a recent consideration of the impact of judicial review on homeless persons,[109] addressed the issue of whether:

> the process of judicial review should develop as what might be labelled a common or mass procedure, widely available as a means for the citizen to challenge official decisions and resolve citizen grievance; or as what may be labelled an elite process, available on a limited basis only for the special case where something has gone wrong, where there is a need for a particularly authoritative review of an issue of law whether of legal interpretation or the setting of procedures.[110]

This is an issue which the courts themselves must address,[111] but it would appear that, from the government's point of view, the 'common' procedure may (increasingly?) be internalised, leaving judicial review itself as an elite procedure. It will—and should—thus concentrate, for example, on 'macro-issues', such as the susceptibility of bodies to judicial review (particularly important in the context of the privatised and regulatory state),[112] the respect for fundamental rights and freedoms, the relationship between European Union law and domestic law,[113] and other issues of major constitutional importance.[114]

The courts must also—if only through utilisation of their residual role in, for example, Social Fund, prisoners or homelessness cases—continue both to interpret the meaning of at least those laws or regulations which are central to the particular administrative scheme and also to formulate the principles of fair—and transparent—public decision-making. Through such cases it is essential that the principles of review continue to develop, not least with regard to the concepts of proportionality and (more generally) abuse of power. The role of a court—with all that the panoply of judicial power entails—as a ventilator of grievances (especially where the issue is expedited and immediately pertinent) or for strategic purposes is also important in terms of a dialogue (or symbiosis) between the judicial and executive branches of the state.

In the discharge of these functions and in the very essence of this dialogue lies the distinction between what Sir John Laws has termed 'political sovereignty' (which relates to elective power) and 'constitutional sovereignty',[115] in all its manifestations. He writes that:

> Ultimate sovereignty rests, in every civilised constitution, not with those who wield governmental power, but *in the conditions under which they are permitted* to do so. . . . For its part judicial power in the last resort rests in the

guarantee that this framework [of fundamental principles which include both democracy itself and fundamental freedoms] will be vindicated.[116]

Notes

1. HL Debs, 5 February 1985, vol. 459, col. 945. Technically, the leave application is renewed in the Court of Appeal.
2. HL Debs, 19 March 1985, vol. 461, cols 443–64.
3. See n.1, above, cols 940–43.
4. *R. v Medical Appeal Tribunal, ex p. Gilmore* [1957] 1 QB 574.
5. [1979] 1 All ER 701.
6. [1982] 1 All ER 892.
7. *IRC v National Federation of Self-employed and Small Businesses* [1981] 2 All ER 93, at p. 104: '. . . progress towards a comprehensive system of administrative law that I regard as having been the greatest achievement of the English courts in my judicial lifetime'.
8. See n. 1, above, col 943.
9. Lord Hewart, *The New Despotism* (London, 1929) pp 11–12.
10. See also his prefatory note (op. cit., p. v): 'An exhaustive examination of the pretensions and encroachments of bureaucracy—the new despotism—must await greater leisure and another occasion. Yet it seemed to be high time that, at any rate, a note of warning should be offered. *Est quadam prodire tenus, si non datur ultra*.'
11. Although outside the remit of this chapter, it is nevertheless worth noting that parliament itself usually addresses these issues in a most limited fashion. One recent worthwhile development is the institution by the House of Lords of the Delegated Powers Scrutiny Committee with these terms of reference: 'To report whether the provisions of any bill inappropriately delegate legislative power; or whether they subject the exercise of legislative power to an inappropriate degree of Parliamentary scrutiny.' For a consideration of the general principles which inform its work, see HL Paper 57, 2 March 1993. In its first appendix to this report, the Committee provides the terms of reference of the Australian Senate Committee on the Scrutiny of Bills which require the Committee to report whether clauses in the (proposed) legislation, by express words or otherwise: '(i) trespass unduly on personal rights and liberties; (ii) make rights, liberties and/or obligations unduly dependent upon insufficiently defined administrative powers; (iii) make such rights, liberties and/or obligations unduly dependent upon non-reviewable decisions; (iv) inappropriately delegate legislative power; or (v) insufficiently subject the exercise of legislative power to parliamentary scrutiny'. Westminster, please note. See further, C. Himsworth, 'The delegated powers scrutiny committee', [1995] PL 34.
12. [1941] 3 All ER 338, at p. 361: 'I view with apprehension the attitude of judges who, on a mere question of construction, when face to face with claims involving the liberty of the subject, show themselves more executive-minded than the executive . . . [The] judges are no respecters of persons, and stand between the subject and any encroachments on his liberty by the executive, alert to see that any coercive action is justified in law.'
13. [1964] AC 40; [1968] AC 997; [1969] 2 AC 147; and [1968] AC 910 respectively. See also *Re HK (An Infant)* [1967] 2 QB 617, and (particularly with the benefit of hindsight) *R. v CICB, ex p. Lain* [1967] 2 QB 864.
14. Op. cit., n. 9 above, p. 165.
15. [1915] AC 120.
16. Op. cit., n. 9 above, p. 167.
17. [1924] 1 KB 171.

18. Op. cit. n. 9 above, p.172. The preclusive clause in the relevant legislation contained the words 'shall have effect as if enacted in this Act', although the case also concerned the nature of the function under scrutiny ('judicial' or 'executive') and the timing at which the case had been brought.

19. See e.g. *R. v Secretary of State for Foreign Affairs, ex p. World Development Movement* [1995] 1 All ER 915, and specifically Lord Griffiths in *R. v Horseferry Road Magistrates Court, ex p. Bennett* [1993] 3 WLR 90, at p.104: 'If the court is to have the power to interfere with the prosecution in the present circumstances it must be because the judiciary accept a responsibility for the maintenance of the rule of law that embraces a willingness to oversee executive action and to refuse to countenance behaviour that threatens either basic human rights or the rule of law . . . The great growth of administrative law during the latter half of this century has occurred because of the recognition by the judiciary and Parliament alike that it is the function of the High Court to ensure that executive action is exercised responsibly and as Parliament intended.' See further the chapter by Peter Osborne.

20. See, e.g., *Anisminic v Foreign Compensation Commission* [1969] 2 AC 147, at p. 207, per Lord Wilberforce: 'Although, in theory perhaps, it may be possible for parliament to set up a tribunal which has full and autonomous powers to fix its own area of operation, that has, so far, not been done in this country. The question, what is the tribunal's proper area, is one which it has always been permissible to ask and to answer, and it must follow that examination of its extent is not precluded by a clause conferring conclusiveness, finality, or unquestionability upon its decisions.' See also *R. v Herrod, ex p. Leeds City Council, sub. nom. Walker v Leeds City Council* (HL) [1978] AC 403, Lord Salmon at p. 424. For recent extra-curial judicial comments on *Anisminic*, see Lord Woolf, 'Droit Public—English Style', [1995] Public Law 57, at p. 69, and Sir John Laws, 'Law and Democracy', [1995] PL 72, at pp 75–6.

21. *In Re M. (M. v Home Office)* [1993] 3 WLR 433, per Lord Templeman, at p. 437: 'the argument that there is no power to enforce the law by injunction or contempt proceedings against a Minister in his official capacity would, if upheld, establish the proposition that the executive obey the law as a matter of grace and not as a matter of necessity, a proposition which would reverse the result of the Civil War'.

22. *Burmah Oil v Lord Advocate* [1965] AC 75.

23. *R. (Hume) v Londonderry Justices* [1972] NI 91. See B. Hadfield, 'A Constitutional Vignette', 1990, NILQ (vol. 41) pp 54–63.

24. *R. v Secretary of State for Social Services, ex p. Lambeth LBC* 1980 (79) LGR 61. There are, of course, other more 'prosaic' ways of removing or confining the impact of the courts in judicial review.

25. The role of parliament and specifically that of the MP as the forum and conduit (as assisted by the Parliamentary Commissioner for Administration) for the redress of citizens' grievances is outside the remit of this chapter, although of importance. Lord Hewart in *The New Despotism* (n. 9, above, at p. 179) refers to a quotation from Hallam, provided by Lord Shaw of Dunfermline in *Scott v Scott* [1913] AC 417 (at p. 477): 'Civil liberty in this kingdom has two direct guarantees: the open administration of justice according to known laws truly interpreted, and fair constructions of evidence; and the right of Parliament, without let or interruption, to inquire into, and obtain redress of, public grievances. Of these, the first is by far the most indispensable . . .'

26. For a recent judicial (but extra-curial) exposition of the 'high ground' role of the judges, see Sedley J., 'Governments, Constitutions and Judges' in G. Richardson and H. Genn (eds) *Administrative Law and Government Action* (1994). A recent case of considerable constitutional significance in terms of the powers of parliament and of the executive is *R. v Secretary of State for the Home Department, ex p. Fire Brigades Union* [1995] 2 All ER 244

27. (1765) 19 State Tr. 1029.

28. Cmnd. 218, 1957.

29. ibid., para. 5. Emphasis added.
30. The Report of the Committee on Ministers' Powers, Cmd. 4060, 1932, s. III, para. 10, p. 97.
31. Op. cit., n. 29, above, para. 38. The Franks Committee, however, stated that 'a decision should be entrusted to a court rather than to a tribunal in the absence of special considerations which make a tribunal more suitable', (para. 38). They were also aware of the need to avoid overburdening the courts.
32. ibid., para. 42.
33. Op. cit., n. 30 above, s. III, para. 2, p. 73.
34. ibid., p. 74.
35. In terms of the concentration of power in the hands of the executive, as mentioned earlier a strong role for the courts in judicial review is only one element in the overall debate on constitutional reform. Similarly, when consideration is given specifically to the value of judicial review itself in terms of balancing the interests of the individual with that of 'efficiency of administration' (as per Franks), the importance of parliamentary procedure, the MP, the Parliamentary Commissioner and tribunals should not be neglected. Judicial review is only one, albeit probably the highest profile, instrument in the individual's armoury—and arguably the one least attuned to considering administrative efficiency. On this, see further, e.g. N. Lewis and P. Birkinshaw, *When Citizens Complain: Reforming Justice and Administration* (1993).
36. The equivalent Acts for Northern Ireland are now the Social Security Administration (NI) Act 1992 and the Social Security Contributions and Benefits (NI) Act 1992.
37. Guidance is issued by 'area district managers' of the Social Fund concerning local high, medium and low priorities in terms of applications to the Social Fund. Direction 40 requires SFOs to 'control and manage the amounts allocated to them so as to give priority to high priority needs throughout the period of the allocation'. See also n. 38 below.
38. See the Administration Act 1992, s. 168(5): 'The Secretary of State may give general directions to social fund officers or groups of social fund officers, or to any class of social fund officers, with respect to the control and management by social fund officers or groups of social fund officers of the amounts allocated to them under this section.'
    S. 140(2) of the GB 'Benefits' Act: 'An [SFO] *shall* determine any question *in accordance with* any general directions issued by the Secretary of State and in determining any question *shall take account of* any general guidance issued by him.'
39. Unreported, nos CO/1026/89, 536/89 and 1901/89, February 1990. See further Purchas LJ. in the CA (3 July 1990) in this case: 'It is clear from the judgment of Woolf LJ. that he felt surprise and concern at such a delegation by Parliament of its powers of supervision which, for my part, I also, with respect, share. It may be that in this case in the execution of the legislative process that "Homer nodded" with the result that wholly exceptional and it might be thought by some objectionable, powers without any Parliamentary fetter or supervision other than the Annual Report was achieved by the Secretary of State. On the other hand, it may be an unwelcome feature of a dominating executive in a basically two-party democracy'. See also Hidden J. in *ex p. Connick*, June 1993, CO 2083/92: 'The directions are not, of course, primary legislation. They are not even secondary legislation.'
40. See further below.
41. The Administration Act 1992, s. 65(3) and (4).
42. Quoted in para. 11 of the Special Report by the Council on Tribunals, *Social security— Abolition of independent appeals under the proposed Social Fund,* Cmnd. 9722, 1986.
43. ibid., para. 12. See also R. Drabble and T. Lynes, 'Decision-making in Social Security: The Social Fund—Discretion or Control?' [1989] PL 297.
44. See, e.g. Sainsbury, 'Internal Reviews and the Weakening of Social Security Claimants' Rights of Appeal', ch. 12 in Richardson and Genn (eds) op. cit., n. 26 above.

45. In Northern Ireland, the SFIs office is known as 'The Office of the Social Fund Commissioner for Northern Ireland'.
46. The Annual Report of the Social Fund Commissioner for 1992/1993, published by HMSO, 1994, bears on its 'spine' the letters 'DSS'.
47. In the six years of the Independent Review Service as at 1993/1994, 91,850 Inspectors' decisions had been delivered in Great Britain. During this time 15 cases were examined by the courts on judicial review. See the SFC's Annual Report, n. 46 above, para. 1.5.
48. There is no statutory duty on an SFI to give reasons, although if such reasons were not volunteered their decisions might, on a judicial review, be caught anyway by the rapidly evolving law on this matter. Such a duty, however, is contained either expressly or by implication in various parts of the guidance to both SFOs and SFIs. See T. Buck, 'The duty to give reasons', *IRS Journal,* Spring 1995, pp 10–11, 19.
49. Op. cit., para. 1.3. This last-mentioned power of an SFI is, of course, essentially not available to a court on a judicial review application.
50. ibid., paras 2.4, 2.10. Team leaders also carried out monitoring of some 1,369 cases of which 86.6 per cent were of an acceptable standard—para. 2.11.
51. These cases tend not to reach the official law reports. For a discussion of some of the earlier cases, see e.g. T. Buck, 'The Social Fund and Judicial Review', JSWFL 1993, pp 159–73; and B. Hadfield and L. Lundy, 'Ex parte Fatima Ahmed Mohammed', JSWFL 1993, pp 277–81. See also *R v SFI, ex p. Ledicott, The Times,* 24 May 1995
52. November 1992, CO 1649/90, 825/90, 1421/90, 170/92, 2486/92. One advantage of SFI decision-making as against that of the courts on judicial review is the speed of the former. In *ex p. Waris Ali,* Brooke J. said of that case: 'It is a *melancholy fact* that that application, once leave was granted, took two years to come before this court.' Emphasis supplied.
53. See further on this point the decision of the House of Lords in *Chief Adjudication Officer v Foster* [1993] 2 WLR 292, that a Social Security Commissioner had jurisdiction, whenever it was necessary to do so in determining whether a decision under appeal was erroneous in law, to determine whether or not a provision of the relevant regulations was *ultra vires* the Secretary of State. Lord Bridge of Harwich stated at p. 301: 'I am pleased to reach that conclusion for two reasons. First, it avoids a cumbrous duplicity [*sic—sc* duplication] of proceedings which could only add to the already overburdened list of applications for judicial review awaiting determination by the Divisional Court. Secondly, it is, in my view, highly desirable that when [the CA or HL] are called upon to determine an issue of the kind in question they should have the benefit of the views upon it of one or more of the Commissioners, who have great expertise in this somewhat esoteric area of law.' The expertise of an SFI and a Social Security Commissioner, however, are not of course identical.
54. Note also the value of s. 66(5), mentioned in the text, in the context of threatened judicial review where the SFI believes there is merit in the applicant's contentions. From April 1994 to December 1994, 543 cases were reopened under s. 66(5) (although it is not implied in any way that all these were connected with threatened judicial review proceedings). See *IRS Journal,* op. cit., n. 48 above, p. 8. For the parliamentary background to this provision, see Baroness Trumpington, Under-Secretary of State in the Department of Health and Social Security on the House of Lords' debates on the Commons' Amendments to the Social Security Bill: ' . . . we have taken the opportunity of this change to the provisions relating to [SFIs] to correct a minor defect in the Bill as drafted. Before amendment there was no power in the Bill to change an inspector's decision. We concluded that this was too rigid . . . [so] we have brought forward an amendment to give [SFIs] the power to review their own decisions so that problems can be avoided.' HL Debs, 24 July 1986, vol. 479, col. 431.
55. See n. 52 above.
56. See also McCollum J. in *In Re Friel* (NI, unreported, February 1993): 'I make the general comment that this type of case does not readily lend itself to judicial review for

the reason that the extensive code of directions . . . [the SF] manual and the guidance issued by the area [office] are together directed to investing a great deal of discretion in the officers and inspectors in whose hands the duty of administering the Fund is statutorily placed. It will be a very rare case, it seems to me, that a court will be entitled to interfere in any way with a decision made, unless it can be clearly shown that the officer or inspector has gone right outside the statutory powers that he is given, or has failed to comply with the directions, or has failed to understand and properly apply the guidance that is given in the various regulations that are provided for his use.'

57. The exception to this is (probably) *ex p. Stitt*, see text and n. 39, above, which involved a challenge to the validity of directions, issued by the Secretary of State.

58. The SFC and SFIs are not subject to the Parliamentary Commissioner for Administration. They are not mentioned in the schedule to the Parliamentary Commissioner Act 1967, as amended; nor, in general terms (if their independence is to be respected) could they be said to be carrying out 'action taken by or on behalf of a government department'. The SFC does, however, aim to provide standards of service consistent with Citizen's Charter principles; see e.g. Annual Report 1993/94, ch. 7.

59. See particularly Lord Donaldson for the partnership approach in *R. v Lancashire CC ex p. Huddleston* [1986] 2 All ER 941, at p. 945: ' . . . a new relationship between the courts and those who derive their authority from the public law, one of partnership based on a common aim, namely the maintenance of the highest standards of public administration'. See also *R. v Monopolies and Mergers Commission, ex p. Argyll Group* [1986] 1 WLR 763.

60. Baroness Trumpington in the House of Lords (see n. 54, above, op. cit., loc. cit.) said: 'The [SFC's] job is managerial and his responsibilities are to ensure that [SFIs] act impartially and carry out their functions to the highest standard.'

61. Statutory Rules of Northern Ireland, SR 1995, No. 8. The rules were made on 10 January 1995 and came into operation on 1 March 1995.

62. The positions in Northern Ireland and England are not identical. For example, in Northern Ireland, the boards of visitors continue to hear the more serious disciplinary charges (unlike the current position in England); see rule 40, SR 1995, No. 8. There is no prisons ombudsman for Northern Ireland; specific complaints of maladministration in the administration of the prisons, falling within the responsibilities of the Northern Ireland Office, should be made to the UK Parliamentary Commissioner for Administration (currently Mr William Kennedy Reid) and not to the NI Parliamentary (or Assembly) Commissioner within whose remit fall the six Northern Ireland departments. There are very few complaints made by NI prisoners to the PCA, probably averaging out at around one per annum. The material in the text above is deliberately kept at a general level; for the substantive law more fully considered, see the chapter by Stephen Livingstone.

63. 1987 MLR 432.

64. ibid., at p. 441, Table 4.

65. M. Sunkin, L. Bridges, G. Mészáros, 'Judicial Review in perspective', *Public Law Project,* 1993, at pp. 4, 7.

66. See B. Hadfield and E. Weaver, 'Trends in Judicial Review in Northern Ireland', [1994] PL pp 11–16.

67. For fuller detail, see B. Hadfield and E. Weaver, 'Judicial Review in perspective', Summer 1995, NILQ forthcoming. See also in this context and in the context of what follows in the text, the Law Commission's Report on Administrative Law, LC No. 226, 1994, para. 2.23: 'In principle the fact that a particular jurisdiction throws up a large number of judicial review cases is an indicator that a right of appeal or other supervisory review is needed, or that, if one exists, it is not regarded as satisfactory by those who use it.' Earlier, at para. 2.18, the Law Commission stated: 'The absence of an internal mechanism of review by a senior official, which can be effective and just, was

also identified as contributing to the problems in many types of case where there is no right of appeal.'

68. See e.g. for 1991–1992 the total of 1,827 provided on p. 10 of the Report on the Work of the Northern Ireland Prison Service 1991–1992, HC 331, 1992–1993. Deliberately, no attempt is made here to use figures from the years which overlap with the years covered by the NI PLP research. These figures are provided not only with regard to the incidence of judicial review, but also as background information to the 1995 rules themselves.

69. The Annual Reports on the Work of the Northern Ireland Prison Service for 1989–90, 1990–91 and 1991–92 at respectively HC 2, 1990–91, p. 9, HC 46, 1991–92, p. 12 and HC 331, 1992–93, p. 13.

70. Cf. the *specialist* cadre of the Social Fund Inspectorate, and the back-up they receive and the monitoring provided by the SFC.

71. Draft Prison and YOC Rules (NI). Draft published by the Prison Service Northern Ireland, 11 April 1994, p. xiv.

72. Emphasis added.

73. [1985] 6 NIJB 6 (NICA).

74. ibid., at p. 23. Lord Lowry here is in effect analysing the judgment of Glidewell J. in the DC in *R. v Camphill Prison, ex p. King.* [1984] 3 All ER 897 gives the CA judgments. Lord Lowry in the immediately preceding sentences to the quotation above said: 'Glidewell J. rightly said that the absence of an alternative remedy is an "argument in favour of the court being able and willing to review a decision", but the furthest, again rightly, in my opinion, that he puts the contrary proposition is that the existence of an *adequate* remedy (emphasis per Lord Lowry), even when the decision is of a kind which is clearly reviewable, is a matter which the court may decide justifies it in exercising its discretion not to grant relief.'

75. [1988] 1 All ER 485.

76. ibid., at p. 500.

77. Cf. the more general r. 79(1) of the 1995 rules: 'A prisoner may petition the Secretary of State about any matter relating to his imprisonment.' Rule 36(6) provides: 'Every charge against a prisoner shall be dealt with by the governor or, in a prison where a deputy governor has been appointed, by the deputy governor; but where neither the governor nor the deputy governor is available the governor may delegate the inquiry [into the charge] to another governor authorised by the Secretary of State to deal with charges.' Cf. the previous r. 29(3).

78. See e.g. Lord Oliver in *Leech*, n. 75, above, at p. 510: 'An alternative remedy for abuse or excess, whether effective or not, may be a factor, and a very weighty factor, in the assessment of whether the discretion which the court undoubtedly has to grant or refuse judicial review should be exercised. But it cannot, as I see it, bear on the question of the existence of the jurisdiction.'

79. [1983] 3 All ER 257, at p. 262. See also *R. v Chief Constable of Merseyside Police, ex p. Calveley* [1986] 1 All ER 257, *R. v Birmingham CC, ex p. Ferrero* [1993] 1 All ER 530 and (quoted with approval in *Calveley*) *R. v Hallstrom, ex p. W.* [1985] 3 All ER 775, at pp 789–90, per Glidewell LJ.: 'Whether the alternative statutory remedy will resolve the question at issue fully and directly, whether the statutory procedure would be quicker, or slower, than procedure by way of judicial review, *whether the matter depends on some particular or technical knowledge which is more readily available to the alternative appellate body*, these are amongst the matters which a court should take into account when deciding whether to grant relief by way of judicial review when an alternative remedy is available.' Emphasis added.

80. See e.g. Lord Donaldson MR in *R. v Panel on Take-overs and Mergers, ex p. Guinness* [1990] 1 QB 146, at pp 177–8: 'it is not the practice of the court to entertain an application for judicial review unless and until all avenues of appeal have been

exhausted, at least in so far as the alleged cause of complaint could thereby be remedied . . . it is not for the court to usurp the functions of the appellate body.'

81. n. 75, above.
82. At p. 500.
83. ibid., pp. 500–501.
84. Emphasis supplied; words also appropriate in the context of Northern Ireland, to the NIO's Prison Service Headquarters.
85. Op. cit., at p. 501.
86. ibid.
87. ibid., at p. 512.
88. It is interesting to note, albeit in a different context, the contents of this letter from Treasury Solicitor to Legal Advisers' Branch of the Home Office in December 1983 (before governors' disciplinary decisions in England had been held to be susceptible to judicial review): 'You will remember the recent decision in the case of Mr Ewing when, although we had a strong case on the facts, it was decided to concede the case in order to avoid a decision that governors' adjudications are reviewable.' Quoted by M. Loughlin and P. Quinn, 'Prisons, Rules and Courts', 1993 MLR 497, at p. 515, n. 122.
89. See B. Hadfield and E. Weaver, 1995, op. cit., n. 67. The *absence* of interim relief may, of course, also cause difficulties for the prisoner applicant.
90. HL Debs 1989–90, vol. 514, col. 949, 23 January 1990. On this also see further below.
91. HC 64, 1990–91.
92. ibid., para. 1.8 and 1.9.
93. ibid., para. 2.18. See also para. 2.22: 'As matters stand, however, the internal review system now being advocated by the Government for adoption by local authorities represents, in our view, perhaps the least satisfactory arrangement which could be devised in terms either of its adequacy as an appeal mechanism or of its perceived independence.'
94. See most notably—and most often cited—the dictum of Lord Brightman in *R. v Hillingdon LBC, ex p. Puhlhofer* [1986] AC 484: ' . . . in the end the local authority will have to balance the priority needs of the homeless on the one hand, and the legitimate aspirations of those on their housing waiting list on the other hand . . . I am troubled at the prolific use of judicial review for the purpose of challenging the performance by local authorities [of their statutory functions] . . . I think that great restraint should be exercised in giving leave to proceed by judicial review . . . I express the hope that there will be a lessening in the number of challenges which are mounted against local authorities who are endeavouring, in extremely difficult circumstances, to perform their duties [under the Act] with due regard for all their other housing problems.' At pp 517–18.
95. pp 2–3 and pp 13–15 particularly.
96. ibid., pp 14–15. Emphasis supplied. One problem facing the homeless regarding use of judicial review is that of delay. See pp 49–53 and 56–61. See also n. 52. For judicial differences of opinion concerning a duty to give reasons in this general area, cf. *R. v Lambeth BC, ex p. Walters* 26 HLR 170 and *R. v Royal Borough of Kensington and Chelsea, ex p. Grillo* (CA), *The Times,* 13 May 1995.
97. *In re O'Neill* [1990] 3 NIJB 1, and *In re Canavan,* judgment delivered by Murray LJ. 28 June 1991.
98. See B. Hadfield and E. Weaver, op. cit. n. 67 above.
99. Where complaints of maladministration against the Housing Executive are made to the Commissioner for Complaints (the 'ombudsman' responsible for investigating complaints of maladministration by local and public bodies) under the terms of what is currently the Commissioner for Complaints Act (NI) 1969, the Commissioner refers these complaints to the Executive to be dealt with under its own complaints procedure. See e.g. Annual Report of the Ombudsman for NI 1994, HC 252, March 1995, pp 32–3.
100. See B. Hadfield and E. Weaver, op. cit., n. 67, above.

101. This appeal is usually processed within ten working days, as is the second stage of the appeal procedure.
102. Details kindly provided by the NI Housing Executive.
103. See also Lord Donaldson in *R. v Legal Aid Board, ex p. Hughes,* 1992 CA: '[There is a] need for an independent specialist tribunal to deal with homeless persons' cases. If such a tribunal existed, it would only be rarely that the *inherently inappropriate* judicial review jurisdiction of the High Court would be involved.' Quoted by M. Partington, 'Reforming Judicial Review: the impact on homeless persons' cases' JSWFL 1994 47, at p. 59. Emphasis supplied by Partington.
104. Quoted by the Law Commission, op. cit., n. 67 above, para. 2.26.
105. The Law Commission's own preference is the creation of a right of appeal to a court or independent tribunal: ibid. See also M. Partington, op. cit., n. 103 above, at pp 59–61, and the Council on Tribunal's arguments in text above.
106. See R. Cranston, 'Reviewing judicial review', ch. 3 in G. Richardson and H. Genn (eds) op. cit., n. 26 above, at p. 45: '[This] chapter . . . argues that administrators can develop an expertise in, and a detailed overview of an area which the courts may never acquire.'
107. Prisoners cases have frequently faced less difficulty here, either through being expedited or through the grant of interim relief.
108. In terms of the NIO and rule 45, however, it should not be assumed that the NIO is simply an administrative extension of the adjudicating governor. Also, as from 1 April 1995 the NI Prison Service becomes an executive agency.
109. See n. 103, above.
110. ibid., pp 54–5. On p. 55 he lists six purposes to judicial review, namely: 'ensuring the legitimacy of government through controlling acts of administrative bodies; interpreting the law; controlling procedures; reviewing decisions taken by the administration; providing remedies; and protecting fundamental values'.
111. See, e.g. Sedley J. in *Public Law* 1993, at p. 544: '. . . odd though it may seem, judicial review has not yet made up its mind what it is or where it is going'. See also the chapter by Andrew Le Sueur.
112. On this topic, European Union/Community law on the meaning of an 'emanation of the State' may be particularly valuable.
113. This will be of increasing importance given the expanding reach of European law after the Treaty on European Union, for example, with regard to the concept of European citizenship and aspects of political union (such as justice and home affairs, including immigration and combating international crime and terrorism, social policy, education, consumer policy, health and the environment). Also of importance here is, for example, art. F(2) of the Treaty on European Union: 'The Union shall respect fundamental rights, as guaranteed by the [ECHR] . . . and as they result from the constitutional traditions common to the Member States, as general principles of Community Law'.
114. e.g. as in *ex p. Fire Brigades Union* [1995] 2 All ER.
115. Sir John Laws, 'Law and Democracy', op. cit., n. 20, above, at p. 92.
116. ibid., emphasis supplied.

Chapter 10

Judicial Review in Scotland

C.M.G. Himsworth

Introduction

A feature of legal scholarship in Scotland, well known even to those outside the jurisdiction, has been the attention given to asserting the autonomy of the Scottish legal order in the face of the domineering pretensions of its larger neighbour to the south. There have been a variety of motivations for this which have ranged from quite overt legal nationalism (whether or not also accompanied by political nationalism) to a more disinterested concern about relationships between legal systems, mixed systems of law, their historical origins and their probable future development. It is, however, true to say that most of the scholarly energy in this field has been devoted to the study of Scots law as a body of private law and much less to public law issues and the explanation for this must lie, quite uncontroversially and unsurprisingly, in the historical predominance of doctrinal concern for private law rules and principles. The civilian inheritance of Scots law is primarily to be found in the doctrine shared by the institutional writers of ancient Rome and Holland and Scotland. What are now recognised as public law issues maintained a very low profile in these sources and have, since the Union of 1707, in any event, been assumed to run very much in parallel in England[1] and in Scotland[2]. This similarity of development should not be overstated. Despite a long period of quietism, it was the Union Treaty itself which was invoked in *MacCormick v Lord Advocate*[3] to establish the basis of a challenge to 'the distinctively English principle'[4] of the unlimited sovereignty of parliament. The credibility of such a challenge has been kept alive in a number of cases in the Court of Session since *MacCormick*—most recently in legal campaigns against the poll tax.[5] None of these has registered any clear success in establishing a significant inroad into parliamentary supremacy—but, as an aside, it has also been interesting to see an attempt to invoke the Acts of Union in England in the case where the (Scottish) Lord Chancellor's legal aid regulations were judicially reviewed on grounds including conflict with the Treaty.[6] The application was not successful.

Whatever the formal status of the Treaty, however, there is no doubt that the institutions of government which were continued (and arguably entrenched) in Scotland under the terms of the Union have produced a different environment within which public law could develop. The system of local government (in particular, the burghs which survived as authorities until the reorganisation of 1975) is often held up as one of the distinctive characteristics of Scottish society. Although the Local Government (Scotland) Act 1973 removed much that was distinctive about the structure of Scottish local government and the 1996 reorganisation will bring another major change—though one which, in its restoration of single-tier government in the cities and the re-creation of authorities in many of the old county areas, may in some small respects appear to revive older traditions— central government in Scotland, in particular the Scottish Office, does certainly have a different character from south of the border. Intermediate government by quango has taken a different direction with the creation, for instance, of Scottish Enterprise and Highlands and Islands Enterprise and to be demonstrated again from April 1996 with the addition of the three new water and sewerage authorities. The administration of the police service in Scotland has also developed rather differently.

Beyond the institutions, much of Scots public law doctrine has, especially in those areas where common law rules predominate, been quite different from equivalent English rules, the best example probably being that of police powers and civil liberties, where earlier common law differences have been joined by differences in modern statutory codes.[7] Elsewhere the divergences between Scots and English law appear more sporadic, although a different approach by courts to the Crown and the exercise of prerogative power may be sufficient to explain and then link, for instance, a more enlightened (that is, more restrictive) attitude to claims of Crown privilege in the days preceding *Conway v Rimmer*[8] and a historically relaxed approach to delictual (tort) actions against public bodies including the Crown. Nineteenth-century differences in the House of Lords in relation to non-Crown authorities were eventually resolved in favour of holding them liable in reparation, the view originally adopted in the Court of Session,[9] and it was well into the twentieth century before that court abandoned earlier authority according to which the Crown could be sued in reparation in Scotland.[10] Since then, the Crown Proceedings Act 1947 has statutorily reimposed civil liability, although interpretations of the different impact of the Act upon Scottish procedures have recently led the Second Division to deny the application of *M. v Home Office*[11] and to continue to protect the Crown from interdict proceedings.[12]

A recent analysis[13] of the divergence of the rules on Crown privilege/ public interest immunity has reminded us of Professor John Mitchell's insistence on the 'merits of disharmony'[14] between rules in the two neighbouring jurisdictions—the merits of one set of rules can show up the defects of another—but the bigger question of how far a system of rules of public law could subsist alongside another within the same state, in the same way that the systems of private law are said to coexist, is more difficult. What indeed does it (or would it) mean for a single state to have two systems of public law?

This is a question which must, in its generality, be addressed on some other occasion. It does, however, provide the backdrop to the more specific issues to be discussed in the remainder of this chapter and which are confined to judicial review in administrative law. In presentational terms, the chapter is a study of a series of suggested differences between judicial review in Scotland and in England. These include differences of constitutional function; differences in the practice of judicial review by reference to reviewable institutions and procedures; and differences in the substantive and procedural rules of judicial review. First, however, at the heart of the chapter is an account of the one characteristic of judicial review in Scotland which in recent writing has begun to mark it out as sharply different from English practice—the rejection of a public/private test as the determinant of the limits of the Court of Session's supervisory jurisdiction and thus of the scope of judicial review.

The Supervisory Jurisdiction of the Court of Session

The rules of the Court of Session have recently been reissued in a consolidated new version[15] and, since 5 September 1994, it is rule 58.3 which requires that 'an application to the supervisory jurisdiction of the court . . . shall be made by petition for judicial review'. Thus, the scope of the application for judicial review, first introduced under that name in 1985,[16] is defined by reference to the court's 'supervisory jurisdiction', to which it provides exclusive access. The procedure was created in the aftermath of *Brown v Hamilton District Council*[17] in which it was finally decided that judicial review (and, in particular, the remedy of reduction— which quashes an act or decision) was available only in the Court of Session and not in the sheriff court. In the course of his speech in that case Lord Fraser urged that there would be advantages in the adoption of a special procedure in the Court of Session which would make speedy and cheap remedies available but also protect public authorities from unreasonable actions.[18] In the report of the working party established to consider such a procedure, and chaired by Lord Dunpark, it was recommended that a new form of application should give access to the 'supervisory jurisdiction of the

Court of Session *in relation to acts or decisions of inferior courts, tribunals, public authorities, public bodies, or officers acting in a public capacity*[19] (emphasis added). In the form of the rule eventually promulgated, however, these qualifying words referring to tribunals and public bodies were dropped, with consequences which cannot have been anticipated at the time. The term 'supervisory jurisdiction' is not one of long standing in the law of Scotland. Early references are instead to the 'supervisory powers' of the court, its 'superintending' authority and its 'supereminent jurisdiction', and it may have been only in the 1970s that 'supervisory jurisdiction' began to be used.[20] This is not a merely terminological issue but one which makes it far from clear what, in the modern law, is included within the supervisory jurisdiction and what is beyond its reach. There is, for instance, an ancient power known as the *nobile officium* which, whilst once described as a part of the court's supereminent jurisdiction,[21] is today exercised quite separately from judicial review proceedings and must, therefore, be assumed not to be an aspect of the modern supervisory jurisdiction.

Because the scope of the jurisdiction is itself uncertain, the failure to demarcate the boundaries of that area of the jurisdiction to which an application for judicial review should relate (whether by restriction to public authorities, as suggested by Dunpark, or whatever) has given rise to many of the problems which have become very familiar in England. It has also, however, provided the opportunity for a very different response. Some commentators have celebrated this response as a means of escape from the misguided rigidity of the present English rules.[22] There are, however, many reasons to be sceptical about this and it is to this debate that this section is devoted.

The primary focus is the decision of the First Division in *West v Secretary of State for Scotland*,[23] a case in which the court, in the opinion written by Lord President Hope, sought, quite deliberately, to stake out the boundaries of the supervisory jurisdiction and the principles applicable within it. In so doing, the court went much further than was necessary to decide that a prison officer who complained that he had been unreasonably denied removal expenses on transfer from one prison to another could not do so by means of judicial review. It was simply, the court said, a private dispute between employee and employer which was not reviewable under the supervisory jurisdiction.

This question of the reviewability of employment decisions is one of those which are similarly difficult to resolve in England but, although the particular result in *West* might well have been the same there, the court's purpose was to draw important distinctions between the principles applicable in the two jurisdictions. In cases prior to *West*[24] the impression had been given that, in employment cases at least, susceptibility to judicial review depended, very much in the English mode, on establishing a 'public law' element in the decision under review. This approach had been modified by the First Division in *Watt v Strathclyde Regional Council*[25] where, in particular, Lord Clyde insisted[26] that the test of reviewability did not turn on the public/private distinction familiar in England. The historical emergence of the supervisory jurisdiction, he argued, denied this distinction.[27]

It was this idea that Lord President Hope (who was also part of the court in *Watt*) developed much more fully in *West*, both by analysis of principles underlying decisions since the sixteenth century and in relation to contemporary issues.[28] The breadth of this survey enabled Lord Hope to go far beyond what was necessary to decide *West* itself and to lay down some more general principles governing judicial review and the supervisory jurisdiction as a whole. It may be most convenient to proceed first to the exposition of those principles and indeed to set them out at some length before turning more critically to their origins in the judgment and to their implications for the future development of judicial review in Scotland.

Lord Hope first offered three propositions (expressed by reference to the old Rule of Court 260B):

(1) The Court of Session has power, in the exercise of its supervisory jurisdiction, to regulate the process by which decisions are taken by any person or body to whom a jurisdiction, power or authority has been delegated or entrusted by statute, agreement or any other instrument.

(2) The sole purpose for which the supervisory jurisdiction may be exercised is to ensure that the person or body does not exceed or abuse that jurisdiction, power or authority or fail to do what the jurisdiction, power or authority requires.

(3) The competency of the application does not depend upon any distinction between public law and private law, nor is it confined to those cases which English law has accepted as amenable to judicial review, nor is it correct in regard to issues about competency to describe judicial review under Rule of Court 260B as a public law remedy.[29]

He then went on to set out, by way of explanation, certain further 'important points':

(a) Judicial review is available, not to provide machinery for an appeal, but to ensure that the decision maker does not exceed or abuse his powers or fail to perform the duty which has been delegated or entrusted to him. It is not competent for the court to review the act or decision on its merits, nor may it substitute its own opinion for that of the person or body to whom the matter has been delegated or entrusted.

(b) The word 'jurisdiction' best describes the nature of the power, duty or authority committed to the person or body which is amenable to the supervisory jurisdiction of the court. It is used here as meaning simply 'power to decide', and it can be applied to the acts or decisions of any administrative bodies and persons with similar functions as well as to those of inferior tribunals. An excess or abuse of jurisdiction may involve stepping outside it, or failing to observe its limits, or departing from the rules of natural justice, or a failure to understand the law, or the taking into account of matters which ought not to have been taken into account. The categories of what may amount to an excess or abuse of jurisdiction are not closed, and they are capable of being adapted in accordance with the development of administrative law.

(c) There is no substantial difference between English law and Scots law as to the grounds on which the process of decision making may be open to review. So reference may be made to English cases in order to determine whether there has been an excess or abuse of the jurisdiction, power or authority or a failure to do what it requires.

(d) Contractual rights and obligations, such as those between employer and employee, are not as such amenable to judicial review. The cases in which the exercise of the supervisory jurisdiction is appropriate involve a tripartite relationship, between the person or body to whom the jurisdiction, power or authority has been delegated or entrusted, the person or body by whom it has been delegated or entrusted and the person or persons in respect of or for whose benefit that jurisdiction, power or authority is to be exercised.[30]

It will be noticed that included among these principles and points of explanation are some extraneous but fairly uncontroversial comments on grounds of review and the like. The principal points of interest, however, are the rejection of the distinction between public and private law as the basis for determining the competence of judicial review; the need instead to identify a reviewable 'jurisdiction' (which might, for other purposes, be regarded as being within the scope of either public or private law); and, thirdly and most controversially, the identification of a 'tripartite relationship' as the defining characteristic of such a jurisdiction.

Clearly these ideas are closely related and the impact of their combined effect is going to be difficult to interpret for some time. As we shall see, that process of interpretation has already been the cause of some confusion in cases which have followed *West*. Some points are, however, reasonably clear.

The first is that it is now beyond doubt that decisions made by arbiters, however 'private' the context, are reviewable. The court in *West* deliberately overruled the 1989 decision in *Safeway Food Stores Ltd v The Scottish Provident Institution*[31] in which a contrary position had been adopted and, on this, *West* has been followed in subsequent cases.[32]

This position on arbiters was taken in reliance upon the nineteenth-century case of *Forbes v Underwood*[33] which was no doubt clear on that specific issue. The decision, however, in that case was also heavily relied on by the court in *West* to support the wider proposition, already referred to, that 'the public or private nature of the inferior body or tribunal is not decisive'.[34] The fact that two 'private' contracting parties submit an issue for decision by arbitration does not exempt such a decision from review. The force of *Forbes v Underwood* as a buttress to such arguments as they extend beyond arbitration is, however, much less clear. Lord Inglis, in that case, compared the rule requiring arbiters to remain within their jurisdiction with a rule which similarly 'applies to a variety of other public officers, such as statutory trustees and commissioners'[35]—a formula which tends rather to support the idea that it is the arbiter as 'public' official rather than the arbiter as 'privately appointed' official who is reviewable.

If the thrust of *Forbes* is, in this respect, problematic—although it should be confessed that the First Division in *West* are not alone in using the case to try to demolish the relevance of the public/private distinction at this point in Scots law[36]—then so too are some other authorities crucial to the court's reasoning. One emerging distinction between England and Scotland which has already been asserted is that, in Scotland, the decisions of religious and sporting bodies are reviewable[37]—another consequence claimed for the escape from the need for a 'public law element'.

The principal authorities for this argument were given prominence in *West* and were clearly viewed as supportive of the court's general line of reasoning. They are by no means, however, without difficulty. The 'religious bodies' case is *McDonald v Burns*[38] which involved quite extraordinary facts and then legal consequences which are very distant from the typical circumstances of judicial review. In no conventional way did *McDonald v Burns* involve an application to the supervisory jurisdiction of the court. It was not a case in which reduction or a related remedy was sought. It was an action for a decree of removal (eviction) and associated remedies of declarator and interdict brought by the authorities of the Roman Catholic Church against certain sisters then resident in a convent in Edinburgh following a lengthy dispute on matters of doctrine and church authority.

The principal ground on which the defenders relied in resisting their enforced removal was that deprival of their religious status as 'extern sisters' had been brought about by irregular means and, thus, one of the main questions was how far the Church's procedures could be brought into issue in the civil courts. As the Lord Justice-Clerk (Lord Aitchison) said: 'The internal discipline of any such [church] body is a matter of domestic concern, notwithstanding that status, or civil rights, may be involved, and it is only in extraordinary circumstances that the Courts will regard it as within their competence to intervene.'[39] He went on to say that those extraordinary circumstances might arise in either of two situations and it is important that these be set out in full. They were

> (first) where the religious association through its agencies has acted clearly and demonstrably beyond its own constitution, and in a manner calculated to affect the civil rights and patrimonial interests of any of its members, and (secondly) where, although acting within its constitution, the procedure of its judicial or quasi-judicial tribunals has been marked by gross irregularity, such fundamental irregularity as would, in the case of an ordinary civil tribunal, be sufficient to vitiate the proceedings. But a mere irregularity in procedure is not enough. It must be so fundamental an irregularity that it goes beyond a mere matter of procedure, and becomes something so prejudicial to a fair and impartial investigation of the question to be decided as to amount to a denial of natural justice, as, for example, if a conviction of an ecclesiastical offence were to take place without an accusation being made, or without allowing the person accused to be heard in his defence. In short, the irregularity alleged must not be simply a point of form, or a departure from prescribed regulation, but must go to the honesty and integrity of the proceedings complained of.[40]

There is room for some ambiguity in the interpretation to be placed on this exposition—ambiguity which was discussed in *Scottish Football Association*,[41] considered below. What is plain, however, is that under his first head, Lord Aitchison was including only those circumstances in which the body acted beyond its own constitution *and* in a manner calculated to affect the civil rights and patrimonial interests of its members. It is equally plain that in *McDonald* the civil rights and patrimonial interests of the defenders were at stake. They were seeking to protect their right to carry on living in their convent. The possible ambiguity which arises, however, is as to whether or not the 'civil rights and patrimonial interests' qualification applies also to the second head. The phrase is not repeated. It might, though, be thought quite extraordinary if Lord Aitchison did not himself assume that the same qualification did apply. If it applied to the stronger case of the clear and demonstrable breach of the body's constitution, why should it not apply also in the weaker, though still important, circumstances of gross irregularity of procedure?

The opposite view was, however, taken by Lord Kilbrandon in *Scottish Football Association*. The circumstances with which he was dealing were, on their face, very different. A football club had been summarily fined for infringing a rule of the association, but in breach of the rules of natural justice. What the two cases had in common, of course, was that both involved governing bodies of private or voluntary associations and their reviewability. It was for this reason that *McDonald* was invoked. Lord

Kilbrandon quoted the passage from Lord Aitchison's judgment and then went on:

> In the second of these situations the Lord Justice-Clerk makes no mention of the civil rights and patrimonial interests of the members, and in my judgment this case is authority, by which I am bound, for the proposition that this Court will entertain actions arising out of the 'judgments' of the governing bodies of private associations, whether or not the civil rights and patrimonial interests of its members have been interfered with by the proceedings complained of, where a gross irregularity, such as a departure from the rules of natural justice, has been demonstrated.[42]

In *Scottish Football Association* the fine imposed was, in any event, treated as involving patrimonial loss and judgment given for the pursuers.

This reasoning in the two cases must now be followed as it is taken forward into *West* by Lord Hope because it is principally upon *McDonald* and *Scottish Football Association* that he relies in the era since *Forbes v Underwood* to establish the unimportance for the purposes of defining the scope of the supervisory jurisdiction of any distinction between public and private law. Describing *McDonald* as a case in which 'the Court of Session was willing to entertain an action as to whether the proceedings by which sisters were expelled from a convent in Edinburgh were regular and in conformity with the law and constitution of the Roman Catholic Church'[43] Lord Hope observed, without reference to the ambiguity noted in the judgment of Lord Aitchison, that Lord Kilbrandon had followed *McDonald*.

Drawing together the instruction to be derived from all three cases— *Forbes* on arbiters, *McDonald* on the Catholic hierarchy and *Scottish Football Association*—how are we to evaluate the strength of the proposition so forcefully propounded in *West* that the supervisory jurisdiction is as readily invoked in relation to a private as a public body? Perhaps as follows:

1. *Forbes*, though powerful in relation to arbiters themselves, seems to contribute little to the wider question. To establish the reviewability of arbiters, Lord Inglis's comparisons were with judges and other *public* officers.

2. *McDonald* and *Scottish Football Association* appear to allow challenge by members of 'private' organisations to irregular decisions of those organisations where, *pace* Lords Kilbrandon and Hope, patrimonial interests are at stake. Whatever the precise basis of this challenge, it does appear very limited. The plight of the nuns in *McDonald* was acute and they were defenders in an ordinary action. The treatment of a member club in *Scottish Football Association* was abrupt but the complaint was one of breach of natural justice. It is to go a long way from both cases to

claim that they render religious and sporting organisations open to judicial review and, even more, private bodies at large.

If private bodies *are* to be admitted to the general fold of the supervisory jurisdiction, their presence adds to the next problematic aspect of *West*—the function of the test of tripartism in determining the conditions of competent judicial review.

It will be recalled that it was in one of his points of explanation in *West* that Lord Hope mentioned the importance to his analysis of the decisions amenable to judicial review of the idea of a tripartite relationship—the relationship 'between the person or body to whom the jurisdiction, power or authority has been delegated or entrusted, the person or body by whom it has been delegated or entrusted and the person or persons in respect of or for whose benefit that jurisdiction, power or authority is to be exercised'.[44] At that point in the judgment Lord Hope was talking specifically of employer and employee relationships and it was, in part at least, the lack of any complication of the direct relationship between West and his prison service employer by such an element of tripartism that decided the case against him. There was no separate 'jurisdiction, power or authority conferred on some third party who could be separately identified from his employer'.[45] The court's long analysis of *Tehrani*,[46] another employment case, proceeded along similar lines. In so far as that case had implied the incorporation into Scots law of the question of whether a matter of public law had been raised in the application, it was wrong. The use of expressions such as 'public law remedy', 'public law areas' and 'public administrative law' was inappropriate.[47] It was, instead, in the court's view, the direct employer/ employee character of the relationship between health board and consultant which precluded judicial review.

Further questions relating to tripartite relationships in employment cases will be raised below, both as regards cases surveyed in *West* and in a later case. In the meantime, it should be explained that Lord Hope did not at all confine the concept of tripartism to employment situations. It was made to work much harder and apparently across the whole range of the supervisory jurisdiction. With English doctrine pushed back across the national border, something else was needed to distinguish the reviewable from the unreviewable. The jurisdiction entrusted to the arbiter was a clear expression of the tripartite relationship. Much more problematically, the *Scottish Football Association* case was also described by Lord Hope as a 'clear example' of a tripartite relationship. This was created by virtue of the allocation by the Scottish Football Association to its council, under its articles of association, of its powers to discipline members. Such an internal and necessary delegation (how else could a body such as the association do its business?) was sufficient to create a reviewable jurisdiction. Only because the council acted contrary to the rules of natural justice, in the exercise of that jurisdiction, did the decision affecting the club become reviewable. Presumably, if the association had had some means of acting directly against the club, that action would not have been reviewable. The same sort of question may equally be posed in relation to *Tehrani*. The court made it clear that, whilst a decision made by a health board which directly affected an employee could not be reviewed, the reference by the board of an issue to an internal committee of inquiry might well render the decision of that committee subject to the supervisory jurisdiction.[48]

These are some of the situations where the concept of tripartism seems insufficiently clearly developed to be put to effective use. It has been argued, however, that in some respects they are beyond the heartland of judicial review within which the more obvious susceptibility to review of abuse of statutory power is unchallenged.[49] Within that heartland there is room for two views on the relevance of a test of tripartism. On one view, the test becomes unnecessary and there are hints of this in *West* where Lord Hope, still discussing employment cases, seemed to imply that if there was breach of a 'special statutory provision'[50] or if the decision of an authority 'cut across' a statute[51] then, in these exceptional cases, there was no need, as a pre-condition of review, to establish a tripartite relationship. If that is true in these employment cases then it may be even more self-evidently true in the great range of non-employment cases, where action by an authority which breaches a statutory provision or 'cuts across' a statute is the normal circumstance of judicial review.

The alternative view is that it was indeed the court's intention in *West* to establish the need for a tripartite relationship as a general pre-condition of review; that conferring a jurisdiction, a power to decide, necessarily implies such a relationship. The problem with this approach is that the 'triangles' of the tripartite relationship are not always very easy to identify and there is a danger of the emergence of a new formalism as attempts are made to classify functions by reference, not to the dichotomy of the public and the private but to the three points of a triangular relationship. There are too many such triangular legal relationships which could never, by virtue of their geometry alone, render resulting acts or decisions subject to the supervisory jurisdiction.[52] Other triangles are difficult to construct in a rational way. If the triangle including an arbiter has, as its other two points, the two contracting parties who have referred the matter for decision, what sense does it make to call the judge in a tribunal exercising not a consensual but a compulsory jurisdiction part of a triangle constructed by reaching down from the judge to an affected party, but also up to the source of his or her power—which would presumably be parliament? As would also presumably be the case with virtually all reviewable statutory powers.

Many of these comments on the tripartite aspects of the *West* judgment could have been, and indeed were, made at the time it was delivered. What was going to be of most interest was how the decision would be interpreted and applied in subsequent cases. We have already seen that, on the specific issue of the reviewability of arbiters, *West* has been taken to have resolved a difficult issue which had arisen in earlier cases; but the reinstatement of *Forbes v Underwood* without the triangular aspect of the case attributed to it by the Lord President was sufficient to achieve that. The more interesting question will be how *West* contributes to the analysis of employment cases. In particular, there will be the question of whether analysis by triangles rather than by dividing public and private will produce a greater divergence in practice between Scotland and England and Wales. It is plain that pre-*West*, there was some judicial sympathy towards the adoption of English reasoning where this appeared helpful. The assistance obtained from *McClaren v Home Office*[53] in the *Watt* case is a good example of this. In *West* itself, although many of the English influences on the decision in *Tehrani* had to be viewed with suspicion, the relevance of some specific decisions was acknowledged. It would, for instance, be important in Scotland as well as in England to acknowledge the distinction drawn by Purchas LJ. in *R. v East Berkshire Health Authority, ex parte Walsh*[54] between 'the rights and remedies enjoyed by an employee arising out of a private contract of employment [and] the performance by a public body of the duties imposed upon it as part of the statutory terms under which it exercises its powers'.[55] *Does* this distinction, however, whatever may be the difficulties of its application in England, survive in Scotland once the wider innovations of *West* are accommodated? In England it must still be the 'public' nature of the statutory powers of the 'public' body referred to which raises the question of review at all and at least enables the distinction between those powers and the effects of the 'private' contract to be posed. If the public/private distinction is withdrawn in Scotland and the 'public' character of a body or its powers is irrelevant to their review, can the form of analogous reasoning between jurisdictions, such as that used in *West* to adopt *Walsh*, survive?

Looking beyond employment, there will also be much interest in the general impact of tripartism. Lord Hope's project in *West* was, on the one hand, very conservative in the sense that he sought to place his analysis of the supervisory jurisdiction firmly within a tradition of very long standing.[56] It was, on the other hand, potentially very radical in its attempt to break new ground, although also ambiguous, as we have seen, in some of its key aspects. In the Outer House, at the coal-face of judicial review, the case may have been seen to pose more questions than answers.

Although, in a number of cases, there has been a passing reference to *West*, only in a very few has there been the need for serious interpretation of it. Three cases stand out. Two were the related cases of *Naik v University of Stirling*[57] and *Joobeen v University of Stirling*.[58] Both cases concerned the termination of a student's participation in a course of study. In both cases, the student sought judicial review on the grounds, *inter alia*, of breach of the rules of natural justice and unreasonableness. In both cases, the competence of judicial review was raised as an issue by the university and the application of *West* was argued. The outcome in each case was, however, different. Although the case was not finally decided in the proceedings as reported, in *Naik* the competence of review was granted (Lord MacLean). In *Joobeen*, the case was held to be one involving only a contractual relationship and review denied (Lord Prosser).

In *Naik*, the university argued that it was in the same position as the prison service in *West*. The decision to exclude the student from the course was not one which had been made in the exercise of a jurisdiction, power or authority which had been delegated or entrusted to it by any statute, agreement or other instrument. The decision was not made by a body or person which was identifiably separate from the respondent. In terminating the student's membership of the university, the university had acted in the context of only a 'bipartite relationship' in which it exercised its own rules which governed one aspect of its legal relationship with one class of its members—students. There was no tripartite relationship of the sort explained in *West*.[59] In response to these arguments, Lord MacLean confessed that he had 'very considerable difficulty in understanding that in every case in which application is made to the supervisory jurisdiction of the Court of Session there must exist such a tripartite relationship. That seems to me to impose an inflexible and over formal restraint upon the court's jurisdiction.'[60] He went on to say, however, that in this case, he did consider that such a relationship could be discerned. The case was one which was not a simple case of non-payment of fees by a student but which raised wider issues. It involved the relationship of the Queen as the granter of powers (by charter) to the university and the fulfilment of those powers to one of its members. The university had been empowered by Her Majesty to prescribe rules for the discipline of its students but it had then failed to observe them when excluding this particular student. 'That failure', he said, 'in the circumstances . . . falls comprehensively in my view within the principles of *West*.'[61] In summary, then, Lord MacLean expressed some scepticism about the comprehensive (and thereby inflexible) claims made for *West* tripartism as the determinant of the scope of review but also held that, in this instance, the use of a university's disciplinary powers fell within the *West* principles—although it is not made absolutely clear which 'principles' are being invoked.

In *Joobeen* Lord Prosser heard evidence from both parties about the emergence of the circumstances in which the student had been dismissed from the course. It was plain that the situation had not been ideally handled by the university but Lord Prosser made it equally plain that he found the petitioner a most unsatisfactory witness. In the result, he also found that judicial review was not competent. In his view, the university *had* failed validly to terminate its contract (of registration) with the student. In a difficult passage, however, he went on to explain that denial of rights of one kind did not mean that a person could be afforded a remedy as if wronged in a quite different way. Submissions, in a contractual case of this sort, made in terms of denial of legitimate expectations or of decisions based on irrelevant considerations, were 'quite unreal'. The university was simply in breach of the terms of the ordinance and fee regulations which governed the situation with which it was faced. Thus the petitioner's remedy, if any, would have to lie in contractual proceedings rather than judicial review and these would be proceedings in which breach of contract based on breach of the ordinance and regulations could be argued—but not that the decision was based on irrelevant considerations.

Although this conclusion was sufficient to decide the case, Lord Prosser did offer some thoughts in response to arguments presented to the court on *West*. It had, he said, been urged (for the petitioner) that a contractual origin did not prevent a relationship becoming subject to judicial review in certain circumstances, and that the requirement of a tripartite relationship which appeared to be laid down in *West* must not be given too narrow a meaning and was satisfied in this case. It had been suggested, further, that the reason why this requirement should not be given too narrow a meaning was evident from the fact that a large number of, and indeed the classic, examples of disputes subject to judicial review involved issues between the citizen and local or central government, where the 'third' party must apparently be merely parliament, as the body conferring the powers. In the present case, it was argued, the university's royal charter produced a comparable tripartite background. In response, the university had argued that, although the proceedings had started with the remedy of reduction as the primary aim, they had developed into what was really an action for damages.

This was not, in itself, however, enough to persuade Lord Prosser of the inappropriateness of judicial review. A demand for damages was a perfectly appropriate part of that process and it would be 'highly ironic, and paradoxical, if in Scotland we began to define competency in terms of pigeon holes'. There was, however, a real issue as to competency and Lord Prosser said that he would be perturbed if the 'tripartite' principle were to be transformed into some technical test. He did not understand the Lord President in *West* as having intended any such result. The opinion of Lord MacLean had been referred to, but he accepted the university's view that, whilst one could say that there was a tripartite relationship wherever a third party had created one of the actual parties, if the tripartite test was to mean anything, it could not cover every case where one party had been created by another party. Lord Prosser did, however, acknowledge that sometimes a contract did create a new legal relationship, different from that of mere contracting parties and that this was perhaps more likely where one of the parties had been created with special powers, by parliament or royal charter. The creation of a university, with members, seemed to be an example. With or without the tripartite test, membership of a university might well produce situations in which judicial review was appropriate. He did not, however, find it necessary or appropriate to move towards a universal statement of principle covering the whole area. Reviewable situations might be (or include) cases where the created body had delegated particular quasi-judicial functions to others. 'In the present case', he said, 'it seems to me that the real issues were not of a kind suitable for judicial review, but were matters of simple right and obligation, requiring the court's ordinary, and not its supervisory jurisdiction.'

We shall return briefly to the *Naik* and *Joobeen* cases, but first we should note a third, more recent decision drawn this time from an employment relationship. In *Blair v Lochaber District Council*,[62] the council's chief executive sought to challenge by judicial review his suspension from duties on full pay. Lord Clyde held, however, after a debate involving detailed examination of *West* and its implications, that judicial review was not competent. For the chief executive it was argued that, in order to understand the Lord President's explanatory point (d) quoted above, it was necessary to reconcile it with *Watt v Strathclyde Regional Council*,[63] a case in which the council's decision unilaterally to amend the terms and conditions in teachers' contracts was held to be reviewable and which was held in *West* to have been correctly decided. This, it was suggested, was possible only if one or other of two alternative approaches was adopted. According to the first, it was necessary to treat parliament as the third party in a relationship also involving the council itself and its chief executive. The council would thus be exercising a discretion, capable of being reviewed, whenever it made a decision such as the suspension. Such an approach would have the effect, however, of making everything done under statutory powers subject to review—an analysis, it was argued by the respondent council, which was too wide and which lacked utility.

The second possible construction was that the concept of tripartism was intended to deal, at least primarily, with the situation in which a private employer has conferred a jurisdiction on an independent quasi-judicial body, thus extending the scope of the supervisory jurisdiction to the private sector, as well as the public sector. In response to this, however, it was argued by the respondents that it was illogical to confine the concept of tripartism to the private sector, given that the court had already discarded the utility of a distinction between actings in the public and in the private sectors.

It was the third submission, argued on behalf of the council, which was adopted by Lord Clyde. It was an interpretation which insisted on a similarity of treatment between the public and private sectors, such that in employer/employee disputes the tripartite test was conclusive. Lord Clyde acknowledged some of the difficulties with this approach. It does not fully explain the other ways in which a tripartite test may operate in non-employment situations. It may remain curious, despite the justification offered by the court in *West*, that the involvement of the tripartite test may make reviewable a defective decision entrusted by an employer to another body whilst a decision taken by the employer himself would not be. 'However that may be', said Lord Clyde, 'I must follow the guidance given in *West*.'[64]

Because he did not regard that part of *West* which appeared to make satisfaction of the tripartite test a necessary pre-condition of review in employment cases as absolutely definitive, however, Lord Clyde went on to show some willingness to explore exceptions. Although this is not directly acknowledged in his judgment, Lord Clyde may have felt under some obligation to do this since he played a major part in *Watt*, a case which displayed no tripartite characteristics but which, as already noted, was approved in *West*.

The alternative test mooted in *Blair*—one which appeared to have attracted support from both parties and also the sympathy of Lord Clyde—was that of the 'administrative character' (or, in other circumstances not relevant to this case, the 'judicial character') of the decision. Indeed the court was invited to define the characteristics of such an administrative decision but Lord Clyde declined to offer a comprehensive definition. Factors suggested by counsel for the chief executive as pointing in the direction of an administrative decision included the imposition of specific statutory requirements on the contract, a statutory restraint on the exercise of an authority's powers or a contract relating to the holding of a public office.

Without offering a final decision on these possibilities, Lord Clyde was clear that none applied to the case in hand. Mr Blair's suspension fitted none of the special cases and he concluded that

> properly regarded, this case is essentially concerned with the regulation of the contract between the petitioner and the respondents and . . . it is not a matter for the exercise of the supervisory jurisdiction. Even if the tripartite principle is not to be one of absolute application so that cases may be found . . . which only concern one employee and his employer which yet may be open to judicial review, although there is no third party involved I do not consider that the considerations individually or cumulatively put forward by [counsel for the petitioner] should cause the present case to qualify as such an exception. To take a different approach, the circumstances here do not seem to me sufficient to justify resort to the supervisory jurisdiction where a contractual remedy remains. The priority to be given to a contractual remedy should be recognised equally in relation to contracts by public bodies as well as private ones and ordinary judicial processes may be expeditious enough to provide rapid remedies.[65]

Of these three cases looked at in some detail it must be *Blair* which contains the most pointers to the boundaries of judicial review in Scotland in this post-*West* world. All three cases demonstrate that it is not just early academic commentaries which have found *West* difficult to interpret. It is quite plain that judges in the Outer House are puzzled, above all, by the meaning, the scope and the status of the tripartite test. It is in *Blair,* however, that the tensions are most fully revealed, and this is a case which, because it involved public employment, might have been expected to be best illuminated by *West.* Lord Clyde, however, was, despite his proclaimed willingness to defer to the higher authority of the First Division in *West*, no better equipped, it seems, to decide whether judicial review was competent than he was in *Watt*. True, lip-service was paid to the need to identify a tripartite situation but with evident scepticism about the significance of the 'third party' involvement in such disputes for the reviewability of proceedings. It then becomes clear, however, that tripartism does not and should not resolve every issue even in the employment field. There remains the need for tests involving references *inter alia* to the statutory framework within which certain offices are created or otherwise regulated and to the availability of other 'ordinary' procedures and remedies. The justification, in both *Joobeen* and *Blair,* for the denial of judicial review on the grounds of the 'essential' nature of the dispute or of the remedy sought—without explanation of what constitutes that 'essence' in either case—shows the continuing poverty of the analysis.

What is perhaps most revealing, however, is the difficulty resulting from the explicit rejection in *West* of the relevance of public/private distinctions in this area. We have yet to see major assaults on the territory represented in the past by 'religious and sporting bodies' but, even in the field of employment, there is more confusion than light. Insistence on the rejection of a public/ private distinction at one point in *Blair* still allowed discussion to focus on the exercise of 'administrative power' as a primary test. A body's employment decisions (and presumably also any other contractual decisions) are reviewable if, in some undefined sense, they are 'administrative'. If that is not the readmission of a public law test, it is not at all clear what it is.

The Grounds of Review

One of the less significant aspects of the *West* case was, as already noted, the opportunity that the Lord President took to reaffirm the view already expressed by Lord Fraser in *Brown v Hamilton District Council*[66] that there is no substantial difference between English and Scots law as to the grounds of judicial review.[67]

This is a position which seems well supported in the case law of the Court of Session. Judges use much the same language in their decisions as is used in the English High Court and cite many of the same cases. English landmark cases such as *Wednesbury*[68] and *GCHQ*[69] figure prominently in Scottish debate and decisions.

Simply to declare that the grounds of review are the same in the two jurisdictions does not, however, remove certain signs of divergence, some more important than others. Least important may be a tendency among Scottish judges to be rather more conservative and less innovative than their English counterparts, a tendency to follow rather than to lead. This may, in part, be a consequence of the unilateral declaration of similarity between the systems. The English judges have never declared the systems the same and never committed themselves to monitoring developments in the Court of Session—nor do they do so in practice.

Be that as it may, the Court of Session, whilst willing to follow a lead from England—for instance, in relation to the circumstances in which reasons may be expected to accompany administrative decisions[70]—has shown little enthusiasm for pioneering in developing areas such as 'legitimate expectations'[71] or proportionality. One issue on which it was a Scottish judge who did appear to strike out on his own is the, now rather confused, question of the alleged restrictions (on invoking irrationality as a head of challenge) which should apply in the review of delegated legislation which has been subject to scrutiny before its promulgation by one or both Houses of Parliament. In *City of Edinburgh District Council v Secretary of State for Scotland*[72] Lord Jauncey held that whilst 'patent defects' and some procedural defects could be reviewed, alleged irrationality could not—a position subsequently adopted, it seems, in *Nottinghamshire County Council v Secretary of State for the Environment*,[73] although probably retreated from in *Hammersmith and Fulham*[74] and also in later Scottish decisions.[75] If that is one area in which there is an apparent convergence between the rules of the two systems, one point at which a firm resistance to reconciliation with England is being maintained seems to be in the matter of the jurisdictional error of law. In *Watt v Lord Advocate*[76] the significance of a distinction was maintained between errors within and outwith the decision-maker's jurisdiction in some reliance on *Anisminic v Foreign Compensation Commission*[77] but, whereas in England *Anisminic* may now be seen as marking the end of the road for the usefulness of the distinction, its value has been reaffirmed in several Scottish cases since.[78] It may be that one of the effects of *West*, despite its assertion of no substantial differences between the systems, will be to further accentuate this one. The language in the case tends to reinforce the jurisdictional basis of review.

Whilst these may be examples of differences which have developed almost fortuitously within the substantive rules of judicial review, there are also certain more systemic problems about the pursuit of a completely common line on grounds of review. One factor, extraneous to judicial review itself, is the apparently different significance attributed by the Scottish courts to the European Convention on Human Rights. In England there is room for the argument that the terms of the Convention will enable new avenues of judicial review to open up,[79] but the Court of Session has taken a much more restrictive approach to the use of the Convention as a source of law,[80] and this has had an effect on review cases[81] although, on at least one occasion, the possible use of the Convention as a test of reasonableness in the exercise of a discretionary power has been acknowledged.[82] Presumably the general hostility of the Court of Session will, in due course, subside but, in the meantime, it does seem to stand in the way of the serious use of the Convention in judicial review.

Locus Standi, *Procedure and Remedies*

In contrast with its position on the grounds of review, the Court of Session has always attached importance to the differences between Scotland and England in matters of *locus standi*, procedure and remedies. Certainly the historical development of the rules in these areas has been quite different[83] and many differences, including those of terminology, remain. The tests of 'title and interest' may well not resolve questions of access in quite the same way as that of 'sufficient interest'; the lack of a preliminary requirement of leave is a clear procedural difference; and the use of the same remedies as are used in ordinary 'private law' actions rather than special remedies like the prerogative orders has a continuing importance.[84] Without wishing, however, to underestimate the significance of these differences for practitioners, it may fairly be concluded that they do not at present pose anything like the challenge to interjurisdictional comity as that of the *West* decision.

Judicial Review in Operation

The similarity just demonstrated between both the grounds of review and procedures in Scotland and England point strongly towards an impression of general equivalence of function and operation of judicial review in the two jurisdictions. No doubt that impression is generally accurate but it must be qualified in certain respects, the most important of which requires us to return, in a concluding section, to *West* and the scope of review. First, however, certain other matters of comparative practice.

One obvious consequence of enabling, under broadly similar conditions, the review by courts in two jurisdictions of decision-making under identical or very similar powers provided to statutory authorities by the Westminster Parliament is that review may arise, on the happenstance of a litigation initiative, in either jurisdiction. The Court of Session may easily find itself deciding issues which have either never fallen to be resolved in England, or else where, despite the general tendencies towards uniformity of practice, the Scottish court has had some reason for striking out in a different direction. Generally this is not the case. The sheer size of the jurisdiction and high level of activity in the English courts force the Court of Session into the subordinate role of a satellite. It seems, however, to take a small instance of independent activity, to have fallen to a Scottish judge to decide the only (reported) challenge by judicial review to a local authority's decision-making under the compulsory competitive tendering regime in the Local Government Act 1988.[85] An area of emerging comparative practice is in relation to the Social Fund where, despite the English base, decisions of the Social Fund Inspectors have come under review in the Court of Session.[86]

Of greater significance is the example of review of decision-making under the Immigration Acts. Activity in the Court of Session has increased in this area and it has been interesting to see the Scottish judges being prepared to adopt a rather more liberal approach than that of their English brethren to the question of granting liberty to the applicant pending final decision of the case.[87] This has been a difference of approach which applicants have spotted, and some of the more imaginative among them have sought to achieve some rather crude forum-shopping between the jurisdictions—an initiative which has, however, been frowned on by Scottish judges.[88] Of course, the question of choice of appropriate jurisdiction may arise in many different situations. In *Bank of Scotland v IMRO*[89] the issue was resolved under the terms of the Civil Jurisdiction and Judgments Act 1982 in favour of declining jurisdiction in Scotland. On the other hand, the high-profile case of *Monckton v Lord Advocate*[90] is an example of a question, in that instance the lawfulness of payments under the Maastricht Treaty, which might legitimately be raised in either jurisdiction.[91]

Viewed more systematically, however, there are no general reasons for the pattern of judicial review in Scotland to develop differently from England. It performs the same function as a procedure operating residually and often only in default of other forms of redress—whether judicial or otherwise. Although this is not an issue which has been addressed directly in Scotland in the same way that it has in England,[92] there is room for a similar debate about the relationship between statutory forms of appeal to the Court of Session and 'common law' judicial review.[93]

There are, of course, *some* differences produced by institutional variations between the jurisdictions. One example is the rather different role allocated to the Accounts Commission in Scotland in relation to the audit of the accounts of public authorities in comparison with that of the Audit Commission.[94] Not only does this produce different mechanisms for the resolution of *vires* questions by the Controller of Audit and by the Accounts Commission, involving reference as necessary of questions by case stated to the Court of Session, but it provides opportunities for the direct challenge of the Accounts Commission by judicial review which enables, in turn, the testing of the limits of the powers of both auditors and local authorities which are not available in England.[95]

Another point of institutional contrast between Scotland and England, which is of longer standing and which has an important bearing on the context of judicial review and especially on questions of reform, is the role in Scottish local administration of the sheriff.[96] Certain issues which, in England, may make their way on appeal from local authorities to a minister, go instead to the sheriff. An example is the sheriff's role in relation to appeals by parents from choice of school decisions. This has three effects relevant to present purposes. One is simply the redirection of grievances away from administrative appeal to a minister (and leading potentially to judicial review) to a sheriff appeal. A second is to provide a credible alternative to judicial review if, in a process of reform, it were thought desirable to divert some substantial appellate business towards a locally based statutory forum. Presumably the strongest candidate would be appeals under the homelessness legislation, which have provided much judicial review business on both sides of the border. Whereas, in England, it might be necessary to contemplate establishing a new specialist housing tribunal, it is usually, in Scotland, an extension of the sheriff's jurisdiction which is thought of. This is especially true because of a third feature of sheriff appeals which is that, although they build on an established institution, there have been developed, in recent years, some quite sophisticated styles of appeal. Starting with the Licensing (Scotland) Act 1976, but adopted also into other legislation, have been forms of statutory judicial review which confine the grounds on which the sheriff may review the decisions of licensing boards and local authorities to *inter alia* breach of natural justice and unreasonableness.[97]

If certain of these institutional differences between Scotland and England affect the context within which judicial review operates and especially within which any proposals for reform have to be considered, they do not dictate actual patterns of use of the procedure in practice. There has been an impression in Scotland supported by the results of an early study made in the period following the procedural reforms of 1985[98] that, although there has been an increase in the numbers of applications for review, this has not had the same swamping effect as in England and that the distribution of types of case (in terms of subject matter) has been different. Those are conclusions which are borne out in the preliminary results of a more recent study of all applications for judicial review in Scotland in the period from 1988.[99] What the study shows is that, with applications for review totalling some 418 in the period 1988–92, there has been a much lower rate of use per head of population in Scotland than in either England and Wales or Northern Ireland. As to the subject matter, the most interesting finding is that, despite a slow start in Scotland in this area, immigration cases lead the field in terms of numbers of petitions—followed by licensing, housing (mainly homelessness) and planning and land use. Principal respondents have been local authorities (44.7 per cent of petitions) and central departments (33.7 per cent). Delay in the processing of applications for review is confirmed as much less of a problem in Scotland than in England and Wales. Precise comparisons are difficult but, excluding immigration cases which tend to distort because of the number which cease to progress once interim relief (that is, liberation) has been granted, an average time in Scotland from application to disposal of 149 days has to be set against the position in England where nearly a half of the applications took more than 540 days.

Harmony and Diversity

The sort of evidence produced by studies which throw light on the actual use made of judicial review and, more problematically, on the eventual impact of review on the authorities subjected to it, is clearly of very great importance—not least in the ways it may be used to reveal differences in practice between the jurisdictions of the United Kingdom.

Viewed in terms of narrower doctrinal issues, two main questions in comparative law arise. One is about how far a system of judicial review in Scotland, which appears at some points to claim a strong similarity of approach to that adopted in England but at others strikes out on its own, is sustainable in terms of coherence and stability of doctrine. The other question is about how far divergence of doctrine within the United Kingdom and then within the European Union is, in any event, justifiable and sustainable. As a conclusion to this paper, both questions will be considered, though much more briefly than they deserve.

Sufficient has already been said about recent developments in judicial review in Scotland to reveal that it is a system (a) which includes certain rules of procedure and remedies which have a clear historically based distinctiveness but whose differences (from England) in practice may not be very great; but (b) which also claims a close similarity with England as to the grounds of review; and (c) which, in *West*, has asserted a distinctiveness in the scope of the supervisory jurisdiction—especially in the rejection of a public/private test—but a distinctiveness which neither commentators nor judges appear yet to have understood and one which, on the evidence of *Blair* (and perhaps some parts of *West* itself) appears to be rejected in the retention of tests which continue to refer to the 'administrative' character of the decision reviewed.[100] Final judgment must be suspended but it seems likely that the tensions resulting from the attempt to merge two systems— one a system of administrative law in which the regulation of the exercise of public power is a defining characteristic and within which ideas of abuse of such power have developed, and the other a supervisory jurisdiction which denies that defining characteristic—will prove too great to survive. It is one thing to acknowledge, as in England, that there are difficulties at the margins of the public and the private, difficulties in the identification and treatment of special cases at those margins, but very much more difficult if the distinction is, from the start, denied.

Even if this conclusion is wrong and a distinctive system in Scotland capable of producing major differences between England and Scotland can be developed, the second question is whether that should be encouraged or permitted, given emerging pressures towards harmonisation in both a United Kingdom and European context. It was interesting, in another context, to see Lord President Hope himself stressing the need for a similar position to be maintained between Scotland and England on the recovery of tax payments made under error of law:' . . . we will be achieving the same result [as in England] by reference to the principles of Scots Law. I regard that as satisfactory, because it would be inequitable that a remedy which is now available in England in this important field of transactions between the citizen and a public authority should be denied here on the ground that it was not permitted by our law.'[101] If there are questions of interjurisdictional equity which may arise in that relationship between citizen and public authority, why not also in other such relationships including that between citizen employees and public authority employers or other citizens entering into contracts with public bodies? Equity may not require the application of identical rules and principles but it may prove very difficult to ensure equitable treatment at all if fundamental divergences begin to emerge about the significance, for this purpose, of distinguishing public from private authorities. Recognition of the general advantages of convergence in this area extends widely. It was the Scottish Law Commission, writing of administrative law, which said that 'where problems are common it is clearly desirable that they should be addressed in both jurisdictions and that our respective rules should produce solutions which are in harmony'.[102]

An even stronger harmonising force in administrative law may be the European Union. Under its legal order there are not merely gentle principles of equity inviting equivalence of treatment but the imperative of the level playing field which underpins the entire operation, and it is becoming apparent that harmonisation of procedural and remedial matters may be of great importance. It is no longer a question of observing tendencies in the direction of common rules[103] but of an increasingly prescriptive approach to uniformity. The *Factortame*[104] and *EOC*[105] cases are perhaps the strongest evidence of this so far and, whilst in European matters it may be that the incoming tide of harmonisation will yet be ordered back by the Canute of subsidiarity, further pressure towards harmonisation must still be assumed to be the most likely way forward. Nor is this pressure to be confined to questions of procedure (or indeed of grounds of review) narrowly construed. The project of defining 'emanations of the state'[106] and the legal controls to which they may be subjected is still incomplete but may have important implications for a jurisdiction now set to deny that its procedures for judicial review take account of a distinction between public and private. When high water comes, it will be interesting to see how much of *West* is still showing.

I wish to acknowledge the help of Mark Himsworth in the production of this chapter.

Notes

1. An early confession should be made that, at many points in this chapter, references to 'England' should be interpreted as references to 'England and Wales'.
2. Although, as will be (too briefly) shown in what follows, much of what is now described as administrative law did develop very differently in the two jurisdictions. For a full account of the subject see A.W. Bradley, 'Administrative Law' in the *Stair Memorial Encyclopaedia*, Vol. 1 (1987).
3. 1953 SC 396.
4. ibid., at p. 411.
5. For discussion see N. Walker and C.M.G. Himsworth, 'The Poll Tax and Fundamental Law', 1991 JR 45.
6. *R. v Lord Chancellor, ex p. the Law Society*, 21 June 1993.
7. See, for instance, the Civic Government (Scotland) Act 1982 and the selective application of the Public Order Act 1986.
8. [1968] AC 910. See *Glasgow Corporation v Central Land Board* 1956 SC (HL) 1.
9. See *Virtue v Police Commissioners of Alloa* (1873) 1 R 285; *Mersey Docks and Harbour Board v Gibbs* (1866) LR 1 HL 93.
10. *MacGregor v Lord Advocate* 1921 SC 847.
11. [1993] 3 All ER 537.
12. *McDonald v Secretary of State for Scotland* 1994 SLT 692.
13. F.M. McShane 'Crown Privilege in Scotland: the Demerits of Disharmony Pt II' 1993 JR 41 at 47.
14. [1956] PL 6.
15. Act of Sederunt (Rules of the Court of Session 1994) 1994 SI 1994, No. 1443.
16. SI 1985 No. 500 which inserted the then R. 260B.
17. 1983 SC (HL) 1.
18. ibid., at p. 49.
19. Report of the Working Party, p. 7.
20. For fuller discussion of this point, see C.M.G. Himsworth, 'Public Employment, the Supervisory Jurisdiction and Points *West*', 1992 SLT (News) 257, at 259. For another comment on the case see W.J. Wolffe, 'The Scope of Judicial Review in Scots Law', [1992] PL 625.
21. See Lord Inglis in *Forbes v Underwood* (1886) 13 R 465.
22. See in particular H.W.R. Wade and C.F. Forsyth, *Administrative Law* (7th edn, 1994) vii, 667 and 682.
23. 1992 SLT 636.
24. See in particular the Outer House case of *Connor v Strathclyde Regional Council* 1986 SLT 530 and then the difficult Second Division case of *Tehrani v Argyll and Clyde Health Board (No. 2)* 1990 SLT 118.
25. 1992 SLT 324. For discussion of the case, see C.M.G. Himsworth, 'Public Employment and the Supervisory Jurisdiction', 1992 SLT (News) 123.
26. As he had earlier in 'The Nature of the Supervisory Jurisdiction and the Public/Private Distinction in Scots Administrative Law' in W. Finnie, C.M.G. Himsworth and N. Walker (eds) *Edinburgh Essays in Public Law* (1991)
27. For an introduction to judicial review in Scotland written after *Watt* but before *West* see C.M.G. Himsworth, 'Judicial Review in Scotland' in M. Supperstone and J. Goudie (eds) *Judicial Review* (1992).
28. For fuller discussion of the Lord President's argument, see C.M.G. Himsworth, 'Points *West*', n. 20 above.
29. *West*, op. cit., at p. 650.
30. ibid. at p. 650–1.
31. 1989 SLT 131.

32. See *Shanks and McEwen (Contractors) Ltd v Mifflin Construction Ltd*, 1993 SLT 1124. Other cases on arbiters have included *Haden Young Ltd v William McCrindle & Son Ltd* 1994 SLT 221 and *Witan Properties Ltd v Lord Advocate*, 1 July 1993, unreported.
33. (1886) 13 R 465.
34. *West*, at p. 643A.
35. (1886) 13 R 465, at p. 468.
36. See also Lord Clyde, op. cit. n. 26 above and Judge David Edward in 'Administrative Law in Scotland: The Public Law/Private Law Distinction Revisited' in D. Curtin and D. O'Keefe (eds) *Constitutional Adjudication in European Community and National Law* (1992).
37. See Wade and Forsyth, n. 22, above at p. 667.
38. 1940 SLT 325.
39. ibid., p. 331.
40. ibid., pp 331–2.
41. *St Johnstone Football Club Ltd v Scottish Football Association* 1965 SLT 171.
42. ibid., p. 174.
43. 1992 SLT 636, at 643.
44. 1992 SLT 636, at 651.
45. ibid.
46. *Tehrani v Argyll and Clyde Health Board (No. 2)* 1990 SLT 118.
47. n. 44, at p. 649.
48. ibid., p. 647.
49. On this and on tripartism in general in *West*, see W. Finnie, 'Triangles as Touchstones of Review', 1993 SLT (News) 51.
50. The phrase used in relation to *Malloch v Aberdeen Corporation* 1971 SLT 245.
51. As in *Watt v Strathclyde Regional Council* 1992 SLT 324.
52. See Finnie, n. 49, above and Himsworth, n. 20.
53. [1990] ICR 824, IRLR 338.
54. [1985] QB 152, at 176.
55. *West*, p. 649.
56. Though, for doubts about the validity of the analysis of that tradition and the coherence claimed for it, see Himsworth, n. 20, above.
57. 1994 SLT 449.
58. 1995 SLT 120 (note).
59. 1994 SLT 449, at 451.
60. ibid., 451–2.
61. ibid., 452.
62. 1994 SCLR 1070.
63. 1992 SLT 324.
64. 1994 SCLR 1070, at 1073.
65. ibid., at 1075.
66. 1983 SC (HL) 1, at 42.
67. 1992 SLT 636, at 651. The same position is affirmed in the government's *Judge Over Your Shoulder* (2nd edn, 1994) 5.
68. *Associated Provincial Picture Houses Ltd v Wednesbury Corporation* [1948] 1 KB 223.
69. *CCSU v Minister for the Civil Service* [1985] AC 374.
70. See e.g. *Lawrie v Commission for Local Authority Accounts* 1994 SLT 1185.
71. But see *Lakin Ltd v Secretary of State for Scotland* 1988 SLT 780.
72. 1985 SLT 551. For critical discussion of the case, see C.M.G. Himsworth, 'Defining the Boundaries of Judicial Review', 1985 SLT (News) 369.
73. [1986] AC 240, discussed at [1986] PL 374.
74. *R. v Secretary of State for the Environment, ex p. Hammersmith and Fulham LBC* [1991] 1 AC 521, discussed at [1991] PL 76.

75. *Leech v Secretary of State for Scotland* 1991 SLT 910 and *East Kilbride District Council v Secretary of State for Scotland*, 3 August 1993, unreported.
76. 1979 SC 120.
77. [1969] 2 AC 147.
78. See e.g. *Cooper v City of Edinburgh District Licensing Board* 1990 SLT 246 and 1991 SLT 47. For discussion see Himsworth, op. cit., n. 27 above. See, with regard to the Northern Ireland position, the chapter by Peter Osborne, above.
79. See A.E. Boyle, 'Administrative Justice, Judicial Review and the Right to a Fair Hearing under the E.C.H.R.' [1984] PL 89 and 'Sovereignty, Accountability and the Reform of Administrative Law' in G. Richardson and H. Genn (eds) *Administrative Law and Government Action* (1994).
80. *Kaur v Lord Advocate* 1980 SC 319.
81. See e.g. *Hamilton v Secretary of State for Scotland* 1990 GWD 10–624.
82. *Budh Singh, petitioner,* 13 July 1988, unreported, discussed in J.L. Murdoch, 'The ECHR in Scots Law' [1991] PL 49.
83. For the fullest account, see Bradley, op. cit., n. 2, above.
84. ibid. and see Himsworth, op. cit. n. 27, above.
85. *Colas Roads Ltd v Lothian Regional Council* 1994 SLT 396.
86. *Murray v Secretary of State for Social Security* 1994 GWD 23–1436; *McKim's Curator ad litem v Collinge* 1994 GWD 13–864.
87. See M. Bovey, 'Judicial review of immigration cases: the Scottish dimension' [1990] *Immigration and Nationality Law and Practice*, 94.
88. *Sokha v Secretary of State for the Home Department* 1992 SLT 1049. In *Sokha*, Lord Prosser agreed, by reference to a line of cases to *Re Serif Maybasan* [1991] ImmAR 89, that the practice of the English courts was indeed different (pp 1051–2) but not in ways sufficient to displace normal rules about choice of suitable jurisdiction and forum (p. 1054).
89. 1989 SLT 432.
90. 5 May 1994, unreported.
91. Cf. *R. v Secretary of State for Foreign and Commonwealth Affairs, ex p. Rees-Mogg* [1994] QB 552.
92. See Law Commission, *Administrative Law: Judicial Review and Statutory Appeals,* Consultation Paper no. 126 (1993).
93. The same applies to the statutory regulation of judicial review—a process which has not always elicited a sufficient sensitivity to differences between Scotland and England. See e.g. s. 13 of the Extradition Act 1989 which assumes, in both jurisdictions, a procedure starting with application for leave.
94. On local authority audit, see C.M.G. Himsworth, *Local Government Law in Scotland* (forthcoming, 1995) ch. 7.
95. See *Grampian Regional Council v Commission for Local Authority Accounts* 1994 SLT 1120.
96. See G. Little, 'Local Administration in Scotland: the Role of the Sheriff' in W. Finnie, C.M.G. Himsworth and N. Walker (eds) *Edinburgh Essays in Public Law* (1991); C.M.G. Himsworth, *Local Government Law in Scotland* (forthcoming, 1995) ch. 9.
97. See also the Betting, Gaming and Lotteries Act 1963 and the Gaming Act 1968 (both as amended) and the Civic Government (Scotland) Act 1982.
98. A. Page, 'Judicial Review in the Court of Session' in M. Adler and A. Millar (eds) *Socio-Legal Research in the Scottish Courts,* vol. 2 (1991).
99. See T. Mullen, K. Pick, T. Prosser, 'Trends in Judicial Review in Scotland' [1995] PL 52.
100. It is at least a symptom of the problem that both Lord Clyde (n. 26, above) and Judge Edward (n. 36), whilst writing strongly in rejection of a public/private distinction, nevertheless claimed, in the titles of their articles, to be writing about *administrative* law.

101. *Morgan Guaranty Trust Company v Lothian Regional Council* 1995 SLT 299, at 315.
102. *27th Annual Report* 1991–92, Scot. Law Comm., No. 139, para. 2.5.
103. Cf. J. Schwarze 'Tendencies towards a Common Administrative Law in Europe' (1991) 16 Eur L3 and *European Administrative Law* (1992).
104. *R. v Secretary of State for Transport, ex p. Factortame No. 2* [1991] 1 AC 603.
105. *R. v Secretary of State for Employment, ex p. Equal Opportunities Commission* [1994] 1 All ER 910.
106. See e.g. *Kincardine and Deeside District Council v Forestry Commissioners* 1992 SLT 1180.

Chapter 11

Judicial Review —
The Law of the Republic of Ireland

Gerard Hogan

Introduction

A leading commentator has recently observed that British public lawyers 'regard excursions into United States jurisprudence as an academic day trip to foreign climes. The legal flora is very interesting, but there is no point digging it up and trying to grow it at home because the constitutional environments are so dissimilar.'[1] Even though the Republic of Ireland is much closer to home, the average British public lawyer would probably find contemporary Irish constitutional[2] and administrative law[3] to be equally exotic. While it is true that the gap between Irish and British constitutional law is almost as great as that prevailing between the United States and the United Kingdom, there is still a great deal of similarity between the two systems of administrative law. To that extent, a chapter on judicial review of administrative action as it presently obtains in the Republic of Ireland probably requires little justification.

Apart from the fact that the modern Irish administrative law developments are in themselves full of interest, there is, however, an important practical dimension to this exercise. As is well known, major principles of English constitutional and administrative law have suffered modification in the light of the emerging general principles of Community law[4] and the increasing influence of the jurisprudence of the European Court of Human Rights. No one can doubt but that even further changes would be necessary if the United Kingdom were ever to adopt the European Convention of Human Rights as part of its own domestic law. Accordingly, the Republic of Ireland provides an excellent example of how a common law system of administrative law has been required to change and adapt in the presence of a written constitution providing for judicial review of legislation.

The Constitution and Irish Administrative Law

The enactment of the Constitution in 1937[5] following a plebiscite had important implications for Irish administrative law. From the perspective of administrative lawyers, the most important features of the Constitution can be summarised as follows:

- the vesting in the High Court and Supreme Court of express powers of judicial review of legislation;[6]
- the strict (although not complete) separation of powers;[7]
- the protection of individual constitutional rights via a Bill of Rights.[8]

Despite this important development, the Constitution did not in its early years impact greatly on the principles of Irish administrative law. There were two major decisions which were exceptions to this. In the first of these, *Buckley v Attorney General*,[9] the Supreme Court invalidated legislation which purported to direct the High Court to dismiss a pending case. The court held that such a legislative direction offended against the principles of judicial independence contained in article 34 and was 'an unwarrantable interference by the Oireachtas with the operations of the courts in a purely judicial domain'.[10] The other major decision saw the invalidation of those provisions of the Solicitors Act 1954 which allowed the Incorporated Law Society (the statutory body governing the solicitors' profession) to strike off a solicitor for alleged misconduct. The power to strike off a solicitor represented the exercise of judicial power (reserved to the courts under article 34) and the case was not a 'limited' one within the exception provided by article 37, as it was a sanction of such severity that it approached that of a term of imprisonment.

These decisions were isolated ones and the possibilities the Constitution might afford of the development of Irish public law only became evident from the early 1960s onwards. Since then developments bearing directly on administrative law have been rapid, if at times uneven. In 1970, in the seminal *East Donegal* case[11] the Supreme Court held that the presumption of constitutionality carried with it the ancillary presumption that all powers and discretions granted by statute to an administrative body would be exercised fairly and reasonably. In 1971 the Supreme Court, affirming that the right to fair procedures was one of the unspecified personal rights protected by article 40.3 of the Constitution,[12] invalidated legislation which denied the right of an accused person to cross-examine his accusers before a statutory tribunal.[13] In the same year, the court held in *Byrne v Ireland*[14] that the old common law whereby the state was immune from suit was inconsistent with the obligations to vindicate the twin constitutional rights of the right to sue and to recover damages in respect of a justiciable controversy protected by article 40.3. This decision subsequently formed the basis for the Supreme Court's momentous decision in 1993 where a majority held that the rule, whereby it was presumed that the state was exempt from the application of statute, was unconstitutional.[15]

These and similar developments notwithstanding, Irish administrative law is still heavily influenced by the traditional common law principles. Nevertheless, Irish administrative law has acquired a dynamic of its own and in recent years the interaction of both administrative and constitutional law has led the Irish courts into new areas, such as the 'constitutionalisation' of the right to fair procedures;[16] the right to sue for damages for breaches of constitutional rights[17] and the principle of proportionality.[18] As we shall presently see, it is the interaction of these novel principles with the traditional common law rules which makes a study of contemporary Irish administrative law so interesting.

Scope of Judicial Review

Irish practice and procedure relating to judicial review was substantially reformed in 1986 with the introduction of a new consolidated version of the rules of the Superior Courts.[19] The new version of Order 84 of the rules introduced reforms which in very large measure correspond with Order 53 of the English rules which had been introduced some nine years previously.[20] While it is undoubtedly true that the new rules removed some tiresome anomalies[21] and that judicial review practice may be said generally to have streamlined as a result, the fact remains that there seems to have been considerably more arguments after 1986 about aspects of judicial review procedure than had occurred theretofore. In other words, the procedural change designed to minimise disputes about the technical features of judicial review seem—just as in England—to have produced exactly the opposite result.

It must immediately be admitted that these difficulties have not been as pronounced in Ireland as they have been in England and this may partially be attributed to the unwillingness of the Irish courts to follow the decision in *O'Reilly v Mackman*.[22] Moreover, since much of the case law in this area is concerned with the extent and scope of judicial review, it is probably fair to surmise that these difficulties stem not so much from the 1986 reforms, as from arguments about the limits of public law in an increasingly complex and sophisticated state.

Just as in England, there is now much uncertainty regarding the proper scope of judicial review. In one of the first cases where the point arose in the wake of the new rules, *Murphy v Turf Club*,[23] the applicant sought to challenge by way of judicial review a decision of the Turf Club not to renew a trainer's licence on the ground that the decision had been arrived at in breach of fair procedures.[24] While the Turf Club enjoys certain statutory powers,[25] these powers were held by Barr J. to be immaterial in this context as the Turf Board's disciplinary jurisdiction in respect of trainers was derived from contract. In the event, the applicant could not proceed by way of judicial review, but could only proceed in the ordinary way for breach of contract. As Barr J. said:

> I have no doubt that the relationship between the applicant and the [Turf Club] derives from contract . . . and the [latter's] duty to regulate the sport of horse-racing in Ireland, though having a public dimension, is not a public duty as envisaged by the Court of Appeal in *R. v Take-Over Panel, ex parte Datafin plc*[26] and in purporting to revoke the applicant's training licence the respondent was not exercising a public law function. On the contrary, its decision was that of a domestic tribunal exercising a regulatory function over the applicant, being an interested person who had voluntarily submitted to its jurisdiction.[27]

This passage prompts a number of observations. First, it would seem anomalous that the Turf Club can be amenable to judicial review in respect of some of its functions (for example, excluding the members of the public from racecourses) and not of others. This is not simply a matter of procedure: if judicial review does not lie then it would appear that the decision itself can only be challenged on the private law ground that the Turf Club was in breach of contract as opposed to the wider public grounds based on reasonableness, irrationality and so forth. Secondly, is it not altogether unrealistic to regard the Turf Club's jurisdiction as 'voluntary' given that it enjoys a monopoly in respect of the granting of a horse trainer's licence?[28] Thirdly, the *Murphy* judgment fails to take account of the argument that in reality the Turf Club was exercising a governmental function.

The private law/public law boundary has also been explored in a series of subsequent decisions and the following three cases may be taken as representative. In the first of these, *Beirne v Garda Commissioner*,[29] the applicant was a probationer Garda (policeman) who was dismissed for alleged misconduct. While all members of the Supreme Court were agreed that fair procedures had not been observed, a majority of the court held that such a decision was amenable to challenge by way of judicial review. Finlay CJ. laid down the following test:

> The principle which, in general, excludes from the ambit of judicial review decisions made in the realm of private law by persons or tribunals whose authority derives from contract is . . . confined to cases or instances where the

duty being performed by the decision-making authority is manifestly a private duty and where his right to make it derived from contract or solely from consent or the agreement of the parties affected. Where the duty being carried out by a decision-making authority, as occurs in this case, is of a nature which might ordinarily be seen as coming within the public domain, that decision can only be excluded from the reach of jurisdiction in judicial review if it can be shown that it solely and exclusively derived from an individual contract made in private law.[30]

While it was true that the applicant's terms of employment provided that the Commissioner might dismiss him for misconduct, this jurisdiction was not one 'which is solely or purely or even mainly derived from contract' but it is 'a clear jurisdiction necessarily vested in the Commissioner by reason of the office which he holds and the statutory powers which are attached to it'. In the circumstances, the decision was amenable to judicial review.

The principles in *Beirne* were applied in a very sophisticated manner by Barr J. in *Browne v Dundalk UDC*.[31] Here the representatives of the Sinn Féin Party had contracted to hire a hall for their annual conference from the respondents. When the elected councillors learnt of this development, they passed a resolution recommending that the town clerk rescind the contract. The town clerk then sought to rescind the contract and the applicants sought judicial review of that decision. At the hearing it was not seriously disputed that the respondents were in breach of contract. While the applicants could well have sought specific performance of the contract, Barr J. held that judicial review would lie:

> In the instant case there is no doubt that the hiring of the town hall to the applicant by the town clerk with the authority of the county manager constituted a valid administrative contract in private law made on behalf of the local authority. *Prima facie*, therefore, it is outside the realm of judicial review.[32]

Applying the *Beirne* test, however, Barr J. held that there was an element in the purported rescission of the contract which was not derived 'solely and exclusively' from the contract itself:

> I am satisfied that there is a crucial element in the transaction which brings it into the realm of public law and subject to judicial review. . . . The resolution of the council was successful in procuring the unlawful rescission of the hiring contract by the town clerk acting on behalf of the local authority. As the Council's resolution was in terms politically motivated, it was clearly in the public domain.[33]

This is a most interesting example of where political motives can be regarded as being sufficient to give a particular case a public law dimension.

While it might be tempting to treat this case as being purely private law in character, it would have to be conceded that the political motivation rendered the council's decision unreasonable in the administrative law sense of that term and, accordingly, amenable to quashing by way of judicial review.[34]

On the other hand, *Rajan v Royal College of Surgeons in Ireland* [35] is a decision which is on the other side of the line. Here the question was whether decisions taken by the respondents with regard to the exclusion of medical students from its college were amenable to judicial review. Keane J. held that they were not, since the decisions in question derived not from public law, 'but from the contract which came into being when the applicant became a student in the College'. The fact that RCSI derived its existence in law 'from a charter or Act of Parliament is not a sufficient ground for bringing matters relating to the conduct and academic standing of its students within the ambit of judicial review'.[36]

Murphy J. took a similar view in the case of *Geoghegan v Institute of Chartered Accountants*.[37] Here the applicant was facing disciplinary charges and sought judicial review seeking to prohibit the Institute from proceeding with these charges. Even though the evidence demonstrated that the Institute had been created by charter and supplemented by private Act of the Oireachtas and, furthermore, that the Institute's disciplinary code had been submitted to the government for its approval, Murphy J. held that its decisions were not amenable to judicial review. In his view, the decisions in question were purely private decisions governed by consent and not amenable to judicial review. This is questionable, since the evidence showed that the disciplinary code in question had been agreed as appropriate in the absence of legislation.[38]

The rejection of O'Reilly v Mackman

The Irish courts have to date shown no enthusiasm whatever for *O'Reilly v Mackman* and, indeed, in the one reserved judgment where the matter was fully argued—*O'Donnell v Dun Laoghaire Corporation*[39]—that decision was not followed. Costello J. explained that he could not follow the House of Lords' decision because:

> Firstly, as a matter of construction, I cannot construe the new rules as meaning that in matters of public law, O. 84 provides an exclusive remedy in cases where the aggrieved party wishes to obtain a declaratory order and that such a person abuses the courts' processes by applying for such an order by plenary action. Secondly, I do not think that the court is at liberty to apply policy considerations and conclude that the public interest requires that the court

should construe its jurisdiction granted by the new rules in the restrictive way suggested . . .[40]

Costello J. went on to hold that the safeguards contained in Order 84 should be applied, *mutatis mutandis,* to actions against public authorities commenced by plenary summons (writ of summons):

> In considering the effects of delay in a plenary action there are now persuasive reasons for adopting the principles enshrined in Ord. 84, r. 21 relating to delay in applications for judicial review, so that if the plenary action is not brought within the three months[41] from the date on which the cause of action arose, the court would normally refuse relief unless it is satisfied that, had the claim been brought under Ord. 84, time would have been extended.[42]

Because he felt that the Order 84 safeguards could be applied to plenary actions against public authorities, Costello J. concluded that:

> The apprehended use of plenary actions as a device to defeat the protections given by Ord. 84 is not a real danger and does not justify the court in concluding that the proceedings by plenary action for declaratory relief must be an abuse of process.[43]

Apart from the different legal cultures prevailing in both jurisdictions— Irish judges seem to have a distaste for technical arguments of this kind— the fact that a majority of constitutional actions have been begun by plenary proceedings, and not by judicial review, must also have influenced this conclusion. In many of these cases the plaintiff simply attacks the constitutionality of the impugned legislation and there is no administrative law 'decision' which lends itself to being quashed.[44] At all events, this approach seems certainly preferable to the inherent difficulties posed by *O'Reilly,* although this private/public dichotomy will remain so long as the Rules of Court contain in-built safeguards for public authorities, since for so long as these safeguards remain, litigants will seek to circumvent them by resorting to plenary actions.[45]

Legislating for O'Reilly v Mackman: the 1992 Planning Act

Despite the practical difficulties which *O'Reilly v Mackman* has caused the courts in England and Costello J.'s studied refusal to follow this decision, it would have to be recognised that there are certain circumstances where the avoidance of the judicial review procedure could give rise to an abuse of process. The main objection to *O'Reilly* lies in the fact that the House of Lords apparently insisted that every public law matter must be commenced by way of judicial review.

Planning law is one area where the possibility of such an abuse is manifest. This is well illustrated by the decision of Costello J. in 1983 in *Cavern Systems Dublin Ltd v Clontarf Residents Association*[46] where a Residents Association had issued plenary proceedings challenging the grant of a planning permission within the two months statutory time limit. The Association did not, however, serve the summons on the planning authority within that period, but claimed that it was entitled to do so at any time within the twelve months prescribed by Rules of Court.[47] Costello J. held that, in the absence of a compelling reason, the omission to serve the summons within the two month statutory period prescribed for planning cases was an abuse of process, as otherwise 'the objector will have consciously rendered the [statutory time limit] useless and have flouted parliament's will'.[48]

What is interesting is that the Oireachtas (Parliament) has now expressly legislated for a form of the *O'Reilly v Mackman* rule in planning matters. Section 82(3A) of the Local Government (Planning and Development) Act 1963 (as inserted by section 19(3) of the Local Government (Planning and Development) Act 1992) now provides as follows:

> (3A) A person shall not question the validity of a [planning permission or planning decision] otherwise than by way of application for judicial review under Ord. 84 of the Rules of the Superior Courts, 1986.
>
> (3B) (a) An application for judicial review [under Ord. 84] shall –
>
> (i) be made within the period of two months commencing on the date on which the decision is given, and
>
> (ii) be made by motion on notice . . . to [all interested parties].[49]

Even if this section did not contain the express prohibition on proceeding otherwise than by way of the Order 84 judicial review procedure, this would have been the very type of case calling for the application of an *O'Reilly v Mackman* type rule. The section provides for a special time limit[50] and the requirement as to leave is more stringent than in the case of judicial review in non-planning matters.[51] These safeguards are designed to ensure that development projects are not held up pending lengthy legal challenges which have little prospect of eventual success and as Finlay CJ. said in *KSK Enterprises Ltd v An Bord Pleanala*:[52]

> . . . it is clear that the intention of the legislature was greatly to confine the opportunity of persons to impugn by way of judicial review decisions made by the planning authorities and, in particular, one must assume that it was intended that a person who has obtained a planning permission should at a very short interval after the date of such decision in the absence of a judicial review be entirely legally protected against subsequent challenge to the

decision that was made and therefore presumably left in a position to act with safety upon the basis of that decision.[53]

In such circumstances, it would make little sense if an applicant could circumvent these particular statutory requirements by resorting to plenary proceedings where a declaration of invalidity could be sought without the need for leave and where the plaintiff's case would not have had to be put on affidavit. These considerations do not apply, however, to every type of administrative law proceedings. There is thus a strong argument to be made that *O'Reilly v Mackman* should be made the exception and not the rule and that, if it is considered desirable that particular types of case must be commenced by way of judicial review proceedings, any such innovation should be created by statute and not by the courts.[54]

Administrative Law Remedies and the Constitution

One especially interesting feature of Irish administrative law is the extent to which the availability and scope of remedies have been influenced by constitutional considerations. In the case of damages, the most notable development is the extent to which the Irish courts have been prepared to depart, where occasion warrants, from the limitations imposed by the ordinary law of torts. The practice in relation to injunctions has also been modified, especially in regard to the courts' willingness to grant injunctions to protect apprehended infringements of constitutional rights.

Interim Relief Pending the Outcome of a Constitutional Challenge

It is now clear that in an appropriate case the Irish courts are prepared to grant an injunction restraining the operation of a statute pending the outcome of a constitutional challenge. It is perhaps indicative of the extent to which Irish administrative law has been transformed by the influence of the Constitution that such a development—which was hailed as a milestone in the United Kingdom context in the *Factortame case*[55]—has been regarded in Ireland as merely the inevitable concomitant of the availability of judicial review of legislation.

By a coincidence the facts of the leading Irish case on this topic are very similar to those in the subsequent *Factortame* case. In *Pesca Valentia Ltd v Minister for Fisheries*[56] the plaintiffs had sought to challenge the constitutionality of certain provisions of the Fisheries (Amendment) Act 1983 on the ground that the nationality conditions attached to their fishing licences were too restrictive and interfered with their constitutional right to earn a livelihood. The Supreme Court granted an injunction restraining the defendants from seeking to enforce the relevant provisions of the 1959 Act pending the outcome of the constitutional challenge. Finlay CJ. said:

> It is . . . the duty of the courts to protect persons against the invasion of their constitutional rights or against unconstitutional action. It would seem wholly inconsistent with that duty if the Court were to be without power in an appropriate case to restrain by injunction an action against a person which found its authority in a statutory provision which might eventually be found to be invalid having regard to the Constitution. In particular, it seems to me that this power must exist in an appropriate case where the form of action is under a penal section and involves conviction and the imposition of a penalty for the commission of a criminal offence.[57]

The plaintiffs had a stateable constitutional action and might well suffer irreparable damage if the injunction were not granted. The court went on to conclude that on the facts the balance of convenience clearly favoured the plaintiffs notwithstanding the fact that the granting of interim relief put 'into suspension' the relevant portion of the 1959 Act.[58]

While the *Pesca* principle has weathered unevenly in practice,[59] the existence of the jurisdiction to grant interim relief cannot be doubted. The most spectacular example of this came in *Crotty v An Taoiseach*,[60] where the government was restrained[61] from ratifying the Single European Act pending a challenge to the constitutionality of such ratification. Finlay CJ. explained that if the interim relief sought were not granted, then 'the Government's act of ratification would deprive this Court of its jurisdiction or power to grant to the plaintiff the remedies necessary to protect his constitutional rights'.[62] Although the criteria governing the granting of such relief were not addressed in any of these cases, the various judgments do appear to proceed on the assumption that the standard principles—arguable case, balance of convenience and adequacy of damages—will apply, albeit, perhaps, with some modifications.[63]

Injunctions to enforce public rights

The law in relation to injunctions and public rights has been developed in two significant respects. In the first place, the Irish courts have not accepted the principles inherent in *Gouriet v Union of Post Office Workers*,[64] namely, that the Attorney General has a monopoly in the enforcement of public rights and that a private citizen can only sue to enforce those rights *ex relatione* the Attorney General. Secondly, the courts have been willing to allow private citizens to sue to enforce the law where either it could be shown that constitutional provisions would otherwise be set at naught or where they can show that they have a personal interest in its enforcement.

The first sign of what was subsequently to come may be found in the judgment of Kenny J. in *Macauley v Minister for Posts and Telegraphs*.[65] Here the plaintiff had attempted to sue the defendant to compel him to provide an adequate telephone service, but section 2(1) of the Ministers and Secretaries Act 1924 required that the Attorney General grant a fiat before a minister could be sued in that capacity. In this case the Attorney had (quite exceptionally) refused the fiat—he evidently considered the action a frivolous one, but Kenny J. held that the subsection was unconstitutional in that the fiat rule impeded free access to the courts.[66]

This approach was strongly endorsed by the Supreme Court in *Society for the Protection of Unborn Children (Ire.) Ltd v Coogan*.[67] Here the plaintiff sought to restrain certain student organisations from distributing abortion information contrary to article 40.3.3[68] of the Constitution. The student organisations maintained that the plaintiff had no standing to seek such an injunction and that the enforcement of public rights was committed exclusively to the Attorney General. This proposition was initially upheld by Carroll J. in the High Court, but the Supreme Court held that the Attorney did not enjoy a monopoly in the vindication of a public right and that a *bona fide* plaintiff had standing to secure the enforcement of this constitutional provision. Were it otherwise, the Attorney's inaction might lead to the inability of the courts to restrain unconstitutional activities and, as Walsh J. stressed, every citizen has the right to ensure 'that the fundamental law of the State was observed'. It is true, of course, that this decision concerned the special and very sensitive subject of abortion, but the principle underlying this decision can probably be applied to other instances of actual or threatened breach of the Constitution where in the nature of things it is unlikely that any plaintiff suffering special loss and damage (above and beyond that suffered by other citizens) will come forward.[69]

Another constitutional dimension—on this occasion, the constitutional right to earn a livelihood—has featured in another series of cases. In *Parsons v Kavanagh*[70] the plaintiff was a licensed bus operator who faced competition on the same bus route from an unlicensed competitor. O'Hanlon J. first rejected the contention that the Road Transport Acts 1932–1933 were to be construed as statutes passed for the benefit of a limited class of the public, namely, licensed operators under the terms of the Acts. O'Hanlon J. felt, however, that cases such as *Cutler v Wandsworth Stadium Ltd*[71]—which would dictate that the plaintiff would have had no cause of action—would have to yield to constitutional considerations:

The right to earn one's living by any lawful means was recognised by Kenny J. in *Murtagh Properties Ltd v Cleary*[72] [where] he granted an injunction to restrain picketing of licensed premises on the basis that it amounted to an unlawful interference with the constitutional right of the bar maids employed therein to earn their livelihood. . . . The Supreme Court in *Byrne v Ireland*[73] was primarily concerned with the enforceability of civil claims against the State in situations where a right of action would arise against a private individual but the judgments also stress that rights derived from the Constitution must be safeguarded by remedies to be provided by the courts.[74]

O'Hanlon J. then concluded that:

> The constitutional right to earn one's livelihood by any lawful means carries with it the entitlement to be protected against any unlawful activity on the part of another person which materially impairs or infringes that right.[75]

In the event, therefore, as the defendant had thus engaged in unlawful activity which significantly impaired the plaintiff's exercise of her constitutional right to earn a livelihood, O'Hanlon J. granted an injunction restraining the defendant from carrying on business as an unlicensed operator.

This approach was expressly endorsed by the Supreme Court in *Lovett v Gogan*,[76] a case with facts practically identical to those in *Parsons*. A further gloss was put on this emerging doctrine, however, when the court held that the traditional equitable maxims governing the granting of injunctive relief were not necessarily applicable in a case of this kind. The defendants had contended that the plaintiff's own breaches of its licence under the Road Transport Acts 1932–1933 disentitled him from obtaining an injunction restraining the defendant's unlicensed activities. Finlay CJ. responded thus:

> I am not satisfied that the right of the plaintiff to an injunction in this case, deriving . . . as it does from an invasion and threatened continued invasion of his constitutional rights must be approached in the same manner as may generally apply to the discretion of a Court to grant the equitable relief of injunction and the doctrine that a plaintiff seeking that must come with clean hands. Where the Court . . . is prepared to grant an injunction in order to protect his constitutional right the enquiry must rather be as to whether he has got a constitutional right and whether it is that right which is being threatened.[77]

The question thus reduced itself to the issue of whether the plaintiff's breaches of the licence were so manifest as to render his activities illegal. As this claim failed on the facts, the plaintiff was duly granted the injunction sought. Whether this subtle recasting of the traditional rules governing injunctions in cases involving a threatened breach of constitutional rights presages a general re-evaluation of the law of remedies in the light of such developments remains to be seen.

Damages

The willingness of the courts to countenance a reshaping of remedies in the light of the Constitution is nowhere more evident than in the context of the law of torts.[78] Here there are essentially two schools of thought. The first is that the Constitution gives the courts a general licence to engage in an entire rebalancing exercise of the competing rights involved so as to shape the existing contours of tort law[79] (and, where necessary, to create entirely new torts)[80] in the light of constitutional considerations. The second and more conservative view is that the courts are entitled to intervene 'only where there has been a failure to implement or where the implementation relied on is plainly inadequate to effectuate the constitutional guarantee in question'.[81]

One may begin with the leading statement of Walsh J. in *Meskell v CIE*:[82]

> It has been said on a number of occasions in this Court . . . that a right guaranteed by the Constitution or granted by the Constitution can be protected by action or enforced by action even though such action may not fit into any of the ordinary forms of action in either common law or equity and that the constitutional right carries within it its own right to a remedy or for the enforcement of it. Therefore, if a person has suffered damage by virtue of a breach of a constitutional right, that person is entitled to seek redress against the person or persons who have infringed that right.[83]

This statement of principle has been subsequently widely approved and has formed the basis for the courts' preparedness to depart from the conventional limitations of the law of administrative law remedies. A few examples will suffice to illustrate how this has occurred in practice.

In *Byrne v Ireland* [84] the Supreme Court invalidated the common law rule whereby the state was deemed to be immune from suit. The plaintiff had suffered personal injuries as a result of the alleged negligence of officials of the Department of Posts and Telegraphs.[85] The court held that (i) none of the prerogatives which had hitherto attached to the Crown had survived the enactment of the Constitution,[86] and (ii) any such immunity would be inconsistent with the plaintiff's constitutional rights to have access to the courts and to recover damages in respect of a legal wrong. As Budd J. observed, the constitutional rights given to citizens 'would be quite meaningless, in so far as suing the State is concerned, unless they were in some way enforceable against the State'.[87] This decision has had enormous repercussions. Not only did it abolish at one fell swoop a long-standing immunity of the state and thus raised doubts about the constitutionality of other immunities conferred by statute,[88] but it raised the prospect of the 'constitutionalisation' of the entire law of torts, at least as far as actions against the state and public officials were concerned.[89]

There have been a number of cases where damages have been awarded for breach of constitutional rights, even though such an action would not lie at common law. In *Kearney v Ireland* [90] a prisoner was awarded (admittedly nominal) damages against the state for breach of his constitutional right to communicate when his mail was stopped by reason of industrial action taken by prison officers. Substantial damages[91] were awarded in *Kennedy v Ireland*,[92] where Hamilton P. concluded that agents of the state had deliberately engaged in irregular phone-tapping of the plaintiff journalists' telephones. This was an actionable violation of the plaintiffs' constitutional right to privacy, even if such an action would not have sounded at common law. In *Conway v Irish National Teachers' Organisation*[93] the Supreme Court awarded exemplary damages for breach of the plaintiff's constitutional right to education. The court found that the defendant union had recklessly engaged in industrial action which had left a class in a small village bereft of education for six months. The court concluded, having regard to the supreme importance of the right to education, that the defendants were aware of the importance of that right and that the breach was an intended, as distinct from inadvertent, breach of that right. A further example of the interaction of traditional tort rules and constitutional principles is supplied by *The La Lavia*.[94] In this multifaceted case Barr J. awarded damages to the plaintiffs under the rubric of the tort of misfeasance of a public office in circumstances where he found that the Commissioners of Public Works had made an order restraining the finders of the wrecks of ships from the Spanish Armada from conducting an inspection survey of the wrecks in circumstances where they either knew 'or had good reason to suspect that it did not have such power'.[95] Barr J., however, declined to hold that the plaintiffs were entitled to damages for breach of their constitutionally protected property rights, as he had already found that they had no salvage rights in respect of the wrecks. The implication, however, is that, had such salvage rights been established in law, the plaintiffs would have been entitled to damages on a strict liability basis for breach of their property rights by reason of the illegal administrative action in question.

It will be immediately appreciated—especially having regard to the large number of individual rights which merit constitutional protection and the relative ease with which these rights can be infringed both by the state and private individuals[96]—that these developments could readily lead to the complete circumvention of the traditional restrictions imposed by the law of torts (for example, limitations requiring proof of negligence and so forth). Accordingly, it might not be altogether surprising if, in order to avoid the creation of an alternative system of quasi-tort law with the action for breach of constitutional rights as its main vehicle, we were to witness some form of judicial checks on the emergence of such a strict liability system. In particular, it may be that the courts will move away from the present strict liability system in actions for breach of constitutional rights in favour of some *via media* requiring proof of fault or knowledge of illegality.[97]

One qualification already existing in the present law, however, is that the consitutional right in question must be one which is genuinely personal to the plaintiff. An example here is supplied by the judgment of Murphy J. in *Greene v Minister for Agriculture*[98] where the minister was found to have breached article 41.3.1 (by which the state pledges 'to guard with special care the institution of marriage') by imposing discriminatory conditions[99] on the payment of certain EC headage payments to farmers. The judge concluded that this constitutional breach did not entitle the plaintiff farmers to damages, even though they had clearly suffered as a result:

> What has happened is that the Minister as an agent of the State has neglected to perform his constitutional duty to safeguard the institution of marriage. There is evidence of damage suffered by the plaintiffs by reason of the neglect by the Minister of that constitutional duty . . .[100]

This suggests that whereas a plaintiff may recover damages for a breach of a purely personal constitutional right (such as the right to liberty or to earn a livelihood), no such action will lie where the breach is of a general constitutional duty or prohibition (such as article 44.2.2 whereby the state guarantees not to endow any religion). The full dimensions of this problem remain to be judicially explored.

Liability of the State for Breach of Community Law

A related question is the liability of the state for breach of Community law. As is well known, the Court of Justice ruled in the *Francovich* case[101] that a member state might be liable in damages in respect of the loss and damage suffered by a private individual which was directly caused by the state's failure to implement a directive which conferred directly enforceable rights. The court further indicated that a plaintiff's entitlement to damages must be determined in accordance with national procedural rules, which must not be less favourable than those relating to similar domestic claims and must not be framed so as to make it virtually impossible or excessively difficult to obtain compensation. Although these principles are currently in the course of evolution, to judge from the latest decision of the Court of Justice in *Wagner Miret v Fondo de Garantia Salarial*,[102] liability would appear to be strict and not dependent on a deliberate or culpable failure to implement the directive in question. In this case Spain had taken no steps to implement a particular directive, since it considered that its own national law was adequate for this purpose. While this view transpired to be incorrect, there is no discussion in the judgment as to whether the interpretation adopted by Spain was a reasonable one. It would thus seem that such a consideration is immaterial in this context.[103]

Some of these issues were explored by Carroll J. in her judgment in *Tate v Minister for Social Welfare*,[104] a case arising from the state's failure adequately to transpose the Equality Directive into national law. Carroll J. rejected the submission that the plaintiffs' claim for damages by reason of the failure to implement the directive derived from the Constitution,[105] and also said that the concept of 'the duty of care under the law of negligence is not applicable'. Rather, the plaintiffs' entitlement to sue 'was a wrong arising from Community law which has domestic effect' and was a 'breach of duty to implement the Directive and it approximates to a breach of constitutional duty'. Carroll J. nevertheless concluded that the six year limitation period contained in section 11 of the Statute of Limitations Act 1957 applied to actions seeking damages for breaches of Community law. Just as the word 'tort' in the section captured breaches of statutory duty and breaches of constitutional rights, so also 'the word "tort" is sufficiently wide to cover breaches of the obligations of the State under Community law'. It is noteworthy that Carroll J. regarded this cause of action as an autonomous one arising under Community law, and not necessarily conforming to any of the established domestic causes of action.

The State in Administrative Law Litigation

The decision in *Byrne v Ireland* has also meant that certain other residual prerogatives or privileges hitherto enjoyed by the state (formerly the Crown) have disappeared. Thus it has been held that mandamus (or other similar remedies) can lie against both ministers[106] and the government,[107] although it has been said that it is inappropriate to grant an injunction against Ireland[108] (i.e. the state) *as such*.[109] Finally, in *Howard v Commissioners of Public Works*[110] the Supreme Court held that the common law rule whereby there was a presumption that the state was exempt from the application of statute was held to be unconstitutional. Effectively, a majority of the Supreme Court held that this common law rule was so bound up with the former Crown prerogative that it was felt that the rule could not live, as it were, in the pure republican air created by the Constitution.[111]

Judicial Review: Fundamental Principles and Emerging Trends

Since a fully comprehensive account of judicial review of administrative action as it presently operates in the Republic of Ireland would be outside the scope of this chapter, it is here intended only to highlight some of the fundamental principles for the benefit of the outside observer. Considerations of space require selectivity of treatment and, hence, particular emphasis is placed on some of the new emerging trends such as the 'constitutionalisation' of the rules of natural justice and the increasing influence of the new concepts of proportionality and legitimate expectations.

The constitutionalisation of the Rules of Natural Justice

While the right to fair procedures has been held to be one of the personal rights guaranteed by article 40.3 of the Constitution,[112] the courts have, in general, been prepared to follow and employ the standard common law rules of *nemo iudex in causa sua* and *audi alteram partem*. In practice—whatever may be said about the strict theory—it seems to be that it is only where these common law rules are inadequate to satisfy this constitutional principle that the courts will fall back on the Constitution. There have, however, also been strong indications that legislation which seeks to exclude the rules of natural justice will be found to be either ineffective for this purpose (in that the courts will read in the rules of natural justice) or, if this is not possible, found to be unconstitutional.[113]

Since it would be quite impossible to give a comprehensive account of the large number of cases involving fair procedures and natural justice, it is proposed to highlight some of the more interesting recent decisions so as to give the outside reader some indication of how the Irish courts deal in practice with these issues.

Nemo iudex in causa sua

The decision of the Supreme Court in *Dublin Well-Woman Centre Ltd v Ireland*[114] provides an interesting illustration of the application of the rule against bias in a case with unusual facts. In this case the plaintiff applied in the High Court to have an earlier injunction restraining them from providing information about abortion services abroad lifted in the light of the enactment of the 14th Amendment of the Constitution Act 1994.[115] When the action came on for hearing before Carroll J. in the High Court, counsel for the Society of Unborn Children (Ireland) Ltd (a notice party to the action) applied to her to discharge herself from the hearing of the action on the ground that in her capacity as Chairwoman of (the official) Second Commission on the Status of Women she had made submissions regarding the availability of abortion information. When Carroll J. refused, the notice party appealed successfully to the Supreme Court. Denham J. observed that:

> ... where many reasonable people in our community hold strong opinions, it is of particular importance that neither party should have any reasonable reason to apprehend bias in the courts .... Further, once the question of a possible perception of bias has been raised reasonably on the grounds of pre-existing non-judicial position and actions, it would be contrary to fair procedures to proceed with a trial.

O'Reilly v Cassidy[116] is another example of alleged judicial bias. Here the respondent trial judge had allowed an appeal against a District Court order renewing the applicant's intoxicating liquor licence. At one stage during the course of the hearing counsel for the applicant commented on the fact that counsel for the state was the daughter of the respondent. The respondent replied that the comment was an impertinence and that he would report counsel for the applicant to the Bar Council. Flood J. would not accept that the 'mere fact of the judge's daughter being brief before him is sufficient to give rise to the possibility of a reasonable man considering that bias could follow'. Such, however, were the circumstances prevailing in court on the day that the complaint made by the applicant's counsel as to the relationship between the judge and opposing counsel 'got so inextricably entangled with other factors that there was a real possibility that the [decision] could give rise to a fear in a reasonable person that the outcome of the proceedings' could have been affected by that relationship.

Most of the modern cases have involved allegations of prejudgment on the part of the decision-maker. *O'Neill v Beaumont Hospital Board*[117] is a prime example: in this case the Supreme Court restrained three members of a hospital board—who had previously expressed strong views concerning the continued employment of the plaintiff consultant—from adjudicating on the question of whether to dismiss him or not. On the other hand, the courts have been more sympathetic to the interests of the administration in cases where it has been contended that the decision-makers have an in-built loyalty to the institutions they serve. In *O'Brien v Bord na Mona*[118] the plaintiff challenged the constitutionality of land acquisition procedures operated by a statutory board. It was said that the procedures contained an in-built bias in favour of acquisition. While the Supreme Court agreed that such procedures would be unconstitutional if the body in question were exercising judicial powers (because of the stringent standards of impartiality required in such cases), it held that a lesser standard was to be tolerated where (as here) the powers were simply administrative in character. This result had been anticipated by Keane J. in *The State (Comer) v Minister for Justice*[119]—a case where the prison authorities had been required to adjudicate on whether a prison officer had been guilty of neglect of his duties—when he said that the *nemo iudex* principle 'could not be literally applied in such circumstances'.

Audi alteram partem

Two subcategories of the *audi alteram partem* rule may be taken as representative: the adequacy of notice and the form of the hearing.

Adequacy of Notice

The leading case in this area remains *The State (Gleeson) v Minister for Defence*[120] where the Supreme Court held that the dismissal of a soldier from the Defence Forces was invalid in circumstances where he was not told of the reason for his dismissal, nor was he given any adequate opportunity to make representations in advance of that decision.[121] This principle was applied in another context in *TV Three Ltd v Independent Radio and Television Commission*,[122] which provides a notable example of where an administrative body acts unilaterally to cancel a right or interest which they had conferred on the person affected. The Commission had awarded the franchise for the third television channel to the applicants and the Supreme Court confirmed that this right or interest (however it was classified) could not be unilaterally cancelled or revoked without 'some form of prior hearing'. Since this opportunity had not been afforded to the applicants in the present case, Egan J. held that this amounted to a breach of fair procedures. Nevertheless, there are limits to the principle and specific notice need not be given where the applicant has had ample time to make representations[123] or where he already knows *aliunde* the grounds of complaint.[124]

Form of the Hearing

Most of the case law has been concerned with the right to counsel and the right to cross-examine adverse witnesses. In the leading case of *In Re Haughey*[125] the Supreme Court held that the constitutional rights to good name and to fair procedures would be meaningless unless the deciding tribunal was prepared to abide by the following procedural safeguards:

(a) that he should be furnished with a copy of the evidence which reflected on his good name; (b) that he should be allowed to cross-examine, by counsel, his accusers; (c) that he should be allowed to give rebutting evidence; and (d) that he should be permitted to address, again by counsel, the [tribunal] in his own defence.[126]

It must be stressed that these words were spoken in the context of a Tribunal of Inquiry at which Mr Haughey[127] was a key witness. It was on this basis that the Tribunal refused Mr Haughey the right to cross-examine witnesses and so forth, but the Supreme Court stressed that as in substance he was the defendant in proceedings in which his good name had been seriously impugned, he was constitutionally entitled to these essential safeguards. This does not mean that these standards are applicable to all administrative decisions and much will turn on the gravity and complexity which the applicant is required to meet.[128] Nevertheless, where the charges are serious in character, the trend has been towards insisting on these protections.

In *Flanagan v University College, Dublin*[129] the applicant was a student who had been found guilty of cheating by a disciplinary panel. She had made several attempts to discover what had been alleged against her and was orally informed of this some six days before the hearing. The procedure followed was deficient in several other respects, for as Barron J. stated:

> . . . the procedures must follow those of a court hearing . . . The applicant should have received in writing details of the offence. . . . At the hearing itself, she should have been able to hear the evidence against her, to challenge that evidence on cross-examination and to present her own evidence. Unfortunately, there was a total failure on the part of the College to allow her these rights. There was no attempt to make the applicant aware of the exact nature of the charge against her . . . The refusal to permit her representation of her own choosing was a virtual denial of the former and the absence of anyone to give evidence against her at the hearing before the committee was a denial of one aspect of the latter. It gave her no opportunity either to discover how the case against her was being put to the test or to test its strength by cross-examination.[130]

A further dimension to this aspect is illustrated by the judgment of Geoghegan J. in *Goodman International v Hamilton (No. 2)*.[131] Here the makers of a television programme—which made certain serious allegations against the applicant company—had declined to give evidence before a Tribunal of Inquiry which was investigating the allegations. The applicant claimed that the failure on the part of the Tribunal to procure these witnesses amounted to a breach of fair procedures, but Geoghegan J. could not accept this submission:

... the Tribunal is carrying out its obligation to vindicate the applicant's good name if it does not permit hearsay evidence to impugn that good name and if it accedes to reasonable requests for the availability of particular witnesses considered necessary for the vindication of a good name provided that it is possible to obtain such witnesses or evidence.[132]

Proportionality

The doctrine of proportionality does not appear to have been examined in any Irish case prior to about 1988. The concept of proportionality has subsequently won at least a foothold in Irish constitutional and administrative law. In the last few years the concept has been principally employed as a means of judging whether the restrictions imposed by legislation on the exercise of any given constitutional right are excessive in the circumstances.[133]

In the first case where the concept was expressly[134] employed—*Hand v Dublin Corporation*[135]—Barron J. acknowledged the European origins of the doctrine. Here the plaintiffs were street traders who had been convicted of two or more offences under the Casual Trading Act 1980. By virtue of section 4(6) of that Act any person convicted of two or more such offences within a given five year period may not be granted a street trading licence. The plaintiffs—who had been thereby disqualified from holding a licence— claimed that this disqualification was disproportionate and, hence, that it constituted an unjust attack on their constitutional right to earn a livelihood.[136] Barron J. seemed prepared to admit the existence of the doctrine of proportionality, but considered that it applied only to the exercise of discretionary powers and not to cases such as the present, where the validity of a statutory disqualification was at issue:

> The principle of proportionality exists in the administrative law of other member states of the European Community . . . The principle itself, that there should be an obligation on an administrative authority when exercising a discretionary power to maintain a proper balance between any adverse effects which its decision might have on the rights, liberties or interests of persons and the purpose pursued by that authority, is one annexed to Recommendation No. R(80)2 adopted by the Council of Ministers of the Council of Europe on 11th March 1980. Nevertheless, this principle, even if adopted in this jurisdiction, applies only to the exercise of administrative powers. . . . Different considerations apply in relation to [the present case] since it is the Oireachtas itself which has imposed the sanction.[137]

The distinction drawn here between the exercise of administrative discretion and the imposition of a statutory disqualification in the context of the possible application of the proportionality doctrine seems unsound. What is interesting, however, is that despite the above passage, Barron J. was prepared to apply the doctrine in assessing whether to invalidate the statutory disqualification:

> Treating the grant of a licence under the Casual Trading Act 1980, as a certificate of fitness to trade under the provisions of that Act, it seems to me that it is appropriate that the statute itself may set out the circumstances in which the privilege may be lost.
>
> Such circumstances must, however, be reasonable. Can it be said to be unreasonable on the part of the Oireachtas to provide that a casual trading licence shall not be given to a person who has already at the date of application two convictions for offences under the Act?
>
> It is said to be unreasonable because the penalty is out of proportion to the offence. The offence is the commission of two offences, which may be trivial in their nature, whereas the penalty is the right to earn one's living. Undoubtedly some of the offences which may bring the [statutory disqualification] into effect may be relatively unimportant and its effect may have serious consequences in individual cases. However, the right to earn one's living by casual trading is given by the Act. It does not seem unreasonable for the Oireachtas, having granted the privilege, to deprive persons of it for conduct referable to the fitness of the person concerned to exercise that same privilege.[138]

Thus, although the contours of the doctrine remained uncertain, what was significant is that the High Court was willing in principle to apply the principle of proportionality. The potential utility of the principle was further enhanced as a result of the important Supreme Court decision in *Cox v Ireland*.[139]

In this case, the plaintiff was a schoolteacher who had been convicted of certain firearms offences before the Special Criminal Court. By virtue of section 34 of the Offences against the State Act 1939, a public servant convicted of certain scheduled offences before the Special Criminal Court[140] was automatically disqualified from all public servants' posts for a seven year period and forfeited his or her pension entitlements. The plaintiff protested that the disqualification orders were disproportionate in character and, accordingly, that the section constituted an 'unjust attack' on his personal rights within the meaning of article 40.3 of the Constitution. This proposition was accepted by the court which held the section to be unconstitutional.

Finlay CJ. first observed that the task of the court was to examine whether a fair balance had been struck between the duty of the state to vindicate and protect the constitutional rights of citizens (including the right to earn a livelihood and property rights) and the state's duty to protect public peace and order and to ensure 'the maintenance and stability of its own authority'.[141] He then drew attention to the anomalies produced by the section. It did not apply to non-public servants; nor did it apply if the person was convicted before the ordinary courts[142] and persons convicted of relatively trivial offences (such as the non-renewal of a licence for a sporting gun) might nonetheless attract the drastic sanctions of section 34, because these offences are nonetheless scheduled offences. The Chief Justice continued:

> A citizen charged with one of the less serious offences coming within a category scheduled . . . and tried for such offences by such Court and convicted, if he happens to be the holder of an office or employment funded by the State has no protection against the mandatory imposition of the forfeiture provisions contained in s. 34. This is so even though he might be in a position to establish . . . the fact that his motive or intention in committing it, or the circumstances in which it was committed, bore no relation at all to any question of the maintenance of public peace and order or the authority and stability of the State. . . . For these reasons . . . notwithstanding the fundamental interests of the State which the section seeks to protect, the provisions of s. 34 of the Act of 1939 fail as far as practicable to protect the constitutional rights of the citizen and are, accordingly, impermissibly wide and indiscriminate.[143]

The significance of this judgment, given that the court held that the section constituted a disproportionate attack on constitutional rights, is that one may, therefore, read the judgment 'as implicitly disapproving Barron J.'s holding in *Hand v Dublin Corporation* that proportionality is not a test of statutory validity'.[144]

The extent to which the doctrine of proportionality has been adopted into Irish constitutional law may be judged from the fact that it has been applied in three major cases in 1994. The first of these is *Re Article 26 of the Constitution and the Matrimonial Homes Bill 1993*.[145] Here the Supreme Court was required to examine the constitutionality of a Bill[146] which proposed automatically to confer equal ownership in the family and chattels on both spouses jointly, irrespective of existing ownership arrangements. If either or both spouses were unhappy with this, the Bill proposed to grant them the right to request a court, in effect, to disapply the provisions of the Bill in their own particular case. The Supreme Court held that the measure was a disproportionate interference by the State with the rights of the family and ruled that the measure contravened article 41.1.2 of the Constitution.[147] The court's reasoning is of interest, as it shows the extent to which the proportionality doctrine has quickly jumped to the forefront of Irish judicial techniques.

Finlay CJ. first drew attention to the likely effect of these legislative proposals:

> In some instances the net effect of these legislative proposals would be automatically to cancel a decision freely made by both spouses as part of the authority of the family and substitute therefor a wholly different decision unless the spouses can agree to a new joint decision to confirm the earlier agreement or unless the owning spouse can succeed in obtaining a court order . . .[148]

In these circumstances, the court concluded that the measure would constitute an unconstitutional interference with family decision-making since 'such provisions do not constitute a reasonably proportionate intervention by the State with the rights of the family' and amounted to 'a failure by the State to protect the authority of the family'.[149]

Perhaps the most elaborate statement by an Irish court of the proportionality doctrine is to be found in the judgment of Costello J. in *Heaney v Ireland*.[150] Here the High Court was required to examine the constitutionality of section 52 of the Offences against the State Act 1939 in the light of article 38.1[151] of the Constitution. This section requires persons arrested under the provisions of the 1939 Act 'to give an account of their movements' and failure to do so gives rise to a maximum penalty of six months' imprisonment. The plaintiffs in this case were arrested within the territory of the Republic of Ireland shortly after a large bomb explosion in Northern Ireland had killed six persons. When, following their arrest under section 30 of the 1939 Act, they failed to give an account of their movements they were convicted of an offence under section 52 and sentenced to six months' imprisonment.

Costello J. accepted that the right against self-incrimination was a right protected by article 38.1. In the light of the *Cox* case he was required to consider whether this constitutional right had been validly abridged by the Oireachtas when enacting section 52:

> In considering whether a restriction on the exercise of rights is permitted by the Constitution the courts in this country and elsewhere have found it helpful to apply the test of proportionality, a test which contains the notions of minimal restraint on the exercise of protected rights and the exigencies of common good in a democratic society. This is a test frequently adopted by the European Court of Human Rights (see, for example, *Sunday Times v United Kingdom*)[152] and has recently been formulated by the Supreme Court in Canada in the following terms. The objective of the impugned provision must be of sufficient importance to warrant overriding a constitutionally protected right. It must relate to concerns pressing and substantial in a free and democratic society. The means chosen must pass a proportionality test. They must:
>
> (a) be rationally connected to the objective and not be arbitrary, unfair or based on irrational considerations;

(b) impair the right as little as possible; and

(c) be such that their effects on rights are proportional to the objective: see *Chaulk v R.*[153]

Costello J. then proceeded to apply this test to the facts of the present case and concluded that:

> Recalling that the object which s. 52 has been enacted to achieve, namely, the investigation and punishment of serious subversive crime, and having regard to the legal protections which exist which will minimise the risk involved in the operation of the section . . . it seems to me that the restriction on the right to silence imposed by the section cannot be regarded as excessive and that it is proportionate to the objective which it is designed to achieve.[154]

While some might query the balancing exercise conducted by Costello J. as far as the impugned section was concerned, in many ways this is not germane to our discussion. What matters is that the High Court was willing explicitly to apply the principle of proportionality and, having acknowledged the European provenance of the principle, was prepared to lay down an elaborate test for its application. The significance of this development cannot really be overstated, since, as we have seen, the doctrine lends itself to ready application to the area of Irish constitutional law. Much of the fundamental rights provisions of the Irish Constitution (article 38 and articles 40–44) are couched in subjective language, for example, article 40.3.2 commits the state by its laws to protecting 'as best it may from unjust attack' the life, person, good name and property rights of every citizen. The very subjectivity of what constitutes an 'unjust attack' has troubled Irish constitutional lawyers for many years[155] and while it would be wrong to regard the principle of proportionality as a solution to every such difficulty, the great advantage of this new doctrine is that it will help to provide a badly needed analytical framework and, hence, reduce otherwise subjective judicial appraisals in important areas of constitutional law.

The Doctrine of Reasonableness

Just as in the case of their English counterparts, the Irish courts have always enjoyed a residual discretion to interfere to quash an administrative decision which is plainly at variance with common sense or which is absurd or which disproportionately interferes with legal rights. Prior to about 1975, this doctrine was rarely invoked by litigants in judicial review matters, still less applied by the courts. It is, of course, important to stress that the doctrine of reasonableness is not to be equated with an administrative appeal and the Irish courts will not interfere simply because they do not agree with the impugned decision. Undoubtedly, however, one of the difficulties with this doctrine is its very subjectivity.

In the leading case, *The State (Keegan) v Stardust Victims' Compensation Tribunal*,[156] the applicants were a husband and wife who were awarded substantially differing sums by the respondent tribunal. The husband (who actually received nothing) sought to have the decision in his case quashed, but the court refused to intervene, saying that there were (unspecified) differences between his case and that of his wife which explained this apparent discrepancy. The test enunciated by Henchy J. has since become canonical:

> I would myself consider that the test of unreasonableness or irrationality in judicial review lies in considering whether the impugned decision plainly and unambiguously flies in the face of fundamental reason and common sense. If it does, then the decision-maker should be held to have acted *ultra vires*, for the necessarily implied constitutional limitation of jurisdiction in all decision-making which affects rights or duties requires that the decision-maker must not flagrantly reject or disregard fundamental reason or common sense in reaching his decision.

It is interesting to note that in arriving at this view Henchy J. had expressly declined to adopt the following test which had been expressed by Lord Diplock in *Council of Civil Service Unions v Minister for the Civil Service*:

> It applies to a decision which is so outrageous in its defiance of logic or of accepted moral standards that no sensible person who had applied his mind to the question to be decided could have arrived at it.[157]

On this Henchy J. said that he 'would be slow to test unreasonableness by seeing if it accords with logic'. He observed that:

> Many examples could be given of reputable decisions and of substantive laws which reject logic in favour of other considerations.[158]

Henchy J. was equally unimpressed with the 'accepted moral standards' criterion:

> The concept of 'accepted moral standards' represents a vague, elusive and changing body of standards which in a pluralist society is sometimes difficult to ascertain and is sometimes inappropriate or irrelevant to the decision in question (as it is to the decision in question in this case). The moral or ethical postulates of our Constitution will, of course, make certain decisions invalid for being repugnant to the Constitution, but in most cases a decision falls to be quashed for unreasonableness, not because of the extent to which it has departed from accepted moral standards (or positive morality), but because it is indefensible for being in the teeth of plain reason and common sense.[159]

Henchy J.'s criticism of the limitations inherent in the *GCHQ* test is probably well taken. What is not clear, however, is whether this formulation yields significantly different results. In particular, it would have to be conceded that the *Stardust* test is no less subjective than its British counterpart. Perhaps the lesson of these formulas is that subjectivity is inevitable in any form of administrative review and that irrespective of the test actually adopted it is both futile and impossible to avoid this.

At all events, the Irish courts have sought to stress the limited nature of the judicial review function, especially in the context of challenges to decisions taken by specialist tribunals. In *O'Keefe v An Bord Pleanala*[160] the Supreme Court indicated unease at the increasing number of judicial review applications whereby it had been sought to impugn administrative decisions on the grounds of unreasonableness and it sought to stress that judicial review could not be regarded as a form of statutory appeal. As Finlay CJ. emphasised:

> The Court cannot interfere with a decision of an administrative decision-making authority merely on the grounds that:
> (a) it is satisfied on the facts as found that it would have raised different inferences and conclusions; or
> (b) it is satisfied that the case against the decision made by the authority was much stronger than the case for it.[161]

Thus, the Supreme Court concluded that the specialist Planning Appeals Board (An Bord Pleanala) was entitled to grant planning permission for a large television mast, despite the reservations which had been expressed by a planning inspector appointed by the Board about the possible negative consequences of such a decision.

While it is probably true to regard the *O'Keefe* test as being especially applicable to specialist tribunals[162] (such as the Planning Board), this cautious approach has had an influence in other areas of administrative law. Thus, another example along these lines is supplied by *Stroker v Doherty*,[163] where a member of the Garda Siochána (police) had received a relatively minor disciplinary penalty in respect of an incident which had occurred in a public house. The garda in question—who was off duty at the time—had suggested to an acquaintance that his wife was available for sexual favours. The Supreme Court refused to quash this decision of a (police) disciplinary panel as being unreasonable in law, with McCarthy J. explaining that the decision was one which the disciplinary body was *entitled* to come to, even if his words contain a hint that the court was unhappy with the result.[164]

This trend was continued by the Supreme Court in *Garda Representative Body v Ireland*.[165] In this case the applicants sought to quash a decision which had been made by a civil service conciliation body regarding an aspect of Garda overtime. The Supreme Court found that the decision was not manifestly unreasonable according to the *O'Keefe* formulation and continued:

> Judicial review is what it says it is, namely, a review and not an appeal and for the courts to give to the plaintiff a declaration that the chairman of the council had been incorrect in his interpretation, as distinct from declaring that his interpretation was void or invalid, would be to conduct an appeal from his decision.[166]

This prompts two comments. First, the decision under challenge was effectively that of a specialist body, so that the applicant's task of establishing unreasonableness was all the more exacting. Secondly, there is, of course, a very fine line to be drawn here, since it has been judicially accepted that the incorrect interpretation of relevant legislation may amount to an error of law which, of course, would be susceptible to judicial review.

Recent examples where the courts quashed decisions as being unreasonable in law

While many of the cases are truly myriads of single instances not readily lending themselves to systematic analysis, it may be nonetheless useful to chronicle three contemporary examples of where administrative decisions were quashed on grounds of unreasonableness.

In *Dumbrell v Governor of Mountjoy Prison*[167] the applicants (who were prisoners) were found guilty of certain disciplinary offences in the following circumstances. A prison officer inspected a recreation hall and found it to be in good order. The three applicants were subsequently admitted to the hall, but after they had departed, it was found that the snooker table had been damaged. All three denied the charge of malicious damage and there were no other witnesses. The governor concluded that 'as they were the only prisoners to use the hall during the period of the damage, I concluded that they were responsible for the damage'.

The Supreme Court quashed the decision as being unreasonable in law. Blayney J. agreed that the governor was entitled to conclude that one of the three had damaged the table, but 'there was no evidence on which he could find which of them had done it, nor was there any evidence on which he could conclude that all three had caused the damage'. Since there was no such evidence, it 'was not reasonable to find all three guilty of having damaged the table'.

Another example of this residual power is provided by *Matthews v Irish Coursing Club Ltd.*[168] The respondents (who are given statutory responsibility for greyhound meetings) found that the winning dog at a coursing meeting had been illegally doped. Having found the owner of the winning dog guilty, the club simply imposed a fine, but allowed her to keep the trophy. The owner of the runner-up dog was successful in his application to have this decision set aside as being unreasonable in law. O'Hanlon J. described this case as 'one of the infrequent cases where the intervention of the court may legitimately be invoked to challenge the validity of a decision made by an administrative tribunal'. In their desire to be lenient towards the owner of the doped dog, the club was 'manifestly unjust in relation to the applicant's rights in the matter' and further lost sight of its statutory obligations. Accordingly, the decision to allow the doped dog to retain such a premier award was so at variance with those statutory obligations as to be unsustainable.

The final example is provided by the decision of Barr J. in *The La Lavia*[169] where he quashed as unreasonable the refusal of the Commissioners of Public Works to grant an excavation licence to a group of expert divers and marine historians who had discovered certain wrecks from the Spanish Armada off the Sligo coast. The judge stigmatised this refusal as 'extraordinary' and one 'going far beyond petty bureaucracy' and reading between the lines of the judgment it seems that he concluded that the Commissioners were actuated by a sense of dislike of the group and that they were determined not to co-operate with them.

Are There Unreviewable Discretionary Decisions?

Despite the huge expansion in the scope of judicial review over the last thirty years or so, there have been nonetheless some recent indications that there are limits to the court's powers of review. Some decisions—such as the Director of Public Prosecution's decision whether to prosecute[170] in any given case or the government's delay in bringing a statutory provision into force[171]—will only be reviewed on a limited basis, that is, proof of bad faith or improper motive seems to be required. In other instances the courts have signalled that certain administrative decisions are practically immune from review. Thus, in *McKenna v An Taoiseach*[172] Costello J. refused to condemn as either unconstitutional or unreasonable in law the government's decision to spend public monies supporting the 'Yes' campaign in the Maastricht Treaty referendum in June 1992. While it was true that the plaintiff—as a representative of the 'No' campaign[173]—had a legitimate political grievance, Costello J. warned that:

> . . . not every grievance can be remedied by the courts. And judges must not allow themselves to be led, or, indeed, voluntarily wander into areas calling for adjudication on political and non-justiciable issues. They are charged by

the Constitution with exercising the judicial power of government and it would both weaken their important constitutional role as well as amount to an unconstitutional act for judges to adjudicate on such issues.[174]

Another example of this tendency is supplied by the judgment of Murphy J. in *Duff v Minister for Agriculture and Food*[175] where the plaintiff farmers claimed that the minister had acted unreasonably in law in failing to create a national milk quota reserve as permitted by article 3(1) of (EC) Regulation 857/84 so as to cater for the special needs of farmers who had lodged development plans prior to 1 March 1984. Murphy J. drew attention to the fact that the article 'gave no indication as to what criteria might be considered appropriate' in implementing it:

> The regulations deliberately chose to confer a discretion which though not absolute, not unfettered and not capable of being exercised unreasonably does not appear to have been restricted by any identifiable objective or in any purposeful fashion. I can only infer that the discretion was granted to each member State to be exercised in accordance with the national policy of that State rather than the attainment of particular objectives within the Council regulations.[176]

Murphy J., however, concluded that he was not at liberty to review an administrative decision taken for reasons of national policy:

> Even leaving aside any question of the application of the doctrine of the separation of powers it seems to me impossible for the Courts to review decisions based on questions of national policy. To do so would involve the State disclosing publicly details of highly confidential national and international planning and strategy and even if that were done some yardstick would have to be found by which the Courts could be invited to say that such policies were irrational. I do not think that the first of these propositions is desirable or that the second is possible. . . . Political decisions of a policy nature are inherently far removed from the relatively compact arguments concerning the legal or constitutional rights of parties. . . . Accordingly I take the view that whilst the Minister's discretion was not unfettered and was not capable of being exercised in an arbitrary fashion, it was a decision based on national policy for which the Minister . . . is answerable politically and not to the courts of law unless . . . the policy infringes the constitutional rights of the citizen or is shown to involve the abuse of a fiduciary function, which is not the case [here].[177]

This judgment—which finds echoes in two other contemporary decisions refusing to adjudicate on the constitutionality of the alleged failure of the Oireachtas to provide adequately via taxation policies for certain disadvantaged groups[178] and large families[179]—shows that while the boundaries of judicial review have expanded greatly, there are nonetheless limits to the courts' powers of review.

Duty to Give Reasons

Administrative bodies exercising quasi-judicial powers or even administrative powers affecting legal rights and interests are now under a general duty to give reasons for their decisions, even in situations where they are not under a statutory duty to do so. This development is mixed up with the doctrine of reasonableness itself since the courts consider (a) that any reasonable administrator will provide reasons for his decision, and (b) the reasons given will enable the courts to assess the reasonableness of the decision under review. This is illustrated by the leading decision, *The State (Creedon) v Criminal Injuries Compensation Tribunal*.[180] Here the Tribunal rejected without explanation the applicant's claim for compensation under the scheme, despite the fact that all the evidence pointed towards the conclusion that her husband died in the course of attempting to save human life. The Supreme Court set aside this decision as being unreasonable in law. The Chief Justice added:

> Once the courts have a jurisdiction ... to enquire into and, if necessary, correct the decisions and activities of a tribunal of this description, it would appear necessary for the proper carrying out of that decision that the courts should be able to ascertain the reasons by which the tribunal came to its determination.

The subsequent decision of Blayney J. in *International Fishing Vessels Ltd v Minister for Marine*[181] makes it clear that the ambit of the *Creedon* decision is not confined to quasi-judicial decisions (such as that which was at issue in the *Creedon* case). The minister had refused to give reasons in respect of his decision to refuse to grant a fishing licence, but Blayney J. held that this was incorrect in law:

> While the functions of the Minister in the present case are not quasi-judicial, it seems to me none the less that the reasoning of the Chief Justice [in *Creedon*] is equally valid here since the Minister has the obligation of acting fairly and judicially in accordance with the principles of constitutional justice. What the Minister did here was precisely what the Chief Justice criticised the tribunal for doing ... Just as the tribunal's silence was not consistent with the administration of justice, I consider that the Minister's silence was not consistent with the proper discharge of his obligations to the applicant ...[182]

Despite the broad principles which might be thought to underlie the judgments in *Creedon* and *International Fishing* some limitations have more recently been imposed by the courts on the obligation to provide reasons. In *H. v Director of Public Prosecutions*[183] the Supreme Court distinguished the *International Fishing* case on the ground that that case had proceeded on the premise that the minister's decision was open to full judicial review. In *H.* the applicant had sought to compel the Director to initiate a particular prosecution,[184] but he declined to do so without giving reasons for his decision. O'Flaherty J. stressed that in contrast with the position of the minister in *International Fishing*, the Director's decisions were amenable to review in very limited circumstances only, namely, where he had been influenced by an 'improper motive or improper policy'.[185] O'Flaherty J. continued:

> It would seem then that as the duty to give reasons stems from a need to facilitate full judicial review, the limited intervention available in the context of the Director's decision obviates the necessity to disclose reasons.[186]

This proposition is by no means self-evident. Even accepting that the Director is amenable to judicial review only on the grounds of improper motive or improper policy, one must ask how an applicant can ever successfully establish such grounds if the Director does not furnish reasons for his decision. Certainly, the absence of any necessity on the Director's part to give reasons serves only to place obstacles in the way of any litigant wishing to challenge such a decision.

A similar approach had been taken by Barron J. in *Manning v Shackleton*[187] where the applicant sought to challenge a decision of a statutory arbitrator where his award did not recite the reasons for the decision. Barron J. referred to the earlier authorities such as *International Fishing* and said:

> These cases indicate that the giving of reasons by a person or body required to act judicially may be compelled by this court when such reasons are necessary to determine whether such a power has been validly exercised. It is not an essential obligation and arises only when required to prevent an injustice or ensure that not only has justice been done but is seen to have been done. The absence of reasons in this award itself does not invalidate it. The question is, whether, if reasons are not now given, justice will neither be done nor be seen to be done.[188]

Barron J. concluded on the facts that, with regard to one aspect of the award, the applicant would suffer prejudice if reasons were not given.

It will be seen, therefore, that while the duty to give reasons applies generally to persons exercising quasi-judicial and administrative powers, it is subject to exceptions. There thus remain certain islands of immunity (such as, for example, certain types of academic decisions and decisions governing the exercise of prosecutorial discretion) in respect of the giving of reasons.

Legitimate Expectations

The principle of legitimate expectations is one which was not known to Irish law prior to December 1987 when its existence was acknowledged by the Irish Supreme Court in *Webb v Ireland*.[189] While the court did not deal with the provenance of this doctrine, it is impossible to doubt but that the Irish judiciary were much influenced by the (then) recent decision of the House of Lords in the *GCHQ* case, *Council of Civil Service Unions v Minister for the Civil Service*[190] and, more generally, by developments in the administrative law of the European Community and its member states. Lord Mackenzie Stuart's statement is at least as true of Ireland as it is of England:

> Can one here [in *GCHQ*] detect the influence of Community law or at least some of the Member States? It is at least possible to suggest that the answer is yes. The concept of recognising that a failure to respect legitimate expectations may give rise, in public law, to a remedy is a novelty in English law and lacks discernible English parentage. To find the true ancestry one does not have to go far beyond the channel.[191]

The facts of *Webb* were as follows: the plaintiffs were the finders of an exceptionally valuable hoard of treasure containing unique specimens of early Christian art. The plaintiffs handed over the hoard to the Director of the National Museum who assured the plaintiffs that they would be honourably treated. The plaintiffs' claim for recovery of the treasure from the Museum failed, since the Supreme Court rather dubiously concluded that article 5 of the Constitution entitled the state to claim the find as a form of treasure trove.[192]

The plaintiffs, however, succeeded on their alternative claim, namely, that the circumstances of the case gave rise to a legitimate expectation that they would receive some form of reward. Finlay CJ. observed:

> It would appear that the doctrine of 'legitimate expectation', sometimes described as 'reasonable expectation', has not in those terms been the subject of any decision of our courts. However, the doctrine connoted by such expressions is but an aspect of the well-recognised concept of promissory estoppel . . . whereby a promise or representation as to intention may in certain circumstances be held binding on the representor or promisor.[193]

The plaintiffs had argued that the long-standing practice of the National Museum of paying rewards to finders of antiquities was enough to create a legitimate expectation to fair compensation in their favour, but Finlay CJ. did not find it necessary to rule on this point. In his view this was enough:

> The plaintiffs' claim for compensation rests solidly on the fact that the assurance given to Mr Webb that he would be honourably treated (which should be held to mean that he would be reasonably rewarded) was an integral part of the transaction whereby he deposited the hoard in the National Museum. It would be inequitable and unjust if the State were to be allowed to repudiate that assurance and give only a meagre and disproportionate award.[194]

In a way, the implications of *Webb* were distorted by the very special facts of that case. Hogan and Morgan comment thus:

> . . . the *Webb* decision would seem to have been an instance of a generous application of the doctrine of promissory estoppel, rather than presaging a radical new development in the law. Moreover, this judgment was given in the context of a case in which no new statutory powers of the State were involved, and, accordingly, there was no potential conflict between the plaintiff's legitimate expectation and the doctrine that the exercise of statutory powers may not be fettered by estoppel.[195]

While the subsequent case law has been fitful and somewhat inconsistent, the principle is nonetheless well established. The major difference between Irish and European law in this regard would appear to be that the former very largely confines the application of the principle of legitimate expectations to the sphere of *procedural* as distinct from *substantive* rights, at least where the granting of substantive rights would conflict with the principle that the donee of a statutory power may not fetter by estoppel his freedom of action.[196]

The rationale of the legitimate expectations doctrine

There appear to be two distinct rationales underlying the principle of legitimate expectations in Irish law. The first—which would appear to apply equally to private as well as public law—is that there are circumstances in which it may be unfair or inequitable to permit an administrator to renege on a promise or representation made. As noted already, this rationale does not seem to add much to the existing law, since viewed in this way, the principle of legitimate expectations would appear to approximate very closely to the traditional doctrine of promissory estoppel. The *Webb* case is indeed itself an example of this rationale in application.

The other line of authority is a more radical one, but there are already signs of judicial unease with this approach. This line of authority has it that, in the absence of a conflict with the exercise of a statutory power or some other exceptional circumstances, a solemn promise given by or on behalf of an administrator should be held to be binding. In *Fakih v Minister for Justice*[197] a number of Lebanese immigrants had illegally arrived in Ireland. Their applications for refugee status were summarily rejected and they were refused permission to enter the state. They asserted that their applications should have been dealt with on the basis of procedures privately agreed between the Irish Minister for Justice and the United Nations High Commissioner for Refugees in 1985 prior to the making of any deportation order.[198] Unlike *Webb,* there was no question that the applicants had received any promise or representation that they would be treated in this fashion before they arrived in Ireland, so that the issue of acting to one's detriment—an essential feature of the promissory estoppel doctrine—simply did not arise.

O'Hanlon J. nevertheless held that the applicants had acquired a legitimate expectation that they would be dealt with according to the terms of the 1985 agreement and he quoted the following passage from the speech of Lord Fraser in *Attorney General of Hong Kong v Ng Yuen Shiu*[199] with approval:

> The justification [for the principle of legitimate expectations] is primarily that, when a public authority has promised to follow a certain procedure, it is in the interest of good administration that it should act fairly and should implement its promise, so long as the implementation does not interfere with its statutory duty.[200]

O'Hanlon J. then continued by saying:

> As the law has developed it has come to be applied in situations where the conventional plea of estoppel by conduct might not be available since the party seeking to rely on the plea of legitimate expectation may not be able to establish that he has been induced by the conduct of the other party to act to his own detriment.[201]

The judge, therefore, concluded that the applicants had acquired a legitimate expectation that their request for asylum would be dealt with in accordance with the 1985 procedures, even though, of course, they could have had no knowledge of these arrangements prior to their arrival in the state. This, perhaps, is not so much an example of a legitimate expectation—since expectation is usually dependent on prior knowledge—but rather an application of the principle that it is in the interests of good administration that, in the absence of good reasons to the contrary, an administrator should be bound by agreed procedures.

This precise issue surfaced again in a subsequent immigration case, *Gutrani v Minister for Justice.*[202] On this occasion the minister agreed not to deport an illegal immigrant save in accordance with the terms of the 1985 scheme and this concession was adjudged by the Supreme Court to have been properly made. McCarthy J. commented:

> Having established such a scheme, however informally, so he would appear to be bound to apply it to appropriate cases, and his decision would be subject to judicial review. It does not appear to me to depend on any principle of legitimate or reasonable expectation; it is, simply, the procedure which the Minister has undertaken to enforce.[203]

The other line of authority reflects the more conventional and orthodox common law perspective and this is illustrated by two decisions in particular, *Wiley v Revenue Commissioners*[204] and *Tara Prospecting v Minister for Energy*.[205] In the former case the applicant was a partially disabled driver who, pursuant to a statutory scheme, obtained on separate occasions in 1983 and 1985 substantial repayments of excise duty otherwise due on motor vehicles. In 1986 the Revenue Commissioners, conscious that a scheme designed for the benefit of wholly disabled drivers had been availed of by ineligible persons, introduced more stringent evidential requirements. The applicant was not aware of this when he purchased a new motor vehicle in 1987 and he subsequently found that the medical certificates as to the extent of his partial disability were not accepted. He then claimed that he had acquired a legitimate expectation that the pre-1986 arrangements should be continued in his case, or, failing that, that 'if there was to be a change in the requirements of the Revenue Commissioners, he should have been told in advance of his purchase of a new motorcar'.[206]

It is scarcely surprising that this application was rejected by the Supreme Court.[207] The views of O'Flaherty J. may be taken as representative:

> [The applicant submits] that he should continue to have conferred on him a substantive benefit by way of exemption in the circumstances that he was not informed in advance of the more stringent requirements that the Revenue Commissioners had put in place to satisfy themselves so that they could properly discharge their duty in accordance with the scheme that they had set up under the relevant legislation.
>
> It will be clear immediately that acceptance of this submission would involve a radical enlargement of the scope of legitimate expectations. It would involve the courts saying to the administration that it was not entitled to set more stringent standards so that it might discharge its statutory obligations, without giving notice to anyone who might have benefited in the past from a more relaxed set of rules. Stated thus, I believe that it would involve the courts in an unwarranted system of interference with the actions of administrators.[208]

The claim was also rejected on the basis that the claim would conflict with the principle that the donee of statutory powers may not fetter the exercise of those powers.[209] What is interesting, nevertheless, is that while

O'Flaherty J. was prepared to allow for further expansions of the doctrine, he also signified his willingness to draw on the jurisprudence of the Court of Justice in this area.[210]

Hamilton P. expressed similar sentiments in *Carbury Milk Products Ltd v Minister for Agriculture*[211] when he said that 'the principle of the protection of legitimate expectations is well recognised in Irish law and in Community law'. In this case the plaintiffs had manufactured a certain type of milk product which they submitted to the defendants. The defendants classified the product as a milk protein product for Common Customs Tariff Classification purposes and this meant that the company was entitled to export refunds for third country sales. On the strength of this classification the plaintiffs entered into contracts with third parties based outside the European Community in the expectation that such export refunds would be payable.[212] Some two years later, however, the defendants realised that, through no fault of the plaintiffs, an error had been made: the product was, in fact, to be classified as a whey powder which did not attract export refunds. The plaintiffs then claimed an entitlement to export refunds for the two years during which the product had been wrongly classified as being entitled to such payments. Hamilton P., in a judgment which provides a good example of the interaction of promissory estoppel and legitimate expectations, held that in these circumstances the minister was estopped from denying the plaintiffs' entitlement to the export refunds:

> Having regard to the circumstances in which the product was classified by the Revenue Commissioners at the request of the Department of Agriculture, the conduct, including the fixing of its prices, by the company in its export of products in the legitimate expectation based on such classification that it would be entitled to export refunds in respect thereof . . . and the fact that the company was in no way at fault or contributed in any way to the situation, it would be unjust and inequitable if the company were held not to be entitled to the export refunds on the product exported by them [for the years in question].[213]

Whether one classifies this case as an example of promissory estoppel or legitimate expectations, it is plain that the company deserved to succeed in their claim. As other cases—such as *Webb*—demonstrate, the Irish courts have no difficulty in such circumstances in drawing on European concepts of legitimate expectations in order to bolster a conclusion that a plaintiff was entitled to relief where it had been misled into altering its position to its detriment by a representation by an agent of the state. Difficulties arise, however, where the effect of the legitimate expectation would be to fetter the exercise of a statutory power by a minister or other statutory body. This principle emerges clearly from the most elaborate exposition of Irish law to date on the doctrine of legitimate expectations.

In the *Tara Prospecting* case the applicant companies had been awarded mining prospecting licences under the Minerals Development Act 1940 in 1981 and 1984. The companies found some gold deposits in the areas covered by their licences and they reapplied for a renewal of their prospecting licences. These licences were granted, but large areas of territory included in the earlier licences were excluded. The minister justified this exclusion on environmental, cultural and religious grounds.[214] The applicants challenged this aspect of the decision on the ground that it violated the principle of legitimate expectations: they asserted that the minister had represented that their licences would be renewed in full if the prospecting had proved to be successful.

Following a review of leading English[215] and Australian[216] authorities, Costello J. concluded that in cases involving the exercise of statutory powers the doctrine of legitimate expectations was limited to procedural matters. In other cases, the doctrine might exceptionally (as in the *Webb* case) include substantive rights, but such cases really represented an application of the principles of promissiory estoppel rather than legitimate expectations as such. He summarised his conclusions on the present state of the law as follows:

(1) There is a duty on a minister who is exercising a discretionary power which may affect rights or interests to adopt fair procedures in the exercise of the power. Where a member of the public has a legitimate expectation arising from the minister's words and/or conduct that (a) he will be given a hearing before a decision adverse to his interests will be taken or (b) that he will obtain a benefit from the exercise of the power then the Minister also has a duty to act fairly towards him and this may involve a duty to give him a fair hearing before a decision adverse to his interests is taken. There would then arise a co-relative right to a fair hearing which, if denied, will justify the court in quashing the decision.

(2) The existence of a legitimate expectation that a benefit will be conferred does not in itself give rise to any legal or equitable right to the benefit itself which can be [judicially] enforced. However, in cases involving public authorities, other than cases involving the exercise of statutory discretionary powers, an equitable right to the benefit may arise from the application of the principles of promissory estoppel to which effect will be given by appropriate court order.

(3) In cases involving the exercise of a discretionary statutory power the only legitimate expectation relating to the conferring of the benefit that can be inferred from words or conduct is a conditional one, namely, that a benefit will be conferred provided at the time the Minister considers that it is a proper exercise of the statutory power in the light of current policy to grant it. Such a conditional expectation cannot give rise to the benefit should it later be refused by the Minister in the public interest.

(4) In cases involving the exercise of a discretionary statutory power in which an explicit assurance has been given which gives rise to an expectation that a benefit will be conferred no enforceable equitable or legal right to the benefit can arise. No promissory estoppel can arise because the Minister cannot estop either himself or his successors from exercising a discretionary power in the manner prescribed by Parliament at the time it is exercised.[217]

On the facts Costello J. agreed that the applicants could reasonably have expected that, if prospecting was successful, their licences would be renewed until such time as they were in a position to apply for a mining lease:

> But this expectation could only be a conditional one as the Minister was exercising a discretionary power and the applicants should have been aware that the renewal of the licence was conditional on the Minister concluding at the time of renewal that renewal was in the public interest. This was the only 'legitimate expectation' that the applicants could entertain. As the Minister concluded that the renewal of licences was not in the public interest no enforceable right to them could possibly arise.[218]

This decision—representing as it does the distilled wisdom and experience of the Irish courts with regard to the legitimate expectations doctrine— makes an interesting contrast with the celebrated judgment of the Court of Justice in *Mulder v Minister van Landbouw en Visserij*.[219] As is well known, the Court of Justice found parts of Community milk marketing regulations to be invalid on the ground that they violated the applicants' legitimate expectations. Certain milk producers had opted out of milk production for a five year period in return for payment of a premium by the Community. At the end of this period, the applicants found themselves unable to resume milk production because the subsequent milk quota regulations did not take account of their special position.[220] The court said that where a producer

> has been encouraged by a Community measure to suspend marketing for a limited period in the general interest and against payment of a premium he may legitimately expect not to be subject, upon the expiry of his undertaking, to restrictions which specifically affect him precisely because he availed himself of the possibilities offered by the Community provisions.[221]

At the same time the European Court has placed sensible limitations on the scope of the legitimate expectations doctrine. In this respect, the judgment in *Tomadini* [222] is representative of the limits of the doctrine:

> The field of application of this principle cannot be extended to the point of generally preventing new rules from applying to the future effects of situations which arose under the earlier rules in the absence of obligations entered into with the public authorities. . . . This is particularly true in a field such as the common organisation of the markets, the purpose of which

involves constant adjustment to the variations of the economic situation in the various agricultural sectors.

It would seem unlikely—at least to judge by reference to *Tara Prospecting*—that the Irish courts would have approached the *Mulder* problem in the same way. *Mulder* is a legitimate expectations case involving substantive rights and the exercise of statutory powers (in this instance, the allocation of milk quotas) and *Tara Prospecting* appears to insist that in the context of statutory powers, the principle of legitimate expectations must yield to the overriding principle that the discharge of such powers may not be fettered by estoppel.

Conclusions

Just as with the United Kingdom, administrative law in the Republic of Ireland has evolved at a rapid pace over the last thirty years or so. This evolution may broadly be ascribed to four main influences. First, Irish society is undergoing a rapid and profound social and cultural transformation. This has led to an increasingly complex form of society, requiring greater legislative regulation and control while at the same time a new individual rights consciousness has emerged. Secondly, Irish constitutional law has been transformed: there is now in existence a vast corpus of case law covering areas (such as the separation of powers and personal rights) of immediate relevance for administrative law. We have thus witnessed the 'constitutionalisation' of substantial areas of administrative law, such as state liability and fair procedures. Thirdly, the administrative law of the United Kingdom has itself evolved at a rapid pace and this in itself has also influenced the development of Irish law. Finally, there is the influence of European law which has witnessed the emergence of certain common principles of administrative law throughout the European Union.[223] The emergence of principles such as legitimate expectations and proportionality may certainly be ascribed—whether directly or indirectly—to this European influence.

In summary, therefore, Irish administrative law is currently in a state of rapid evolution, but it still has some way to go before it could be said to have acquired the systematic coherence which is characteristic of continental administrative systems. Nevertheless, it is the presence of the Constitution which gives Irish public law its distinctive flavour. The Irish legal system has long since come to terms with the abandonment of parliamentary sovereignty and it can quickly absorb Court of Justice decisions such as *Factortame* without difficulty. Moreover, the Constitution has given the Irish courts a cutting edge when it comes to dealing with common law rules or presumptions which are no longer appropriate in a modern state (such as state immunity and the exemption of the state from the application of statute) and employing principles such as proportionality and fair procedures to invalidate legislation which are considered to impinge on individual constitutional rights. It is these distinctive features which make Irish administrative law at once so interesting and yet so relevant for the administrative lawyers in the United Kingdom in that it provides an example of how a common law system has been obliged to change and adapt in the light of a written Constitution providing for judicial review of legislation.

Notes

1. Loveland, 'Positive Discrimination and Fair Electoral Representation in the United States' [1994] PL 332, 343.
2. See generally Kelly, *The Irish Constitution* (Dublin, 1994) and Casey, *Constitutional Law in Ireland* (London, 1992).
3. See generally Hogan and Morgan, *Administrative Law in Ireland* (London, 1991).
4. In this respect it is scarcely necessary to look any further than the seminal decisions in *Factortame Ltd v Secretary of State for Transport* [1990] 2 AC 85; *Factortame Ltd v Secretary of State for Transport (No. 2)* case C–213/89 [1991] 1 AC 603 and *Equal Opportunities Commission v Secretary of State for Employment* [1994] 1 All ER 910.
5. This replaced the earlier Constitution of the Irish Free State, 1922. That Constitution had proved to be unsatisfactory for two main reasons. First, it had originally contained many elements (such as the presence of a Governor-General and the oath of allegiance required to be sworn by Members of Parliament) which were unacceptable to Irish public opinion. Secondly, the Constitution could be amended by ordinary legislation, thus defeating the object of the clauses providing for the principle of judicial review of legislation. See generally Ward, *The Irish Constitutional Tradition* (Dublin, 1994) at pp 212–38
6. Article 34.3.2. See generally Kelly, op.cit., pp 421–93.
7. See generally arts 6,15, 28 and 34 of the Constitution. Art. 37 permits non-judicial personages (i.e. generally administrative tribunals) to exercise judicial powers in limited non-criminal cases: see Kelly, op.cit., pp 560–71.
8. Arts 40–44. See Kelly, op.cit., pp 671–1116.
9. [1950] IR 67.
10. ibid., at p. 84 per O'Byrne J. The Oireachtas is the name of the Irish Parliament.
11. *East Donegal Co-Operative Development Ltd v Attorney General* [1970] IR 317.
12. This provides that the state 'guarantees in its laws to respect and, as far as practicable, to vindicate, the personal rights of the citizen'. The 'personal rights' of the citizen are not confined to those rights expressly enumerated elsewhere in the Constitution: see *Ryan v Attorney General* [1965] IR 294.
13. *Re Haughey* [1971] IR 217.
14. [1972] IR 241.
15. *Howard v Commissioners of Public Works* [1994] 1 IR 101.
16. See Hogan and Morgan, op.cit., 409–20.
17. See e.g. *Kennedy v Ireland* [1987] IR 587; *Conway v Irish National Teachers' Organisation* [1991] 2 IR 305.
18. See *Cox v Ireland* [1992] 2 IR 503, where the Supreme Court invalidated s. 34 of the Offences against the State Act 1939—which, *inter alia*, forfeited the superannuation

entitlements of public servants convicted of certain offences—on the ground that it constituted a disproportionate interference with the plaintiff's property rights.

19. SI No. 15 of 1986. These rules correspond in broad terms with the English Rules of the Supreme Court.

20. The essential features of the judicial review procedure are that the applicant is required to verify his case on affidavit (Ord. 84, r. 20(2)(b)), obtain prior leave of the High Court (Ord. 84, r. 20(1)) and move expeditiously, at all events within six months of the decision in question (Ord. 84, r. 21(1)), although this period may be extended. It would seem that, in practice, the Irish courts are less strict in comparison with their English counterparts on the issues of the granting of leave and undue delay. In *G. v Director of Public Prosecutions* [1994] 1 IR 374 the Supreme Court emphasised that leave should be granted *at the preliminary stage* if the applicant could demonstrate that he had an 'arguable' or 'stateable' case. On the issue of delay, the Irish courts will generally only refuse relief if this has been prejudicial to the respondents or third parties: see, e.g. *O'Donnell v Dun Laoghaoire Corporation (No. 2)* [1991] ILRM 301; *O'Flynn v Mid-Western Health Board* [1991] 2 IR 223 and Hogan and Morgan, op.cit., pp 597–603; and delay *in itself* is not a ground for refusing relief: see *The State (Furey) v Minister for Defence* [1988] ILRM 89 and *Eurocontainer Shipping plc v Minister for Marine*, High Court, 11 December 1992.

21. e.g. the rule whereby an applicant could not in the same proceedings seek damages along with certiorari. The deficiencies in the old system were comprehensively set out in the (Irish) Law Reform Commission's Working Paper No. 8, 'Judicial Review of Administrative Action: The Problem of Remedies' (1979). The new rules very largely follow the scheme of reform proposed by the Commission in their working paper.

22. [1983] 2 AC 237.

23. [1989] IR 172.

24. The applicant would seem to have had a good case on the merits. Inspectors called to the applicant's stables and, as a result of their complaints, the licence was revoked without any form of hearing some two days later: see [1989] IR 171, 172.

25. Such as the power to exclude certain persons from race meetings: Racing and Racecourses Act 1945, s. 39.

26. [1987] QB 815.

27. [1987] IR 172, 174–5. This proposition also emerges from the judgment of Geoghegan J. in *Walsh v Irish Red Cross Society Ltd*, High Court, 3 February 1995, where he held that the purported expulsion of a member was invalid. The society was established by the Irish Red Cross Act 1938 and Geoghegan J. held that statutory instrument prescribing its rules did not, as of the date of the purported expulsion, allow for such a course of action. The judge indicated that the right to expel was 'a sufficiently public law issue to enable it to be litigated by way of judicial review proceedings'. Although Geoghegan J. was not required to deal with the subsidiary argument that the expulsion was also invalid by reason of an alleged breach of the rules of natural justice, he added that such an issue 'was a matter of private law and involving an autonomous private society, albeit created pursuant to a public statute and statutory instrument'.

28. It is true that in the not dissimilar *Aga Khan* case, *R. v Jockey Club, ex p. Aga Khan* [1993] 2 All ER 853, 873 Farquharson LJ. dismissed this objection with these pithy remarks: 'Mr. Kentridge has referred to the lack of reality in describing such a relationship as consensual. The fact is that if the applicant wished to race his horses in this country he had no choice but to submit to the Jockey Club's jurisdiction. This may be true but nobody is obliged to race his horses in this country and it does not destroy the element of consensuality.'

29. [1993] ILRM 1.

30. ibid., at p. 2.

31. [1993] ILRM 328.

32. ibid., at pp 333–334.

33. ibid., at p. 334.
34. Cf. *Re Cook's Application* [1986] NI 242.
35. [1994] 1 ILRM 233. Cf. in contrast the comments of Sedley J. in *R. v Manchester Metropolitan University, ex p. Nolan, The Independent,* 15 July 1993 where he said that as the respondent university was a 'public institution discharging public functions and having no visitor, it is subject to judicial review of its decision on the normal grounds'. See Carroll, 'Enforcing Students' Rights in Irish and English Law' (1994) 12 *Irish Law Times* 259.
36. Op. cit., at p. 239. Cf. the comments of Kelly LJ. in *Malone v Queen's University, Belfast* [1988] NI 67, 82 where he said that the fact that a university had been established by way of royal charter was 'so remote and indirect that it cannot realistically be said to bring in any significant element of public law'.
37. High Court, 9 July 1993.
38. But compare the approach of the Court of Appeal in *R. v Take-over Panel ex p. Datafin* [1987] 1 All ER 564 and *R. v Visitors of Inns of Courts, ex p. Calder* [1993] 2 All ER 876. On the other hand, in *R. v Jockey Club ex p. Aga Khan* [1993] 2 All ER 853 the English Court of Appeal held that decisions of the Jockey Club were not amenable to judicial review, even though the court accepted that 'if the Jockey Club did not regulate this activity the government would probably be driven to create a public body to do so'.
39. [1991] ILRM 301. See generally Hogan, 'The Scope of Order 84 Remedies' (1990) 12 DULJ 114.
40. [1991] ILRM 301, 314. A further consideration is that Ord. 84 has not been given statutory backing—there is no Irish counterpart to s. 31 of the Supreme Court Act 1981—and in the absence of equivalent statutory provisions, the Superior Court Rules Committee would probably have been acting *ultra vires* had it purported to prescribe an exclusive procedure for challenging the validity of an administrative decision.
41. In this case the plaintiff had sought a declaration that a decision to levy certain services charges was invalid. The time limit in such instances is three months: Ord. 84, r. 21(1). If the plaintiff had sought certiorari, the time limit would have been six months. It is not easy to discern why the different remedies should themselves have differing time limits.
42. [1991] ILRM 301, 314.
43. ibid., at p. 315.
44. But cf. now *Equal Opportunities Commission v Secretary of State for Employment* [1994] 1 All ER 910.
45. Cf. the speech of Lord Lowry in *Roy v Kensington and Chelsea FPC* [1992] 1 AC 634.
46. [1984] ILRM 24.
47. Now Ord. 8, r. 1 of the Rules of the Superior Courts 1986 (SI No. 15 of 1986).
48. [1984] ILRM 24, 29–30.
49. The details of the parties who must be served are set out in s. 3B(ii) and include (depending on the circumstances) the planning authority, the Planning Appeals Board and the developer.
50. The application must be moved within two months (s. 3(B)(a)(i)) and time cannot be extended. In contrast, other applications for judicial review must be moved within six months and time can be extended where there is good reason to do so: Ord. 84, r. 20(1).
51. S. 82(3B)(a) provides that leave to challenge the validity of a planning decision shall not be granted 'unless the High Court is satisfied that there are substantial grounds for contending that the decision is invalid or ought to be quashed'. In contrast, in *G. v Director of Public Prosecutions* [1994] 1 IR 374, 381 Denham J. said that an applicant for judicial review was merely required to show at that stage that he had 'an arguable case in law', although she conceded that on the actual application for judicial review 'an applicant has an altogether heavier burden of proof to discharge'.
52. [1994] 2 ILRM 1.
53. ibid., 5.

54. There is already a strong hint of this in the speech of Lord Lowry in *Roy* ([1992] 1 AC 624, 653) when he said that he much preferred the 'broad approach' to *O'Reilly v Mackman*. By this he meant that the rule 'did not apply generally against bringing actions to vindicate private rights in all circumstances in which those actions involved a challenge to a public law act or decision, but that it merely required the aggrieved person to proceed by way of judicial review only when private law rights were not at stake'. Lord Lowry added that he much preferred the broad approach 'which is both traditionally orthodox and consistent with the *Pyx Granite* principle [1960] AC 260. . . . It would also , if adopted, have the practical merit of getting rid of a procedural minefield . . .'

55. Case C-213/89, *R. v Secretary of State for Transport , ex p. Factortame Ltd* [1990] ECR I-2433.

56. [1985] IR 193. See generally Kelly, op.cit., pp 431–4.

57. [1985] IR 193, 201.

58. The terms of the injunction actually granted, however, did permit fishery officers to inspect the plaintiffs' vessels to ascertain whether they were actually complying with the terms of their licence.

59. In *Cooke v Minister for Communications, The Irish Times Law Report*, 20 February 1989, the Supreme Court (in an *ex tempore* judgment) refused to grant interim relief restraining interference by the authorities with the activities of an illegal radio operator. Although Walsh J. recognised that the plaintiff had made out an arguable case that the legislation was unconstitutional and the inconvenience manifest (the minister had made an order under the Radio and Television Act 1988 directing that the plaintiff's electricity supply be disconnected), interim relief was refused. *In Grange Developments Ltd v Dublin County Council (No. 4)* [1989] IR 377 Murphy J. recognised that there was some 'apparent discrepancy' between *Pesca Valentia* and *Cooke*, but nevertheless, applying 'ordinary grounds of balance of convenience, stateable case and irreparable damage', refused to grant an interlocutory injunction in a case where the defendants wished to challenge the constitutionality of legislation requiring them to pay compensation to the plaintiffs.

60. [1987] IR 713. For the background to this case, see Hogan, 'The Supreme Court and the Single European Act' (1987) 22 *Irish Jurist* 55; Temple Lang, 'The Irish Court Case which delayed the Single European Act' (1987) 24 CML Rev. 709 and Casey, 'Crotty v An Taoiseach: A Comparative Perspective' in O'Reilly ed., *Human Rights and Constitutional Law: Essays in Honour of Brian Walsh* (Dublin 1992).

61. The original injunction had been granted by Barrington J. on Christmas Eve 1986. This meant that as the instruments of ratification of all member states had not been deposited by the end of year deadline, the Single European Act did not come into force on 1 January 1987. The plaintiff succeeded in the Supreme Court on the merits of his case and, following a referendum in May 1987 to amend the Constitution so as to permit ratification, the government finally ratified the Single Act on 24 June 1987.

62. [1987] IR 713, 763.

63. In *Society for the Protection of Unborn Children (Ire.) Ltd v Grogan* [1989] IR 753, 765 (a case where an injunction was sought in respect of unconstitutional activities which had been engaged in by private persons), Finlay CJ. said that with regard to the balance of convenience 'where an injunction is sought to protect a constitutional right, the only matter which could properly be capable of being weighed in a balance against the granting of such protection would be another competing constitutional right'.

64. [1978] AC 435. For an extended discussion of relator actions in Ireland and the extent to which they have been superseded by constitutional principles, see Hogan and Morgan, op, cit., pp 626–32.

65. [1966] IR 345. See generally Kelly, op. cit. , pp 386 and 1149–51.

66. Kenny J. identified this right as one of the general personal rights of the citizen protected by art. 40.3 of the Constitution and it also seemed to him to be a 'necessary

inference' from Art. 34.3.1 which vests the High Court with 'full original jurisdiction in and power to determine all matters and questions whether of law or fact . . .'

67. [1989] IR 734.

68. This originally provided that 'The State acknowledges the right to life of the unborn and, with due regard to the equal right to life of the mother, guarantees in its laws to respect and, as far as practicable, by its laws to defend and vindicate that right.' In 1992, following referenda, two further clauses were added guaranteeing the right to travel and freedom of information respectively. The constitutionality of legislation permitting medical practitioners and others to give specific information concerning the availability of information services outside the State has been upheld by the Supreme Court following a reference of the Bill to the Court by the President; see *Re Article 26 and the Regulation of Information (Services outside the State for Termination of Pregnancies) Bill, Supreme Court,* May 12, 1995.

69. See also *Crotty v An Taoiseach* [1987] IR 713 (plaintiff had sufficient standing to challenge constitutionality of ratification of the Single European Act); *McGimpsey v Ireland* [1990] 1 IR 110 (plaintiffs had sufficient standing to challenge ratification of the Anglo-Irish Agreement) and see Kelly, op, cit., pp 438–48.

70. [1990] ILRM 560.

71. [1949] AC 398.

72. [1972] IR 330.

73. [1972] IR 241.

74. [1990] ILRM 560, 566. This result had already been anticipated by Barrington J. in *Irish Permanent Building Society v Caldwell (No. 2)* [1981] ILRM 242, 254 where the judge rejected the suggestion that the 'parliamentary intent' test could determine whether a particular plaintiff could recover damages for breach of statutory duty: 'But in our jurisdiction the citizen would appear to have a remedy, by virtue of the provisions of Article 40.3, if he has or may suffer damage as a result of a breach of the law in circumstances which amount to an injustice.'

75. ibid.

76. [1995] 1 ILRM 12.

77. ibid., 21.

78. The best analysis of this problem is found in Binchy, 'Constitutional Remedies and the Law of Torts' in O'Reilly ed., *Human Rights and Constitutional Law: Essays in Honour of Brian Walsh* (Dublin 1992) at pp 201–225. See generally Kelly, op. cit., at pp 707–708.

79. See e.g. *Byrne v Ireland* [1972] IR 241 (state immunity from suit inconsistent with constitutional obligation to vindicate legal and constitutional rights); *Ryan v Ireland* [1989] IR 177 (any common law rule preventing soldiers suing the state for negligence would be unconstitutional) and *McKinley v Minister for Defence* [1992] 2 IR 333 (common law rule confining loss of consortium actions to husbands only would infringe equality guarantee in art. 40.1 and, hence, the cause of action must be extended so as to permit wives to sue for loss of consortium).

80. See e.g. *Kennedy v Ireland* [1987] IR 587 (State liable in damages for improper invasion of plaintiff's privacy).

81. *Hanrahan v Merck, Sharp and Dohme (Ireland) Ltd* [1988] ILRM 629, 636. The same judge took a similar view in *Hynes-O'Sullivan v O'Driscoll* [1988] IR 436, 450 where he said that any reformulation of the law of qualified privilege 'must reflect a due balancing of the constitutional right of freedom of expression and the constitutional protection of every citizen's good name' but that the 'articulation of public policy on such a matter would seem to be primarily a matter for the Legislature'. There is more than a hint of this in *Walsh v Family Planning Services Ltd* [1992] 1 IR 496, 522 where McCarthy J. cautioned against using the personal rights guarantees in Art. 40 'to elevate the status of a trifling cause of action' (here, a technical assault), implying that the plaintiff should be left to his remedy in tort. See also the pithy comments of Barron J. in

Sweeney v Duggan [1991] 2 IR 274, 285 to the effect that art. 40.3 involved 'no more than a guarantee of a just law of negligence'. On the other hand, in *Walsh v Ireland,* Supreme Court, 30 November 1994, Hamilton CJ. described the wrongful arrest of the plaintiff as 'a breach of his constitutional right to liberty and to his good name' and that the courts were thereby obliged to vindicate that right by means of a substantial award of damages.

82. [1973] IR 121.
83. ibid., at pp 132–3. Other courts have taken a similar view. Thus, in *Bivens v Six Unknown Federal Narcotic Agents,* 403 US 388 (1971) Brennan J. said that 'where federally protected rights have been invaded, it has been the rule from the beginning that courts will be alert to adjust their remedies so as to grant the necessary relief'. More recently, in *Simpson v Attorney General* [1994] 3 NZLR 667 the New Zealand Court of Appeal expressly followed *Meskell* when the court held that an infringement of the New Zealand Bill of Rights gave rise to a cause of action. The following comments of Hardie Boys J. ([1994] 3 NZLR 667, at 702) are of interest:
'The New Zealand Bill of Rights Act, unless it is to be no more than an empty statement, is a commitment by the Crown that those who in the three branches of the government exercise its functions, powers and duties will observe the rights that the Bill affirms. It is, I consider, implicit in that commitment, indeed essential to its worth, that the Courts are not only to observe the Bill in the discharge of their own duties but are able to grant appropriate and effective remedies where rights have been infringed. I see no reason to think that this should depend on the terms of a written constitution. Enjoyment of the basic human rights are the entitlement of every citizen, and their protection the obligation of every civilised state. They are inherent in and are essential to the structure of society. They do not depend on the legal or constitutional form in which they are declared. The reasoning that has led the Privy Council and the Courts of Ireland and India to the conclusions reached in the cases to which I have referred . . . is in my opinion equally valid to the New Zealand Bill of Rights Act if it is to have life and meaning.'
84. [1972] IR 241.
85. She had fallen into a trench which had been dug by state employees and negligently refilled.
86. See generally Kelly, op. cit, pp 1134–55; Kelly, 'Hidden Treasure and the Constitution' (1988) DULJ 1 and Lenihan, 'Royal Prerogatives and the Constitution' (1989) 24 Irish Jurist 1. This aspect of the decision has had wide implications: the Supreme Court has subsequently held that neither the common law prerogative of treasure trove (*Webb v Ireland* [1988] IR 353) nor the presumption of the state exemption from statute (*Howard v Commissioners of Public Works* [1994] 1 IR 101) has survived the enactment of the Constitution.
87. [1972] IR 241, 292.
88. e.g. the immunities provided in the Postal and Telecommunications Services Act 1983 for An Post (s. 64) and Telecom Eireann (s. 88) in respect of actions for loss and damage arising out of the postal and telecommunications systems respectively. Note that in *Ryan v Ireland* [1989] IR 177, 183 the Supreme Court held that in so far as the common law provided for an immunity from suit in respect of an action for negligence taken by a soldier on active service, such a rule had not survived the enactment of the Constitution 'since it would be inconsistent with the guarantees by the State to respect, defend and vindicate the rights of the citizen contained in Article 40.3 of the Constitution'. The state, however, has been held not to be liable (whether vicariously or otherwise) in respect of the actions of a judge 'because no action is maintainable for anything said or done by a trial judge in the exercise of a jurisdiction which belongs to and is exercisable by him': *Deighnan v Ireland* [1995] 1 ILRM 88, 93 per Flood J.
89. See Cooney and Kerr, 'Constitutional Aspects of Irish Tort Law' (1991) DULJ 1.
90. [1986] IR 116.

91. Totalling IR£50,000 to three separate plaintiffs. Hamilton P. said ([1987] IR 587, 594) that in assessing damages he had had regard to the fact that the infringement 'was carried out deliberately, consciously and without justification by the executive organ of the State which is under a constitutional obligation to respect, vindicate and defend that right'.
92. [1987] IR 587. See Hogan, 'Free Speech, Privacy and the Press in Ireland' [1987] PL 509.
93. [1991] 2 IR 305.
94. High Court, 26 July 1994.
95. See also *Pine Valley Developments Ltd v Minister for Environment* [1987] IR 23 (no liability for misfeasance, as minister at all times acted pursuant to legal advice, even if that advice later proved to be mistaken); *Duff v Minister for Agriculture* [1993] 2 CMLR 969 (similar principle) and *Callinan v Voluntary Health Insurance Board*, Supreme Court, 28 July 1994 (defendants liable under rubric of misfeasance for deliberate abuse of power).
96. A plaintiff may, of course, recover damages in an appropriate case against a *private defendant*, for 'uniquely the Irish Constitution confers a right of action for breach of constitutional rights against persons other than the State and its officials': *PH v John Murphy & Sons Ltd* [1987] IR 621, 626, per Costello J.
97. There is already a hint of this in some judgments: see e.g. *Moyne v Londonderry Port and Harbour Commissioners* [1986] IR 299, where Costello J. said (without elaborating) that the infliction of pecuniary loss by a state agent in the course of an illegal act did not of itself establish an infringement of the constitutional right to earn a livelihood. In this regard the Irish courts might well be influenced by the attitude taken by the Court of Justice in the *Factortame* litigation with regard to state liability for infringement of the Treaty of Rome. It should be noted, however, that in (the admittedly very different) context of the exclusion of unconstitutionally obtained evidence, liability is strict and there is no good faith exception: *The People (Director of Public Prosecutions) v Kenny* [1990] 2 IR 110.
98. [1990] 2 IR 17.
99. Eligibility for payments depended on household income and the income of a spouse (but not an unmarried partner) was taken into account for this purpose. This was found by Murphy J. to constitute a discrimination against married couples.
100. Op. cit. at p. 29.
101. Case C-6/90 [1991] ECR I–5357.
102. Case C-334/92 [1993] ECR I–6911.
103. Contrast the differing approach of the Supreme Court in *Pine Valley Developments Ltd v Minister for Environment* [1987] IR 23.
104. [1995] 1 ILRM 507.
105. 'The function of [art. 29.4.5 of the Constitution] was to allow the entire body of European Community law to have effect in Ireland in spite of any provision in the Constitution. It did not confer any new constitutional right; rather, its tendency is to qualify those rights'; at p. 520.
106. *The State (King) v Minister for Justice* [1984] IR 169. A minister can be found guilty of contempt of court: see *Desmond v Glackin (No. 1)* [1993] 3 IR 1.
107. *The State (Sheehan) v Government of Ireland* [1987] IR 550. Costello J. said (at p. 555) that the argument that mandamus would not lie was apparently based on the proposition that 'in English law since a prerogative order emanates from the Crown it cannot lie against the Crown', but, as Costello J. observed, there was 'no analogy' between the 'law of Ireland and England on this topic', since under the Constitution: 'the Government which it establishes is not the successor to the Crown. There is no constitutional reason, therefore, which would prohibit the making of an order of mandamus against the Government.' In *Dudley v An Taoiseach* [1994] 2 ILRM 321 the applicant sought leave to challenge the failure on the part of the government and the

Dáil to hold a by-election in compliance with what (was contended) were constitutional requirements. Geoghegan J., following *Sheehan*, granted leave in respect of the government's alleged failure to comply with constitutional obligations but refused to grant leave in respect of the Dáil (the lower House of Parliament) because: 'No enforceable order can be made by the courts as against Dáil Éireann as such. Dáil Éireann can only give the direction if the majority of the members vote for the motion but the courts cannot mandamus the body of members of the Dáil as such to vote in a particular way on a particular motion.'

108. This immunity seems difficult to justify, for as has been noted (Hogan and Morgan, op. cit., 723): 'If Ireland can be liable for damages, why should it enjoy an immunity for another form of remedy, such as an injunction? This is especially so, given that it now seems mandamus (a very similar form of remedy to an injunction) will lie against Ireland.'

109. *Pesca Valentia Ltd v Minister for Fisheries* [1985] IR 193. The practice instead is to grant an injunction against some agent of the state, such as the government or a minister. Thus, in *Crotty v An Taoiseach* [1987] IR 713 both Barrington J. and the Supreme Court granted the plaintiff an interlocutory injunction restraining the government from ratifying the Single European Act.

110. [1994] 1 IR 101. See generally Hogan, 'The Mullaghmore Case' (1993) 15 DULJ 243.

111. As Denham J. said in her judgment ([1994] 1 IR 101, 157): '[This] rule is in fact so rooted in the prerogative and the Crown as the personification of the State that it is in fact inseparable from that concept . . .'

112. See e.g. *East Donegal Co-Operatives Ltd v Attorney General* [1970] IR 317; *Re Haughey* [1971] IR 217; *Goodman International v Hamilton (No. 1)* [1992] 2 IR 542; *Goodman International v Hamilton (No. 2)* [1993] 3 IR 307.

113. *O'Brien v Bord na Mona* [1983] IR 256 (where statute does not contain any set or fixed procedures, the presumption of constitutionality requires that an administrative body must 'create and carry out procedures. . . which are fair and in accordance with natural and constitutional justice'); *S. v S.* [1983] IR 68 (common law rule which precluded parties giving evidence as to the true paternity of a child born to a married woman inconsistent with the constitutional guarantee of fair procedures and held not to have survived the enactment of the Constitution); *Jaggers Restaurant Ltd v Aherne* [1988] IR 305 (Supreme Court rejected as unconstitutional an interpretation of the Licensing (Ire.) Act 1833 which confined right to object to renewal of licence to members of the civil parish in question as such an interpretation would be 'clearly contrary to fair procedures'). See generally Hogan and Morgan, op. cit. , at pp 409–20, Kelly, op. cit., pp 357–59 and Hogan, 'Natural and Constitutional Justice: *Adieu to Laissez-Faire*' (1984) 19 *Irish Jurist* 309.

114. [1995] 1 ILRM 408

115. This provides that nothing in art. 40.3.3 (for the text of which see n. 68) shall limit 'freedom to obtain or make available, in the State, subject to such conditions as may be prescribed by law, information relating to services lawfully available in another State'.

116. [1995] 1 ILRM 311. See further Hogan and Morgan, op. cit., pp 420–27 and *Connolly v McConnell* [1983] IR 172; *Dublin and County Broadcasting Ltd v Independent Radio and Television Commission*, High Court, 12 May 1989 and *Chestvale Properties Ltd v Glackin* [1993] 3 IR 35.

117. [1990] ILRM 419. See also *O'Neill v Irish Hereford Breed Society Ltd* [1992] 1 IR 431 (several members of a disciplinary committee held to be disqualified by reason of their involvement with the case at an earlier meeting where views gravely prejudicial to the plaintiff had been expressed by them).

118. [1983] IR 255.

119. High Court, 19 December 1980. See also *The State (McEldowney) v Kelliher* [1983] IR 289 and *Collins v Co. Cork Vocational Education Committee*, High Court, 26 May 1982.

120. [1976] IR 280.
121. For other examples, see *Gallagher v Corrigan*, High Court, 2 February 1988 (where Blayney J. held that prison officers who were disciplined for alleged negligence had no reason to construe a letter from the prison authorities asking them to explain their conduct as giving them sufficient notice that they would be facing disciplinary charges); *Beirne v Garda Commissioner* [1993] ILRM 1 (where a probationer policeman was held to have been unfairly dismissed in circumstances where he was not given notice of the existence of witness statements so that, said Egan J., he had no opportunity 'of contradicting any specific allegations or eliciting any facts of a mitigating nature from the makers of the statements') and *O'Shea v Garda Commissioner* [1994] 2 IR 408, [1993] ELR 239 (dismissal of garda for gross misconduct quashed in circumstances where, per Carroll J., he was simply given the 'bare charge' and 'did not get a summary of the factual background to support the accusation against him').
122. [1994] 2 IR 439.
123. *The State (Duffy) v Minister for Defence* [1979] ILRM 65 (where, somewhat dubiously, seven days' advance warning was held to be sufficient in the context of a proposed dismissal on grounds of incompetence from the Navy).
124. *Lang v Government of Ireland* [1993] ELR 234 (civil servant 'well aware for some years before his dismissal of the matters causing concern to his superiors' and express notice had already been given on several occasions).
125. [1971] IR 217.
126. ibid., 263, per Ó Dálaigh CJ.
127. This was Mr Padraic Haughey, the brother of Mr Charles Haughey who was subsequently Taoiseach between 1979–1981, 1982 and 1987–1992.
128. See e.g. *The State (Boyle) v General Medical Services Board* [1981] ILRM 14. Where one side is afforded an important procedural advantage (such as the right to cross-examine witnesses), however, it will be a breach of fair procedures to deny that right to the other side: *Kiely v Minister for Social Welfare (No. 2)* [1977] IR 287.
129. [1988] IR 724.
130. ibid., 731. See also *Gallagher v Revenue Commissioners* [1991] 2 IR 370 (civil servant facing 'extremely serious' and complex disciplinary charges entitled to legal representation at the hearing) and *Gallagher v Revenue Commissioners (No. 2)* [1995] 1 ILRM 241 (same civil servant entitled to cross-examine witnesses giving adverse evidence against him at the inquiry).
131. [1993] 3 RM 307.
132. ibid., 317.
133. This principle has also been used to invalidate an administrative decision purportedly taken pursuant to an EC regulation. In *Bosphorus Hava Yollari Turizm Ve Ticaret Anonim Sirketi v Minister for Transport* [1994] 2 ILRM 551 the High Court quashed a decision of the minister to impound, pursuant to reg. No. 990/93 (the Serbian sanctions regulations), an aircraft which was about to leave from Dublin airport. The evidence showed that the aircraft, owned by Yugoslav Airlines, had been leased to a Turkish airline. The lease was entirely bona fide and Murphy J. held that the minister's action was disproportionate in the circumstances ([1994] 2 ILRM at 559–560): 'To impound an asset for the possession and enjoyment of which a wholly innocent party has paid a substantial sum of money simply because another party has a theoretical right to receive a nominal rent must be absurd . . . As long as the position is that no citizen of Serbia and Montenegro has any use or control over the aircraft in question or the opportunity to receive any income derived from it, then it would seem to me that the regulations have achieved their purpose fully and the impounding of the aircraft would constitute a wholly unwarranted intervention in the business of Bosphorus.'
134. For discussion of a few earlier cases where something like the doctrine of proportionality appears to have been applied, see Hogan and Morgan, op. cit., at 541–2.
135. [1989] IR 26.

136. Art. 40.3.1 of the Constitution of Ireland 1937 provides that: 'The State guarantees in its laws to respect, and, as far as practicable, by its laws to defend and vindicate the personal rights of the citizen.' The right to earn a livelihood is regarded as one of these unspecified personal rights which falls to be protected by art. 40.3.1: see *Murphy v Stewart* [1973] IR 97 and Kelly, op. cit., 761–6.

137. [1989] IR 26, 31.

138. [1989] IR 26, 32. This decision was upheld on appeal to the Supreme Court: see [1991] 1 IR 409. Barron J.'s characterisation of the right to earn a living by casual trading as having been granted by the 1980 Act seems questionable. As Kelly, op. cit., observes (at p. 633): '. . . it seems wrong to present a fortfeiture, revocation or disqualification as a "regulation" or "withdrawal" of a statutory right. The truth, historically, in this State or in any other, must be that once upon a time everyone was free to sell drink, lay bets, travel in a vehicle; only when the State perceived a potential public injury in this uncontrolled liberty . . . was it proposed to avert this injury, or reduce the risk of it, by a regime of licensing.'

139. [1992] 2 IR 503. In *Fajujono v Minister for Justice* [1990] 2 IR 151, 166 Walsh J., speaking for the Supreme Court, said that any attempt to deport a married couple who were illegal aliens—but whose children were Irish citizens—would contravene art. 41 of the Constitution (which protects family life) unless the minister was satisfied that: '. . . the interests of the common good of the people of Ireland and of the protection of the State and its society are so predominant and so overwhelming in the circumstances of the case, that an action which can have the effect of breaking up this family is not so disproportionate to the aim sought to be achieved as to be unsustainable'.

140. The Special Criminal Court is expressly provided for by art. 38.3 of the Irish Constitution and was established by the Offences against the State Act 1939: see Kelly, op. cit., at pp 642–9. It is a non-jury court composed of three judges and deals almost exclusively with terrorist-type cases. The offences which are scheduled under the 1939 Act are all offences (firearms offences, explosives offences etc.) which tend to be committed by terrorist offenders rather than 'ordinary' criminals.

141. [1992] 2 IR 503, 522.

142. The venue for the trial of the offences is determined solely by either the Attorney General or by the Director of Public Prosecutions.

143. [1992] 2 IR 503, 523–4.

144. Humphreys, 'Blacklists and Shortcuts' (1991) 13 DULJ 118, 126.

145. [1994] 1 ILRM 241.

146. Art. 26 of the Irish Constitution provides for a form of abstract judicial review, whereby following the decision of the President of Ireland to refer the Bill, the Supreme Court must consider the constitutionality of the proposed measure. This procedure is not frequently invoked—only on some ten occasions since 1937—and the overwhelming majority of constitutional actions are commenced in the High Court, with a right of appeal to the Supreme Court: see Kelly, op. cit., at 212–19.

147. Which provides that 'The State. . . guarantees to protect the family in its constitution and authority, as the necessary basis of social order and as indispensable to the welfare of the Nation and the State.'

148. [1994] 1 ILRM 241, 254.

149. ibid.

150. [1994] 2 ILRM 420.

151. This provides that: 'No person shall be tried on any criminal charge save in due course of law.' See generally Kelly, op. cit., pp 572–623.

152. (1979) EHRR 245.

153. (1990) 3 SCR 1303, 1335–6.

154. [1994] 2 ILRM 420, 434. Costello J., however, reserved the question of whether the section could validly be applied in the case of persons arrested for an 'ordinary non-subversive type of offence'. Note also the comments of Denham J. in *Director of Public*

Prosecutions (Stratford) v Fagan [1994] 2 ILRM 349, 367 when she restated the test in the following way: 'In legislating for the limitation of a [constitutional] right the legislature has to reconcile the common good with personal rights and its decision should prevail unless it is oppressive or unless there is no reasonable proportion between the benefit the legislation will confer on the community and the interference with the personal rights of the citizen.' In addition, in *The People (Director of Public Prosecutions) v WC* [1994] 1 ILRM 321, 325 Flood J., relying on the *Cox* decision, applied the 'constitutional principle of proportionality' to sentencing: 'The imposition of a particular sentence must strike a balance between the particular circumstances of the commission of the relevant offence and the relevant personal circumstances of the person sentenced.'

155. See Kelly, op. cit., pp 1076–83.
156. [1986] IR 642; see especially p. 658.
157. [1985] AC 374, 410.
158. [1986] IR 642, 657.
159. [1986] IR 642, 657–8. Likewise in *P. & F. Sharpe Ltd v Dublin City and County Manager* [1989] IR 701, 708 O'Hanlon J. said that the requirement of 'overwhelming proof' of unreasonableness demanded by Lord Greene in *Associated Provincal Picture Houses Ltd v Wednesbury Corporation* [1948] 1 KB 223, 230 was no longer necessary.
160. [1993] 1 IR 39. See also *O'Donoghue v An Bord Pleanala* [1991] ILRM 750 and *Schwestermann v An Bord Pleanala* [1995] 1 ILRM 269 (where O'Hanlon J. described the onus resting on an applicant seeking to challenge a planning decision as being 'very heavy').
161. [1993] 1 IR 39, 71. Of course, the definition of statutory requirement is a matter for the courts and 'no other body has the authority to usurp the powers of the court in performing that function': *Shannon Regional Fisheries Board v An Bord Pleanala* [1994] 3 IR 449, per Barr J. On the other hand, this principle does not imply that the planning authority is not entitled to conclude that a particular development conforms with a statutory obligation, since this 'is a matter which is peculiarly within the competence of the planning authority and the court ought not to interfere unless there is no reasonable basis on which the decision of the authority might be upheld'.
162. See also e.g. *Madigan v Radio Telefís Éireann* [1994] 2 ILRM 472 (decision as to the manner in which the television authority discharged its statutory duty of impartiality to all candidates held not to be unreasonable on the facts having regard, *inter alia*, to RTE's acknowledged expertise in the matter) and *PL v Registrar - General*, High Court, 7 April 1995 (determination of administrative officer re status of foreign divorce 'need not be treated with the same deference as the determination of a specialised tribunal on an issue of fact').
163. [1991] 1 IR 23.
164. 'There are, no doubt, many who would consider the incident in question as tasteless and offensive but irrelevant to An Garda Síochána as such . . .'
165. [1994] 1 ILRM 81.
166. ibid., 89. See also the similar comments of O'Hanlon J. in *Rajah v College of Surgeons* [1994] 1 IR 384, 388: '. . . it is important that the High Court should not be turned into a court of appeal from decisions of administrative tribunals generally and that the tendency to invoke the jurisdiction of the High Court by way of judicial review proceedings in every case where a party is dissatisfied with the decision of such a tribunal is one which must be resisted'. It may be significant that these comments were made in the context of an application to review a decision of a medical school to exclude a student for want of academic progress.
167. Supreme Court, 20 December 1993.
168. [1993] 1 IR 346.
169. High Court, 26 July 1994. See also *Kajli v Minister for Justice*, High Court, 21 August 1992 (ministerial decision requiring illegal immigrants to be deported held to be

unreasonable in the circumstances as it was probable that no other country would accept them and they might be condemned to indefinite travel between various third countries) and *Twomey v Minister for Transport,* Supreme Court, 12 February 1993 (minister's failure to deal with application for licence prior to statutory 'cut-off' date held to be unreasonable in law).

170. *The State (McCormack) v Curran* [1987] ILRM 225; *Foley v Director of Public Prosecutions, The Irish Times Law Report,* 25 September 1989.

171. *The State (Sheehan) v Government of Ireland* [1987] IR 550; *Rooney v Minister for Agriculture and Food* [1991] 2 IR 539.

172. High Court, 8 June 1992.

173. The plaintiff is now a Green Party MEP.

174. Costello J. also refused to grant an injunction restraining the dissemination of a guide to the Maastricht Treaty, which had been published by the government, which the plaintiff asserted was partisan and lacked objectivity, but whether this was so was a matter 'for others' and was 'entirely inappropriate' for judicial resolution.

175. [1993] 2 CMLR 969.

176. ibid., 984.

177. ibid., 984–5.

178. *O'Reilly v Limerick Corporation* [1989] ILRM 181. For further discussion of the non-justiciability question in Irish constitutional law, see Kelly, op. cit., pp 347–8.

179. *MhicMhathuna v Attorney General* [1995] 1 ILRM 69. See also *Murtagh v St Emer's National School* [1991] 1 IR 482 (doubts expressed by Supreme Court as to whether three-day suspension from national school was amenable to judicial review).

180. [1988] IR 51.

181. [1989] IR 149. See generally Collins, 'The Obligation to Give Reasons for Administrative Decisions' (1992) 86 *Gazette ILSI* 195.

182. ibid., 157. See to like effect the judgment of O'Flaherty J. in *Breen v Minister for Defence* [1994] 2 IR 34.

183. [1994] 2 ILRM 285. See also the comments of Keane J. in *Rajah v College of Surgeons* [1994] 1 IR 384, 395 where he said that a decision to exclude on academic grounds a student from medical school was not 'of a nature which necessitated the giving of reasons'. Keane J., however, did not elaborate on this and his conclusion does not seem self-evident. See also the judgment of O'Hanlon J. in *Doran v Garda Siochána* [1994] 1 ILRM 303 (formal necessity to give reasons does not arise where the applicant 'knew at all material times about the case he had to meet').

184. She alleged that her former husband had sexually abused her son.

185. *The State (McCormack) v Curran* [1987] ILRM 225, 237, per Finlay CJ.

186. [1994] 2 ILRM 285, 291. Cf. the decision of the English High Court in *R. v Higher Education Funding Council, ex p. Institute of Dental Surgery* [1994] 1 All ER 651 where a similar approach appears to have been taken.

187. [1994] 1 IR 397.

188. ibid., 403–4.

189. [1988] IR 353. See generally Hogan and Morgan, *Administrative Law in Ireland* (1991) at pp 671–96; Kelly, 'Hidden Treasure and the Constitution' (1988) 10 DULJ 1; Delany, 'The Doctrine of Legitimate Expectations in Irish Law' (1990) 12 DULJ 1.

190. [1985] AC 374.

191. Mackenzie Stuart, 'Recent Developments in English Administrative Law—The Impact of Europe?' in Capotorti (ed.) *Du droit international au droit de l'integration, Liber amicorum P. Pescatore* (Baden Baden 1987) at p. 417. Note also the comments of Murphy J. in *Duff v Minister for Agriculture* [1993] 2 CMLR 969, 983: 'There has been a notable evolution in administrative law in the State over the past thirty years. No doubt membership of the European Community and closer ties with those countries having a civil as opposed to a common law system will accelerate further the changes in this regard.' The adoption by the Irish courts of the principles of proportionality and

legitimate expectations seems to have been a direct consequence of this increasing European influence.

192. Art. 5 of the Irish Constitution provides that: 'Ireland is a sovereign, independent, democratic state.' Finlay CJ. said (at p. 383) '. . . a necessary ingredient of sovereignty in a modern state . . . is and should be an ownership by the State of objects which constitute antiquities of importance which are discovered and have no known owner'.

193. [1998] IR 353, 384.

194. ibid., 385. This principle was applied in somewhat similar circumstances by Barr J. in *In Re The La Lavia*, High Court, 26 July 1994. Here the plaintiffs had discovered three vessels from the Spanish Armada and Barr J. said that in the circumstances they had acquired a legitimate expectation that they would be treated honourably: 'The general tenor of negotiations . . . created a legitimate expectation in the minds of the [plaintiffs] that they would be fairly treated by the State and would receive a reasonable reward for the discovery which they made.'

195. Hogan and Morgan, op. cit., p. 679.

196. In *Wiley v Revenue Commissioners* [1993] ILRM 482, O'Flaherty J. described (at 493) *Webb's* case as one involving a claim for substantive relief based upon a legitimate expectation, but this case did not involve any potential clash with the exercise of a statutory power.

197. [1993] 2 IR 406.

198. The agreement set out the steps (such as personal interviews etc.) that would be taken by immigration officers in respect of applications for refugee status.

199. [1983] 2 AC 629.

200. ibid., 638

201. [1993] 2 IR 406, 414.

202. [1993] 2 IR 427.

203. ibid., 436.

204. [1993] ILRM 482.

205. [1993] ILRM 771.

206. Op. cit. 491.

207. The Court of Justice would scarcely have taken a different view, for as was said in case C-350/88 *Delacre v Commission* [1990] ECR I-395, 462: 'Traders cannot have a legitimate expectation that an existing situation which is capable of being altered by the Community institutions in the exercise of their discretionary powers will be maintained.'

208. [1993] ILRM 482, 494.

209. As Finlay CJ. also noted ([1993] ILRM at 488): 'This applicant could not pursue on the basis of expectation a remedy which would involve the carrying out by . . . the Revenue Commissioners, of activities which they were not empowered to carry out, and the . . . repayment of monies which they were not entitled . . . to repay.'

210. Although he commented that he did not think ([1993] ILRM at 493) that the case law of the court went further than 'our experience' and 'did not extend the boundaries of this remedy to a point which has not already been established in our jurisprudence'.

211. (1988–1993) 4 *Irish Tax Reports* 492.

212. Hamilton P. found that the prices fixed by the plaintiffs for these contracts 'were based on their entitlement to such refunds and that were it not for such classification they would have exported their product to and developed a market for such product in EEC countries'.

213. (1988–1993) 4 *Irish Tax Reports* 492, 503.

214. Some of the lands were particularly scenic. One licence had also included Croagh Patrick, a traditional place of pilgrimage.

215. Including *R. v Liverpool Corporation, ex p. Liverpool Taxi Fleet Operators' Association* [1972] 2 QB 299; *Re Westminster County Council* [1986] AC 668.

216. Costello J. quoted extensively from the judgment of the Australian High Court in *Attorney General for New South Wales v Quin* (1990) 170 CLR 1. In this case a former magistrate claimed that the Attorney General's failure to recommend him for appointment to a local court constituted a breach of his legitimate expectations. Brennan J. held that the doctrine of legitimate expectations could not apply to the present claim, since the applicant was seeking a *substantive* rather than a *procedural* right (i.e. a judicial appointment). If the law were otherwise, it would mean (at 39–40) that: 'A legitimate expectation not amounting to a legal right would be enforceable as though it were, and changes in government policy, even when sanctioned by the ballot box, could be sterilised by expectations which the superseded policy had enlivened.'

217. [1993] ILRM 771, 789. This passage was approved and followed by Morris J. in *Dempsey v Minister for Justice* [1994] 1 ILRM 401. Here a prisoner claimed that he had acquired a legitimate expectation that he would not be transferred from one prison (with a more favourable regime) to another (with a less favourable regime). The claim failed on the facts, but Morris J. added that even if this were not so, the claim would be bound to fail as a matter of law. The minister was given very broad statutory powers in relation to the transfer of prisoners and she could not be estopped in the exercise of such powers. See also to like effect the comments of Lardner J. in *Devitt v Minister for Education* [1989] ILRM 639, 651.

218. Op. cit. 789. Cf. the very similar test enunciated by Stuart-Smith LJ. in *R. v Jockey Club, ex p. RAM Racecourses Ltd* [1993] 2 All ER 225, 236–7. Costello J. had previously expressed similar sentiments in *Hempenstall v Minister for the Environment* [1993] ILRM 318. In this case the minister had rescinded a previous moratorium on the grant of new taxi licences in the light of a new departmental report on the subject. Costello J. held (at p. 328) that no plea of legitimate expectations could prevail in such circumstances: 'It seems to me that the law should not trammel the exercise by a minister of his statutory functions even if, in the light of new information and advice, he exercises them in a manner contrary to an earlier statement of intent.' This issue also surfaced in a curious manner in the confidence debate in the Dáil in November 1994 arising out of the appointment of the then Attorney General as President of the High Court. The then Taoiseach (Mr A. Reynolds TD) had asserted that by convention the Attorney had first claim on any judicial vacancy and that this convention was in the nature of a condition of employment of the Attorney General. This contention was, it is submitted, convincingly countered by the Tánaiste (Deputy Prime Minister) (Mr R. Spring TD) speaking in the same debate: (447 *Dáil Debates* 352, 16 November 1994): 'Our Constitution reserves the right of appointment of members of the judiciary to the President of Ireland, acting on the advice of the Government . . . Any promise of "condition of employment" which guaranteed an appointment to the judiciary, thereby pre-empting the free and unfettered decision of the Government in the matter, would clearly have to be null and void . . .'

219. Case 120/86 [1988] ECR 2321.

220. The milk quota regulations were based on milk production by producers in reference years. The gravamen of the plaintiffs' complaint was that they had been prevented under the terms of their undertaking from producing milk in those years.

221. Op. cit. 2352.

222. Case 84/79 [1979] ECR 1801.

223. See generally Schwarze, 'Tendencies towards a Common Administrative Law in Europe' (1991) 16 ELRev 3; Schwarze, 'Developing principles of European administrative law' [1994] PL 229.

Appendix

The Procedure for Judicial Review in Northern Ireland

Paul Maguire

Introduction

The grounds for judicial review and its function are little different in Northern Ireland from those in England and Wales. There is a shared embracing of Lord Diplock's synthesis of the grounds for intervention.[1] Both jurisdictions, moreover, reflect the essential policy that the courts in judicial review are not courts of appeal and exercise only a supervisory role.[2] In matters of procedure also there is a high degree of commonality. While procedural reform in the late 1970s was effected in a different manner in Northern Ireland, fears that this would promote divergence from England and Wales have not materialised.[3] On the contrary, English cases, though technically not binding on the courts in Northern Ireland,[4] are followed almost without exception.

As in England and Wales, there has been a marked growth in the number of judicial reviews in Northern Ireland and, as had been commented upon elsewhere,[5] there has been a specialisation among the judges in Northern Ireland in this area to a much greater degree than in England and Wales. It has been calculated that over a period of some five years, Carswell J. (as he then was) heard two thirds of the substantive applications for judicial review[6] and, more recently, the mantle of leading judge at first instance has fallen on Kerr J., though, of course, other judges also hear judicial reviews. This specialisation probably has more advantages than disadvantages, but the matter will not be explored here. In what follows, it is proposed to concentrate on explaining the procedure for judicial review in Northern Ireland primarily by reference to the case law it has generated. For discussion of the substantive law readers will be referred elsewhere.[7]

Procedural Reform

The present law in relation to the procedure for judicial review in Northern Ireland is contained in sections 18–25 of the Judicature (Northern Ireland) Act 1978 (hereafter 'the 1978 Act') and Order 53 of the Rules of the Supreme Court (Northern Ireland) 1980 (hereafter 'the Rules'). These provide for a procedure called 'an application for judicial review'.[8] This procedure, which came into use in 1980, replaced procedural arrangements for challenging in the courts the acts or omissions of public authorities on grounds of illegality, which had been the subject of extensive criticism.[9] Prior to 1980 the litigant had had available to him two separate procedures which could be used for this purpose, but they were mutually exclusive and an invidious choice had to be made between them.

The traditional method of invoking the court's supervision of public authority behaviour had been through the procedure to obtain a prerogative order. Three orders had long been associated with this task. Certiorari was the order used by the court to call up the record or decision of an inferior jurisdiction for the purpose of quashing it. Prohibition restrained an authority from acting or continuing to act unlawfully. Mandamus was the order of the court commanding the authority to carry out its legal duty.

Prerogative order procedure involved two stages: an application for leave and, if granted, a substantive hearing. As evidence was given by way of affidavit, the procedure was ill suited to resolving disputed matters of fact. Interlocutory facilities, such as discovery, were not available. Each of the orders, moreover, was surrounded by an intricate substantive law. In addition, as between the orders, there were differing locus standi requirements and time limits.

This regime made applicants and their advisers uneasy and it was understandable that they looked to exploit other procedural avenues by which to challenge public authorities. A ready alternative, which had the great merit of familiarity, was at hand in the form of private law procedure (by means of writ or originating summons). Through this procedure, declarations of the legal rights of the plaintiff *vis-à-vis* the public authority could be obtained without the need to combine this with any other remedy and, where it was desired to restrain an unlawful act or course of action, an injunction could be sought against public authorities, except the Crown. To a substantial extent, this route had advantages over prerogative order procedure. There was no need for leave; disputed facts, at least in the context of writ procedure, could be resolved through the adducing of oral evidence and cross-examination; and interlocutory facilities, including discovery, were available.

Not all the features of private law procedure were advantageous, however. The locus standi requirement for these private law remedies was generally stricter than for prerogative orders and, like the prerogative orders, each of the private law remedies was subject to an elaborate substantive law. The courts readily accepted that either of these procedural routes could be used[10] but, nonetheless, the situation was unsatisfactory. The late Professor S. A. de Smith summed up the matter in these words:

> Until the legislature intervenes, therefore, we shall continue to have two sets of remedies against the usurpation or abuse of power . . . remedies which overlap but do not coincide, which must be sought in wholly distinct forms of proceedings, which are overlaid with technicalities and fine distinctions, but which would conjointly cover a very substantial area of the existing field of judicial review.[11]

It was clear that reform would have to come.

The matter attracted the attention of the Law Commission which published influential reports in 1970[12] and 1976.[13] In Northern Ireland, it also attracted the attention of the Committee on the Supreme Court of Judicature of Northern Ireland, which reported in 1970.[14] Both of these bodies supported procedural changes enabling the different remedies to be combined.[15]

Reform came in England and Wales in 1977 when a new Order 53 of the Rules of the Supreme Court was devised.[16] Later, the changes made in England and Wales were given a statutory foundation in the Supreme Court Act 1981. In Northern Ireland, however, reform was given a statutory basis from the outset with the rules of court following afterwards. The provisions in both jurisdictions were modelled on the recommendations of the Law Commission in 1976.

The Application of Judicial Review

Section 18(1) of the 1978 Act provides that under the aegis of an application for judicial review 'application may be made to the High Court for one or more of the following forms of relief, that is to say, relief by way of: (a) an order of mandamus; (b) an order of certiorari; (c) an order of prohibition; (d) a declaration; (e) an injunction'.

The law which establishes the function and remit of each of these remedies is unaffected by the procedural changes effected by the 1978 Act. Lord Lowry expressed this point in an interesting way in *In Re McNally's (A Minor) Application*.[17] He said:

> Apart from the new procedural advantages, a homely way of describing the change is to say that, notwithstanding the new *remedies* mentioned in section

31(5) of the 1981 Act and sections 21 and 25 of our 1978 Act, having started with five golf clubs, we can now put them in one bag, but we cannot play any shots with them we could not play before and cannot obtain an order of certiorari on any *grounds* which were not already available.[18]

A sixth remedy, damages, can be conjoined with an application for judicial review. They can be awarded 'in lieu of or in addition to any other relief'.[19] The applicant must claim them as part of his application[20] and, before they can be awarded, the court must be satisfied that the applicant would have been entitled to them if such claim had been made in a separate action begun at the time of making the application.[21]

Prior to 1980, a claim for damages could not be joined with an application for a prerogative order, though it could be joined with private law proceedings for an injunction or declaration.[22] The effect of the change is that where today an unlawful act of a public authority gives rise to a cause of action sounding in damages, for example, where, without the cloak of statutory authorisation, a public authority commits a tort such as trespass to property,[23] these may be recovered as part of an application for judicial review without the need to initiate a separate action. It should be noted, however, that damages are not available simply to make good losses caused by unlawful administrative action *per se*.[24]

The Sphere of Judicial Review

Prerogative orders have long been associated with the task of judicial supervision of the duties and powers of public authorities and inferior jurisdictions. While it used to be thought that they were available only against persons or bodies with judicial or quasi judicial powers, since *Ridge v Baldwin*[25] it has been clear that they are also available against public authorities exercising administrative powers. Prior to 1980, if a definition was required of the public, as opposed to the private, law sphere one would have looked to the scope of the prerogative orders as the touchstone. After 1980, the application for judicial review was intended to operate within the public law sphere, though not necessarily exclusively, and, as has been noted, procedural reform was designed to ensure that the remedies formerly associated with private law procedure could be obtained as part of the application for judicial review. The legislation consequently addresses the availability of these remedies.

Section 18(2)(b) of the 1978 Act states that leave to apply for judicial review (a prerequisite to obtaining a substantive hearing of the application, as will be discussed in detail below) shall not be granted if, having regard to the nature of the persons and bodies against whom relief may be granted by an order of mandamus, prohibition or certiorari, the court is satisfied that the case is one in respect of which relief could not be granted by way of any such order. This anchors the application for judicial review to the sphere of public law. In Northern Ireland, moreover, this is achieved by wording which is rather more confining than is the case in England and Wales. While under the 1978 Act the application may only proceed provided it is one in respect of which relief by way of prerogative order could be granted, in England and Wales, the Supreme Court Act 1981 offers the court more latitude. A declaration or injunction may be granted in any case where the court considers it 'just and convenient' having regard to the nature of persons and bodies against whom, and the matters in respect of which, relief may be granted by prerogative order and all the circumstances of the case.[26] Whether the difference in language between the governing statutes in each jurisdiction will produce differences in the scope of cases susceptible to review is an open question. It does not appear to have done so to date, but if circumstances arise where doubt surrounds the availability of a prerogative order,[27] and where nonetheless it is viewed as just or convenient to proceed by judicial review, there is plainly a danger of divergence of response as between the jurisdictions. The danger, however, as it depends on a positive conclusion by the court that a prerogative order is not available, may not materialise. As Craig has observed, there is a tendency to see the ambit of such orders as fixed, but there is little justification for this and, historically, the orders were used flexibly to provide a remedy against institutions not covered by existing forms of redress.[28] The ability to avoid divergence, if this is viewed as of importance, may, therefore, be greater than at first sight may appear.

When in 1976 the Law Commission proposed the application for judicial review procedure, it was made plain that it was not proposing that this procedure would be an exclusive one for challenging public authorities on grounds of legality.[29] The private law procedure, referred to earlier, was not to be closed off for this purpose, and after the reform the new Order 53 and the old private law procedure for seeking injunctions or declarations co-existed.[30] From 1980, therefore, there were two means of seeking supervisory declarations or injunctions against public authorities: either as part of an application for judicial review or as part of private law procedure.

The decision of the House of Lords in *O'Reilly v Mackman*[31], however, changed all this. In effect, their Lordships held that, as a general rule, claims for declarations or injunctions relating essentially to public law matters must be brought as part of an application for judicial review.[32] The rationale for this general rule, which was subject to exceptions, was that as the new judicial review procedure contained specific provisions for the protection of public authorities (for example, the need to obtain leave to apply for review and protection against tardy applications), these could be evaded if private law procedure was invoked and this was undesirable in circumstances where, after the reform, all necessary remedies for rights protected by public law could be obtained through the application for judicial review procedure.[33] A premium was, therefore, placed on the identification of issues as either being within the province of public or private law. A considerable case law, which it is not practicable to explore here, has grown in the judicial attempt to sketch the boundaries of public law.[34] Much of this has been 'unprofitable'[35] and the problems engendered by the need to categorise issues have given rise to talk of the need to reform the reforms.[36] The reality, however, is probably accurately expressed by Craig in his remark that 'no simple test exists to determine the meaning of public law'.[37]

One is left to ponder possible tests. Two may usefully be mentioned here, in addition to the test of the scope of the prerogative orders, mentioned above. First of all, a court will usually have regard to the source of the authority's power in addressing this issue. Where that power is derived from statute this will point towards the question being one of public law. Conversely if the source of the power is contract, this will point towards the question being one of private law.[38] Secondly, the nature of power being wielded will, on occasions, be influential. The more governmental the nature of the power is, the more likely it will be that the question will be viewed as one of public law.[39] Any test along these lines will have an open-ended quality and the language deployed will often be elusive: is there a sufficient public element or is there an implied devolution of governmental power, for example.[40]

In Northern Ireland the divide between public and private law in the context of judicial review has attracted judicial comment in a small number of cases, mostly relating to the problematical area of employment by public authorities. In *In Re Lyle's Application*[41] the decision sought to be reviewed was that of a political party. Carswell J. (as he then was) had little difficulty, as the party was a body based on private contract without statutory regulation, in concluding that judicial review did not lie. In *In Re Malone's Application*[42] a female employee of Queen's University, Belfast, sought a judicial review of the university's decision to retire her at sixty when men employed by the university could work on to sixty-five. It was argued that this was unlawful discrimination and that her public law rights, based on the university charter and a Community law directive, were at issue. On analysis of these rights, however, both at first instance and in the Court of Appeal, it was held that the rights at issue were private law rights suitable for vindication at common law or in industrial tribunals, but not through judicial review. The source of the power being exercised was the ordinary contract of employment, which was not buttressed by statute or statutory provisions. In *In Re Carroll's Application*[43] a director of a health and social services board sought review of disciplinary steps taken against him by his employer. These steps involved, in the court's view, issues both of public and private law. His terms and conditions of employment, which the employer had sought to alter, had the necessary statutory underpinnings to engage a public law element and, even though this element was not dominant in the proceedings, the court was prepared to proceed with the judicial review because of the urgency of the matter. The learned judge, moreover, considered that to hear it would do no great violence to public policy. Notably this review was decided before the rules in Northern Ireland were amended to include an 'anti technicality' rule under which proceedings begun by judicial review, if unsuitable to review, could be allowed to continue as private law proceedings.[44]

Finally in *In Re McGrotty's Application*[45] Campbell J. regarded the decision of the Northern Ireland Prison Service to discharge a prison officer from his employment on medical grounds as amenable to judicial review. While the applicant did have a contract of service and his relationship with his employer was one of ordinary master and servant, it was not a 'pure employment' situation.[46] His dismissal in substance had arisen from the decision of an independent medical board which had been established under an official code and, in reality, it was the medical board's decision which was under scrutiny. This engaged the second of Woolf LJ.'s principles set out in *McClaren v Home Office*[47] and it was this feature that rendered the decision subject to judicial review.

Leave

The application for judicial review is a two stage procedure. Leave of the court must be obtained to apply for review. If granted, this will lead on to a substantive hearing of the review. Only the Attorney General, acting on behalf of the Crown, when seeking certiorari does not require leave.[48]

To obtain leave the applicant makes an *ex parte* application to the court. He must lodge in the Central Office a statement and a grounding affidavit or affidavits. The statement is an important document. It must set out the name and description of the applicant and must specify: (a) the relief sought and (b) the grounds on which it is sought.[49] It would be wise under the heading of relief to claim together or in the alternative each of the particular forms of relief considered appropriate. Likewise, care should be taken to separate from one another the different grounds on which the application is based. Kerr J. in *In Re Austin and Others Application*[50] has stated that an applicant should set out his case with some definition and should commit himself to a reasonably precise case. A failure to do so may lead to difficulty later, for example, in obtaining an order for discovery.

If leave is granted, the applicant will be confined to the ground of challenge set out in his statement,[51] but this is subject to the court's powers of amendment. The court hearing an application for leave[52] or at the substantive hearing[53] may direct or allow the applicant's statement to be amended, whether by specifying different or additional grounds or otherwise. The grounding affidavit(s) will be the medium of adducing evidence in support of the application. All the facts relating to the issue to be decided by the court will need to be put before it. As the application for leave is *ex parte*, there is a duty on the applicant to make full and frank disclosure.[54] The applicant must show *uberrima fides* and, if there is any false disclosure or non-disclosure of relevant matters, a remedy may be refused on this ground alone.[55]

The application for leave is dealt with by a judge in chambers.[56] The papers are considered without a hearing but, if the judge is so minded, he may direct that the applicant appears before him.[57] The rules, moreover, provide that no application for leave will be refused without the applicant first being given an opportunity of being heard.[58] Presumably this envisages an oral hearing. In considering the grant or refusal of leave the judge must have regard to the sufficiency of the applicant's interest in the matter to which the application relates.[59] As this matter also arises at the stage of the substantive application, it will be discussed later. The judge, before granting leave, must also be satisfied that, having regard to the nature of the persons and bodies against whom relief may be granted by prerogative order, the case is one in respect of which relief could be granted by way of any such order.[60] The effect of this provision has been discussed above.

The principal test to be applied in granting or refusing leave is whether or not the application discloses an arguable case.[61] Leave may, therefore, be viewed as a mechanism for sifting out cases which have no prospect of success.[62] If the applicant's case appears weak but the judge is left with an uneasy feeling and would like to know more, or if the applicant's case appears strong but the judge thinks there may be a quick and easy explanation for what has occurred, there is English authority to the effect that it would be reasonable to adjourn the application for leave in order that it may be further heard *inter partes*:

> At such a hearing it is not for the respondent to deploy his full case, but he simply has to put forward, if he can, some totally knock-out point which makes it clear that there is no basis for the application at all.[63]

An example of a reported case in which leave to apply for judicial review was refused is *In Re Madden's Application* [64] where it was held that the applicant's challenge to decisions of the Director of Public Prosecutions and the police not to disclose to him notes of police interviews with him failed as there was no arguable case. Where leave is refused, the applicant may renew his application before the Court of Appeal which itself may grant leave.[65] A refusal of leave was successfully renewed before the Court of Appeal in *In Re McKerr's Application*[66] and the application went on to be successful. Where leave has been granted a respondent may mount an application to have it set aside, but the burden resting on the respondent will be a heavy one. Such an application was successful in *In Re Savage and Others' Application*.[67] This application arose out of the shooting dead by soldiers of three IRA members in Gibraltar. Following the deaths, the relatives of the deceased began civil proceedings for damages against the Ministry of Defence. The Foreign Secretary issued a certificate in each action under the Crown Proceedings Act 1947 (as applied to Northern Ireland) certifying that 'any liability of the Crown alleged in (each action) . . . arises neither in respect of Her Majesty's Government in the United Kingdom, nor in respect of Her Majesty's Government in Northern Ireland'. In view of these certificates, the defendant in the civil actions sought to have them struck out as disclosing no reasonable cause of action. Before it could do so, however, the applicants obtained leave to apply for judicial review of the certificates. Counsel for the Foreign Secretary applied to have the grant of leave set aside on the basis that, as a matter of law, the applicants had no arguable case, as the certificates by statute were conclusive as to the matter so certified. Carswell J., who himself had granted leave, set it aside since he considered that legally the certificates were determinative of all matters of fact and law contained in them. In face of this, the applicants, it was held, had no arguable case.

Time Limits and Delay

The 1978 Act is silent on the question of time limits and delay. Order 53 rule 4, however, provides that an application for leave to apply for judicial review 'shall be made promptly'. In any event, it must be made within three months from the date when grounds for the application first arose 'unless the court considers that there is good reason for extending the period within which the application shall be brought'.[68] According to the Supreme Court Practice, promptly means 'as soon as practicable or as soon as the circumstances of the case will allow'.[69] It is clear, moreover, that in England and Wales there have been cases where an application for leave made within the three months period has not been viewed as being made promptly.[70] Time, therefore, would appear to be of the essence.

In *In Re Shearer's Application*[71] an application for leave was received one day before the expiry of the three months period. The application related to a challenge to a health authority's decision to establish a controversial advice service. Carswell J. (as he then was) noted that no sufficient reason had been put forward to explain the delay despite the fact that the applicant had clearly been contemplating the possibility of judicial review for some time. Endorsing the decision of the English court in *R v Stratford on Avon District Council ex parte Jackson*[72] the learned judge stated that 'applicants should not assume that they have three months in any event in which to make an application'. He went on: 'Where a major project may be held up because an application for judicial review is pending, it may be quite unwarranted to take three months to launch the application'.[73] As the application, at substantive hearing, failed on its merits the learned judge did not reject it on time grounds,but had it been otherwise he would, he stated, 'have had to give serious consideration to the issue of delay'.[74]

An instance of the court allowing an application to proceed, notwithstanding the fact that it had been brought nearly four months after the decision under challenge had been taken, is *In Re Black's Application*.[75] The applicant had been convicted in a magistrates' court of a variety of offences and had been disqualified from driving in relation to one of them. Through his own fault he had not appeared before the magistrate but, on learning of the outcome, he appealed his convictions to the county court. When the county court appeal came on, for technical reasons the county court judge declined jurisdiction, a course of action accepted by the applicant as correct. Judicial review proceedings, aimed at overturning the magistrates' court decision, on a number of grounds, were then initiated. Carswell J. (as he then was) took the view that as the applicant had been pursuing an appeal to the county court, there was good reason for extending the period for making the application. Where leave has been granted and there is an issue concerning delay, this can be reconsidered on the substantive hearing of the application.[76]

In *In Re Aitkin's Application*[77] a judicial review was rejected on the grounds of delay in applying for it. The applicant was a full time member of the RUC Reserve and his appointment was for a fixed term of three years. After serving four successive three year fixed terms his contract was not renewed. He was informed of this on 1 April 1992. He then asked his police authorities to reconsider the matter but on 6 April 1992 the police refused to rescind their original decision. Later, on 16 September 1993, after more than seventeen months, he sought judicial review. It was accepted that it was for the applicant to show that there was good reason to extend the period for review. No information was available to the court, however, to explain or justify the apparent inaction on the applicant's part after June 1993. Prior to this last date the applicant had been seeking redress through a variety of channels. Kerr J. emphasised that a tardy challenge may create formidable problems of administration 'not least because it may have an effect well beyond the particular circumstances of the individual case'.[78] Promptness, the learned judge stated, was particularly necessary because of the nature of judicial review which 'involves an examination of the procedures leading to a decision rather than the merits of the decision itself'. Where the issue was whether there was good reason for extending time, the reasons for the applicant's inaction and the effect that this will have on good administration required consideration. In general the court 'would expect a cogent explanation to be presented which dealt with the entire period of delay'.[79] In the absence of this, delay, as here, was fatal.

Finally in *In Re O'Neill's Application*[80] an extension to the time period in which to apply for review was granted by Kerr J. The review concerned the decision of a district council not to allow the council's leisure centre and swimming pool facilities to open on a Sunday. A motion which, if passed, would have enabled Sunday opening was defeated in mid June 1993, but review of the decision was not sought until a considerable time (unspecified in the judgment) later. No reason for the delay was proffered, a fact which 'save in exceptional circumstances'[81] must be fatal to an application. The learned judge stated 'it will usually be necessary, therefore, for an applicant for judicial review who has failed to observe the requirements of O.53 r.4 to put forward convincing and acceptable reasons for his failure to act promptly and to persuade the court that such default does not operate unfairly to the person or body whose decision he seeks to challenge'.[82] The extension was granted, however, because, if the application was rejected on grounds of delay, it was thought that a further motion to open the facilities on a Sunday would be put forward. As it was virtually certain that the vote on such a motion would produce the same result, judicial review of this decision, it was thought, would ensue.

Interim Relief

Section 19 of the 1978 Act and rule 3(13) deal with the subject of stays of proceedings and interim relief. Section 19 simply states that 'on an application for judicial review, the High Court may grant a stay of proceedings or of enforcement of an order or may grant such interim relief as it considers appropriate pending final determination of the application'. This language may be wide enough to enable the court to grant interim relief, if it was so minded, even before leave was obtained or pending a decision on the grant of leave.[83]

The rule deals specifically with the position once leave has been granted. Where the relief sought is an order of prohibition or certiorari, if the court so directs, the grant of leave shall operate as a stay of the proceedings[84] to which the application relates until the determination of the application or further order. Where other forms of relief are sought, the court has discretion and 'may at any time grant . . . such interim relief as could be granted in an action begun by writ'. In the granting or withholding of interim relief the court will look to the balance of convenience as the primary test.[85] It should be noted that as a result of the decision in *M v Home Office*[86] injunctions and interim injunctions are now available against the Crown, contrary to earlier authority on this point. Interim declarations may also be available.[87]

Examples of the use of interim relief in Northern Ireland are the lifting of a driving disqualification pending the outcome of judicial review[88] or the suspension of a disciplinary award imposed by a prison governor under the Prison Rules.[89]

Discovery

One of the most commented on shortcomings of the old prerogative order procedure was the absence of the facility for discovery.[90] Prior to 1980, a positive incentive for litigants to use private law procedure was the availability of discovery. This had proved of importance in some cases.[91] The Law Commission in 1976 proposed that as part and parcel of the application for judicial review procedure, irrespective of the relief sought, there would be access to discovery.[92] Order 53 rule 8, accordingly, provides that Order 24, which deals with discovery, applies to proceedings for judicial review. The key rules in Order 24 are rules 3 and 9. Rule 3(1) provides:

> . . . the court may order any party to a cause or matter (whether begun by writ, originating summons, or otherwise) to make and serve on any other party a list of documents which are or have been in his possession, custody or power relating to any matter in question in the cause or matter, and may at the same time or subsequently also order him to make and file an affidavit verifying such a list and to serve a copy thereof on the other party.

Rule 9 provides:

> On the hearing of an application for an order under Rule 3, 7 or 8, the court, if satisfied that discovery is not necessary, or not necessary at that stage of the cause or matter, may dismiss, or as the case may be, adjourn the application and shall in any case refuse to make such an order if and so far as it is of the opinion that discovery is not necessary either for disposing fairly of the cause or matter or for saving costs.

Rule 7 relates to applications for orders of discovery of particular documents. Rule 8 is not relevant in this context.

The combined effect of these provisions was summarised by Kerr J. in *In Re Austin and Others' Application*.[93] He said:

1. The court has a general discretion to order discovery in judicial review applications.

2. It *may*—but it is not required to—refuse an application for discovery if the party opposing discovery satisfies the court that it is not necessary.

3. It *must* refuse discovery if the party opposing satisfies the court that it is not required for disposing of the cause or matter or for saving costs.[94]

The time for seeking discovery in judicial review will be after leave has been granted and after the respondent's case is known. An application for discovery before the respondent's case is known may be premature and, therefore, be an occasion for the refusal of discovery as not being necessary at that stage.[95] It will only be when the respondent's case has become known that the issues will crystallise.

Discovery applications in judicial review in Northern Ireland have given rise to several decided cases,[96] out of which a number of general propositions may be gleaned. First of all, there appears to be general acceptance, at least as a matter of practice, of Glidewell LJ.'s view expressed in the English Court of Appeal in *ex parte Harrison*[97] that 'discovery in judicial review will be appropriate in far fewer cases and will frequently, even when it is ordered, be more circumscribed in its extent than it commonly is in relation to an action begun by writ'. Secondly, it appears clear that the court will only grant discovery where it is required in the resolution of some issue arising in the application.[98] Attention, therefore, needs to be devoted to defining what issues do arise in the application and then as to whether any given issue requires discovery for its resolution. Thirdly, in the face of the respondent's affidavit(s), which will usually, at least in general terms, reveal the decision making process, the court will not grant discovery if 'the applicant is unable to point to any material which suggests the respondent's affidavit is incorrect or insufficient'.[99] In other words, discovery sought merely in the hope that it will provide material to attack the accuracy or good faith of the respondent's affidavit (sometimes referred to as contingent or Micawber discovery[100]) will be viewed by the court as a fishing application and will be refused. The court's opposition to contingent discovery was reaffirmed by the Court of Appeal in *In Re McGuigan's Application*.[101] Hutton LCJ. considered that this stance was consistent with the undoubted fact that the onus of proof in judicial review rests on the applicant.[102] He also endorsed the view of Nolan LJ., as expressed in *ex parte London Borough of Islington*,[103] that to grant discovery 'by way of a fishing licence' would be oppressive.

Where the issue before the court has been whether the respondent has acted 'wholly unreasonably', there is authority to the effect that the court will not order discovery.[104] This is because in these circumstances the court is considering merely the 'terminus' of the decision making process and not the route to it. To examine the terminus, it has been asserted, does not require discovery of documents relating to the route. This analogy may, however, need to be treated cautiously. Kerr J. in *In Re Austin and Others' Application*[105] quoted, with apparent approval, reservations expressed about it by Dillon LJ. in the *Islington* case. Dillon LJ. stated that 'there are many cases of judicial review where the whole issue turns not on the terminus but on whether the decision maker has followed the correct route or procedure in reaching the terminus, e.g. where it is claimed that a decision which might have been reached legitimately has been reached unfairly because the decision maker has got the relevant facts significantly wrong'.[106] To this, Kerr J. added that there were also cases where the issue will be whether the decision maker 'took a particular factor into account or was influenced to a decision by a factor which was irrelevant or extraneous to the issue to be decided'.[107] In these sorts of cases, the production of contemporaneous documentation would be welcomed by the court[108] and examination of the route would seem appropriate.

In many cases in Northern Ireland discovery has not been ordered[109] and it may be of value to set out, in short form, by way of illustration, the court's analysis of the discovery issue in a reported case. In *In Re Glor Na nGael's Application*[110] the judicial review concerned a challenge to a decision by the Secretary of State to withdraw funding (under the ACE scheme) to the applicant. The grounds of the challenge, in summary, were: (1) breach of natural justice; (2) unfairness; (3) *Wednesbury* unreasonableness; and (4) denial of a legitimate expectation. An application was made by the applicant for production and inspection of documents. The court held that no discovery was necessary. It viewed grounds (1), (2) and (4) as being concerned with aspects of procedure. On procedure, discovery was unnecessary as the facts concerning the procedure employed were not in dispute. If fairness was being raised by the applicant as a criticism of the substance of the decision, this related to its merits, a matter inappropriate to judicial review. Finally, on the issue of unreasonableness, discovery was unnecessary because, if the allegation was one of perversity, the decision (the terminus) spoke for itself and there was no issue of fact in dispute. On other matters which might relate to unreasonableness, there was nothing to suggest that the evidence relied on by the Secretary of State was inaccurate or false so that the seeking of discovery was on a contingent or Micawber basis.

As with other interlocutory matters in judicial review, the decision of the judge on a discovery application is appealable to the Court of Appeal.[111]

Cross-Examination of Deponents

Another useful interlocutory order which may be sought in the context of judicial review, but which, prior to 1980, had effectively been unavailable in the context of applications for prerogative orders,[112] is that which requires the attendance of a deponent for the purpose of cross-examination. This is governed by Order 38 Rule 2(3) and Order 53 Rule 8. As with discovery applications, the granting of such an order will depend on the issues before the court and the extent to which facts relating to those issues require clarification or resolution. In *In Re McCann's Application*[113] an application was made to have all of the respondent's witnesses attend and be available for cross-examination. Carswell J. (as he then was) deferred ruling on the application at the interlocutory stage, but took the opportunity to offer some general guidance in this area. After quoting Lord Diplock's view that, though cross-examination of deponents should be allowed whenever the justice of the particular case so required, normally, by reason of the nature of the issues in judicial review, it would be rarely required,[114] he went on to assert that 'the party seeking cross-examination must make out a case that in the particular circumstances there is something specific which requires such further investigation'.[115]

Some issues would be more appropriate for exploration in this way than others. Allegations of procedural unfairness or breach of natural justice might more often be suitable for cross-examination than a challenge based on unreasonableness where it is the terminus not the route that is being scrutinised. Carswell J., moreover, repeated a warning first given by Lord Diplock: 'that to allow cross-examination presents the court with a temptation, not always easily resisted, to substitute its own view of the facts or the merits of the decision . . . for that of the decision making body . . .'.[116] Notwithstanding the suggestion that cross-examination in judicial review will rarely be required, examples may be found of deponents having undergone cross-examination. This occurred in *In Re McManus's Application*,[117] *In Re Keenan and Others' Application*[118] and *In Re McCann's Application*.[119] It may not, therefore, be as rare as might be supposed.

Interrogatories

This interlocutory facility is available in judicial review proceedings in accordance with Order 26 and Order 53 Rule 8. It is sought in the same way as discovery and, it is thought, will be granted in accordance with the principles relating to discovery, which have been discussed above.

The Substantive Hearing

After leave has been granted, the application for judicial review itself is made by originating motion which shall be grounded on the original statement and the affidavit(s) lodged in support of the application for leave.[120] The notice of motion must be served on all persons directly affected.[121] Where the proceedings concern a court or tribunal and the object of the application is either to compel the same to do any act or to quash an order made, notice must also be served on the clerk or registrar.[122] If the conduct of a judge or the president or chairman of a tribunal is being impugned, the impugned party should also be served (by way of the appropriate clerk or registrar) with the proceedings.[123] The notice of motion must be issued within fourteen days after the grant of leave or else leave will lapse.

Save in cases of urgency where at the leave stage the court has directed an early hearing, there must be at least ten days between the service of the notice of motion and the day named for hearing.[124] At the hearing, any person who desires to be heard in opposition to the application and who appears to the court to be a proper person to be heard, shall be heard, even if he was not served with the notice of motion.[125]

At hearing, after the affidavit evidence has been opened, legal submissions will be made to the court. These will primarily encompass the issue of the merits of the application but procedural issues, and, in particular, that relating to the standing of the applicant, may also arise.

Sufficient Interest

As noted above, Order 53 rule 5 requires the court to consider whether the applicant has a sufficient interest in the matter to which the application relates prior to granting leave. A grant of leave does not, however, dispose of the issue and it is clear that, in accordance with section 18(4) of the 1978 Act, the court shall not grant any relief on an application for judicial review unless the applicant has a sufficient interest. Carswell J. (as he then was) in *In Re Hogan's Application*[126] explained that at the leave stage the court will form a *prima facie* view on the material then available to it. At this threshold, sufficient interest is a test designed to turn away only hopeless or meddlesome applications.[127] The court's *prima facie* view may alter at the substantive hearing on further consideration in the light of further evidence or, it may be, fuller argument.[128]

Until 1980, different locus standi requirements had existed for each of the prerogative orders and for the private law remedies, with the requirements themselves being broadly viewed as more liberal in the case of the prerogative orders (especially certiorari) than in the case of private law remedies. It was hoped, however, that the new test of sufficient interest would both simplify and unify standing requirements.[130] Much inevitably would depend on judicial interpretation. When the matter first came before the House of Lords in the *Inland Revenue Commissioners case*[131] in 1982, judicial opinions diverged on a range of issues.

In Northern Ireland, in the case of *Hogan*, Carswell J. reviewed these opinions and sought to offer some general guidance. In *Hogan* the applicant claimed that her local district council was acting unlawfully as it was adjourning its meetings in protest against the Anglo-Irish Agreement without transacting its business. Her interest in the matter was as an elector, resident in the council's area. Carswell J. considered that the requirement of locus standi 'has to be approached in a substantially more flexible manner than before the introduction of the present Order 53'.[132] He also thought that, in considering locus standi, 'the merits of the case are more directly relevant than before'.[133] Standing was to be judged in its legal and factual context. Applying these considerations, the conclusion arrived at was that the applicant did have standing in her capacity as a local elector and maybe also as a resident of the borough.

A similar conclusion had been arrived at in *In Re Cook and Others' Application*[134] where there were four applicants together challenging a variety of actions of Belfast City Council. Three of the applicants were members of the council but the other, Mr Cook, was merely a ratepayer. All four were viewed by the court as having a sufficient interest to obtain declarations that the council was acting unlawfully in adjourning its meetings in protest at the Anglo-Irish Agreement. All the applicants, moreover, were viewed as having standing to obtain an order of mandamus commanding the council to hold meetings and fix a rate. Interestingly, though, the court did not regard Mr Cook as having standing to obtain an injunction to restrain the council from continuing to display a banner on the City Hall building without planning consent. The court's view was that where a private citizen was seeking, by injunction, to enforce a public right, he would need to show either that a private right of his was affected or that the interference with the public right at issue caused him special damage.[135]

Mr Cook was unable to bring himself within either limb of this test but the other applicants were viewed as having a 'particular and special interest in ensuring that the council does not break the law'.[136]

There are relatively few cases in Northern Ireland where the issue of standing has been raised by respondents. This may be because it is generally understood that the court will approach the issue flexibly, but it may also be because most judicial reviews have involved individuals who have clearly been affected by the decision at issue. In Northern Ireland, pressure groups, a controversial class of applicants whose standing has been questioned in England and Wales,[137] do not appear to have invoked the court's supervisory jurisdiction. In one case, in 1988, the court held that the Equal Opportunities Commission for Northern Ireland had standing, because of its statutory anti-discrimination remit, to raise by judicial review public authority conduct which amounted to unlawful discrimination.[138] In other reviews, bodies which were entitled to procedural rights of consultation were viewed as having standing to vindicate these rights through judicial review.[139] In a recent judicial review, moreover, several bookmakers were viewed as having standing to question a magistrate's decision to grant a competitor a temporary move of premises, despite the fact that the statutory provisions governing the competitor's application for this purpose to the magistrate did not confer on trade rivals any right to be heard and probably any such right was impliedly excluded under the statutory scheme.[140]

Discretion

It is well established that the remedies of judicial review are discretionary and that even where a public authority has been guilty of unlawful conduct, the court may, in its discretion, refuse to grant to an applicant a remedy.[141] This situation, as Wade notes, 'may make inroads upon the rule of law' and discretion, accordingly, must 'be exercised with the greatest care'.[142] Why might the court refuse in its discretion to grant a remedy? An argument which may arise, particularly in procedural unfairness cases, though it may also arise in other cases, is that unlawful conduct of the authority (for example, in failing to provide a hearing or an adequate hearing) has had no effect on the outcome of the decision making process and that if the decision making process was gone through again—this time with the authority acting lawfully—it would make no difference. It is argued, therefore, that in these circumstances it is in vain to grant any remedy or relief. In Northern Ireland, this argument has been accepted in a number of cases. In *R (McPherson) v Ministry of Education*,[143] while the court held that there had been procedural failings in the respondent's decision making process, Lord MacDermott considered that 'the applicant, even if given the rights of reply she claimed and did not get, could not have brought about a different decision'. In his view, to grant an order of certiorari to quash the Ministry's decision 'will beat the air and confer no benefit on the person seeking it'.[144] No order, therefore, was made.

A similar approach was adopted where the same arm of government was found to have considered an irrelevant matter in the course of decision taking in *R (Campbell College) v Department of Education*.[145] Kelly J. (as he then was) was satisfied that if he quashed the original decision the respondent's reconsideration of it 'will inevitably have the same result'. In the circumstances, no remedy was granted as there was 'no possibility of any benefit accruing to the school'.[146]

In *In Re NUPE and COHSE's Application*[147] Carswell J found that the applicant trade unions had not been adequately consulted over a health board's action plan but as he considered that proper consultation would have made no difference to the course the unions would have adopted or their reaction to the proposals, his view was that the unions had 'lost nothing by the lack of consultation'.[148] No order, accordingly, was made.

In all these cases, the judge was satisfied that reconsideration could not produce a different result. This was not the case, however, in *R (Hennessy) v Department of the Environment*[149] where O'Donnell LJ. found a breach of the rules of natural justice. His view was that 'it must be a very rare case where a departure from the principles of natural justice, in failing to give a hearing on an appeal, would disentitle the applicant to judicial review by way of certiorari'.[150] On the facts, he did not think that the respondent, if acting lawfully on a reconsideration of the matter, 'must inevitably take the same view'.[151]

In *R (Smyth) v Coroner for County Antrim*[152] a procedurally irregular inquest was quashed by Kelly J. (as he then was) notwithstanding that 'it may well be that another coroner's jury hearing the same evidence assisted by a proper and adequate summing up of it by the coroner will come to exactly the same verdict'. The learned judge considered that 'the next of kin, at least, are entitled to have their unhappiness tempered by the knowledge that such a verdict was reached by considered and regular inquiry'.[153] In his view, to grant a remedy would not be of no benefit to the applicant.

Lastly, in *R (Snaith) v The Ulster Polytechnic*,[154] where Hutton J. (as he then was) found that the respondent had acted unlawfully as judge in its own cause, certiorari was granted. In these circumstances, Hutton J.'s view was that 'certiorari should issue unless there are special reasons to cause the court to decide not to issue the order. This was so even if, in the future, a lawfully constituted decision taker would very probably have come to the same decision'.[155]

A second argument which may cause a court to refuse, in its discretion, to grant relief is that an adequate and effective alternative remedy is open to the applicant and that in the circumstances it is not appropriate to grant judicial review. In *In Re Gribbon's Application*[156] a challenge had been mounted to a school's failure to provide a place to the applicant who was seeking admission to it under the transfer procedure then operating. Against the decision not to admit her there was an appeal available through a specially constituted tribunal. Carswell J. (as he then was) considered that in substance the applicant's challenge failed. He indicated, however, that even if he had been in favour of the applicant on the substance, he would not, in the exercise of his discretion, have quashed the decision. The learned judge's view was that the appeal tribunal was better equipped to deal with the issue which was before him and that, as the applicant had lodged an appeal and the tribunal could direct the school governors to admit the applicant, the matter was best dealt with in that jurisdiction. In these circumstances, he thought, 'the court should not ordinarily grant judicial review'.[157]

To similar effect is the decision in *In Re McNally's Application*.[158] A judicial review had been mounted by the applicant to a county court judge's decision in a criminal matter. Hutton LCJ. dismissed the application on its merits but he made it clear that even if his view on the merits had been otherwise, he would not, in his discretion, have quashed the decision. As the review had related to a point of law, the matter should have been raised not by judicial review but through a case stated.

Before discretion is exercised in this way, however, it ought to be established that the alternative remedy is, in fact, an adequate and effective one. In *In Re McKenna and Another's Application*[159] the applicants sought judicial review of a senior police officer's decision to defer their statutory right of access to a solicitor while in police custody. Counsel for the police argued that any abuse of the applicants' statutory rights could be remedied before the Crown Court at any subsequent criminal trial. Judicial review, in face of this alternative remedy, should, it was submitted, be withheld in the exercise of the court's discretion. Hutton LCJ. and Kelly LJ. disagreed. The possible consideration of the legality of the deferral which might occur in the Crown Court could not be viewed as a remedy for breach of the applicants' statutory right of access. Having carefully examined what possibly might occur in the Crown Court Kelly LJ. concluded: 'These matters confirm for me that the possibility of correction at the criminal trial does not constitute a remedy and, if it does, provides only a remedy which may be inadequate and ineffective. I consider that effectiveness and adequacy are necessary elements in an alternative remedy'.[160]

In similar vein, in *In Re Cook and Others' Application*[161] Hutton J. (as he then was) was prepared to grant the remedy of mandamus to command the defaulting district council to hold meetings and strike a rate. In reaching this conclusion, the learned judge rejected a submission on behalf of the respondent that he ought not to grant the remedy in his discretion because an alternative remedy, in the form of a general central government default power,[162] was available. On analysis of the section conferring this default power, Hutton J. concluded that it did not provide 'a sufficient, effective or appropriate remedy to the applicants'.[163]

A third argument for the refusal of relief as a matter of discretion holds that unmeritorious conduct or behaviour on the part of an applicant should preclude the granting of relief. In *In Re O'Neill's Application*[164] the applicant sought review of a decision of the Northern Ireland Housing Executive that she was intentionally homeless within the meaning of the Housing (Northern Ireland) Order 1988. On its merits, the review failed but Murray LJ. indicated that in any event he would have been inclined to exercise his discretion against giving the applicant a remedy. The reason for this view was that 'in the ways I have explained, she both misled the Executive as to the relevant facts and attempted to mislead the Court as to the facts'. The court, he went on, 'should be very slow to help an applicant who, instead of being completely frank and honest with the Executive about her situation, creates difficulties for the Executive in the ascertainment of the true facts by misstatements which inevitably hinder their investigations and their ascertainment of those facts'.[165]

Conduct which does not deserve or merit serious criticism would be unlikely to engage the court's censure in this way. In *In Re E.O.C.'s Application (No2)*[166] the court granted a remedy notwithstanding that the issue raised in the review could have been foreseen and could have been raised in an earlier review in relation to the same subject matter. This failure, however, was not viewed by Hutton LCJ. as serious and the scale and importance of the crucial issue for the second review, through no fault of the Commission, had not been known to it until after the first review.

Other arguments which may influence the court to withhold a remedy will depend on the particular circumstances of the case. Occasionally the court may have regard to whether the granting of a remedy will be conducive to the interests of good administration.[167] The court may, moreover, wish to discourage a certain type of application where no discernible benefit accrues to the applicant by the grant of a remedy.[168] The categories of circumstances where a remedy may be withheld are not closed.

Other Disposals

The Act and Rules of Court provide the court with a degree of flexibility in the way it may ultimately choose to dispose of a judicial review. Two powers in particular should be noted. First, in relation to applications where an order of certiorari is sought, if the court is satisfied that there are grounds for quashing the decision it *may*

(i) remit the matter to the lower deciding authority concerned with a direction to reconsider it and reach a decision in accordance with the ruling of the court;

(ii) reverse the decision of the lower deciding authority; or

(iii) vary the decision of the lower deciding authority.[169]

In *In Re McKinney's Application*[170] the court made plain that as there were no grounds to quash a magistrate's decision regarding the granting of legal aid, it had no power to direct the magistrate in accordance with section 21 of the Act. By way of contrast, the court itself granted the applicant legal aid, making use of section 21, in *In Re McAuley's Application*,[171] but in this case the court had concluded that the magistrate had failed to have regard to a relevant factor and, therefore, there were grounds for quashing the decision. Cases where the court has remitted the issue to the lower deciding authority for reconsideration include: *In Re Patricia Murphy's Application*[172] and *In Re Leeper's Application*.[173]

A more controversial use of the power may be found in *In Re McKee's Application*.[174] In this case the issue which had to be decided by the Secretary of State was whether the applicant, who had fled from lawful custody in Northern Ireland, could be credited on his return to custody in Northern Ireland against the balance of his sentence with a period of imprisonment spent in the Republic of Ireland. The Secretary of State decided that no account would be taken of this period despite the fact that in extradition proceedings for the return of the applicant to the North some years previously he had given an undertaking to give credit to the applicant for his time in custody in the Republic. The extradition, however, had been unsuccessful and it was only as a result of recapture that the applicant was returned to custody in Northern Ireland. The court considered the Secretary of State's decision unreasonable in the *Wednesbury* sense and decided to quash it but, rather than leave it to the Secretary of State to make a fresh decision, the court declared that the applicant was entitled to have his period of imprisonment in the Republic count for the purposes of the sentence he was then serving in Northern Ireland. This course was adopted, said Murray LJ., 'in view of the highly unusual facts of this case'. The factual situation which had come about led the learned judge to believe that it was not possible 'that the Secretary of State could approach this matter in the objective, impartial and fair way required'.[175]

A second flexible disposal power available to the court is that which enables the court to transform proceedings begun as judicial review into proceedings begun by writ. Under rule 9(5) where the relief sought is a declaration, an injunction or damages and the court considers that it should not be granted as part of the application for judicial review, but that such relief might be granted if it had been sought in an action begun by writ, it may, instead of refusing the application, order the proceedings to continue as if they had been begun by writ.

This has been described as 'an anti-technicality rule'[176] the general effect of which, according to Wade, is that 'the court may thus transfer the proceedings from the public law to the private law channel, but not vice versa'.[177] Rule 9(5) in Northern Ireland was introduced only in 1989 after its absence was noted in *In Re Malone's Application*.[178]

Criminal Causes

Where a criminal cause or matter is concerned, the procedure for judicial review is modified or altered in a number of respects. Initially the decision on the grant of leave is one for a judge sitting in chambers only (not a master).[179] If refusal of leave is contemplated, the applicant must first be given an opportunity of being heard. This, however, will be before a two or three judge court.[180] If leave is refused, no appeal against this decision is available. In interlocutory applications, a single judge will deal with the matter in the ordinary way.[181]

No appeal, however, lies in relation to the order of the judge. Instead an application may be made within five days to a two or three judge court to set aside or discharge the order and to substitute such other order as the court may think fit.[182] The substantive hearing of a judicial review in a criminal cause or matter goes before three judges sitting together[183] but, where the Lord Chief Justice so directs, such jurisdiction may be exercised by two judges.[184] The only appeal available against the decision at the substantive hearing is to the House of Lords and certification and leave as required by section 41(2) of the Judicature (Northern Ireland) Act 1978 must be obtained. A point of law of general public importance must be involved.[185] An example of an appeal in Northern Ireland in a judicial review in a criminal cause or matter directly to the House of Lords under the above provision is *Neill v North Antrim Magistrates' Court*.[186]

Conclusion

It is unlikely that the procedure for judicial review in Northern Ireland will remain static and, as in England and Wales, overhaul of existing procedures is in prospect. The Northern Ireland Law Reform Committee has been considering the judicial review procedure. Its conclusions are not yet known but the views of the Law Commission, recently expressed for England and Wales,[187] will no doubt be an important factor in their deliberations. As in procedural matters in the recent past a common path has very largely been followed, it would be unexpected if Northern Ireland procedure in this field suddenly diverged onto a different course in the near future.

Notes

1. For example, Carswell J. refers to Lord Diplock's synthesis of the grounds of review in *In Re Glor Na nGael's Application* [1991] NI 117 at 130.
2. See, for example, Hutton LCJ. in *In Re Murphy's Application* [1991] 5 NIJB 88 at 103 and Carswell J. in *In Re Glor Na nGael's Application* [1991] NI 117 at 129.
3. Graham, 'Judicial Review: The New Procedures in Northern Ireland' (1980) vol. 31 NILQ 317 at 338.
4. See, Dickson, *The Legal System of Northern Ireland* (1993) at 66.
5. Hadfield and Weaver [1994] PL 12 at 15.
6. ibid.
7. The major texts are Wade and Forsyth, *Administrative Law* (1994), and Craig, *Administrative Law* (1994), hereafter referred to as 'Wade' and 'Craig'. For a discussion of judicial review in Northern Ireland, see Hadfield, 'Judicial Review in Northern Ireland: A Primer' (1991) vol. 42 NILQ 332.
8. S. 18(1) of the 1978 Act.
9. As expressed in Law Commission Working Paper No. 40 (1971); and Law Commission No. 73, Cmnd 6407 (1976). The following discussion of reform is largely based on the analysis contained in the latter report.
10. See *Barnard v National Dock Labour Board* [1953] 2 QB 18; *Vine v National Dock Labour Board* [1957] AC 488; and *Pyx Granite Co Ltd v Ministry of Housing and Local Government* [1960] AC 260.
11. Quoted in the Law Commission's 1976 paper (n. 9 supra) at para. 32.
12. See n. 9.
13. See n. 9.
14. Report of the Committee on the Supreme Court of Judicature of Northern Ireland (1970) Cmnd 4292.
15. Cmnd 6407 (1976) para. 59; Cmnd 4292 (1970) para.116.
16. SI 1977 No. 1955.
17. [1992] 11 NIJB 100.
18. ibid., at 118.
19. S. 20 of the 1978 Act.
20. S. 20(a) of the 1978 Act; Rule 7.
21. S. 20(b) of the 1978 Act.
22. Cmnd 6407 (1976) para. 21.
23. A situation such as occurred in *Cooper v Wandsworth Board of Works* (1863) 14 CB (NS) 180.

24. *R v Knowsley MBC ex p. Maguire* [1992] 90 LGR 653; *Dunlop v Woollahra Municipal Council* [1982] AC 158.
25. [1964] AC 40.
26. S. 31(2) Supreme Court Act 1981.
27. For example, see *R v Secretary of State for Employment ex p. EOC* [1994] 1 All ER 910.
28. Craig, 565.
29. Law Commission No. 73 at para. 34.
30. For an example of the use of private law procedure after 1980 in this context, see *Royal College of Nursing of the UK v DHSS* [1981] 1 All ER 545.
31. [1983] 2 AC 237.
32. ibid., at 285.
33. ibid.
34. See, Wade pp 686–692 for a summary.
35. Wade, 685.
36. Craig, 588.
37. ibid., 564.
38. For a discussion, see Craig, 564.
39. See, Craig pp 565–566.
40. An example of the analytical difficulties in this area is *R v Panel on Take Overs and Mergers ex p. Datafin plc* [1987] QB 815.
41. [1987] 1 NIJB 24.
42. [1988] NI 67.
43. [1988] NI 152.
44. Rule 9(5) introduced in 1989.
45. Unreported 22 June 1994.
46. Such a situation would not normally be subject to judicial review: *R v BBC ex p. Lavelle* [1983] 1 WLR 23 at 30.
47. [1990] ICR 824 at 836. This principle holds that where, in the context of employment by a public body, there exists some disciplinary or other body established under the prerogative or by statute to which the employer or employee is entitled or required to refer disputes affecting their relationship, the procedure for judicial review can then be appropriate.
48. Rule 3(1).
49. Rule 3(2).
50. Unreported 25 November 1994.
51. Rule 5(1).
52. Rule 3(4).
53. Rule 6(2): see S.R. 1993 No. 143.
54. *R v Kensington Commissioners ex p. Polignac* [1917] 1 KB 486; *R v Barnes ex p. Vernon* (1910) 102 LT 860; *R v The Jockey Club Licensing Committee ex p. Wright* [1991] COD 306.
55. ibid.
56. This means that a master can deal with it: see, Order 32 Rule 11. Note that a master has no power to deal with (i) matters relating to criminal proceedings; (ii) matters relating to the liberty of the subject. The master may, in his discretion, refer the matter to the judge: see, Order 32 Rule 12.
57. Rule 3(10).
58. ibid.
59. Rule 3(5).
60. S. 18(2)(b) of the 1978 Act; Rule 3(6).
61. *R v Secretary of State for the Home Department ex p. Rukshanda Begum* [1990] COD 107.
62. As the Law Commission regarded it; see Cmnd 6407 (1976) at para. 38.
63. *R v Secretary of State for the Home Department ex p. Doorga* [1990] COD 109 at 110.

64. [1991] 1 NIJB 99.
65. Order 59 Rule 14.
66. [1993] 5 NIJB 18, see p. 21.
67. [1991] 4 NIJB 78.
68. Rule 4.
69. Supreme Court Practice (1995) Vol. 1, at p. 865.
70. *Hilditch v Westminster City Council* [1990] COD 434.
71. [1993] 2 NIJB 12.
72. [1985] 1 WLR 1319. It should, however, be noted that while the Rule of Court in England is the same on this subject as in Northern Ireland, statutory provision, which has no counterpart in Northern Ireland, also impinges: see, s. 31(6) Supreme Court Act 1981.
73. [1993] 2 NIJB 12 at 27.
74. ibid.
75. [1993] 2 NIJB 63.
76. This was the view of Shiel J. in *In Re Leeper's Application* (Unreported 29 November 1991) relying on Lord Lowry's judgment in *In Re Hughes's Application* [1986] 13 NIJB 1 at pp 5–6 and on the judgment of Carswell J. (subject to further argument) in *In Re Wilson's Application* [1989] 10 NIJB 96 at 99. In *Leeper* the respondent accepted at the substantive hearing that there was good reason to extend the time and the court, therefore, extended it.
77. Unreported 13 January 1995.
78. ibid.
79. ibid.
80. Unreported 20 March 1995.
81. ibid.
82. ibid.
83. Indicators to this effect were given, in the context of the wording of the English provisions, in *M v Home Office*, n. 86 below, at p. 564.
84. Rule 3(13).
85. See *R v Secretary of State for Transport, ex p. Factortame Ltd (No.2)* [1991] AC 603.
86. [1993] 3 All ER 537.
87. See *R v Secretary of State for the Environment ex. p. Royal Society for the Protection of Birds*, Feb 1995 (HL).
88. As in *In Re Black's Application* [1993] 2 NIJB 63.
89. As in *In Re James McCabe's Application*, unreported. Leave granted 26 April 1993. See also *In Re O'Hare* (CA) [1989] 1 NIJB 1 at p. 3 re Board of Visitors.
90. See, for example, Lord Diplock's speech in *O'Reilly v Mackman* [1982] 2 AC 237 at 280B.
91. Examples are *Barnard v National Dock Labour Board* [1953] 2 QB 18 and *Anisminic v Foreign Compensation Commission* [1968] 2 QB 862 in both of which discovery had a significant impact on the outcome of the litigation.
92. Cmnd 6407 (1976) at para. 49.
93. Unreported 25 November 1994.
94. ibid., at p. 6.
95. ibid., at p. 15. See also: *In Re Gilgan Limited's Application*, unreported 20 February 1991 at p. 14 where Carswell J. stated that he would defer consideration of applications for discovery until the respondent's evidence had been filed.
96. *In Re Glor Na nGael's Application* [1991] NI 117; *In Re Gilgan Limited's Application*, unreported 20 February 1991; *In Re McGuigan's Application*, unreported 29 April 1994; *In Re Austin's Application*, unreported 25 November 1994; *In Re Atkin's Application*, unreported 12 January 1994.
97. *R v Secretary of State for Home Affairs ex p. Harrison*, unreported 10 December 1987.
98. *In re Glor Na nGael's Application* [1991] NI 117 at 129.

99. *In Re McGuigan's Application* unreported 29 April 1994 at p. 11. See also, *In Re Glor Na nGael's Application* [1991] NI 117 at 132.
100. Per Henry J. in *Re Cemi Limited* (unreported 1988).
101. Unreported 29 April 1994.
102. ibid., at pp 15–16.
103. *R v Secretary of State for the Environment ex p. London Borough of Islington* (unreported 19 July 1991).
104. *In Re Glor Na nGael's Application* [1991] NI 117 at 132.
105. Unreported 25 November 1994.
106. *R v Secretary of State for the Environment ex p. London Borough of Islington* (unreported 1991) at p. 19 of transcript.
107. Unreported judgment 25 November 1994 at p. 14.
108. ibid., at p. 15.
109. It was not ordered in any of the cases cited at n. 96 *supra.*
110. [1991] NI 117.
111. Order 58 Rule 4. If a master takes the decision his decision is appealable under Order 58 Rule 1 to a judge.
112. Cmnd 6407 (1976) para. 15 citing *R v Kent Justices ex p. Smith* [1928] WN 137 and *R v Stokeley, Yorkshire, Justices ex p. Bartram* [1956] 1 WLR 254.
113. Unreported 13 May 1992.
114. Speaking in *O'Reilly v Mackman* [1983] 2 AC 237, 283.
115. Unreported judgment p. 4.
116. ibid., p. 3.
117. Unreported 4 May 1990. This was a case of a senior police officer, exercising powers to regulate public processions under Article 4 of the Public Order (Northern Ireland) Order 1987. The officer, who was cross-examined on his affidavit, had re-routed a proposed procession. Despite a challenge that he had *inter alia* acted unreasonably, the court held that he had acted lawfully.
118. Unreported 26 August 1993. This case concerned a challenge to the legality of the Poultry Feedingstuffs Order (Northern Ireland) 1991 mainly on grounds that it was contrary to Community law. 39 affidavits were filed on behalf of the applicants and 22 on behalf of the respondent (the Department of Agriculture). The number of witnesses cross-examined is not stated in the judgment but the cross-examination and legal argument occupied 55 days. The court upheld the Order.
119. [1992] 9 NIJB 1. This case concerned a challenge by a Sinn Féin councillor to the operation and composition of sub-committees of Belfast City Council, from which he, and other Sinn Féin councillors, had been excluded. A senior official of the council was cross-examined on his affidavit mainly as to the role, function and purpose of these sub-committees, which the applicant alleged were a device to exclude Sinn Féin councillors from fully participating in the work of the council, a claim upheld by the court.
120. Rule 5(1).
121. Rule 5(3).
122. ibid.
123. ibid. It should be noted that review is not available of the conduct of a High Court judge: see *In re A Company* [1981] AC 374, 384.
124. Rule 5(4).
125. Rule 9(1).
126. [1985] 5 NIJB 81.
127. ibid., at 91.
128. ibid.
129. Craig pp 479–485.
130. Per Lord Diplock in *O'Reilly v Mackman* at 198.
131. *R v Inland Revenue Commissioners ex p. National Federation of Self-Employed and Small Businesses Ltd* [1982] AC 617.

132. [1986] 5 NIJB 81 at 96.
133. ibid.
134. [1986] NI 242.
135. ibid., at 272 quoting Lord Fraser in *Gouriet v Post Office Engineering Union* [1978] AC 435 at 518.
136. See n. 134, at 273.
137. See, for examples, *R v Inspectorate of Pollution ex p. Greenpeace (No.2)* [1994] 4 All ER 329 and *R v Secretary of State for Foreign Affairs ex. p. World Development Movement Ltd* [1995] 1 All ER 611.
138. *In Re EOC's Application (No.2)* [1988] NI 278.
139. *In Re Police Association for Northern Ireland's Application* [1990] NI 258, *In Re NUPE and COHSE's Application* [1988] NI 255.
140. *In Re McLean and Others' Application* unreported 24 November 1994.
141. *In Re McManus's Application* unreported 4 May 1990 at p. 7.
142. Wade, 718.
143. [1980] NI 115. The application was decided in 1973 but not reported until 1980.
144. ibid., 121.
145. [1982] NI 123.
146. ibid., at 142.
147. [1988] NI 255.
148. ibid., at 267.
149. [1980] NI 109.
150. ibid., at 113.
151. ibid.
152. [1980] NI 123.
153. ibid., at 125.
154. [1981] NI 28.
155. ibid., at 45.
156. Unreported 11 July 1990.
157. ibid., at p. 17.
158. [1993] 4 NIJB 64.
159. [1992] 1 NIJB 1.
160. ibid., at 46.
161. [1986] NI 242.
162. S. 129 Local Government Act (Northern Ireland) 1972.
163. [1986] NI 242 at 267.
164. [1990] 3 NIJB 1.
165. ibid., at pp 33–34.
166. [1988] NI 278.
167. *In Re Police Association for Northern Ireland's Application* [1990] NI 258 at 285.
168. *In Re Hunter's Application* [1989] 1 NIJB 86.
169. S. 21 of the 1978 Act; Rule 9(4). Note also, in this context, s. 18(5) of the 1978 Act which gives the court power to validate any decision or determination of a lower deciding authority where the sole ground of relief established is a defect in form or a technical irregularity and where no substantial wrong and no miscarriage of justice has occurred or no remedial advantage could accrue to the applicant.
170. [1992] 9 NIJB 86.
171. [1992] 4 NIJB 1.
172. [1991] 7 NIJB 97.
173. Unreported 29 November 1991.
174. Unreported 6 August 1993. The judgment does not, in terms, refer to section 21 of the 1978 Act but the power used would appear to be that conferred by it.
175. ibid.
176. *R v East Berkshire Health Authority ex p. Walsh* [1985] QB 152 at 166.

177. Wade, 678.
178. [1988] 3 NIJB 8.
179. Order 32 Rule 11.
180. Order 53 Rule 3(10) and (11).
181. Order 53 Rule 8(3).
182. ibid.
183. Order 53 Rule 2(2).
184. Order 53 Rule 2(3). The norm, in fact, is a two judge court.
185. S. 41(2) of the 1978 Act.
186. [1992] 1 WLR 1220.
187. Law Commission Report No. 226 Administrative Law: Judicial Review and Statutory Appeals, HC 669 (1994).

Index